ALSO BY VICTORIA JOHNSON

*Backstage at the Revolution: How the Royal Paris Opera
Survived the End of the Old Regime*

*American Eden: David Hosack, Botany,
and Medicine in the Garden of the Early Republic*

GLORIOUS COUNTRY

HOW THE ARTIST
FREDERIC CHURCH
BROUGHT *the* WORLD
to AMERICA *and*
AMERICA *to the* WORLD

VICTORIA JOHNSON

SCRIBNER

*New York   Amsterdam/Antwerp   London
Toronto   Sydney/Melbourne   New Delhi*

Scribner
An Imprint of Simon & Schuster, LLC
1230 Avenue of the Americas
New York, NY 10020

First Scribner hardcover edition May 2026

SCRIBNER and design are registered trademarks of Simon & Schuster, LLC

Simon & Schuster strongly believes in freedom of expression and stands against censorship in all its forms. For more information, visit BooksBelong.com.

For information about special discounts for bulk purchases, please contact Simon & Schuster Special Sales at 1-866-506-1949 or business@simonandschuster.com.

The Simon & Schuster Speakers Bureau can bring authors to your live event. For more information or to book an event, contact the Simon & Schuster Speakers Bureau at 1-866-248-3049 or visit our website at www.simonspeakers.com.

Interior design by Kyle Kabel

Manufactured in the United States of America

1   3   5   7   9   10   8   6   4   2

Library of Congress Cataloging-in-Publication Data is available.

ISBN 978-1-9821-9629-5
ISBN 978-1-9821-9631-8 (ebook)

Scan here to get book recommendations, exclusive offers, and more delivered to your inbox.

For Markley,
who improves everything quietly and constantly—
broken tools and kitchen drawers,
gardens and landscapes, villages and cities,
and all my days

See for yourself this glorious country where we reside. I cannot do it justice either with pen or pencil.

—Frederic Church,
May 16, 1875

We have already, in our glorious country, a vast and almost boundless territory. . . . Is it not the height of ingratitude to Him, to seek, by war and conquest, indulging in a spirit of rapacity, to acquire other lands, the homes and habitations of a large portion of his common children?

—Henry Clay of Kentucky,
November 13, 1847

We still have a country—a glorious country—a country that may have a more glorious future than it could have had had slavery continued to exist.

—Frederick Douglass,
July 24, 1872

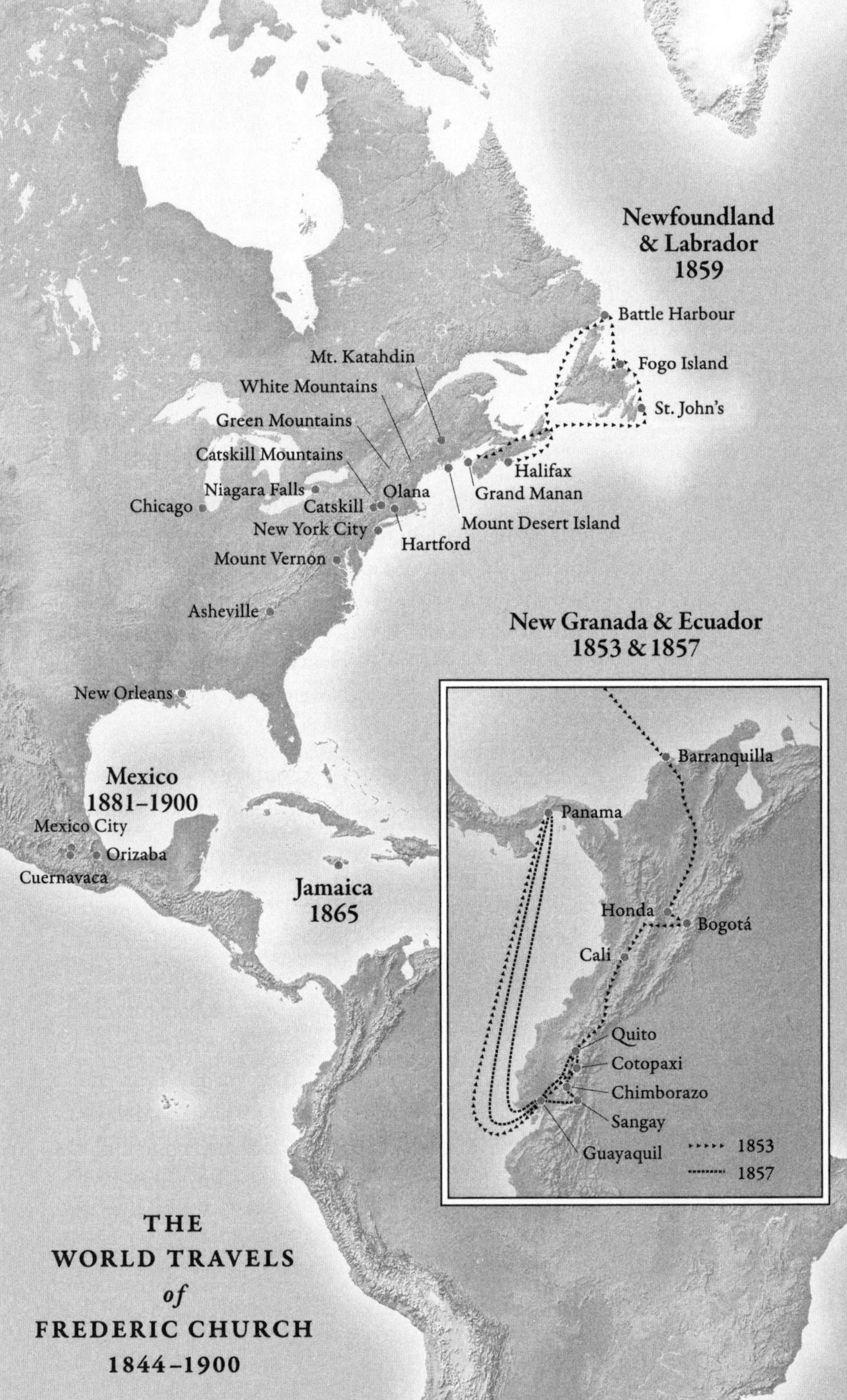

Newfoundland
& Labrador
1859

Battle Harbour
Fogo Island
St. John's
Halifax
Grand Manan
Mount Desert Island
Mt. Katahdin
White Mountains
Green Mountains
Catskill Mountains
Niagara Falls
Chicago
Catskill
Olana
New York City
Hartford
Mount Vernon
Asheville
New Orleans

New Granada & Ecuador
1853 & 1857

Mexico
1881–1900
Mexico City
Orizaba
Cuernavaca

Jamaica
1865

Barranquilla
Panama
Honda
Bogotá
Cali
Quito
Cotopaxi
Chimborazo
Sangay
Guayaquil

1853
1857

THE
WORLD TRAVELS
of
FREDERIC CHURCH
1844–1900

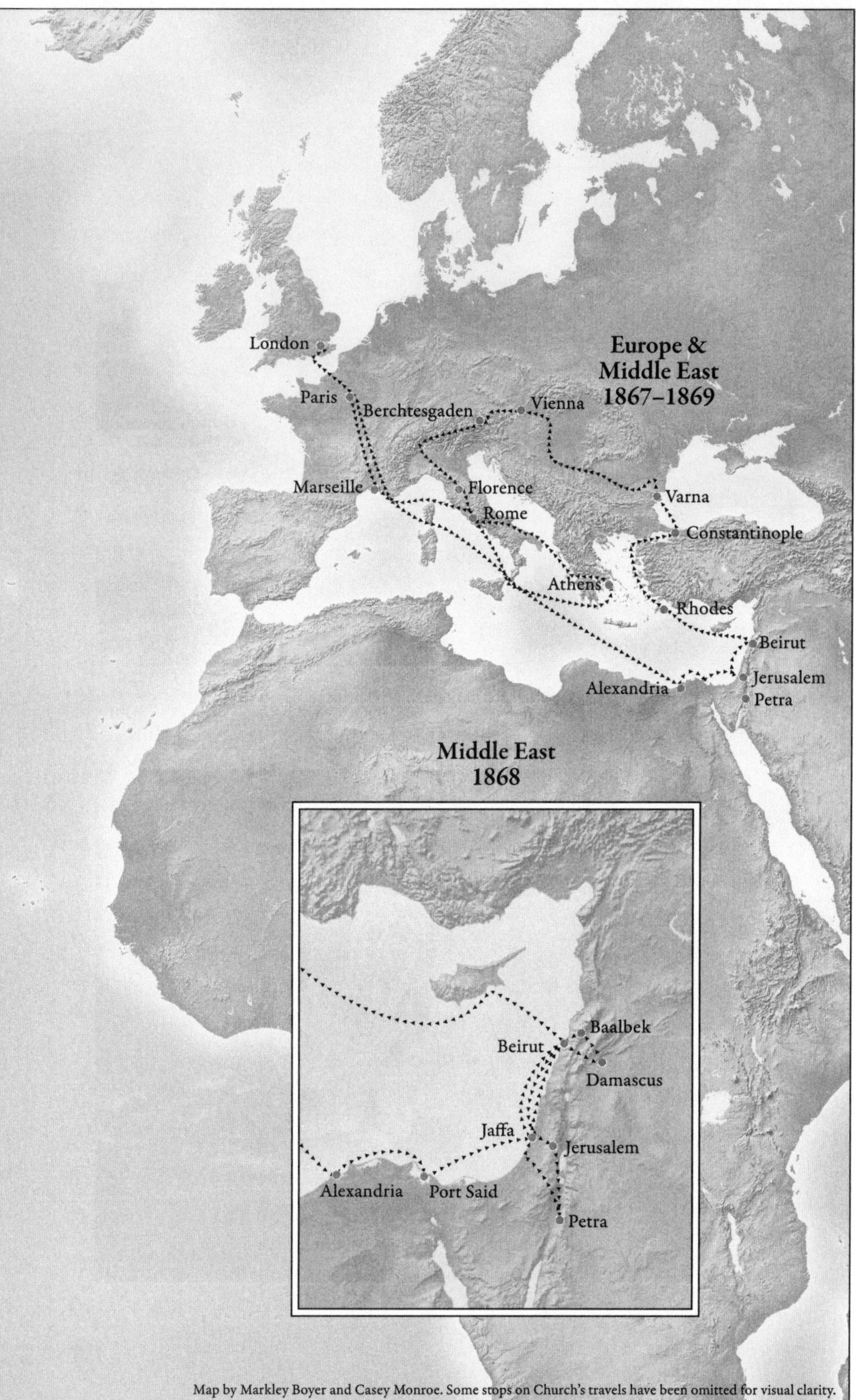

Map by Markley Boyer and Casey Monroe. Some stops on Church's travels have been omitted for visual clarity.

Contents

To the Reader

Frederic Church left behind more than a thousand pages of letters and diaries along with thousands of images. Quoted remarks I attribute to him come from his surviving written documents, as is the case for everyone else quoted in this book. Church often wrote his letters and diary entries in a hurry and habitually omitted punctuation marks. I have preserved his style throughout this book, except in a few cases where his meaning is difficult to follow. Church's spelling also occasionally looks odd to our eyes, sometimes because of nineteenth-century convention and sometimes because he simply got it wrong. I have preserved his spelling, adding a "[*sic*]" only when it seemed necessary to avoid the impression of a typo.

While I almost always refer to Church by his last name, I refer to his wife, Isabel Mortimer Carnes Church, exclusively by her first name. In doing so, I mean no disrespect to this soulful, intelligent, and creative woman. I have chosen to use her first name to preserve for her some independence from her identity as Church's wife and to distinguish her from Church's mother, the first "Mrs. Church" in his life.

In attempting to access Church's interior life, I rely in large part on the documents he left behind. Yet Church was a visual artist, not a writer, and he therefore expressed himself above all in his paintings and sketches, pouring into them his ideas about the relationship between human beings and the vast cosmos, and about the specific time and place in which he lived. The literary and visual culture in which he painted is not our own, however, which means that some of the symbols and meanings readily grasped by his contemporaries are not obvious to us today. The challenge is to try to see his work with nineteenth-century eyes as well as with our own. For example, Church some-times painted an elm in a landscape where elms were not common, because Boston's Liberty Tree—an elm under which the Sons of Liberty met to protest British policies—held special significance as a symbol of the North Ameri-can colonists' struggle for self-government. Engravings of the Liberty Tree were ubiquitous in the United States in the early nineteenth century, and many viewers of Church's paintings would have grasped the political import of an elm. The same was true for Church and oak trees. Early in his career, he painted two pictures of the Charter Oak in Hartford, Connecticut, another tree whose role in colonial history gave it anti-monarchical connotations. When Church placed oaks or elms in prominent and incongruous spots in his paintings, he was evoking a treasured part of his New England upbringing: an anti-monarchical fervor for self-determination.

As Church matured, his symbolic language became more abstract, and he developed an original visual style that injected political symbolism not merely into oaks and elms but into all manner of events and processes unfolding in the natural world. In the fraught 1850s and during the Civil War, for example, he often painted ominous sunsets over North American landscapes to evoke the tension and violence threatening the United States.

In the pages of this book, I transport readers to these vanished cultural and political moments that gave rise to Church's art and won him international fame. At the same time, I aim to show how and why, two centuries after his birth, his work continues to thrill and move people at home and around the globe.

More information about this book and more Church-related resources can be found at gloriouscountry.org.

GLORIOUS COUNTRY

"Mr. Church Likes to Undertake the Impossible"

They came to see the world.

In New York City in the spring of 1859, women swept down the steps of townhouses toward waiting carriages. Stiff crinolines swayed under skirts of organdy and taffeta, making trim black boots appear, disappear, appear. Men emerged from offices and social clubs, buttoning up frock coats and clapping on top hats. Nursemaids hurried along broad bluestone sidewalks flanked by girls with ribbons on their braids and boys in sailor caps. They flowed from all over the city to a single block of Tenth Street, between Fifth Avenue and Sixth Avenue, where they lined up by the hundreds. The block was so mobbed for three weeks, through cold rain and spring sunshine, that policemen were called in to keep the street clear for traffic. There were people waiting on the sidewalk from eight o'clock in the morning until ten o'clock at night.

The city had been anticipating this event for six months, since the day the New York papers reported that a famous painter had returned to the city after a death-defying journey and had gotten to work in a room on Tenth Street. The waiting crowds could have gone to Barnum's Museum, down by City Hall. They could have watched wild animals jump through flaming hoops. They could have listened to strange human figures—giants, pygmies, gnarled women older than time—recount their improbable histories from the stage. But these people wanted to be here, even if footsore and chilled. Over three weeks in May 1859, more than twelve thousand of them came to wait on Tenth Street, and after they had paid their twenty-five cents and gone inside, many people came back to stand in line again. Two thousand arrived on the last day alone, frantic not to miss their chance.

Their destination was an elegant building sandwiched into a row of townhouses. The building was not the same size or shape as its neighbors. Constructed of red brick and trimmed in sandstone, it stood three stories high and stretched the width of three or four townhouses. Large windows covered much of the façade. Over the door, gilt letters spelled out one word:

STUDIOS

As the line inched toward the building, it blocked the front steps of town-houses and the doors to the offices of lawyers, bankers, doctors, jewelers, butchers, saddlers, astrologers, undertakers, and daguerreotype makers. Some of those who were waiting had brought opera glasses, just as the newspaper advertisement had recommended. From the first time the doors had opened, it was clear that the crush of people would make it difficult to see.

When they reached the entrance, the visitors were ushered into a large, high-ceilinged room where benches had been lined up as in a theater. The clatter of horses' hooves and iron wheels was replaced by the hum of human voices. Standing against the far wall was a massive structure of black walnut, fourteen feet wide and twelve feet high. The structure had been designed to resemble an ornate window frame. Heavy draperies were affixed to the top, so that they cascaded to the floor on either side. Through this strange window, people saw what they had come for. Although they were seated, they also seemed to be floating above a river in a luminous landscape. Flowers, vines, and trees grew along the rocky riverbanks. At a great distance, beyond a range of dark hills, a snow-covered volcano rose into a pale blue sky—and who among them had ever seen a volcano? They were looking at some faraway part of the globe, yet they also knew with certainty that they had entered this room from a New York City street.

This otherworldly vision was the inspired creation of a painter in love with the whole cosmos, a man who, when he came face-to-face with the eternities of time and space, felt not fear or alienation but the thrilling connection of humans to all other beings and matter. His painting was called *The Heart of the Andes*. It filled many of its viewers with reverence and awe, not only for nature but for the painter himself. One critic wanted to kiss his feet.

Mark Twain—he was still Samuel Clemens then—found a single viewing inadequate when, two years later, the painting was exhibited in his home state of Missouri. He went a second time, and then once more. Afterward he wrote a dazed letter to his brother. "Your third visit will find your brain gasping and straining with futile efforts to take all the wonder in . . . and understand how such a miracle could have been conceived and executed by human brain and human hands."

In London that summer, Queen Victoria was given a private viewing of the picture and predicted further great feats from the brush of its young creator. British critics who usually found American art clumsy and backward stopped their carping and searched for words of sufficient praise. It was as clear to them as it was to the ladies and gentlemen of New York. Thirty-three-year-old Frederic Edwin Church was the greatest landscape painter in the Western Hemisphere.

BORN IN 1826 INTO a New England commercial family, Church knew by the age of ten that he was meant to be an artist. He loved nature fiercely and had a photographic memory for all its details, from the dappled gray-green of a mossy rock to the tender pink underbelly of a cloud bank at dawn. By fifteen, he was the drawing instructor in his own school. By twenty, after two years of study with the eminent artist Thomas Cole, Church had sold his first landscape painting and moved to New York City, the emerging center of American art. Cole himself had studied the work of the greatest artists from the Renaissance forward, and still he marveled that "Church has the finest eye for drawing in the world."

As a young man, Church packed his rucksack and set out from New York every summer in search of stunning landscapes to master on canvas. He loved to hike and camp and thought nothing of covering fifteen miles in a day and then catching his own dinner with a fishing rod. Another artist observed that if a view inspired Church, he captured it "with a rapidity and precision which were simply inconceivable by one who had not seen him at work. I think that his vision and retention of even the most transitory facts of nature passing before him must have been at the maximum of which the human mind is capable." Church came back to the city every autumn browned and fit from his summer travels. Then he spent the winter months holed up in his studio, painting so intensely that he emerged in the spring pale and exhausted.

At first Church's summer trips took him to landscapes frequented by other artists, as he tramped with friends or on his own through the mountains of New Hampshire, Vermont, and Maine. But he was too intensely curious about the wider world to stay so close to home. He was Meriwether Lewis in a painter's body. Over and over, Church raced toward adventure and danger in far-flung lands. Critics at home and abroad remarked on how ambitious he was in his headlong pursuit of new landscapes to paint. They compared him to Alexander the Great, Hannibal crossing the Alps, and Michelangelo designing St. Peter's. "Mr. Church likes to undertake the impossible," one critic wrote, and he almost always succeeded.

Church steamed to South America to explore jaguar-filled jungles and climb smoldering volcanoes, and then he returned to create *The Heart of the Andes*. He chartered a boat off the coast of Newfoundland and chased icebergs that cracked and crashed into the sea while he sketched them. Chronically plagued by seasickness, he would rush to the side of the vessel, vomit into the water, and go back to work. One explorer, in awe of his iceberg paintings, named an Arctic mountain for him: Church's Peak. When other artists started painting the American West, Church departed for the opposite side of the world, risking injury or death at the hands of Bedouin warriors as he rode a camel across a Syrian desert. When he finally toured Europe, the cherished destination of generations of artists, he found it too tame.

Church came back to his New York studio after each trip with dozens or sometimes hundreds of sketches that inspired and guided him as he painted. In his plein air (or outdoor) oil sketches, he condensed sky, water, and landscape into their purest elements, producing pulsing images that in hindsight seem to prefigure the experiments of Claude Monet, Vincent van Gogh, or Edvard Munch. The same energy that sent him around the world allowed him to stand at his easel for ten hours a day. Slender and nearly six feet tall, Church cut a graceful figure as he worked. He preferred suits from Brooks Brothers, a luxury he could afford, because he came from money and was making more. "He was fortune's favorite from the beginning," a friend said.

Although Church sometimes struck strangers as quiet and reserved, in private he was often merry and mischievous. He excelled at telling funny stories and happily did so at his own expense. "Mr. Church's capacity for entertainment is perfectly inexhaustible," his host at a monthlong house party observed one summer. A female journalist who met him when he was in his forties was charmed by his "boyish playfulness." Despite his international fame, he seemed to her "entirely unconscious of his distinguished position. I like him the best of all the men of note I have ever met."

Church was lighthearted with his friends, but he was deadly serious about his art. He wasn't offended by criticism of his work, seeing it as an opportunity to improve his technique and composition. As he traveled the world and honed his eye, his paintings became increasingly bold and unusual. Many of the American painters around him turned out bucolic, peaceful scenes, but while he was still in his twenties, Church's pictures began to explode with color, light, and drama. He used landscape painting to tell stories in a way no artist had ever before done, turning clouds, water, light, plants, rocks, and earth into his protagonists.

Church arrived at this powerful new language of painting because he didn't accept clear distinctions among science, art, and religion. Botany, geology, and astronomy helped him to see and capture the world around him. Art allowed him to express his feelings about being alive and human in that world, and he felt the presence of the divine when he was surrounded by nature.

His parents sat on the hard pews of the First Congregational Church and prayed to a severe God, and their dutiful son likewise attended church, read the Bible daily, and abstained from painting on the Sabbath. But for Frederic, a friend observed, "Christianity was above all the gospel of love," and he extended that love to the natural world, worshipping the crystalline rapids of a river in Maine, the snowy heights of an Andean peak, and the sun-pierced thunderheads over the Caribbean Sea.

Early in his career, his paintings of nature often included approving hints of human enterprise such as bridges, barns, and sawmills. In his thirties, however, he began to develop a new sensitivity about the place of humans in nature. The material signs of human life in his paintings became smaller and subtler, and sometimes they vanished completely. The landscapes he loved best were the grandest ones, because by making him feel like a tiny part of a huge, impossibly complex planet, they connected him to the whole cosmos. "He is the only landscape-painter living who has anything cosmical in aim and idea," a critic wrote in 1870.

Church did more than any other painter to usher the young United States onto the world cultural stage. His pictures articulated an exuberant new national identity. He showed Americans that they were much more than an inferior model of European, urging them to see themselves as a nation defined by their relationship to nature, not just physically but also spiritually. He infused his paintings with wonder at the natural world of North and South America. The so-called New World, Church insisted at the peak of his fame, "affords every variety known on earth"—soaring mountains, spectacular skies, and untold numbers of plants and animals.

To Church, the capacity to be spiritually moved by nature was the essence of what it meant to be human, making him the visual-artist counterpart to the literary giants of his era—Emerson, Thoreau, and Whitman. And like them, even as he grappled with what it meant to be human in a vast cosmos, his more immediate concern was the fate of his young nation.

Church's New England ancestors had rebelled against political and religious tyranny, and he grew up understanding that a government could either help its people to lead free, creative, meaningful lives, or it could prevent them from doing so. Church believed that to live in a republic was a rare privilege, even as he recognized how flawed the republic of the United States was. Coming of age as a painter in the late 1840s and early 1850s, he watched with anxiety as Americans struggled over the future of slavery. But Church didn't *write* about political issues—he *painted* about them. Before, during, and after the Civil War, he poured his hopes and fears for his troubled country into virtuosic landscape paintings. Emerson, the most influential American thinker of Church's young adulthood, inspired landscape painters to think of nature as a source of symbols through which to converse with other human beings. "Every appearance in nature corresponds to some state of the mind," Emerson wrote in *Nature* in 1836; Church mined the natural world for metaphors to express his state of mind concerning the nation.

Yet Church's intense personal connection with nature meant that even his most politically charged paintings retained the ambiguity of meaning that gives art enduring resonance. The great commitment of his art was to provoke wonder—about the world and about being human in it. A fiery sunset over a North American lake could flash a warning to a nation on the verge of civil war, but it also could celebrate the sublime beauty of the world's wildest places. An Arctic iceberg could speak of the North's unity and strength but also of nature's glittering indifference to human ambition. An exploding volcano could depict the moral cataclysm of slavery but also the ungovernable forces that shape the cosmos.

FREDERIC CHURCH WAS BOTH DEEPLY American and utterly original. He embodied the contradictions of his country in the nineteenth century but used them to create a new kind of art and a new vision for his young nation. He was a rule follower in his personal life and a rule breaker in his work. Friends often commented on his quiet, refined manners, but critics recognized that he had a dash of Barnum in him. With his blockbuster single-painting shows, he invented the now-familiar figure of the American celebrity artist. Men wrote to ask for his autograph. Women wrote to ask for his photograph.

Creative tensions permeated Church's life and art. He found the pace and impact of technological change disturbing but counted railroad men and industrialists who were responsible for that change among his patrons and closest friends. He was fascinated by advances in photography and collected thousands of photographs even as photography began to challenge the primacy of his own medium. He told friends he wasn't interested in party politics but painted some of the most powerful and influential political imagery of the Civil War era. He loved the United States with a robust patriotism but had a profoundly open and cosmopolitan mind. He spent his whole adulthood studying the cultures of other lands, and he admired them tremendously—Egyptian, Babylonian, Aztec, Ottoman Syrian, Renaissance Italian, and more—yet he never doubted the promise of his own rising nation. He was lumped together with other painters into the so-called Hudson River School (a term coined in the 1870s), but in his subject matter and thematic concerns he was a global artist.

When a crippling illness threatened his ability to paint, Church increasingly used the earth itself as his canvas, fashioning a dramatic landscape high above the Hudson River. Crowning that landscape with a villa of his own design, Church took inspiration from Middle Eastern domestic architecture he had seen on his travels and in books. He filled the rooms of the new house with art and artifacts from around the world, creating a kaleidoscope of cultures that reminded him every day of the universal human capacity to create beauty and meaning.

He often sat with his wife and children on the piazza of their house as the day waned, watching the sky above the Hudson River blaze red and gold. He constantly urged friends to come visit the "glorious country" where he had made a home. Humbled by the beauty around him, he wrote, "I cannot do it justice either with pen or pencil." But he could, and he did—not only on the Hudson, but around the globe.

CHURCH WAS A PRIVATE AND modest man, even at the height of his celebrity. He wrote hundreds of personal letters but filled them mainly with puns and anecdotes, news of family and friends, and questions for his correspondent. "When you write me you never tell me anything about yourself or what you are doing now," one friend complained. "I wish the next time you write you would give an account of yourself." During the New York exhibition of *The Heart of the Andes*, Church sometimes positioned himself where the crowds wouldn't notice him.

I believe that Church deserves to be seen, and in these pages, I aim to lead him back out into the world that he loved to roam and that inspired his art. I've spent the past six years retracing his life and adventures through his paintings and sketches, through thousands of pages of archival documents, and through a wealth of indispensable art-historical scholarship. I've also tracked him through the Maine woods, up the slopes of Andean volcanoes, and across a Middle Eastern desert. Church's stamina and courage amazed me as I traveled under far more comfortable conditions than those he endured. Some of the places he ventured are still so perilous that I had one chilling brush with my own mortality in the Ecuadorian Andes. I was caught in a lightning storm at the glacier line on Cotopaxi, an active volcano that rises to nearly twenty thousand feet. A full hour after the descent, my body was so charged with electricity that my hair still stood on end. That terrifying experience made plain to me why Church felt most alive when faced with nature's titanic power.

What Church felt—about the human place in nature, about art, about his family and friends, about his political times—informed what he painted. *Glorious Country* tells the life story of an epoch-making artist whose bravery, curiosity, and talent changed the way his contemporaries saw art and themselves. Moving with Church through his days as he responded to the world illuminates how and why he created his extraordinary paintings.

Although Church was born two hundred years ago and died when the twentieth century was only a few months old, his oil sketches and paintings have something vital and urgent to convey to us in the twenty-first century. *The Heart of the Andes*, the painting that astounded the United States and Britain in 1859, hangs today in the Metropolitan Museum of Art, which Church helped to found, and his reverence for the natural world suffuses the entire massive canvas. Yet his legacy derives not only from his love of nature and his towering talent. More than any other artist of his century, he harnessed his talent to address threats to the republic that he loved. In his most powerful works, Church fused nature and nation to create art both universal and particular in its concerns. Humans wield little power in the cosmos, his paintings suggest, but through our political ideas and institutions we author other powers, including the power to safeguard or savage one another.

"I Scarcely Dared Hope"

On an early-summer day in 1844, eighteen-year-old Frederic Church crossed the Hudson River with his art supplies and his ambitions in tow. He had traveled from his hometown of Hartford, Connecticut, through sunlit valleys and hardwood forests until he reached the eastern shore of the Hudson. On its far side, he saw blue mountains scalloping the western sky. Beyond them lay a whole continent.

Church had recently turned lanky, and he was heading toward six feet, although he would never quite arrive there. His thin face and angular cheekbones were softened by a full mouth and large hazel-gray eyes; his hair was dark brown. He carried himself with the confident posture of a young man with important things to do. His older sister, Elizabeth, teased him for it, calling him "your own tall Majesty."

He was almost one hundred miles from home. There was no bridge across the Hudson here, only a ferry that slid slowly toward the opposite shore, bisecting the paths of sloops and steamboats heading to and from New York City. Once he reached the village of Catskill on the western bank, he walked toward a large house on a hill. It had green shutters and white trim and was painted a buttery yellow. Though not as formal as his family's home in Hartford, it was fronted by a wide veranda with white balustrades, and a delicate fanlight crowned the front door. Even the privy in the yard was large and topped by a cupola.

The yellow house was the home of painter Thomas Cole.

Greenery enveloped Church as he approached the house. Cedars and honey locusts shaded the yard. Flower borders and vegetable gardens gave way to

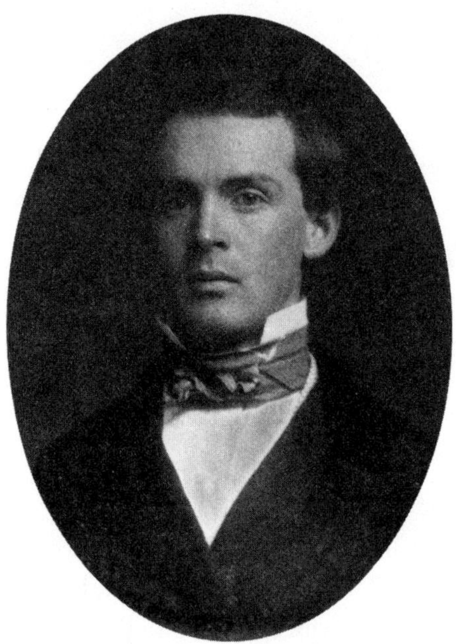

Frederic Church at about
eighteen years old

meadows where cows, horses, and sheep grazed. A breeze was blowing from the south that day, ruffling and righting the tall grasses.

Church owed his presence here to his father's friend Daniel Wadsworth, who had written to Cole on Church's behalf. Wadsworth was one of Cole's chief patrons, and Church knew Cole's paintings firsthand from visiting Wadsworth's home with his parents. Frederic Church, Wadsworth had informed Cole in his letter, was affable, well-mannered, and bursting with artistic talent, and Church deserved a mentor equal to his great promise. As Wadsworth's letter had made its way west from Hartford to Catskill, Church had steeled himself for rejection. Cole rarely accepted students. When the answer came back—*yes*—Church had dispatched a breathless note of thanks. "I scarcely dared hope," he wrote. "My highest ambition lies in excelling in the art."

CHURCH COULD NOT HELP HIMSELF. By the time he was five or six years old, it was clear to everyone that he was different. The ancient human urge to make pictures, to capture the world in miniature on a cave wall, surged through him with irresistible force. He inhaled light and lines and color, and he exhaled pictures. It didn't matter what kind of paper—a torn scrap of a bill, the margin of a schoolbook, the back of an envelope—just so long as he had a blank space on which to preserve the scenes that whirled and jostled in his mind.

Gripping a quill pen in his small fingers, Church fixed the world on paper. He embellished his schoolbooks. A bestiary escaped the confines of his imagination and raced across the pages of his sketchbook. "Gentlemen & Ladies this is an Owl," he wrote in fancy lettering beneath an ink cartoon of a huge-eyed bird. He drew fish, dogs, rodents, eagles, and people. He drew sailing ships, clouds, and lyres. When President William Henry Harrison died, he drew a picture of a tiny coffin and another of a tiny White House seen through parted stage curtains. While practicing his penmanship, he stopped to draw a picture of a pen, a man, and a ship, and then half a dozen pictures of quill pens.

Nothing seemed to escape his eye, except perhaps what his teachers wrote on the blackboard. He often gazed out the window at the leafy, light-shifting world beyond. Noticing his dreaminess as well as his talent, one of Church's earliest teachers sat him in front of the class and asked him to draw pictures to amuse the other children. The theatricality of this moment, when he first held an audience spellbound, stayed with him for the rest of his life. Later, another schoolteacher hired him to replace a departed drawing master, so that Church found himself teaching his classmates. For the first time, he was earning money with his artistic skill, and his father, he later recalled, "advised me with impressive seriousness to deposit it in the Savings Bank after deducting a small sum for pocket money." The delight Church felt at being rewarded for the pastime he loved best left a lasting impression. He decided he wanted to be a great artist.

AS A BOY, CHURCH WAS fascinated with the latest scientific and industrial innovations. He possessed what Wadsworth described in his letter to Cole as "mechanical genius." A close friend would note decades later that Church "had that aggressive trait peculiar to the Connecticut Yankee and known as 'the enquiring mind', and there was never the most commonplace utensil about the house or in his studio or on his farm that he did not scan with a keen eye to see if something could not be invented which would do the work better or could be made more beautiful." When he wasn't drawing, tinkering, or amusing his sisters and friends—he loved to make people laugh—Church composed stories in which he behaved heroically in the face of life-threatening danger. "We were wrecked on a little island but I saved my mother and myself," he wrote in one tale.

Mrs. Eliza Church was a serious woman who wore simple gowns, devoid of flounces and lively patterns. Frederic's father, Joseph Church, ran a prosperous silver and jewelry business and later served as a director of an insurance company. He built a handsome house and made successful investments in local industry and real estate. He and Mrs. Church looked forward to an equally respectable future for their son, who would have liked to comply with their wishes, but couldn't. The only office that enticed him was a meadow with a ceiling made of sky. When he managed to break free from four walls, he ran to the green banks of the Connecticut River, where he lay on his back studying the clouds and then tried to re-create their shapes using paper and pencil. He took off his hat and piled his drawings in it to carry them home.

Church's parents found life weightier than did their effervescent son. They both issued from the seventeenth-century Puritan founders of Connecticut and had the fear of God to prove it. They had also been chastened by terrible losses. Their first two sons had died in infancy before Church was born; his middle name, Edwin, was in honor of one of these brothers he had never met. Joseph and Eliza Church gazed with the eyes of their pious ancestors upon the mournful world and their surviving children. On Sundays, they ushered the children into a pew at the old Congregational church: forthright Elizabeth, dreamy Frederic, and frail, pretty Charlotte.

Frederic's obsession was vaguely disreputable. If he had to make art, his parents' sort of New England piety leaned toward portraiture or historical scenes. Portraiture was both lucrative and respectable, and history paintings performed a public service by reminding the nation that it owed its existence to brave forebears. But what Frederic loved best was art that captured the natural world. His father complained about Frederic's fixation; he would rather see his son go into business. Despite their misgivings, his parents recognized his gifts, as did their cultivated friends. Mr. Church finally bowed to his son's stubborn, joyful creativity and agreed to pay for lessons with two local artists.

In the spring of 1844, as Church neared his eighteenth birthday, he went outdoors one day and tried to paint in oils. It was the first time he had painted directly from nature—as opposed to sketching in pencil—and he found it the "most delightful" experience of his young life. But he saw plainly that he could not yet do justice to the world around him.

Within weeks, he was preparing to leave Hartford to study with Thomas Cole, packing his suits and his pencils and paints. His mother, not sharing Frederic's view that he was almost a man, exhorted him, "Be a good boy!" Church's father saw him off with money and his reluctant blessing. For the straitlaced Mr. Church, it was a gesture akin to helping his son run away to sea by bankrolling his apprenticeship with a captain.

FREDERIC LEFT CHILDHOOD BEHIND THE day he set out from the gentle Connecticut River Valley for a village at the edge of the American wilderness. The blue peaks he could see in the distance were the Catskill Mountains, a range rising to the west of the river. As a child he had passed through this region on a family trip, and he still had a misty memory of the "beautiful and romantic scenery" with its "abrupt bluffs and lofty heights." Here, the Esopus and Mohican people had once hunted deer, bear, and wolves. The bones of mastodons lay buried in the muddy depths of the ponds where they had fished, and the lace skeletons of ancient sea creatures decorated the boulders along their high trails.

The Native American families were mostly gone now. In a bloody campaign in the late eighteenth century, white settlers had exiled or killed many of them; disease and hunger did the rest. Their fertile bottomlands had been taken over by the farms of settlers descended from first Dutch and then British colonists; tanneries and mills now pockmarked their hills and hollows. Still, immense swaths of the mountains remained pristine and wild.

By the time Church arrived there in June of 1844, readers in North America and Europe knew that this was a landscape so wild and haunted that a man could storm out of his house after a fight with his wife, take his dog hunting in the hills, and be lost for twenty years. It was Washington Irving who had told the world about the Catskills—"these fairy mountains," he called them in his 1819 short story "Rip Van Winkle," which had made him the most famous American writer. Irving's undeniable literary talent persuaded many skeptical Europeans that the raw, young United States might one day rise above cultural mediocrity.

The beauty of the Catskills was everywhere you looked. It was in a backlit field of goldenrod and meadowsweet, in the cataract that frothed down a moss-lined gorge before relaxing into a languid stream, and in the hundred-mile views from a cliff higher than the clouds—a panorama that embraced the mighty Hudson River, the Taconic Mountains of New York, and the distant Berkshire Hills of Massachusetts.

If the beauty of this place was blinding, its menace was subtler. It lay with the rattlesnake coiled beside a path, and it perched on the crumbling mountain ledge where a misstep meant death. Some locals believed the devil himself lived in the Catskills, and that he could use local witches to ruin a crop, break an arm, or sicken a newborn baby. When he struck, people summoned a witch doctor, who would try to vanquish the evil with charms and incantations passed down from their Dutch ancestors. One of the last Catskills witch doctors, Jacob Brink, had died only a year before Church arrived.

A bright young man seeking his fortune in Church's day often made for a more cosmopolitan city than the one where he grew up—New York or Boston, or better yet London or Paris—but Church had headed in the opposite direction. Hartford, his hometown, was a "city of pleasant faces and office chairs," as he would later describe it to his closest childhood friend, Aaron Goodman. A commercial and shipping center of about ten thousand people, Hartford boasted one of the first art museums in the United States, the Wadsworth Atheneum. Founded by the Churches' family friend Daniel Wadsworth, the museum opened the same summer Church left to study with Cole. Catskill, by contrast, was a rural village surrounded by farms, mills, and tanneries. Much of the village's meager share of cosmopolitanism was concentrated in the person of forty-three-year-old Thomas Cole, who was considered the greatest landscape painter in the United States.

COLE HAD GROWN UP UNDER the coal-blackened skies of northern England, but his family had emigrated to the United States when he was seventeen. He had discovered the Catskills as a struggling New York artist in his mid-twenties, when an early patron in Manhattan, recognizing Cole's talent at rendering landscapes, had suggested he explore the Catskill region for inspiration. Cole hiked day after day, stopping to open his sketchbook and record a gnarled tree, a glacial boulder, a creek plummeting over a cliff. The first paintings he created from his mountain adventures drew acclaim in New York City, and he soon had patrons up and down the East Coast buying his canvases and commissioning new ones.

Wanting to improve his eye and art, Cole made two extended trips to Europe to see the great architecture of England, France, and Italy and to study the original sketches and paintings of Claude Lorrain, Constable, Rembrandt, Michelangelo, and other masters. In London, Cole had met Britain's most celebrated painter, J. M. W. Turner, and viewed

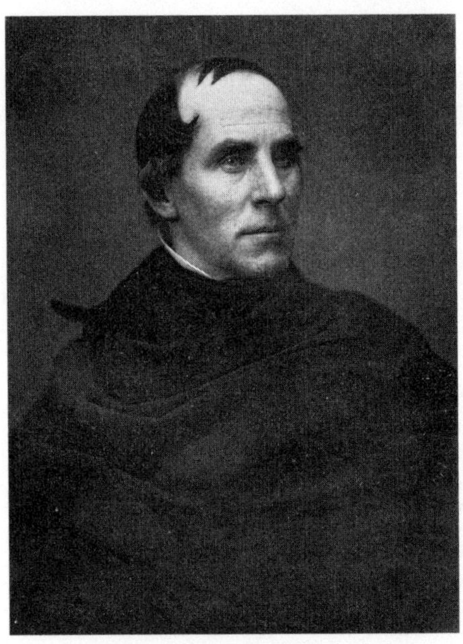

Thomas Cole, by Mathew Brady, c. 1845

his light-suffused canvases. In Italy, as he wandered among Etruscan ruins, an idea for a new series of paintings had taken shape in his mind.

Comprising five paintings he called *The Course of Empire*, the series depicted the beauty of unspoiled nature, the ingenuity and destructive avarice of human beings, and the triumph of resurgent nature after the collapse of human civilization. The paintings were wildly ambitious and technically stunning. The American writer James Fenimore Cooper declared Cole's achievement "the work of the highest genius this country has ever produced."

Cole spent several years moving up and down the Hudson River between New York City and Catskill, where he rented a cottage. The Hudson, also known in Cole's day as the North River, was originally called the Mahicannituk—"the river that flows both ways"—by the Mohicans who lived on its shores, because the Atlantic tides reverse the prevailing current some 150 miles inland. It was as magnificent a river as any on earth, according to one awestruck European traveler after another. Along Manhattan Island, the river was filled with rowboats, sailboats, fishing vessels, tall sailing ships, and steamboats, but the traffic thinned as Cole's ferry steamed north toward Catskill. On the western shore, ribbed cliffs rose toward the sky, their summits blanketed in forests of chestnut, hickory, and oak. Osprey sheered out over the water in search of fish. Sometimes a whale or dolphin followed the incoming tide from the Atlantic, swimming past villages and country estates. Small factories and warehouses clustered along the river near many towns, including Catskill.

Cole's landlord in Catskill was a farmer and storekeeper named John Alexander Thomson, whose farm was called Cedar Grove. For Cole, the Catskills region in summer was heaven on earth. He was in love with the "glorious scenery," and soon he was also in love with Thomson's pretty niece Maria Bartow. They married in 1836, and Thomson, known in the family as Uncle Sandy, invited Cole to move into the house at Cedar Grove. Cole set up a painting studio in a high-ceilinged farm building near the house and commenced life as a family man. By the time Church arrived in the summer of 1844, Thomas and Maria* were the parents of three young children.

When Church entered the house at Cedar Grove for the first time, he discovered a shrine to nature and art—the two things he loved best. Cole's

---

* Pronounced "Mar-*I*-uh."

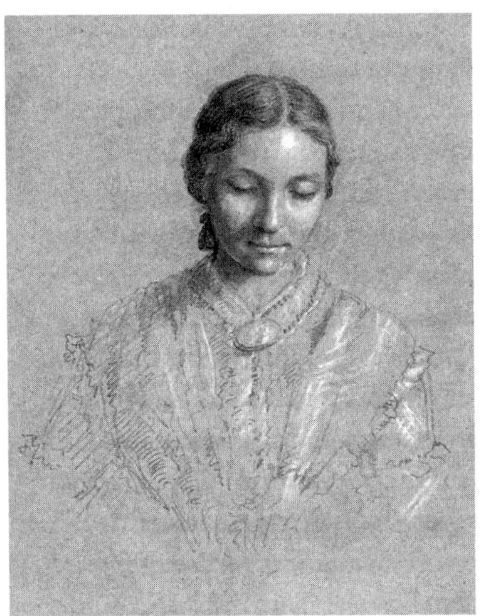

Maria Cole in a sketch by her husband,
Thomas Cole, c. 1840

spectacular canvases graced many of the walls, and some of them depicted the same mountain peaks Church could see out the parlor window.

Cole welcomed Church to Cedar Grove. Two decades spent hunched over an easel had left Cole with a stooped posture and a gait that a friend described as "a peculiar rising and sinking motion." His blue-gray eyes were pale and intense, his face bare of whiskers. Deep lines ran across his forehead, and he wore his thinning black hair swirled up and over his skull, with a few longer locks fluffed out over his ears. Grave and courteous, he dressed in sober clothes.

In a leather-bound account book, Cole wrote out the terms he had fixed with Church's father. Cole would receive $300 for one year of instruction, and Church was to board in a small white farmhouse on the grounds of Cedar Grove. Church and his parents had hoped that he could rent a room in the main house, but it was already filled with Cole's large family. Thomas and Maria shared a tiny bedroom on the second floor, with their children installed in a nursery close by. A large bedroom on the other side of the hall housed Maria's three unmarried adult sisters. Their Uncle Sandy, the patriarch, slept in a small bedroom on the first floor. There was simply no room for a boarder.

Church felt humble before Cole, but his teacher quickly set him at ease. His arrival coincided with the season when Cole's spirits were at their highest. Most years, the harsh winter stretched into early May. When the late snows veiled the mountains, Cole felt that the cold winds and gray skies had lodged deep in his soul. He exulted each year when summer finally blossomed.

Cole took Church out into the June sunshine to begin their lessons. Cole had a folding stool equipped with an umbrella to cut the glare on his canvas and palette, but sometimes he just perched on a rock while he sketched. As they explored and worked, Cole sometimes talked to Church, sharing both technical advice and a grander sense of art's purpose and power; Cole had written at length about the latter in diaries, letters, and essays. American art was still in its infancy, and Cole wanted to teach his adopted nation to "sow seed in the fields of the Beautiful which for ourselves and the coming generations shall grow and ripen into abundant harvests."

Cole believed that the artist's highest calling was to celebrate nature, which he thought of as God's creation. The artist must master all of its details—plants, sky, rock, water, light—in each of their varied moods. To become a great artist, Church would have to learn to see nature clearly, and to do that, he would have to draw it, over and over. "Genius has but one wing," Cole said, "and unless sustained on the other side by the well-regulated wing of assiduity, will quickly fall to the ground." Church's assignment was disciplined daily sketching.

First came the trees. Not trees in general, but particular trees. "Trees are like men," Cole explained— they had different personalities and characters depending on the circumstances in which they grew. Using a graphite pencil, Church learned to capture chestnut, hickory, oak, sassafras, pitch pine, white pine, elm, and maple. He practiced their distinctive leaves, bark, branches, stumps, and roots, until he was proficient.

He found human figures harder. He tried sketching pictures of the three Cole children, but he knew his work was clumsy; he described a drawing he did of Cole's daughter Emily as "very rude." He turned to sketching the barnyard animals and

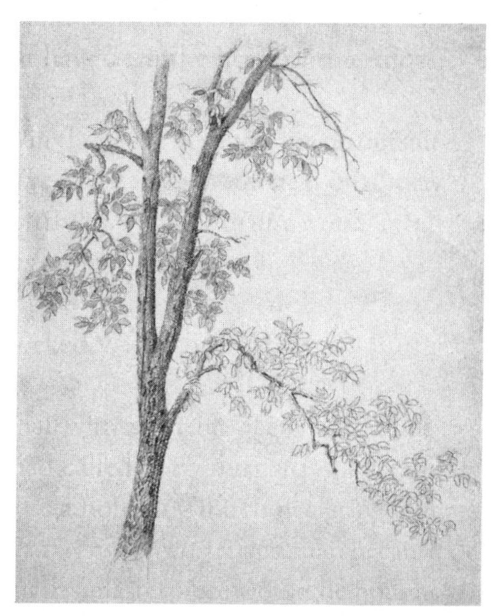

Hickory tree sketched by
Church in June 1844

discovered he was better with them. He drew cows grazing, resting on the ground, and yoked to wagons. He drew horses standing still, running free, and with mounted riders. Cole looked through Church's sketchbook and was impressed. His young charge was talented.

But drawing wasn't painting.

CHAPTER 2

"What Are the Forms the Clouds Take"

All that summer of 1844, Church passed his days and evenings with his adopted family, who drew him into their domestic whirl of meals, music, reading aloud, and parties.

Maria's sisters helped care for the three Cole children. Theodore (known as Theddy) was six years old, Mary was four, and Emily was ten months old. Although twelve years apart in age, Theddy and Church developed a close friendship. Theddy liked to trail around behind Frederic chattering about the farm dog or the new litter of kittens he longed to keep. Theddy and Mary sometimes included Church in the tea parties that they held with their baby sister at a child-size table. He was a skinny giant hobnobbing with sprites in pinafores and pantaloons.

One warm summer day, Church and Cole climbed into a stagecoach that rattled and bounced its way into the mountains. On the way up, wild roses and black-eyed Susans gave way to twisted boughs of mountain laurel and the Christmas scent of balsam firs. Cole and Church settled into rooms at the Catskill Mountain House, a grand hotel high above the Hudson. They stayed there for five days, talking, hiking, and sketching.

At sunrise, rosy clouds of mist floated and snagged on the crags below the summit. Cole had watched the sun come up over the ruins of French castles and Roman temples, but for him nothing surpassed the magnificence of Hudson Valley skies. After a storm, he thought the clouds looked like "crimson bands interwoven with feathers of gold, fit for the wings of angels."

Above those clouds stretched an endless sky "whose color is too beautiful to have a name."

Cole showed Church how the sky gave birth to light and color, and how a painter might work to reproduce those effects. Cole felt a poet could be rather vague and still achieve great things, but a painter could not. He explained that when "the Poet describes a sky—he says—'the morning sky was beautiful / Light rosy clouds floated across the purple vault of heaven.'" The painter, by contrast, "must know what are the forms the clouds take in the morning—when light & rosy—he must know too that there are no two parts in the whole sky alike." Like people, clouds could wander, change, and vanish. Cole shared this passion for clouds with his fellow Romantics, among them Emerson, the English painters Turner and Constable, and the English poet Wordsworth.

At Cole's side, Church began to understand clouds in all their variations. There was the cumulus humilis that perched above a sun-drenched field. The sheer cirrostratus that lightly veiled the sun. Or the towering cumulonimbus that bloomed into a black rage of rain punctuated by lightning. Church sometimes grew euphoric as he sketched the sky. One evening he tried to capture "the most beautiful sunset that ever was seen." He wrote on his sketch, "This cloud rests on top of the mountain." Another day, the clouds were "broken into innumerable lines and threads [and] tufts." He tried to memorize their heft and their shadows, and the way they sometimes seemed to be lit from within.

Church's Puritan forebears had believed that the sky was the dominion of an angry God. Deadly storms or floods expressed divine judgment. On occasion, God used Satan as an agent of the weather, as the Reverend Increase Mather had told his flock in 1703: "Yea, and sometimes by Divine Permission, Evil Angels have a hand in such *Storms* and *Tempests*, as are very hurtful to men on the Earth." In the Bible, Satan was the "prince of the power of the air." Since those austere times, however, Enlightenment men such as Benjamin Franklin and Thomas Jefferson had changed the way many Americans thought about the weather, and by the early nineteenth century, the U.S. Army was leading an effort to gather the first systematic American meteorological records. Private science academies joined the crusade, with many of the most dedicated collectors of weather data based in upstate New York.

As Cole and Church watched the sky together, American meteorologists were locked in a bitter fight over the varieties and causes of storms. What caused clouds and rain? Why did tornadoes spring up, and what kept them—and whirlwinds and waterspouts—in motion? Among the contending answers, electricity and gravity increasingly pushed aside Divine Providence. Cole was deeply interested in science, finding no contradiction between it and his sense that the world was a gift from God. He believed that more than anything else it was the sky—"the soul of all scenery"—that made the world beautiful.

He set his pencil to the cream-colored pages of his sketchbook and showed Church how to use darkness to make light. To Cole, light was as variable as the growth habits of trees. Take the play of light on water. A waterfall, he thought, looked like a "gush of living light from Heaven." Diamond light sparkled off Catskill Creek in the sunshine, while solid light pooled on a quiet pond in the woods. Broken bits of light skittered across the Hudson on a windy day.

Sun, moon, lightning, fire. Spark, firefly, star. Church began to seek out the many species of light that flourished around him. A stretch of dark-green water seemed to him shot through with "needles of light" where it reflected the sky. The weathered gray flank of an empty barrel in the farmyard curved around an ink-black void. Certain leaves of an oak tree blanched in the sunlight, while others stayed hidden in shadow. Church tried to work out these effects in his sketchbook.

To get closer to the light, he went toward the sky. After his first trip with Cole to the Catskill Mountain House, he frequently hiked into the mountains, walking so many miles that he had to take his shoes to the cobbler repeatedly. Sometimes he hiked alone, sometimes with Cole; occasionally, Cole's friend Louis Legrand Noble joined them.

Noble, who soon became one of Church's dearest friends, was the new rector of St. Luke's Episcopal Church in Catskill, where Cole and his family worshipped. Noble was an energetic, witty man in his early thirties whose romantic outlook on faith and nature mirrored Cole's. One day Noble, Cole, and Church hiked up into the mountains, and on their way home, they gathered armfuls of

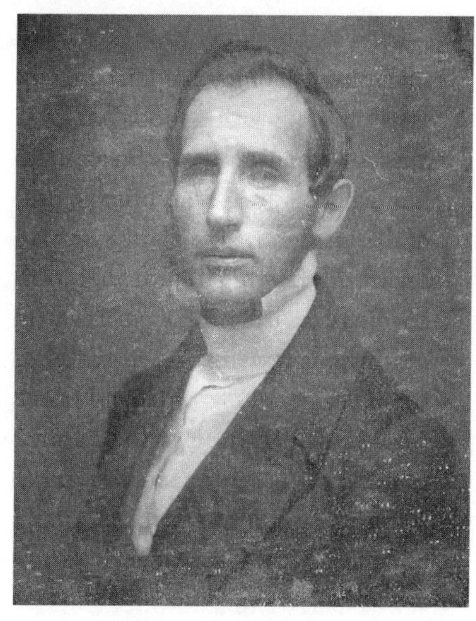

The Rev. Louis Legrand Noble

flowers. They could bring back flowers, but they couldn't bring back the colors of the sky. Instead, Church wrote tiny numbers across his penciled sunset clouds and left himself verbal clues at the corners of his sketches:

2 Bright light
3 Brightish
4 Dark, bluish thundery appearance
5 Darkish slightly warm indescribable color

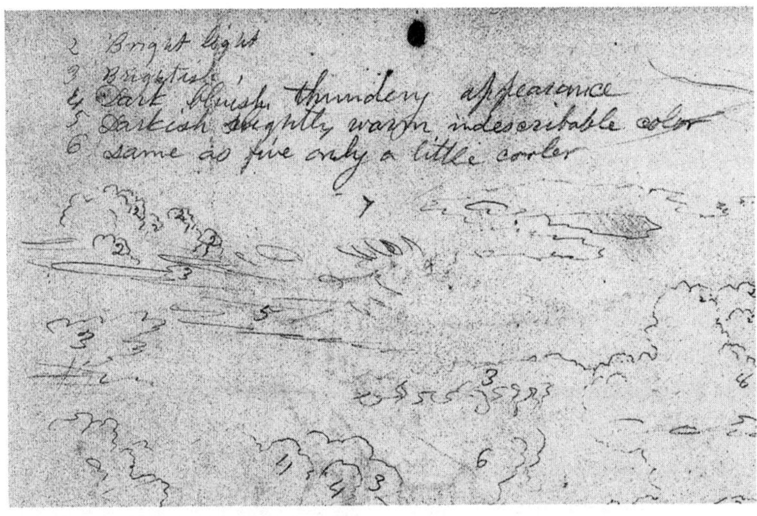

Church's color labels on a cloud study, Catskill, August 1844

AS CHURCH CAME TO KNOW Cole better, he saw that, although his teacher was often quiet and gentle, inwardly Cole was on fire. His moods were so tightly coupled with those of the natural world that at times he felt an "indescribable . . . melancholy" and at other times a searing exaltation. Celebrating the arrival of spring, Cole noted in his journal, "Regrets that it will so soon pass invade the actual enjoyment." He thought that no sight was more stunning than autumn in the hardwood forests, yet as summer slipped away, he sank into sadness.

One day when Cole was away on a painting trip, Maria wrote to him that she, Church, and Theddy had all dreamed about his imminent return. "Theddy saw you arrive in a four horse stage, with another stage following with your baggage. Mr. Church . . . saw you returning with an immence [*sic*] quantity of

Band Boxes. I too saw you, but you looked tired and care worn & said nothing to me." In Theddy's and Church's dreams, Cole came home surrounded by signs of prosperity, but Maria knew better. She knew about her husband's difficult negotiations with rich, sometimes tight-fisted patrons, and she understood how deeply he longed to paint only what *he* wished.

Working by his teacher's side that year, Church began to learn something of Cole's struggles. Even for an extraordinarily talented painter, life could be filled with as much pain as joy. Noble said of Cole that he lived on the "gloom and glory" of the world, and what made Cole most wretched was the sight of nature being destroyed. It was happening all around him. Tanneries felled hemlock trees for the tannins in their bark and vomited foul sludge into the streams, killing the fish. Railroads were being built along the Hudson from Albany to New York City; Cole's favorite woodland walk, along Catskill Creek, had recently been destroyed this way, and he was sick about it: "The copper-hearted barbarians are cutting all the trees down in the beautiful valley on which I have looked so often with a loving eye."

As he watched the destruction unfolding around him, Cole's pictures grew plaintive. He begged the world to stop and feel wonder. He wanted to tell stories with paint, to warn against what people were doing to the sublime beauty of the landscape. Before Cole, the most celebrated American painters were men such as John Trumbull, with his famous canvas of the presentation of the Declaration of Independence to the Continental Congress, or Rembrandt Peale, with his portraits of George Washington and Thomas Jefferson. But Cole found more drama and emotion in the country's landscape. "The most distinctive, and perhaps, the most impressive characteristic of American scenery is its wildness," he wrote. Cole warned of a catastrophe unfolding in the way Anglo-European settlers treated the land. He used his artistic gifts to convey ominous signs of the future: denuded bottomlands seen from atop a forested mountainside, a locomotive spewing smoke as it passed through a once-lush valley in the Catskills.

"We are still in Eden," he told a New York audience in 1835. "The wall that shuts us out of the garden is our own ignorance and folly."

COLE, AFTER WATCHING CHURCH'S PROGRESS for a while, decided the time had come for him to practice with oil paints. Church had been preparing for this moment. He had an easel, an umbrella, and pieces of paperboard on which to create quick oil sketches in the field. These plein air oil sketches would help nudge his memory back in the studio, when Cole finally let him loose on an actual canvas. Church had turpentine, paintbrushes, a palette knife, and linseed oil to mix with his dry paints. A British company had recently patented a tin paint tube with a screw top, but those tubes weren't yet widely available in the United States, so colormen still sold their paints either as dry powder or as wet pigment stored in little pigskin bladders tied tightly to keep the paint moist.

Church kept his dry paints in small bottles with cork stoppers. He had brought some colors with him from Hartford and purchased others during his stay in Catskill, including Krems white, a lead-based paint prized for its opacity, and chrome yellow, a brilliant hue that would help him capture sunsets. He also bought Paris green, an emerald pigment containing arsenic, which was currently wafting poisonous gas into the air of many wallpapered homes in the United States and Britain.

Church would need additional paint colors. From a distance the Catskill Mountains looked blue, but now he knew that they contained a thousand different hues, and also that a sky that looked entirely blue to most people might actually range from yellow to pink through many different shades of blue. Cole would be able to lend him more paints: Roman ochre, Naples yellow, raw and burnt sienna, vermilion, ultramarine, Antwerp blue. Cole's portable sketch box, in which he carried his palette, his brushes, and his paints, was a work of art in itself; he had painted a scene of Sicilian ruins on the inside of the lid.

Church's earliest efforts in oil that summer focused on humbler subjects than ancient ruins. He painted a small picture of a mullein, a stalwart wildflower that grew in the ditches and meadows around Cedar Grove. Earlier he had made beautiful pencil sketches of mulleins, and now the heft of his painted leaves showed how much he had learned from his early assignments. But the relationships of

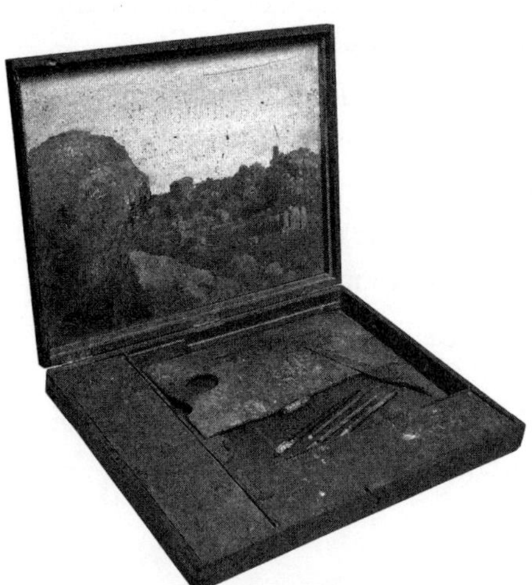

Thomas Cole's sketch box
(Courtesy of the Bronck Museum,
Greene County Historical Society)

the colors, the contrasts of light and dark, weren't right. He soon tried an elm tree in oils, with more promising results. And most exciting, he depicted water in motion—a swirl of rapids on Catskill Creek as it rushed toward him. Then he decided to paint one of Cole's favorite views: looking west from the village toward the Catskills. Church considered the way the undulating mountains glowed on their flanks, and how certain treetops in the valley caught the sun while others remained dark. He chose his colors, arrayed them on his palette, and began to work on his first real landscape painting.

AUTUMN ARRIVED, AND WITH IT a piercing new cast to the light. Haystacks hulked in the meadows, and ripe apples tumbled to the ground. The evening air around Cedar Grove pulsed with the noise of katydids. Unlike Cole, Church looked forward to winter, when he could go skating and sledding and watch fleets of iceboats racing over the frozen river. In his lodgings he set up a winter studio in a room that had good light. He invited Theddy to help him prepare his dry paints, which they did by mixing the powdery pigments with linseed oil to create smooth pastes.

Cole nurtured hopes for Theddy's future as an artist, and when Cole went down to New York to meet with patrons that winter, he asked Church to take charge of the boy's drawing lessons in his absence. Church was making progress in his own drawing; a pencil portrait he did of Cole looked so alive that his teacher might have looked up to speak at any moment.

Working from his nature sketches, that winter Church used his numbered notes and his prodigious visual memory to bring the colors of summer to canvas. By April 1845, when the Hudson had thawed and the swallows were diving through the skies at dusk, he had completed his painting. In this serene and golden scene, a child—probably Theddy— stood on the banks of Catskill Creek,

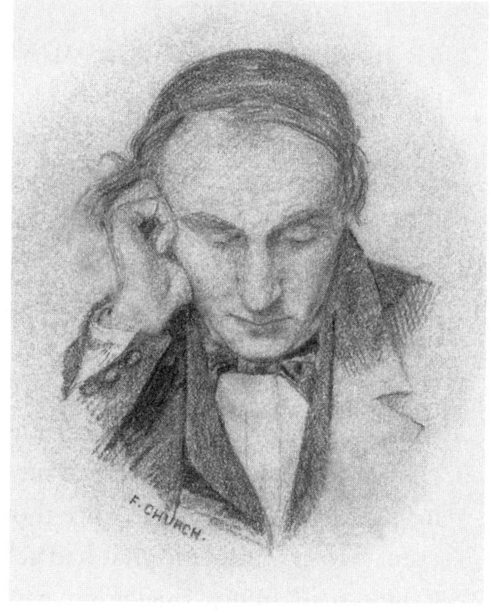

Thomas Cole, sketched by Church, c. 1845

gazing westward toward the blue-violet Catskills. Church called the painting *Twilight Among the Mountains*. More than anything else, the way he handled the light in this painting revealed how much he had learned during his ten months with Cole. Before coming to Catskill, Church had painted in dark, muddy hues, but in *Twilight Among the Mountains* he expertly juxtaposed purple and yellow—complementary colors—so that the scene shimmered and the white-hot sun seemed to burn right through the canvas.

Cole was so pleased with Church's work that he arranged for this and another of his paintings to be displayed at the National Academy of Design, an institution Cole had founded in 1825 with a group of New York painters, sculptors, architects, and engravers. The main function of the National Academy was to nurture American art through an annual spring exhibition, and being included in this show was a highly visible debut for a young artist. Noticing Church's work, the *Broadway Journal* proclaimed the arrival of a striking new talent: "These little pictures give evidence of genius in the painter."

At the age of nineteen, Church was launched. During a visit to New York City shortly after his works went on display at the National Academy, he bought painting supplies and noted confidently in his account book that they were for "my profession." He was no longer a nervous, hopeful student. He was a painter.

AROUND THIS TIME AN OMINOUS idea came rumbling at Church like the first ragged thunderclaps of a violent storm. His father, he learned, wished him to attend college. Church would face years of schoolbooks and forced camaraderie—years away from his art. He had to find a way to show his father that he didn't need polishing and credentialing by a New England college.

If landscape paintings weren't enough to persuade his father, he would prove himself as a history painter. Even the most moralizing of elders could freely embrace celebratory depictions of great events from American history. With a splendid history painting, Church could show his parents that his chosen career promised both earnings and dignity.

Church's choice of historical subject was inspired. In fact, it was probably inspired by Cole, who had once thought of painting it himself—a historical event two centuries old that had achieved an almost mythological status in Connecticut. In 1636 the Puritan pastor Thomas Hooker and his congregation had journeyed out of the Colony of Massachusetts Bay to unknown lands on the Connecticut River, where they founded the Connecticut Colony and the town of Hartford. After his apprenticeship with Cole, Church believed he could do justice to this subject, set as it was in the landscape of his childhood.

He began making preparatory sketches in the fall of 1845, and the following spring he finished *Hooker and Company Journeying through the Wilderness from Plymouth to Hartford, in 1636*. Almost half of the large canvas was devoted to a glowing sun and a clear, radiant sky, but Church was too talented at painting clouds to resist including a few dark wisps, lit on their underbellies by the sun. The rest of the canvas was given over to water, trees, and rocks, all painted with intense precision. Church rendered Hooker and his companions as graceful, tiny figures bathed here in open light and there in forest shadow. The picture fused religious fervor, British imperialism, and patriotic sentiment in a celebration of the American landscape. It went on display at the National Academy just as Church celebrated his twentieth birthday.

Church painted another politically charged canvas that year, but this time he dispensed with the literalism of *Hooker and Company* in favor of a subtler approach. He painted a small picture of the Charter Oak, a tree in Hartford that had been a gathering place for the Wampanoag people long before the seventeenth-century events that made it part of New England history. In 1687, the British governor tried to seize the Connecticut Charter in order to revoke it, but Captain Joseph Wadsworth—an ancestor of Church's benefactor Daniel Wadsworth—reportedly hid the charter in the trunk of the great oak. A century and a half later, Church had grown up just blocks away from this venerated symbol of self-government. In both his 1846 *Charter Oak* and a second version he made the following year, he included human figures clothed in red, white, and blue, and also an American elm, a widely understood symbol of liberty thanks to the tree under which American revolutionaries had gathered in Boston. With his Charter Oak paintings, Church began to experiment with the ways he could harness his passion for nature to explore ideas about the nation.

In late June, Church said goodbye to the Coles and returned to Hartford, but his bonds with his adopted family were too strong to unravel just because he was going home. That fall he wrote a long letter to Cole. "The recollection of the blue mountains is as fresh and vivid to me as the day I last saw them; neither does it require any very powerful effort of memory to see you all engaged in your respective employments." Church had good news to report: Hartford's new museum, the Wadsworth Atheneum, wanted to buy his painting of Thomas Hooker and his band of settlers. The Atheneum agreed to a price of $130, almost half the amount Church's father had paid Cole for a full year of art lessons. His father was so pleased with his son's achievement that he donated $30 for the painting's frame. Talk of college died away.

Church was grateful for the warm reception in Hartford, but he lasted only a few months in his hometown before bolting.

CHAPTER 3

"A Vast Amount of Good and Evil"

To his parents' dismay, Church left Hartford for New York—to them, an unwholesome city that thrived on greed and vice.

During an 1842 visit to New York, Charles Dickens, brutally enlightened by his time as a child laborer in a London factory, had perceived the urban misery beyond the city's resplendent galleries and mansions. "Nor must it be forgotten that New-York is a large town, and in all large towns a vast amount of good and evil is intermixed and jumbled up together."

Church, unlike Dickens, arrived in the city optimistic and unguarded. He had grown up free from want and cherished by his family, and he felt buffered from the scourges of racism, poverty, and violence that plagued the more vulnerable members of society. Church was unschooled in the ways a young man in his enviable position might be targeted. A policeman on the take might create a distraction while a confederate picked someone's pocket. A well-dressed gentleman in a saloon might send over a drink as a prelude to befriending a naïf whom he would eventually defraud. Then there was the stealthy slither of moral corruption. In the saloons and restaurants and theaters—even in a fellow artist's studio—a gentleman might find himself in the seductive company of worldly women, or of men who saw nothing wrong with an occasional excursion to a brothel.

The latest New York guidebook warned of the city's threats to young fellows like Church. "It would be folly to deny that hundreds of youth, flocking to New-York from various sections of the Union, are annually drawn into those whirl pools of vice with which a large city abounds. Educated perhaps in correct principles, but inexperienced in the wiles of those who trade in vice, the new comer rushes into the vortex, and is ruined."

It was some consolation to Church's parents that Mrs. Church's brother lived near Union Square with his family, so Frederic could commence his New York life in the protective embrace of a familiar household. His uneasy mother cautioned him from Hartford, "Let not the pleasure of the world, the vanities, fill your mind and you lose the Pearl of great price"—a place in heaven. But Church saw the city differently. To him, New York was a giant emporium filled with patrons and fellow painters. It was unthinkable that he live anywhere else.

He rented a studio on lower Broadway in the American Art-Union. Housed in a former mansion, the Art-Union offered an exhibition gallery on the ground floor and artists' studios upstairs. He unfolded his easel, arranged his brushes and palette knives, and got to work. Other artists began to drop by his studio, curious about the only protégé of the exalted Cole.

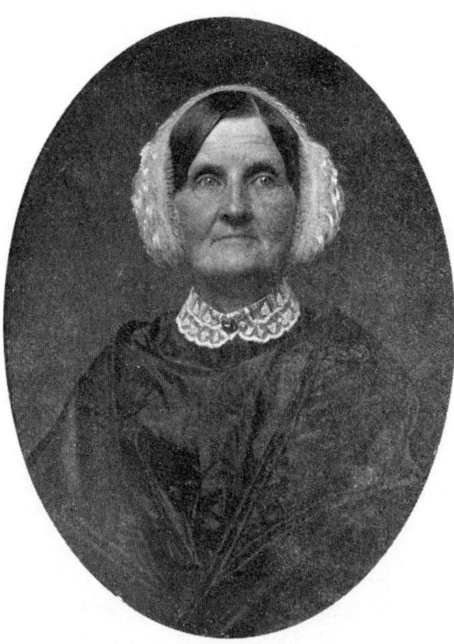

Church's mother, Eliza Church, c. 1855

Church's new acquaintances soon came to admire him for what one described as "his extreme conscientiousness, his absolute integrity, his reliability," but they flocked to his studio because he was amusing, clever, and talented. One day, Jervis McEntee, an aspiring artist from a village twenty miles south of Catskill, called at Church's studio to ask for painting lessons. McEntee was only two years younger than Church, who was surprised that anyone wanted to study with him. "I thought it was like being one of the old masters and had visions of a train of pupils," Church would reminisce two decades later. "Luckily he did not stay long or otherwise I might have spoiled a good artist."

Church and McEntee became close friends instead. McEntee showed promise as a landscape painter, but he was shy and insecure, and he appreciated

Church's unflagging kindness. McEntee marveled at the ease with which Church moved among the New York artists and patrons. "He thoroughly believes in himself and has no end of energy and ambition."

Church loved living in the world-liest city in the United States. In January 1848, he joked in a letter to Aaron Goodman, his childhood best friend, about having a medical condition that required him to indulge in New York's culinary riches. "Oyster pie helps me occasionally when beef fails but I am often obliged as a dernier resort to try pastry and even fruit. My complaint is common and generally results in expanding the figure to uncouth dimentions [*sic*] thus..." At this spot in his letter Church drew a skinny man and a fat man. "Fortunately the last symptoms have not as yet made their appearance." Church urged his friend to come to New York; before long, Goodman moved to the city, set up as a paper purveyor, and started a family.

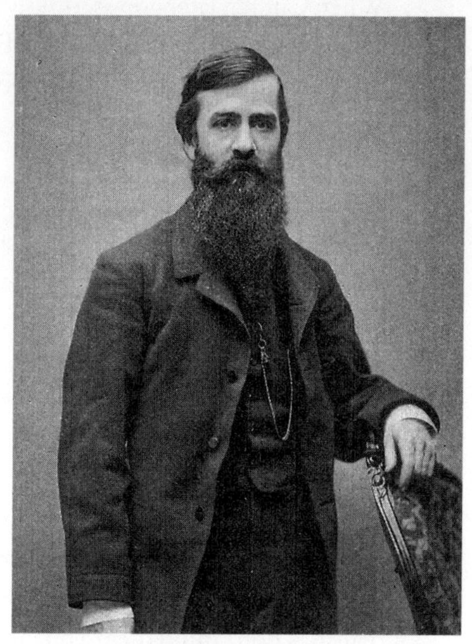

Jervis McEntee

Church spent his days painting, except Sundays, when he observed the Sabbath. After sampling different churches, he found a pastor he liked: George Washington Bethune, who preached at the Dutch Reformed Church in Brooklyn Heights. Bethune was a famously witty man who adored art, poetry, nature, and fishing. Church found Bethune's worldview so appealing that he traveled by ferry each Sunday from Manhattan to Brooklyn to hear his sermons.

Every other day of the week, Church spent long hours in his Art-Union studio. He concentrated hard, his brush pressing grooves in the pads of his fingers, the toasty smell of linseed oil floating on the air. As he painted, he shifted his weight on his feet, stepping forward, backward, and forward again in an unconscious little dance. He leaned close to the canvas and laid on a foundation of the white paint that set his skies alight. Like the sun itself, this paint was beautiful but deadly; it was lead that made it so bright and opaque. "CAUTION TO ARTISTS," the Art-Union's *Bulletin* warned Church and his fellow painters in 1849. "Mr. A. F. West, a young artist of London, died on the 23rd of May, and after a post mortem examination, a jury returned a verdict 'that the deceased died from the effects of carbonate of lead.' It appeared that he was in the habit of drawing his brushes through his lips."

When Church later grew seriously ill, doctors wondered whether to blame it on his exposure to toxic pigments. But for Church in his twenties, painting was urgent and vital, and it was impossible to fathom danger in what made him feel so alive.

IN THE AUTUMN OF 1847, Church managed to place four paintings on the crowded, coveted walls of the Art-Union gallery. One was his 1846 *Charter Oak*, and the other three were Catskills pictures: *Scene on Catskill Creek*, *Storm in the Mountains*, and *Kauterskill* [*sic*] *Clove, Catskill*. An anonymous reviewer for the *Literary World* praised this intriguing young artist, fresh from Cole's studio. "If his future career redeems the present promise, he will be one of our finest landscape painters." But the critic also had a warning: "He must beware of being merely an imitator, even of the best." Church's paintings looked too much like Cole's. They lacked originality, without which even fine technique mattered little. Church always read his reviews, including the negative ones. Years later, he would tell a journalist, "I don't mind them a bit; and after all I learn a good deal from them."

He knew better than anyone else the depth of Cole's influence on him, but he wasn't yet ready to claim his artistic independence. He had barely begun working through all that he had learned from his teacher. Every time he picked up his brush, Cole was with him in spirit. Carriages rattled down Broadway beneath the studio window; Church heard the roar of a mountain storm snapping the trees in its path. A slice of yellow sunset glared from between drab brick buildings; he saw gilded heavens above a green valley. A drunkard stumbled out of a city saloon and toward the nearest brothel; Church painted Christian, the hero of John Bunyan's 1678 religious saga, *The Pilgrim's Progress*, arriving in the Valley of the Shadow of Death.

The compositions he painted emerged from his own imagination, but they conformed closely to his teacher's driving passions. Wild nature, sublime in its ferocity; the pastoral countryside, hospitable to humans and not yet ruined by their greed; the soul's lifelong struggle between good and evil.

Church hadn't yet made his way out of Cole's shadow, but at least he was already showing his work at the two venues that counted most: the National

Academy of Design and the Art-Union gallery. The National Academy was the older and more exclusive institution; the Art-Union was a recent upstart but reached a larger audience. When Church arrived in New York, the president of the National Academy was Cole's friend Asher Brown Durand, a fifty-year-old former engraver and accomplished landscape painter. The National Academy occupied plush, mirrored rooms in a Greek Revival building at the intersection of Broadway and Leonard Street, which it rented from the New York Society Library. Readers streamed in and out of the library all day, among them Henry David Thoreau (visiting from Massachusetts) and Herman Melville (who borrowed a book on whaling). In the evenings, men and women settled into the building's large auditorium for lectures and performances—an abolitionist lecture one night, a minstrel show another. In 1842, Ralph Waldo Emerson delivered a speech there, with Walt Whitman in the audience.

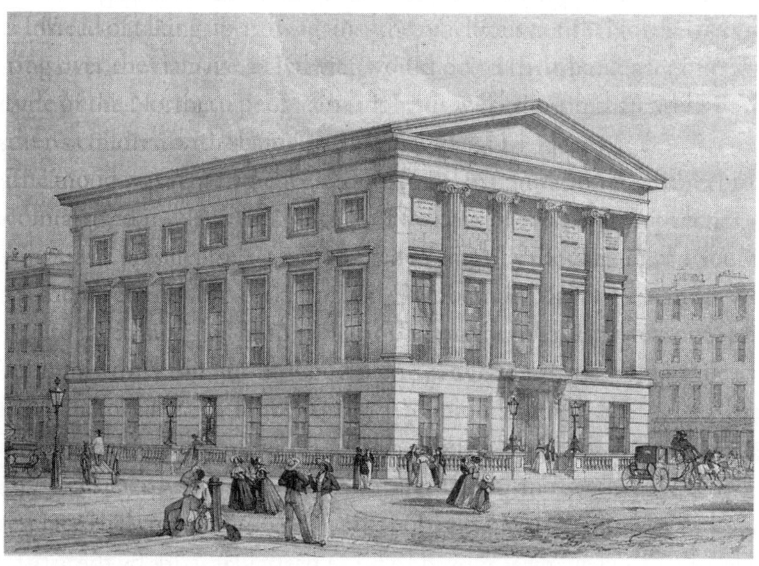

The National Academy of Design rented the top
floor of the New York Society Library.

The opening of the National Academy's spring exhibition was one of the great events of the New York social season. A steep twenty-five-cent admission fee ensured that the exhibition was what one guidebook called "a very fashionable place of genteel resort." But before the showcase opened to the public, a small group of artists chosen from among the academy officials allocated wall space to the accepted pictures. These men made up what was at first called the Committee of Arrangements and later the Hanging Committee. The men were the source of great anxiety and bitter jokes among the artists. When the artists were eventually granted entry, they shuffled around searching for their works. A critic for the *Broadway Journal*, a monthly cultural magazine coedited by Edgar Allan Poe, tried to imagine what they must feel: "That modest little canvass [*sic*], bearing upon its surface a remote likeness of a kitten ... insignificant as it may appear to you or me, is an object of immense importance to somebody ... and you may be sure that the obscure position in which the merciless 'hangers' have placed his *chef d'oeuvre* has caused him a cruel palpitation of the heart." Other unlucky artists found their work hugging the crown molding or "on a level with one's boots, as though spectators carried their eyes in their ankles."

For two decades the National Academy had been anointing new artists, and in the process it had made New York an important center of the American art world, along with Boston and Philadelphia. Church intended to keep submitting work there, but he also turned to the Art-Union for a more regular source of income. The Art-Union had been created in 1839 as an alternative to the National Academy by a group of merchants, bankers, lawyers, and editors. Their ingenious scheme was to link the New York art world to a national audience of subscribers, each of whom paid $5 annually, in return for which he or she was guaranteed to receive an engraved copy of a painting chosen by an Art-Union committee. Subscribers' names were also entered in a drawing to win one of hundreds of paintings in an annual Christmas Eve lottery that drew thousands of attendees. The grand prize for 1848 was all four paintings of Cole's celebrated series *The Voyage of Life*.

The money raised through the annual subscriptions gave the Art-Union managers a reliable way to pay artists. At the National Academy, an artist made money only if a viewer was moved to buy a particular work by the artist, but the Art-Union bought works *before* they went on display. Church's primary income in his early years in New York came from the sale of about two dozen paintings to the Art-Union. Having grown up watching his father's commercial dealings, he was unafraid to negotiate with the Art-Union managers for higher fees. "Gentlemen," he wrote in one terse note, "I am sorry that I cannot accept your offer for my picture of the 'Plague of Darkness.' $500.00 with the frame is as low as I wish to sell it for."

The pictures and sculptures purchased by the Art-Union were displayed at a gallery on the ground floor of its building at 497 Broadway. Unlike the National Academy, the place was free to the public until late in the evening, and it drew hundreds of thousands of visitors each year. Even the most established National Academy artists, among them Cole and Durand, overcame any qualms about selling to the Art-Union. The economic security it offered helped offset the fickleness of wealthy patrons, who occasionally died before paying for commissioned work.

Young and recently arrived artists vied to rent studios at the lively Art-Union. Church moved in just as a lavish new gallery more than one hundred feet long was opening on the ground floor. While he painted in his studio, the gallery downstairs hummed with visitors. The tableau changed by the hour. In the morning, businessmen dropped by on the way from their art-filled homes on Union Square and Washington Square to their downtown offices. Sometimes a few "b'hoys" strolled in—stylish working-class men from the Bowery and Five Points neighborhoods. By midday, finely dressed women in gloves and bonnets were gliding through the gallery, and the afternoons brought swarms of children chaperoned by nursemaids and teachers. It was a tableau tailor-made for the sensibilities of Walt Whitman—who occasionally joined the throng.

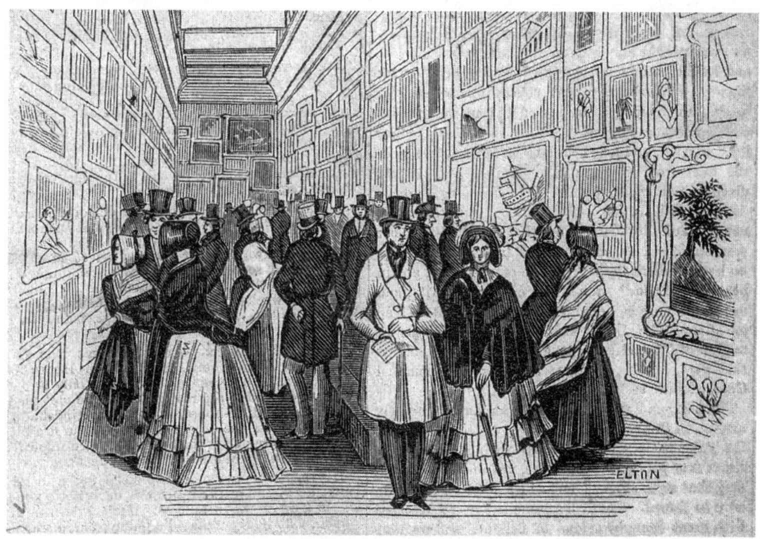

The gallery at the Art-Union, downstairs from Church's studio

Democracy created opportunity. It threw people together and blurred old social boundaries. The bustle and freedom of the Art-Union enticed lovers, who arranged to meet among the crowds for assignations. Amorous behavior became such a problem that the management removed the sofas for a time.

THE MUSIC TO WHICH CHURCH painted, he told Goodman, was "the roar of Chariot Wheels over Cobble Stones." When Church stepped out onto Broadway, hoofbeats ricocheted around the canyon of hotels, stores, and apartment buildings. Newsboys yelled, dogs barked, and shopkeepers called out as he passed beneath awnings that sheltered crates of oysters from the harbor and vegetables from the farms up the island. Shop windows shimmered with rows of apothecary bottles and bolts of silk. Far below Church's feet, fresh water from upstate rushed through buried pipes stretching from the new reservoir at Forty-Second Street to a fountain at City Hall Park. Along the way it burbled into bathtubs and recently installed toilets in the fancier townhouses and hotels.

On rainy days, the low clouds were stained yellow with coal smoke, but on bright, breezy days, banners of boarding-house laundry crisped on lines slung across the alleyways. The white billows lazing in the sky were the city cousins of the clouds that Church had sketched upstate. Forests had once covered the hilly island the native Lenape people had called Mannahatta, but most of the Lenape had been killed or displaced, and there was no longer any dense forest on the island—just an occasional grove where farmers hadn't cleared the land for crops. In the lower quarter of Manhattan, where Church spent most of his time, there weren't many trees at all.

Most of the city's buildings were no more than six stories high, for fear of collapsed walls, and of flames that might rage beyond the reach of fire hoses. The spire of Trinity Church, on Broadway just south of Barnum's Museum, was the tallest structure for miles. Although Trinity towered over its neighbors, its message of Christian godliness was drowned out by the shrill din of commerce, manufacturing, and entertainment. Giant circus-sign letters painted on brick and brownstone blared about top hats, saloons, bowling alleys, and daguerreotypes.

Trains rolled in and out of the Lower Manhattan terminals day and night, sometimes maiming or killing animals or people as they tried to cross the tracks. The central post office was open twenty-four hours and processed tens

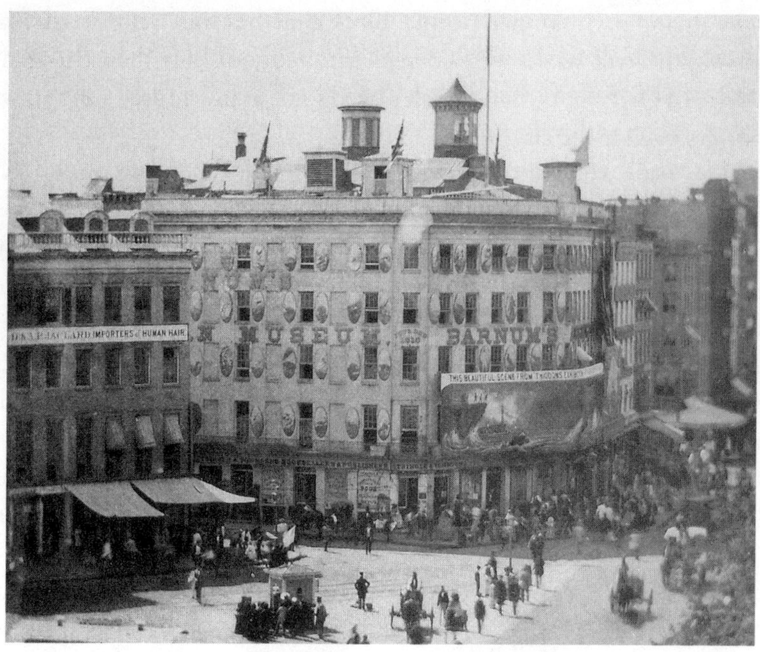

Barnum's American Museum

of thousands of letters and newspapers each day. When dusk fell, men came to light the gas lamps along Broadway and Fifth Avenue. The side streets remained "dark as grave vaults," in the words of a contemporary novelist, giving cover to evildoers. But even daylight didn't always protect the innocent.

Some of the city's worst treatment was reserved for African Americans. White men were allowed to vote regardless of their economic status; free Black men had to own substantial property, a path closed off to most of them by educational inequality and bigoted banks, courts, landlords, and employers. When Church moved to New York City in 1847, slavery had been illegal there for two decades, but Black people suffered near-constant physical and psychological aggression.

Southerners were allowed to hunt down runaways from slavery who had made it to New York City, emboldening kidnappers who captured free Black men on the streets and sold them into bondage. Barnum purchased an elderly enslaved woman and put her on display at his museum as George Washington's 161-year-old nurse. Phrenologists on Broadway examined the skulls of white people and came up with absurd theories about why they were superior to animals and dark-skinned people. Black churches were vandalized. Black parents in difficult straits were coerced into relinquishing their children to the Colored Orphan Asylum, which placed some as indentured servants with employers outside the city.

In May 1849, when the writer and orator Frederick Douglass came to New York for a meeting of the American Anti-Slavery Society, he strolled down Broadway flanked by two white Englishwomen. People stared angrily at the sight of a Black man behaving as though on equal footing with the white women, and several men assaulted them. Douglass wrote of the incident in his antislavery newspaper, *The North Star*. "Persons who at a distance of thirty or forty yards, appeared the very pictures of health, were found, on a nearer approach, most horribly cut and marred" by racism.

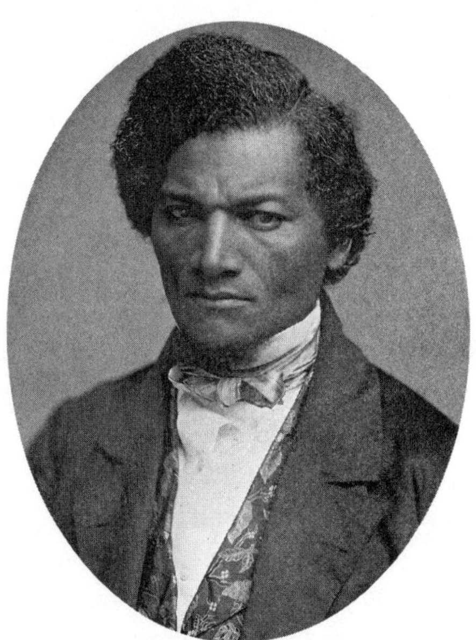

Frederick Douglass, c. 1847

People also clashed over labor relations, class status, ethnicity, immigration, and the place of women. Tens of thousands of immigrants, among them exhausted refugees from Europe's failed crops and failed revolutions, arrived on steamships each year, endlessly shifting the composition of the city and the nation.

But what *was* the nation? When Church arrived in New York, the United States was on the verge of victory in the Mexican War. The treaty Congress ratified in May 1848 expanded U.S. territory by more than 525,000 square miles and ignited a struggle over the legality of slavery in these vast new holdings. Meanwhile, a generation of West Point men were coming home from the war with invaluable battlefield experience, among them talented soldiers such as Ulysses S. Grant and Robert E. Lee—men who would be ready to lead the United States in its next foreign conflict. The Mexican War had given Henry David Thoreau in Massachusetts the chance to practice a different kind of maneuver. He had gone to jail for civil disobedience after refusing to pay taxes in support of a government that might expand the reach of slavery. For Thoreau, love of country meant agitating for a United States unstained by slavery.

Church had grown up among New Englanders who embraced this kind of patriotism, and in New York he gravitated toward such people. But there was another vision of the nation under discussion in Church's New York circles. Some argued that the United States would realize its true greatness only when its boundaries stretched to the Pacific Ocean, fulfilling the nation's "manifest destiny," a concept championed by John O'Sullivan, editor of the influential *Democratic Review*. For those who subscribed to this doctrine, patriotism meant supporting national expansion.

Church didn't enjoy talking or writing about politics. He could never harangue another man to think or vote a certain way. He wasn't ever going to run for office or deliver a political speech. Yet he had already painted pictures on overtly political themes, and while he assured his friend Goodman in 1848 that he wasn't thinking about what he called the "approaching political crisis" over slavery, his mention of it suggested that the opposite was true. Church could tell himself and his friends that he wasn't interested in politics, but he couldn't help tinkering in his pictures with ideas about the nation—especially about the land and the way people lived, farmed, and built on it.

For now, however, he was more concerned with the state of the New York art world. Early in 1848, after he had been in the city for about a year, he concluded that New York's "painters need a good stirring up," as he told Goodman.

One National Academy official would later criticize what happened next as disruption for its own sake, so typical of newcomers and the young. Church was both.

CHAPTER 4

"Blessed Are the Dead"

Church waited in his studio. It was January 19, 1848, and the mercury had been stuck in the low twenties all day. On the street below—Broadway—the pale roofs of omnibuses slid through the darkness behind teams of shivering horses, men and boys swaying on the back steps like undisciplined footmen. Now and then an omnibus stopped and disgorged a few passengers, who commenced a strange series of stops and starts as they aimed for the safety of the sidewalk. There they melted into throngs of pedestrians heading home for supper or out to clubs, restaurants, and theaters. The crystallized breath of beasts and people hung in the air. Faces glowed briefly in gaslight, faded, then shone once more under the next lamp before vanishing into side streets or houses. At the Art-Union building, a fanlight of red glass spilled a gash of garish color down the front steps.

Church was excited about his evening's plans. His parents, had they known, would have been horrified. In Hartford, they were praying that he would be able to resist the city's temptations and focus on his work. The restaurants and shops and theaters teemed with offerings that drew bills from a man's pocket like filings to a magnet. His father had already scolded Church for running out of funds only weeks after arriving in New York. "I have no money to spare for this unprofitable business," Mr. Church snapped.

Mrs. Church tried a different approach, appealing to her son's conscience: "If you have a habit of industry and economy, with your health you will not only take care of yourself, but you will be able to taste of the luxury of doing for others—which I know you would if you were able, for I do not think you selfish by any means." But wastefulness was a minor transgression compared to what Church was contemplating. He was a co-conspirator in a plan that, should it succeed, would set him on what his parents considered a path to damnation.

Men began to appear at the threshold of Church's studio. Shaking off the cold, they greeted one another in the rich accents of the city: Irish, English, German, Yankee. By the time the meeting started, about forty men had crowded into the room. Most were older than Church—some by a few years, others by more than a decade. It would have been hard for any of them to be younger; he was only twenty-one years old. He saw with satisfaction that many artists of what he considered the "better class" had joined his cause.

Church was no Walt Whitman. He would never dream of clambering up on the front of a hackney cab to consort with the driver, much less of publicly defending prostitutes as "good-hearted" women. But he had decided that there was more artistic talent to be discovered and nurtured among Americans than the National Academy could or would embrace. The doors could safely be opened to more aspirants, as long as they evinced commitment, aptitude, and respectability. Hadn't he himself been such an aspirant a few years earlier? His passion for painting had come close to dying a slow death in a Hartford insurance company or law office. Only the opportunity to take art classes, first in his hometown and then with Cole, had saved him from professional misery.

When the meeting came to order, it wasn't Church who spoke. His preference would always be to organize things quietly and competently and then fade into the background while flashier men did the talking. A fierce-looking painter in his mid-thirties stepped forward: Tompkins Harrison Matteson. The son of an upstate sheriff, Matteson had taken his first art lessons as a boy from a Native American man in jail on a murder charge. He reminded the men around him why they had all braved this bitter January night to assemble at Church's studio. They needed bodies—bodies that could stay as still as death but weren't actually dead.

As Matteson spoke, a faint whiff of betrayal wafted through the room. They had gathered at the Art-Union, but a number of the older men were elected fellows of the National Academy, which already offered life-drawing classes.

Several evenings a week, a small group of students who had passed a difficult drawing test—some said an arbitrary and unfair test—were admitted to a room where gaslight played over the skin of a model imported from licentious Paris. This handful of initiates thereby gained invaluable practice sketching the human body. They, and only they, were authorized by the National Academy to gaze at naked flesh long and often enough to master on paper the soft swell of a buttock or a breast. These fortunate few were thus enabled to paint portraits, history scenes, and even populated landscapes with the help of the anatomical knowledge that endowed the greatest European works with life. All the other artists were stuck at their easels speculating about what lay beneath the clothes of their subjects.

There were many other places in New York to see naked bodies, but even the venues that tried hard to appear respectable drew censure. In 1847, a troupe called Dr. Collyer's Model Artistes had begun performing tableaux based on paintings, sculptures, and books. The audience was heavily male. Women were not allowed to buy tickets for themselves, and few thought of attending even with their husbands. Among the most popular of these performances was a shackled and nearly naked woman posing as *The Greek Slave*, a famous contemporary sculpture by the American sculptor Hiram Powers. Another scene that cheered male audiences was "Adam's First Sight of Eve."

These performances were racy but not illegal, except on Sundays. The month before the meeting at Church's studio, police had raided a Sunday performance at a saloon near the Art-Union, and the panicked actors had had to scramble for their clothing before they were paraded to the police station, a crowd trailing them. "Arrest of the Model Artists—Rich Scene in Broadway," the *National Police Gazette* reported.

Nudity was more scandalous onstage than in an artwork, but sometimes only just. After the Art-Union commissioned sculptor Henry Kirke Brown to create a work on a Native American subject, he presented the managers with a bronze sculpture of a nude young hunter whose hands were busy with a bow and arrow, leaving his penis exposed. A critic complained, "The bronze is so near to the natural copper of the skin, that there is nothing to modify the complete disgust with which its undisguised nakedness must be looked upon." When they made a set of copies for sale, the gallery managers pasted fig leaves made of tinfoil over the phalluses, but they kept falling off.

Powers's marble sculpture *The Greek Slave* could be put on display in 1847 at the eminently respectable National Academy only because one of the enslaved woman's hands blocked the prime view. This was not modesty enough for a local Baptist newspaper, which blasted the work as "an indecent sculpture" that should be sealed in a room with no doors or windows. In such a climate, it was difficult to persuade any Americans to sit as nude models for artists, unless they were a "low" sort of person, which meant that art students risked being thrust into contact with prostitutes. Yet American art would never reach the world stage if its artists remained unpracticed at drawing the human body, and few had access to life-drawing classes.

The men gathered in Church's studio intended to rectify the situation. They agreed that a small committee would approach the academy to ask for the use of a classroom. It was a bold idea, given that their proposal challenged the primacy of the academy—unless you believed that reasonable men could agree that the greater good mattered more than institutional squabbles. A week later, the artists reconvened in Church's studio to hear that the academy's directors had generously yielded to the groundswell of interest in a new drawing class and would indeed provide a room. On January 27, an editorial praising the artists' initiative and the academy's largesse ran in the *New York Evening Express*, although the piece included a reference to the recent scandals involving nude tableaux performers.

CHURCH'S FATHER WAS PERUSING a newspaper at home in Hartford when his wife heard him cry out. He had just encountered his son's name in the *New-York Daily Tribune*, named as the host of a meeting about nude drawing. His mother composed a sober warning to her son: "Have you thought what effect such a course as you purpose will have upon your character and morals and those associated with you? . . . Your uncle wrote you that the eyes of the world were upon you, but I will say that the eyes of a pure and holy God are upon you. And do you realize that you are his property under his moral government, indebted to him for the genius and talent you possess, and must appear at last before him to give an account how you employed them and how you have influenced others?"

His parents clearly didn't understand. Even if Church painted only saints and angels, he would need to study the human body, both clothed and naked. How could there be anything ugly or sinful about depicting God's own cre-ation? Even the devout Cole had taken life-drawing classes in Florence, which had formed the basis for a great religious painting called *The Angel Appearing to the Shepherds* and had shaped his painting of human and divine figures ever since. Although Cole was Episcopalian—not of Puritan stock like the Churches—he was as deeply Christian a person as Mr. and Mrs. Church could ever hope to meet this side of the grave. In his quest to master the human form, Church was simply following his teacher's example. He had already completed several paintings on religious themes featuring human figures, and he had more in mind. He would also need to be able to paint people convincingly in historical scenes and even in some of his landscapes. If this meant defying his parents, so be it. He ignored both public opinion and parental censure, and on January 31, twenty-eight male artists attended the first session of the new life-drawing course in a borrowed classroom at the academy.

THAT SAME NIGHT, IT SNOWED heavily upstate. At Cedar Grove, Cole awoke the next day—his forty-seventh birthday—to a bright sky that scattered sunlight across the snow, which reflected it back into the shimmering air. Across the yard from the main house, Cole's new painting studio beckoned. The large, airy space had windows twice as tall as a man. Noble later recalled that when a friend called there to see how a picture was coming along, Cole opened the door holding his palette and brush, his face flushed, and exclaimed, "Oh, go away!" The new studio was a haven in a period of relentless loss and strain. Uncle Sandy, the jovial patriarch of Cedar Grove, had died in the summer of 1846, leaving Cole to shoulder responsibility for the entire household. The following April, Maria had given birth to a girl, who had died almost immediately. By early February 1848, Maria was pregnant again, but Cole was exhausted and ill.

He minimized his condition to himself and his family, blaming it on a lack of exercise. The winter had been brutally cold; a few weeks before his birthday, the temperature dove to thirteen below zero. Cole was pushing hard to complete a series of paintings called *The Cross and the World*, inspired by John Bunyan's *The Pilgrim's Progress*. This new series depicted two young men taking divergent paths. One of the men would choose the path of the Cross and spend his life seeking salvation; Cole had nearly finished the painting of this man's arrival at the glowing edge of heaven. The other man would choose the path of the World and spend his life seeking riches and pleasure. Cole had completed an oil study for the last painting of this man, which would show him stranded in a bleak, empty landscape. The sky was eclipsed by a black wall of cloud from which a winged death's-head grinned down at the doomed pilgrim.

On the Sunday after his birthday, Cole went with his family to the morning service at St. Luke's, about a mile down the hill from Cedar Grove, in the heart of Catskill. After the service, he felt shaky and depleted. By late evening, he was suffering from a "bilious attack"—fever, headache, intestinal distress. The doctor was summoned. After this Cole seemed to improve briefly, but then his breathing grew painful and labored. He asked that Theddy, Mary, and Emily be brought to his bedside. When four-year-old Emily saw him, she blurted, "Pa, you're sick and you'll never get well, you'll never get well." Cole gently instructed the children to be good to their mother.

Five days after he had taken to his bed, he let his friend Noble know that he wished to receive the last rites. Noble prepared the bread and wine and intoned the mournful phrases of the Communion of the Sick. When he had finished, Cole said, "I want to be quiet." After a brief silence, he died.

The news reached New York City by telegram the next day. The funeral was to be held in Catskill on February 15. With steamboat travel on the Hudson River blocked by ice, Cole's friends among the New York artists began planning their own memorials in the city.

In Catskill on the afternoon of February 15, Cole's body was placed in a coffin and driven to St. Luke's. Maria and the children followed, accompanied by other family members and friends. The sun was shining brilliantly again, the light refracted by the white fields and frozen river. Out of grief and respect, much of Catskill had suspended the business of daily life, and the coffin rolled past empty shops. The villagers crowded into St. Luke's, a building Cole himself had designed. They jammed the pews on the floor and overflowed into the balcony. Maria and the children filed into the front pew, and Cole's dog sat beside the coffin.

The bell began tolling, but the sound of each stroke died quickly on the wind. "Blessed are the dead," the choir sang. Noble stepped forward to the black-draped altar and looked out at Cole's family, friends, and neighbors. He spoke the blunt words of his faith. "The Lord gave, and the Lord hath taken away."

The funeral procession traveled slowly up the steep hill out of the village, passing Cedar Grove before coming to a halt in a snow-covered field. There, at the family vault, in view of the mountains, Noble led the burial service.

Afterward, Maria walked through the rooms of Cedar Grove, contemplating life without her husband. The coming months and years would be made more wretched by poverty; she had no source of income beyond the meager earnings of the farm. Theddy, her only son, was still too young to work. As she moved through the house, she saw her husband's pictures on the walls around her. He lived on in the flesh and bone of color and canvas. Out in his studio, a painting of a stone cross lit by a wilderness sunset awaited his finishing brushstrokes.

CHURCH, HAVING ENJOYED ALMOST TWO years in New York as the confident young protégé of a famous mentor, faced his first profound personal loss. He would never again talk with Cole about light and clouds and water, never get to show him his work. One of Church's uncles, upon seeing the obituary in the paper, wrote a sympathetic note to Church's father. "I noticed the death of Mr. Cole—I think Frederic will feel that very much." Mrs. Church held Cole up to her son as a moral exemplar: "Do you sometimes ask yourself—'Am I prepared to follow; am I treading in his footsteps so far as he followed Christ and duty?'" Church might be young, his mother told him, but death could take the young, too.

Cole's absence from the world felt unnatural. Some of his friends and family reflected that the landscapes he had loved must feel as desolate as they did. To Cole's friend William Cullen Bryant, publisher of *The Evening Post* and a noted poet, it was as if the highest peak in the Catskills had simply disappeared overnight.

The National Academy convened a special meeting at which its president, Asher Brown Durand, spoke feelingly of his late friend. With Cole's death, Durand had become the new dean of American landscape painters. He was liked and respected by the best artists of the rising generation, among them Church, John Frederick Kensett, Jasper Cropsey, George Inness, Sanford Gifford, Jervis McEntee, and Worthington Whittredge. Durand's exquisite paintings of woodland scenes from the Catskills and Adirondacks graced the walls of discerning collectors from Boston to Washington, DC, and engravings of his canvases hung in thousands of humbler American homes, thanks to Art-Union subscriptions. Cole might have been a more imaginative and original painter than Durand, but Durand was a patient administrator as well as an accomplished artist, and in the coming years he would preside as elder statesman of the New York art world.

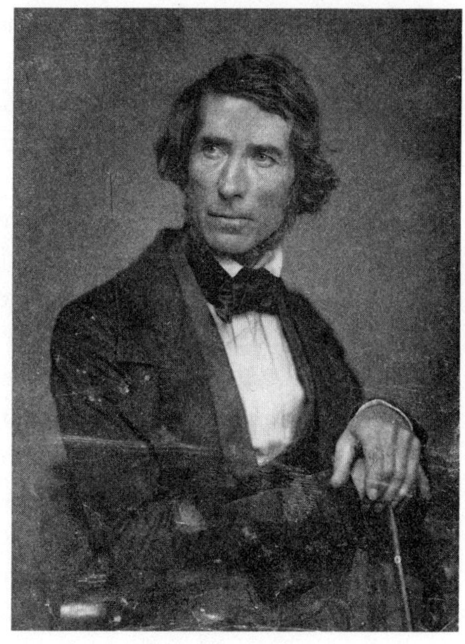

Asher Brown Durand,
by Mathew Brady, c. 1848

As they mourned Cole, the New York artists agreed that his life's work should be assembled before the public as soon as possible. The National Academy and the Art-Union pledged to collaborate on a memorial exhibition, with the proceeds going to Maria Cole and her family. The Art-Union volunteered to host the show, which presented eighty-three of Cole's paintings, while ten more—including his five-part *Course of Empire*—went on view at another New York gallery. In a typically generous gesture, Durand took the lead organizing role.

The Art-Union gallery became a shrine to Cole. A handsome oil portrait of him by Durand hung in the center of one long wall. For weeks beginning in late March, the Art-Union gallery was filled with Cole's admirers, Church among them. Walking through the exhibition was like watching his ideas shape-shift from his first Catskills rambles in the 1820s until the recent winter day when he had cleaned his brushes for the last time. Maria Cole had permitted her husband's unfinished series *The Cross and the World* to be included, giving the public an intimate look at the spiritual preoccupations of his final months.

Observing the crowds in the Art-Union gallery as they examined Cole's paintings, Church saw firsthand how powerfully a great painter could shape the way people viewed the world. His sorrow began to mingle with something like excitement. While visitors continued to throng the Cole show, upstairs Church began working on a new painting. He touched the tips of his brushes to the wet pigments, transferring dabs of pure colors to bare spots on his palette and swirling them together until he had the subtler shades he wanted: soft green, chalky violet, cool blue, pink gold.

By the end of April, when the dirty snow had melted and the earliest trees were starting to leaf out, his picture was finished. On May 4, a warm day of the sort that saw women dressing in muslin after a long season of wool, Church turned twenty-two. By coincidence, the National Academy had chosen this day for a public memorial service in honor of Cole. At the Church of the Messiah on Broadway, William Cullen Bryant stood before the members of the academy and delivered a funeral oration. He asked his listeners to imagine "a sound of lament for him who we have lost in the voices of the streams and in the sighs of the wind among the groves, and an aspect of sorrow in earth's solitary places." The deep friendship between Bryant and Cole, forged by their shared love of nature, would be immortalized by Durand the following year in his most famous picture, *Kindred Spirits*.

A week later, Church welcomed the public to his studio to see his new painting. *To the Memory of Cole* depicted his mentor's favorite view of the

Catskill Mountains, with Catskill Creek meandering through the valley in the middle distance; some of Cole's works in the gallery downstairs featured the same view. At the center of Church's canvas stood a pale stone cross, bathed in a splash of sunlight and entwined with climbing roses in full bloom. Above the mountains, Church had painted a layered, complex sky, at once mournful and celebratory. The low-slung clouds blanketing the familiar peaks were dark on their undersides but copper-colored on top. Higher still, white cumuli swelled into the blue sky, silhouetted against a pale mass of cloud that floated heavenward as if it were Cole's spirit.

In the lower left, Church had painted a large tree stump, a symbol that a monumental life had been cut short. Near the bottom right, he had signed and dated the painting on the face of a rock, at the base of which a spring flowed out of the ground. A spring promised life and renewal—as did a talented young protégé. Church was boldly and confidently declaring his intention to become the nation's next great landscape painter.

Not long after Church gave the public its first glimpse of his tribute to Cole, the *New-York Daily Tribune* published a sonnet about the painting. The closing couplet anointed Church as Cole's heir: "Nor is thy dream to COLE'S renown alone: / It prophesies, O gifted CHURCH, thine own."

Church was also causing excitement that spring at the National Academy, where he had two more paintings on display at the annual show. A critic raved about Church's *The River of the Water of Life*, "This is a glorious landscape; one of the best, if not the very best, in the collection, and the artist is gradually following in the footsteps of Cole."

Church's other submission, *View near Stockbridge, Mass.*, also drew praise, although one critic joked that the cow in the foreground did not look as if it could fit inside the barn down the hill. Church hadn't actually painted a barn at all; it was a house, complete with smoke wafting from the chimney. But this was the kind of clever insult with which critics often spiced their reviews. The general opinion was that Church was hugely gifted, a judgment echoed in his election that month as an associate member of the National Academy—the first step on the way to becoming a full academician and an extraordinary honor for so young a painter.

The question Church faced now was how to use what he had learned from Cole to move beyond him. He would become Cole's heir not by imitating him, but by creating his own visual language and exploring his own grand themes. Cole had earned renown for harnessing Hudson Valley landscapes to depict the struggles of civilizations and the human soul. What landscapes, Church asked himself, should *he* seek out? What struggles would be *his*—to witness, to endure, and to paint?

CHURCH WASN'T THE SORT TO indulge in sorrow. He was so naturally cheerful that one day when he ran into a friend from Hartford who was depressed and homesick, Church laughed and insisted his friend would be over it by the next week. To his childhood friend Aaron Goodman, Church wrote blithely of the encounter, "Oh how comical people appear under the influence of the Blues." The best approach, in his view, was to get on with life. That summer, while his tribute to Cole was still on display, he left the noise and grime of the city in search of landscapes to sketch in pencil and oils, having "right good fun" on the way, as he wrote Goodman.

All over New York, artists' studios stood empty in the baking summer heat, their occupants having scattered across the countryside to unpack easels next to waterfalls or in shady woodlands. Durand had fled to the Adirondacks and the Catskills with fellow painters John Frederick Kensett and John William Casilear. Thomas Addison Richards was visiting Lake George and Lake Champlain, while George Inness had gone to Peekskill, on the eastern shore of the Hudson about forty miles north of the city.

Church chose to travel hundreds of miles by railroad and stagecoach to reach the Green Mountains of Vermont. From the town of Rutland, he crowed to Goodman, "All my hopes have been realized as far as the scenery is concerned." After the long winter in the city, he reveled in the outdoors. He haunted the borders between human settlements and the forested mountains, collecting ideas for his next studio paintings. He sketched a cornfield, a kitchen garden, farmhouses, and wooden fences, recording placid, optimistic images of a New England where farmers, having tamed the wilderness, lived and worked against backdrops of stunning beauty.

When Church wasn't sketching, he was fishing. He wrote from Vermont to Theddy Cole, "I sometimes go to the mountain streams, and fish for trout, which you know are the best of all fishes, and catch a great many at a time, enough to make a nice breakfast for a dozen people perhaps." Church's letter to ten-year-old Theddy was dated exactly seven months after Cole's death. As always with his young friend, he tried to include useful guidance, although he was tactless this time: "As you will never see your kind father while you live you ought to remember and make the most of all the good advice that he has given you."

Church promised to visit in a few weeks. In the meantime, he urged Theddy to practice drawing every day and included one of his Vermont sketches as a gift.

Reaching Cedar Grove in October, Church found that Maria had given birth a few weeks earlier to a baby she had named Thomas Cole Jr. Although the boy was healthy, life at Cedar Grove was sad and strained without Cole. Theddy was trying to grow up fast so he could take his father's place as chief breadwinner.

The month of Church's return to Catskill was marked by long stretches of clear, cool weather. The trees were tinged with scarlet and yellow. One day Church walked across the lane into the field, where he stopped and turned to look back. He sketched the scene before him: the low stone walls along the lane, the yellow house with its gracious veranda, the cupola and weather vane atop the privy, and Cole's elegant studio. Maria had left its interior alone; it seemed Cole had simply stepped out for lunch. An unfinished picture was on the easel, and the brushes he had been using still lay nearby. Sketches were scattered around the floor and propped against the walls.

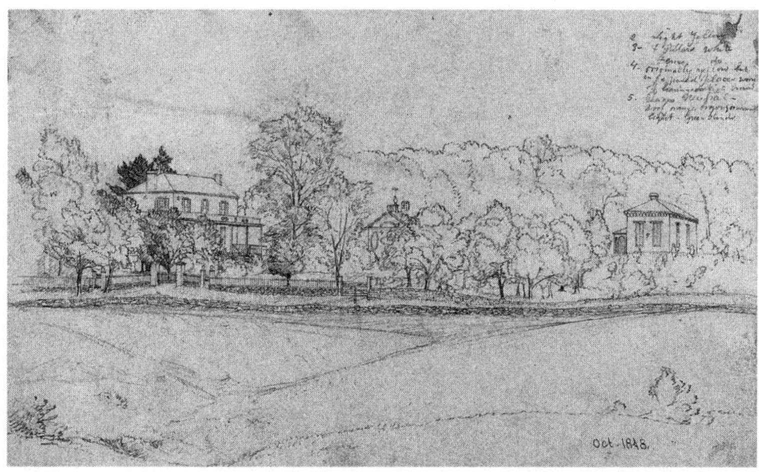

Cedar Grove sketched by Church, October 1848

Church returned to New York and resumed painting. His mentor was gone, but the light he had taught Church to see still flooded the sky and gave life to the land.

Church would never stop looking for that light.

CHAPTER 5

"A Sensation Wherever I Go"

Bright white clouds floated in the summer sky, dappling the thick crowns of the trees with shadow and playing over the glassy river. A wagon stood in the shorn field. One man worked nearby, while another balanced atop the wagon, smoothing out a slippery heap of hay. The white of their shirts was echoed by that of a steeple rising from the treetops beyond. In the farthest distance, a solitary, red-cliffed hill arced against the sky like the rounded back of a sleeping animal.

Church had worked in this Connecticut field on a July day in 1848, sketching the elms and willows and apple trees and memorizing the ruddy tints of the cliffs. In the city the following winter, he turned his carefully numbered and labeled pencil sketch into a painting whose effect was somehow both tranquil and majestic. A summer day gleamed forth from Church's easel, as if he had invented a scientific method for boxing up sunlight and releasing it indoors.

Church's picture, *West Rock, New Haven*, opened a new epoch in his work and life. The painting honored Cole's twin passions—grand moral questions and fidelity to nature—but from this picture forward, Church's technical prowess would serve his own vision, not his teacher's.

West Rock was a natural landmark with a strong historical identity for New Englanders. In the 1660s, two British exiles, signatories to the death warrant of Charles I, had fled to the American colonies to escape execution. Hunted by agents of the restored monarchy, they had hidden in a cave on West Rock, surviving on food and water brought to them by anti-royalist locals. Someone—maybe one of the exiles, maybe a local—had scratched a message into the face of the rock: OPPOSITION TO TYRANTS IS OBEDIENCE TO GOD.

Cole had once thought about painting West Rock, imagining it as a conventional history painting, with one of the exiles standing on the rock proclaiming his political credo. Church let the landscape speak for itself, trusting that the meaning of West Rock would be obvious. Yet he also made one critical addition that layered in his own ideas about the United States. He hadn't sketched any men harvesting hay in the meadow on the summer day in 1848 when he sat looking at West Rock. Church invented these figures at his easel to serve as symbols of the republic, suggesting that the true harvest of the New England way of life was the bucolic serenity he pictured in *West Rock, New Haven.* The whole painting celebrated the principles of agrarian republicanism: self-reliance, political independence, and a distaste for aristocracy.

West Rock, New Haven went on view at the National Academy's spring show in 1849. It dazzled critics with its virtuosic rendering of clouds, sunlight, rocks, fields, woods, and river. "Church has taken his place, at a single leap, among the great masters of landscape," wrote one. "The sky and water in this piece are truly admirable. Seldom have we seen painted water which fulfills so well as this the 'Oxford Graduate's' conditions of excellence."

The "Oxford Graduate" was the British critic John Ruskin, as everyone who knew anything about art was aware. The first volume of Ruskin's *Modern Painters* had been published anonymously in England in 1843 by "a graduate of Oxford." By the time the first U.S. edition appeared, in 1847, Ruskin was already famous, even notorious. In a tour de force of iconoclastic argument, he had attacked cherished beliefs about landscape art. He insisted that a landscape painter could achieve greatness only through fidelity to nature. Any painter—no matter how revered an Old Master—who merely approximated elements of the natural world was an arrogant desecrator of God's works, "which it is the pride of angels to know, and their privilege to love." Ruskin thought the English artist J. M. W. Turner was the supreme living painter of nature, and *Modern Painters*, which eventually stretched to five volumes published over seventeen years, was Ruskin's ardent, influential defense of Turner's art and what he called its "truth to nature." Church found Ruskin's ideas attractive, and it was extremely gratifying to be praised by the New York press in Ruskinian terms.

To be sure, Church was not the only artist working in New York in the late 1840s who excelled at painting nature. With Cole gone, Durand reigned as the unmatched painter of trees and forest scenes, while John Frederick Kensett, a Connecticut-born landscape painter a decade older than Church, was starting to earn favorable comparisons with Durand. Jasper Cropsey, a painter from Staten Island three years older than Church, was developing a specialty in colorful New England autumn forests. Sanford Gifford, an upstate New Yorker also three years older than Church, had recently shown accomplished Catskills landscapes at the Art-Union and National Academy shows.

Despite this wealth of New York talent, the effusive praise for Church and *West Rock* kept coming. On May 3, 1849, the day before his twenty-third birthday, a critic declared him "without doubt among our best landscape painters." His parents were among his many new admirers. "We should like, *if it is possible for you to spare the time*, to have you get up one or two pictures suitable for our humble mansion," his father wrote. People who came to call on Mr. and Mrs. Church expected to find their son's paintings on the walls. Church's father, who had previously been short-tempered with Church about money, now asserted that he had always planned to offer financial support when his son got started in a profession or a business. He was prepared to do so, he said, anytime Church desired.

The previous autumn, as Church had shouldered his way down Broadway through crowds of pedestrians, he had thought up an amusing remark to put in a letter to his friend Goodman. "I cannot avoid creating a sensation wherever I go," he joked, pretending he was such a famous man that strangers gathered around him when he stepped outside. "Oh! the miseries and annoyances of being known." By the spring of 1849, however, praise for Church's extraordinary talent was "in everybody's mouth," as one critic put it. The idea that he might be recognized on the street by strangers was starting to seem less ludicrous.

CHURCH'S SUCCESS AT THAT SPRING'S National Academy show clinched his place on the ballot for promotion to full membership in the academy. If elected, he would be the youngest academician in its history.

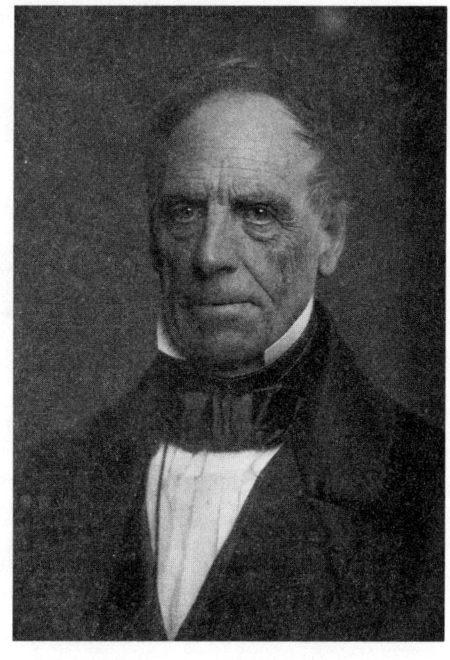

Church's father, Joseph Church, c. 1855

The vote was scheduled for May 9, but before it could take place, the city erupted in a bloody cultural war. The trouble began at a theater. On May 7, the English actor William Charles Macready was showered with rotten eggs and vegetables during a performance of *Macbeth* at the Astor Opera House. Someone threw a chair from an upper gallery as men screamed and cursed at the players, who tried to keep acting even though no one could hear them. The assailants were devotees of Macready's American rival Edwin Forrest, who was appearing at the Broadway Theatre in the same role on the same night. Some of Forrest's partisans had come to the Astor Opera House expressly to ruin Macready's show.

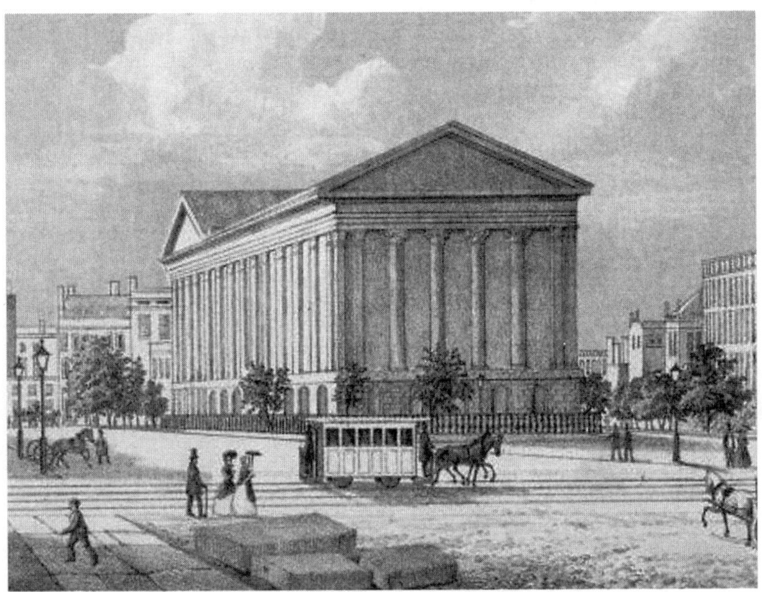

The Astor Opera House

The Astor Opera House stood at Astor Place, an easy walk from posh Washington Square. It was the theatrical resort of the city's elite, and Macready performed Shakespeare in the refined old style they loved. The cheaper Broadway Theatre, located half a mile south of Church's Art-Union studio, held more appeal for Bowery b'hoys and Irish immigrants. Forrest, their hero, gave them a brash and smoldering Macbeth. They despised Macready and the unpatriotic Anglophiles who applauded him with kid-gloved hands. To

Forrest's admirers, running Macready off the Astor Opera House stage and out of town was an act of political resistance.

Later that night, Macready, bruised in body and ego, slipped out of the Astor Opera House in disguise and packed his bags to leave the country. He was dissuaded at the last minute by nearly fifty business-men, publishers, and writers who published a letter in *The New York Herald* assuring Macready that it was safe to practice his art in New York City. Washington Irving, old and famous, and Herman Melville, still young and obscure, were among its signatories.

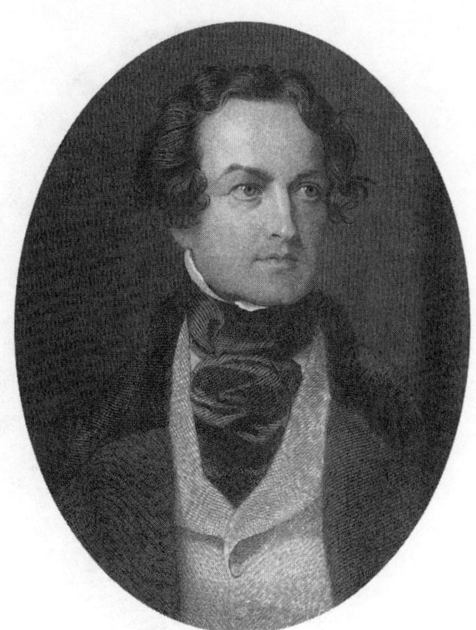

William Charles Macready

Macready decided to brave the stage again. A group of sailors from a British ship pledged to defend him, which galvanized Forrest's supporters to plaster posters on the sides of buildings: "WORKINGMEN, SHALL AMERICANS OR ENGLISH RULE IN THIS CITY? . . . We advocate no violence, but a free expression of opinion to all public men! WORKINGMEN! FREEMEN! STAND BY YOUR LAWFUL RIGHTS!" At this, some of the men who had signed the letter in support of Macready boarded up their townhouse windows and hid their paintings and jewelry. The new mayor, Caleb Woodhull—a Macreadyite—ordered the police and military to prepare for civil unrest.

A few blocks down Broadway from the Astor Opera House, the National Academy decided to proceed with its annual membership vote. On May 9, the same day the pro-Macready letter appeared in the *Herald*, Church was promoted from associate to full academician.

When he woke up the next morning, the mood in the city was angry and tense. Manhattan was covered by a thick, clammy fog. Macready was set to reappear onstage that evening. In an ominous development, men from the Bowery and the Five Points began picking up free tickets to the show, paid for by Democratic opponents of Mayor Woodhull.

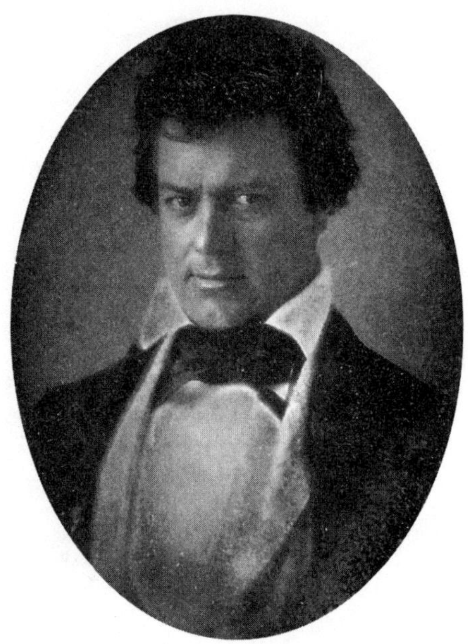

Edwin Forrest

By midday, the sun had burned through the fog, leaving the air fresh and clear. In the spring sunshine, militiamen and policemen hoisted their weapons and practiced battle maneuvers. By curtain time, the Astor Opera House was packed with hundreds of rowdy ticket holders and a twitchy force of 150 policemen. When Macready made his entrance and began delivering his lines, he was instantly greeted by jeers and screams from the Forrest men. Macready and his fellow actors persevered, while roving policemen arrested protesters and enforced the peace.

Outside, at least ten thousand people had converged on Astor Place. Some had come to protest peacefully, some for the fun of stirring things up. Others simply wanted to see what would happen. Philip Hone, an elderly former mayor of New York, was among the merely curious. He strolled up from his townhouse to Astor Place, but when he saw the seething crowd, he fled, and on his way back down Broadway he noted hundreds of militiamen marching in orderly formation toward the opera house. This pleased Hone, who was disgusted by the "vulgar, arrogant" Forrest and the "pack of kindred rowdies at his heels."

The sun set, and darkness intensified the confusion on Astor Place. Here and there a gas lamp or a flaming torch illuminated the moving mass of bodies. The soldiers reached the opera house and positioned themselves in front of the crowd. Paving stones began reeling through the air toward them. An order was shouted, and the soldiers fired into the air to disperse the crowd. Their explosive volley had the opposite effect. Enraged men and women raced toward the soldiers, who now fired straight at them. Eighteen people died almost immediately, and the wounded were everywhere. Lines of bloody footprints had tapped a macabre Morse code across the broken pavement. The soldiers held their positions as people tended to the injured.

The next day, Hone returned to find the façades around Astor Place gouged by bullets. Soldiers and policemen remained on high alert as they patrolled the streets of the city, but an uneasy calm prevailed. "Although the lesson has been dearly bought, it is of great value," Hone reflected. "Law and order can be maintained under a Republican form of government"—not only in a monarchy. Across the Atlantic, he knew, especially in Great Britain, many people were waiting for the American experiment to fail.

Like a lightning bolt suddenly illuminating the topography of a landscape at night, the Astor Place Riot, as it came to be known, revealed the fault lines in American political and cultural life. Yet as frightening as the mayhem was, it also showed how much New Yorkers cared about cultural matters. Across social classes and ethnicities, people argued passionately and sometimes violently. At stake was nothing less than the right to define the national character.

NO ONE WAS FIRING GUNS over pictures, but the New York art world was also embroiled in an intense struggle. The profitable, populist Art-Union, with its packed walls, free exhibitions, and lottery system for distributing art nationally, had long irritated partisans of the older, more exclusive National Academy. Some argued that the Art-Union's democratic spirit was doing far more to nurture American art than the staid gatekeepers at the National Academy. Others countered that the National Academy exposed New Yorkers to a better class of art and thereby contributed more to their cultural education. Newspapers and magazines ran editorials attacking or defending the Art-Union, and soon artists and journalists alike were calling the contretemps the Art-Union War.

Church was among the artists who continued to participate in both institutions. He watched as his adopted city boiled, exploded, and settled into an unstable peace. His letters to friends and family remained as apolitical and lighthearted as ever. It was through painting, not writing, that he expressed himself.

That winter, Church worked on several canvases based on his travels of the previous summer. He had created his sketches of New England farms and woods in an optimistic mood, but as he worked on his new paintings, the material took on a darker tone. The city remained tense. Worse still, the principles holding the entire nation together were straining dangerously.

By now, it had become clear to many Americans that a violent conflict over slavery might erupt. In the streets and in the press, enslavers and abolitionists raged at one another, while both groups attacked proponents of gradual emancipation. Congressmen and senators brandished weapons and fists in the halls of Congress. Southerners challenged Northerners to duels. Telegraph lines crackled day and night with frenzied updates.

In Washington, DC, one tired old man was trying to forge a compromise that would keep the Union intact. Henry Clay, the senior senator from Kentucky, knew that sectionalism was what President George Washington had feared most when he had retired from political life. Those in power, Washington had argued, must always help Americans see and pursue their shared interests, or the Union would collapse. He had agonized that geographical differences would be exploited by "designing men" who hoped to provoke Americans into sectional conflict. Now, with Washington dead for half a century, the disaster he had dreaded seemed imminent.

In January 1850, Clay presented a rescue plan to Congress in the form of eight separate bills. After months of wrenching debate, Congress enacted a revised package of five laws. A compromise had been struck—but like a flint throwing off sparks. California would enter the Union as a free state. Texas, a slave state, would give up some of its territorial demands, receiving debt relief in exchange. The new territories of New Mexico and Utah would decide for themselves whether to allow slavery. The District of Columbia became off-limits for slave trading. And the law protecting fugitives from slavery who made it to free soil was toughened in favor of slaveholders.

This new Fugitive Slave Law not only authorized but explicitly required federal officials to pursue suspected fugitives and arrest them without due process. Anyone found to have aided their escape risked fines and prison. When news of these harsh new measures reached the North, people argued furiously about them over supper tables and at town meetings. Abolitionists were livid. Horace Greeley's *New-York Daily Tribune* published a searing editorial arguing that only an unjust system would punish "a quiet, respectable man guilty of no crime—unless, indeed, it be a crime to prefer Liberty to Slavery, unless it be a crime to believe in that sublime truth which the men of '76 tell us is 'self-evident.'" Emerson, reacting to the brutal capture in Boston of a fugitive from slavery, told an audience, "There is infamy in the air," which "robs the landscape of beauty, and takes the sunshine out of every hour."

Despair and anger swept through African American communities around the country. Many African Americans, particularly in Northern cities, already lived in constant fear of white kidnappers who seized men, women, and children under the pretext that they were runaway slaves. A rare few managed to prove they weren't runaways, but far more disappeared into the dreaded Southern slave markets. After word of the new law reached New York City, thousands of African Americans went into hiding or fled to Canada. Whether they were fugitives from slavery, had at some earlier point been set free, or had been free from birth, they knew they might be ensnared at any moment and ripped from their families forever.

"The land will be filled with violence and blood till this law is repealed," Frederick Douglass prophesied.

AT THE NATIONAL ACADEMY SHOW that spring, Church debuted a strange new picture. It had the same bucolic elements as his earlier New England sketches and paintings—a farmhouse, a winding river, forested mountains in the distance—but now the mood was threatening. The sun had just slipped out of sight, shrouding the fields and mountains in darkness. The farmhouse huddled behind a hill, its lit upper windows staring like wide eyes into the gloaming. Church had filled more than half the canvas with high, ragged clouds of purple that gave way to a wall of burning orange near the horizon. A huge boulder thrust inward from the right edge of the picture, where it hung like an empty pulpit over the landscape.

Church gave the painting a pointed name: *Twilight, "Short Arbiter 'Twixt Day and Night."* As the well-read among his viewers would have known, this was a quotation from John Milton's *Paradise Lost*, drawn from the moment when Satan, having been chased from the Garden of Eden by the angel Gabriel, slipped back under cover of darkness to plot the destruction of humanity.

Church, along with many in his familial and intellectual circles, thought of New England, the birthplace and bulwark of American republicanism, as a new Eden. In the early months of 1850, slavery was the paramount sin troubling that Eden. It threatened both the North's peace and the integrity of the United States as a whole. Church's painting was a warning issued in the manifold colors of an ominous sunset. Just as Emerson had urged in *Nature* in 1836, Church was using nature to convey human emotions. In *West Rock, New*

Haven, he had pushed himself to use realism to express abstract republican ideals, but now, in *Twilight, "Short Arbiter 'Twixt Day and Night,"* he made a further leap. He suffused his painted landscape with the anxiety, dread, and fear that so many people felt for the nation itself.

THAT SUMMER, CHURCH AGAIN FLED the city in search of new material. He loved New York, loved that it was "full of dust and excitement," as he wrote to his friend Goodman. The city's hectic pace whipped him into a pleasant frenzy that drove him forward in his work. But every May, after a winter spent indoors, painting madly for the spring exhibitions, he would feel a tugging at his sleeve. Mountains and meadows, ponds and streams were waiting for him, and when they called, he would quickly get his affairs in order and go. He told Goodman that his philosophy was simple: "When a notion strikes me 'I ups and does it.'"

Church's traveling companions that summer of 1850 were two other landscape painters, Régis Gignoux and Richard Hubbard, both about ten years older than Church, although he was the only one who was already a fellow of the National Academy. The three men crossed Massachusetts to reach New Hampshire, then worked their way north on foot and by stagecoach until they arrived in the White Mountains. Cole had visited this region in the 1820s and had reveled in scenes of "the sublime melting into the beautiful" and "the savage tempered by the magnificent." Church, Gignoux, and Hubbard hiked through forests of beech, hemlock, and birch to a "notch," where the mountains sloped down to cradle a stream. Each man chose a spot from which to sketch the view—and was instantly besieged by clouds of mosquitoes and biting blackflies. They fashioned makeshift fans out of branches and tied handkerchiefs around their faces, and then they tried to carry on with their pictures, one hand flailing at the insects and the other keeping pencil to paper.

Despite the annoyance, Church thought the White Mountains were the "most splendid country I ever beheld," as he wrote in an account of their travels for the Art-Union's *Bulletin.* But Church felt a ceaseless compulsion to push onward toward new kinds of light, earth, and water. From Portland, Maine, a steamer carried the trio across moonlit waters to the town of Belfast, where they boarded a sloop and crossed Penobscot Bay to the village of Castine. There they transferred to a fishing schooner that would drop them on an island at the edge of the North American continent, a place known as Pesamkuk to the Wabanaki people who had inhabited it for thousands of years.* The French explorer Samuel de Champlain, seeing the island from the water in 1604, had been struck by the stark, treeless mountains. "I named it Isle des Monts Déserts," Champlain wrote. Mount Desert Island.

NO WONDER COLE HAD COME here to paint. Church scrambled up the last stretch of sun-warmed rock and looked out over the world in awe. A forest of spruce and fir lapped at the edges of the bare summit. Below him—he was more than a thousand feet above the sea—the forest hitched up at a boulder-strewn coastline trimmed with the white lace of waves. Out on the water, far from the boat-crushing rocks and well past a scattering of small green islands, he saw pieces of white pinned to the blue ocean. These were the sails of fishing vessels, and he thought there must be a hundred of them.

Church spent more than a month on the island that summer. He walked and hiked everywhere—along the rocky shores, through the cool woods, and up the mountains toward the sky. He sketched endlessly, writing careful notes on his drawings. He admired the "fine rich green" of the vines that grew at the edges of the mossy rocks and, as the summer waned, the "beautiful reddish orange tinge" of the foliage atop the cliffs. He saw seals lounging on the shore and a whale spouting. He fished for cod, haddock, and halibut, and he watched as the local men hauled in their lobster traps. He found the "amphibious islanders," as he called them, courteous and warm. On Sundays he enjoyed the novel sight of worshippers from the smaller islands sailing toward Mount Desert to attend church.

He loved everything about the island. The scenery was "magnificent both land and seaward" and the fishing was "glorious." He wondered why "some shrewd Bostonian" hadn't built a hotel there yet. He wrote to Goodman about how much fun he was having and tried to lure him from Connecticut with an extravagant description of the island's natural riches. "Berries are so abundant that I must try to give a list of the kinds although I am aware that I shall omit a number. Huge quantities of blueberries and whortleberries Strawberries and blackberries Partridge berries & wintergreen berries Raspberries and Blackberries. Bear berries and Deerberries. Highland cranberries and lowland cranberries, squaw berries & Redberries. Thimbleberries & wild gooseberries." Even the place names on the island charmed Church. He informed Goodman

---

* The Passamaquoddy also used the word Pemetic, or "a range of mountains," for the island.

gleefully that the address of the house where he was renting a room was "Wm Lynams Schooner Head near Devils oven by Thunder Hole Frenchmans Bar Town of Eden, Mount Desert Island, Maine."

One day Church settled himself near where the waves dashed against the rocks. He watched in fascination. Although he excelled at painting inland waterways, this unquiet ocean was to Catskill Creek as a thundering locomotive to a gentle old horse. "There is no such picture of wild, reckless, mad abandonment to its own impulses, as the fierce, frolicsome march of a gigantic wave," he mused.

He studied the water carefully. It wasn't one thing only, he saw; it came in as many varieties as the grasses and wildflowers in a summer meadow. As the water moved toward the rocks, it looked smooth and green as glass, but at the instant of impact, it exploded into chunks and shards of white foam. Rushing back out in a pale sheet, it gave glimpses of reddish-brown rock just below the surface. As Church watched, he felt a mild despair.

He began experimenting with different brushstrokes for the water's varied moods. He touched his brush to the squeeze of white paint on his palette and then to the canvas. He used fluid, swirling strokes to create the foam of the breaking waves. Mixing a blue-green to match the calmer expanse of ocean beyond the rocky shore, he painted a large patch toward the top third of his paper, making it opaque enough to keep a schooner afloat. With a greener tint laid down in alternating thin and thick strokes, he captured the wash of the water as it neared the rocks. The fogbank in the far distance was a pale violet shroud unfurling over land and sea.

The skies of that summer were new to Church, too. The light danced from the sky to the water and made the air shimmer. He left his bed before dawn to watch the sun rise over the Atlantic; at sunset he saw the clouds aflame. In quick, brilliant oil sketches, he captured orange-streaked skies and lakes turning to liquid gold in the dying light.

Other painters might go to Europe in search of sublime subjects, but Mount Desert gave Church all the drama and symbolism he needed. The sea could turn swiftly from placid to fatal, and the fiery skies above could provoke wonder and fear.

THE FOLLOWING SPRING, TWO GENTLEMEN stood talking before a small picture at the National Academy. It depicted an old boat abandoned on a grassy, flowery shore. Out on the water, the painted fog was so thick as to obscure the line between water and air. An artist standing near the two men heard them praising the picture, one of Church's Mount Desert scenes.

Not far from it hung a larger painting, also by Church, as stark and bright as the little one was soft and diffuse. It showed the sun hanging low over the Atlantic, igniting the underside of the clouds into burning pinks and reds. A stone day beacon stood atop a pile of rocks in the water, trying to warn a tiny, distant ship of danger. Entitled *Beacon, off Mount Desert Island*, it was an unsettling picture. George William Curtis of the *New-York Daily Tribune* wrote that, as he looked at it, he felt "the sea and the shore and their eternal mystery and sadness."

The next sunset seascape Church painted was even more disturbing—the ship in this picture had foundered. He called it *The Wreck*.

CHAPTER 6

"In Your Own Secret Souls"

June 1851. Church was having trouble with his sketch.

He had positioned himself so that he could see through a metal gate meant to keep pilgrims and grave robbers at bay. Two marble sarcophagi—of husband and wife—lay behind it, in the antechamber of a family vault.

The bones in the right-hand sarcophagus had once belonged to George Washington. From the moment of the former president's death in 1799, however, they had become the spiritual property of the nation. North and South, awkwardly conjoined at the birth of the republic, could at least agree on their reverence for a great general who had been a Southerner by birth and a Northerner by adoption. Washington, a Virginia planter and enslaver, had fought his Revolutionary battles in northern British colonies and had lived in New York and Philadelphia during his presidency.

In the decades after the first president's death, thousands of Americans had made pilgrimages to his tomb. Now it was Church's turn, but upon his arrival he found that Mount Vernon was slowly crumbling around Washington's descendants, who still owned it. The portico roof was sagging, and dark splotches of rot bloomed across its white trim.

Church examined his sketch of the tomb. Brick wall, dark gate, pale marble. This much he had deftly captured, along with the trees and shrubs that sheltered the tomb. But something essential had gone awry. He looked up at the façade of the vestibule, with its arch and marble plaque, and back down at his sketch. Now he understood—he had drawn the side wall at a strange angle.

It looked as if the tomb had been thrown together hastily by two different masons following incompatible blueprints.

Church made a brief, annoyed note: "All wrong."

IN THE PAST YEAR AND a half, Church had climbed ever higher in New York's cultural world. Only a few weeks before he sketched Washington's tomb, he had been elected to the Council of the National Academy and to the committee in charge of its annual spring exhibition. The previous year, he had been elected to the Century Association, a men's club for accomplished New York artists and writers and well-heeled admirers of the arts. The Century had been launched in 1847 by Bryant, Durand, and other New York luminaries who had for years been gathering to eat, drink, talk, and sketch. Kensett had joined in 1849, and nearly all the landscape painters in Church's circle would eventually join: Cropsey, Inness, Gignoux, Gifford, McEntee, Whittredge, Hubbard, and others. For the rest of his life, Church would remain a member of the Century, which Mark Twain later called "the most unspeakably respectable Club in the United States." But in the summer of 1851, Church left his fellow artists in search of new landscapes. He had been invited on a tour of the American South by the wealthy New York merchant Cyrus Field and his wife, Mary.

Field was much shorter than Church and even thinner. He had a narrow face with a slightly protruding upper lip that gave him an avian air, as if he were a sparrow in human form. Sickly as a child, he still looked frail, but this was misleading. At thirty-one years old, the energetic Field had

Cyrus Field, by Mathew Brady, c. 1860

already made a fortune as a paper merchant and was building a palatial home on Gramercy Park. He was the owner of Church's *West Rock, New Haven*, and he had organized this trip with Church in part as a chance to commission new paintings on subjects of his own choosing. Church, who had spent his whole life in the North, was ready to see the land of cypress swamps, Spanish moss, and slavery.

FROM MOUNT VERNON IN JUNE, Church and the Fields traveled a hundred miles, moving slowly toward Richmond. As they neared the James River, the deep stands of chestnut, hickory, and oak gradually disappeared. Here the earth and water were pinned down by an endless sky. This low landscape was the opposite of the dramatic scenery Church loved to sketch and paint—the Catskills, Mount Desert Island, and the cliffs along the Hudson. When Frederick Law Olmsted, Church's distant cousin from Hartford, visited the James River a year or so later, he dismissed the landscape as "uninteresting." But Olmsted saw the James River in winter, and Church was traveling in early summer, when yellow primroses dotted the fields and butterflies clustered on milkweed blooms. There was subtle beauty in this landscape. Weeping willows arched from the riverbanks, and the marshes were thick with cordgrass, cattails, and duckweed. Osprey and marsh hawks flew overhead, their eyes trained on the water.

From Richmond, the river twisted its way toward Jamestown and then on toward the Chesapeake Bay, but Church and the Fields stopped long before Jamestown. About twenty-five miles southeast of Richmond, they reached a cluster of red-brick buildings set a few hundred feet from the river. Expanses of corn, wheat, and cotton stretched in every direction. Small figures moved about among the crops.

Church and the Fields had arrived at the oldest plantation in Virginia. The main house would have been impressive even among the mansions of London, and on this rural American river, it stood out like a royal residence. Designed in the Georgian style, it had a two-story portico, a row of five dormer windows, and two tall chimneys. The massive front door faced into a courtyard formed by several smaller buildings.

The plantation was known as Shirley, after the surname of its earliest English owners. Established in 1613, only six years after the founding of the Jamestown colony, its present mansion dated from the early eighteenth century. When Church and the Fields arrived in June 1851, Shirley belonged to descendants of the Hill family, who had owned the estate since 1660. Their host was the fifty-five-year-old planter Hill Carter. Having inherited Shirley at the age of ten, Carter was the standard-bearer of a powerful clan with close ties to several other Virginia dynasties. His wife, Mary, was a Randolph, while an aunt had married Revolutionary War hero Henry "Light-Horse Harry" Lee in the Shirley parlor in 1793, when Lee was governor of Virginia. One of their sons, Robert E. Lee, had recently returned from service in the Mexican War.

As Church stepped into the front hall, he saw a broad staircase that rose and turned above him for three stories in a miraculous feat of eighteenth-century craftsmanship. Generations of Carter family wealth, derived from the labor of the enslaved, had produced splendid interiors. Marble-topped tables, rich carpets, and ancestral portraits adorned the ground-floor rooms.

Guests at Shirley were waited on by a select few of the Carters' enslaved people. An earlier visitor recalled Mrs. Carter's thoughtfulness in sending "two little black boys" to his room to serve him "as fine a cup of coffee as you ever tasted." Enslaved men brought male guests hot water for shaving each morning, while enslaved women set the mahogany table in the dining room with plates of ham and corn cakes. At suppertime, enslaved people served course after course, then cleared the plates and set out bottles of champagne, port, and Madeira.

Church's visit to Shirley constituted his first intimate encounter with slavery, although the wealth of many prosperous Northerners derived from the labor of the enslaved in the sugar and textile industries, and even more directly from the trade in enslaved people. Two years after Church's stay at Shirley, the company of which his father was a director, Aetna Fire Insurance, would create a new firm that insured the lives of enslaved people, with payments for any loss of life going not to their families but to their owners.

Hill Carter considered himself an enlightened and benevolent man, and he had published his views on slavery in the hope of persuading other enslavers that humane treatment was in everyone's interest. He occasionally sold children away from their parents, but no more often, he insisted, than he felt absolutely necessary. He allowed his people to grow their own vegetables and to raise chickens. He explained that he extended these privileges because he believed it was the right thing to do, adding that a side effect was to bind his people emotionally and financially to his estate, making them less likely to run away.

When the Carters retired to their beds at night, they felt safe, even though the big house was surrounded by dozens of men and women whose muscles were strong from long days in the fields. Sometimes news reached Shirley of uprisings in states where slaveholders were more brutal—Mississippi was especially notorious—but Carter wasn't worried. The enslaved of Virginia,

Carter asserted, "are the happiest people in the world, unless tampered with by fanatics," by which he meant abolitionists.

Just as Church and the Fields were enjoying the Carters' hospitality, the first installment of a new serialized novel, *Uncle Tom's Cabin*, appeared in a newspaper in Washington, DC. Its author, a New England minister's wife named Harriet Beecher Stowe, sought to thrust readers into the daily struggles of enslaved people and thus engender sympathy for their plight. Over the next months, as the novel appeared in forty installments, it gripped readers and changed minds. When the entire book was published the following March, it sold three thousand copies on the first day. Frederick Douglass met with Stowe, whose message of universal compassion touched people across the nation and around the world. *"God bless her for that word!"* Douglass wrote. Soon after his Southern trip, Church would acquire a copy of *Uncle Tom's Cabin*, at one point writing to his sister Charlotte to ask her to find the book in his room in Hartford and mail it to him in New York.

Stowe had conjured a complex and shattering account of American slavery. In an afterword, she posed a question to people such as the Carters: "To you, generous, noble-minded men and women of the South—you, whose virtue, and magnanimity, and purity of character, are the greater for the severer trial it has encountered—to you is her appeal. Have you not, in your own secret souls . . . felt that there are woes and evils in this accursed system far beyond what are here shadowed or can be shadowed?"

If Church was troubled by what he saw at Shirley, he didn't reveal it in the note he wrote to Mrs. Carter after he and the Fields had left the plantation. In gratitude for all the "kind hospitality" they had received, Church enclosed a sketch he had made of the mansion.

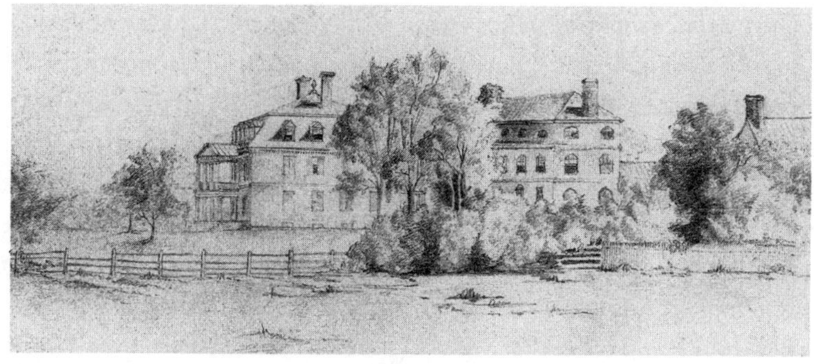

The mansion at Shirley, sketched by Church in June 1851

Later, Church would have powerful reasons for changing his language about the South. The word that would occur to him then was not "hospitality" but "inhumanity."

CHURCH AND THE FIELDS NEXT traveled west toward the Blue Ridge Mountains, which rose ahead of them in soft layers. When they had traveled about 120 miles west of Shirley, they descended into a wooded ravine and followed a winding creek. Coming around a bend, they encountered a sight that had struck travelers with awe since long before the English had arrived at Jamestown. More than two hundred feet above them rose a huge bridge made of rock, with tall trees growing from its top span. It was known as the Natural Bridge, and a glimpse of it was said to make believers of atheists.

Washington had surveyed this site in the 1740s, and his initials were still visible on the rock. Jefferson, who in 1774 had bought the land on which the arch stood, had called it "the most sublime of nature's works." He had felt an overwhelming joy in the presence of this extraordinary geological formation, which seemed to be "springing as it were up to heaven."

Jefferson had steered many friends and visitors to the Natural Bridge over the years. The flow of sightseers, American and European alike, had not stopped with his death in 1826. In a novel Herman Melville would publish in October 1851, five months after Church saw the Natural Bridge, Melville conjured the mysterious natural force of the white whale he called Moby-Dick. "But soon the fore part of him slowly rose from the water; for an instant his whole mar-bleized body formed a high arch, like Virginia's Natural Bridge, and warningly waving his bannered flukes in the air, the grand god revealed himself, sounded, and went out of sight."

Field was enchanted with the Natural Bridge and told Church he wanted to commission a painting of it. Church paced the ground below, trying to decide on the best angle for a picture. He positioned himself almost in the creek bed and sketched the cedars clinging to the ravine and the black walnut trees growing along the creek. He studied the arch's walls and its great span, noticing shades of brown, gray, black, white, and most of all the dominant rusty-orange hue of the rock. He gave these colors numbers on his sketches. Climbing through the woods to the vertiginous heights of the arch, he sketched the view: crisscrossing lines of foothills and coves that drew his gaze onward to a far range of the Blue Ridge Mountains. Field tried to hand Church a small piece of the orange rock, thinking it would be difficult to recapture from memory back in New York. But Church refused the rock, and Field pocketed it as a souvenir.

From the Natural Bridge, they traveled west into Kentucky. Now only Missouri lay between them and the frontier; Church sketched a covered wagon he saw rolling past one day. In Kentucky, they toured Mammoth Cave, the longest known cave in the world. It was the inverse of the Natural Bridge, requiring descent into a chilly gloom. One of the first caverns was customarily filled with thousands of hibernating bats during the winter, but they had already left for the spring. Mammoth Cave was not a congenial place to sketch, but Church was fascinated by the pale, eyeless fish that populated the underground rivers, and he collected a few to take home as natural history specimens. Then he parted company with the Fields, who continued by steamboat to St. Louis. Once home, Church wrote to Field, "I am telling marvellous stories here of our adventures to gaping audiences, and exhibiting my blind fishes with tremendous effect."

WHILE CHURCH AND THE FIELDS were visiting the Natural Bridge and Mammoth Cave, other tourists were admiring painted versions of them in London, courtesy of George Brewer, a British artist who had traveled widely in the United States. Brewer was welcoming audiences to his "Grand Moving Mirror of American Scenery." Through a trick of the sun, a large mirror, and a painted canvas, Brewer had re-created several celebrated geographical marvels—not just the world-famous Niagara Falls, but also Virginia's Natural Bridge and Kentucky's Mammoth Cave.

The Great Exhibition of the Works of Industry of All Nations had opened in London that spring, after Queen Victoria had invited countries around the world to send their treasures and inventions for display in what was soon being called the Crystal Palace, a pavilion of iron and glass covering eighteen acres of Hyde Park.

The United States had much to prove at the Great Exhibition. Americans were widely and frequently mocked across Europe for their crudeness and cruelty. Dickens had been disgusted by the way American men spat tobacco juice on the carpets even in the finest interiors because they were too inept or lazy to hit the spittoon. When he visited Congress, Dickens had heard the same men who invoked the Declaration of Independence speak with passion of their right to buy, sell, and abuse chained human beings. To many Europeans, especially after the passage of the Fugitive Slave Law, Americans seemed stupid, greedy, and violent, and their vast territory too sparsely settled for a refined society to emerge. The nation's literature and art were undistinguished, and its cities were ugly. The New York publisher Horace Greeley summed up the prevalent British attitude: "We are a rude, clumsy people, inhabiting a broad, fertile domain."

Some educated Americans believed that cosmopolitan critics had a point about the general backwardness of their country, and the wealthy strove to associate themselves with the Old World instead. They wore European fashions, bought European paintings, and wrote their letters on European stationery. This last predilection was one Field had cannily exploited in his paper business. Touring Great Britain and the Continent in 1849, he had contracted with suppliers in London and Paris to become the exclusive New York agent for their bleaches and dyes.

When Queen Victoria invited the United States to participate in the Great Exhibition of 1851, she presented a chance for the American people to improve their international standing. The federal government issued an appeal in the nation's newspapers for contributions to the exhibition. Within a week, ambitious men—and a few bold women—were dispatching boxes and packages, some small enough to fit in a child's palm, others enormous. One contraption, Cyrus McCormick's reaper, appeared to combine elements of a "chariot, a flying machine, and a treadmill," in the words of a reporter who later witnessed it in action.

In early 1851, the winning American entries were loaded onto a ship in New York Harbor. After almost a month at sea, the ship reached England in time for the goods to be transferred to London and installed in the American display space at the Crystal Palace. Greeley went over as a special correspondent for his own paper, the *New-York Daily Tribune*.

On May 1, Queen Victoria, resplendent in a pink silk dress with silver brocade trim, arrived at Hyde Park to open the Great Exhibition. Multicolored flags ornamented the length of the immense building, and the displays in the central hall and galleries stretched for a cumulative eight miles.

Greeley thought that the Crystal Palace made Castle Garden, a grand New York theater seating five thousand people, look like a dog kennel. All around him, he saw elegant sculptures, ingenious machinery, strange rocks and minerals, sumptuous textiles, and thousands of other interesting objects. In the India display, a stuffed elephant draped in red and gold trappings towered above the crowds, and the Koh-i-Noor diamond glittered inside a tall cage like

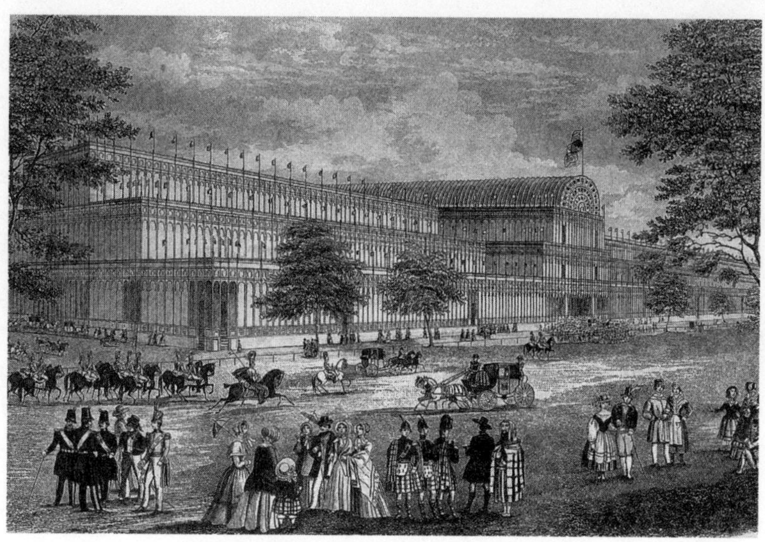

The Crystal Palace in London, 1851

an exotic bird at risk of escape. Believed to be the largest diamond in the world, the Koh-i-Noor—or "mountain of light"—had been presented to Queen Victoria by the East India Company after a treaty wrested it from a doe-eyed child maharaja in Punjab. The cage, fashioned by locksmith Jeremiah Chubb, featured a hidden safe into which the diamond descended at night. During the day, the contraption was rigged so that any touch on the protective glass would instantly lock the diamond in the safe.

The British had given continental Europe far less room than they had reserved for themselves, but France, Italy, Austria, and other European countries vied fiercely with one another to showcase their most exquisite craftsmanship. When Greeley finally came to the United States's display, he saw instantly that the American commissioners had booked far too much space. After the ivory, gold, ermine, and silks of the other countries' displays, the American section resembled an understocked country store deep in the Oregon wilderness.

The British press gloated that the display perfectly captured the United States: thinly populated and primitive. While the British Empire had its giant festooned elephant, the United States offered a small stuffed squirrel from Ohio. Several Americans had contributed autumn leaves in assorted colors; others had sent false teeth, hams, and cod-liver oil. High above the American exhibit space, a pasteboard bald eagle stretched its broad wings, but *Punch* magazine observed that "the gigantic bird soars over next to nothing."

One American showpiece, *The Times* of London noted, did offer a titillating respite from the "desolate prairie" of the rest of the display. It came from the manufacturer Samuel Colt, a Hartford native who moved in the same circles as Church's family. Colt had invented an innovative weapon that could dispense six bullets in succession without reloading. Colt's six-shooter had recently earned praise in a Senate report for its efficiency in killing "savages." *The Times* ventured to suggest additional uses. "Have you a difference of opinion with a rival legislator?" it inquired. "Would you clear your path of a troublesome competitor in the walks of art or literature?" The British marveled at the American attachment to weapons. Queen Victoria, seeing a collection of bowie knives at the exhibition, observed in her private diary that Americans "never move without one."

Greeley went to the Crystal Palace every day for a week and was chagrined to hear some Americans openly expressing their sense of national shame. The whole enterprise had worked against the United States, as its most spectacular possessions couldn't be packed up and shipped over for display in the Crystal Palace. Not Niagara's thundering waters; not the prairies that seemed to stretch to the end of time; not the setting sun gilding a cliffside cypress above the Pacific Ocean.

Nonetheless, American photographers, led by Mathew Brady, were responsible for the most sophisticated and extensive array of daguerreotypes on view. Most were portraits of people, but in one image Niagara Falls had been frozen in streaks of light spray and dark water. In another photograph, using a telescope at Harvard University, John Adams Whipple of Boston had captured the pitted, shadowy surface of the moon.

When the Council Medals were awarded, five American contributors were among the approximately 170 recipients. Cyrus McCormick won for his reaper, which was soon harvesting crops on a wildly successful demonstration tour around England, and Charles Goodyear won for a

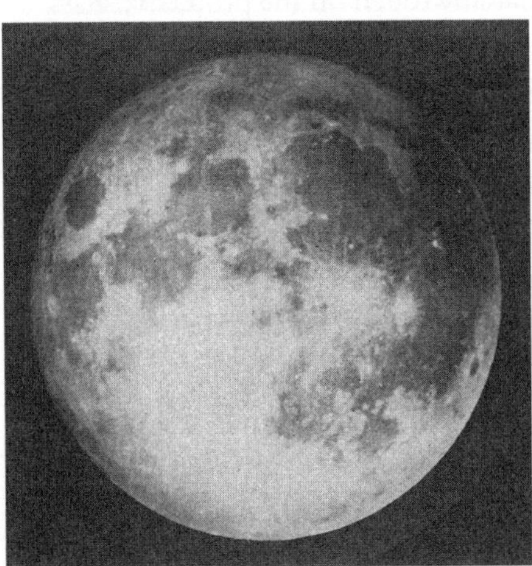

The Moon, by John Adams Whipple, 1851

collection of products made from India rubber. Another medal went to Gail Borden Jr., a food engineer who had invented a long-lasting "meat biscuit" for sailors, soldiers, gold prospectors, and pioneers. This nutritious food could speedily be prepared on the trail with no need for a campfire, which, one testimonial stated, so often betrayed the traveler's position to marauding Indians.

Greeley apologized in print to his fellow Americans for his early critical reaction. His country had done a creditable job, after all—not spectacular, but not embarrassing. Soon, confirming the British judgment that Americans were shameless self-promoters, a Louisiana man named Charles Rodgers began work on a book called *American Superiority at the World's Fair*.

IN 1852, CHURCH COMPLETED THE painting Field had commissioned during their Southern trip. Field's daughter later recalled that when Church delivered *The Natural Bridge, Virginia*, Field hunted down the rock he had taken from the Natural Bridge and compared it to the color Church had painted from memory. It was, she said, a perfect match.

Church had decided on a vertical orientation for his canvas, depicting the Natural Bridge from an angle that made it look less like a bridge and more like a triumphal arch. The Roman Republic, whose representative government had been a source of inspiration to Washington, Jefferson, Hamilton, and their fellow founders, had celebrated its victories with grand marble arches. Church's painting suggested that the American republic had no need of man-made arches. The great monuments of the young nation sprang from her soil and rose to the heavens. Ancient forces, not human hands, had built the Natural Bridge and ornamented it with native plants and trees rather than with the carved soldiers who marched across Roman arches.

Church had included two small figures in his painting. A woman sat on a grassy outcropping beside the creek, clad in a flowing dress of a warm rust color, as though she were a sister to the rocks, with white cuffs gathered around her hands and a white collar at her neck. Church painted a blue shawl around her shoulders and a red scarf lying on the ground next to her, so that her costume united the colors of the American flag. She gazed up at a man standing before her, who was gesturing at the arch. The woman was white, and the man was Black.

The Natural Bridge, Virginia was Church's first engagement with slavery. He had never included a Black person in any of his paintings before. After seeing slavery firsthand, he had stood at his easel in New York and imagined this Black man speaking to this white woman. The new picture was the latest in Church's series of warnings about the nation, but this time he was more direct. Instead of expressing his fears through an oncoming night or a wrecked ship, he painted a human figure pointing out the danger. The Black man was an unmistakable representative of slavery, and through him Church warned that the American republic, like the Roman Republic before it, was at risk of collapse. Church had begun his Southern excursion with a misbegotten sketch of Washington's tomb and had concluded it with a virtuosic portrait of his magnificent but troubled country.

With Field's blessing, Church sent the painting to London in the summer of 1852 for exhibition at the Royal Academy of Arts. He was proud enough of his work to hope it might impress the British press, which had been so scathing about the recent American showing at the Great Exhibition. But the British critics took no notice.

WHILE *THE NATURAL BRIDGE* WAS in London, Church left New York again. After a visit to his parents and sisters in Hartford, he went farther north than he had ever been before, to Maine's Mount Katahdin, one of the tallest peaks in New England. Guided by a group of lumbermen, he tried to climb the mountain, but the weather was so wet and cold that he decided he would have to return someday under better conditions. He did make some useful sketches, and at the National Academy's 1853 spring show, he debuted a painting called *Mt. Ktaadn.*

It was another in his series of New England sunset pictures, but far more serene than the last few. The plein air sketches on which Church based his painting had no signs of human life, but after his recent trip through the South, Church was in the mood to celebrate the agrarian republicanism of his native New England. Mount Katahdin, a wild and sometimes dangerous peak, here served as a regal backdrop to the main subject: a farm carved out of the Maine woods. The farmhouse stood at the edge of a rose-tinted lake; nearby a small herd of cows watered themselves and grazed. In the foreground, instead of the region's ubiquitous evergreens, Church had painted an oak and an elm, symbols—via the Charter Oak and the Liberty Tree—of New Englanders' struggles for self-government. A man sat at the base of the elm, contemplating the peaceful scene. *Mt. Ktaadn* went on display at the

National Academy in May 1853 along with *The Natural Bridge*. Together the pictures showed what Church loved about his country and what he feared would destroy it.

By the time the exhibition opened, though, Church had already left the city on a new trip with Cyrus Field. This time they went by ocean steamer. Before their departure, Field prudently increased his life insurance.

CHAPTER 7

"I Am Terrified"

They arrived at the hottest hour of the day. It was nearly one hundred degrees and the sweat was running down Church's back. The sandy soil radiated heat into the air, and all around him mud houses baked in the sun. Eight malnourished horses, their bones protruding sharply, stood in a group nearby. Church despaired at the sight of them. He and Field had a fifteen-mile ride ahead on two of these sad creatures. After three weeks of sitting idle on the deck of a steamship, Church felt unfit for the grueling trek to the town of Barranquilla, where they would begin their journey into the jungle.

They had landed in the Republic of New Granada, on the northern coast of South America, on April 28, 1853.* Wrested from the Spanish colonial authorities in the early nineteenth century and officially created in 1831, the country was dominated by gold and silver mines, coffee and tobacco plantations, and caste-based discrimination. It had only recently freed its enslaved people.

Church and Field each had his own reasons for coming here. Field was interested in the commercial potential of South American metal mines, and he also wanted to see some of the continent's great natural attractions. Church's primary motive for making the trip was his fascination with a man he had never even met: Baron Alexander von Humboldt. In 1799, Humboldt had left behind the luxurious life of a young Prussian nobleman and sailed for South America with a French botanist, Aimé Bonpland. They had spent nearly four years floating on rivers, camping in jungles, exploring towns and cities, and climbing the great

---

* The country stretched from the Caribbean to the Pacific mainly across territory that is today Colombia and Panama.

volcanoes of the Andes. They had studied plants, animals, geology, weather patterns, religion, art, artifacts, and languages. In the half century since Humboldt's return to Europe, he had published volume after volume filled with thrilling accounts of his South American adventures, experiments, and discoveries. His writings had made him one of the most famous men in the world.

Church had pored over English translations of Humboldt's work, bewitched by the ideas of this brave, brilliant man who had gazed into the heart of nature. As Humboldt had traveled and studied and talked with local people, he had come to the revolutionary realization that plants and animals existed in a global web of complex relations shaped by climate and geology. Humboldt wrote of nature's intricate balance, primal power, and exquisite beauty. Instead of putting human beings at its center, he showed how the natural world carried on with no regard for human interests. His five-volume masterwork, *Cosmos*, which began to appear in 1845, was Humboldt's "attempt to delineate nature in all its vivid animation and exalted grandeur."

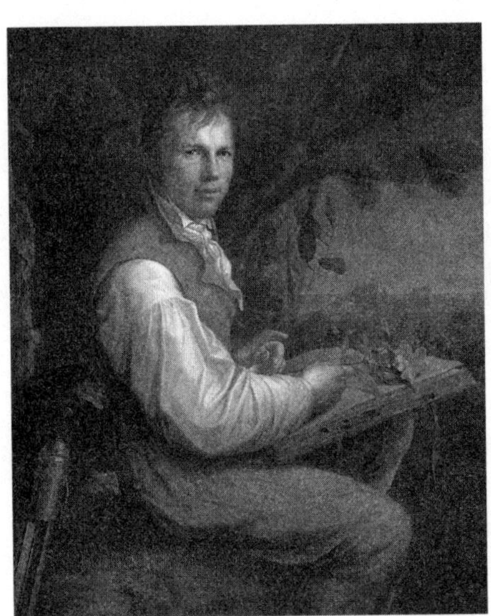

Humboldt in South America

Humboldt's love and respect for nature moved Church, who discovered passages in *Cosmos* that could have been written for him personally. Humboldt argued that landscape painters were critical to sharing the wonder of nature with the world. Scientists could collect, catalog, and hypothesize, but only a painter could capture "the azure of the sky, the form of the clouds, the vapoury mist resting in the distance," and all the other natural details that came together to give a landscape its special character. Church had drawn a careful line in pencil down the side of Humboldt's passage about landscape painters. Reading on, he had found Humboldt complaining that the artists who were generally assigned to government-funded expeditions fell painfully short. Humboldt longed for a landscape artist endowed with the extraordinary technical skill required to reproduce every aspect of flora, fauna, geology, and climate.

Church wondered if he could become the kind of artist Humboldt dreamed of. He had a good eye for details and years of practice painting water, rocks, air, and clouds. But he saw that for Humboldt technical skill was not enough; the ideal artist would also possess a "boundless depth of feeling." Technique must be guided by passion. Only then could what Humboldt called "the great enchantment of nature" emerge on canvas.

There was one destination above all others that Humboldt urged painters to see: the tropics. "Are we not justified in hoping that landscape painting will flourish with a new and hitherto unknown brilliancy," he asked, if "artists of merit" dared to make the perilous journey to the tropics? There they would find "the nobler and grander forms of nature." The landscapes of South America ranged from palm-lined beaches to lush rainforests to bare plateaus to undulating foothills to soaring volcanoes. A daring painter who wasn't killed en route by disease, predators, or hostile locals might manage to capture for humanity the most stupendous sight of all—the Andes.

Humboldt's words fired Church with ambition. They were why he had come to South America.

WHEN CHURCH SET FOOT IN New Granada, he was young, lean, and sinewy. He thought of himself as an outdoorsman. He had walked hundreds of miles through the New England wilderness carrying a pack laden with food, cooking utensils, sleeping gear, and art supplies. Still, every day of the next six months would challenge his strength, patience, and tenacity.

Barranquilla lay at the wide mouth of the Magdalena River, the lifeblood of New Granada. For millennia before Spanish invaders saw the river in 1501 and named it for Mary Magdalene, the river had been home to Indigenous peoples who had known it by other, older names. The Magdalena flowed north into the Caribbean from deep in the interior, and Church and Field were planning to travel upstream toward Bogotá, the capital city, which perched in the eastern chain of the Andes—the Cordillera Oriental. From Bogotá they would proceed southwest along the Cordillera Central until they reached the Andes' western chain, or Cordillera Occidental, home to the greatest volcanoes Humboldt had climbed half a century earlier, Cotopaxi and Chimborazo. Each of these two peaks was more than three times as high as the tallest mountain in New England—Mount Washington, in the White Mountains of New Hampshire. If Church made careful sketches along the way—and survived the trip—he might return to New York prepared to paint the landscape of Humboldt's dreams.

In Barranquilla, Church learned that the steamboat that plied the river would not be back for a week, but he was so excited to be in South America he didn't care. He found every building, person, animal, and plant "novel and singular" or "quaint and odd." People spoke rapidly in an accent that stumped him. He had tried to learn some Spanish, and he could read and write a bit, but he couldn't converse at all. He used a phrase book to ask directions but then couldn't understand the answers.

At meals during his first week in New Granada, Church discovered that foods he was accustomed to eating at home seemed more flavorful here. "I can't sufficiently praise the rice in this country," he wrote to his sister Charlotte. "The grains are small and dingy but the flavor is vastly better than the rice in the States." The coffee tasted richer; so did the hot chocolate. Other foods were entirely new to him. He loved the cumin-spiced breakfast meats and sampled a papaya dessert he found so delicious he arranged to send a jar of it to Hartford. The only local food he did not enjoy was an avocado: "to me it is perfectly insipid." He began to keep a running list of new foods, among them banana, guava, pomegranate, breadfruit, cassava, tamarind, pineapple, okra, and tacos.

As Church roamed that week with his art supplies, he marveled at the animal life. On the Caribbean coast, he had seen birds of "monstrous size" including pelicans, frigate birds, and cranes, and in Barranquilla, he saw parrots and parakeets wheeling and darting overhead. Small, shy lizards skittered across the walls. After he found a skin shed by a scorpion, he enclosed it in his first letter to his sister Charlotte. He made a quick oil sketch of one of the burros he saw everywhere; the sheer strength of these pack animals amazed him. "Sometimes a little fellow will come trotting along," he wrote, "nothing but his legs and ears visible[,] with two huge nets on each side crammed with oranges and a great stout woman in some unaccountable manner poised on top." More than the houses, people, or animals, it was the plants that astonished him. On his very first day in South America, he had seen cacti as big as trees and flowering plants more than twenty feet tall.

Only one thing truly bothered him during the wait in Barranquilla. When the mail arrived, Field received a whole packet of letters, but there was not a single letter for Church. On his twenty-seventh birthday, he began a letter to Charlotte by noting his disappointment. He was so wounded at the lack of family letters that he chastised even his father, toward whom he usually took a deferential tone: "I am very sorry that I have not heard from home but as you are all notoriously negligent of writing I don't feel surprised. I am sure that no fault can be found with me as this makes the seventh or eighth [letter] since I started."

Church kept on dispatching letters to Hartford, and he wrote frequently in a travel diary, as Humboldt had done. His first entry was a wry little dig at himself: "Today I begin a diary in Spanish, but like so many of my other resolutions I expect to give up this practice soon." But he stuck with it for months.

WHEN THEIR STEAMBOAT ARRIVED, FIELD and Church boarded along with a few other foreigners and a crowd of locals. Despite Church's excitement about following Humboldt's route, he was feeling apprehensive about the river trip. He had been warned in Barranquilla that they would be plagued by swarms of sand flies and mosquitoes and that the temperatures could reach 120 degrees.

Still, he knew that he and Field could expect a more pleasant time than Humboldt and Bonpland, who in April 1801 had walked sixty miles from Cartagena, a coastal city to the south of Barranquilla, to the Magdalena, where they had embarked against the current in a canoe. In addition to supporting a glorious welter of plant life, the Magdalena attracted predators. Sharp-toothed caimans—reptiles of the alligator family—slid into the river, the spikes on their spines jutting above the murky surface. Jaguars lurked in the thickets, invisible from the boat. Poisonous snakes whipped through the water and slithered up tree trunks. It had taken Humboldt and Bonpland two months to travel upstream to the town of Honda, where the Magdalena became unnavigable.

From the deck, Church watched the jungle slip by. He was relieved to find that the temperatures remained unexpectedly comfortable, with frequent cooling rains. One night thunder and lightning exploded, and the next morning Church delighted in the refreshed scenery. Thick, low clouds blocked out the distant mountains, but he knew he was moving ever closer to them. His spirits were high, and he felt strong and healthy. Ever since his arrival in Barranquilla, he had been drinking straight from the warm river—he guessed it was about eighty degrees—even though he had been warned that it wasn't safe. "I drink enormous quantities every day and find that it agrees with me perfectly."

As the steamboat thrummed upriver, Church saw coconuts dangling from palm trees, drifts of flowers covering the shore, and vines trailing in the water.

This tropical region struck him, as it had many others before, as a kind of Eden. All around him, Church saw the same lushness of plant life that had thrilled Humboldt a half century earlier. "You can form no idea of the wonderful luxuriance of vegetation," he wrote to his father. "Magnificent trees which spread out their immense branches to a prodigious extent are loaded down with vines[;] in fact everything is covered with vines."

In *Cosmos*, Humboldt had advised artists who made it to the tropics to get down all possible botanical and geological details: leaves, stems, tree trunks, vines, flowers, rocks, even the textures and colors of the soil. Church recorded the minutiae of nature in page after page of sketches and notes. "Monstrous tree," he wrote. "Alligator." Next to a dense mass of pencil lines: "Trees entirely smothered in vines"; he drew their reflection in the water. "Network of vines— dead," he labeled another tiny picture.

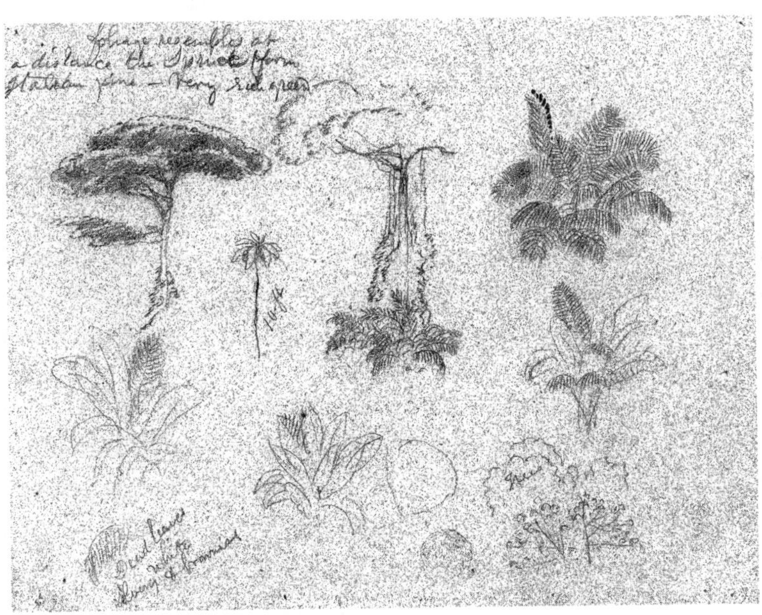

Botanical sketches by Church on the Río Magdalena, Colombia, 1853

About a week into the river journey, Church killed a six-inch tarantula. "I have been delighted with my trip," he wrote in his diary two days later when they reached the village where they would be transferring to a canoe for their next leg, toward the town of Honda. Church missed his family and longed for letters from home, but he remained rapturous about all the new sights, including a grove of "chocolate trees."

HONDA, FOUNDED IN THE SIXTEENTH century by Spanish colonists, was filled with shady squares and Baroque churches. In 1805, four years after Humboldt and Bonpland had passed through on their way to Bogotá, an earthquake had killed more than one hundred people and damaged hundreds of buildings. Almost fifty years later, Church rambled along the cobblestone streets between whitewashed houses, serenaded by the rushing Magdalena. He wandered among picturesque ruins entwined in the exposed roots of rubber trees that had sprouted atop the rubble left by the earthquake. It was a poignant, powerful sight: the fleeting works of mortals being slowly devoured by inexorable nature. Church found Honda "singular and beautiful," and in this dreamy mood, he thought that the jagged mountains surrounding the town looked like cathedrals.

He and Field now faced another difficult stretch of their journey. They were still at least a hundred miles from Bogotá, which was almost eight thousand feet higher than Honda. Neither man had any idea how his body would respond to the thinning air as they hiked and rode mules up into the mountains and across the high savanna on which Bogotá stood. They would have to ride for days on rocky bridle paths that wound along what an earlier French traveler had described as "horrifying precipices" that made people "faint with fear." One misstep by a mule could plummet beast and rider to their deaths. Humboldt had written to his brother that the trail was "awful beyond all description." In places it dwindled to "little steps carved into the rock" and became so narrow that the mules "could barely squeeze their bodies through."

Before they braved this journey, Church and Field made a detour to see a silver mine that Humboldt and Bonpland had also visited. They rode for six hours amid palms, flowering jacarandas, and ceiba trees whose dense canopies cast great pools of shade. Dismounting at one point, Church was fascinated to encounter a so-called sensitive plant that folded its leaves defensively when he touched it. But when they reached the silver mine, they found that Eden had been scraped bare; plants and trees would have hampered the movement of laborers. The mine was marked by a cluster of raw wooden buildings, along with a precarious swinging bridge, a smokestack, and a waterwheel. This was not the landscape Humboldt had urged painters to capture.

They rode on, up into the mountains. Church and Field were now traveling with a guide, who was on foot, leading the mules that were carrying their bags. Imprudently, Church and Field rode ahead, far outpacing the only member of their party who knew the way. At sunset they reached a crest overlooking the town of Guaduas, and as they descended the other side, night fell. They lurched down the slope, hoping the mules would not lose their footing in the dark, and were relieved to reach the valley floor. Once there, however, the mules wandered into a swamp and got stuck in thorn-spiked thickets. Church and Field tried to guide their mounts back toward the right path, but neither they nor the animals could find it. Dejected, the men lowered themselves to the ground right where they were. There was nothing to do but wait out the night.

They rode into Guaduas the next day disheveled and exhausted, but in his next letter to his father, Church spared his family any knowledge of the perilous descent and the grim night he and Field had spent in a swamp. "Our course was continually up one mountain and down another. I was delighted with everything," he wrote. "The flowers by the roadside would have enchanted a Botanist."

It had taken them five weeks to get this far, and Bogotá finally seemed in reach. They set out with renewed energy and optimism. For two days, as their mules soldiered on, they gained over five thousand feet in elevation. Neither Church nor Field seemed to be suffering from the thinning air. On June 4, they switched their mules for horses, galloped for twenty-four miles across a fertile plateau, and arrived at Bogotá in time for supper. There were no letters waiting for either of them.

BOGOTÁ LOOKED AND FELT LIKE a different country. The city was more than eighty-five hundred feet above sea level, with the mountain of Monserrate looming about fifteen hundred feet above, a white monastery clinging to its summit. It was nearly forty degrees cooler here than it had been in Barranquilla, and it felt to Church as though there were ten times as many people as in Honda. When Humboldt had visited Bogotá in 1801, he had remarked on how rare foreign visitors were, but now the streets were crowded with locals and foreigners alike. Church saw the same panama hats and colorful cloaks, or ruanas, that he had noticed earlier on his journey, but other people were dressed more like New Yorkers, in broadcloth suits and tall beaver hats or in fine dresses and carrying parasols.

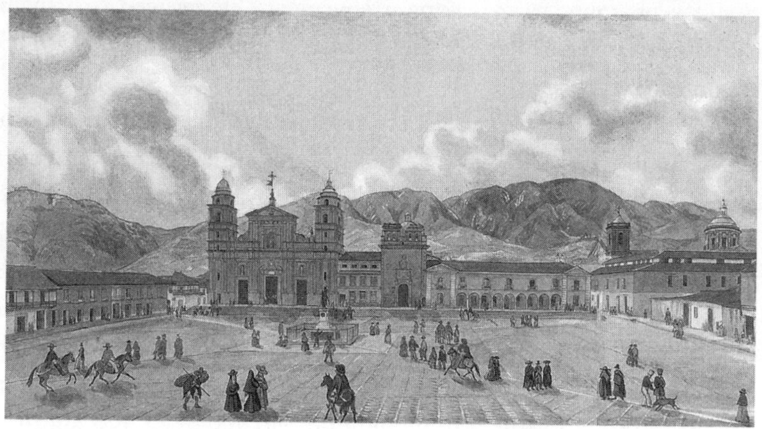

Plaza de Bolívar, the main square in Bogotá

Church and Field settled into a guesthouse and discovered that they had arrived in the middle of a political drama. Three weeks earlier, working-class men (known as *artesanos* or *ruanas*) had clashed violently with young conservatives (*cachacos*) in front of the Congress. A mason had died in the melee. Two days later, tensions had risen higher still upon the publication of the country's controversial new constitution, which had introduced universal male suffrage. Over the next weeks, artisans in cloaks and dandies in frock coats eyed one another warily, looking for the hint of an insult or the flash of a knife. Pamphlets calling for resistance circulated on both sides.

Church explored Bogotá anyway. Two days after he and Field arrived, he attended a bullfight, but he soon departed in disgust. "It is a spectacle I consider to be cruel and miserable," he wrote in his diary.

The next day, Field fell ill. A physician tried to determine whether Field had contracted malaria or another tropical fever, while Church—ever the optimist—ran errands in preparation for their upcoming trip south to the volcanoes. The following day, after a small group of *cachacos* were surrounded by *artesanos* hurling stones, rumors of fatalities spread across the city. *Cachacos* armed with guns and swords faced off against a swarm of *artesanos*—two thousand of them, according to one newspaper. A squadron of soldiers was mobilized to break up the fighting, and in the ensuing fracas a soldier was killed.

To any *artesano* looking for a well-dressed gentleman to harass, Church would have been an obvious target, but he was blithely unconcerned for his safety and went around town making arrangements. He engaged a man named Tomás (whose last name has not survived) as a guide, confident that Field's condition was temporary.

By June 20, Field was well enough to accompany Church on a short trip to see what Humboldt had described as "one of the wildest scenes" in the Cordilleras. The men rode southwest across the high savanna, toward the foothills of the Andes. Acres of corn alternated with grassy bottomlands on which cattle and sheep grazed. Here and there agave plants taller than Church sent thorny spears reaching toward the sky. After about twenty miles, they came to a dwelling near the Bogotá River and arranged to stay there for several nights.

As they approached the river, they heard a noise that grew ever louder until it was exactly the "dreadful roar" Humboldt had described. Just ahead, the river was throwing itself over a precipice. Church saw with wonder that even as the water fell "in one unbroken sheet," half its volume seemed to melt into billows of prismed mist. The other half of the river slammed into the rocks below and then careened over ledges and boulders for hundreds more feet.

This was the Salto de Tequendama—Tequendama Falls. As Church gazed, he saw "huge and gaudy Macaws and other birds of brilliant plumage" wheeling through the vapor. He found the place almost unbearably sublime. "I am terrified by the beauty and grandeur of the Falls," he wrote. He felt intensely connected to Humboldt, for whom Tequendama Falls had epitomized the tropics' fusion of natural splendor, ancient myth, and scientific fact. Humboldt had found the falls "sublimely picturesque" and was fascinated by the local legend of its origin. The Muisca people, who had lived in the region for thousands of years before the Spanish invasion, had spoken of a divine old man whose beautiful but evil wife had flooded the Bogotá savanna, killing the inhabitants. The old man had punished her, exiling her so far from home that she became the moon. Then he had smashed a channel through the mountains that encircled the savanna, creating a spectacular cataract that drained the farmlands his wife had inundated.

Humboldt had noticed that the plant species growing at the top of the waterfall were dramatically different from those at the bottom, and Church saw the same contrast as he stood looking down from the plateau. "At the top of the fall," he told his mother, "you are in what is called the cold country with the trees and plants and fruits of the temperate climates; at the bottom grow palms, oranges etc."

For the next several days, he sketched in pencil and oils, trying to capture the shifting effects of water and light. On the third day, he climbed a mountain three miles away to see an "enormously splendid" view of the falls. Far to the south, he could just make out a snow-crowned volcano jutting into the sky.

Church knew that the most exciting view of the waterfall would be from below, but the steep jungle that plunged down the hillsides looked impenetrable. In 1801, Humboldt had made the three-hour descent to the ravine to take scientific measurements, but even he, a seasoned traveler, had found it a treacherous undertaking. Reluctantly, Church accompanied Field back to Bogotá.

There he found two letters awaiting him, but his joy was tempered when he read that his mother was ailing. She had been ill off and on for years, sometimes confined to bed. Church wrote to her saying that if he could magically whisk himself home, he would gladly cancel the rest of his trip. But even if he had departed for Hartford that day, the journey would have taken him at least two months. For now, he could only write that when he did finally see her, he hoped she would be "better than ever."

The next day he decided to attempt the descent to the river below Tequendama Falls. Field elected to stay in Bogotá, but Church found a new acquaintance who was willing to go with him. They rode out to meet a local landowner, who rounded up some strong men for the excursion. They all mounted mules, and as they began edging downward, Church discovered why the sure-footed mules were far preferable to horses. The path was a series of steep steps cut into the rock face. Church jumped down from his mule—not because he was scared, he told himself, but because he was impatient and could go down the steps faster than his mule could.

He made it to the river a half hour earlier than the others and stood alone, contemplating the river, the mossy green of the perpetually wet rocks, and the sunlight reflecting off the spray. When the others caught up, the hired men took the lead, slicing through the thick underbrush with machetes. Their progress was slow and difficult as they all picked their way along the shore, trying not to fall on the slippery boulders. At last they emerged onto a ledge about seventy-five feet above the river, but thick tree branches blocked much of the view. Church asked the men to cut away some of the branches, waiting impatiently as they swung their machetes over and over.

Suddenly he was face-to-face with the falls. As he gazed in astonishment, he was pleased to hear exclamations from the hired men; until now he had found the locals shockingly unmoved by the beauty of their country. Staying just beyond the spray, Church began to sketch. A painting was taking shape in his mind.

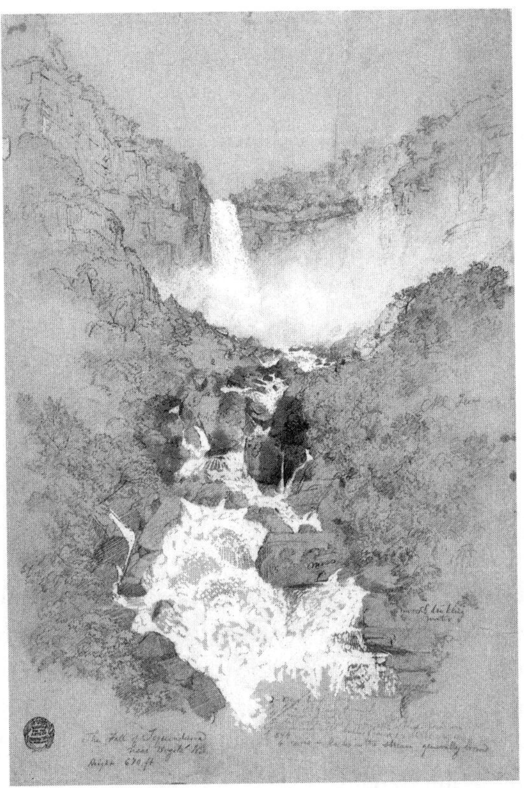

Tequendama Falls, sketched by Church in June 1853

"Unparalleled Magnificence"

Back in Bogotá, Church worked on arrangements for the next leg of their trip, which would cover more than eight hundred miles of riding and hiking. Their route would take them from New Granada into Ecuador as they crossed the three Andean mountain chains, or cordilleras, which ran roughly north-south. For the next weeks or months—they had no idea how long—they would descend from the Eastern Cordillera, cross the valley of the upper Magdalena River, and climb into the Central Cordillera, along which they would travel south until they reached the volcanoes Cotopaxi and Chimborazo.

Early on the morning of July 9, they rode southwest out of Bogotá, accompanied by their new guide, Tomás, and his fourteen-year-old son, Marcos. Church considered Marcos "as efficient as the majority of grown persons here." Field had hatched a plan to take Marcos back to the United States after their trip, thinking that such a bright boy would prosper under the refining influence of the educated, wealthy Field family.

The route through this part of the Central Cordillera was so difficult that when Humboldt and Bonpland came here in October 1801, they had encountered stretches that not even mules could traverse. The path often threaded through deep, dark crevasses barely a few feet wide—too narrow for any beast of burden. Humboldt had been appalled to find that, in such circumstances, men of means hired young men to carry them and their belongings like pack animals. These young men walked for hours each day over slippery rocks and sharp roots, bent under the weight of men sitting in chairs strapped to their backs. Sometimes their employers referred to the young men as "little horses." Church and Field, like Humboldt and Bonpland, chose instead to go on foot.

Up and down they moved, conquering one steep slope after another. They gasped in the thin air, and when they remounted and rode, their thighs ached from gripping the flanks of their mounts. In a valley between the Eastern and Central Cordilleras, they crossed the Magdalena for the last time. They had dropped eight thousand feet in altitude since Bogotá. Ahead, rising to more than fifteen thousand feet, was the Nevado del Quindío, the first volcano they planned to climb in the Central Cordillera. Humboldt had described the approach to the foot of this volcano as "the most difficult passage in the Cordilleras of the Andes. It is a thick uninhabited forest, which in the finest season cannot be traversed in less than ten or twelve days." Here he and Bonpland had admired passionflowers and a striking shrub with bright pink blooms six inches long. Palm trees rose in pencil-thin lines above the dense thickets.

Church, Field, and their guides moved slowly up the Nevado del Quindío. Church had decided to make the ascent on foot. He inhaled the misty air of the cloud forest as he picked his way around tangled masses of exposed roots. At about ten thousand feet, the expedition emerged above the tree line and entered a grassland where hundreds of strange-looking plants—strange to Church and Field, at least—stood like soldiers at attention. Some were taller than Church. Each had a single shaggy trunk from which a cluster of pale green leaves burst in a beautiful crown. These were *Espeletia* plants, also known as *frailejones* or "big monks."

They had ascended to an altitude higher than Bogotá, but still the volcanic rim was far above them. Frigid night was descending, forcing the men to set up camp well beneath the summit. Church piled on blanket after blanket in an attempt to fall asleep. The next day, as the men labored up the slopes, plant and animal life dwindled, then disappeared completely. Beneath Church's boots, the earth was a grainy volcanic debris. He reached the summit with an icy wind ripping at his skin. From here, he could see the peaks of the Central Cordillera, some shrouded in snow. They rose and dipped in an astonishing display of ancient geological forces.

Climbing down toward the temperate Cauca Valley, Church removed one layer after another to cool off. Back among the farms and fields of the valley floor, he thought he could have been in New England, except for the plantain trees waving their giant leaves. "The plantain is so universal a food in New Granada," he wrote to his sister Elizabeth, "that the sudden deprivation of it would cause a greater famine than the failure of potatoes in Ireland."

In the town of Obando, he encountered his first sloth, which he thought "resembled exceedingly an old man with white hair on his head." A villager tried to give him a baby sloth, but he turned the offer down, "having luggage enough without adding to it a Menagerie."

In Popayán, a city of seventeenth- and eighteenth-century buildings still bullet scarred thirty years after the struggle for independence, Church sketched the elaborate cathedral nestled among the tiled roofs. Above the towers of the many churches, he could see the volcano Puracé, from which a huge plume billowed. Residents lived in constant wariness of this volcano, which had killed many people when it had erupted four years earlier.

One morning in early August, Church and Field rode to a village at the foot of Puracé through scenery Church found "marvellously beautiful and pictur-esque." In a wooded valley, they came to a river known as the Río Vinagre, where Humboldt had sampled the awful-tasting water. It was sour as vinegar, which he had attributed to the river's origins in sulfuric volcanic rock. Church tried mixing it with sugar to make a sort of lemonade, which he found "delicious."

The village nearest the volcano of Puracé was "perched on the table of a rocky mountain surrounded by huge cliffs and mountains," Church wrote. From there, they set out on horseback with four guides, who raced up the slopes on foot. After hours of hiking and riding, first through the forest and then across grassland, they made their way among craggy outcroppings through a scene of "perfect desolation." Everywhere Church looked he saw only "grey ashes and rock," made bleaker still by the heavy clouds that clung to the slopes. The rain turned to hail, and a bitter wind sliced through his thick layers of clothing.

As they climbed ever higher, the rock began to alternate with slabs of glacier. The hail turned to snow. The smoke surging from the crater rolled downward, and even in his discomfort Church admired the "vaporous undu-lations &c. melting into a smoky light." When the clouds drifted apart briefly, he caught a thrilling glimpse of the summit, swathed in snow. At this altitude, he could barely take ten steps without losing his breath. The horses trudged forward, often coming to a standstill as they snorted and gasped in the thin air.

Soon, not a single horse would take another step. Church and Field dis-mounted to continue on foot. Field was so limp that two guides had to hold him upright as he staggered along, but Church marched doggedly upward to inspect a hole blasting forth sulfurous steam. He picked up a nearby stone, and it seared his hand "like a hot iron." He longed to push on to the edge of the vast crater, but none of the guides would accompany him in the strengthening snowstorm. Wet and cold, Church decided to warm up by hiking down the mountain instead of riding. He set off with a guide, and they reached the village an hour and a half ahead of the others.

FOR THE NEXT WEEK, CHURCH and Field rode south on mules toward the border between New Granada and Ecuador, passing through mountains and valleys that Church found even more stunning than the landscapes behind them. This region of New Granada was known for its fine cloaks, and Church saw women spinning wool on handheld bamboo spindles while they walked along the road. With their pale skin and poor Spanish, Church and Field were objects of curiosity to the local people, who rarely saw foreigners. "Wherever we stopped, men and women would flock into the house and deliberately stare at us whether eating or doing anything else, made no difference, and as seldom any of the huts have windows we were often much annoyed by their blocking up the door."

They rode across a windswept plateau, at whose southern edge a seemingly endless valley unfurled before them. Humboldt had reveled in the primeval beauty here, where "the vallies [*sic*] of the Cordilleras, deeper and narrower than those of the Alps and Pyrenees, present scenes of the wildest aspect and fill the soul with astonishment and terror."

Now it was Church's turn to gape. "A view of such unparalleled magnificence presented itself that I must pronounce it one of the great wonders of Nature," he exulted. He felt utterly unequal to capturing the scene but made a few "feeble sketches" before they descended and crossed into Ecuador. Ahead stretched the long corridor of volcanoes Humboldt had described, which ran southward to the capital city of Quito and beyond. Now and then, they caught sight of peaks floating amid the clouds, and Church sketched whenever he could steal a transient view. "Remember the ashy lights," he noted on a picture of the volcano Cotacachi.

On August 30, they rode into Quito, where Church visited the studio of Ecuador's most prominent landscape painter, Rafael Salas, and then strolled among the city's churches, convents, and handsome plazas. Church soon found someone to take him up Pichincha, the volcano nearest to the city. Humboldt had tried to climb it in 1801 but had fainted from altitude sickness on his first attempt. Church's climb was also ill-fated. "Having a guide who was not a guide[,] we were a long time in accomplishing the ascent," he grumbled in his diary. When they reached the summit, it was enveloped in thick clouds and they couldn't see a thing—not Quito, not the massive forest sloping toward the Pacific coast, not the scattered volcanoes to the north, south, and west. Disappointed, Church made the descent under a heavy barrage of hail. Back in Quito, he sought comfort by the fireplace at his host's house. "Only think!" he mused. "A hail storm and a fire agreeable under the equator." What a land of contrasts this was, just as Humboldt had written.

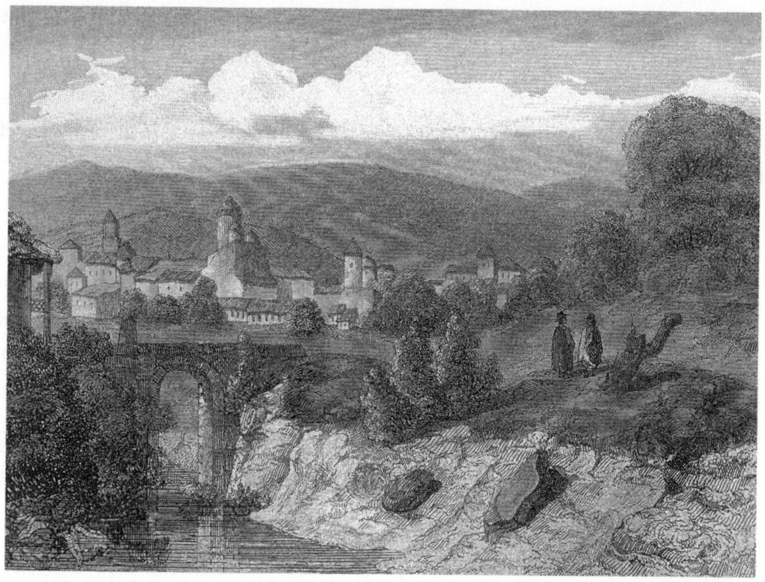

View of Quito, Ecuador, c. 1850

The last leg of their journey would take them to Cotopaxi and then Chimborazo. As they traveled south, they caught tantalizing glimpses of Cotopaxi, a snow-topped peak so perfectly conical that it looked like a child's drawing. Rising to more than 19,000 feet above sea level, it was surpassed in Ecuador only by Chimborazo. Humboldt had tried to summit Cotopaxi, reaching 14,500 feet before he gave up, thwarted by snow.

For five months Church had slogged through jungles and over mountains to get to Cotopaxi, whose peak was often scoured by cold winds and wrapped in clouds that crackled with lightning. In the past three centuries, it had erupted almost a dozen times, and no one knew when it might again spew a deadly river of boulders, lava, and mud. No European or American had reached the summit since Humboldt's effort, and Church had no intention of trying, but he desperately wanted to see the volcano long enough to sketch it for a future painting.

On September 10, he and Field rode across the volcano's base, but to their frustration, they couldn't see much of it through the heavy clouds. The terrain around them looked utterly different from the forested lower slopes of Puracé. Cotopaxi, Church noted, "grimly secludes itself in an immense circle of volcanic and comparatively barren country." It was rivetingly inhospitable, offering nothing to humans except its austere, godlike presence. Two days later, from an estate reputed to have a good view, Church kept watch all day, willing the sky to clear. At sunset, he was rewarded, and Cotopaxi shone above him, its glaciers dazzlingly white. He sketched this magnificent mountain that, for generations to come, only a few of his countrymen would see.

Church wasn't sure exactly how he would use his plein air sketches in future paintings; the process usually took him months of thought and experimentation. But he was finally feeling confident that he would return to New York with a trove of original studies on which he could draw for a long time.

All that was left now was to see and sketch Chimborazo, sixty miles to the southwest. When Humboldt and Bonpland had climbed nearly to Chimborazo's summit, it was thought to be the highest point in the world. Cotopaxi was sharp and steep, but as Church caught glimpses of Chimborazo over the next days, it looked like a floating dome, so distant from the valley below that it belonged to the sky. The mountain, he wrote, "rears its white and lofty head most grandly."

On September 19, guides awakened him at two in the morning to climb as far up Chimborazo as the weather and thin air would permit. They made it almost to the snow line—not as far as Humboldt, but close enough to the top to feel both awe and pride.

During six months of travel, Church had seen and recorded the stirring tropical and Andean landscapes he had read about in Humboldt's works, and he felt ready to return to New York. He and Field headed west for the coastal city of Guayaquil, where they boarded a steamship bound for Panama. They crossed the isthmus (which was still a part of New Granada) by train, as no canal existed yet. The day after they reached the Atlantic coast, a brief notice appeared in the local paper: "Among the passengers arrived yesterday in the

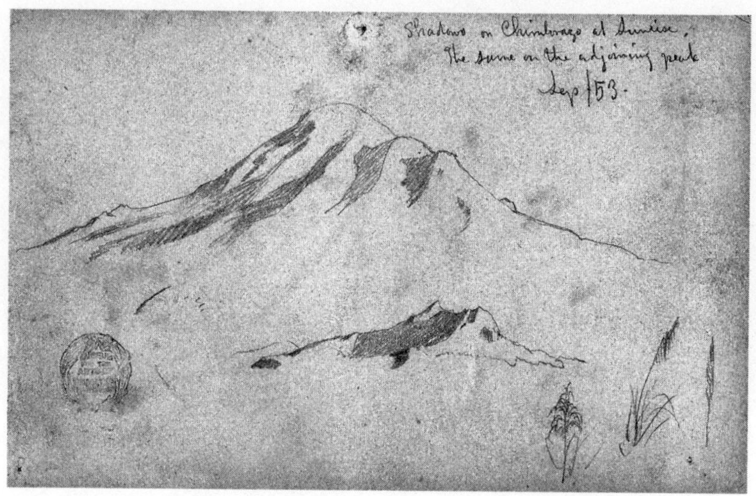

Chimborazo at sunrise, sketched by Church, September 1853

steamship *Bogota* from Guayaquil are Messrs. Cyrus W. Field and F. E. Church, of New York, who have been travelling for the last six months in South America. They say that the scenery in some parts of the Andes is grand and beautiful beyond description."

Field was bringing back two dozen live parakeets, a live jaguar, and an Indigenous boy—Marcos, the son of their guide Tomás. Church was bringing back a new vision of heaven and earth. Now he would find out if he could get it down on canvas.

CHAPTER 9

"A True American"

As the chill of late autumn settled over New York, Church unpacked his sketches of South American scenes in the Art-Union building. It was quieter than in years past. The studios were still occupied, but the gallery downstairs was no longer jammed with visitors. In the spring of 1852, the Supreme Court of the State of New York had ordered the Art-Union to cease operations, after *The New York Herald* had led a public campaign against it as an illegal lottery. New York State law barred lotteries, yet people subscribed to the Art-Union in part because they hoped to win a valuable painting at the annual drawing. After losing an appeal, the managers of the Art-Union had held an auction in December 1852 of artworks still in their possession. All four of its pictures by Church had sold, with his large canvas *New England Scenery* fetching $1,300—a record for an American landscape painting.

Church spent most of 1854 working from his memory, notes, and sketches of South America. He was trying to master entirely new plant species, atmospheric effects, and geological formations. He painted the jungle-lined waters of the Magdalena River, the prismatic mist of Tequendama Falls, and the glinting icy peaks of Andean volcanoes. He showed no new works in the spring 1854 National Academy exhibition; instead, he sent *A Country Home* and *A New England Lake*, both from the phase of his career he was leaving behind.

He was gratified by what he saw emerging on his easel that year. In December, he boasted to a client that one of his new canvases, *The Cordilleras: Sunrise*, was "unquestionably the finest picture I have painted." It combined tropical lowlands, rolling foothills, and the high Andes, all bathed in golden light. Church was so energized by his new material that by the following spring, he had completed five South American paintings. He was saving one for a show in Boston, but he planned to send the other four to the National Academy's upcoming show.

On March 12, 1855, the New York critics and public would get their first look at the results of Church's trip to the Andes—if, that is, they could be made to focus on art. As the exhibition's opening day approached, the city was in an uproar about the murder of William Poole, a famous and controversial businessman known as Butcher Bill, who died at his Manhattan home on March 9 of a gunshot wound sustained two weeks earlier. Poole had been a vocal partisan of the Know-Nothings, a political party opposed to immigration and immigrants' rights. So many foreigners had arrived in recent decades that the population of New York City was ten times what it had been in 1800. In some wards, people born abroad outnumbered native-born Americans three to one, and nativists such as Poole saw a tide of squalor, disease, and criminality rising to engulf the city.

Poole had been shot at a Bowery saloon by friends of the Irish political operative John Morrissey, a man with whom Poole had a long-standing feud. The day he died, *The New York Times* charged that he had been assassinated by foreign thugs. Poole's enterprises had been butchery, boxing, and saloons, but qualms about his rough and debauched life were quickly forgotten in the united rage at immigrants.

The National Academy's annual exhibition was supposed to open the day after Poole's funeral, but now no one could think about anything but murder and politics. Many artists were desperate to find buyers for their paintings—an awful winter had slowed art sales—and the academy, itself in financial straits, urgently needed to sell tickets.

On March 11, the day of the funeral, Butcher Bill's wife allowed a photographer to take a daguerreotype portrait of her dead husband, who was to be buried in a black suit with a loose white collar in the style made fashionable by Lord Byron. "He was in an excellent state of preservation," the *Herald* wrote, with "only slight indications of decomposition being visible on his forehead." The pallbearers loaded the coffin onto a black hearse pulled by four white horses. Painted on either side of the hearse were Poole's last words: I DIE A TRUE AMERICAN.

By early afternoon, when the funeral officially began, the temperature was still only in the thirties, but the streets were clogged with mourners anyway. Not since the funeral of Alexander Hamilton a half century earlier had the city seen such intense public grieving. Nearly a hundred thousand people lined the sidewalks, leaned out windows, and even clung to tree branches to watch the cortège. It moved slowly along Bleecker Street to Broadway, then turned south toward the dock at the tip of Manhattan; from there a ferryboat carried the hearse and a large contingent of mourners to Brooklyn, where Poole was buried in Green-Wood Cemetery.

The next day, the city papers ran front-page stories elaborating on the funeral and speculating about the coming trial of Poole's assassins. Few people showed up at the National Academy's exhibition opening. A critic for a new magazine called *The Crayon* stopped by and saw "many poor portraits and *absolutely bad* pictures," but he was intrigued by Church's four South American paintings, which he planned to review in detail later.

New York art lover George Templeton Strong also went to see the National Academy offerings. A brilliant, opinionated lawyer in his mid-thirties, Strong was keeping a diary about his personal life, New York affairs, and national politics that would eventually run to over 4 million words. He was a loyal patron of the National Academy, although his diary was often scathing about the art he encountered there.

The academy had recently moved, and at first, Strong was grateful to find the new "space smaller than usual and consequently the number of bad pictures less." Then he caught sight of Church's paintings. He was completely disarmed by their "warm, rich, hazy air, copious masses of brilliant, many-colored equatorial foliage, with outlying festoons and draperies of tangled vine-growth and great pendant clusters of fruit and flowers." Church's work was "strong, real, and true," Strong wrote. "I think him our most promising artist."

With the Poole murder dominating the news, reviews of the academy exhibition came out slowly. The most thoughtful piece appeared in

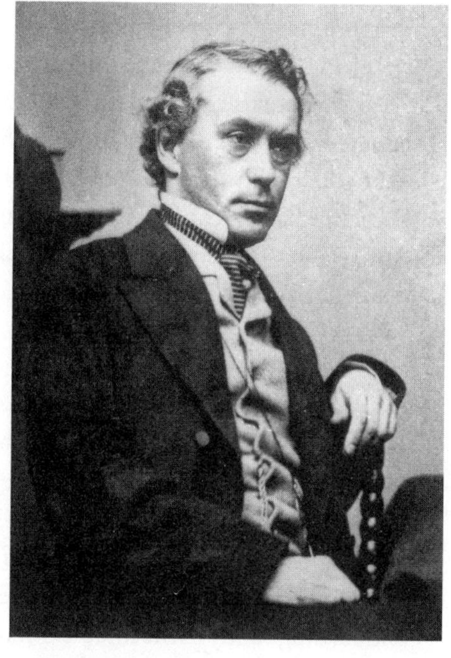

George Templeton Strong

The Crayon, recently founded by John Durand (son of Asher Durand) and the painter and critic William James Stillman. They hoped *The Crayon* would help improve American art criticism and thereby, perhaps, American art.

The anonymous *Crayon* critic complained about the poverty of the New York art scene, especially compared to the Old World. London had six annual exhibitions and, on average, rejected two paintings for every one accepted; New York had only one exhibition and accepted almost every painting, just to fill the wall space. There was no real "American school" yet, no real "indications of a national and peculiar greatness." Landscape painting seemed the most promising genre, but many landscape painters substituted "blank spaces" or "masses of paint" for the true details of nature. There were, of course, a few exceptions: Asher Durand knew how to paint trees, Jasper Cropsey could render a foreground believably, and John Frederick Kensett excelled at panoramas of the White Mountains. But Church rose above them all, the *Crayon* critic wrote, as "the most remarkable and complete exception to this general fault of American painters." He had an uncanny ability to recollect the tiniest details of a landscape he had seen months or even years before. *The Cordilleras: Sunrise* showed his "absolute knowledge" of natural elements such as clouds, rocks, and plants. To the *Crayon* critic, "this faculty of his is one of the most extraordinary things in modern Art."

The critic for *The New York Times*, which had been founded only four years earlier, also singled out *The Cordilleras: Sunrise*. "The atmospheric effects in this picture are superb; the tropical foliage luxuriant and well defined." The *Knickerbocker* critic wrote, "CHURCH shows, this year, that his genius is not confined to painting northern scenes." The skies of South America shimmered on the gallery walls. "See the clearness, the brilliancy, the depth of atmosphere, and then say that CHURCH is not a great painter—if you can."

THAT SAME SPRING, AT THE Boston Athenaeum's exhibition, Church presented the most daring picture he had ever painted. At four feet by over six feet, it was also the largest. With *The Andes of Ecuador*, Church seemed to have traveled not just to the Andes but to the dawn of time. Under a white-hot sun, barren foothills filled much of the canvas, rising darkly in the foreground, and turning ruddy in the middle distance, before vanishing on the horizon. In the far distance, Cotopaxi soared. Church had felt the extremes of this wild place in his body. He had baked under the Andean sun one day and shivered in a snowstorm the next, and this hard-won experience animated every inch of *The Andes of Ecuador*. Among the crowds who came to see it was Humboldt's ardent admirer Henry David Thoreau. The painting did pay homage to Humboldt, yet Church had endowed it with a spiritual awe entirely his own. He had included a tiny wayside cross and a remote church, explicitly linking his faith in a divine Creator with his wonder at the beauty and drama of the New World.

A young railroad executive named William Henry Osborn bought *The Andes of Ecuador* for his townhouse on Fifth Avenue. W.H., as Osborn's friends called him, was only five years older than Church, but he had already made a fortune. Church later joked about his own dependence on rich patrons, remarking, "We who can draw everything but checks are always ready to have less talented people draw the checks for us." In truth, he respected and liked Osborn and Osborn's wife, Virginia. Mrs. Osborn was the daughter of another of Church's patrons, the merchant Jonathan Sturges, and she had grown up surrounded by books and art. Now Virginia and W.H. were filling their home with cultural treasures of their own. Virginia told her sister that she often came down in the morning to find her husband standing in front of a Durand sketch he loved, "drinking in large draughts of forest coolness. . . . I suppose he exclaims a dozen times 'how beautiful, how perfect it is.'"

Compared to these new friends, Church had no wealth or power. He had recently raised his prices, so that a two-by-three-foot canvas had gone from $400 to $500 and a four-by-six-foot canvas from $1,000 to $1,200. But he still roomed in a boarding house near lumberyards and a piano factory. What Church had instead of money was talent, and the Osborns were interested in talent. They also soon came to prize what Church's closest friends loved about him: his easy, unpretentious air and his gift for

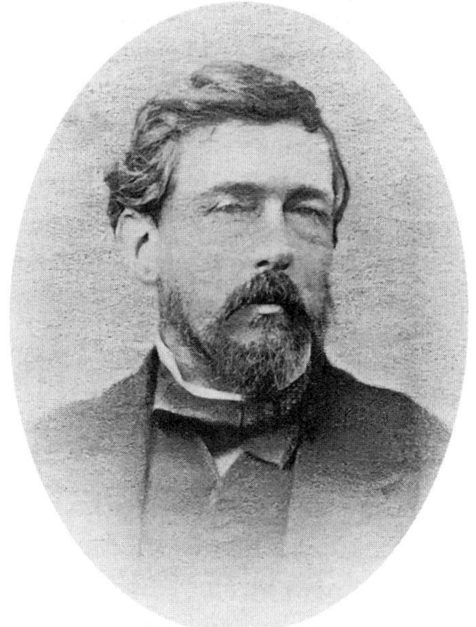

W. H. Osborn

devoted friendship. For his part, Church found that the Osborns managed to be worldly without being impious—the very balance he was trying to strike.

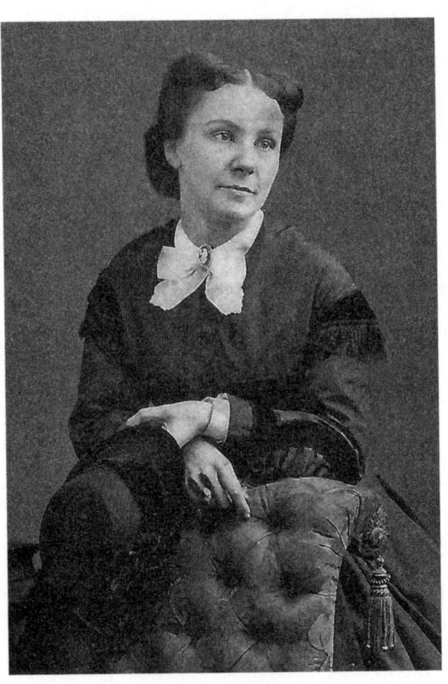

Virginia Osborn

Two years after *The Andes of Ecuador* debuted in Boston, W. H. Osborn gave Church permission to display it at the 1857 National Academy show, and New York audiences were as dazzled as Boston's. The picture, one critic later recalled, "seemed a quivering haze upon the wall. It was a picture of heat itself." Strong was again impressed. "Magnificent, sultry-tropical landscape by Church, in the neighborhood of which I think a sensitive thermometer would rise rapidly," he wrote in his diary.

The reviewer for *Harper's Weekly* was effusive. "Let me stand with bare head and expanding chest upon one of Church's mountain-peaks, gazing over a billowy flood of hills; at my feet, torrents flashing, half-seen, through clouds; while from the rifted heavens the southern sunshine pours, like God's benediction on my temples." At last, here was a New World artist who had painted a virtuosic picture of a quintessentially New World landscape. Cole had celebrated American landscapes, of course, but he had been born in England and studied in Europe as a young man, and his work often engaged with Old World artistic and architectural traditions. Church had been born in Connecticut, studied in the Catskills, and ranged up and down the New World for his vistas. He had never even been to Europe. He struck many critics and viewers as the first great landscape painter who was truly an American.

The eminent Philadelphia portraitist Rembrandt Peale, now nearly eighty, went to see *The Andes of Ecuador*. His ecstatic reaction reached Church in a letter from a friend: "Rembrandt Peale said . . . that he had seen all the good pictures in the world and your 'Andes' was the best landscape ever painted."

CHAPTER 10

"Daring and Insolent Men"

The horse careened around the bend, rocking the wagon dangerously, and a moment later Church was thrown from his seat. He somersaulted through the air, hitting the ground hard, but quickly jumped to his feet and climbed back into the wagon, reassuring his friends that he was fine. After his death-defying adventures in the Andes, a tumble from a wagon on a summer day in New England couldn't rattle him.

It was August 1855, and Church was back on Mount Desert Island in Maine, this time with his sisters Elizabeth, thirty-one, and Charlotte, twenty-three. He welcomed the chance to spend time with them; he usually only saw them on his infrequent visits to Hartford. As the sole boy in the family, Church had been allowed to go seek his fortune; his sisters, although educated at an excellent girls' school, still lived with their parents. Elizabeth was a strong-willed woman who, lacking a professional outlet for her intellect and drive, behaved like a second mother to the whole Church family. Charlotte was meeker; she suffered from some unspecified chronic illness that frequently left her exhausted.

Church and his sisters had come to Mount Desert to join a monthlong house party at the invitation of Charles Tracy, a genial lawyer Church knew from the Century Association. Traveling by train, sailboat, and wagon, more than twenty-five people had converged on three houses at the northern end of Somes Sound, a fjord-like inlet stretching from the heart of the island to the sea. The day after they arrived, a piano had joined them by sailboat.

Twenty-nine years old and fresh from his triumph with *The Andes of Ecuador*, Church was brimming with high spirits. The two things he loved most—exquisite natural surroundings and the company of witty, joyful people—were both in abundance that summer on Mount Desert. He raved to his new companions about the island, with its blazing sunsets and serene lakes, and he took pleasure in showing them his favorite haunts. The spirit of the happy days with Cole at Cedar Grove hovered over Church as he settled into an extended surrogate family whose members, like the Coles, loved music, stories, games, and mountain hikes.

Each morning began with prayers and hymns in the parlor. Then, if the weather was fair, the guests set out in groups to roam the island, tramping through mossy forests up to bare summits where they could see for miles. At night they gazed up at the Milky Way and watched for meteors. Casually, much as colonial settlers had done, Church and his friends tried out new names for geographical features, although they had been named long ago by the Wabanaki who had lived on the island for millennia. Church bestowed the name Eagle Lake on a lake frequented by bald eagles, but to the Wabanaki the lake was Wiwonotonet, or "surrounded by mountains." Church's name was the one that stuck with European American residents and visitors.

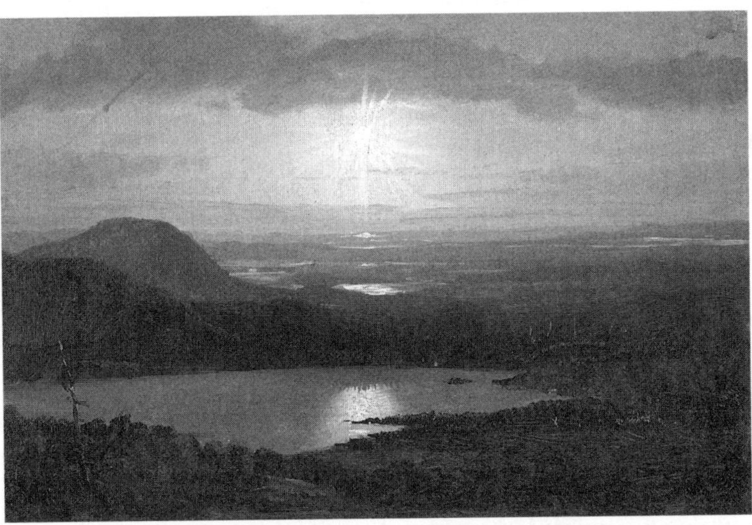

Oil sketch of Eagle Lake by Church, c. 1855

On one outing, the hikers unfurled blankets in the whipping wind and pinned them down with picnic baskets and their own tired bodies. Church kept the wind at bay by pulling on a cloak he had brought back from South America. He carried a siphon coffeepot and passed around steaming cups of coffee. When the party headed back along the grassy lanes that wound through the forest, Church was seized by an impulse to jump from the wagon and race home on his own. He was propelled by the same ebullient energy that had sent him hurtling on foot down volcanoes ahead of his guides in the Andes two years earlier. Walking and running for five miles, he reached the house before the rest of the picnickers, who arrived to find him, in Tracy's words, "fresh as morning."

One week after all the other houseguests had arrived, Theodore Winthrop joined the party. A lawyer-in-training at Tracy's firm, Winthrop's true passion was literature, and Church discovered in him a kindred spirit who combined the emotional depths of Cole with the energetic playfulness to which Church himself inclined. When Winthrop walked through the countryside on a beautiful day, he was sometimes overtaken by an exuberance that made him turn somersaults on the grass or vault back and forth over fences like a schoolboy.

But Winthrop was also plagued by melancholy and self-doubt. He carried the name of a dead older brother whom his parents had revered, a psychological burden compounded by more tragedy when twelve-year-old Winthrop lost his adored father. Longing for a male role model, he was drawn to Church. Though only two years Winthrop's senior, Church was by nature far more self-confident and already occupied an exalted position in American cultural life.

Like Church, Winthrop knew firsthand the romance and challenge of traveling in South America. A few years earlier, he had signed on with a U.S. expedition seeking the best route for a planned canal across Panama. Several men in his party had died of starvation after getting lost for more than a month. Both Winthrop and Church had seen scorpions, feasted

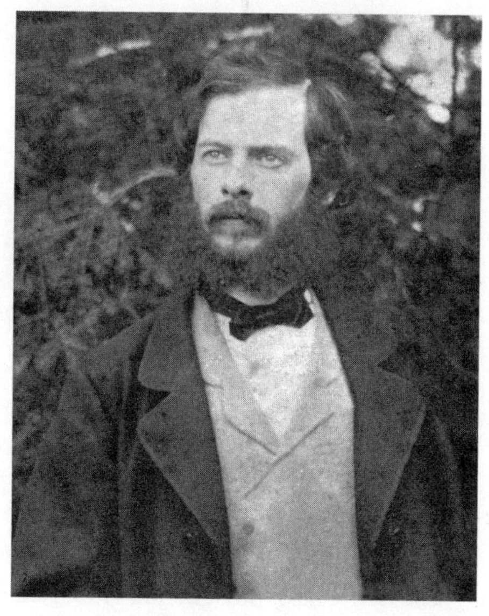

Theodore Winthrop

on plantains, and trekked through jungles where jaguars hunted. Together that summer, they became the ringleaders of excursions on Mount Desert.

Occasionally, Church went fishing with one or two of the other men, bringing home mackerel to add to the supper spread on the long dining table. Other days, he assembled a few of the children and drove them around the island in a wagon. He drew cartoons of the group's adventures to entertain everyone and dreamed up a coat of arms for the house party. In the evenings, the guests acted out charades by candlelight or played another game called the Dumb Orator, in which one person read a dramatic speech while another conveyed its meaning in histrionic gestures. With his quick wit and elastic body, Church excelled at such pastimes.

One day he made a gorgeous sketch of a lake edged with spruces and firs and titled it "Loch Annie." Church had taken notice of Charles Tracy's eldest daughter, Annie, a pretty girl of seventeen.

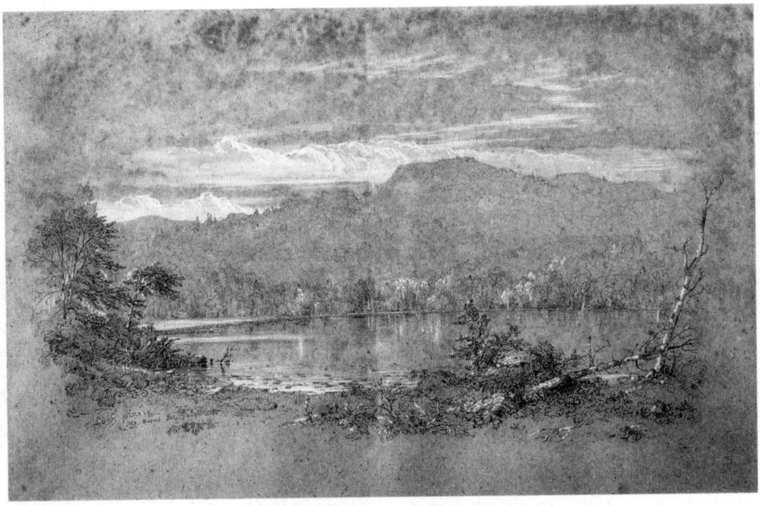

"Loch Annie," sketched by Church, 1855

Sometimes, if a sunset proved too dramatic or a lake too misty to resist, he slipped away from the house alone to sketch and paint. When the wind and rain pummeled the trees and the fishing boats bobbed at their moorings amid the whitecaps, most of the guests sat by the fireplace, sang around the piano, played backgammon, or read aloud. But Church went out into the storm to watch the waves slamming against a rocky promontory called Schooner Head, ten miles away on the eastern side of the island. He was fascinated by water in motion.

CUT OFF FROM THE MAINLAND, the houseguests received news of the wider world only when a packet of newspapers arrived for Tracy in the mail from New York. Among the advertisements promoting hair-growth tonic, pianos, and a shipment of twenty thousand live Swedish leeches for medical use, the broadsheets brought distressing news of the national struggle over slavery. After the passage of the Kansas-Nebraska Act in 1854, violence had broken out on the border between Missouri, a slave state, and the Kansas Territory, whose status was to be determined by a vote of its qualified residents. Would Kansas be admitted as a slave state or a free state? Pro-slavery Missourians were staging bloody sorties into Kansas, where they clashed with antislavery emigrants from the Northeast. Men were shooting one another in the streets.

Tracy was no admirer of slavery, but he was desperately worried that abolitionists were going to end up undoing the Union. He had promised himself that he wouldn't think about politics once on holiday from New York, where living in constant anxiety about imminent national disaster was exhausting. "These thoughts have crowded upon me and I feel ugly," Tracy fretted in his journal.

ON THE MORNING OF AUGUST 18, Church and Winthrop set off on a hike with a party made up of two boys and five girls and young women, including Church's two sisters. Later that day, the two boys returned, saying that all the others had decided to hike up a mountain near Somes Sound. By eleven o'clock that night, the parents of the missing children began to panic, imagining a fatal fall in the dark, hypothermia, drowning. Tracy and several other men set out through the woods, shouting for the hikers, to no avail.

Soon after sunrise, Church returned home alone and explained that the young adventurers hadn't been lost at all. He had led the party up the mountain, but their progress had been so slow that the sun had set when they were only halfway to the summit. He and Winthrop had guided the group back down through the pitch-black forest until they came to a little lakeside beach. There they had built a bonfire of driftwood and fashioned a large bed from evergreen boughs. Church and Winthrop had sat up and kept watch while everyone else slept, Church passing the hours in sketching first the silhouettes around the bonfire and then his sleeping friends. When the sky grew light, he raced back through the woods to fetch a wagon in which to bring them home.

Church and Winthrop, both highly experienced outdoorsmen, had misjudged the strength and energy of their companions, but they had proved themselves resourceful in a crisis. The hikers arrived home, tired yet cheerful. "They all declared they had a capital time and that the conduct and skill of the gentlemen was admirable," Tracy noted gamely.

SUMMER, AND WITH IT THE house party, was coming to an end. The leaves in the blueberry thickets began to turn crimson, and plumes of goldenrod waved across the fields and along the lanes. In early September, most of the party scattered to New York, Boston, or Hartford. Church and his sister Elizabeth remained on the island for another week, accompanying Mrs. Tracy and her daughter Annie to a guesthouse at Schooner Head. Church and Annie thus had a whole week to become better acquainted; after leaving Mount Desert, Annie and her mother spent a night in Hartford with the Churches before going on to New York.

The bonds between the two families endured. That fall, Elizabeth came down to New York from Hartford to stay with the Tracys, and she and Mrs. Tracy subsequently exchanged warm letters. The Tracys visited Church in his studio to see his work in progress, and on occasion he dined with them at their home. People began to speculate about Church's interest in Annie. After a winter party at the Tracys' house, one young guest reported to his sister what people were saying: "Miss Annie Tracy, one of the

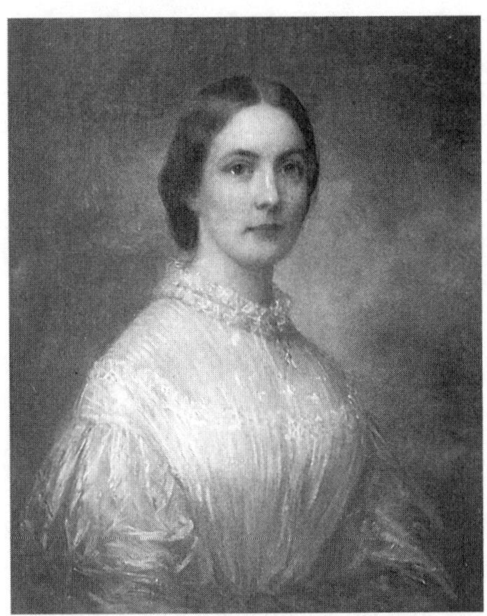

Annie Tracy

prettiest girls in all New York, . . . will one day, if prophets tell the truth be the wife of Mr. Church, the great artist."

WINTHROP AND CHURCH MADE PLANS for a wilderness trek the following summer. In mid-July of 1856, they left New York on the steamer *Isaac Newton*, which Winthrop described as "a great, ugly, three-tiered box that walks the North [or Hudson] River, like a laboratory of greasy odors." From Albany, they headed by train to the Adirondack Mountains—"a compact, convenient, accessible little wilderness," as Winthrop called the expansive range, admiring its beauty but lamenting the crowds of tourists. He and Church thought of themselves as tougher types, bound for wilder lands.

Four years earlier, Church had trekked through central Maine to Mount Katahdin. Now that he had seen and painted the vast Andes under Humboldt's spell, he wanted to see Katahdin again, and this time he wanted Winthrop to join him. He regaled his friend with tales of flying down a river in a birchbark canoe until, as Winthrop wrote, "my life seemed incomplete." Winthrop didn't need much prodding. He had traveled through landscapes Church himself had never experienced, including the American West, but hadn't yet set foot on Mount Katahdin, even though Thoreau, Winthrop's personal hero, had in 1848 published a stirring account of his own trek there. "The tops of mountains are among the unfinished parts of the globe," Thoreau wrote, "whither it is a slight insult to the gods to climb and pry into their secrets, and try their effect on our humanity. Only daring and insolent men, perchance, go there." This was a challenge that Winthrop couldn't resist. He considered adventurousness a moral imperative.

Winthrop and Church traversed Vermont and New Hampshire by train and stagecoach and then began walking the rest of the way to Mount Katahdin. Now and then they paused so Church could sketch and Winthrop could take notes for his travel narrative. Winthrop loved watching Church's fingers fly as he gathered the sky, water, and mountains onto paper. He found Church an ideal companion. "Church of course has made himself popular with all hands," Winthrop wrote his mother from a farmhouse where they lodged one night. Church was even-tempered and relaxed, "totally at peace with himself and the world."

Occasionally, they fell into conversation with a farmer or lumberman, and Winthrop listened with delight to the Maine accent. "People talked as if, instead of ivory ring or coral rattle to develop their infantile teeth, they had bitten upon pine knots." When they heard the lonesome call of a loon on a fogbound lake, Winthrop mused that perhaps the lake and woods were hiding in the mist because they felt too plain to impress Church.

At the edge of Moosehead Lake, they found an experienced guide who agreed to ferry them in his birchbark canoe and then lead them overland to Katahdin. Seeing the peak on the horizon, the two friends talked about the way a mountain linked earth and sky and pulled color and light and darkness into itself. As they moved ever closer over the next days, Church made oil sketches of Katahdin's different moods, capturing them with swift, sure strokes. When the sun shone, the rocky slopes took on the honeyed hue of a cedar plank; at sunset, they turned violet beneath persimmon clouds.

It was a heavenly trip for a friendship forged in a shared love of nature. With the expert help of their guide, they ran rapids that buffeted the canoe among jagged rocks, leaving the young men damp and exhilarated. Katahdin slowly grew sharper and taller on the horizon but remained distant. One day they hoisted a red blanket above their canoe and let the wind carry them across a lake. When they camped by the Penobscot River, Church caught and cooked trout. After supper, he boiled water or, when they had it, milk, to make hot chocolate using cocoa he had brought from Colombia. "What a pity nature spoiled a cook by making the muddler of that chocolate a painter of grandeurs!" Winthrop teased.

When they were forced to portage overland, their guide would carry the canoe on his head, looking, Winthrop thought, like "an elongated and mobile mushroom." As they pushed through the undergrowth, they saw signs of bear and moose: slashing claw marks, discarded antlers, and huge cloven prints. Church and Winthrop began to sense they had entered the wilder lands they craved. The three men finally reached the base of Katahdin, where they set up camp and waited for the sun to come out. After two cloudy days, they rose at dawn to find the world illuminated—except for the mountaintop, which was obscured by fog. Their guide led them partway before giving up, but Church and Winthrop decided to push ahead, praying that the clouds would lift while they climbed.

At the ragged lower edge of the fog that clung to the peak, they paused to survey the world below. They could see all the way to Mount Desert Island, almost 150 miles to the south, on the Atlantic coast. It was a Humboldtian view, encompassing mountain, forest, meadow, and ocean. A decade earlier, Thoreau had stood among these boulders on the slope of Katahdin. In the towns and on the farms and in the wreckage of felled forests below, he had reflected, it was impossible to grasp the fundamental unity of human beings with the natural world. But up here, among the desolate rocks, he had felt that he was made of the selfsame material as the planet itself. "This was that Earth of which we have heard, made out of Chaos and Old Night," he had exulted. "Think of our life in nature,—daily to be shown matter, to come in contact with it,—rocks, trees, wind on our cheeks! the *solid* earth! the *actual* world! the *common sense! Contact! Contact! Who* are we? *where* are we?"

Winthrop, like Thoreau before him, tried to put his impressions of Katahdin in words, but Church captured his reaction in pictures—in the penciled branches of a dying spruce or in the painted scar of an avalanche that had tumbled down the mountain's weathered face. His ideas about nature had changed since his last trip here. In his 1853 painting of Katahdin, he had depicted symbols of pastoral life: a large house, a bridge, grazing cattle, and a boy peacefully contemplating the whole scene. But the plein air studies on which he had based his painting hadn't contained these features, for the simple fact that they didn't exist. *Mt. Ktaadn* had been an optimistic work that celebrated human ingenuity and dreamed of a harmonious balance between wilderness and the farmers who would surely arrive in the wake of the lumberjacks. Now, only three years later, as Church surveyed Katahdin with eyes that had read Humboldt and seen the Andes, he was gripped by the intrinsic beauty of nonhuman nature. This mountain was not some outpost of agrarian New England, but a massive, ancient entity forged by grinding planetary forces. There was a reason the Penobscot called it Katahdin—"the greatest mountain."

Back in New York, Church retreated to his studio and began work on a painting called *Sunset*. He poured his recent revelations into it, blazing a red and yellow sky above a dark lake and forest. Far in the distance, he painted Katahdin rising, eternal and aloof. After Humboldt and the Andes, Church could no longer view nature as a mere backdrop for human events, real or allegorical. His art would continue to reflect on the state of the nation, but his political concerns were now interwoven with reverence for the cosmos.

CHAPTER II

"Fidgety as a Wildcat"

One summer day in the 1850s, two women, three men, and a young boy gathered on the American shore of Niagara Falls. The women shaded their faces with parasols, and they all gazed out at the Niagara River as it poured over the cliffs in silken stripes of cream and dark.

Photographer Platt Babbitt captured the moment, just as he did similar moments each day, weather permitting. He had staked out this spot on Prospect Point as his own. When other photographers tried to work there, he or an assistant waved an umbrella in the air to ruin their pictures. Babbitt sold his pictures to the tourists he photographed. Sometimes he took a picture without their knowledge and hawked it to them afterward; other times the tourists hired him first and then arranged themselves in attentive poses.

Niagara Falls had been tempting photographers almost since the invention of photography. It was among the world's wondrous sights, and it struck many people as equally wondrous that someone had found a way to preserve its likeness using glass, light, and chemicals. Church bought three of Babbitt's Niagara photographs. Two were unpopulated winter scenes; the third showed the group on Prospect Point, one of whom might have been Church himself. He was planning to paint Niagara Falls, and he found that photographs, like his own annotated sketches, helped him recall critical details when he was back in the studio. He wasn't concerned that the rise of photography might lessen the public's appetite for landscape paintings. Photographs drained the world to black and white and captured only what was in front of the lens, but as a painter, he could compose and edit in vivid color. He could take trees he had seen from one vantage point, a mountain seen from another, and a waterfall seen from a third, combining them all to create a landscape greater and more meaningful than its individual features.

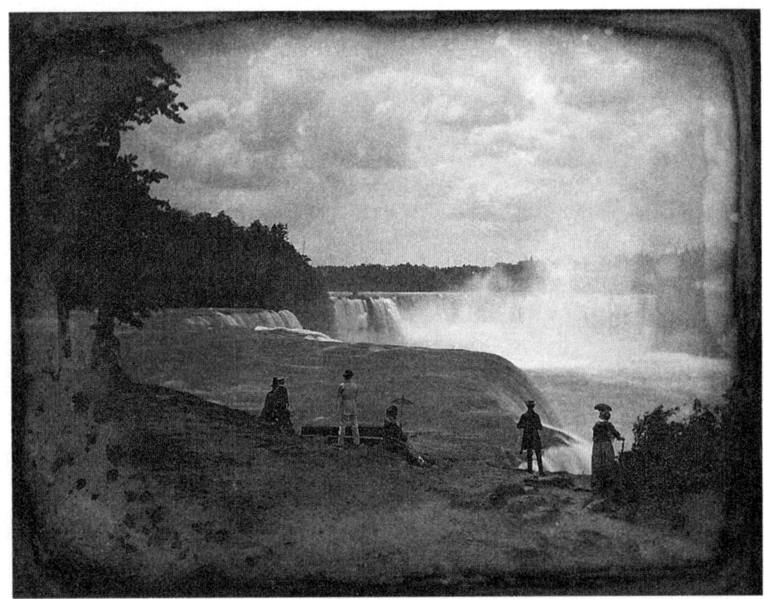

Niagara Falls, by Platt Babbitt

Painting water was one of the most difficult challenges an artist could undertake. Ruskin said that it was "like trying to paint a soul" and that falling water was impossible—"beyond the power of man; to do it even partially has been granted to but one or two." Church had tried with his 1854 painting of Tequendama Falls, but a critic who saw it at the National Academy dismissed the effort: "He should not paint falling water—for he cannot." Church's reaction was to set about painting the most famous falling water in the Western world.

Many artists had already tried to capture the Falls, Cole chief among them. He had first visited the Falls in May 1829, a few days before sailing from New York on a European painting trip. "I wish to take a 'last lingering look' at our wild scenery," he had told a patron. "I shall endeavor to impress its features so strongly on my mind that in the midst of the fine scenery of other countries their grand and beautiful peculiarities shall not be erased." Cole arrived at Niagara to find the cataracts grander by far than he had anticipated. He began making pencil and oil sketches, but he was certain that he would fail to do the scene justice. He made notes about how to try to portray something so impossibly sublime and restless. It was like trying to paint music, he decided. Maybe he could translate the crashing and roaring of the water into pigments of varying intensity, turning sound into color. He could convey the passage of time, as the water plunged and boiled, through the sequence of masses on his canvas. Cole kept trying to capture Niagara, first while in London and then after returning to the United States.

Niagara was endlessly fascinating to all kinds of visitors. Abraham Lincoln, who made a stop there in 1848, wondered, "By what mysterious power is it, that millions and millions, are drawn from all parts of the world, to gaze upon Niagara Falls?" Human beings were so peculiar—even when they knew the scientific cause of a phenomenon, as they did of Niagara, their hearts could surge at its beauty. The profound feelings inspired by the natural world was a theme that Emerson had explored in *Nature*. "Almost I fear to think how glad I am," Emerson wrote of the simple experience of walking across a town common on a gray winter's day. Where did this strange emotional response come from? Emerson located it in an "occult relation" between people and plants and sky and light. Nature, he argued, does far more than provide the farmer with crops and the poet with beauty; it reveals the quintessentially human drive to discover unifying principles and meaning. Nature shows us who we are.

At a time when Niagara was not far from the western frontier of the United States, the Falls counted as the most astonishing natural wonder in North America. Artists, grocers, housewives, farmers, schoolteachers, and stockbrokers felt things there they hadn't felt before. Niagara signified abundance and eternity amid scarcity and death. In a world where food ran out, clothes fell apart, wells went dry, and the human body turned to dust, the Falls spoke of a larger power. For many, that power was God, who had surely created this extraordinary spectacle. Others thought that one didn't need to believe in God to be humbled by a physical force so great that for millennia it had sent thousands of tons of water hurtling down each second.

What the first people here had felt when they contemplated Niagara was of little interest to the tourists who bought trinkets from their descendants. But it was Indigenous people—possibly from the Iroquois Confederacy, possibly from an earlier tribe—who had first called the falls Niagara, a word thought to mean "thunder of waters."

By the 1850s, paintings, engravings, panoramas, and more recently daguerreotypes of Niagara Falls had been seen by hundreds of thousands around the world. To many people, the Falls represented the soul of the United States: wild and ungovernable. The water had claimed countless lives—through boating accidents, slippery rocks, daring stunts gone wrong, and suicide. The Falls' history of violence disturbed some visitors, but for others it heightened the sense of awe. This fearsome beauty, this wild soul of the nation, was what Church sought as he began to make sketching excursions there.

In 1856 and 1857, he took the train from New York City to Niagara Falls repeatedly. Sometimes he stayed at Cataract House, a grand hotel on the American side known to be a stop on the Underground Railroad. Black employees risked their jobs and even their lives to help enslaved servants of the hotel's Southern guests escape to the Canadian side. Southerners began to avoid the hotel; Northerners who abhorred slavery made a point of patronizing it.

CHURCH WAS OUTSIDE AS MUCH as possible; being indoors at Niagara made him "fidgety as a wildcat," he told his friend Goodman. He paced the shores each day making dozens of sketches and sometimes went back out after supper to study the play of moonlight on the cascading water. One day he chartered the *Maid of the Mist* and persuaded the captain to take him to the roaring base of Horseshoe Falls. "I had only one friend with me who got only a little skeered [scared]," he joked to Goodman afterward. The vessel bucked and bounced while Church stabbed wildly with his paintbrush. It took him forty minutes to get a passable sketch.

On the days Church sat sketching on dry land, tourists sometimes peered over his shoulder and gave him advice. He tried to act gruff to discourage them, but it wasn't in his nature, and new gawkers kept stopping by anyway. "As there is but a step from the sublime to the ridiculous," he wrote to Goodman, "I can readily bring myself from the contemplation of the Awful Cataract to the study of human character as developed in the persons of numerous verdants, who full of greenness and conceit, swarm the Hotels."

When he felt he had enough sketches—in pencil, gouache, and oil—from enough vantage points, he went back to his studio and arranged them so he could study their structures, lines, and dramatic effects. Church had a reputation for pacing in his studio. He backed away from a picture to judge it from afar, walked toward it again, distanced himself again, and reapproached. After

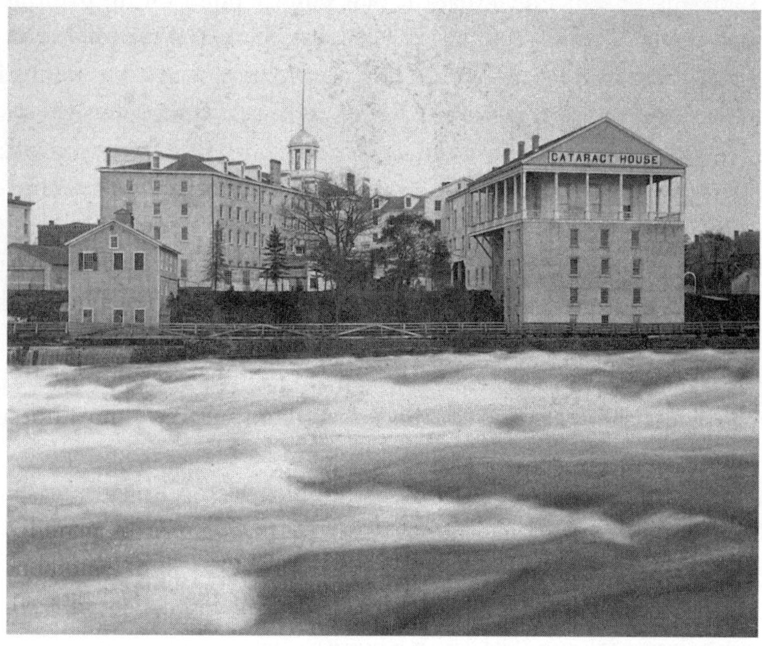

Cataract House, Niagara Falls

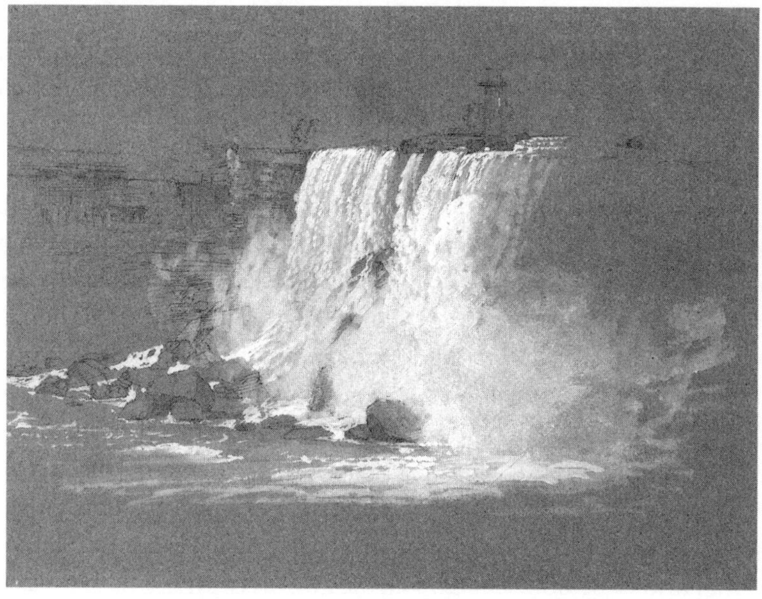

Niagara Falls, sketched by Church in October 1856

weeks of this, he concluded that the best vantage point for his painting of Niagara would be from a spot on the Canadian shore near the top of Horseshoe Falls. A sublime view—beautiful and frightening at once—unfurled from here. The shallow water rolled over smooth rocks before plunging out of sight. In the middle distance, at the center of the horseshoe, the water looked completely different, falling in a thick green sheet. At its farthest point, by the shore of Goat Island, it was a rippling white curtain. It would be a fiendishly complex composition, but if he could capture all these shifting moods of the water in oils, he might provoke the same emotions that the real Niagara did: exhilaration, anxiety, terror, and awe.

He taped two pieces of paper together and painted a long, horizontal oil sketch of Horseshoe Falls. Water dominated his composition. Only a thin strip of earth at the bottom left offered any safety from the torrent as it swept toward the cliff. To gauge the effect, Church put the oil sketch on display in his studio and invited friends and critics to come see it. He was soon crowing to Osborn about "the universal and unqualified satisfaction it gives." Excited reviews of the sketch ran in the New York and Boston papers, drawing attention to his full-scale Niagara painting before he had even put brush to canvas, just as Church intended.

By late February 1857, he felt ready to start painting in earnest. He was as self-assured as he had ever been in the face of a blank canvas. "I shall commence my great Niagara tomorrow I think," he wrote Osborn. "Size 7ft 6 inches by 3 ft 6 inches!!!!" A few weeks later he told another friend he was "hammering away" at Niagara "in a fever of excitement," adding in his offhand way that, otherwise, "New York is quiet except two or three interesting murders etc."

After eight weeks of work, he was done.

Channeling his father's business acumen, Church negotiated a lucrative contract that entailed a sophisticated marketing campaign. His customary approach had been to sell a painting to a patron willing to let him show it later at the National Academy's spring exhibition. For *Niagara Falls*, he struck a new kind of deal. Williams, Stevens, Williams & Co., a New York firm that sold mirrors, picture frames, and art, agreed to pay him $2,500 for the painting—more than twice what he had previously received for a canvas of this size—and to display it in a dedicated room at their store on lower Broadway. The contract stipulated that if the firm later sold the painting for more than $2,500, the difference would be split equally between Church and the firm. For an additional $2,000, Church sold the firm his copyright of the image, so they could produce and sell color lithographs.

About two weeks before the National Academy opened its annual spring show, members of the public were invited to Williams, Stevens, Williams at 353 Broadway, where, for twenty-five cents—the price of entry to the entire National Academy show—they queued up to see a single painting. Church may have been inspired by Cole, who had done something similar with his painting *The Angel Appearing to the Shepherds* some twenty years earlier. More recently, moving panoramas of American scenic landmarks, often installed alone in a room, had drawn paying audiences in New York and elsewhere.

Unlike these scrolling panoramas, Church's new painting didn't move, but it didn't need to. Its impact was instant and dizzying, as the *New-York Daily Times* enthused: "You pass from the bustle of the street into that small back room of the Messrs. WILLIAMS & STEVENS . . . and behold! there is the marvel of the Western World before you!" Church had done away with the sliver of foreground he had included in his preparatory oil sketch. Now the water lapped at the sides and bottom of the huge canvas, threatening to sweep the viewer over the precipice along with a log that bobbed in the waves. The water kept turning into a new version of itself—first streaming in rivulets over rocks in its path, then surging, foaming, and plunging, and finally evaporating into the air. Juxtaposing complementary colors, Church had painted a moody sky that looked violet against the green of the water. Horseshoe Falls curved across the canvas in a sublime arc, conjuring a rainbow in the mist. "It is Niagara, all but the roaring of the waters," wrote *The New York Herald. The Albion* declared it "incontestably the finest oil picture ever painted on this side of the Atlantic."

The critics were so distracted by Church's technical skills that they missed his larger achievement. His mastery of realism allowed him to infuse his landscape and skies with emotions and ideas. As in his New England pictures, he was signaling both wonder and anxiety. The faraway remnants of a storm were succeeded by a brilliant rainbow—a biblical symbol of peace and renewal. Yet the immediate threat of being washed over the fatal edge registered viscerally with viewers.

As a painting of the most famous natural place in the United States, *Niagara Falls* doubled as a portrait of the nation itself. While Church had sketched at Niagara and painted in his studio, the United States had been sliding closer to the brink of civil war. The Kansas Territory had been the blood-soaked epicenter of the struggle over slavery. The election of Democrat James Buchanan to the presidency had cheered slavery's apologists but also energized the nascent, antislavery Republican Party. As Church completed *Niagara Falls*, the Supreme

Court issued its ignominious *Dred Scott* decision, which offered cover for the future spread of slavery.

As the nation careened toward conflict, thousands crowded into Williams, Stevens, Williams's back room to experience the vertiginous thrill of *Niagara Falls*. More than one thousand people, including former president Millard Fillmore, signed up to buy color lithographs. Church gave Williams, Stevens, Williams the right to all profits on those lithographs, but what he got in exchange was far more valuable to him. His precipitous vision of the nation would be witnessed by people who would never get to see *Niagara Falls*—or the real thing—in person.

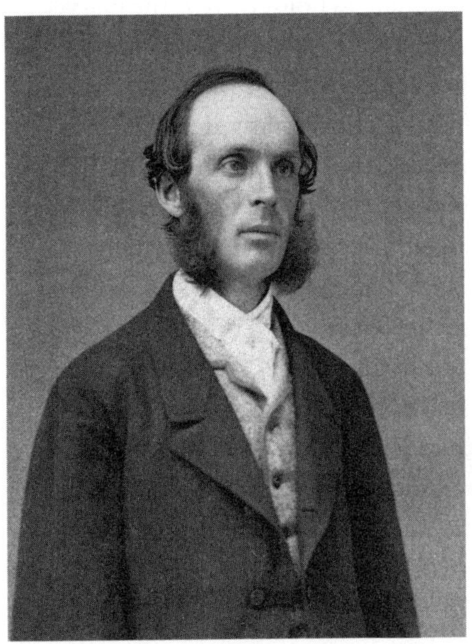

Frederic Church, c. 1860

After the picture had been on view for a month, Church sent it on a steamship to England. He hoped it would make more of an impression on the British than his *Natural Bridge* had done five years earlier. Although American literature had earned more respect in the interim, American art was still regularly ignored or denigrated. Emerson, Irving, Nathaniel Hawthorne, and Henry Wadsworth Longfellow had all garnered praise in the British press. Among American landscape painters, only Cole and Cropsey had received much attention.

When *Niagara Falls* opened in London, John Ruskin went to see it. He inspected the many varieties of water and the rocks they had shaped over eons. He studied the blue-violet sky, the clouds splayed across it, and Church's misty rainbow, which was so true to life Ruskin reportedly thought it a real prism created by the sun streaming through the gallery window. *The Times* of London, too, marveled at this "remarkable picture." Finally, the United States had produced a painter endowed with world-class talent and the patience to master the most difficult subject matter on earth. In Church's hands, "even this awful reality is not beyond the range of human imitation." The *Spectator* urged that the painting "be studied by all who are interested in the future of American Art. It is a work of the best omen, and cannot fail to rejoice them."

At thirty-one, thanks to *Niagara Falls*, Church had become the most famous painter in the United States and the man who had most decisively changed British attitudes toward American art. News of his triumph in London reached New York as fast as a steamship could cross the Atlantic.

CHAPTER 12

"The Grandest Mountain in the World"

In the spring of 1857, while *Niagara Falls* was still on view in New York, Church left the admiring crowds behind and steamed out of the harbor.

He had spent the four years since his last trip to South America constantly improving himself as a painter of landscapes and water. He had also read widely in geology, trying to grasp what volcanoes and valleys and rivers and oceans said about the history of the planet. He had recently astonished New York and Boston with *The Andes of Ecuador*, yet he was convinced he could create even better South American pictures. Having captured Niagara, he was anxious to revisit the great natural features of the Andes.

He was ready for a change, and he thought the public was, too. Scenes of pastoral New England had been painted over and over in the past decade—by Church himself, and also by Durand, Kensett, Cropsey, McEntee, and many others. Among these artists, Church alone had traveled to the Andes and the tropics. His eye and his hand had improved immeasurably since his first trip, and if he could get clearer views of the volcanoes this time, he would go home with dozens of virtuosic sketches to inform highly original paintings about his twin passions: nature and the nation. He would share the stupendous natural wonders of the equatorial New World, while transforming its glaciered peaks and tropical valleys into new metaphors for the North and South of his own country.

Church had seen his friend Kensett use mountains and valleys to great symbolic effect in an 1851 New England canvas called *Mount Washington from the Valley of Conway*. Set in the White Mountains of New Hampshire, the picture looked across a fertile valley of farms and groves toward the highest mountain in the Northeast. Kensett's composition celebrated the same peaceful, agrarian vision that Church had embraced in so many pictures of the late 1840s and early 1850s. With Mount Washington, Kensett cannily invoked George Washington and his legacy of a stable republic without picturing the man himself. The Art-Union, which showed the painting in 1851 and dispatched it as an engraving to subscribers, had helped set off a stampede of artists to Mount Washington.

Church was among them, going a few years later to paint the same view that Kensett had. The first time Church had gone to the Andes, Humboldt had been his dominant inspiration, but by the time he left New York in the spring of 1857 on his second trip, he had incorporated Kensett's vision of Mount Washington as a metaphor for the United States into his imagination. The idea would inform some of his grandest paintings in the decade to come.

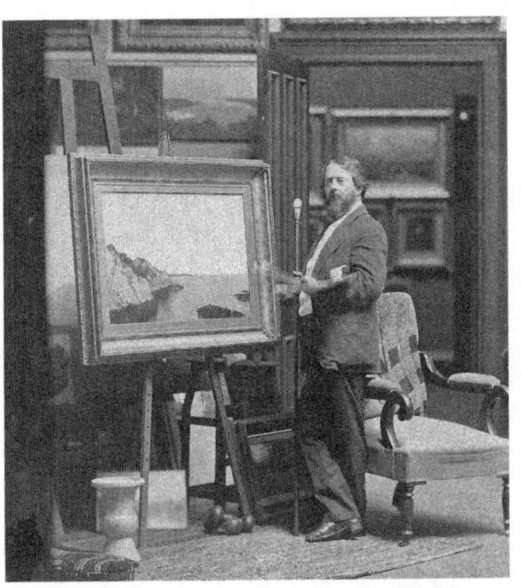

John Frederick Kensett

Winthrop wished he could go to the Andes with Church, but his duties as a lawyer tethered him to the Northeast. "I long with an immense & almost bitter longing for mountains of snow," he complained. Church traveled instead with Louis Rémy Mignot, a younger artist of French extraction who had grown up in Charleston, South Carolina. As they headed east from the South American coast toward the corridor of inland volcanoes, Church was thrilled to see Chimborazo floating "like a white cloud" more than a hundred miles ahead. A year before, Humboldt himself had told Church's friend Bayard Taylor that Chimborazo was "the grandest mountain in the world." Church longed to paint it again, as well as Cotopaxi, and he also hoped to reach the remote peak of Sangay, which he described to Goodman as "the most terrible volcano in the world." Even Humboldt hadn't made it to Sangay, although he had heard it exploding from a distance in 1802.

Church felt even closer to Humboldt on this trip than on his last. He and Mignot visited the house south of Quito where Humboldt had stayed on his way to Chimborazo, and Church was delighted to find a portrait of the young naturalist still hanging on the wall more than fifty years later. He commissioned a copy of it from the Quito artist Rafael Salas to take home with him.

As he rode and hiked through Ecuador, Church was mentally composing a Humboldtian masterpiece. He made close studies of tropical plants, noting their shapes, colors, and sheens. He spent ten days in the town of Guaranda, where he sketched an ever-changing view of Chimborazo, fifteen miles to the northeast. One day in early June, he drew a panorama that encompassed the whole sweep of the Andean landscape, from the hill where he was standing across the miles of olive-green foothills that stretched away before him, and finally up through the clouds to the clear sky above frozen Chimborazo. He described the effects of light and color at the bottom of his paper so he could remember them later. "Snow peak dazzling creamy warm white . . . an exquisite contrast between the cool green blue of the sky, the moon and the low toned smoky warm clouds which surrounded them." He captured exactly these effects in an oil sketch made soon after.

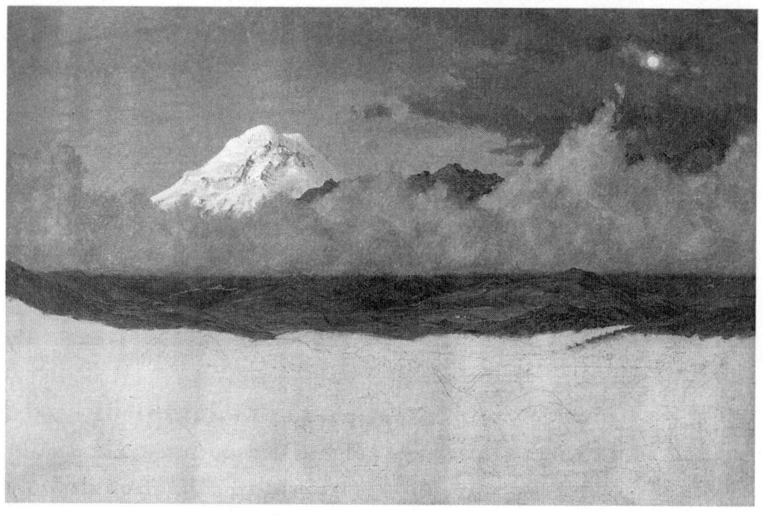

Oil sketch of Chimborazo in mist and clouds, by Church, June or July 1857

Chimborazo looked as serene as when Church had last seen it, but Cotopaxi had turned violent, spewing rocks, ash, and enormous plumes of black smoke. Choking ash had rained down on Quito for three days the previous

December. "The terror stricken faces, the multitude of candles, the loud music, the glittering images—all made supernatural by a dull grey coating of ashes—you can imagine," Church wrote to a friend.

Sketching Cotopaxi, he noted the way the living volcano affected the light and color of the sky. "Dark sullen purple," he wrote of the volcanic rock on one sketch. As the smoke plumed and drifted, the heavens responded. Close to the slopes Church found it "pinky warm" and "blue greenish," and as he lifted his gaze, it became "purple blue beautiful" and then brightened to a "very delicate blue." The scene was as alive with movement as a dance or a battle.

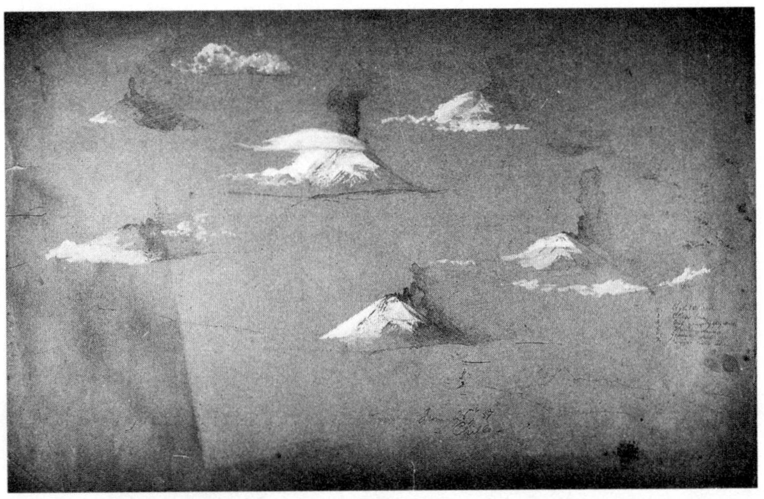

Studies of Cotopaxi erupting, by Church, June 26, 1857

On July 9, Church and Mignot set out from the town of Riobamba for the volcano Sangay, about thirty-five miles to the southeast. Between them and the volcano lay several racing rivers and a warren of foothills. They began the trip on horseback, accompanied by an experienced Indigenous guide named Quipo. Church kept a diary in a pocket-size notebook. "I had a little rat of a horse which didn't promise much from his looks but certainly knew the road for he dashed down the steep hills and through the rough places with a confident rec[k]lessness that excited my admiration." The landscape grew forbidding, even eerie, as they rode east. Boulders pierced the hillsides, and he heard no birdsong. Only the clouds moved, rolling swiftly over the peaks.

The next afternoon, Quipo indicated that the party would stop in a tiny settlement to spend the night and wait for additional local guides for the final twenty miles. When Church awoke the next morning, the mountaintops in every direction had been dusted white by a snowstorm.

They were now about thirteen thousand feet above sea level, and Church found the air painfully thin. The tall grass that blanketed the valleys and the hillsides grew so thick that even the horses couldn't force their way through it, and the guide at the head of the group had to lean over his horse's head to untangle the grass by hand. Every time they reached a river, they had to descend a slick bank and persuade the nervous horses to wade in. After one crossing, Church's mount slipped as he was riding up the opposite bank. He and the animal both plummeted back down the hill to the river. Church hit his face on something, and the horse lay still. Church extricated himself carefully and found that he hadn't broken any bones, and to his relief, the horse soon lumbered to its feet.

Later that afternoon, Quipo, sensing that the incoming weather was going to be foul, insisted they stop and set up camp for the night. Church deferred to Quipo's superior knowledge of the region but was frustrated by the delay. He grabbed his sketchbook, mounted a horse, and set off up the nearest hill. "It seemed not very high but the exertion in working through the grass was tremendous and I toiled and toiled while every little eminence which I gained revealed a still more elevated one above but I persevered and was rewarded finally by planting my feet on the summit" of the highest hill.

Yet he still couldn't see Sangay. It was completely obscured by thick clouds. Disappointed, he turned to sketch a smaller mountain to the southwest. As he worked, the sun found holes in the clouds "and gilded with refined gold every slope and ridge that it could touch." When Church was done, he turned around, "and lo! Sangay with its lofty plume of smoke stood clear before me." A column of steam rose, bright white against the billowing black smoke, and "new beauties revealed themselves as the setting sun turned the black smoke into burnished copper and the white steam into gold. At intervals of two or three minutes an explosion would take place[;] the first intimation was a fresh mass of smoke with sharply defined outline rolling above the black rocks and immediately the dull rumbling sound which reverberated among the mountains."

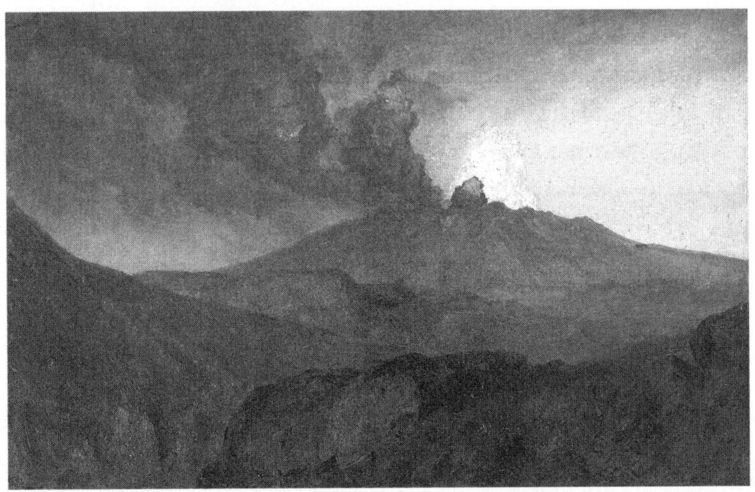

Oil sketch of Sangay erupting, by Church, July 1857

Church was alone in this magnificent landscape, watching and hearing the very pulse of the planet. "I was so delighted with the changing effects that I continued making rapid sketches of the different effects until night overtook me and a chilly dampness warned me to retrace my steps." He hiked back toward the valley and eventually spotted the campfire. Spreading his blanket on the grass, he gazed up at the Southern Cross in the star-speckled sky until he fell asleep.

An hour or so later, he woke up in a pouring rain. Quipo had read the weather correctly. Church, Mignot, and the guides stuffed their warm bedding into waterproof bags. Following the guides' example, Church put on a rubber poncho and sat on the ground with the poncho spread around him. "These Indians always sleep in a sitting position but to a white man it becomes un-indurable [*sic*] without a comfortable seat," he complained in his journal. "Seven mortal hours I counted the minutes. The rain presently turned to snow . . . the largest flakes I ever saw—and shortly everything was white." The mules stood patiently as the snow piled up on their backs.

With dawn came upsetting news from the guides, who said that the melting snow would swell the rivers so much that they might not be able to cross for days. The expedition had enough provisions for only two more meals. They would have to give up and turn around. "We picked our way slowly along[,] our feet in the stirrups dragging through the snow until the cold was almost unendurable," Church wrote. When he looked back, he saw a long line of dark grass snaking through the white fields where their mounts had just cleared a path through the snow.

Church was sorry not to have reached Sangay, but he still thought the trip was "an eminent success for I do not believe that during the cloudless . . . season there could be effects comparable to those I beheld." In the pages of his sketchbook, pillars of smoke and steam rose to the sky, and the sun glinted on the rocky slopes of the volcano.

CHAPTER 13

"All Earth's Riches"

Church and Mignot reached home in September 1857, after nine weeks in Ecuador and a long trip home during which their ship ran aground off Cuba. Soon after his return, Church moved into a second-floor studio in a new building on Tenth Street just east of Sixth Avenue. This studio was much more conveniently located than Church's Art-Union studio had been, being just six blocks south of his rented rooms on East Sixteenth Street, five blocks from the Century Association clubhouse, and three blocks from the Osborns' townhouse.

While the Art-Union had occupied a converted mansion, Church's new studio was in the first purpose-built studio building in the country. The Tenth Street Studio Building, as it was called, had been conceived and bankrolled by James Boorman Johnston, a merchant and art patron who was the brother of railroad executive John Taylor Johnston, the owner of Church's *Niagara Falls*. Designed by Richard Morris Hunt, the nation's foremost architect, the building boasted a large exhibition hall, three floors of studios, and accommodations for those artists who wanted to live where they worked. Demand for the studios quickly exceeded their availability, and beginning in 1858, about two dozen lucky artists, including Church, piled rugs, trunks, easels, and pictures onto horse carts and moved in.

Church was surrounded by good friends in his new quarters: Gignoux, Gifford, and Mignot were part of the inaugural cohort, and McEntee arrived a year later. Worthington Whittredge, a talented painter from Ohio who would soon join Church's inner circle, set up there in 1859 after a decade of study in Europe. A few writers moved in as well; Winthrop rented a room where he slept and wrote, even as he continued to practice law downtown. The sole woman on the scene—the accomplished Anna Mary Freeman—was both a writer and a painter specializing in miniature portraits.

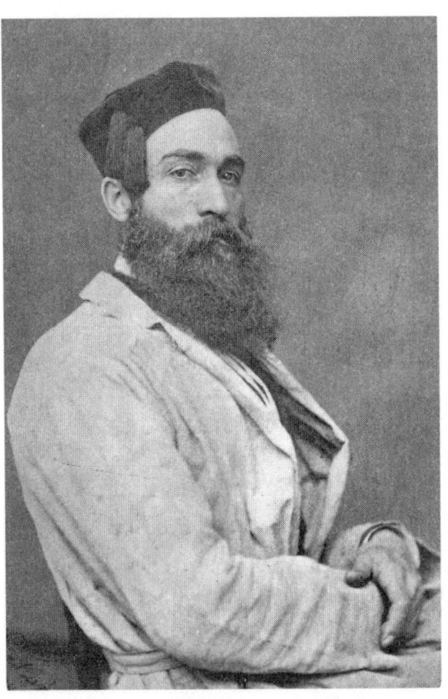

Worthington Whittredge

Thanks to *Niagara Falls*, Church was the most famous artist in the building. He was also one of the most influential. His elegiac, symbol-laden sunset paintings of the late 1840s and early 1850s were inspiring a wave of sunsets from fellow painters, a number of whom had also signed up to buy color lithographs of *Niagara Falls*. But with prominence came criticism. There were those who thought that as a fellow of the National Academy Church should have supported the academy by exhibiting *Niagara Falls* at its spring 1857 show rather than at a private gallery. His comfortable family circumstances, which had allowed him to launch his career without going into debt, also earned him some resentment.

When Martin Johnson Heade, a Pennsylvania-born painter, moved into the Studio Building in 1858, someone assured him that Church was "very unpopular among the artists generally." Heade couldn't make sense of the rumored animosity; he had already met Church and admired him immensely. Heade thought *Niagara Falls* was "the most wonderful picture I ever yet saw" and that Church was "one of the most affable & agreeable men I ever met." Church felt the same way about the witty Heade, who was soon his closest friend among the New York painters.

The Studio Building swiftly became the center of the New York art world. Well-to-do ladies and gentlemen took to visiting on Saturdays, strolling from picture to picture as the artists hovered, hoping for sales. Many callers climbed the broad mahogany staircase to Church's studio, curious about his recent trip and current projects. When he was receiving visitors, they entered his large, high-ceilinged studio to find an oversize easel at one end and items from his travels arranged around the room—a horned animal skull, a spotted jaguar skin, a blue morpho butterfly under glass, and dried palm fronds. There were pencil studies and oil sketches propped up here and there, while a huge chest of drawers held many dozens more. Hanging on one wall was Cole's painting of Prometheus bound to a rock; Church hoped to help Maria Cole find a New York buyer.

A Chickering grand piano in the studio hinted at lively soirées after long days of painting. Church

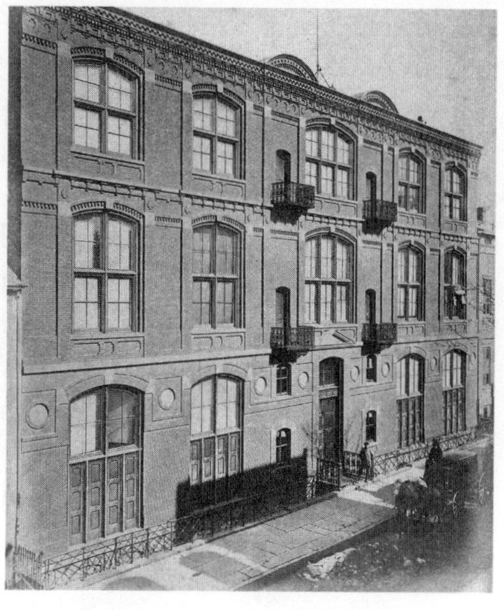

The Tenth Street Studio Building, by Richard Morris Hunt

counted great musical talents among his friends, including the famous composer and piano prodigy Louis Moreau Gottschalk, who dedicated a mazurka to Church, but the latter was modest about his own knowledge. "I

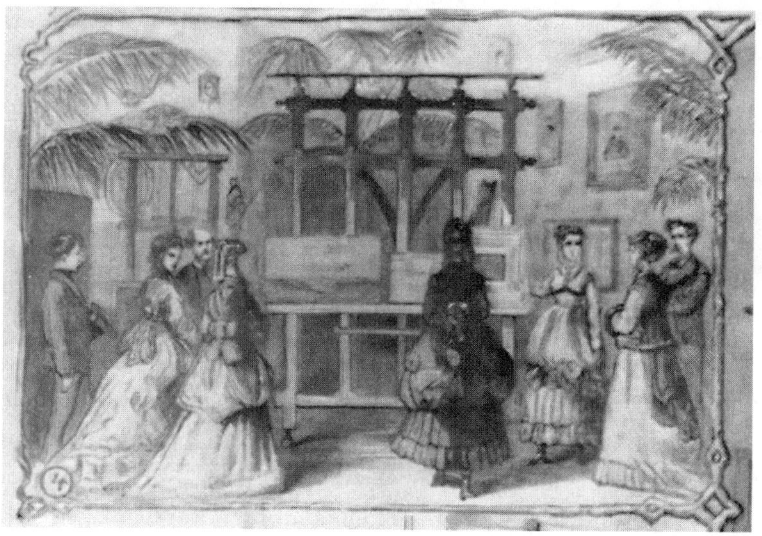

Church's Tenth Street studio, with decorative palm fronds and his enormous easel. (Church is not pictured; his friend Heade is the man closest to the easel at left.)

love music too," he wrote to another composer, "but I fear to speak about that of which I know so little and you so much." Church did bring one novel talent to the Studio Building: making exquisite cups of hot chocolate from his private supply of South American cocoa. Heade found this practice charming: "He is famous in making chocolate as well as in covering canvas. . . . I'm the <u>coffee king</u> of the building & he the chocolate ditto! Tomorrow he's to take coffee with me, & then I'm to <u>retaliate</u> in chocolate."

Most of the time, though, Church was working on a huge canvas, ten feet wide and more than five feet tall. The picture was going to be called *The Heart of the Andes*, and what he hoped to achieve in it far outstripped anything he had attempted before.

He was painting in sight of the man who inspired him most. On a nearby easel he had propped a portrait of Humboldt as a young explorer, arms crossed and a defiant expression on his face, as if challenging Church to impress him.

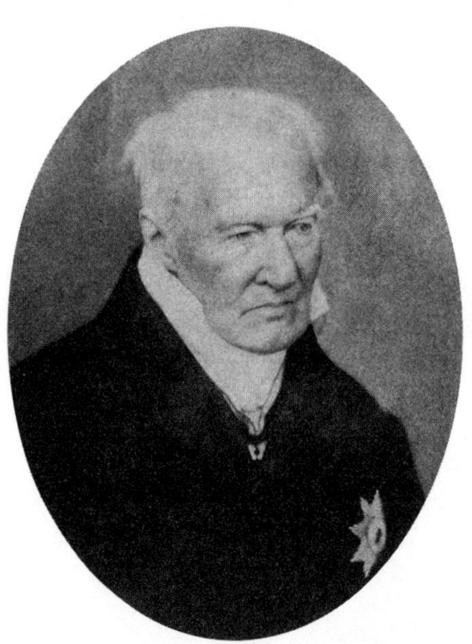

Alexander von Humboldt, 1857

This was the commissioned copy of the 1802 portrait from the house where Humboldt had stayed near Chimborazo. Humboldt was now an elderly man living in Berlin, but as Church worked, the great naturalist's ideas swirled in his mind.

Church's ambitious plan was to conjure on his new canvas Humboldt's revolutionary insight about nature, which had changed almost every field of science. It was in 1802, while scaling Chimborazo, that Humboldt had grasped that nature was an intricate, dynamic web spanning the whole globe—that every small part of nature was a reflection of this totality. He saw with sudden clarity that far-flung parts of the world with similar climates and elevations had developed similar flora, and that, as the earth rose from sea level to the mountaintops, it was blanketed in layer upon layer of vegetation adapted to the moisture, temperature, wind, and soil of the changing terrain.

Working with his friend and fellow naturalist Bonpland, Humboldt had conveyed this insight in an innovative image he called the *Naturgemälde*, or "painting of nature." They had outlined the profiles of Chimborazo and Cotopaxi and inscribed on them the names of the plants and animals they had identified at different altitudes, together with their corresponding climatological data. Further notations compared the Andes with other mountains around the world. The *Naturgemälde* was the schematic representation of Humboldt's epiphany—that nature everywhere on the planet was interconnected, and that humans were only a tiny element in a thrillingly complex system.

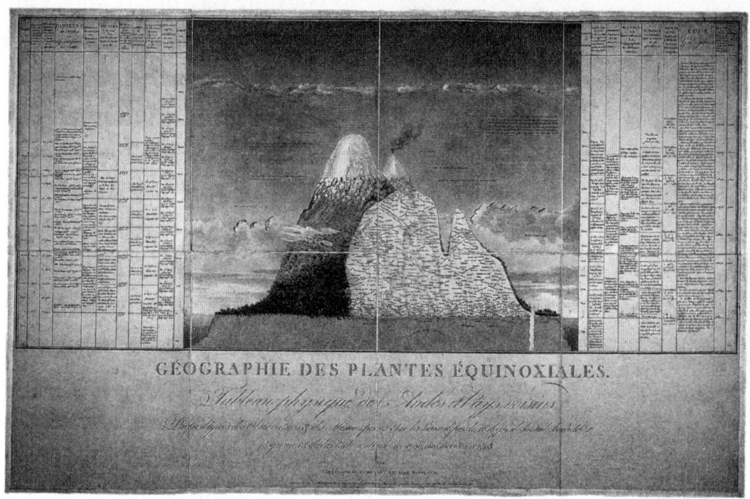

The *Naturgemälde*, or "painting of nature"

Church had first set out for the Andes in 1853 because Humboldt had declared it the richest swath of nature in the world. Church had returned there in 1857 to amass better sketches of the disparate phenomena that had inspired Humboldt's *Naturgemälde*, especially sketches of Chimborazo and Cotopaxi. In his Tenth Street studio, surrounded by his own souvenirs of the Andes, Church was trying to communicate Humboldt's vision of nature—not in the flattened perspective of the *Naturgemälde*, but with the layered depth and true colors of the region he and Humboldt, generations apart, had each spent months exploring.

Church began to dream of sending *The Heart of the Andes* to Berlin once it was finished, so Humboldt could see it. Church's friend Bayard Taylor, who knew Humboldt, offered to write a letter of introduction for the picture explaining that Church had gone to South America because of Humboldt's *Cosmos*. Church's plan to show Humboldt *The Heart of the Andes* energized and inspired him through long months of work until, in the summer of 1858, he put down his brushes. He needed to wander through a landscape that he could feel and smell and hear, so he could get mental distance from the painted landscape in which he had been living. When he returned to his Tenth Street studio in the autumn, he would decide what he thought of his work so far. One day in late July, Church lifted his strained eyes from the bare foothills of the Andean páramo and the icy shoulders of Chimborazo and left the crowded city.

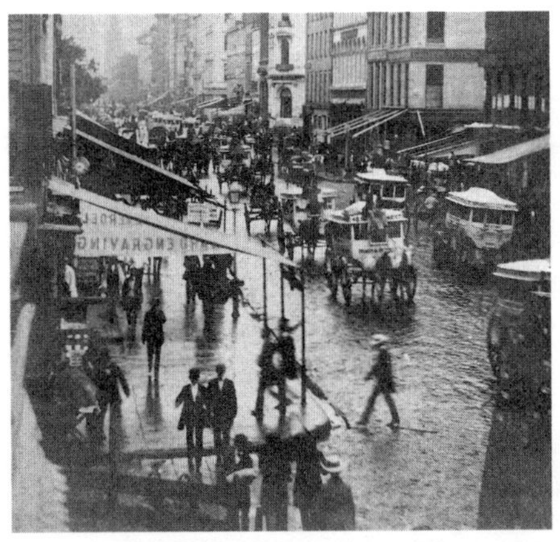

Broadway on a rainy day in 1859

He traveled one hundred miles to the Long Island village of East Hampton, where he rested his gaze on the ocean, the sand, and the slashing vertical lines of beach grass. He sketched in graphite, committing the colors to memory with quick phrases: *smoky yellow, warm blue, dusky dark, brandy.*

He traced the Atlantic horizon and the curves of the rain-swollen clouds above it. He sketched a fishing vessel cresting a swell, and a fisherman trudging along with his heavy net draped over one shoulder. He drew a wooden windmill, left behind by seventeenth-century settlers who had harnessed the ocean breezes for grinding grain and fulling cloth.

AT THE VERY MOMENT CHURCH was sketching this picturesque relic on the Long Island shore, his friend Cyrus Field was wrestling with the technological future two thousand miles to the northeast, in the middle of the Atlantic Ocean. Field was aboard the United States frigate *Niagara*. He had worked toward this day for three years, haranguing investors, consulting with engineers, conducting experiments at sea, and wooing two governments. Field was trying to lay a telegraph cable across the Atlantic. If he succeeded, space and time would be altered forever.

He had already tried twice. After his second defeat, when the cable had snapped and sunk to the ocean floor, several board members of his Atlantic Telegraph Company had resigned in disgust, but Field had been undaunted. He simply tried again—which is what he was doing on July 29 when Church was sketching at East Hampton.

Field watched as men from the *Niagara* and the *Agamemnon*, a British ship floating nearby, spliced the ends of two coils of cable together. Then an order was given, the splice was lowered into the water, and the ships began sailing away from each other, the *Niagara* heading west toward Newfoundland and the *Agamemnon* east toward Ireland.

As they traveled apart, the ships sent electric signals to each other every ten minutes. On the coasts of Newfoundland and Ireland, men waited at telegraph stations to receive their respective ends of the spliced cable. If the cable could be made to transmit a signal from Ireland to Newfoundland and back, Field and his colleagues could take credit for joining two continents.

On August 4, Field saw land from the deck of the *Niagara*. Early the next morning, dozens of sailors hauled the heavy cable to the beach and then over rough, wooded terrain to the Newfoundland telegraph station. Electricians connected the cable to a galvanometer, which would record the strength of the electricity—if any—passing through the cable. As Field watched, the needle suddenly jumped. The current coming from the *Agamemnon*'s end of the cable was strong. From Newfoundland, Field telegraphed the good news to the United States, first to his family and then to President Buchanan.

"The Atlantic is dried up," exulted *The Times* of London the next day. When Queen Victoria was informed, she wished she could confer a knighthood on Field—an impossibility, given that he was an American.

The true test of the cable lay ahead. Electricians at either end began sending signals back and forth as they prepared to receive the official inaugural message from Queen Victoria to President Buchanan. At last, on August 16, the queen's words began pulsing through the cable. The message was transcribed and telegraphed onward to the United States: Her Majesty congratulated the president and expressed her hope that the cable would foster international friendship. Buchanan replied to the queen in similar terms.

New York exploded with joy and gunpowder. Early on August 17, workers blasting rock for the vast new Central Park set off 125 deafening charges in quick succession. They decorated their plows, wagons, horses, and hats with evergreen boughs and flowers, and the park's chief engineer, Frederick Law Olmsted, led more than a thousand of them down Fifth Avenue and then Broadway to City Hall, where they were greeted by the mayor.

When dusk fell, bonfires blazed along the Hudson and the East River waterfronts, and a pyrotechnic show began at City Hall. Colorful sparks formed the Stars and Stripes, then the Union Jack. An American eagle took shape and faded away above huge fiery letters that spelled out HONOR TO CYRUS W. FIELD. The fireworks continued for hours. Sometime after midnight, City Hall caught fire, and the cupola and part of the roof were lost before it could be extinguished.

Field sold the leftover cable from the *Niagara* to Tiffany and Co., which cut some of it into four-inch pieces wrapped in brass ferrules stamped with the Tiffany name. Children wove through the crowds with candy replicas of the Tiffany souvenir between their teeth. With the name of the U.S. frigate *Niagara* everywhere, on posters and souvenirs and in speeches and newspapers, Church's gallerists arranged to re-exhibit his 1857 *Niagara Falls*, which had just returned from a triumphant tour of Great Britain.

The official cable ceremonies took place on September 1. For a brief moment, a divided country united in celebration. Across the nation, villages and towns and cities held church services and parades. Tens of thousands of people streamed toward New York on ferryboats, trains, wagons, and horses. The roads into the city were "one long cloud of dust" for miles, the *Times* wrote. Flags flew on every vessel in the packed harbor, and façades along the city streets were plastered with celebratory signage and draped in colorful bunting.

An estimated half a million people gathered along the parade route. For more than an hour, they watched smartly dressed regiments marching past, followed by members of the city government, officers of the Atlantic

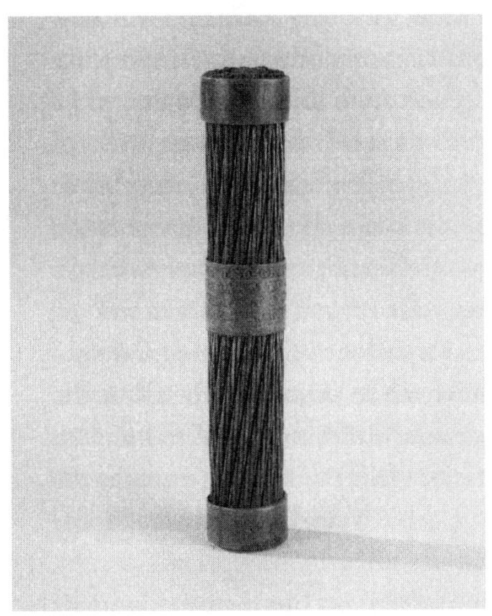

Tiffany's transatlantic cable souvenir

Telegraph Company, the captain and crew of the *Niagara*, and members of dozens of trade and professional associations. When the chief deputation, which included Field, finally arrived at Forty-Second Street for the big ceremony, it was almost six in the evening. An orchestra of several hundred musicians thundered out an excerpt from Haydn's *The Creation*, after which the mayor gave a speech praising Field and his associates. Field thanked the mayor and then performed a previously impossible feat by reading a congratulatory note that had been written in London that very morning.

Church, who was sketching at Niagara Falls once again, missed the celebrations, but he knew he would be seeing the man of the hour soon. Field had somehow found a quiet moment to write, saying he would travel to Niagara with two of his daughters when he could get away. On September 2, as Field was being fêted at a banquet for six hundred, Church wrote to Goodman about his world-famous friend: "I should think that after his labors in laying out the cable . . . he would be glad to get a little comparative quiet." About ten days later, Field reached Niagara Falls by train, having been hailed as a hero at stops along the way.

Field arrived with a painful secret. Since September 1 no message had been received at either end. The telegram he had read to the audience at the ceremony had been the last successful transatlantic communication. The operators had tried over and over, but finally they concluded that the cable had failed. Before the end of September, Field left Church and went back to New York City to inform the public. Some people pitied him; others were derisive. Tiffany and Co. began advertising lengths of genuine Atlantic telegraph cable "by the mile . . . at a very low price."

Field began laying plans for a fourth attempt.

BY NOVEMBER, CHURCH WAS BACK at work in his new studio on Tenth Street. He let it be known through a notice in *The Evening Post* that he wished to paint without interruption until *The Heart of the Andes* was complete. His desire to concentrate was real, but so was his talent for whipping up public anticipation. He hired an agent named John McClure to help organize and publicize the upcoming exhibition of *The Heart of the Andes* and to drum up subscribers for chromolithographs of the picture. He gave McClure permission to advertise the opening, which they set for the end of April. Church had decided to show the picture on its own, using the approach that had worked so well for *Niagara Falls*.

Winthrop—perhaps at Church's request—planned to publish an essay about *The Heart of the Andes* to coincide with its unveiling. With the canvas nearly complete, Church invited him into the studio to take notes. Winthrop studied the picture, then began writing: "The subject is new, the scenes are strange, the facts are amazing." Here was a composite portrait of the forces at work in the natural world. Humboldt had declared in *Cosmos*, "The globe itself reveals at every phase of its existence the mystery of its former conditions." Church made that mystery visible in his painting. In the clouds near the top edge of the canvas, Winthrop recognized the vapors that formed above the Pacific and blew inland to fall as rain on the jungles and grasslands before turning to snow in the high peaks. The white dome of Chimborazo, floating in the distance, spoke of ancient geological forces that had shoved mountains up from the earth's crust. In the softer lines of the foothills, Church portrayed the ceaseless, erosive scouring of rock by wind and rain. Below, in a partly forested plain fed by a winding river and bathed in sunshine, he invoked the elements that helped plants push through soil into air and light. Human beings were here, too; a village nestled between river and forest showed them making a place in the vast natural world.

"All earth's riches are compacted into one many-sided crystal," Winthrop wrote.

Church continued to work on the foreground, where he was representing the warmest and wettest zone of the Andean region, the tropical lowlands. The swaths of canvas to either side of the river were beginning to teem with trees, vines, flowers, moss, and grasses. Church painted thousands of individual leaves, many of them so tiny a single brushstroke sufficed. Among the leaves, he added native butterflies and birds, colorful representatives of Andean fauna. To sign his painting, Church painted his name as though it had been carved into the trunk of a tree that stood next to a sun-dappled path leading in the direction of Chimborazo. He seemed to be offering himself as a guide.

Farther along the path, Church placed two small human figures pausing at a wayside cross. He approached religion with far more certainty than Humboldt and gave God credit for nature's stupendous beauty, not seeing any contradiction between spirituality and scientific curiosity. Some of Humboldt's critics felt that his investigations into the workings of nature stripped away its mystery, but Church disagreed. Like Humboldt, the more he understood about the natural world, the more moving he found it. Church prized this duality in Humboldt—thinking *and* feeling—and with *The Heart of the Andes* he hoped to inspire both.

AFTER MORE THAN A YEAR of work, Church unveiled his new painting. Many critics praised the precisely painted plants in the foreground, but he was much prouder of his skies. He told a journalist that he found the delicate work of painting skies far more taxing than painting thousands of leaves, and that if he had a day of sky painting ahead, he made sure to arrive at his studio in top form, as if ready for a wilderness trek. It was when he rolled thick, gray clouds across a canvas or created a firmament so pale it bordered on translucence that he felt himself most truly an artist. He poured everything he had learned from Cole, Ruskin, Humboldt, and the Andes themselves into this newest sky. His painted landscape might have been the heart of the Andes, but the sky was its soul.

Viewers, egged on by ecstatic reviews in the press, began lining up outside the Tenth Street Studio Building, where *The Heart of the Andes* went on display a few days before Church's thirty-third birthday. One journalist would recall nearly a decade later that the picture "was more than a fashion, it was a rage." Even the picky connoisseur George Templeton Strong averred that "it beats any landscape I ever saw," although he mocked Winthrop's florid essay as "the ravings of Ruskin in delirium tremens."

Fellow artists haunted the exhibition hall with a mixture of envy and admiration. Rembrandt Peale, who in 1857 had called *The Andes of Ecuador* the best painting he had ever seen, now wrote a note to Church declaring that *The Heart of the Andes* had surpassed it. *Harper's Weekly* fretted that, because the city had no public art museum, Church's masterpiece would be bought by a rich man and hidden away at home. Within two weeks of the New York opening, Church did sell the picture to businessman William T. Blodgett for $10,000, the highest price to date for an American landscape painting, but their contract stipulated that Blodgett would not take possession until after a planned tour of the United States and Europe. The painting would also be engraved in Britain for a color lithograph, so that a far larger audience could see a reproduction of it.

Church was the hero of the day, a year after his friend Field had been lionized. People who saw *The Heart of the Andes* understood that, in his own way, Church had also linked two continents. Field had sent electricity flowing through an undersea cable from Ireland to Newfoundland, but Church had connected North and South America personally, risking his life to roam the tropics. He himself was the cable that ultimately brought tens of thousands of people a glimpse of a continent they would never otherwise see.

The Heart of the Andes has also been read by more recent commentators as a painting about the United States. In his first decade as a painter, Church had often celebrated an idea he still hoped would triumph nationally—New England's agrarian republicanism—by painting Northern landscapes. By the late 1850s, partisan bitterness between North and South was so intense that pictures of overtly Northern landscapes couldn't transcend the regional divide to make a national statement. Even if Church had chosen to paint the American South—and aside from *The Natural Bridge* he hadn't—the same would have held for a recognizably Southern landscape. Ecuador offered an unburdened New World landscape, one rife with natural features that could symbolize the North (frigid, snowcapped peaks) and the South (lush tropical lowlands). In this reading, *The Heart of the Andes* represented an ecologically complete but invented landscape in which North and South were symbolically unified into one fertile and peaceful domain. In other words, Church had painted an appeal for national unity.

CHAPTER 14

"Our Beloved Union"

Church took quiet pleasure in the acclaim for *The Heart of the Andes*. One day, as he surveyed the crowds gathered before his picture, he noticed a pretty young woman. Nothing having come of his rumored courtship of Annie Tracy, Church was alert to other prospects. The young woman who drew his gaze wore her light brown hair pinned in glossy waves that threw off golden glints. She had a gently upturned nose and brown eyes set into delicate cheekbones, and her slim, petite frame gave her a doll-like appearance.

Church's friend Worthington Whittredge later recounted the story he heard about that day.

Church watched the young woman, and, when he saw that she and her older female companion were about to depart, he left the gallery through a side door and hurried down the hall to the front of the building. When the two women reached the exit, he abandoned his customary reserve and introduced himself.

The young woman, Church learned, was Isabel Carnes, and she was accompanied by her mother, Emma Carnes, a New Yorker by birth. The family lived in Dayton, Ohio, where Isabel's father was in business. Francis Carnes, who was originally from Boston and had graduated from Harvard in 1805, was the cofounder of a luxury-imports firm that had, for a time, taken him and his wife to Paris, where Isabel had been born. In France, the Carneses had socialized with royalty and aristocrats, counting the old Marquis de Lafayette among their friends. After moving back to the United States, they regularly traveled from Dayton to New York, where Isabel and her mother paid social calls and attended cultural events. This time, they had decided they could not return to

Ohio without visiting *The Heart of the Andes*. They saw the painting; Church saw twenty-two-year-old Isabel.

His obvious interest was flattering. He was one of the most talked-about men in the city. With her parents' consent, Church became better acquainted with Isabel over the following weeks. Initially attracted by her outward appearance, he discovered that she was also intelligent, kind, and pious—possibly more pious than Church himself. He began courting her. She soon drew admiring praise from his friends; one thought she looked like an exquisite marble sculpture.

Church exercised his own attractions. A journalist who visited him in his studio around this time noted, "His manners are polite and easy, and yet have a rural freshness entirely different from the dried up aspect of New Yorkers generally. Add to this the beautiful simplicity of his manners and you have the secret of the charm which he throws upon you." One of Isabel's relatives later recalled that her "whole being was enlisted in admiration" of this "handsome and irresistible" bachelor.

THE NEW YORK EXHIBITION OF *The Heart of the Andes* closed near the end of May. On the last day, Tenth Street was besieged by thousands of people desperate to see the painting before it was too late—or to see it one last time. The gallery was so crowded that many were unable to get into the building at all. Onlookers recognized the elderly Washington Irving when he arrived during the final hours, having traveled down the Hudson from his home in Tarrytown. They stepped back and cleared the way for him as he moved slowly through the hushed room. He studied the painting closely, then declared it "glorious—magnificent!"

Church had succeeded in his Humboldtian ambitions, but Humboldt himself would never see *The Heart of the Andes*. On May 6, 1859, while the picture was still on display in New York, he died in Berlin. Church had never met his idol, yet he had felt his spiritual presence for so many years that the "news touched me as if I had lost a friend."

Soon after the New York exhibition closed, Church's agent, John McClure, sailed with the giant canvas to England. In London, Queen Victoria was given a private viewing. "Her Majesty was greatly pleased with it," an American newspaper reported, and "had no doubt the painter would establish a European reputation inferior to none of his contemporaries." *The Heart of the Andes* was "in every way a triumph," the *London Daily News* proclaimed. More than one critic praised Church as the aesthetic heir of Turner. "On this American . . . does the mantle of our greatest painter appear to us to have fallen," wrote a reviewer in *The Art-Journal.* "Westward the sun of Art seems rolling."

Church's plunge into unknown and dangerous regions struck another critic as a quintessentially American approach. "Coolly to make a trip to South America—to traverse those vast regions where the Awful and the Beautiful are side by side . . . is only to illustrate the principle of the American character, which looks on Nature as an auxiliary and not as an obstacle." With *The Heart of the Andes,* Church had upended the European habit of associating Americans with uncivilized nature. He had shown the Old World cognoscenti that nature provided Americans more than fodder for farming and industry. In the New World, nature was a sheltering hothouse where great cultural creations could take root and flower.

Church pasted the British newspaper reviews into the notebook where he had been collecting notices from the American press. He kept them for the rest of his life.

WHILE *THE HEART OF THE ANDES* was on view in London, Church set out on another painting trip. He had hit upon a perfectly Humboldtian idea—having explored the tropics, he would sketch and paint in a completely different part of the globe. Travelogues and lectures by and about Arctic explorers were wildly popular in the 1850s. A shrewd businessman as well as a hardy voyager, Church envisioned strong public interest in a grand picture of icebergs, and he wouldn't have to go all the way to the Arctic Circle to gather material. In mid-June, he boarded a steamship bound for Newfoundland with his friend Noble, who would document the journey in writing. Church always enjoyed having a congenial companion on his travels, but he also knew that a written account was the best way to publicize his next big painting.

Both men knew that whole expeditions had disappeared in the Arctic, pinned and crushed by pack ice as their crews froze to death, sometimes after desperate acts of cannibalism. "There are the dead in these very waters, I believe," Noble wrote darkly, "whose last earthly experience was among the final thunders of these ices." But seasickness felled Church and Noble before they saw a single iceberg, and they fled to their bunk beds, Noble above and

Church below. Church had come through many dangerous and unpleasant moments unscathed, and he distracted Noble with a long story about the night he and Field had gotten lost in a South American swamp. It had been frightening at the time, but in Church's telling it became so farcical that Noble forgot his nausea for a while.

It was several more days before they suddenly heard a shout and rushed up to the deck to see two icebergs lit up by the sunrise. The larger one looked to Noble like a domed marble mosque, the smaller one like "an Arab's tent" pitched on the "misty desert of the sea." Church quickly gathered his paper and pencils, but fog cut off his view within moments. The next time they saw an iceberg, they headed for it in a fishing boat rowed by six men. The boat moved across choppy waters through a fogbank until Church could see the iceberg well enough to start an oil sketch. He worked rapidly for half an hour, but the oarsmen were so curious about Church's progress that they had difficulty keeping their seats. As the boat drifted, Church pleaded with them to stay put, and Noble passed his opera glasses around to distract them.

After many days at sea, Church's pencil and oil sketches began to pile up, but he wasn't satisfied. When he was gathering new material to take back to the studio, he tried to capture his subject in every possible kind of light and from every possible angle. Icebergs were even more changeable than Katahdin or Chimborazo. They came in different shapes and sizes, and they moved and sometimes broke apart. They refracted infinite combinations of value and hue depending on the weather. An iceberg could look stark white against a dark ocean under a cloudy sky, multicolored on a bright day, or almost black against a sunset.

Eager for more icebergs and more pictures, Church chartered a schooner called *Integrity* to carry them farther north into the Labrador Sea. This expanse of ocean stretched toward ice-covered Greenland, whose glaciers—including one recently named for Humboldt—broke off icebergs from time to time that floated toward Labrador and Newfoundland. If Church and Noble were lucky, the schooner would cross paths with some of these floating behemoths.

On June 30, they departed on the *Integrity*, whose crew was composed of the captain, the first mate, three other sailors, and a young Scottish cook. Church and Noble shared a cabin with the crew. Its ceiling was so low that the tall Church risked a thwack on the head every time he stood up. Bunk beds and storage shelves lined the walls, and a little table stood next to the steep stairs that led up to the deck.

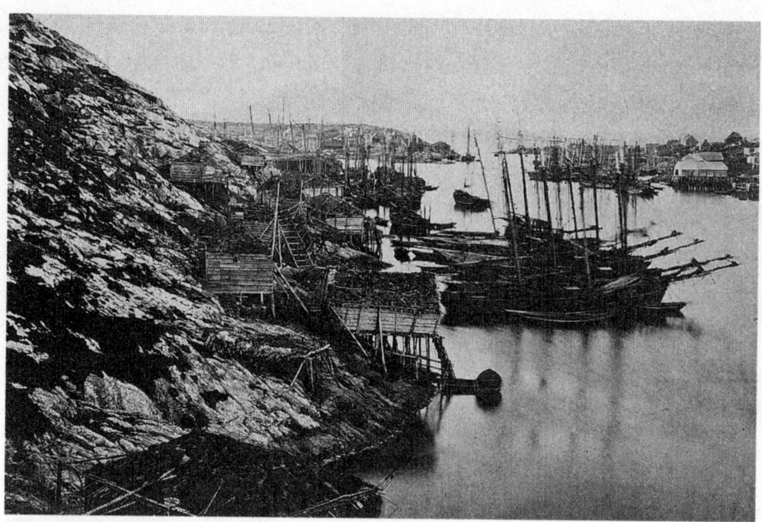

Battle Harbour, Labrador, in a photograph owned by Church, c. 1860

Church was in wonderful spirits. Noble observed that his friend "fairly overflowed with fun and humor." He was exhilarated by his wholly requited love for Isabel, and he adored adventures in the wild. On clear, windy days, the sails of their little schooner billowed and snapped. Sometimes porpoises darted alongside them "like swallows round a barn," Noble wrote. The views back toward the dozens of little islands along the coast reminded Church of his passage through the West Indies on his way to South America. Some nights the ocean shone with luminescence—"the burning of the water," the locals called it. The shimmering on the water was echoed above by the green and pink lights of the aurora borealis.

They sailed on, always in suspense as they kept watch. No one knew where or when they might encounter an iceberg—what Noble called "thou roving Ishmael of the sea," recalling the narrator of *Moby-Dick*. On the morning of July 1, the pale sun pierced the fog to reveal an iceberg, and then another and another. They counted thirteen in all.

With every thrust of the ship toward the icebergs, their colors and contours seemed to change. Church saw violet, rose, blue, green, slate, pearl, and the whitest white. The ocean looked almost black in contrast. In deft oil sketches, he captured the elemental masses of water, berg, and sky. He took brief notes to remind him later of what he was feeling and seeing. "Strange, supernatural," he wrote on one sketch; on another, "exquisite opalescent blue-green." The skies were just as striking. As the sun sank one evening, Noble watched Church, who was looking up at the crimson and gold clouds: "The painter gazes in speechless, loving wonder."

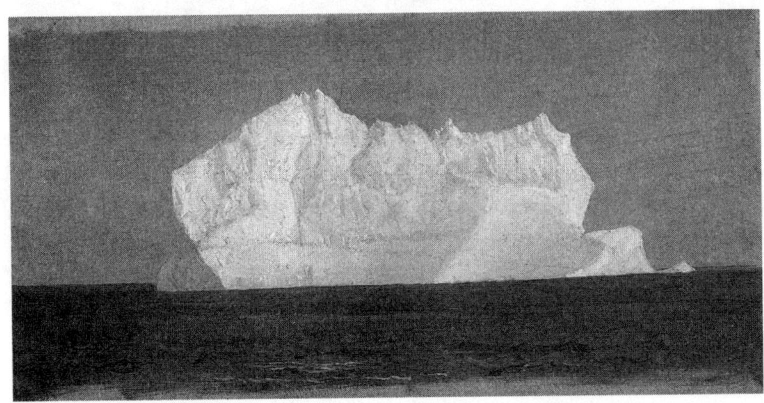

Oil sketch of a floating iceberg by Church, June or July 1859

They sailed among icebergs for a week. Church was trying to draw and paint while the schooner lurched under him. It was, Noble opined, as if Church had perched on a child's swing, placed a canvas on his lap, pumped his legs to send the swing flying back and forth, and then tried to paint a picture of galloping horses in a nearby field. The voyage brought discomfort but also real danger. One day while Church was sketching an iceberg that resembled Windsor Castle, Noble heard him suddenly cry out in surprise. The iceberg had started to crack and explode. Whole towers plunged into the ocean with a sound like thunder as they sent huge waves rolling toward the schooner. Another day, when the men climbed from the boat onto a tame-looking iceberg, Church lost his footing and almost fell into the frigid water. He grabbed the legs of the sturdy captain in time to save himself from hypothermia and drowning.

After five weeks, the two men returned to New York, Church with nearly one hundred pencil and oil sketches. As usual, when his head was filled with images of a new region, he didn't compose a studio picture right away but instead let them ripen in his imagination. When he went back to work in his studio after the trip, the oil paints on his palette were not the colors of icebergs and wintry seas. Instead, they were bright reds, yellows, and greens. His newest painting was to be set among the lakes and mountains of Maine.

CHURCH RENEWED HIS ATTENTIONS TO Isabel. When he took her to dine with the Osborns for the first time, Virginia Osborn found her exquisite. "She is just what you would imagine an artist's wife, with soft curling golden hair, and a sweet face where the colour comes & goes every moment." Church's fame brought press attention to their courtship. By early January of 1860, they were engaged, and the *Boston Evening Transcript* observed that "Church has been successfully occupied with another Heart than that of the Andes." When the couple appeared at the opera one evening, the audience applauded them.

Isabel's mother returned to Ohio, leaving Isabel in the care of relatives and friends in New York. Church took Isabel to Hartford to meet his parents, whom he described to Mrs. Carnes as "plain folks." This was a stretch, unless he was mentally judging them against the Osborns, his wealthiest, most cosmopolitan New York friends.

Mrs. Carnes quickly became an emotional linchpin for the young couple. Isabel confessed to her mother that she despaired of living up to Church's high opinion; Church wrote to Mrs. Carnes about his profound love for her daughter. He sent Mrs. Carnes blank stationery so she would have to write back, playfully signing it for her in advance with "Your devoted mother." She laughed that this was "rather premature!" These early exchanges set the tone for Church's relationship with his mother-in-law, which would be filled for years to come with affectionate ribbing and banter.

Mrs. Carnes wrote Church long, confessional letters that spring. She was happy Isabel had attracted such a fine fiancé, but she mourned the

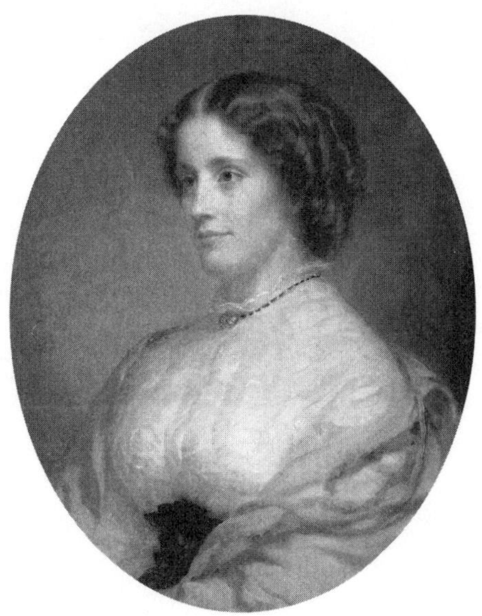

Isabel Carnes, by George A. Baker, 1860

imminent loss of a daughter who was "the light & joy of my life." She begged Church to escort Isabel to Dayton as soon as possible. Church stayed firm. He wanted to have Isabel's picture painted by the society portraitist George A. Baker before the wedding. Mrs. Carnes reluctantly acquiesced.

At last Church accompanied Isabel to Dayton so she and her mother could plan the wedding, which was to take place at the Carneses' home in June. After a brief visit, he returned to New York to continue painting until then.

ONE EVENING IN LATE MARCH, the artists threw open the Tenth Street Studio Building for a reception and exhibition. The whole place was illuminated—gallery, hallways, staircases, and studios. Church's door was the only one closed against the friends and patrons who wandered through the building looking at paintings and sculptures. He had a new painting underway, and until it was done, he preferred not to show it to anyone but his closest friends and the Baltimore collector who had commissioned it.

Church was dividing his time that spring between his work and his preparations for married life. In early April, he went upstate to finalize the purchase of a large farm directly across the river from Cedar Grove. He stayed with the Coles, and he and Theddy spent a few days exploring the new property, which was so hilly and extensive that they "had quite a tramp over it," as Theddy wrote in his journal.

Theddy was now a conscientious young man of twenty-two. He worked hard at Cedar Grove, taking care of the farm animals, planting and harvesting crops, and keeping careful agricultural records. Church asked him to manage the new property; this arrangement would enable Church to take the train up and down the river as his schedule allowed and would also bring extra income to the Cole family.

Although Church was only a renter in New York City, he now owned 126 panoramic acres of the

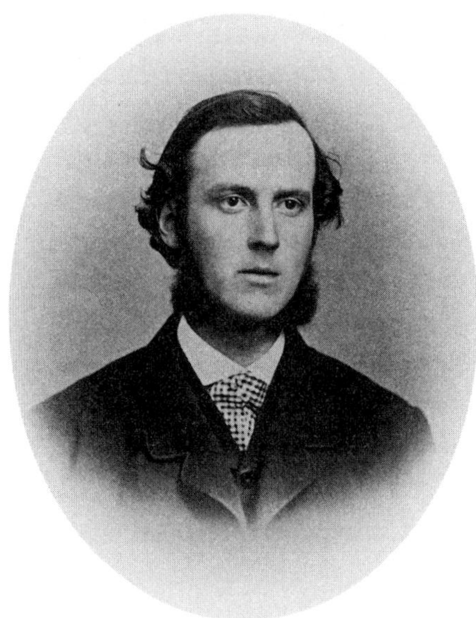

Theddy Cole

Hudson Valley, a region he had come to love while studying with Cole. His land had once been part of the homelands of the Mohicans. Yet if his mind ever wandered to them, his surviving references to previous residents of his property concerned only more recent history, beginning with the farmer who had, in 1794, bought this land from the Van Rensselaer family, whose estate had once totaled a million acres.

Church's new property was three miles south of Hudson, a city of seven thousand people. For over half a century, Hudson had been an important port for whaling ships and a hub for the production of whale oil and spermaceti candles, and its streets were lined with the handsome houses of well-to-do merchants and industrialists. Church and Isabel would soon be frequent visitors to Hudson, shopping on its picturesque main thoroughfare, greeting guests from New York City at the train or ferry, and attending Sunday services at the First Presbyterian Church.

While Theddy hired and supervised farmhands, Church was free to stand at his easel on Tenth Street, completing his new painting of Maine. He unveiled it in early June at Goupil's gallery on Broadway. For twenty-five cents each, visitors found themselves before a moody, complicated picture called *Twilight in the Wilderness.*

Church had covered the top two-thirds of the canvas with a cloud-streaked sky, borrowing drama from a brilliant sunset that, in the summer of 1858, had drawn people in New York City to their rooftops. Ragged sweeps of molten scarlet and orange blazed across a blue-green sky. Church had unspooled the colors seamlessly down to the horizon, passing through aquamarine, pale green, and lemon yellow to reach the white-haloed sun sinking below a ridge of purple mountains. A long, thin lake that reflected the red of the clouds stretched from the foreground into the middle distance. The red lake below and red clouds above compressed the bright light of the setting sun into a narrow band. By covering much of the canvas in darkness, Church intensified the sense of peaceful relief afforded to the eye and the spirit by the cloudless yellow glow on the horizon.

"Mr. Church, like Turner, has mastered the secret of painting spaces," a *New York Times* critic had written in 1859. "He leads the eye into the distance less by lineal or aerial perspective than by his receding gradations of color." When a journalist prodded Church into passing a rare judgment on his own art, he singled out exactly this skill. In the journalist's words, Church's "best efforts had always been directed to those soft blendings of tint with tint which distinguish his skies—one color just dreaming of another, so exquisitely that if a critic only speaks it will awake and vanish."

Church had achieved this effect in *Twilight in the Wilderness* more fully than ever before. A central body of water guided the viewer's eye toward distant mountains and up to the sky. In the foreground, the water was framed on either side by land and trees. There were no signs of human life. The farms, mills, and bridges that had sat at the edge of the wilderness in most of Church's earlier New England paintings were absent. The only life here was wild. One bald eagle sat in a dead tree, and another perched on a tree stump beside a cross formed by two bare branches.

Twilight in the Wilderness was a haunting and ambiguous picture. Was the tone peaceful or uneasy? Even reviewers who praised it as a portrait of a serene, untouched landscape sensed something lonely in it, even gloomy. The ambiguity came from within Church himself. *Twilight in the Wilderness* was an alchemical mix of his love of nature, his deep spirituality, and his growing concern about his country in an age of increasingly fierce sectional rancor. Church shared these commitments with many others, but his particular gift allowed him to transmute his interior life into images at once so virtuosic they seemed to depict real places and so complexly layered they could trigger intense, conflicting emotions.

With this painting more than any other, Church was urging the people of the United States to see theirs as a nation defined by the untamed beauty of the North American continent. The natural cross formed by two branches conveyed his reverence and gratitude for what he considered God's creation. Yet, taken together with the title of the picture, the cross also invoked darker biblical themes. The Israelites had wandered, spiritually lost, in a frightening wilderness. Christ had been tested in the wilderness of the desert. Wilderness was a place of struggle, and struggle could lead to defeat and death or to self-knowledge and redemption.

In the fall of 1859, while Church was working through the composition and ideas that would become *Twilight in the Wilderness*, John Brown's raid on the federal armory at Harpers Ferry, Virginia, intensified fears of a coming national conflagration. In response, on December 19 in New York City, Mayor Daniel F. Tiemann had presided over a large gathering of civic leaders and businessmen. George Templeton Strong had felt extremely ambivalent about attending; he thought slavery was repugnant, yet he abhorred Brown's fanaticism. Strong had found the meeting so packed that he was "happy to extricate myself without broken limbs." But the session resulted in nothing more than a toothless public statement condemning "the idea of an irrepressible conflict existing between the two great sections of our beloved Union."

Two months later, while Church was painting his fiery skies, blood-red water, and descending darkness, Abraham Lincoln arrived in New York to give an almost instantly famous speech at Cooper Union denouncing slavery and those who sought to spread it to new territories and states. Then, on May 18, as Church readied *Twilight in the Wilderness* for delivery to the gallery, Lincoln won the Republican presidential nomination. His candidacy unleashed horrified reactions not only in the South but also among those Northerners certain that a Lincoln victory would provoke a civil war.

That chilling phrase—*civil war*—kept sounding all through the spring and summer of 1860 as viewers contemplated the mysteries of *Twilight in the Wilderness*. The United States, portrayed by Church through one of its most beautiful regions and overtly symbolized by the two bald eagles, was about to face its own dark night in the wilderness.

ON JUNE 14, THE REVEREND Noble presided over Church's wedding to Isabel in a small ceremony at the Carneses' home. Church's parents and sisters rarely left Hartford, and Charlotte was too weak for such a long trip west anyway, but in late September, Church took Isabel, Elizabeth, and Charlotte to Mount Desert Island. He wanted them to spend time together, and he wanted to show Isabel one of his most cherished places. One day, he sketched a playful cartoon showing how much Isabel loved the rugged island. He drew her standing on a cliff over the ocean, her hat ribbons flying and her skirts billowing behind her as she gazed across the water. She looked like the perfect match for Church: a spirited and intrepid young woman who reveled in the natural world. He

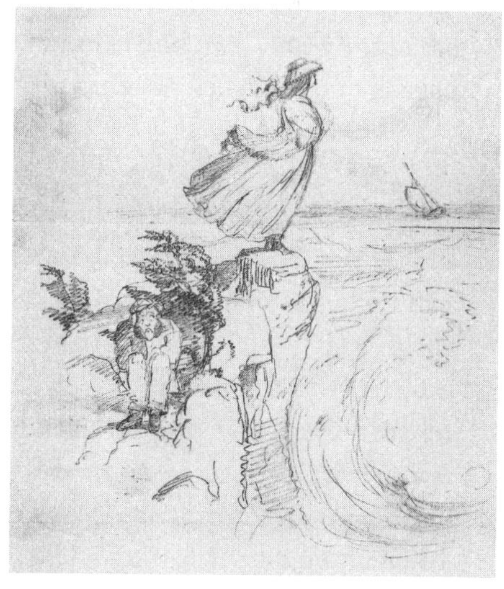

Church and Isabel on Mount Desert Island, sketched by Church, c. 1860

threw these qualities of his young bride into relief by depicting himself cowering in the wind behind a shrub, a miserable expression on his face.

He added a caption:

Mt Desert
Time—two hours past dinner time—
Isabel—Oh Fred, isn't it grand? I feel as if I never wished to go away.
Fred—Teeth chattering—Y-y-y-e-e-s-s ver-r-r-ry.

Church could poke fun at himself without losing face. Over the past year, newspapers in the United States and Britain had made his hardiness the stuff of legend. In truth, as his sister Elizabeth reported to their mother, he was hoping for even wilder weather, so he could study its effects on the sky and water.

"Frederic has been desirous of a violent storm. . . . But thus far there is nothing unusual."

CHAPTER 15

"The Rage of the Wicked"

Church and Isabel returned to Catskill in early October 1860. They stayed at Cedar Grove with Maria Cole and her family, who insisted on it, and Church took the ferry frequently to his new property to check on the progress of a small farmhouse that he was having constructed. He was making a humble start, but he had grand plans for the design of the landscape. He asked Theddy to organize the dredging of a lake in the valley on the property. Church quickly discovered that the pursuit of landscape architecture called for imagination, foresight, and superhuman patience. His lake, which would eventually cover ten acres, would not be finished for nearly two decades.

Four weeks after Church's visit upstate, Abraham Lincoln won the presidential election. In the North, many people celebrated, but ambivalence and anxiety gripped those who feared that Lincoln's election would permanently shatter the fragile union of states, despite his insistence that he would not tamper with slavery in states where it already existed. New York City merchants and bankers saw economic disaster looming, so tightly entwined were their fortunes with Southern cotton. According to Southern newspapers, Lincoln's election was a "calamity" that would lead to "fearful and horrible butcheries."

As the country convulsed, Church was trying to focus on translating his ideas about nature and nation onto canvas. He begged Winthrop to help get him out of jury duty so he could keep working, and he wrote to his paint dealer about which new colors he needed. But few others were thinking about art. On its national tour to Baltimore, Cincinnati, and other cities, *The Heart of the Andes* wasn't drawing many viewers. Church's agent, McClure, who was shepherding the picture from town to town, wrote gloomily, "I sincerely hope confidence will return and that ere long people will cease to wear such long faces." He didn't even bother to take the canvas to Washington.

While Church rarely mentioned politics in writing, he made his political sympathies clear not only through his art but in the company he kept. The people closest to him ranged from cautiously antislavery to passionately abolitionist. Among the more tentative was Church's friend and lawyer Charles Tracy, who was disgusted by slavery yet nervous about abolitionism's possible consequences. Most of Church's other friends longed to see slavery abolished. Noble scoffed at the pretensions of European Americans to moral superiority. W.H. and Virginia Osborn were both strongly opposed to slavery, while Winthrop, Church's closest friend, was the most ardent of all. Throughout the 1850s, Winthrop had repeatedly called in his writings and lectures for the elimination of slavery.

The only man in Church's inner circle who felt allegiance to the South was Mignot, the Charleston-born painter who had accompanied Church to the Andes. Mignot was well-liked in New York, but he came from enslavers, and he identified strongly with the Southern cause. His life among Northern artists became increasingly uncomfortable after South Carolina seceded in late December 1860.

CHURCH KNEW THAT WINTER IN rural upstate New York would be lonely for his cosmopolitan young wife, and the couple settled for the 1860–61 winter season in a boarding house near Madison Square Park. In the evenings, they dined out together and attended lectures, concerts, or the opera.

During long days at his studio, Church sorted through dozens of iceberg sketches, preparing for a new painting. He read the memoirs of Arctic explorers and talked with some of them. He pored over scientific treatises on oceanology, meteorology, and geology. Like Church himself, these works combined faith in science with faith in God. In one of them, *The Physical Geography of the Sea*, explorer-scientist Matthew Fontaine Maury argued that the air and the oceans "are obedient to law and subject to order in all their movements. . . . They teach us lessons concerning the wonders of the deep, the mysteries of the sky, the greatness, and the wisdom, and goodness of the Creator, which makes us wiser and better men."

Church began experimenting with compositions on small canvases. He dragged icebergs over his painted seas, carving a deep cavern here and raising a sharp peak there. The New York press ran bulletins about his progress, and as he worked, people dropped by to steal glimpses of his new project, slowing him down. Eventually he felt ready to launch himself at the final canvas, which was almost as large as the enormous *Heart of the Andes*. He covered the surface in two layers of a chalky white ground, then laid on a translucent film of blue-gray. These underlayers would glow through the colors he painted over them, lending a luminosity he hoped would match the eerie light of the northern seas.

Outside his studio, New York boiled. Shouting and fistfights broke out in saloons and lecture halls. Democrats castigated Republicans for bringing Lincoln to power and provoking the South to self-defense, while Republicans attacked Democrats for pandering to enslavers. They argued bitterly about whether a civil war was really preferable to letting South Carolina go in peace.

On January 9, Mississippi became the second state to secede and was quickly followed by Florida, Alabama, Georgia, Louisiana, and Texas. In early February, the seven secessionist states founded the Confederate States of America. From upstate New York, Frederick Douglass seethed at the cowardice he saw around him. Instead of taking up arms against the rebellious South, Northerners were fretting over the damage a civil war would do to their bank accounts. "The attitude of the Northern people in this crisis will crimson the cheeks of their children's children with shame," he predicted.

The mood was tense when, en route to his inauguration in mid-February, Lincoln arrived in New York City for two days of receptions, speeches, and meetings. The president-elect was hanged in effigy by the captain of a Southern vessel anchored in New York Harbor. Democratic Mayor Fernando Wood refused to meet Lincoln's train, unlike other mayors on the route from Springfield, Illinois, to Washington. Wood bluntly advised Lincoln to find "peaceful and conciliatory means" for restoring the Union.

Strong caught a glimpse of Lincoln riding along Broadway. "The great rail-splitter's face was visible to me for an instant, and seemed a keen, clear, honest face," he wrote, "not so ugly as his portraits." Walt Whitman saw Lincoln as he arrived at the Astor House hotel and feared for the man's life, suspecting that "many an assassin's knife and pistol lurked in hip- or breast-pocket" among the tens of thousands of onlookers. But Lincoln just "looked with curiosity upon that immense sea of faces, and the sea of faces returned the look with similar curiosity," Whitman wrote. When Lincoln departed New York, many people were relieved to see him go—some because they couldn't stand him, others because they held out hope that, once inaugurated, he would save the country from civil war.

On April 12, 1861, Confederate troops fired on Fort Sumter in Charleston Harbor. Major Robert Anderson, the commander of Fort Sumter, had, with a small contingent of soldiers, spent the winter under siege watching provisions dwindle as they waited in vain for federal relief. Coming under Confederate fire, Anderson and his men had fought back until, outgunned, they had been forced to surrender.

On April 15, Lincoln called for seventy-five thousand volunteers to quell the rebellion. Winthrop was one of the New York men who answered the president's call. "I go to put an end to slavery," he told his family. Along with his younger brother, Winthrop joined the elite Seventh Regiment. They and hundreds of other untested young men spent only a few days training. On April 19, one week after the attack on Fort Sumter, the regiment was ordered to depart for a month-long tour of duty. As the soldiers assembled for a parade through the city streets to the New Jersey ferry slip, Winthrop was assigned to guard a twelve-pound howitzer at the rear of the armory. A crowd gathered, and the way they looked at Winthrop made him feel as if they were "taking the measure of my coffin."

At four o'clock that afternoon, the Seventh Regiment marched south from Sixth Street. American flags waved above their heads and tens of thousands of people cheered them from the sidewalks, windows, and rooftops. If many New Yorkers had at first balked at the idea of fighting the Confederacy, the scenes along the parade route persuaded Winthrop that the city was now "utterly united in the great cause we were marching to sustain." Men clapped him on the back as he passed. Women dropped handkerchiefs and gloves from the windows above. "It was worth a life, that march," he decided afterward.

The Seventh Regiment was bound for Washington. Virginia had just become the eighth state to secede, exposing Washington to Confederate attack. Within a week, the Seventh Regiment was quartered in the Capitol, ready to defend the city.

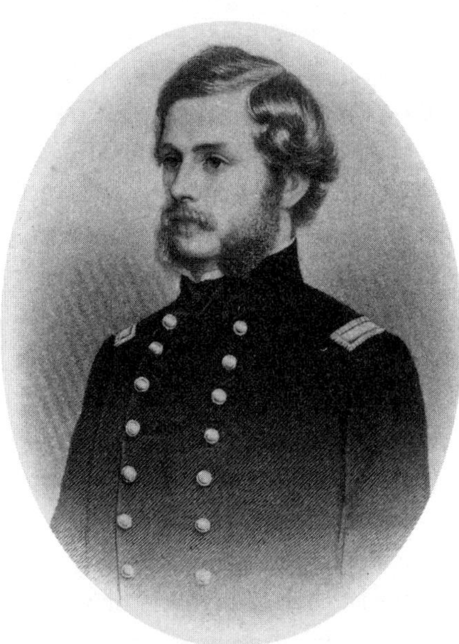

Theodore Winthrop in uniform, 1861

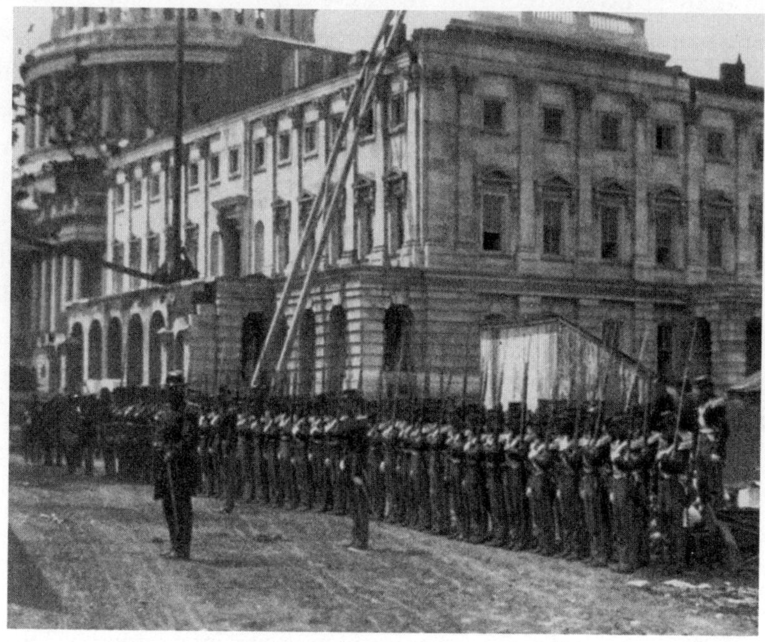

The United States Capitol in May 1861

ON APRIL 20, THE DAY after Winthrop left town, a headline in *Harper's Weekly* announced that "Church's New Picture" was complete and would soon go on display at Goupil's on Broadway. The timing was risky, but Church calculated that the distracting anxiety churned up by national politics would be offset by the topicality of his picture.

Also on April 20, more than one hundred thousand New Yorkers poured into Union Square in what would be described by the press as the largest gathering in the nation's history. In midafternoon, the hero of the hour, Major Robert Anderson of Fort Sumter, appeared. As he climbed up to the speakers' platform, a roar began to spread across the park. "For upwards of twenty minutes the roar of voices sounded more like the dashing of distant waters than articulation of human speech," the *Herald* reported.

Flags and patriotic signs hung from the façades of the houses and hotels fronting Union Square, where an equestrian statue of George Washington— who had died fearing disunion—held the staff of a billowing American flag in one bronze hand. Until a week earlier, that flag had flown over Fort Sumter. Anderson had brought it to New York.

In a letter to her sister-in-law, Virginia Osborn tried to explain how rapidly and profoundly the city had changed. "Four weeks ago people did not hesitate to say 'New York is governed by its pocket, and will never fight against the South if by so doing it endangers its commercial prosperity.'" After the attack on Fort Sumter, "New York was roused from its lethargy and in one week the people were willing to sacrifice their property and their lives if necessary for their beloved country."

Winthrop, a bachelor, had raced off to Washington ready to lay down his life. Church, married for less than a year, stayed with his wife. Isabel's father had died in December, after which Mrs. Carnes joined them in New York. Church was no longer responsible only for himself. He would support the Union not by volunteering to fight, but by donating the fees from his upcoming exhibition to a fund for Union soldiers. In a further tribute, Church changed the title of his painting from *The Icebergs* to *The North*.

He invited friends and members of the press to a preview on the evening of April 23, the day before the exhibition opened to the public. They found a strange and disorienting picture. There was no landscape at all—only water, ice, sky, and a boulder borne from some faraway land by the grinding force of the ice. People who had never seen the frozen north thought of it as a white wasteland, but Church's canvas danced with blue, green, and violet hues. His painting was at once so alien and so beautiful that, as one critic wrote, "you would as soon stretch out your hand to feel the texture of an angel's wing." Somebody published a "Sonnet to F. E. C." that called Church the "Michael Angelo of landscape Art." He pasted it into his book of clippings.

People flocked to *The North*. The picture spoke of the earth's immense and varied beauty, but also of the political survival of the Union. After the fall of Fort Sumter and President Lincoln's mobilization of troops, the Northern symbolism of Church's new picture had grown even more powerful than it had been when he had begun painting it. "There is a North," wrote one reviewer, linking a famous antislavery slogan to Church's new picture. Another wrote, "None need be told that Church is great—that he is national."

Church wasn't as headstrong and fervent as Winthrop, but more than a decade of his paintings attested that he cared deeply about the Union. He went back to his studio and poured his feelings into a new picture that drew on *Twilight in the Wilderness*, his 1860 warning to the nation. Here again were the sweeping red clouds above the forest-lined lake and the mountain range in the distance. Otherwise, this little painting was unlike anything he had ever before painted. In late May, he hung it up on the wall at Goupil's alongside *The North*.

Church called the picture *Our Banner in the Sky*. A tattered American flag dominated the canvas, but the flag was not made of cloth. Its stars were formed by the stars in the night sky and its stripes by thin, red streaks of cloud. A bare tree trunk served as the flagpole. Church let it be known to the press that the time of day was not twilight but the hopeful hour of dawn. He had once again used the elements of nature to speak explicitly of politics. The cosmos and its Creator seemed to be ordaining a Union victory.

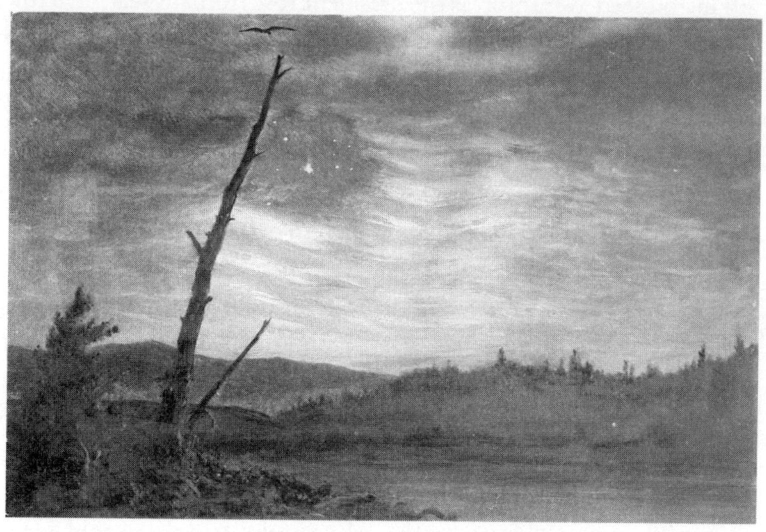

Our Banner in the Sky, by Church, 1861

It was a piece of overt propaganda, one of only two he would ever paint; the other was another wartime flag picture. *Our Banner in the Sky* was devoid of the ambiguity that made Church's best pictures haunting and complex, and the critics were dismissive. They weren't going to suspend artistic judgment simply because a war had broken out. Even the *Hartford Courant*, his hometown paper, joked that "the spacious firmament on high is not gifted in the manufacture of American flags." Nevertheless, the picture was a popular success, inspiring copies, poems, and songs. Church sold the rights to *Our Banner in the Sky* so chromolithographs could be published, and the celestial flag became a familiar beacon on parlor walls throughout the Union.

In Baltimore, William T. Walters, the businessman and art collector who had in 1860 bought *Twilight in the Wilderness*—the inspiration for *Our Banner in the Sky*—found himself the owner of a painting linked in the national imagination with God's plan for a Union victory. Walters was a Confederate sympathizer. Partway through the war, he decided to sell the picture.

WINTHROP, STILL ON DUTY IN Washington, was deputized by a friend in May to take a letter to Secretary of State William H. Seward. Entering Seward's office, Winthrop was surprised to discover President Lincoln sitting on the sofa. Seward introduced Winthrop as the president rose from his seat. "Up towers the Commander in Chief and presents flipper," Winthrop wrote to a friend. "I lose my hand in his." Winthrop affected a nonchalant tone, but he had just met the man who had given him his great purpose in life. Since childhood, he had felt rudderless and ineffectual, but all his self-doubt had evaporated the moment he heard Lincoln's call for men to defend the Union.

When the Seventh Regiment's tour of duty in Washington came to an end in late May, Winthrop accepted an invitation to join the staff of Major General Benjamin Butler at Fortress Monroe on the Chesapeake Bay in Virginia. "We must conquer the South," Winthrop told a friend. "Afterward we must be prepared to . . . police [it] in its own behalf, and in behalf of its black population, whom this war must . . . emancipate."

At Fortress Monroe, Butler promoted Winthrop to military secretary with a rank of major. Butler had taken up his command only a week before Winthrop arrived, but he had already made a decision that would shape the course of the war—and he had done so without first seeking approval from

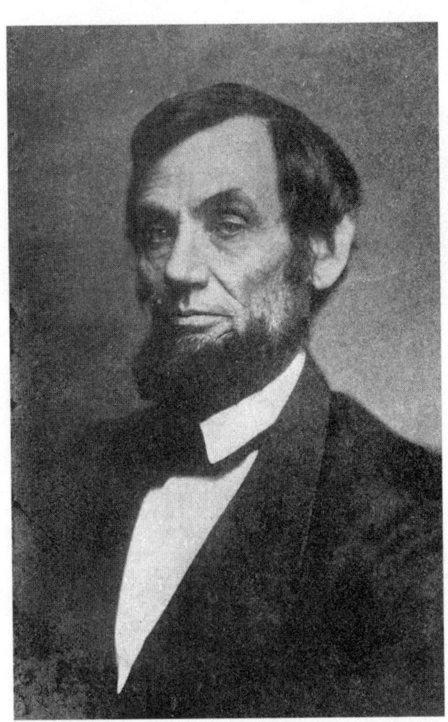

President Lincoln,
by Mathew Brady, April 1861

the Lincoln administration. On May 23, three Black men—the property of a local judge—had appeared at the fort asking for sanctuary. When a Confederate officer came to retrieve the men the next day, Butler refused to hand them over, telling the officer he was confiscating the men as "contraband of war." In doing so, he was defying the Fugitive Slave Law of 1850, but as Butler saw it, Virginia was no longer a part of the United States and therefore wasn't protected by its laws. The news spread from one plantation to another. Over the next weeks, dozens of enslaved people arrived at Fortress Monroe seeking sanctuary.

Winthrop fervently approved of Butler's policy, writing to his sister that he was "in the center of the center!" He appealed to a friend in New York for help collecting clothes for the formerly enslaved and began drafting an essay for the *Atlantic Monthly* entitled "Voices of the Contraband." He wanted Northern readers to know what he was learning firsthand from these refugees about their lives in bondage.

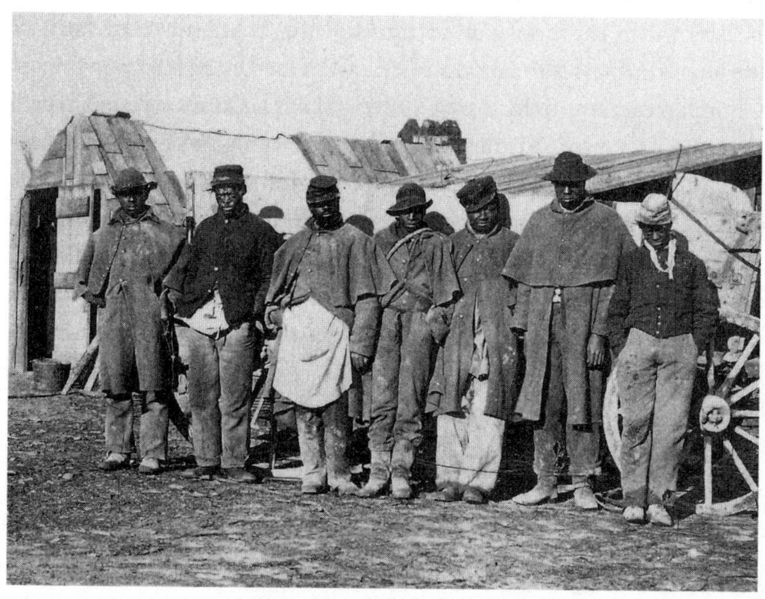

A group of "Contrabands," c. 1862

In early June, Butler made another unprecedented decision regarding enslaved people. Aided by Winthrop, he drew up a plan for an attack on a Confederate position about eight miles away, near a church called Big Bethel.

Included in the plan was the stipulation that one of the Black men now living at Fortress Monroe, a scout named George Scott, would be allowed to carry a revolver during the operation. A Black man armed by the U.S. Army—it was an extraordinary moment in the history of the nation. Winthrop wrote to his mother about the impending strike: "We march at midnight to attack. . . . If I don't come back, dear mother, dear love to everybody."

The mission was a disaster. Eighteen Union soldiers died, some by friendly fire, others at the hands of Confederates. Though outnumbered, the rebels lost only one man. The Union troops made a chaotic retreat, leaving their dead and dying in the field. Winthrop did not return with his fellow soldiers.

Butler learned afterward what had happened to Winthrop from a Vermont private who had been with him on the battlefield. Winthrop had raced toward enemy lines, rallying his fellow soldiers as he went. When he jumped on a log for a better view of the enemy's position, he had been shot. A man in equal parts impulsive and principled, Winthrop had become the first Union officer to die on a battlefield in the Civil War. His family and friends were devastated—yet, as his sister wrote, they took comfort in knowing "that some of the last acts of his life were kindnesses to an oppressed race, a race he never forgot."

Church's reaction to the loss of his best friend has not survived in writing, though two days after Winthrop's body was exhumed to be returned to his family, Church made a substantial donation to a fund supporting the families of Union soldiers. His most recent painting, *Our Banner in the Sky*, was inspired by the Maine woods where he and Winthrop had camped and hiked together. Church had created the picture after Winthrop had enlisted, but before his death. From its inception, *Our Banner in the Sky* had fused national meanings with associations personal to Church, and now those personal associations had turned deeply painful.

Around the time Church's show closed at Goupil's, he and Isabel moved for the summer up to the Farm. The builders had recently completed work on the new farmhouse, which Church and Isabel were soon calling Cosy Cottage. It was modest but pretty, with white walls, diamond-shaped windowpanes, and a gabled roof. Church had chosen the building site with care, setting the cottage partway up the great hillside meadow that rose at the heart of the Farm.

The Farm was a peaceful place, but Church was not at peace. In July, he made a violent oil sketch of a sunset over the Hudson Valley. By the summer of 1861, sunsets had come to mean three things to him: nation, war, and Winthrop. The brushstrokes were thick and rough, and he devoted more than three-quarters of the paper to the sky. A cloud bank the color of fresh blood lay along the horizon; the rest of the sky was the rusty red of dried blood. It was the angriest sunset he had ever painted.

Toward the end of the war, Church would lose another friend, a promising young painter named John Jameson, who was part of the Tenth Street circle. When Church learned of his death, he wrote to Jameson's mother railing against the Confederacy. His anguished letter could have doubled as a furious lament for the loss of Winthrop. "When I think how such a pure, high-minded and talented youth was sacrificed to the rage of the wicked," he fumed, "—I almost feel tempted to rejoice that the direst calamity has visited those regions of inhumanity."

In a letter Church later wrote to Winthrop's sister, he lamented his fallen friend as "your never to be forgotten and always beloved brother Theodore."

"A Moral Volcano"

Church loved children. The friendship he had formed at the age of eighteen with young Theddy had turned out to be one of the lasting gifts of his apprenticeship with Cole. In his twenties, Church had lavished attention on the Osborns' eldest child, Virginia, drawing pictures for her and mentioning her in his letters to W.H. When his friend Goodman became a father for the first time, Church had written to him excitedly, "How is baby????"

Now, at last, it was Church's turn. In early 1862, after almost two years of marriage, Isabel learned she was pregnant. She was twenty-five years old; Church was thirty-five. Noble, knowing how much this turn of events meant to Church, sent him a thoughtful letter. "You are fortunate," he wrote. "I have never known a more fortunate man."

In May, Church and Isabel once again moved to the Farm and settled into Cosy Cottage. As Isabel's petite frame swelled beneath her summer dresses, the world around her burst into bloom. A parade of wildflowers marched through the weeks—bloodroot, violet, chicory, and phlox. The fields in the Hudson Valley turned green with healthy crops of wheat, rye, and oats; only the corn seemed unwell that summer—and, at times, Isabel, whose pregnancy was proving difficult. Virginia Osborn, who had grown close to Isabel, worried that her friend was "so delicate, so frail."

In early August, the crickets began to sing, hinting that autumn was on its way. Church and Isabel thought about when to return to New York City. Giving birth in the country was risky; if something went wrong, they would be far from the most up-to-date doctors. On the other hand, in the country they were much safer from the fatal fevers that stalked the dense city streets—cholera,

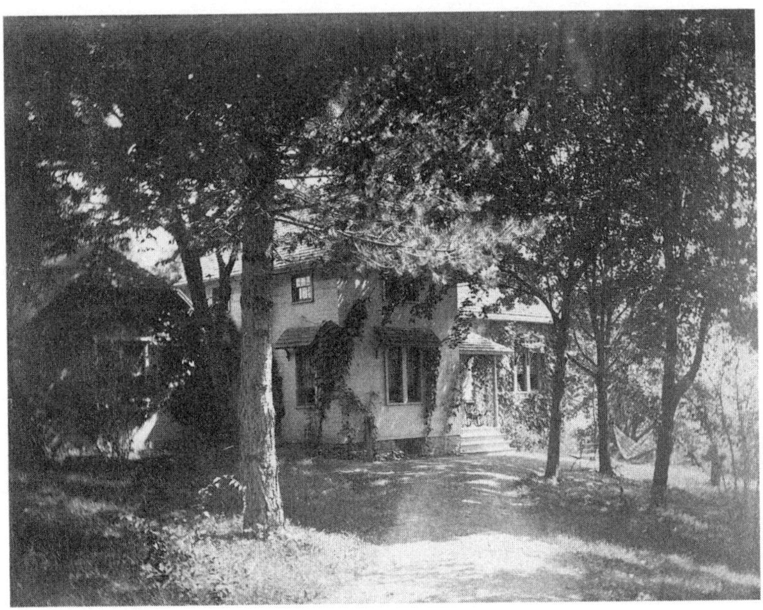

Cosy Cottage in an undated photograph

typhus, diphtheria. They delayed their departure and were rewarded in the fall by blue skies and agreeable temperatures. They left for the city only in mid-October, with the baby due in weeks.

On October 29, Isabel gave birth to a son, Herbert Edwin Church, who would be known as Bertie. Theddy made a note in the journal where he recorded his livestock purchases for the Farm: "Saw Mrs. Churches baby it is a real good specimen." When Church's mother learned she was a grandmother, her Yankee reserve melted. "You and Isabel must kiss baby 20 times and tell him how much I love him," she wrote. "I hope he [will] prove a blessing to you both and to the world and from this moment you must remember that he is living for eternity." A few weeks later Mrs. Church wrote again to her son: "I do want to see the baby I wish you could put him in your pocket." Church's sister Elizabeth sent a request for a photograph of "the young republican."

The Osborns were not in New York to welcome the new baby in person. As president of the Illinois Central Railroad, W.H. was urgently needed at the Chicago headquarters, where he was directing wartime operations in close consultation with General George B. McClellan, formerly chief engineer for the Illinois Central and now a commander of Union forces. The railroad line had become a vital support to the Union, moving tens of thousands of soldiers toward Southern battlefields along with food and weaponry. The return cargo included thousands of captured Confederate soldiers headed for Northern prison camps.

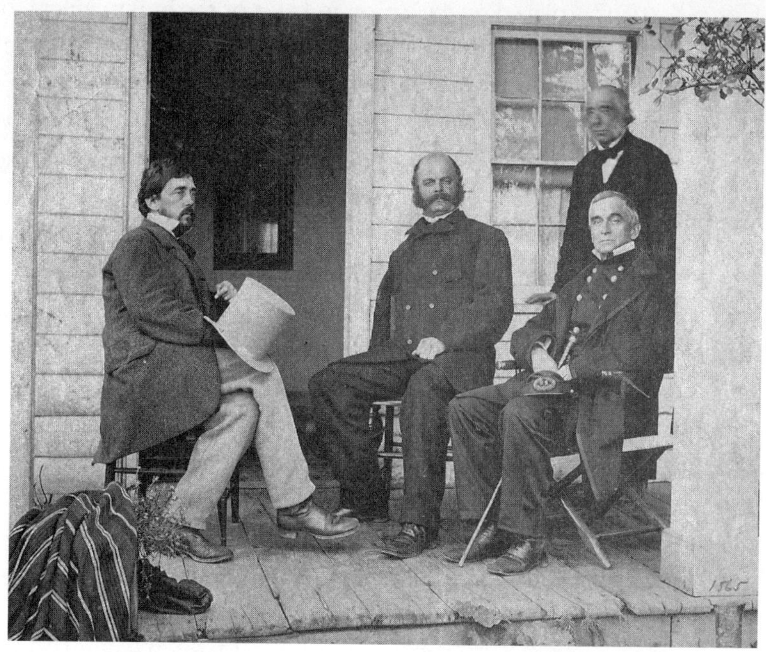

W. H. Osborn with General Ambrose Burnside and former Fort Sumter commander General Robert Anderson (*seated left to right*), 1865

During the Osborns' temporary residence in Chicago, W.H. and Virginia and their three children were camped out in what Osborn described to Church as a "great castle of a House," where the only picture they had bothered to put up was an engraving of *The Heart of the Andes*. When business took W.H. around the state, the family lived in a private railroad car fitted out with a dining room and sleeping compartments. "Mr. Osborn sometimes lives in this car for weeks with his wife and children," a visiting French dignitary observed, "just as a captain would live aboard his ship." Virginia was expecting that autumn; in December she would give birth to her fourth child, whom they christened William Church Osborn.

Virginia was delighted to hear of Bertie's birth, telling her husband, "Nobody in this world will enjoy a baby so much as Mr. Church. . . . How he will tend it—write him and say how glad we are." When Bertie was a few months old, Church and Isabel had him photographed at a Union Square studio owned by George Rockwood, who in later years would photograph such distinguished figures as Charles Dickens, Ulysses S. Grant, and Buffalo Bill Cody. Bertie was placed on a cushion in front of the bulky camera, but he was still too young to sit upright by himself. Mrs. Carnes, sitting so far to one side that she was halfway out of the frame, held her grandson in outstretched hands. She couldn't help beaming down at him. Bertie froze long enough for a clear picture to be taken, except for one fluttering little hand.

Church felt the need to celebrate the birth of his first child in his own way. He painted a small landscape, showing the sun just rising into a pale blue sky above a distant range of hazy mountains. In the foreground, a stream wound its way through soft, green marshland. After a decade of fiery sunsets—portents of national peril—Church had produced a dawn of peace and hope.

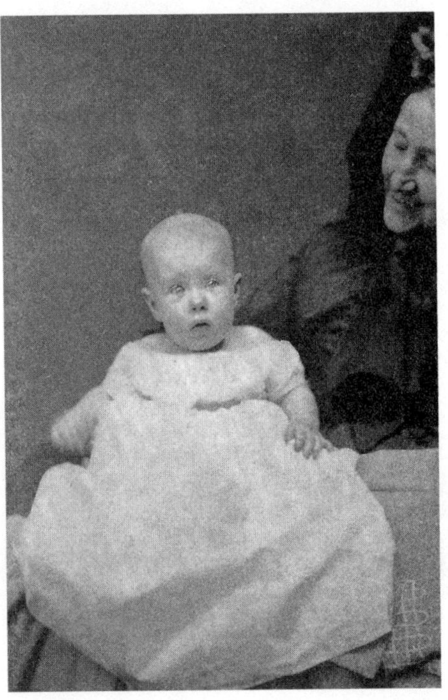

Bertie with Isabel's mother, Emma Carnes

THAT AUTUMN OF 1862, a national peace remained elusive, but there were stirrings of optimism among Union supporters. After a humiliating rout at Bull Run in July 1861 and General McClellan's maddening reluctance to strike the Confederates in fall and early winter of 1861, the first months of 1862 had seen several Union victories. In February, General Grant, with the help of men and supplies moved by Osborn's Illinois Central, had captured two crucial forts in Tennessee. In April, near a church called Shiloh in south-western Tennessee, Union forces led by General Grant, General William

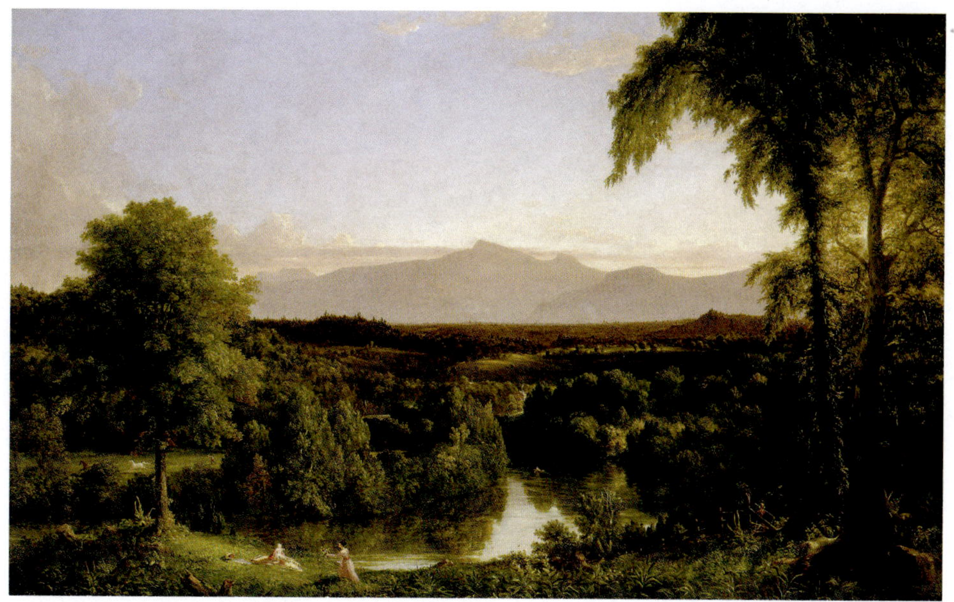

Church's teacher, Thomas Cole, often painted the Catskill Mountains as a backdrop to the Catskill Creek, along whose banks he loved to walk.

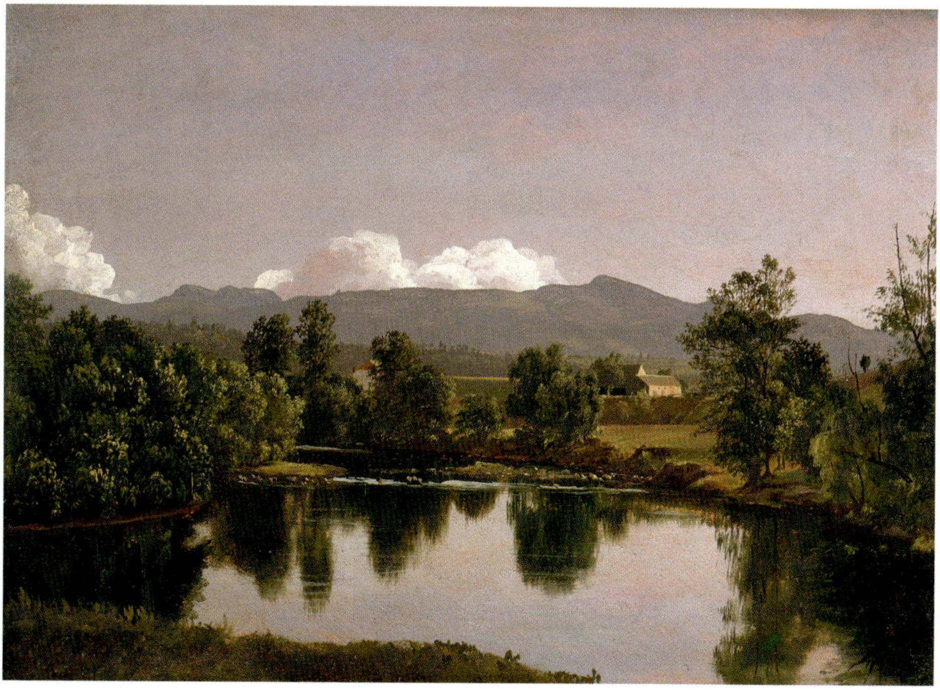

Church painted *The Catskill Creek* (1845) during his studies with Cole, when he was about nineteen years old. In his first few years as a landscape painter, Church hewed closely to his teacher's subject matter and style.

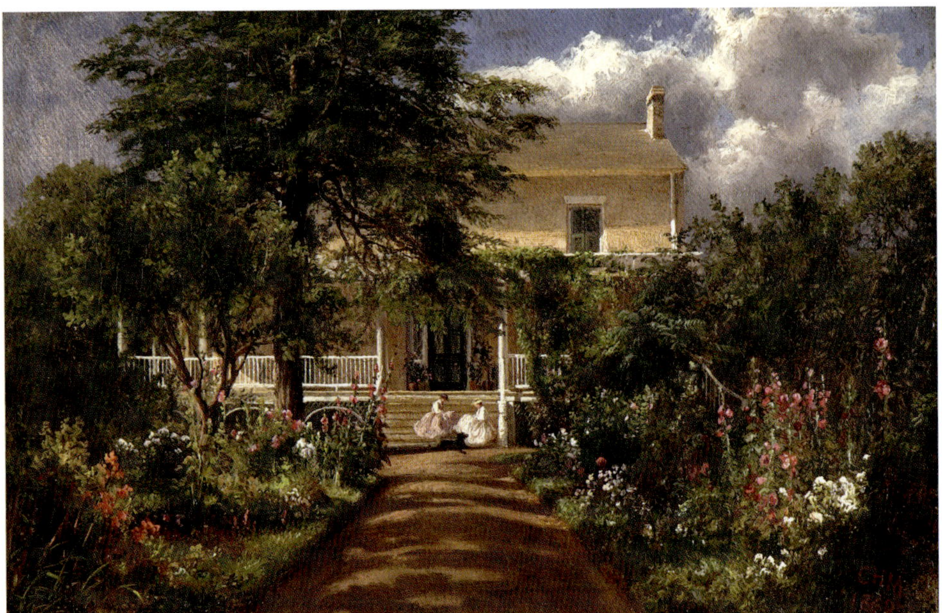

Cedar Grove, the Cole family's house and farm, became Church's home during his studies with Cole. Church grew close to the Cole family and fell in love with the Hudson Valley.

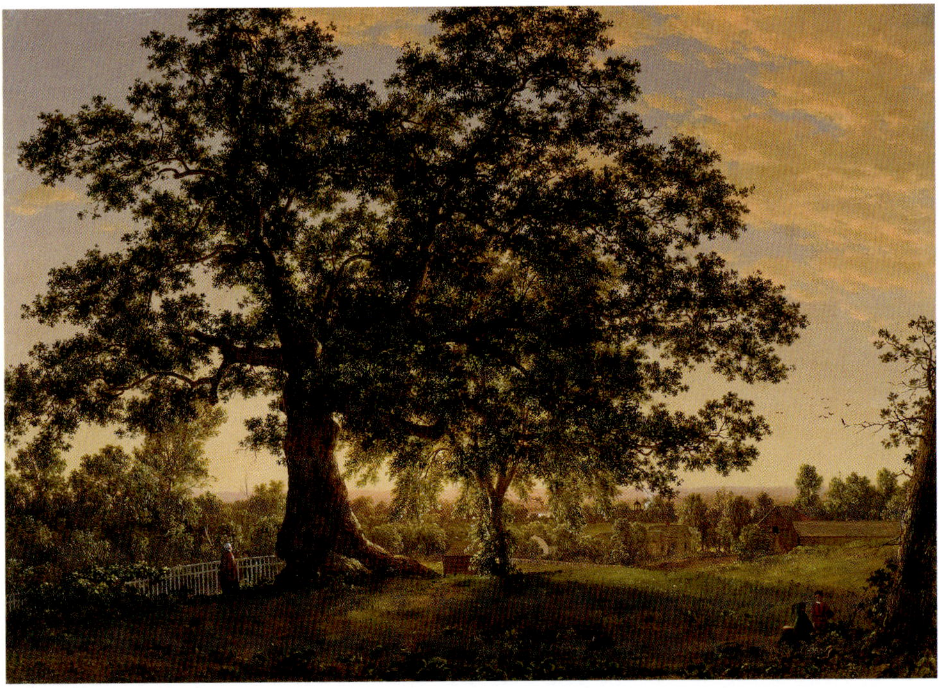

Church painted *The Charter Oak at Hartford* when he was about twenty years old. According to legend, seventeenth-century colonists used a hole in this ancient tree to hide the charter of Connecticut from agents of King James II. Like Boston's more famous Liberty Tree, the Charter Oak symbolized to nineteenth-century New Englanders the anti-monarchical spirit of the nation's founding.

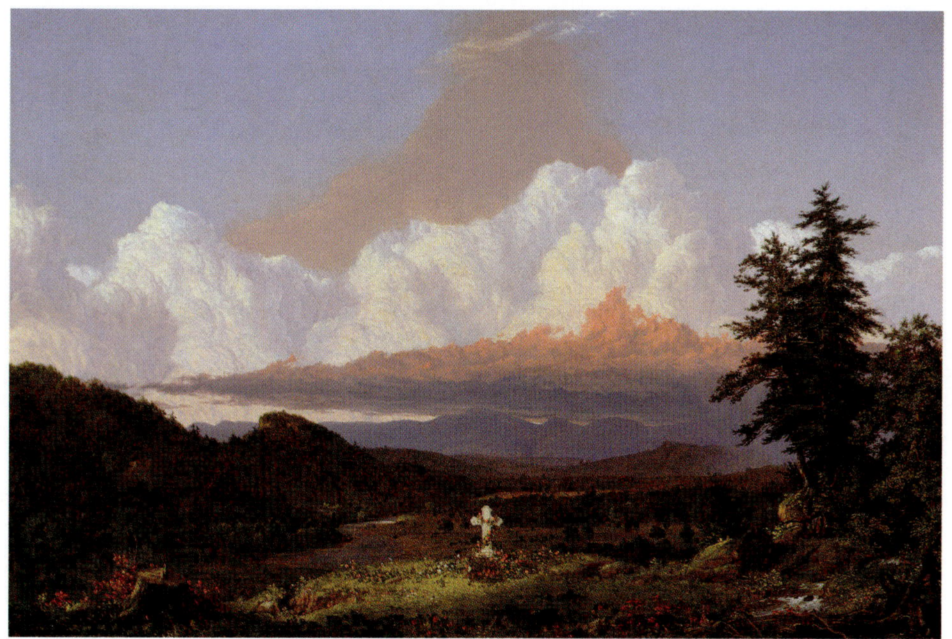

When Thomas Cole died suddenly in 1848, Church poured everything he had learned from his teacher into this tribute, *To the Memory of Cole*, depicting Cole's grave at the center of the landscape he had loved best.

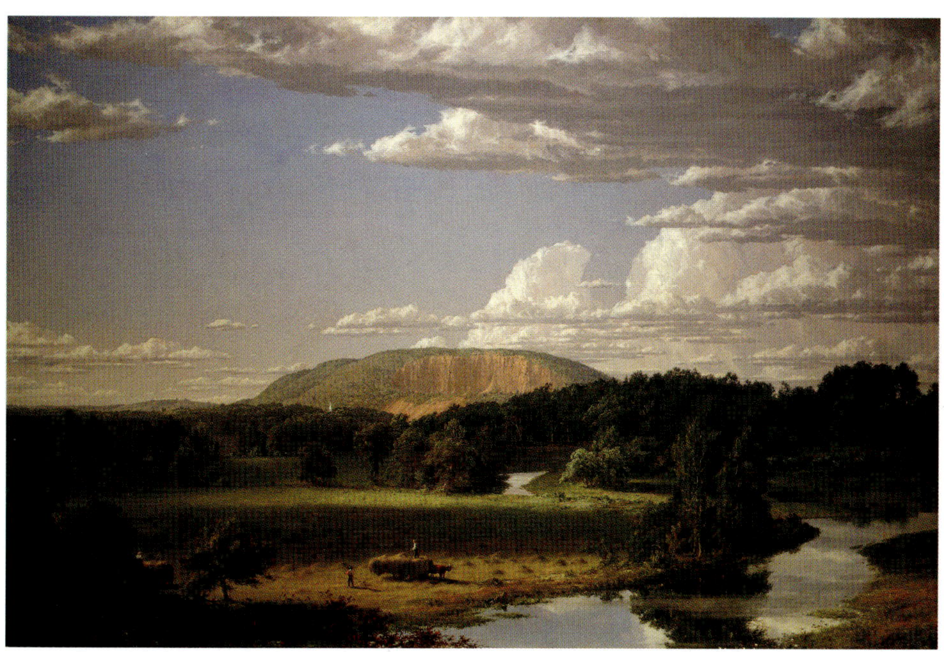

In *West Rock, New Haven* (1849), Church again used a natural landmark to evoke the American colonists' resistance to tyranny. West Rock was famous for having sheltered two English judges sought by royal agents for their role in the regicide of King Charles I. Church, still in his early twenties, drew critical praise for his skill at painting clouds and water.

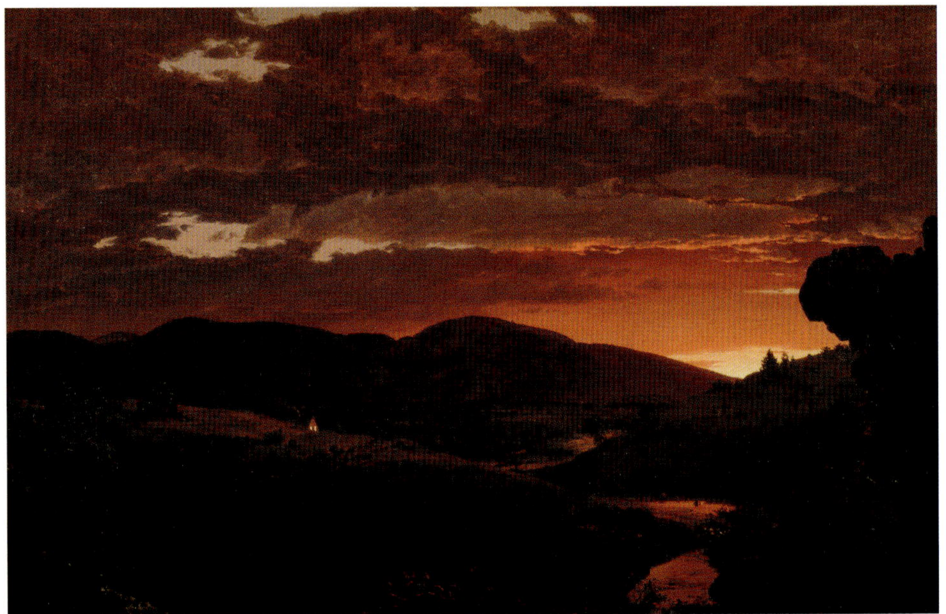

Church's *Twilight, "Short Arbiter 'Twixt Day and Night"* alludes to the moment in Milton's *Paradise Lost* when Satan, banished from Eden, plots the destruction of humanity. Many critics praised Church's rendering of an ominous twilight sky over a shrouded New England landscape. In this 1850 painting, created at the dawn of the fraught decade that led to the Civil War, Church was developing an original visual style that used natural elements to express and provoke emotion.

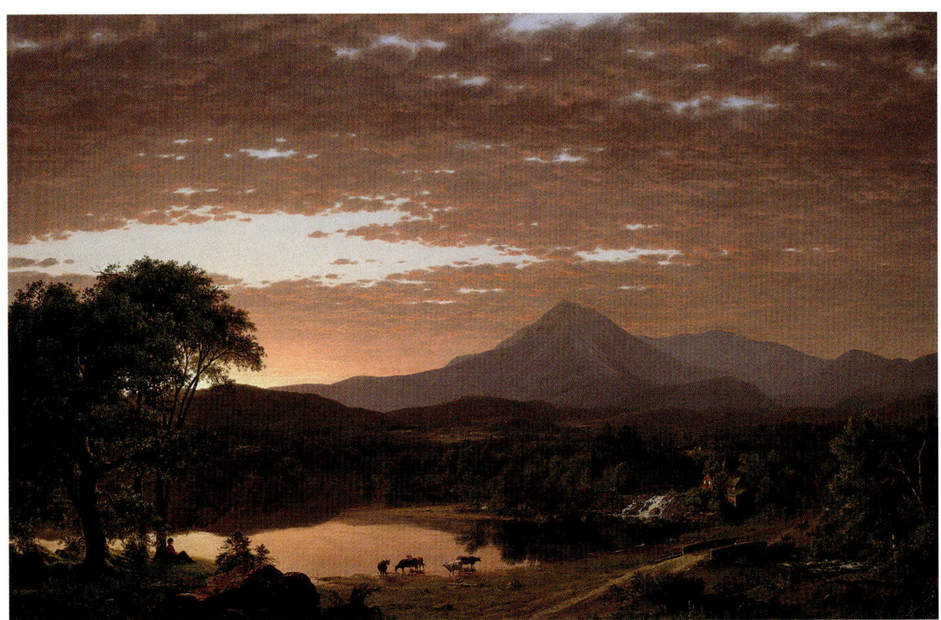

Church first painted Maine's highest mountain in 1853. Expressing pride in what he viewed as New Englanders' rugged self-sufficiency, he used Mount Katahdin as a regal backdrop to his central subject: a farm carved out of the woods. In a region dominated by spruce, pine, fir, and cedar, Church chose to paint an oak and an elm in the foreground. Both trees resonated with his viewers as symbols of the American colonists' struggle to govern themselves.

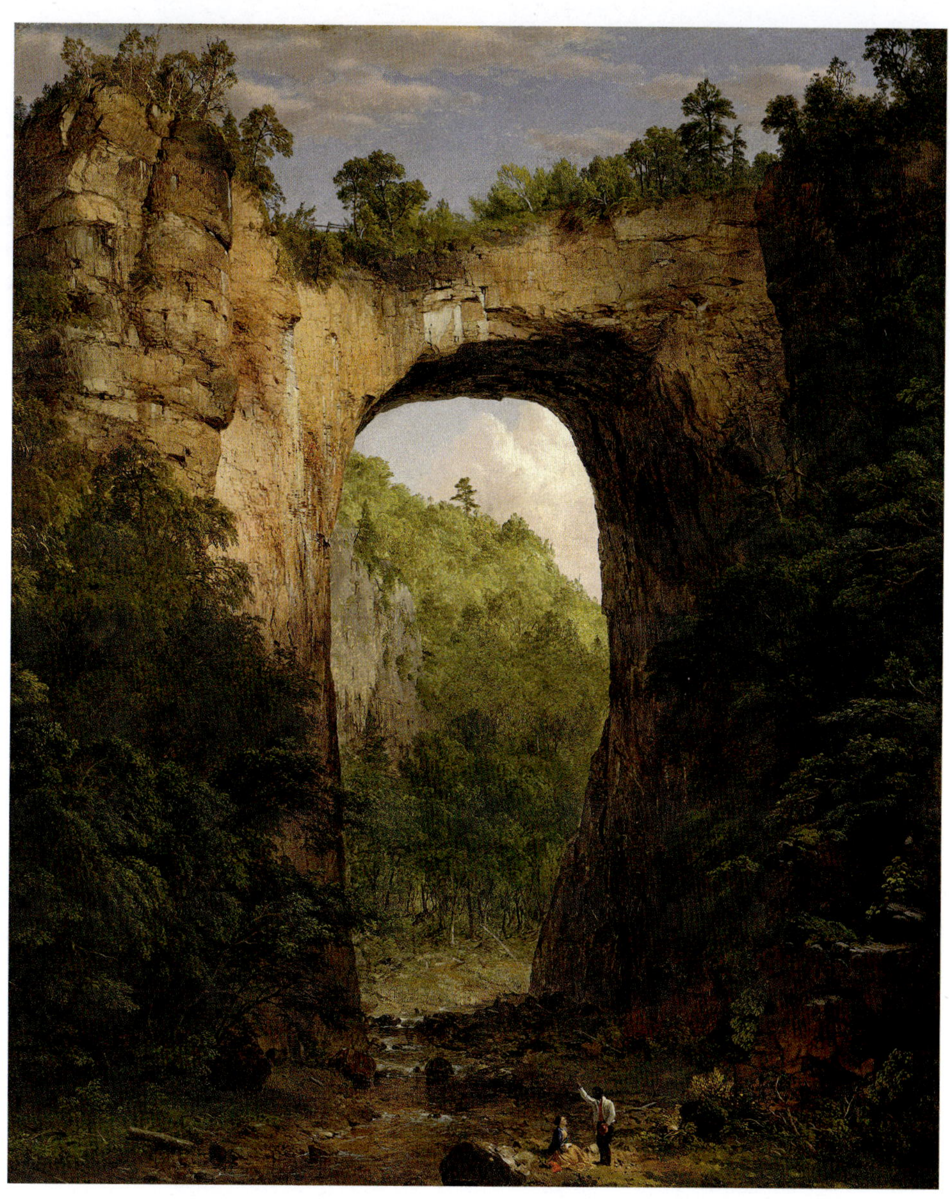

In *The Natural Bridge, Virginia* (1852), Church pictured a Black man declaiming at a famous natural landmark. His composition alluded both to the monumental beauty of North American landscapes and to the centrality of debates over slavery to the future of the nation.

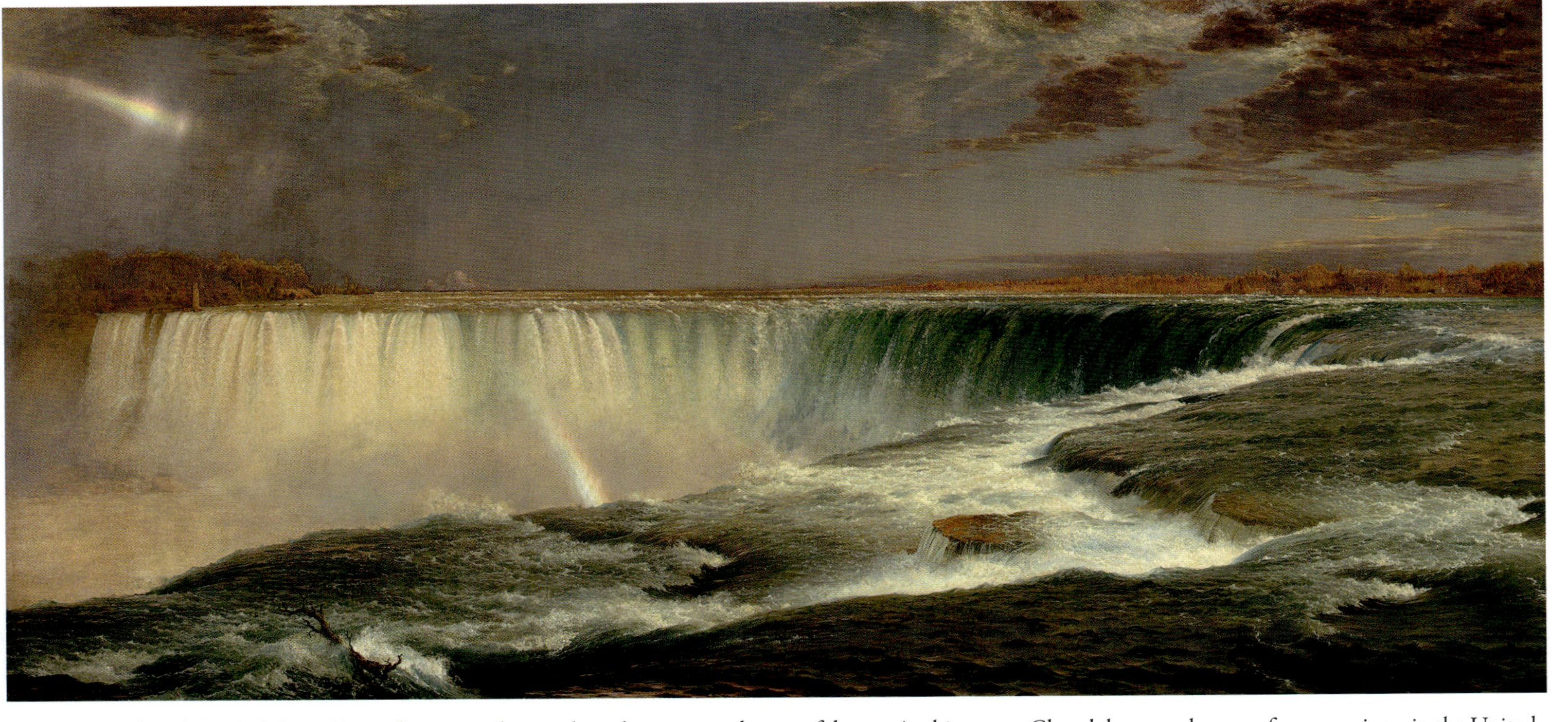

Niagara Falls (1857) dazzled the public and critics with its technical mastery and sense of drama. At thirty-one, Church became the most famous painter in the United States, and when the painting went on view in London, British critics embraced Church as the first great New World painter.

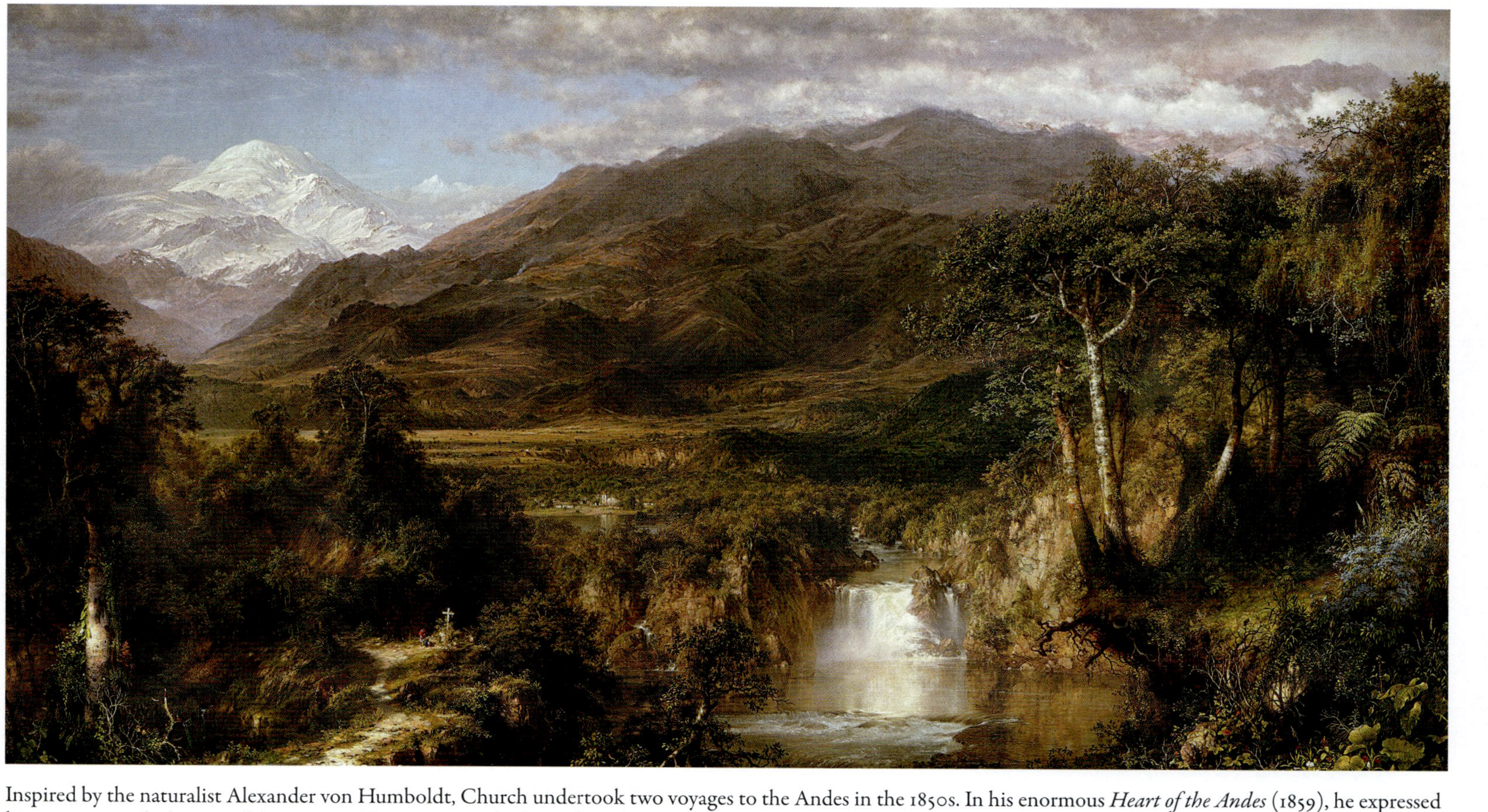

Inspired by the naturalist Alexander von Humboldt, Church undertook two voyages to the Andes in the 1850s. In his enormous *Heart of the Andes* (1859), he expressed his own awe at the beauty of the cosmos. The painting, which combined grandeur with meticulous detail, created a sensation, with twelve thousand people lining up to see it at the building on Tenth Street where Church had his studio.

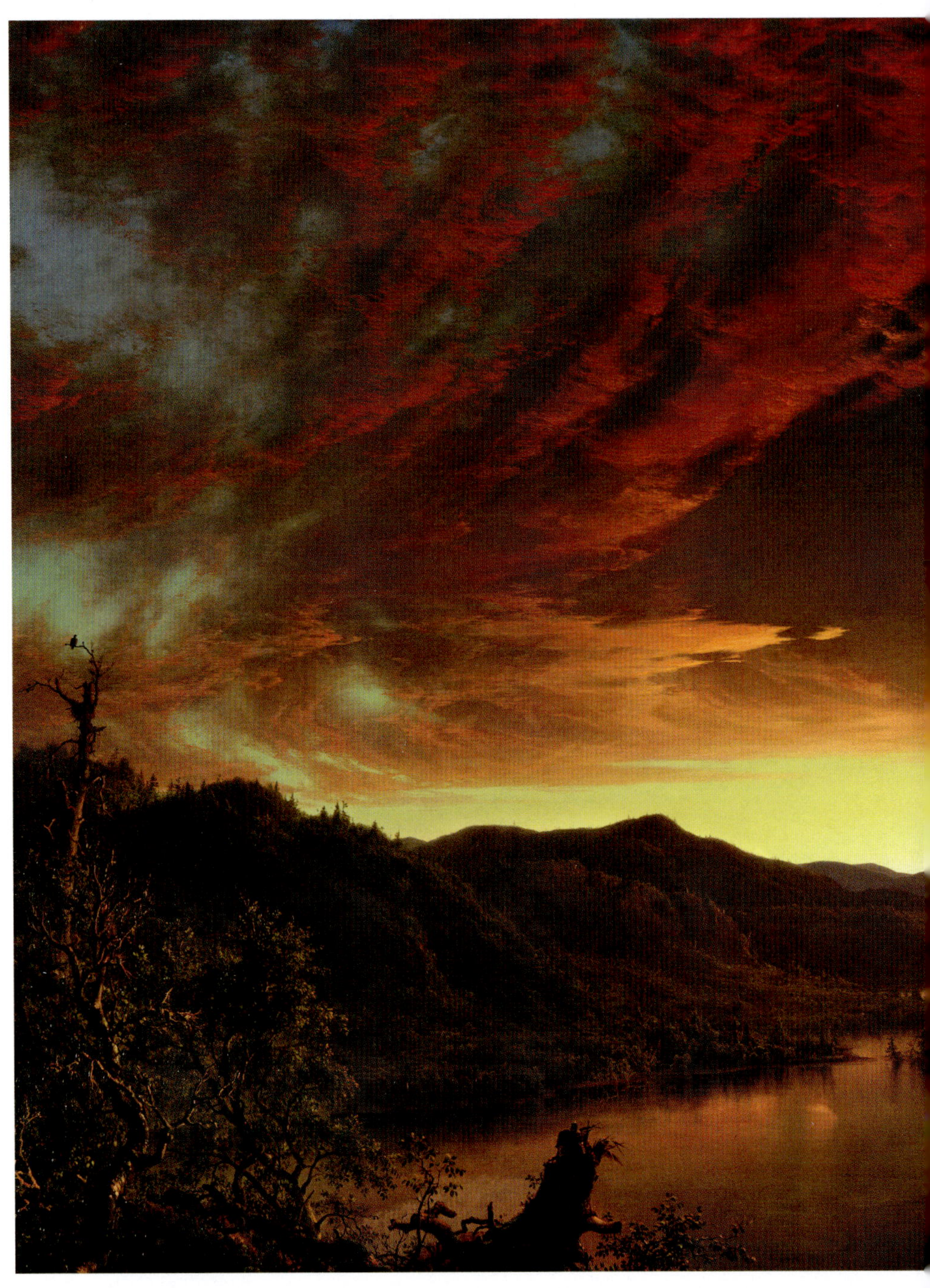

In *Twilight in the Wilderness* (1860), Church harnessed his growing virtuosity as a painter of sunset skies and descending darkness to issue a warning to his troubled nation (symbolized by a pair of bald eagles) in an age of increasingly fierce sectional rancor. For Church's viewers, who were steeped in biblical symbolism, wilderness connoted moral challenge and mortal danger.

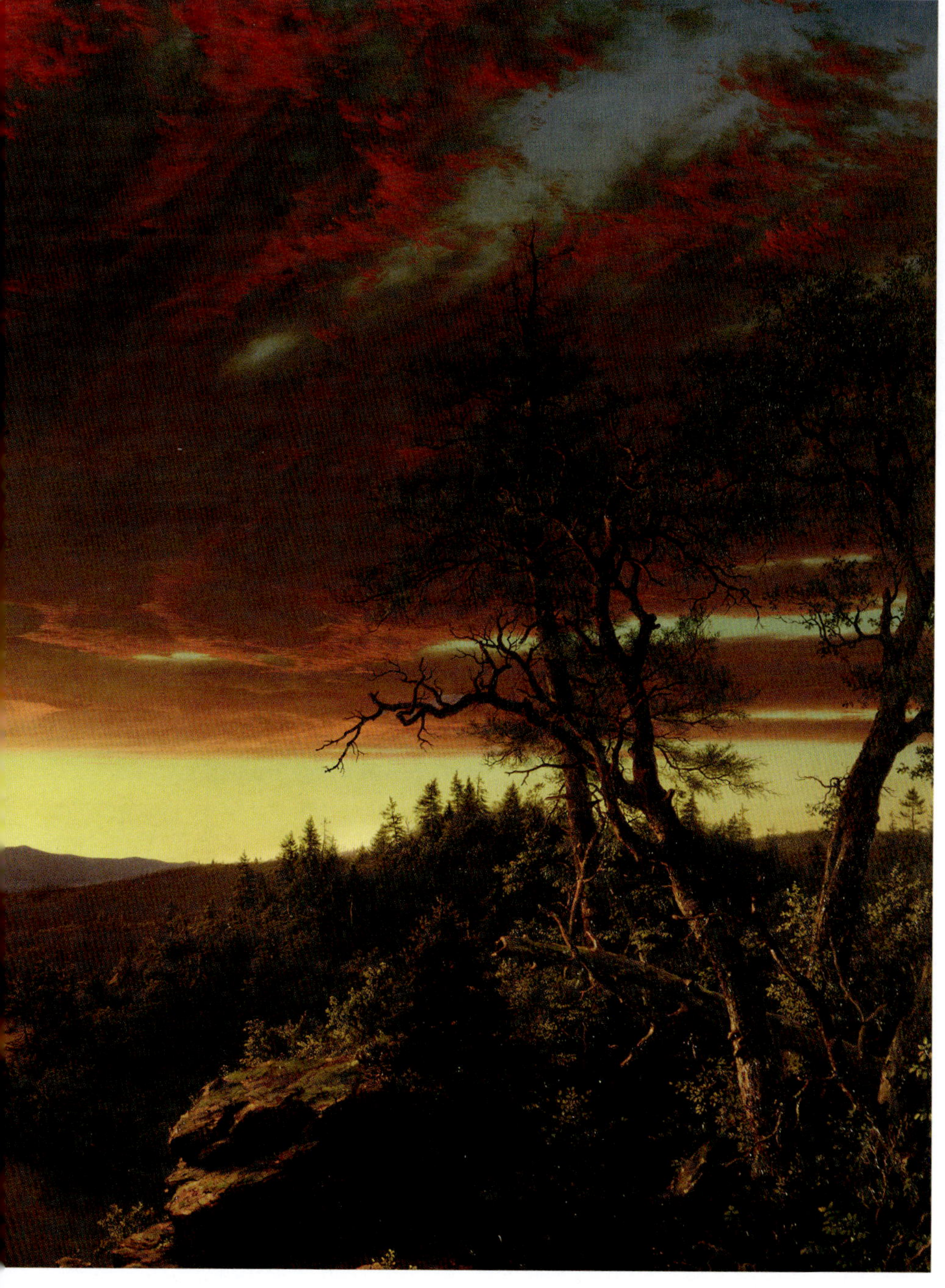

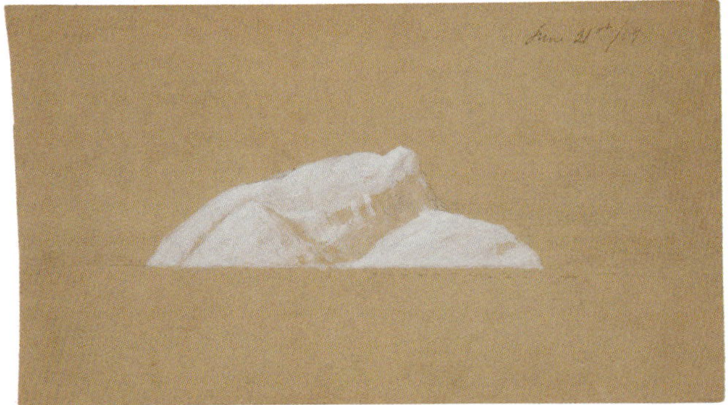

In the summer of 1859, Church sailed to Newfoundland and Labrador, where he sketched and painted icebergs, sometimes using graphite and white gouache to rough out the masses and angles of the ice.

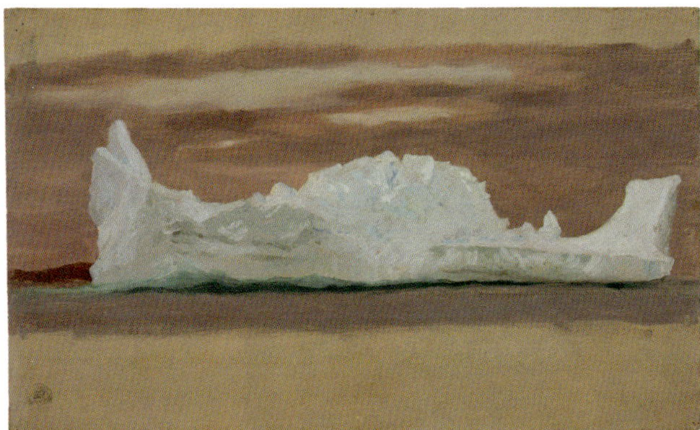

To capture the contrasting and mutable colors of sky, ice, and water, Church painted quickly in oils on paper. These plein air oil sketches would later serve as reminders of the hues and values he wanted to depict on canvas in his studio.

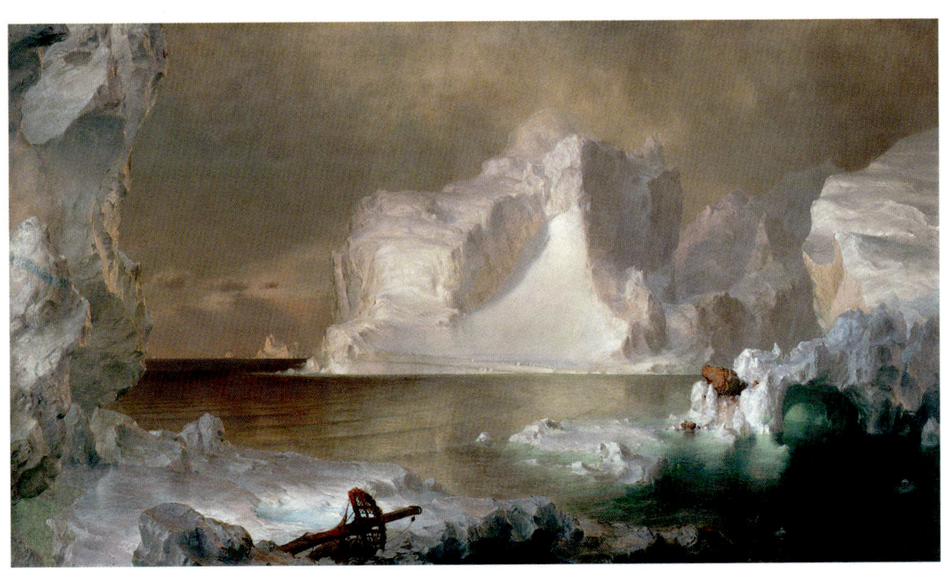

After his iceberg trip, Church used his sketches to compose a large-scale painting. He initially called it *The Icebergs*, but when the painting was exhibited shortly after Fort Sumter fell to Confederate forces, Church changed the title to *The North* and donated his exhibition proceeds to a fund for Union soldiers.

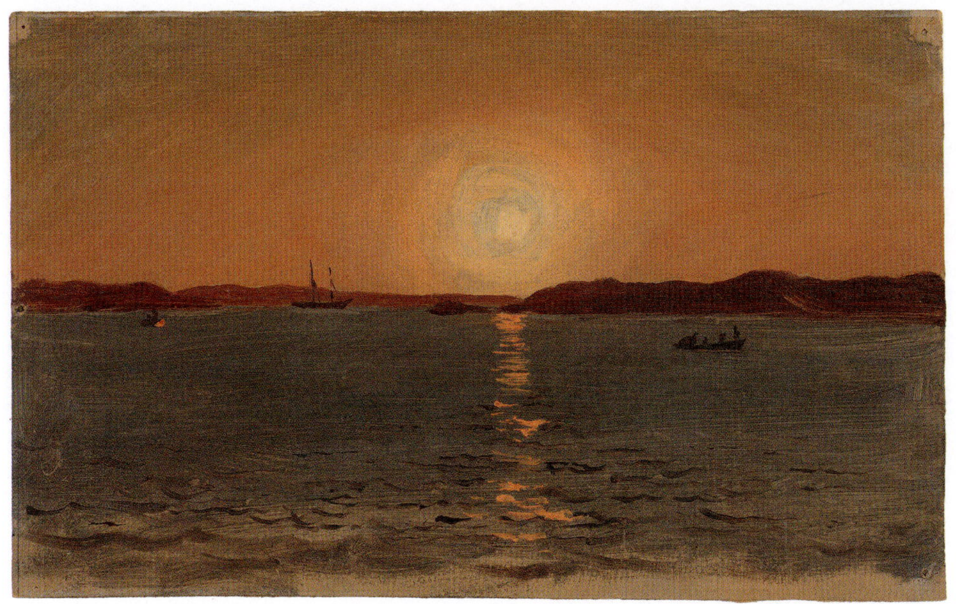

Over the course of his life, Church painted hundreds of plein air oil sketches, distilling momentary effects of color and light into shimmering images that prefigure some of the experiments of later painters such as Monet, van Gogh, and Munch.

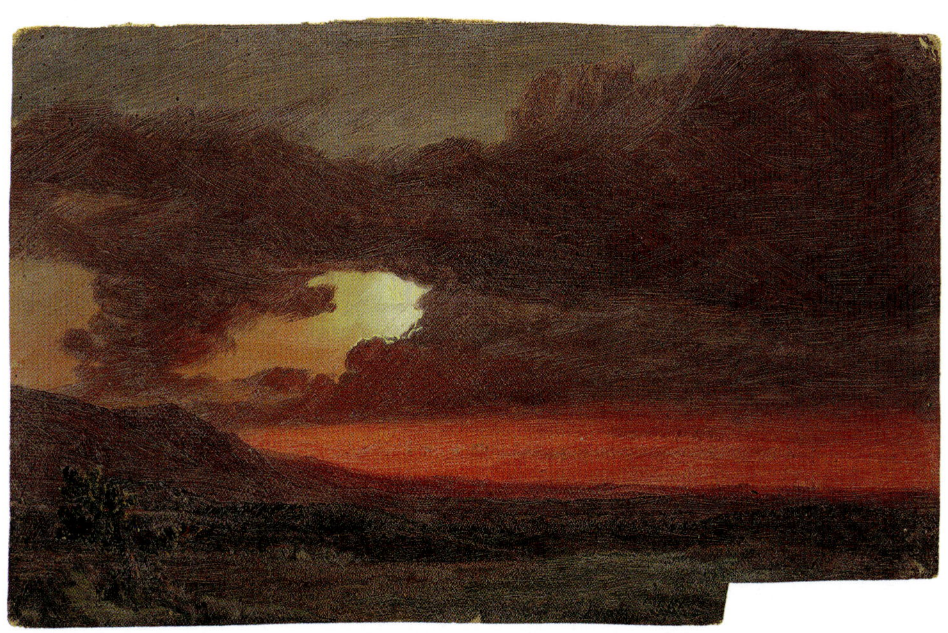

Church often used sunsets in his paintings to create a feeling of uncertainty or threat. In the summer of 1861, just after his closest friend became the first Union officer to die in battle in the Civil War, Church made this searing oil sketch of a Hudson Valley sunset.

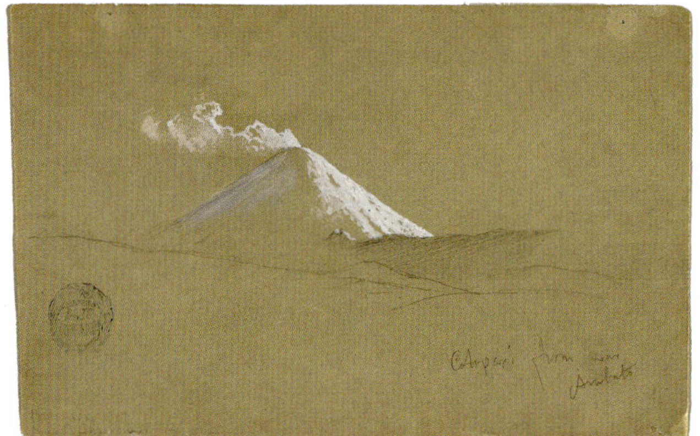

When Church first reached the great Andean volcano Cotopaxi in 1853, it was completely obscured by clouds. After waiting and watching for several days, he was rewarded with this view, which he captured in pencil and gouache.

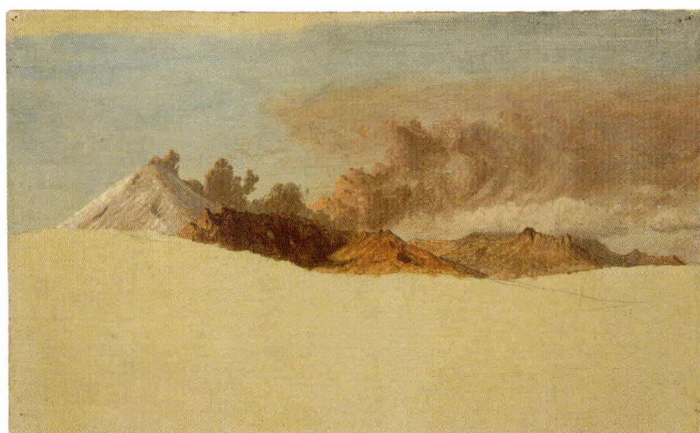

In the spring of 1857, Church embarked on a second trip to the Andes, determined to come back with better sketches of Cotopaxi and other volcanoes. He returned to New York that autumn with a vivid new series of images.

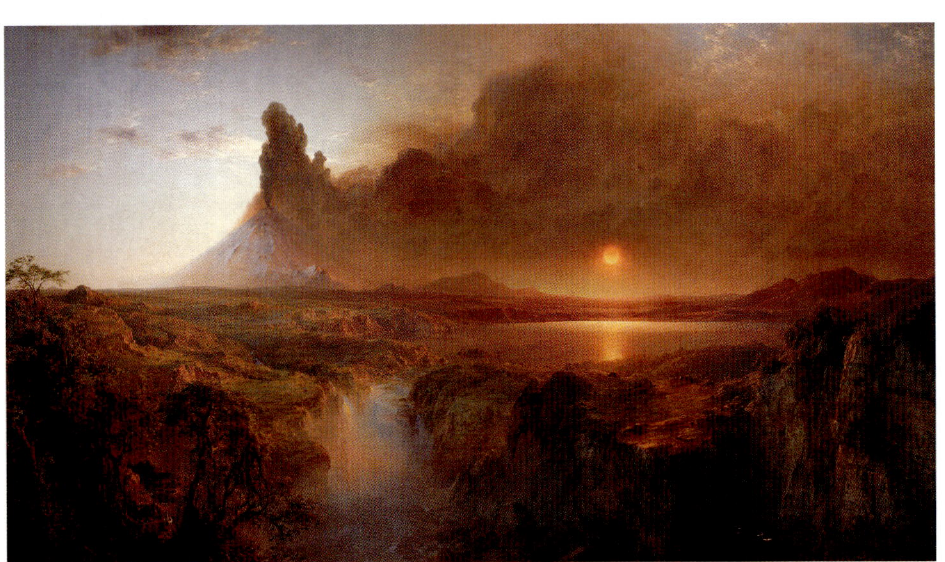

Church's 1862 painting *Cotopaxi*, which drew on his plein air sketches, depicted neither soldiers nor weapons. But, as Church indicated in the accompanying pamphlet, it was a portrait of the Civil War, echoing the explosions and smoke of the battlefields while gesturing toward the possibility of a serene future.

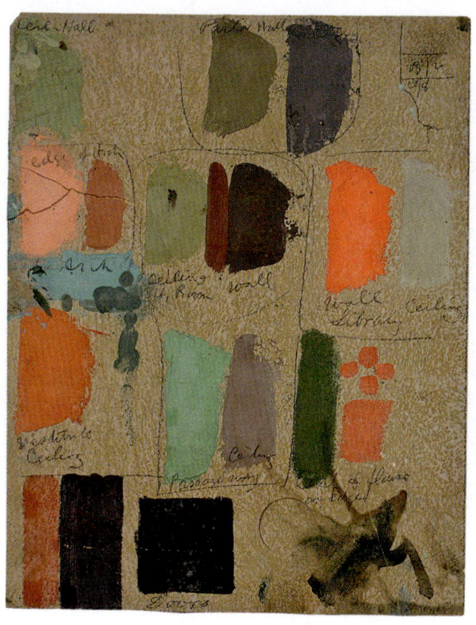

In the early 1870s, Church threw himself into designing a grand villa for his family on his property overlooking the Hudson River. He and his wife, Isabel, drew on architectural and design elements they had admired on a long trip to the Middle East. They named their estate Olana, after an ancient Persian fortress built above another river. Church chose the color schemes of the new house with as much interest and care as he did the paints on his palette.

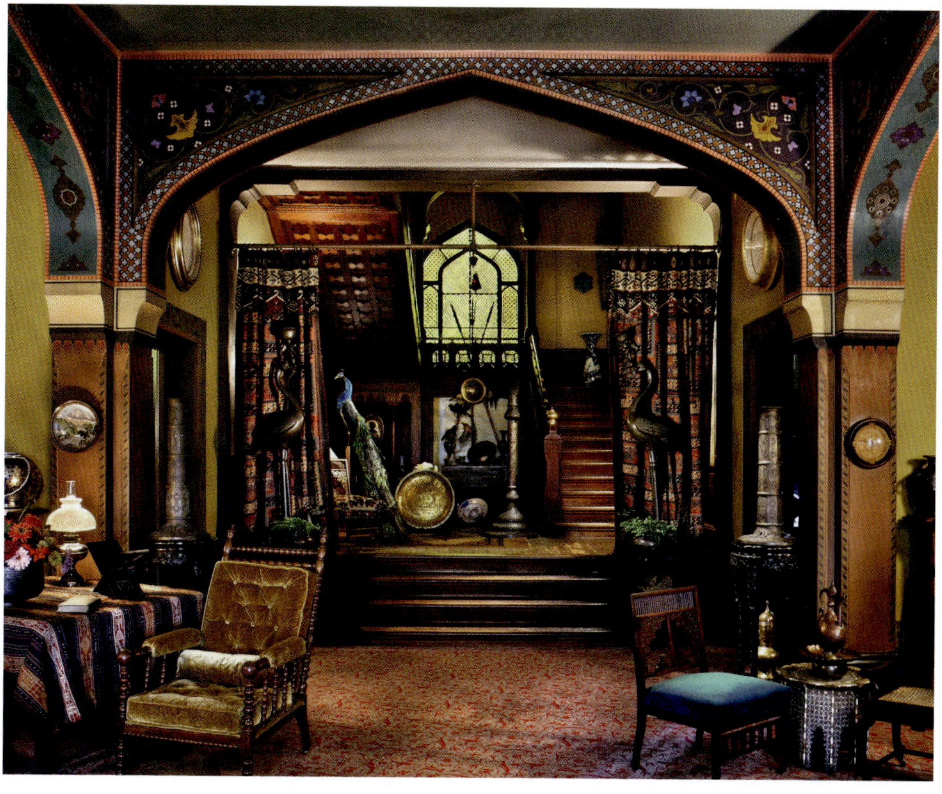

Church and Isabel, inspired by dwellings they had visited in Ottoman Syria, designed Olana's Court Hall to serve as the heart of their home, filling it with treasures from their travels. The Churches loved to entertain houseguests, and their parties sometimes included impromptu theatricals, performed on the curtained landing.

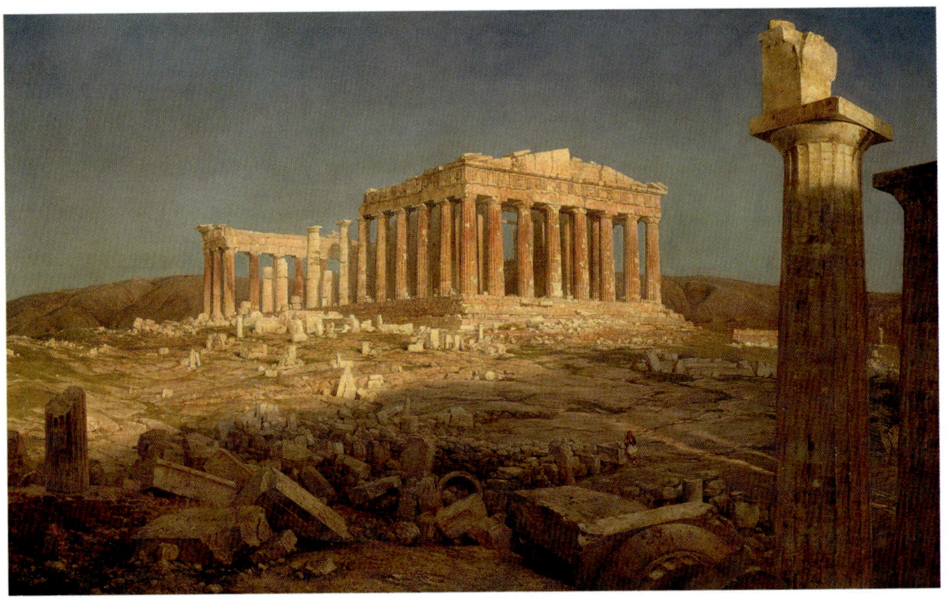

As the United States struggled to recover from the Civil War, Church painted *The Parthenon* (1871), a portrait of the world's oldest symbol of democracy, still standing despite the ravages of time and war.

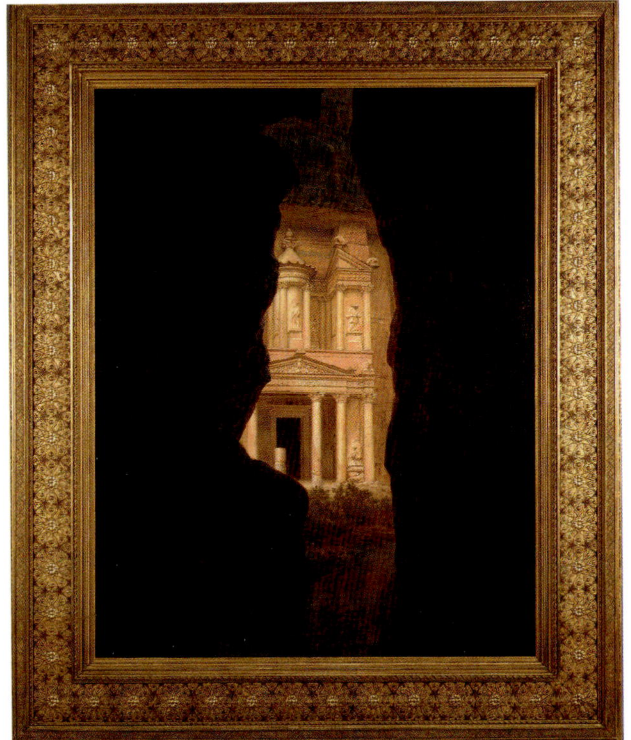

Church's 1868 trip to Petra, the ancient city in what is today Jordan, was one of the greatest adventures of his life. In 1874, he completed *El Khasné Petra*, a painting that captured his increasing respect for the achievements of other cultures.

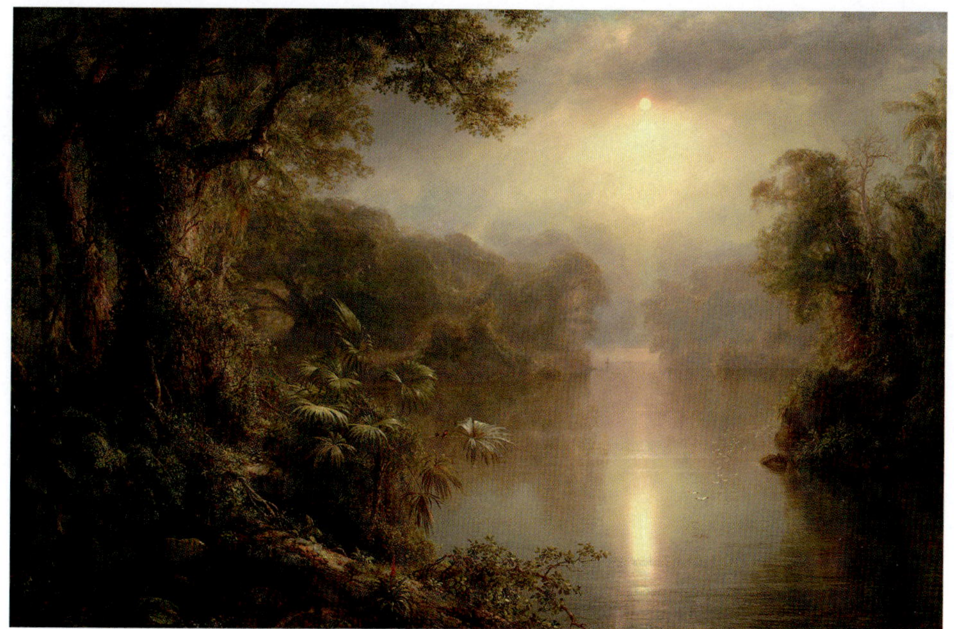

For *The River of Light*, painted when Church was in his fifties and increasingly crippled by rheumatism, he drew on his old South American sketches, but he gave the picture an unusual softness, painting the sun so it barely pierced the hazy air, its pale reflection across the water beckoning the viewer toward an indistinct distance.

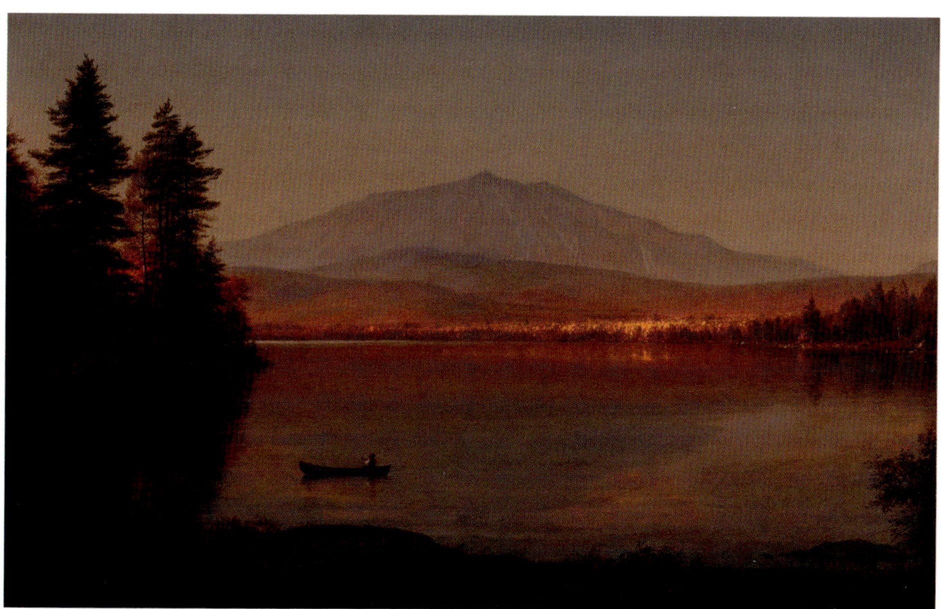

In 1895, for Isabel's fifty-ninth birthday, Church gave her this view of Mount Katahdin in Maine. Ten years older than his wife and in failing health, Church included a poignant note: "Your old guide is paddling his canoe in the shadow, but he knows that the glories of the heavens and the earth are seen more appreciatively when the observer rests in the shade."

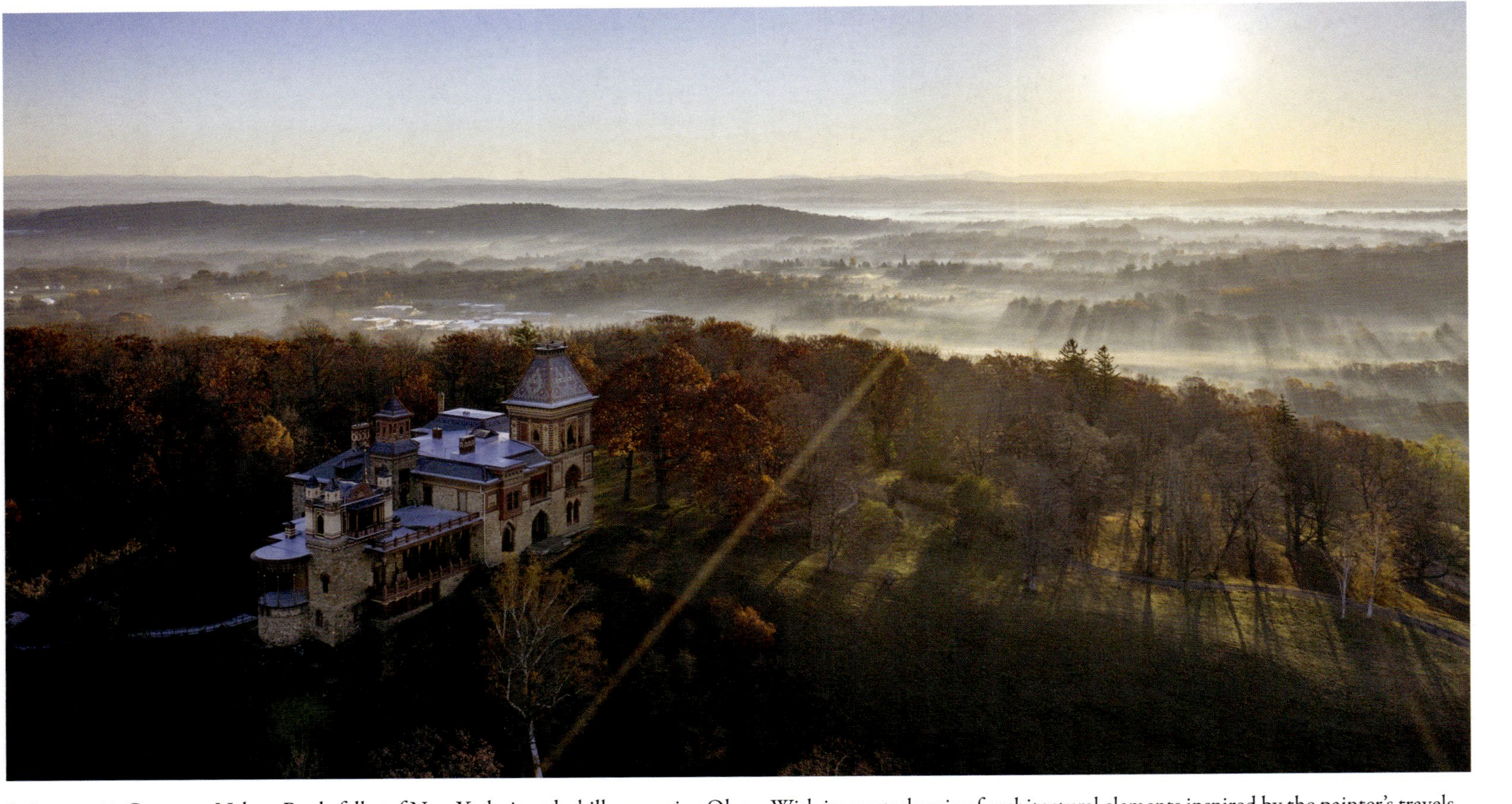

In June 1966, Governor Nelson Rockefeller of New York signed a bill preserving Olana. With its masterly mix of architectural elements inspired by the painter's travels, and an expert landscape design born of his long relationship with the Hudson Valley and the Catskill Mountains, Olana stands two hundred years after his birth as the apotheosis of Church's creative genius.

Tecumseh Sherman, and General Don Carlos Buell had dashed Confederate hopes of blocking a Union advance into Mississippi. Later that month, Flag Officer David G. Farragut had captured New Orleans, the Confederacy's most important port, and Winthrop's former commander, General Benjamin Butler, had been appointed the city's military governor.

Also in the spring of 1862, McClellan had finally felt ready to march on Richmond, the capital of the Confederacy. He moved his Army of the Potomac by boat to Fortress Monroe, and then Union soldiers moved northwest to confront General Robert E. Lee's Confederate forces outside Richmond. As the armies engaged in battle, Olmsted, now general secretary of the U.S. Sanitary Commission—a civilian organization providing critical care for the Union's wounded—met freight cars packed with casualties. "They arrived," he wrote, "dead and alive together, in the same close box, many with awful wounds festering and alive with maggots. The stench was such as to produce vomiting with some of our strong men."

After a week of bloody fighting in late June, McClellan's army defeated Lee at the Battle of Malvern Hill—yet the federal army failed to capture Richmond. As Union troops retreated down the James River, they took thousands of their wounded with them. Seeking food and medical supplies, they stopped at some of the mansions that lined the river. One was Shirley, where Hill Carter, Church's onetime host, noted in his journal, "Negroes running helter skelter owing to the Yankee Army occupying the plantation." Carter's wife, Mary, felt it was her Christian duty to tend to the Union soldiers who were too badly injured to continue south to Fortress Monroe. The Carters' neighbor Edmund Ruffin, who had fired one of the first shots on Fort Sumter, was disgusted by the way the Union army repaid the Carters' hospitality. Mrs. Carter, Ruffin wrote in his diary, cared for the soldiers with as much tenderness "as if they had been our own soldiers, or friends, instead of invaders, plunderers & incendiaries." In return, he sputtered, "the property of Mr. Carter, under his eyes & in the hearing of his angelic wife, (far too good for him or for this world,) was swept off as plunder for the army." Ruffin couldn't countenance the idea that the enslaved who left Shirley with the Union troops might have done so by choice.

In late September 1862, a Union victory at Antietam Creek, Maryland, spurred Lincoln to issue a preliminary Emancipation Proclamation. If the South did not lay down arms, its enslaved people would be declared "forever free" on January 1, 1863. In New York, Strong was one of the many Northerners who welcomed the news, but he worried that Lincoln wouldn't have the courage to go through with the final Emancipation Proclamation in January. "If he postpone or dilute his action, his name will be a byword and a hissing till the annals of the nineteenth century are forgotten."

Frederick Douglass had more faith in Lincoln than Strong did. "We shout for joy that we live to record this righteous decree," he wrote in his newspaper of the preliminary Emancipation Proclamation. "No, Abraham Lincoln will take no step backward." Douglass had found the president's past "slothful deliberation" enraging but believed that slavery was too terrible an evil for Americans to ignore it indefinitely. Slavery "compels us to recognize it, as an ever active, ever increasing, all comprehensive crime against human nature," Douglass argued. "Slavery is felt to be a moral volcano, a burning lake, a hell on the earth, the smoke and stench of whose torments ascend upward forever. Every breeze that sweeps over it comes to us tainted with its foul miasma, and weighed down with the sighs and groans of its victims."

The phrase "a moral volcano" was not Douglass's own. It had been used by British and American thinkers since at least the 1820s to describe spiritual and political struggles between good and evil. But for Douglass and many others, the imagery of an exploding volcano seemed tailor-made for the current crisis. It is not clear whether Church saw Douglass's newspaper or encountered the metaphor in a religious tract, but somehow it floated into his imagination.

WHEN CHURCH BROUGHT ISABEL BACK to New York that autumn, he found the Tenth Street Studio Building changed. His friends Whittredge, Gifford, McEntee, and Kensett were still there, but other close friends were gone. Winthrop was dead. Mignot had gone to England. Heade was traveling around New England sketching; the following year he would leave on a painting expedition through Brazil.

On the whole, though, New York was strangely undimmed by the war. The carriages of the wealthy still rolled through the new Central Park during the day, and at night audiences packed the theaters and concert halls. Fresh fortunes were being made off the war through government contracts and financial speculation, and they were being spent at places such as Tiffany's, Delmonico's, and A. T. Stewart's new cast-iron palace of a department store at Astor Place. The hotels, wrote Church, were "crowded to overflowing."

Still, the daily newspapers were full of war reports, and when urgent bulletins came over the wire on weekends and evenings, editors sent their newsboys out to shriek, "Extry!" War also announced itself in the city when a coffin was carried into a townhouse for a funeral and a line of carriages later rolled away for the burial. More often, however, the dead belonged to immigrant families, whose young men and boys had signed up for the war in droves, eager for a bit of pay and the chance to prove that they were true Americans. There were no carriages or black-edged calling cards for them. The only thing they had in common with the rich was gutting grief.

Two blocks south of Union Square, three different placards announced that a Broadway storefront was now the New York headquarters of the U.S. Sanitary Commission. From there, its officers, among them Olmsted and Strong, organized the removal of wounded soldiers to Northern hospitals. The transport ships steamed into New York Harbor, off-loaded their miserable cargo, and departed immediately to collect the next load. Mutilated men, missing arms or legs, were sometimes seen on the sidewalks, having survived what their comrades had not—bullets, shrapnel, amputations, gangrene. But it was in a building at the corner of Broadway and Tenth Street that the appalling truth of the battlefield was most shockingly revealed. The building's third-floor windows were nearly obscured by a large painted sign reading BRADY'S NATIONAL PORTRAIT GALLERY. At the sidewalk level hung another sign, this one quite small:

THE DEAD OF ANTIETAM

The pictures in the gallery upstairs had been taken by Alexander Gardner and James Gibson, photographers in the employ of Mathew Brady. In the aftermath of the bloodiest day in American history, the Battle of Antietam, they had ranged across the battlefield with their equipment. The scenes they had captured were horrifying: dozens of bodies heaped together in a ditch; bloated corpses baking in the sun; a soldier's arm rising into the air at an odd angle, stiff with death. A shaken reporter for *The New York Times* wrote that if Brady "has not brought bodies and laid them in our door-yards and along the streets, he has done something very like it." War was not the glorious adventure promised in April 1861 when the regiments paraded through the city. After seeing both the battlefield at Antietam and the Brady exhibition, Oliver Wendell Holmes Sr. wrote that war was "a repulsive, brutal, sickening, hideous thing."

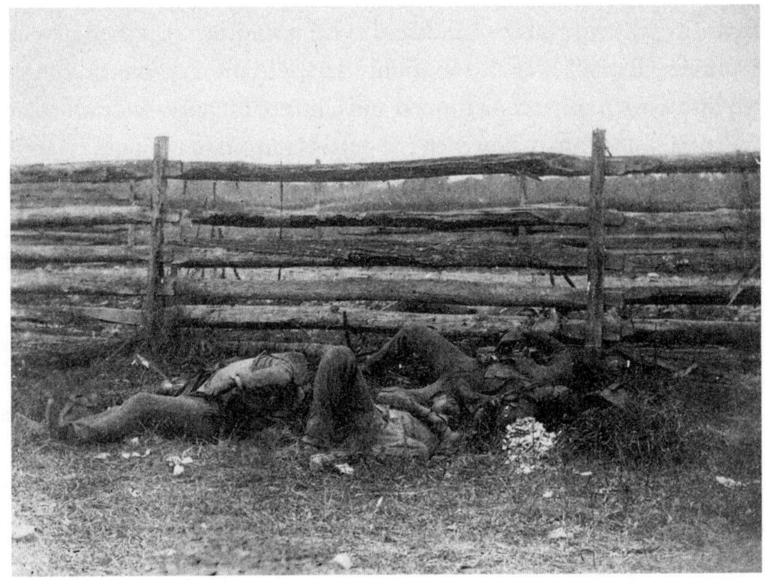

Dead on the battlefield at Antietam, by Alexander Gardner, September 1862

CHURCH WAS PAINTING TWO WAR pictures of his own. Neither of them depicted aspects of the war literally, as the photographs at Brady's studio had done, or as the illustrator and painter Winslow Homer was doing with his images of soldiers for *Harper's Weekly*, or even as Church's friend Gifford was doing in a series of landscape paintings that pictured the Union Army. Instead, Church's interpretations drew on his favored elements: earth, rock, sky, and water.

The first of Church's two new pictures, *Under Niagara*, went on display at Goupil's on December 6, while the Antietam photographs were still on display a few blocks away at Brady's gallery. Church based *Under Niagara* on an 1858 oil sketch he had made from the *Maid of the Mist*, and he let the press know that he had painted the entire final canvas in one day in May—the same month Confederate General Thomas "Stonewall" Jackson was scoring victory after victory in the Shenandoah Valley. Church's 1857 *Niagara Falls* had threatened to sweep viewers over the edge; in *Under Niagara*, painted at a particularly apprehensive time for the Union, Church put viewers near the bottom of the deadly cataract. There was no firm ground, only turbulent surf that dashed against a pile of boulders. High above, rising against a blue sky, an observation tower stood on Goat Island in the middle of the Falls, promising sanctuary but no way to get there.

If *Under Niagara* expressed foreboding, Church's other war picture veered closer to terror. He had started it not long after Winthrop died, but the pattern of his days had shifted with marriage and fatherhood, especially during the months he was spending upstate. He was still not done with it by autumn 1862, when he returned to Tenth Street, where he was constantly interrupted by curious strangers who wanted to meet him and see his studio. He was also plagued by well-meaning women who asked him to donate sketches for the picture albums they were assembling for charity auctions. He had learned to turn these requests down, even when he sympathized with the cause. He vented his frustration privately: "To the World it seems as easy for an Artist to throw off a sketch as for a Millionaire to draw a cheque for a few dollars."

Before Church finished his second war picture, the news came from Washington that Lincoln had signed the Emancipation Proclamation on New Year's Day of 1863. It was a "bolt from the sky," Douglass wrote, and "the dawn of a new day." Church unveiled his new picture about ten weeks later. He had painted the Andean volcano Cotopaxi in full eruption. At seven feet by four feet, the canvas was smaller than *The Heart of the Andes* but still large enough to overwhelm a viewer with its scale and force. A deadly plume of ash and smoke shot straight up to the sky, then plummeted and billowed in choking waves. Two-thirds of the painted sky was shrouded in darkness. Between the conical peak of Cotopaxi and the right edge of the canvas, the orange ball of the rising sun hung close to the horizon, struggling to break through the haze. The sun was reflected in a large lake whose water glowed purple and orange as it took on the colors of the sky. Most artists, the *Tribune* noted, would quail at painting such difficult terrain, let alone traversing it in person. "Mr. Church is an artist who is not easily daunted. Volcanic admonitions seem to have been wasted upon him."

With the exploding peak, smoke-filled sky, and lurid lake, Church had created an apocalyptic scene on the right side of the canvas. An entirely different mood prevailed on its left third. Upwind of the volcano and the smoke, the sky was a pale blue—"clearer than an opal," one critic observed, noting that Church excelled at such translucent skies. "To refine oil-color to the tenuity of air at the summit of a mountain, where the traveler labors for breath and bleeds from the ears, this has not often been compassed, except by the master I speak of." Church's swath of light-filled sky offered viewers respite from the violence and gloom of the volcano and ash. He repeated this effect—the shift from oppression to relief, from drama to peace—in the way he painted the water. Near the foreground, the hot-hued lake narrowed into a rocky channel and fell over a cliff. The churning water threw off a diaphanous mist shot through with cooler tints of blue, yellow, and rose.

Cotopaxi depicted neither soldiers nor weapons, but it was a portrait of war nonetheless. The combatants were light and darkness, and the battlefields on which they fought were the earth, water, and sky. Many who saw the painting recognized and could almost hear the war. The glaciated cone of the volcano was like the white tents used by soldiers, Noble thought, and this tent had been pitched by God on the "great battle-field of nature's forces." Reviewers wrote of "war clouds" and volcanic slopes "torn forever by the unceasing warfare of fire and snow." The peaceful, snow-blanketed slopes (the North) had been ripped open by heat and fire (the South).

Church himself nudged the public to think of war when they saw the picture. The pamphlet describing the painting and announcing the sale of engravings was unsigned, but Church would have approved every word of the text, and he may even have written it himself. The pamphlet noted that Cotopaxi's explosions had reminded Humboldt of "heavy discharges of artillery" and other people of bombs exploding. The allusion to Humboldt, who had repeatedly and famously railed against slavery, also strengthened the link between *Cotopaxi* and the nation's current struggle.

Cotopaxi was a portrait of war, but it was also a prophecy. Church believed God sided with the Union; his spiritual optimism was heartening at a moment when it was far from clear that the Union would prevail. By the grace of God, the smoke would disperse, the sun would rise into a brilliant sky, and the ashen earth would turn green again. A new era of peace and beauty would arise from the devastation.

CHAPTER 17

"The Nation's Future Greatness"

Just after *Cotopaxi* went on view at Goupil's in March 1863, another dramatic painting opened to the public, this one in a gallery near Madison Square. This picture was larger than *Cotopaxi*, larger even than Church's famously large *The Heart of the Andes*, and it depicted a region of greater personal interest to most New York viewers than the volcanoes of Ecuador. The new picture was by thirty-three-year-old Albert Bierstadt, a German American painter from Massachusetts who had a studio on the first floor of the Tenth Street Studio Building. At the gallery reception, Bierstadt basked in the attention of the critics gathered around him.

His painting was entitled *The Rocky Mountains, Lander's Peak*, and it offered a North American counterpart to Church's South American paradise. With technical virtuosity, Bierstadt had conjured up a fertile valley, glassy lake, sunlit waterfall, and ethereal mountain peaks. On the shores of the lake, he had painted a peaceful Shoshone encampment, where children played, dogs romped, and horses grazed among clusters of tepees.

Bierstadt had based the painting on sketches and photographs he made during an 1859 government-sponsored expedition through the Kansas Territory, which lay beyond the western border of the United States and stretched all the way to the Rockies. While Church had chased icebergs with Noble, Bierstadt had been fording rivers, sketching buffalo, and photographing the Shoshone. Bierstadt's studio was decorated with skins, traps, knives, and his own Western sketches and photographs. He was interested in Native people, he said, but only insofar as they were "appropriate adjuncts to the scenery"

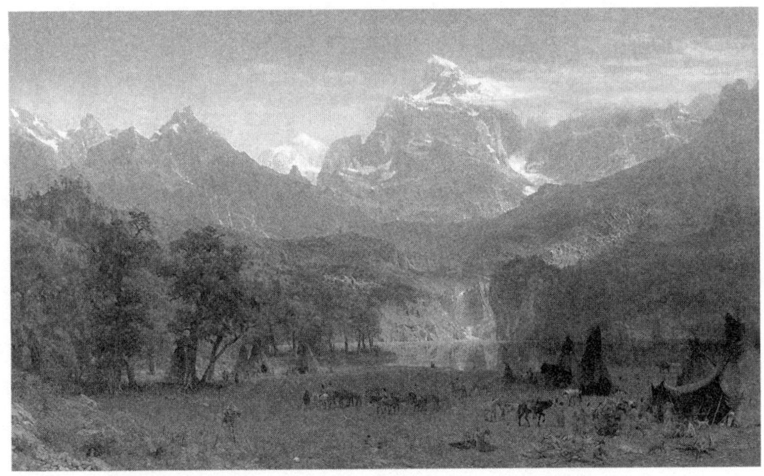

The Rocky Mountains, Lander's Peak, by Albert Bierstadt, 1863

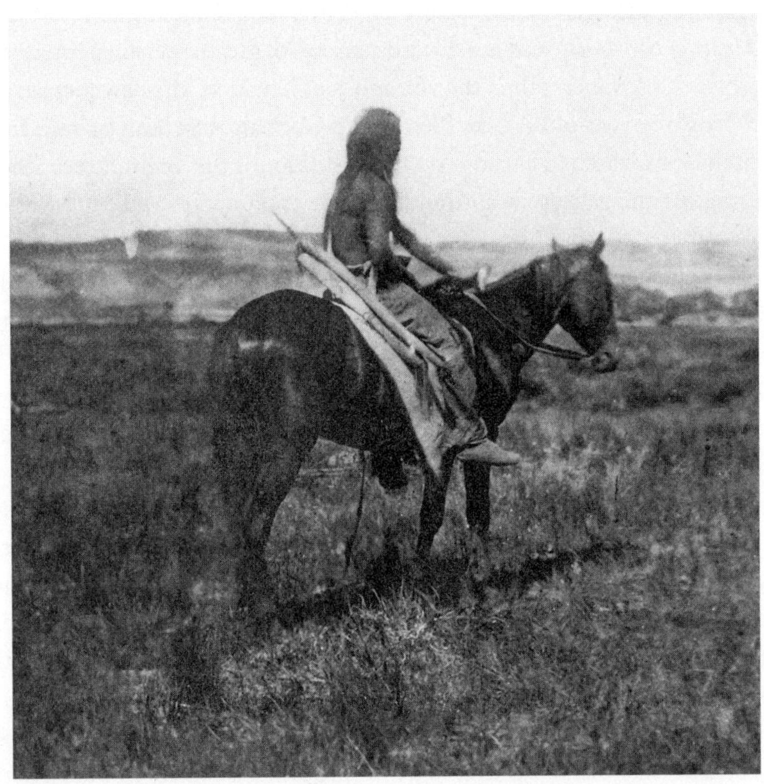

Shoshone man, photographed by Bierstadt, 1859

of the West. They were "rapidly passing away," he observed dispassionately, so "now is the time to paint them."

Bierstadt was a far more literal artist than Church. *Lander's Peak* lacked the Humboldtian ambitions and metaphorical complexity of *The Heart of the Andes* and so many of Church's other works. While Church drew on scenes from Labrador to Ecuador to explore his political concerns about the nation and the spiritual place of humans in the cosmos, Bierstadt used scenes drawn from his Western travels to encourage the United States to expand westward. Bierstadt's vision—an idea that long predated him—was that "civilization" would one day dominate the earth from Europe to the Pacific Ocean; by "civilization," he and many of his compatriots meant what they thought of as "Anglo-Saxon" culture and society. For Bierstadt, unlike Church, a sunset on canvas was not an allusion to human mortality or an impending political crisis. The point of Bierstadt's painted sun was that it was setting in the west, the direction in which white people were—and should be—putting down roots.

The pamphlet Bierstadt approved to accompany *Lander's Peak* articulated this imperialist vision. Someday, he hoped, the bucolic spot by the lake where he had depicted a Shoshone encampment would be the site of "a city, populated by our descendants," in whose "art-galleries this picture may eventually find a resting-place." Critics understood and applauded what Bierstadt was trying to convey. "This is a glimpse into the heart of the continent towards which civilization is struggling," one wrote. "I know that the nation's future greatness is somehow dimly seen in the great West." But there was nothing dim or vague about what this vision meant for the Native people who already occupied the American West. It meant being deceived with toothless treaties and violently expelled from ancestral lands. It meant seeing the life-giving herds of bison slaughtered by white men to provoke mass starvation. It meant being raped and enslaved and murdered until Native people presented no further obstacle.

That spring Bierstadt sent *The Rocky Mountains, Lander's Peak* to Boston, where it went on display in a solo exhibition of the sort that had brought Church fame and wealth. Visitors paid twenty-five cents to see the painting, just as they had for *The Heart of the Andes*. Comparisons were inevitable. One Boston critic predicted, "This painting is destined probably to have as great success before the public as Church's *Heart of the Andes*." It was soon being reported that Bierstadt had turned down an offer of $10,000 for the painting—the precise amount Church had received for *The Heart of the Andes*.

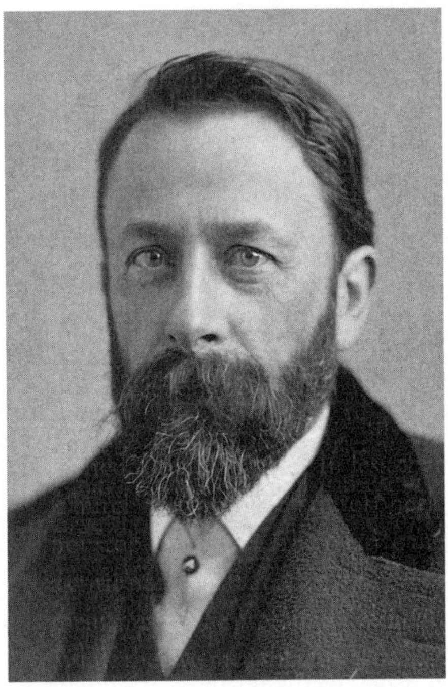

Albert Bierstadt

Bierstadt believed he could paint even better paintings if only he could get out West again. In December 1862, he had seen astounding photographs of the Yosemite Valley by Carleton Watkins at Goupil's, where they had hung near Church's *Under Niagara*. Bierstadt longed to sketch and paint in the Yosemite Valley, and in April 1863, while *Lander's Peak* was earning him money and acclaim in Boston, he left New York by train with several friends. Among them was a novelist and critic named Fitz Hugh Ludlow, who admired Bierstadt's pictures and had written enthusiastic reviews of them in *The Evening Post*. Their arrangement was akin to that of Church and Noble on their 1859 expedition to Newfoundland and Labrador. Bierstadt would sketch and paint; Ludlow would whet readers' appetites for Bierstadt's future paintings by describing their Western adventures together.

Church, meanwhile, hadn't been anywhere new and exciting since the icebergs trip four years earlier. His primary source of subject matter for years now had been his South American sketches, many of which were a decade old. He couldn't mine these Humboldtian veins of inspiration forever. Tastes were changing. If the war ever ended, the Union would surge westward with renewed focus and force, and the public's artistic interests would surely follow. With *The Rocky Mountains, Lander's Peak*, Bierstadt had staked his claim to the West. Even if Church had felt comfortable about leaving Isabel and Bertie to undertake a Western painting trip, Bierstadt now owned the Rockies on canvas. Within a few years, a *Times* critic would note sarcastically that he "has copyrighted nearly all the principal mountains."

CHURCH STILL HADN'T FOUND a buyer for his 1861 iceberg painting, *The North*. In the summer of 1863, he sent it to Great Britain to be shown at the same fashionable gallery where *The Heart of the Andes* had triumphed in 1859. Perhaps it would find a buyer there. But before *The North* left New York, Church altered the title of the picture to improve its appeal to viewers in Britain, where many people were sympathetic to the Confederacy. *The North* became *The Icebergs* again.

He also added a detail to the picture: a broken ship's mast lying on an ice shelf in the foreground. For decades, readers on both sides of the Atlantic had been riveted by stories of Arctic expeditions. Dozens of ships had been lost over the years, the most famous of which were the two ships of the Franklin Expedition of 1845. Sir John Franklin and his crew had disappeared early in their search for a navigable northern passage from the Atlantic to the Pacific. His widow, Lady Franklin, had sponsored multiple efforts to find his ships and his remains, and her steadfast devotion to her husband's memory had captivated the public. In 1854, a British explorer named John Rae had reported in *The Times* of London that he had met Inuit people who had encountered corpses from the Franklin Expedition. The Inuit had told Rae that they had seen unmistakable evidence of cannibalism. In the ensuing uproar, Charles Dickens attacked Rae in print for believing a lie told by "savages," but subsequent research would confirm the terrible truth.

Before *The Icebergs* went to London, Church added the broken ship's mast as a small tribute to the many lost explorers. A crow's nest bisected the mast near its top, so that the mast resembled a fallen cross.

Lady Franklin came to see *The Icebergs* when it was unveiled in late June. A shoal of aristocrats, explorers, and scientists drifted in her wake, murmuring praise for the picture. The *London Morning Star* called *The Icebergs* "the best work by far that has come from Mr. Church's hands," and *The Times* of London ran a long review singling out "Mr. Church's power of painting light and water" as well as his tenacious pursuit of natural wonders "at peril of life and limb." The picture didn't find a British buyer right away, but in July 1863, some of the rapturous London reviews were excerpted in the New York press, further burnishing Church's reputation at home.

THAT SAME MONTH, AT GETTYSBURG, Pennsylvania, the bloodiest battle of the Civil War ended in Union victory and blocked Lee's push into Union territory. Lincoln, feeling briefly hopeful, ventured a few days later, "If General Meade can complete his work . . . by the literal or substantial destruction of Lee's army, the rebellion will be over." At Gettysburg, more than three thousand Union soldiers had been killed, with another twenty thousand wounded, missing, or captured. To Lincoln's frustration, Meade, having failed to destroy Lee's army, did not pursue him.

The war was grinding on, and the Union needed more soldiers. As a married man over thirty-five years old—Church had turned thirty-seven on May 4—he was not subject to the National Conscription Act, the first such act in U.S. history, passed by Congress in March. But two thousand other men from New York City were to be sent to the war after a drawing scheduled for July 11. The National Conscription Act included a provision that some people found deeply upsetting. A man with $300 to spare—almost the yearly wages of a laborer—could pay for a substitute to fight in his place. The official rationale for exemption was that wealthy businessmen were more likely than the poor to be contributing critical services and supplies to the war effort. The side effect was resentment that quickly kindled into murderous rage.

On Saturday, July 11, in a draft office on Third Avenue, federal officials began pulling names from a hollow wooden drum. Around twelve hundred names were read aloud as sympathetic onlookers voiced their condolences. Then the office shut down for the rest of the weekend. On Monday, July 13, thousands of anti-draft protesters began to gather in the streets. Many were Irish immigrants upset that their struggling families would bear the brunt of the draft while the old English and Dutch families carried on with carriage rides and social calls. Yet the protesters' anger went beyond class resentment. Some feared that if the North won the war, hordes of former slaves freed by the Emancipation Proclamation would pour into New York and work for lower wages than white laborers. No matter that the Emancipation Proclamation had authorized the recruitment of Black men as soldiers, thus easing some of the burden on white soldiers.

As the drawing of names resumed, a company of firemen arrived and torched the draft office. Paltry bands of policemen were dispatched to quell the unrest, but they faced sharp resistance from increasingly violent protesters. Class tensions and racial hatred that long predated the war swirled together in a lethal brew. Hearing of the unrest at the Third Avenue draft office, Strong walked uptown to find hundreds of what he called "the lowest Irish day laborers" looting houses and setting them on fire. When he fled downtown to the Sanitary Commission headquarters on Broadway, he learned that the Colored Orphan Asylum on Fifth Avenue at Forty-Third Street had been burned. More than two hundred terrified children had barely escaped out the back of the building and were now huddled in a precinct headquarters under police protection.

All that day and into the night Strong heard fire bells. He was convinced that the unrest had been plotted by pro-Southern elements. "If a quarter [of what] one hears be true," he wrote in his journal, "this is an organized insurrection in the interest of the rebellion and Jefferson Davis rules New York today." That evening Strong met with the mayor and other officials. Troubled by the mayor's ineffectual response, Strong and several friends sent a telegraph to Lincoln pleading for soldiers to be sent back to Manhattan from Pennsylvania.

The riots raged all through the next day, and the mobs attacked African American New Yorkers with special ferocity. Men, women, and children were beaten, lynched, drowned, and set on fire. There were far fewer fatalities among wealthy white New Yorkers; although they, too, were targeted, they mostly lost homes and possessions.

Church and Isabel were upstate at the Farm during the Draft Riots, but a number of their acquaintances were swept up in the chaos, among them the Tracys, Church's friends from the Mount Desert summer party. Charles Tracy was in town with his daughter Annie when the riots broke out. Annie, once rumored to be romantically linked to Church, was now married to a young lawyer named Lindley Miller, and she was pregnant. Her husband and father tried to whisk her out of town, but she was too worried about the family's Black servants to abandon them. "Annie wouldn't leave," Miller wrote his mother, "until she knew they were to be sent from town." The servants disguised themselves, and Miller made a show of handing them into his carriage in front of the house as though they were white family members, before climbing in after them. "I went down Broadway in style with them" and helped them escape the city, he reported to his mother. "The papers do not half describe the fiendish atrocities against the Negroes. But I will not describe any further details."

No one would ever know for sure how many people died in the unrest of that summer. Estimates would eventually range from 120 up to 1,000. After three days of violence, thousands of soldiers arrived, sent at Lincoln's behest by Secretary of War Stanton. The next day, the city seemed calm; Strong ventured out in the evening and found "Gramercy Park in military occupation."

Annie Tracy gave birth to a boy five days after arriving in the sanctuary of the Hudson Valley. About a month later, Theddy recorded in his journal that he and the Tracys had just paid a visit to the Churches at the Farm, where they all had a "splendid walk." But ten days later, Annie was dead, and her baby died a week after that. Annie's husband, suddenly stripped of his young family, sought meaning and purpose in the war, and he was granted the command of a Black regiment, the First Arkansas Volunteer Infantry Regiment (African Descent).

THE CITY RETURNED TO ITS rhythms. In New York for the winter season, Church worked on several commissions. One was a large new picture of Chimborazo, for which he drew on his South American sketches. "I am overwhelmed with work—so much so that I despair of meeting my engagements," he told a friend in November 1863. Yet even as the commissions piled up, he was coming in for increasingly harsh criticism, at least some of which stemmed from jealousy. In December 1863, a friend mounted a defense of Church in *The Evening Post*. "It has recently been somewhat the fashion of inferior artists and critics to attack in all manner of ways Mr. Church, some saying that he is tricky, and others that he is untrue to nature. . . . The *London Times* once said 'that a man will forgive you everything but success,' and there is the cause of many of the attacks on Church."

Around this time, Bierstadt returned to Tenth Street, having sketched and painted all the way from Missouri to California. He and Ludlow had ridden by stagecoach through prairies ablaze with wildflowers and across plains smudged to darkness by herds of bison "reaching without gap to the horizon's edge on every side of me," as Ludlow wrote. They had taken turns sitting next to stagecoach drivers under the open sky, listening to tales of frontier life. In Nebraska they had been welcomed into a log cabin by a pioneer family who served them antelope and bison, an experience that Ludlow found "the nicest possible compromise between Delmonico's and camping out." But it was the Yosemite Valley that Bierstadt called "the garden of Eden," with its giant redwoods, soaring cliffs, and glittering river.

Bierstadt settled back into his Tenth Street studio with a haul of new Western landscape sketches, which he intended to turn into paintings. While he began his first picture of Yosemite, Church labored at his *Chimborazo*. The press began to reach for facile comparisons of the two men. In February 1864, a critic wrote in a weekly cultural magazine, "Mr. Bierstadt's name is now [as] associated with the Rocky Mountains as is that of Mr. Church with the Andes." The review that followed discussed Bierstadt's style and subject matter with reference to Church's. This time, Church came through mostly unscathed, while Bierstadt was chided for the literal, prosaic nature of his work. But in March, *Harper's Weekly* praised Bierstadt's *Lander's Peak* by disparaging Church. "And unlike Mr. CHURCH's pictures of the equatorial mountain scenery of America, which . . . leave an impression of profound sadness and desolation, this work of BIERSTADT's inspires the temperate cheerfulness and promise of the region it depicts, and the imagination contemplates it as the possible seat of supreme civilization."

The critics were trying to stoke a rivalry. Church ignored them and focused on *Chimborazo*. If he sometimes painted desolate pictures, it was because his art responded to his evolving emotions and beliefs about spirituality, nature, and the United States. *Cotopaxi* may have been desolate, even frightening, but it was also tinged with hope, and *Chimborazo* was thoroughly peaceful and optimistic. Church was painting the great volcanic peak floating in the blue sky as if it were more part of heaven than earth, keeping watch over a lush valley where villagers farmed and fished. His composition paid tribute to Kensett's 1851 *Mount Washington from the Valley of Conway*, allowing Church to allude to the principles of self-government that Washington had defended as a general and as president. Church emphasized the political import of *Chimborazo* by dressing two villagers at the river's edge in red, white, and blue clothing, as he and fellow painters had often done in their New England landscapes.

He was interrupted in his work on the picture before the end of winter. "New York is stirred up to the bottom with the great Fair," Church wrote to his father in February 1864. "Nearly everyone seems to be on some committee and all are full of business—I presume that the result will be really stupendous." Church didn't much like committees, but he was involved in the upcoming New York Metropolitan Fair nonetheless. Organized by Sanitary Commission leaders, the fair was officially intended to raise funds for wounded Union soldiers. Unofficially, New York hoped to outshine Brooklyn, Chicago, Boston, and Cincinnati, which had already staged such fairs.

The announcement of the fair unleashed what organizers called "a contagion of kindness." For weeks before the grand opening on April 4, goods poured into cavernous halls on Fourteenth Street and at Union Square. Some of the items donated were intended to lure people to buy admission tickets; others were to be auctioned. Church was arranging to borrow three of his pictures from their owners for display: *The Andes of Ecuador*, *Niagara Falls*, and *The Heart of the Andes*. He was also donating two smaller paintings to the art sale.

When Strong, an officer of the Sanitary Commission, went for a last look around the main building on opening day, he found "the busiest human ant-hill

I ever saw." Satisfied, he went to watch the parade. Over ten thousand soldiers marched through the city streets, some carrying half-destroyed flags from the battlefield. Afterward, people lined up, paid for entry, and streamed inside the fair buildings. An army of young women stood among the display cases, wearing uniform black dresses with white sleeves and collars and diagonal blue sashes.

Women had been vital to the entire project. A group of well-to-do women had been the first to lobby for a New York fair, before their husbands had agreed to become involved. Initially, women from Brooklyn—an independent city across the East River—had joined in the planning effort, but they had suddenly decided to hold their own fair. Strong's wife, Ellie, was treasurer of New York's fair. She and the other women had been working so hard for months that when two of the volunteers died not long after opening day, the papers suggested they had given their lives for the fair. Despite their critical roles, when the female members of the executive committee arrived for the opening ceremony, they found that the man in charge of seating had provided chairs only for the male committee members. Strong recorded in his diary that "Mrs. Astor, Mrs. Belmont, [and] Ellie . . . were almost tearful about it."

THE ART GALLERY AT THE fair occupied a long, well-lit room in the main building. Its walls were covered with hundreds of paintings, yet three pictures in particular commanded attention. One was Emanuel Leutze's massive *Washington Crossing the Delaware*, a celebration of the birth of the United States, dating from 1851. It covered most of the wall at one end of the room. *The Heart of the Andes* had been placed midway along one of the two side walls, with its window-like frame stretching from the floor almost to the ceiling. Nestled in the bunting above the painting were portraits of the first three U.S. presidents, as if to say that artistic genius was as vital to the nation as was political talent.

The third painting was Bierstadt's *Rocky Mountains, Lander's Peak*, which hung directly opposite *The Heart of the Andes*. Comparisons of Church and Bierstadt were being officially encouraged. Viewers could stand in one spot and look back and forth at the two most famous pictures by the two most famous American landscape painters of their generation, and this they did "with a great deal of curiosity," according to the official record of the fair.

But Bierstadt had also hit upon a Barnumesque way to try to get fairgoers even more interested in *Lander's Peak*. He created an exhibit in the main building in which he mounted antlers and animal skins, and he filled display cases

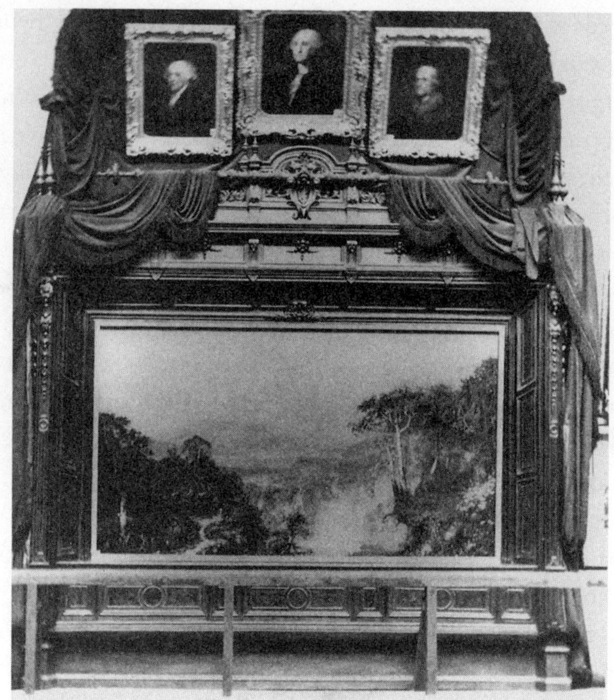

The Heart of the Andes as exhibited at the Metropolitan Fair, 1864

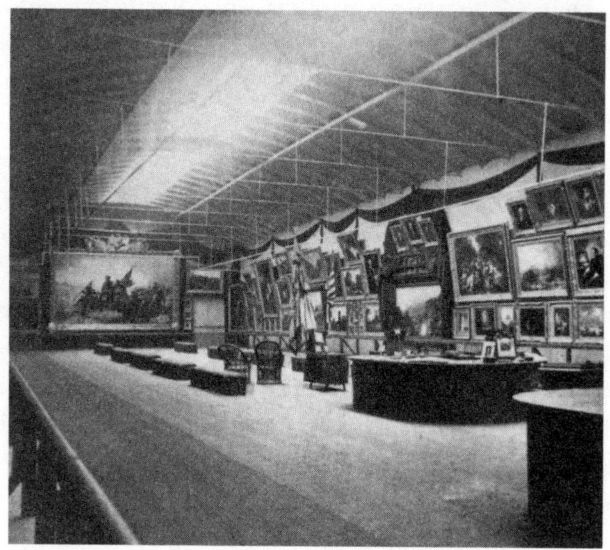

The Picture Gallery at the Metropolitan Fair, 1864

with hundreds of Native "curiosities" (as *The Evening Post* called them)—tools, clothing, jewelry, and other artifacts.

One part of Bierstadt's room was dominated by a stage with a painted Western backdrop and a wigwam. At specified times, a group of Native American men, women, and children came out to perform routines including an Eagle Dance, a Scalp Dance, and a Buffalo Dance. Bierstadt didn't clarify which band or nation the performers hailed from, but it didn't much matter to the enthusiastic crowds who packed the room daily. The job of these performers was to look and act like Indians in general.

The Metropolitan Fair was a triumph for New York and for the Sanitary Commission. When Ellie Strong had prepared her treasurer's report, she announced that the fair had netted over $1 million for wounded Union soldiers, more than twice the earnings of the next most lucrative fair, Brooklyn's. At the sale of donated artworks, Bierstadt's small painting of Yosemite Valley had brought the highest sum of any picture, at $1,600. One of Church's donated paintings reportedly sold for only half that amount.

Before long, Bierstadt would receive an offer of $25,000 for *The Rocky Mountains, Lander's Peak*—more than double the highest fee Church had earned for any picture. In less than a decade, Bierstadt had rocketed past Church to command stratospheric sums and lavish reviews. People could not stop comparing "the relative merits of Mr. Church and Mr. Bierstadt," as a critic noted in 1866. But the comparisons, which would long outlive both of them, missed the profound distinctions between their art and their worldviews. While the two men shared a sense of wonder at the natural world, Church drew on his immersion in science and religion to create landscapes suffused with spiritual and political import. His ultimate aim was not to glorify a particular region or to spur national expansion, in the manner of Bierstadt's spectacular depictions of Yosemite and the Rockies. Politically, Church's commitment was to the preservation of self-government by a free people.

The very real differences between Church and Bierstadt were exacerbated by the press's effort to pit them against each other, and the two never became friends. Years later, Jervis McEntee, who knew both of them well, was relieved not to have been on hand when they ran into each other at a gathering hosted by McEntee's wife. "I don't think they adore each other," McEntee observed in his journal.

CHAPTER 18

"Broken"

In May 1864, Church moved with his family up to the Farm. Bertie, now a year and a half old, toddled around feeding the chickens out of his hand and watching the horses in fascination. "Mother will be shocked to see how brown her grandson is," Church wrote to his father. "He is regularly bronzed." During a visit from Mrs. Church, Bertie sometimes tugged at his grandmother's skirts saying, "Horse," asking her to take him to the barn. Isabel's mother also visited in the early autumn. A cosmopolitan woman who had once socialized with aristocrats in Paris, Mrs. Carnes now enjoyed playing hide-and-seek on a farm. It was helpful that she was there. Isabel was pregnant again.

Church thus had yet another reason not to go to war—even as the chance of his being drafted increased. In July 1864, Lincoln had called for five hundred thousand more soldiers, giving municipalities throughout the Union until September 5 to meet their quotas. But Church was not drafted, and on October 22, Isabel gave birth to a girl. They named her Emma, after Isabel's mother. For her middle name they chose Frances, thus honoring Isabel's late father, Francis. To mark Emma's birth, Church painted a companion piece to the picture he had done upon Bertie's arrival two years earlier. Bertie's picture was *Sunrise*; Emma's was *Moonrise*.

While the Churches celebrated, New York City simmered. The presidential election was approaching, and despite Union military gains that fall, Lincoln remained deeply unpopular in New York, even among many Republicans. A faction of pro-war Democrats hoped to replace him in the White House with McClellan. When the votes were counted, Lincoln had lost New York City decisively, but he had won the presidency.

The Church family returned to Manhattan for the winter, and Church finished *Chimborazo* shortly before the end of the year. The man who had originally commissioned it failed to pay, and W. H. Osborn stepped forward to purchase it, freeing Church to work on a very different kind of painting, which he entitled *Twilight*.

He covered much of his large canvas with a swirl of angry clouds above an expanse of red-tinged water, hiding the only living creature in the picture in near-total darkness on the shore. This was a small deer, a symbol, variously, of renewal, of Christ, of the soul that thirsts for God, and of the defense of Eden against serpents. The deer, defenseless and alone, was under threat by the approaching night. The quieter warnings of Church's prewar sunset pictures had given way to frantic alarm.

Church had started the picture in the summer of 1864, when the outcome of the war was still uncertain. The Union's fortunes had improved by fall, but in December, facing a massive shortfall in troops, Lincoln issued a call for three hundred thousand more soldiers by February 15, 1865. In January, Church's lawyer in Hudson informed him that his name was now on the rolls in the town of Greenport, meaning that he might be picked in the next draft lottery. His lawyer urged him to apply for a substitute as soon as possible; it is not clear from surviving records whether Church did so, or his name simply wasn't picked in the lottery, but he was not drafted.

In early March, Lincoln's second inauguration and recent Union victories unleashed riotous celebrations. Those who despised the president could at least rejoice that the end of the war appeared close at hand. On March 6, two days after Lincoln pleaded in his inaugural address for "malice toward none," New Yorkers turned out to watch a parade nearly seven miles long. The weather was clear and frigid, as if it had been hauled from an icehouse on the Hudson. "A Great and Happy Day," *The New York Times* blared. Dozens of floats celebrated the Union while also advertising the sundry manufacturers who had paid for them. There was an oil derrick in motion, a winemaker throwing tiny bottles into the crowd, and a maker of safes whose float proclaimed OUR COUNTRY'S SAFE. P. T. Barnum was surrounded on his float by stuffed wild animals including a rhinoceros, a walrus, and a lion.

About a week after the celebrations, Bertie fell ill. Judging by his initial symptoms, he might have had a common cold, but far more frightening signs swiftly followed: swollen neck, suffocating lungs. It was diphtheria. He died on March 18, aged two.

The next day, Church asked Horace Robbins, a young artist he knew, to fetch a portraitist to paint Bertie's likeness before the burial. Bouquets of white flowers arrived from friends. Noble, who had officiated at Frederic and Isabel's wedding five years earlier, stood before them once again, this time for a funeral service. Robbins wrote to his mother afterward, "Poor Mr. Church is almost broken down—he and his wife were so 'wrapped up' in their only son." The next morning, Noble baptized five-month-old Emma, who was also showing signs of illness.

Bertie was to be buried in the Church family plot in Hartford. Church and Isabel stayed on afterward with Church's parents and sisters, and they all watched in helpless anguish as Emma grew sicker. She died eight days after Bertie, and they buried her next to him. After starting a family with such joy and promise, Church and Isabel were bereft. Spring was coming, but what had once seemed lovely was now tainted. Cosy Cottage would be as quiet as death. The white apple blossoms would fall to earth, sour and brown.

Church began to plot their escape to some place where they wouldn't be reminded of the children at every turn. He told a friend he wanted to give Isabel a "change of scene, air, and life—believing that we both will be much benefitted by the journey." Longing to paint the tropics again, he settled on the British colony of Jamaica, about fifteen hundred miles from New York by steamer. He hoped Isabel would find some respite from her grief on this wholly unfamiliar island.

DEEP IN MOURNING, CHURCH AND Isabel suddenly found themselves surrounded by celebrating New Yorkers when word arrived of Lee's April 9 surrender at Appomattox. On April 10, despite heavy rain, the city boomed with celebratory cannon fire. Strong exulted in his diary, "Secessia is now conquered, crushed, subjugated, and under our feet."

Then, just as suddenly, the collective joy was obliterated. "*Up with the Black Flag now!*" a stunned Strong wrote in his diary on April 15. That was the morning New Yorkers awoke to learn that President Lincoln had been shot while attending a play in Washington the night before. The New York papers had initially reported that he had remained unconscious all night, but then the terrible news had arrived that Lincoln had died at 7:22 a.m. Shopkeepers locked their doors and draped black cloth in their windows. To Frederick Douglass, the assassination felt "as if some grand convulsion in nature had occurred."

Two days before Lincoln's funeral train arrived in New York on its way from Washington to Springfield, Illinois, Church and Isabel boarded a steamship bound for Jamaica. Church had invited the painter Horace Robbins to join them. Robbins, twenty-two, was sixteen years younger than Church; a lively young man, he would be good company on painting excursions. Isabel, meanwhile, had invited her friend Sarah Hitchcock, a single woman of twenty-five.

Theddy Cole had come down from Catskill to get last-minute instructions. He would be keeping an eye on the Farm while the Churches were out of the country. "We all hope & trust that it may benefit Mrs. C.," Theddy wrote in his diary. "She looks so miserable."

FROM A DISTANCE, JAMAICA LOOKED peaceful and inviting. Coconut palms waved graceful fronds over a pale line of beaches. The green hills were dotted with houses, and beyond them rose the jungle-cloaked Blue Mountains, their tallest peak over seven thousand feet high.

Jamaica wouldn't become a regular tourist destination for wealthy Americans until the end of the century. Even in Church's circle of artists, the island's mountains and seascapes had drawn little attention beyond a rhapsodic *Crayon* article in 1855 about the scenery. In the 1860s, Jamaica was often invoked as a warning to abolitionists by pro-slavery commentators who predicted a miserable future for the American South. Slavery had been abolished in Jamaica in the 1830s; now, thirty years after emancipation, poverty and racial tension blighted the island. Even people sympathetic to the plight of Black Jamaicans, who were still oppressed by white planters economically, legally, and politically, shuddered at the state of the island. "Wreck and ruin, destitution and neglect!" lamented one commentator. But if Church was aware of the warnings about Jamaica in the New York papers, he ignored them.

When the party disembarked at Kingston, they found the town hot and bedraggled—"wretched place," Robbins complained. He was grateful that Church intended to find a place to stay up in the hills, where it was cooler.

In Kingston, Church took Isabel on an errand. He had recently received a letter from an admirer asking for his photograph, but he didn't have one to send. "I have been intending to sit all winter [for a photographer] but have not yet done so." Now he and Isabel posed for tintype portraits. The results were grim. Grief had bruised Isabel's girlish face, leaving dark circles under her eyes. The high spirits of her courtship and early marriage had been extinguished by the loss of her children, and her husband was no longer the dreamy painter she had met six years earlier. A writer who met Church less than a year after the children's deaths found his face "prematurely aged by sorrow."

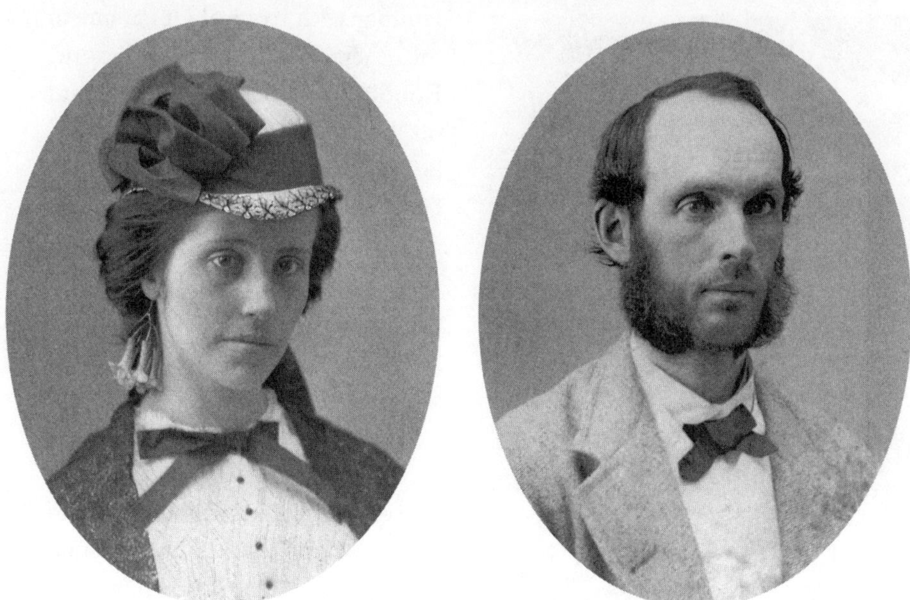

Isabel and Frederic Church, photographed in Jamaica, 1865

Church soon organized lodgings about five miles from Kingston, in the eighteenth-century great house of a plantation called Bellevue. Hundreds of these houses were scattered across the island, many of them surrounded by crumbling stone windmills and weed-filled aqueducts. Hundreds of thousands of enslaved people had labored on Jamaican plantations from the 1600s to the 1830s, and houses such as Bellevue were haunted by misery, violence, and death. Bellevue's owner told them that it had come into his family after the original planter's descendants had run into financial difficulties.

The air around the house was deceptively sweet. Bellevue sat in a fragrant grove of allspice and mango trees. Robbins noticed with relief that there were mosquito nets over the beds; the place was certainly more promising than Kingston. From the house, they could see the coffee estates that blanketed the coastal plains, and beyond them the blue Caribbean. Church and Robbins began going out almost daily on foot or horseback in search of palm trees and ruined windmills to sketch. The moist jungle air had a green tint to it, as if they were underwater, while hummingbirds and parrots flew overhead. Lizards rushed away from their feet, so thin and light they could have perched atop a gentleman's calling card.

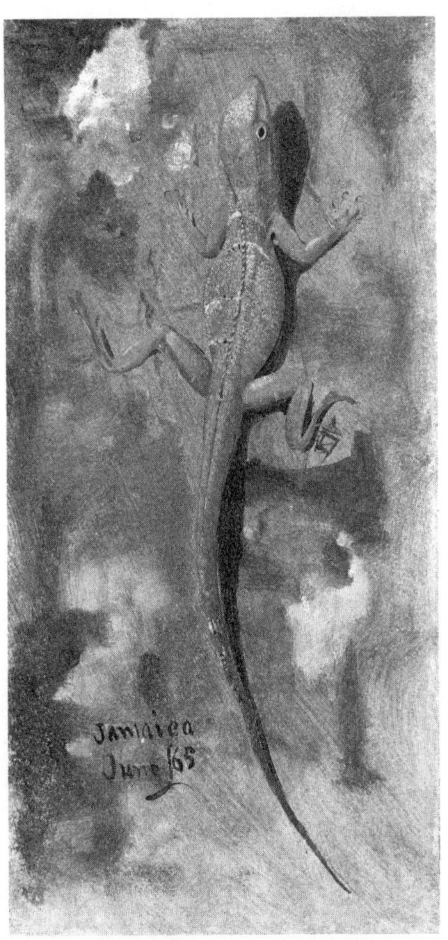

Oil sketch of a lizard by Church, June 1865

Church was already intimately familiar with tropical fauna, but to the others, it was all new and exotic. Robbins was enchanted by a cloud of "beautiful black velvet & gold" butterflies clustered on a single vine. On a visit to a family who lived in a neighboring great house, he was shown a female scorpion that had been trapped in a bottle with over one hundred of her babies, all of which she carried on her back.

Mosquitoes attacked Robbins and Church whenever they stopped to set up their easels. Robbins took to wearing an old blue veil he had found somewhere, pulling it down over his face and ears before he clapped his hat on his head. His right hand was in constant motion as he worked, but over his left hand, the one holding his palette, he wore two gloves for protection. Church seemed unfazed. He waved the mosquitoes away now and then while he kept sketching and painting, and the local flora began to sprout across his pages: arrowroot, cardamom, fern trees, and coconut palms.

He and Robbins sometimes saw trees slowly being killed by a parasitic plant called the strangler fig, which sprouted in the crevices of other trees. Church found the sight disturbing, particularly in his dark mood. More than a decade after this visit to Jamaica, he would still recall "some unusually ferocious monsters which were choking . . . trees whose drooping forms and sickly leaves betokened death—while the juicy flat leaves of the parasite seemed to clap their hands in fiendish joy."

Church never mentioned his dead children to Robbins. Instead, he spent hour after hour making pictures. "He works away as if for dear life," Robbins wrote, "& seems to be trying to forget his trouble by always keeping himself occupied." Isabel's response was different. Sarah Hitchcock told Robbins that Isabel was "very sad" but that she talked frequently about Bertie and Emma.

As Church worked, he turned toward the light. He painted the sun rising into a milky-blue sky and violet stripes of sunlight floating on the surface of the sea. He tried and tried to capture the otherworldly moment when he saw discrete rays fan through the clouds at sunset. He noted how a single vista offered up both light and darkness, life and death. "I have stood on dry parched ground and overlooked valleys intensely green and luxuriant," he marveled in a letter to Theddy.

When Robbins stole glances at Church's easel, he tried not to despair at what he saw. Church completed several gorgeous pictures in the time it took Robbins to complete a single one not nearly their equal. "He works with an energy & constancy unequalled by anyone," Robbins wrote. "Every day of my life I am more & more convinced that he is the only great landscape painter we have."

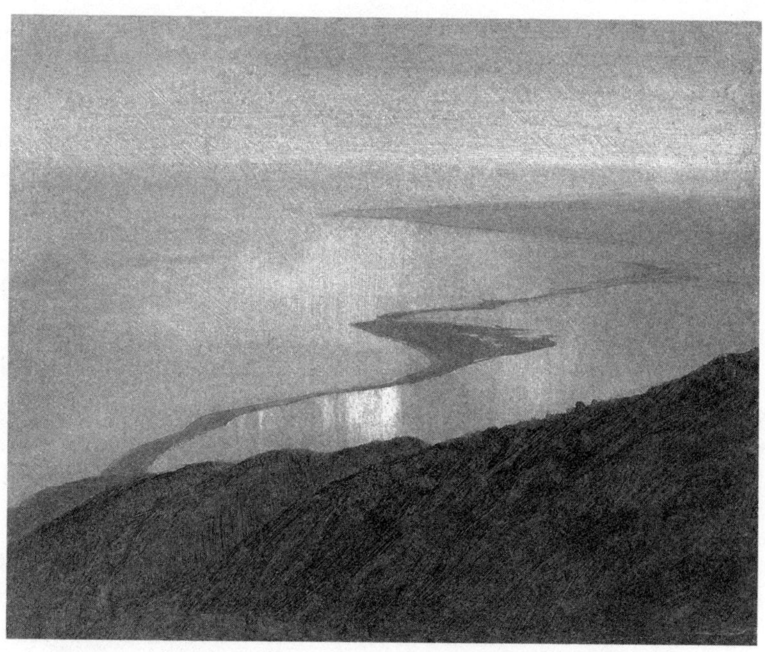

Oil sketch of the Palisadoes near Kingston, Jamaica, by Church, 1865

Church soon grew restless. He wanted to be living and painting higher up, deep in the mountains. Every decent plantation house seemed to insist on an ocean view, which was not at all what he wanted. In early May, he asked Robbins to go with him to Mount Diablo, several days' journey from Bellevue. They rode down to Kingston, boarded the island's single train, and traveled about thirteen miles to Spanish Town, seat of the colonial government. From the windows they saw enchanting sights slide past—orange trees heavy with fruit, blue-green waters, complicated skies that rained and shimmered at the same time. Then they hired a man with a two-horse buggy to drive them into the mountains, and the next day, from the summit of Mount Diablo, Church found the view he had been craving. He studied the mountains and hills, the fog and the sunlight, committing them to his sketches and his visual memory.

"POOR MR & MRS CHURCH I feel very sorry for them," Robbins confided to his mother soon after he and Church had returned to Bellevue. The mood in the house was melancholy. Robbins was sometimes able to interest Church in a game of billiards, but the only thing certain to distract him was painting.

Church soon orchestrated a move of the whole party into the Blue Mountains, to a plantation house called Galloway Hill, near the official residence of Jamaica's British governor. In a letter to Theddy about some business at the Farm, Church turned from instructions regarding manure to a description of the view from thirty-five hundred feet above sea level: "The scenery is superb—grand." In one direction he could see the Caribbean and in another the tallest of the Blue Mountains, rising four thousand feet above them. "I have accomplished a great amount of work—but there is so much to do that I am at a loss to decide day by day what to paint."

Church was starting to feel inspired and energized, and he could see that Isabel's listlessness was ebbing, too. She was going on vigorous treks through the jungle with whichever companions she could corral, as Church reported happily to Theddy. "Mrs. Church is fascinated with the occupation of fern collecting and has already an enormous collection." Hundreds of species grew on the island in thickets that in some spots stretched for miles. As Isabel passed through them, the feathery fronds parted like waves around her long skirts. Now and then, catching sight of a novel specimen, she bent down, carefully clipped a stem, and added it to her green bouquet.

The fern craze was a Victorian phenomenon that had recently reached the United States. It had been sparked by the invention in the 1830s of the Wardian case, a glass box that protected delicate plant specimens as they crossed the seas toward Great Britain from her far-flung colonies. Anyone who could afford a Wardian case could now import tropical ferns to grow in glasshouses at home. Fern lovers also pressed and mounted dried ferns in volumes or framed and hung them on parlor walls.

"Mrs. Church is insane on the Fern question," Church wrote. She was collecting every species of fern she could find "from 1/2 inch to 8 feet in length" and pressing some of them in paper to take home to the Farm.

AFTER THREE MONTHS ON THE island, when Church thought of Cosy Cottage and the Farm he no longer felt aversion. "Notwithstanding this magnificent scenery," he wrote to Theddy, "I cannot think of the Farm and surrounding friends without great longing."

They left Jamaica on the *Montezuma* in early September and arrived to find New York humming with postwar optimism and activity. Merchants and shopkeepers were enjoying their best season in years. The South was desperate to rebuild its ruined houses, businesses, and infrastructure, and it was unable to supply any other region. Buyers from every state and territory combed the city's stores and warehouses for clothes, foodstuffs, home goods, and machinery.

As the South emerged from the wreckage of war, the future of those once enslaved there was a constant topic of speculation. The day Church and Isabel arrived in New York, a front-page story in the *Herald* offered conflicting prognoses. The Freedmen's Bureau was reporting the creation of well-paying jobs for the formerly enslaved, so that "the number of negroes requiring support from the government is reported to be everywhere diminishing." Self-sufficiency and prosperity, it was hoped, would foster the peaceful integration of freed people. A few paragraphs later, however, the *Herald* reprinted an ominous dispatch from Fortress Monroe, Virginia. A disturbance involving armed Black men had reportedly been crushed by a detachment of cavalry from Washington. "Twenty-one negroes were captured, all armed with revolvers, cutlasses and carbines or shotguns." The *Herald*, a paper notorious for its racism, appeared unconcerned that whites were committing atrocities against Black people across the South.

Three weeks after Church and Isabel disembarked from the *Montezuma* in New York, Jamaica erupted. The news reached New York on the *Montezuma*'s return in mid-November. "Eight Miles of Dead Bodies," the *Herald* blared the next day. The British press in Jamaica blamed the rebellion on a small group of Black Jamaicans who had begun attacking and murdering British officials. As the violence spread, the colonial governor declared martial law and dispatched troops, who burned houses and executed men, women, and even children without stopping to sort out who had participated in the uprising. A week later, more than four hundred bodies lay in the fields and roads of southeastern Jamaica, and a thousand buildings had been burned.

THE FOLLOWING YEAR, CHURCH WORKED on a large Jamaica painting. The picture was for Elizabeth Jarvis Colt, the widow of Hartford weapons manufacturer Samuel Colt, whose pistols had helped the Union Army win the Civil War and made his abolitionist wife one of the richest women in the country. Elizabeth Colt had commissioned Church to paint a picture for a large art gallery she was building in her Hartford mansion. That autumn, he wrote to her about his progress on the picture, an idealized view of the Jamaican parish he had seen from Mount Diablo. He told Colt that he would "probably yet indulge in a few earthquakes and heave miles of solid land hither and thither until I am satisfied." The painting was generally going well, but "one part is going to give me a terrible fight," he confessed. It was the sky that was so challenging—and he observed to Colt that the sky was the soul of his painting, echoing Cole's credo.

Church was creating a complex and ambivalent picture, laden with personal and political meanings. Over the past fifteen years, he had conjured skies that signaled his increasing anxiety about the future of the United States, but this time he was trying to paint a sky that was both sunny and stormy, brilliant and muted. He hoped to depict the sun so that it was dimmed by a passing rain shower yet still shone brightly enough to light up the blue sky in the middle section of his picture. He wanted to capture rays of sun struggling through the mist to fall on small passages of landscape.

When the painting went on public display for the first time a few years later, the *New York Evening Post*'s critic found it "grand and impressive" and "vivid and startling." In Church's picture, Jamaica seemed to have weathered its recent storm, and it suggested a guarded optimism for the United States, which had just emerged from a greater trial, although into what new world, no one knew. The sky Church finally achieved in *The Vale of St. Thomas, Jamaica,* spoke of struggle and calm, of darkness and renewed hope, of patience and the passage of time. Church's capacity for optimism came in part from his religious faith. "Thank God afflictions to the Christian can never do harm but good always," he mused to Colt. He and Isabel had soldiered forward through their private pain to find a new measure of domestic happiness.

Church was writing to Colt from the Farm. "I am glad to say that my dear wife is quite well," he told her. "It is delightful to have the daily privilege of witnessing her enthusiasm and pleasure in the wonderful scenery with which we are surrounded." They also had something to look forward to again: Isabel was pregnant. She was now almost thirty years old, he was forty. They were beginning anew.

On September 30, 1866, she gave birth to a healthy boy, whom they named Frederic Joseph, for his father and for his paternal grandfather. When Church wrote to Elizabeth Colt a few weeks after the birth, he shared the good news. She replied, "I know, by a like experience, that nothing can comfort hearts mourning for their children, like another little one."

Cosy Cottage sheltered young life again, but the echoes of the first children's voices heard there would never fade. Seven years after Bertie and Emma died, Church wrote to a friend, "Only we—who have lost little ones—can appreciate what it is to see the unfolded buds wilt away and be powerless to revive them." Almost three decades later, in an 1893 yearbook of daily Christian wisdom, Isabel would inscribe the children's names on the pages corresponding to their deaths, March 18 and March 26.

"Dear Herbert," she wrote. "Dear little Emma."

CHAPTER 19

"Fast Horses"

Having a baby in the house again cheered Church and Isabel immensely. Isabel's mother came up from New York City to help, and everyone settled into a new routine. Most days, Church bade his little family goodbye in midmorning and climbed the steep hill from the cottage to the highest spot on his property, where he had recently built a freestanding studio. The simple wooden structure measured twenty-four-feet square, small enough to keep warm with a woodstove but spacious enough for him to move back and forth between his easel and the piles of sketches that guided him as he worked on his formal compositions. The light poured through the north-facing windows even on overcast days. For six or seven hours at a stretch, the rest of the world faded away while he painted. "I am accomplishing more than I ever did in my life before," he told Osborn.

Church loved the isolation of his studio at the Farm, where no one stopped by uninvited. In December 1866, he reported gleefully to Heade that he'd had only one visitor at his hilltop studio the previous day: one of his farmhands with "a snow plough and oxen preparing to clear the track from studio to house." He pitied Heade, who was renting Church's Tenth Street studio and therefore had to contend not only with Heade's own visitors but also with callers hoping to see Church—who, by contrast, was able to "accomplish four days in one here" at the Farm.

Peaceful and productive as these months were, a shadow was creeping across the landscape. His sister Charlotte, who had been in poor health on and off for the past decade, was declining precipitously. Around the time of Freddie's birth, Church's mother had taken Charlotte to Vermont, where they went horseback-riding every day in the country air, but it didn't help, and Mrs. Church had privately admitted to her husband that Charlotte "gets quite discouraged . . . and is feeling very bad." Charlotte told a relative that she had given up all hope,

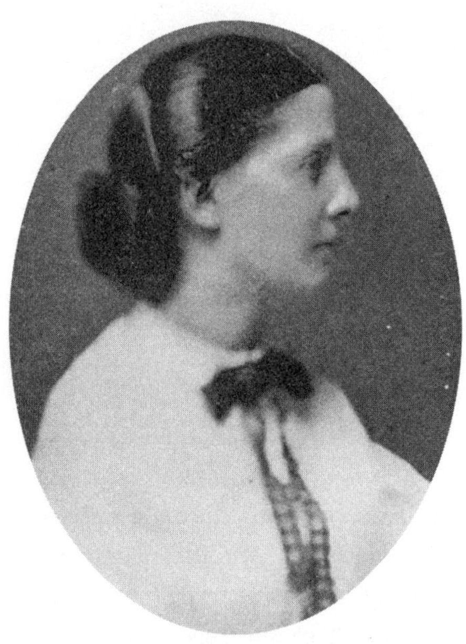

Charlotte Church, c. 1867

and by late 1866, she was desperately ill. Church traveled to Hartford to be at her bedside. Afterward he wrote to his father in despair. "I am constantly thinking of Charlotte's sickness and it distresses me to feel that I can do nothing or think of nothing which might benefit her."

Charlotte died on January 15, 1867, at the age of thirty-four. Church once again poured his grief into painting, creating a fan-burst of golden rays thrown off by the setting sun as it sank behind violet clouds. In what may have been a reference to his family's devastation, he painted a ruined church in the foreground. He named the picture *The After Glow* and sent it to his parents.

"You now have one more chain binding you to the other world," one of Church's cousins told him.

CHURCH FOUND SOLACE IN THE Farm. In early April, he wrote Heade, "We are having spring—nay summer weather—green grass—piping newts— and 46733389,003,675,211,863 birds of various kinds." Now, when he wasn't painting, Church was hauling manure or planting flowers, vegetables, and trees. "I superintended my own hot bed this season and if I planted my seeds right side up I may expect to see them sprout in a day or two," he told Osborn. "Mrs. C. has a digging fit. She flits about with a trowel in one hand and juvenile plants in the other all day." May brought nurturing rains, and Church reported to his friend Erastus Dow Palmer, a sculptor in Albany, "My young trees absolutely laugh to find their toes in the water." In June, the cherry orchard was filled with clouds of pink petals.

Enraptured by country life, Church bought more land, including an eighteen-acre parcel above his studio. It had a stunning view of the Hudson rolling south into the distance and the Catskills rising above the river valley to the west. He began to dream of building a spacious new house at the top of the hill. In the meantime, he oversaw the construction of more outbuildings. "I have nearly broken my neck from looking up and admiring my new barn so much," he told Osborn.

Yet even Church's passion for the Farm and the beautiful Hudson Valley couldn't keep him rooted. He yearned to explore and paint new landscapes. He wanted to see Europe for the first time, and even more than that he wanted to set up his easel among the ancient ruins of Greece and the Holy Land. In recent decades, two-dimensional painted panoramas and three-dimensional architectural models of sites famous from the Bible had drawn crowds throughout the United States. A canny marketer of his own grand pictures, Church crowed to Osborn about the potential of a painting trip to the Levant. "Just think of a series of studies in oil presenting the great features of Thebes, &c., Sinai, Petra, Palmyra, Damascus, Baalbec, Lebanon, Jerusalem, &c., &c. !!!"

As a matter of personal faith, Church and Isabel were both deeply interested in visiting Jerusalem and other biblical sites, and Church hoped that the change of scene would revive Isabel, who was physically and emotionally exhausted after the strain of pregnancy and giving birth to Freddie. Church confided to Osborn, "I am anxious to carry home a plump wife and a plump portfolio even at the expense of an uncommonly lean purse, for with the domestic bliss of a fat wife, and splendid studies I think I could soon replenish the purse." Osborn responded by arranging for Church to have ample financial credit during the upcoming trip. Osborn also decided that he, Virginia, and their children would travel with the Churches as far as Europe.

Word of Church's plans soon spread, and several newspapers ran bulletins about the upcoming voyage of the celebrated painter. Jervis McEntee grumbled, "Any humble individual like myself who goes there hereafter will be playing second fiddle." But it was Sanford Gifford, not McEntee, who would be the next in Church's circle to paint in the Holy Land. McEntee and Gifford traveled to Europe together six months before the Churches, but McEntee couldn't afford to go on to Jerusalem with Gifford.

In late October 1867, Church picked the last grapes from his vines and packed them to savor at sea. In mid-November, he, Isabel, Mrs. Carnes, and one-year-old Freddie sailed for France with the Osborns. The Churches and Mrs. Carnes would spend the winter in Paris, where Isabel had been born, before crossing the Mediterranean.

The Atlantic steamship was filled with Americans going abroad. After the horrors of the Civil War, those who could afford it were flocking to Europe, driven by curiosity, escapism, and a desire for the refining polish of world travel. Europe no longer seemed as far away as it had during the war; in 1865, Cyrus Field had failed yet again to lay a transatlantic cable, but in the summer of 1866, on his fifth attempt, he had finally triumphed. Traveling to Europe no longer meant a delay of weeks or months in communications with loved ones. With the world so much smaller, some Americans who went to Europe felt emboldened to venture all the way to the Holy Land.

Once they reached Paris, Church settled his family in lodgings for the remainder of the year. He toured the Louvre and picked up a medal from the Exposition Universelle for his 1857 *Niagara Falls*, being the only American painter thus honored. Then he made a quick trip to London to see the royal art collections and meet with patrons. He decided he preferred "big and dirty" London to Paris, which "has so much sham and excessive ornament—that it becomes very tiresome." He also voiced a rare judgment on his artistic contemporaries, writing haughtily to Palmer—without singling anyone out—that "Landscape Art in France and England is crude enough."

AT THE END OF DECEMBER, Church took his family to Marseille to board a steamer for the six-day voyage to Alexandria. The ship hugged the European coast before slipping through the Strait of Messina between Sicily and the toe of Italy into the open sea, as Isabel admired the torchlights from the port towns dancing on the water. When they dropped anchor off the Egyptian coast, two sailors rowed Church, Isabel, Mrs. Carnes, and Freddie to shore in a small boat along with their trunks and bags. They made their way through the crowded streets to the Peninsular and Oriental Hotel, one of the city's finest. Alexandria was teeming with foreigners. There were English industrialists on their way to India, French engineers helping to construct the Suez Canal (it would open the following year), and European and American families preparing to cruise up the Nile. Isabel began keeping a diary on their first day, noting that the city was "more than half oriental in its appearance— with a motley assemblage of people from all nations and in many picturesque and curious costumes."

Her husband was less open-minded, complaining to Osborn that Alexandria "is the noisiest and dirtiest place I was ever in, everything talks or gabbles, or squeals, or groans, or screeches, or howls perpetually. The camels only represent silence." Church occupied himself with sketching the locals—men in white robes and red fezzes or blue robes and white turbans. He had intended to take his family up the Nile, but with Isabel unwell, he didn't want to insist. At the same time, he couldn't bring himself to leave her behind and go alone. After coming all this way, he wouldn't get to sketch the Great Pyramid of Giza and the Sphinx, or wander among the ruins at Thebes or in the Valley of the Kings. "I have longed sadly to go up the Nile and make studies of the great monuments of the past," Church told Osborn.

If he could get his family settled somewhere comfortably, he would feel better about leaving on a painting excursion. He decided on Beyrout, as it was then known, where there was a sizable expatriate circle of Americans and Britons. After just three days in Alexandria, the Churches and Mrs. Carnes left by sea for Beyrout, about four hundred miles to the northeast. They reached the city, Isabel wrote in her diary, after "a perfect moonlight night—sea smooth as glass—and air as pure and soft." It was freezing at home in the Hudson Valley, but here roses and almond trees bloomed among the stone houses and along the twisting lanes. In the distance, Mount Lebanon glinted with snow. Church was captivated by the setting: "the loveliest blue sky, with snowy mountains, a sapphire sea, and green trees," he wrote to Osborn.*

They settled into a seaside hotel called the Belle Vue. Church reported to Osborn, "We have enormous rooms, ceilings 30 feet high and marble floors, furniture scant, plenty to eat." The cuisine did not agree with the Churches, at least not yet. "The mode of living here is destructive to Yankee stomachs," Church wrote, although the menu was mostly Western. "Breakfast at 8. Coffee, excellent. Bread, eggs, chops, potatoes. Dinner at 2: Soup, mutton, roast veal, cauliflower, mashed potatoes and asparagus, Bavarian cream, fine large oranges, bananas, Damascus apples, figs, dates. At 7: tea, toast, Lebanon honey, quince jelly. There, don't your mouth water?"

Soon after they arrived, Church bought Persian carpets for their rooms because the floors were cold, then learned almost immediately that he had

---

* The country of Lebanon would not be created until 1920, and the city in which Church settled lay in a vast region known as Ottoman Syria. It stretched from modern-day Turkey, south of the Taurus Mountains, to the edges of Egypt and swept from the Mediterranean across what is today Israel and the Occupied Territories into the deserts of what is today Jordan.

paid too much for them. He also had an easel made. For now, he planned to work on a small South American scene. He would wait for the unfamiliar landscape around him to work its way into his imagination before he attempted to paint it.

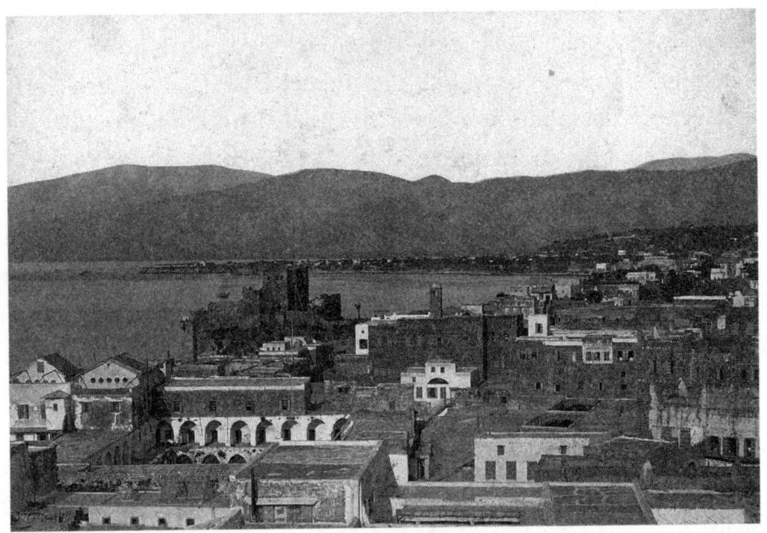

Beyrout, second half of the nineteenth century

The new arrivals were quickly besieged by old acquaintances from New York, the Reverend D. Stuart Dodge and his wife, Ellen. He was a Presbyterian minister in his early thirties who had grown up in New York as the son of a fantastically wealthy merchant; she was the daughter of an American railroad baron. They had come to Beyrout to help another American couple, the Reverend Daniel Bliss and his wife, Abby, establish the Syrian Protestant College, which had opened in 1866 with funding from Dodge's father.*

Ellen Dodge took Isabel donkey-riding on her first day in Beyrout, and Isabel found that she loved it. "These white Bagdad donkeys are wonderful little beasts," Church wrote to Osborn, "untiring and very easy and amiable." Church hired a man to wait outside the hotel with donkeys for Isabel and her mother, and soon Isabel was riding almost daily. "My wife is a celebrated donkey rider," Church told Osborn happily. Freddie sometimes snuggled

---

* Today this is the American University of Beirut.

into his mother's arms and went along. His father called him "a connoisseur of donkeys—some he will ride (of course carried) for hours with delight—others he rejects in a few minutes." Occasionally, Isabel went alone on horseback instead, galloping on the beach and through a forest near Beyrout. Church was delighted to see her so lively. "Isabel enjoys herself—she likes fast horses and fast donkeys."

They saw camels around the city, but were not inclined to ride them. "They are awfully picturesque but all conceived notions of anatomy must be staggered at the legs and gait of the beautiful beast," Church told

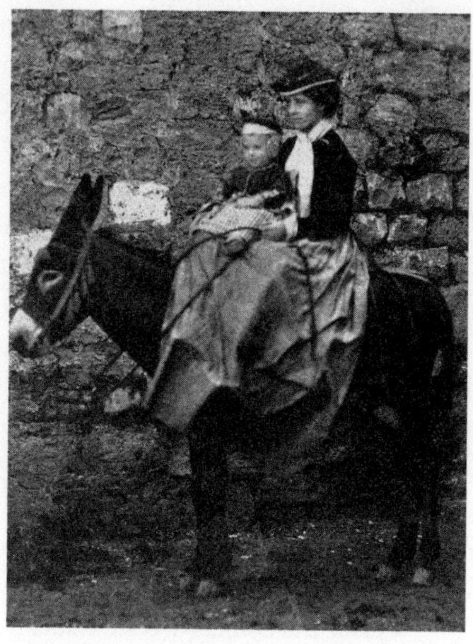

Isabel and Freddie in Beyrout, 1868

Heade. He arranged for a photograph to be taken of himself and Freddie atop a camel. When the photographer snapped the picture, Church was gazing into the distance, but Freddie was staring at the camera, worry stamped on his face. His unconventional childhood had begun.

As they explored Beyrout, Church was intrigued to find that many houses had stairs leading to the roof, so their occupants could stay cool and enjoy the city's spectacular views. He took a strong liking to one of the first houses he saw, whose vast central court struck him as both elegant and meaningful—it was the beating heart of a home. He made mental notes, thinking of the hilltop house he planned to build at the Farm. "The Dwellings are often quite grand," he wrote. "I have got new and excellent

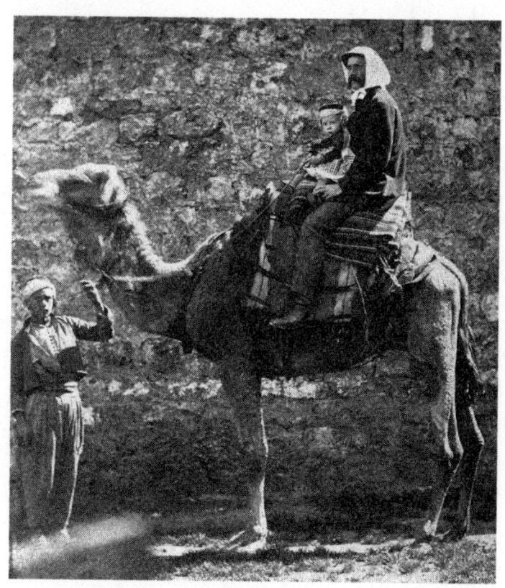

Church and Freddie in Beyrout, 1868

ideas about building since I came abroad." So many houses in New York and New England were constructed of wood, which seemed insubstantial compared to the stone residences of Beyrout. "Here we are in Syria," he informed Heade. "All settled and in rare contrast everything is to the new thin shelled city of New York."

He and Isabel spent their first three weeks in a whirl of social calls and sightseeing. "You can't imagine how kind and devoted our new friends are here," Church told Osborn. He began to feel easier about leaving on an extended painting trip. The Reverend Dodge decided to accompany him, as did a Scotsman named Alexander Fowler. On February 6, 1868, the three men departed for Jerusalem. Isabel was immediately racked with loneliness. "Dear Fred! how I miss his dear bright presence every moment," she lamented in her diary only hours after seeing Church off. Mrs. Dodge, who was pining with equal fervor for her husband, called on Isabel the next day, but the women failed to cheer each other up.

Over the coming weeks, Isabel tried to distract herself by taking Freddie on social calls, receiving visitors, and exploring Beyrout with her mother. At one Sunday prayer gathering, Isabel was embarrassed that she had to read from her hymnal when everyone else knew theirs by heart. She chastised herself in her diary: "I should be most grateful for all my many blessings—but today [I] have been more than usually cross & unkind particularly to dear Mama—God help me, and give me grace to conquer my own evil heart."

Isabel's nerves were jangled by Freddie, who was "a concentrated lump of mischief," according to his father. She chased after her son, trying to keep him from falling down the stairs or burning himself on the stove that heated his nursery. Isabel agonized about him constantly. When he seemed fussy, she worried that he was falling ill. One day the Dodges' young daughter told Isabel bluntly, "You must feel very particular about Freddy [sic] since your other two children are dead!" She was relieved when Freddie's eighth tooth poked through his sore gums and she realized he did not have some exotic fever. She returned to fretting about her husband. "When he is absent more than half the sunshine is gone from my life," she wrote in her journal. "I long for him."

She remained unaware of the danger of Church's expedition.

CHAPTER 20

"I Wasn't Shot"

Church was bound for Petra.

Half a century later, the English adventurer T. E. Lawrence would assure a friend that nothing could prepare one for the sight of this ancient city whose monumental buildings had been carved right into the salmon-colored sandstone—"till you have seen it you have not had the glimmering of an idea how beautiful a place can be."

Since the second century BC, Petra had been the capital city of the Nabataeans, a people made wealthy and powerful by their control of desert trade routes. In AD 106, the city had been acquired by the Romans, but four hundred years later, it had been abandoned to Bedouin tribes. It was rediscovered to the West in 1812 by the Swiss explorer Johann Burckhardt, and in the half-century after that, hundreds of Europeans and some Americans had set out across the desert to see the city. Most had completed the trip safely, but some had returned without comrades who had succumbed to wounds or illness. Others told harrowing stories of narrowly averted catastrophe.

Church had seen lithographs and even some rudimentary photographs of Petra, and he was confident that he could capture on canvas some essence that these flat images could not. He longed to see this fabled city in what had once been the biblical land of Edom, the kingdom of Jacob's brother, Esau. That Petra was so difficult to reach made it all the more alluring. Few artists had yet been there. What a coup it would be if Church could bring this ancient wonder to American audiences in a grand new painting.

Church, Dodge, and Fowler knew they would need help getting to Petra, which lay one hundred miles to the southeast of Jerusalem, and they arranged to meet with a man who had been recommended to them: Michail Hene, who worked as a dragoman, a role that combined the duties of guide, provisioner, and security chief. Hene's skill and experience would help safeguard the travelers against the possible perils of the trip, which included snake bites, scorpion stings, sunstroke, starvation, fever, and attacks by Bedouin tribes. The 1868 edition of Murray's *Handbook for Travellers in Syria and Palestine* emphasized that the Bedouin people who controlled the area around Petra were "a wild and lawless set," yet warned that it was impossible to avoid them. "In fact, it should be adopted, and strictly followed out, as a general rule, that no traveller should ever attempt to pass through the territory of a tribe until he has secured an escort from it, or has obtained the express permission of its chief."

Church knew that his plans to sketch and paint at Petra would place him in special danger. The Petra Bedouin considered it a form of theft for a foreigner to make images of their city without prior agreement and recompense. Church reported to Palmer that "some years ago an artist who ventured there was shot while attempting a sketch." But he was undeterred. "I told Michail that I wanted to go to Petra to work [and] to sketch and that he must arrange it so that I could." Hene agreed to guide Church's party.

On the morning of February 12, Church, Dodge, Fowler, Hene, and several servants set out on horseback for the town of Hebron, where they were scheduled to rendezvous with a pair of Bedouin sheikhs who would, for the right price, escort them to Petra. They were drenched for hours by cold rain, which a strong wind pelted into their faces. Church shivered in his saddle and meditated on the story he'd heard about the artist who had been shot. He was gripped by an uncharacteristic pessimism. The trip had been his idea, and if

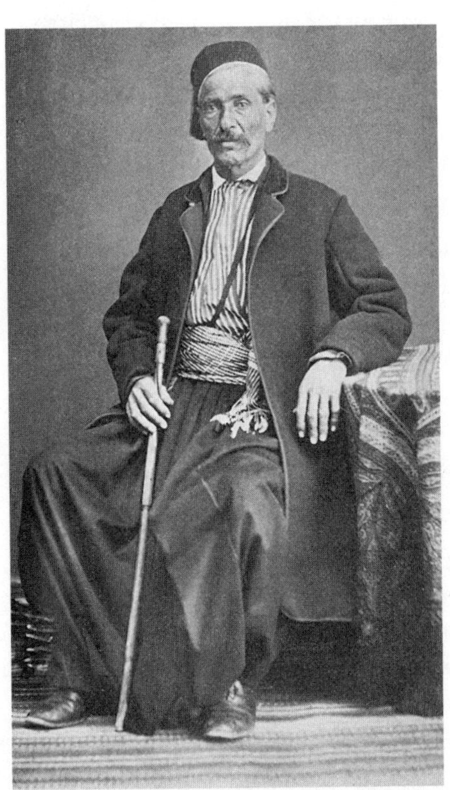

Michail Hene

something terrible happened, he would bear some responsibility for the fates of Dodge and Fowler.

In Hebron, Church, Dodge, and Fowler sheltered in an old quarantine station while Hene went out to buy provisions and negotiate with the sheikhs. Mindful of the physical demands they would face, the travelers devoted some of their day to exercising. "After practicing gymnastics," Church noted in his diary, they all "played hopscotch on the cemented floor," which they had "marked with a piece of charcoal." Then they braved the rain to scramble up a hill behind their quarters.

Hene returned with good news; he had engaged the sheikhs to lead them to Petra. One was an old man called Abu Mousa, who was known to hold great sway with the tribes in and around Petra. The old sheikh might be able to help them gain entrance to Petra so that Church could sketch and paint—although the Bedouin might still decide to shoot him while he worked. Hene, for his part, found Church's art intriguing, not threatening. Church was amused when Hene "requested me to make a sketch of himself when angry and one when peaceful."

The day of departure from Hebron dawned blessedly clear. Hene was everywhere at once, barking orders at the servants as they loaded the mules with tents, food, and baggage. One camel was burdened with two enormous bags of charcoal for fires to keep the travelers warm and ward off wild animals during the cold desert nights. The sheikhs mounted their horses and took the lead as the parade of animals and men began the trek south. Church counted around seventeen horses, mules, and camels.

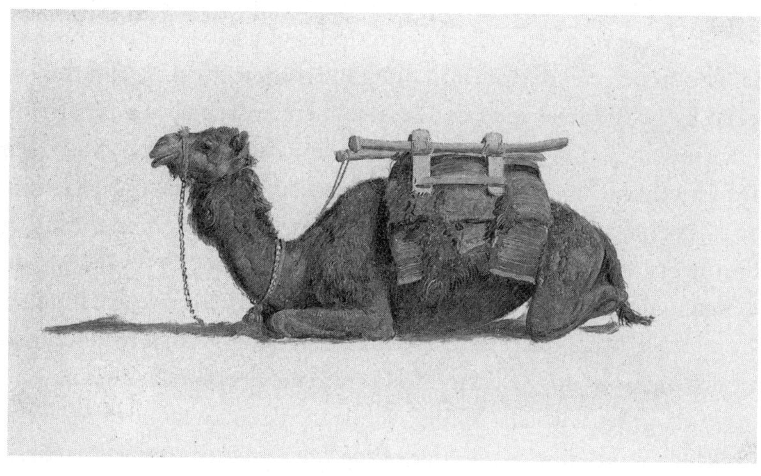

Oil sketch of a camel by Church, 1868

All that day, their third since leaving Jerusalem, they traversed a landscape that to Church looked "wild & lonely." There was no vegetation, not even grass or weeds. In every direction he saw the arid opposite of the verdant tropics and the forest-clad New England mountains. But as the hours passed, his eyes began to adjust to the subtle colors of the Judaean Mountains, and he started to find traces of beauty in the bare earth and rock.

When the caravan stopped for their midday meal, the Bedouin built a fire and sat watching as Hene and the foreigners ate. Church was discomfited to see that Hene would not share any of their food with the Bedouin—not even with the old sheikh. Later, Hene insisted to Church that if they were to share anything, the demands would never end.

That afternoon, the caravan approached an old village high on a ridge. The Arabic name of the village was Semu-a; in the Old Testament it had been called Eshtemoa. Church admired a ruined stone tower and pieces of ornately carved stones scattered on the ground. The romance of the biblical past evaporated when Hene and Abu Mousa began to search for a place for Church, Dodge, and Fowler to sleep. Church longed for a tent, but it had rained too much in recent days. "It is no joke to encamp on ground soaked with water," he conceded. Abu Mousa tried to persuade Hene and the other Bedouin to seize the local sheikh's house at sword point, and as the new arrivals and the local men yelled at one another, Church was amused at the thought of a sword fight. "Although in harmony with the strong walls and loopholes of the castle . . . we could muster but one sword in the party."

Church, Dodge, and Fowler were given shelter in the base of the old stone tower, where they picked their way over piles of garbage into a small, dark cellar. The stench of creosote and dung filled their nostrils, and they were attacked by fleas. Hene tried to alleviate their misery by sending them an elegant dinner. "Strange sight in this blackened dirty vaulted room," Church wrote in his diary, "was the spectacle of snowy table cloth French forks knives spoons—cut glass a bright silver plated soup tureen several *courses* and all the appointments of a good table."

When night fell, rats emerged. Church slept with his riding whip in easy reach and took "occasional cracks at them in the dark." Rain forced the men to spend two nights in this noxious hovel before the Bedouin could finally pitch the party's large tents in a flat hollow. While the Bedouin set up camp, Church couldn't help wandering to the edge of the village to make some sketches. He soon found himself trailed by several local men. Fearing an impending robbery, or worse, Hene sent a guard to protect him. As Church finished sketching a view of the village, several of the men approached him and "seemed disposed to be troublesome but a sharp reproof from the guard silenced them. What a country!"

The caravan had been traveling for five days now but was only one-third of the way to Petra. They were about to enter a vast desert, and Abu Mousa rode off to arrange for camels to replace the mules and the horses, most of which would be sent back to Jerusalem. He returned with about a dozen camels and their owners. Hene, meanwhile, had engaged several dozen men from the village to accompany and protect the caravan.

Church was given a camel named Zraigan to ride. He approached the crouching animal carefully and threw one leg over its hump. Torquing his body awkwardly, he clutched the front saddle horn hard with one hand and with the other grabbed the horn behind him. "At the requisite signal the beast suddenly raised up on his hind legs[;] of course this movement had a tendency to pitch me over his head but I clung on with a good grip—the motion was now reversed as he raised himself upon his foreknees and then upon his feet." As soon as the camel began walking, Church recalled hearing that many people felt seasick from the movement, and he understood why. "The motion was peculiar—exactly like that of a rocking horse compelling an involuntary bowing of the body so we sailed along like a trio of nodding mandarins."

AT AROUND FOUR THAT AFTERNOON they reached a watering hole nestled in a valley and protected from the strong desert winds. The old sheikh halted the caravan, dismounted, and drove his spear into the ground—the sign that they would camp for the night. Church, Dodge, and Fowler climbed a nearby hill and found themselves looking out at the Dead Sea, and, on its opposite shore, a range of bare mountains. Church wrote ecstatically in his journal about the scene. The sunlight illuminated the peaks so that their "infinitely broken sides glittered like gold." His painter's eye parsed the patches of color, finding "strong purple shadows with greenish grey lights—mottled with whitish stones and rocks—from patches of vegetation greener bushes and occasional brilliant gleams of vivid green." A connoisseur of the tropics, Church was falling in love with the desert.

Later that night he slipped out of his tent to observe the Bedouin discreetly. "Never saw so picturesque a scene as these Arabs sitting by the camp fire smoking and the camels lying close by also enjoying the warmth and chewing their cuds. Their huge forms looked still huger in the vague light." He captured the scene in a quick oil sketch, down to the flashing whites of one Bedouin's eyes as he sat near the bright fire. Church had decided it would be wise to let these men see him sketching as often as possible. He made a point of working whenever they stopped to camp and then showing his pictures to them. Maybe they would persuade the Bedouin at Petra not to hurt him.

Church had always been more interested in the Americas' monumental landscapes than in the people who inhabited them, but this journey began to change him. For the first time, he was paying close attention to the people who made their homes in the terrain he had come to paint. He was traveling day after day with dozens of men from an entirely alien culture, watching them talk, argue, and laugh among themselves. As they slouched along on their camels, robes flowing and spears in hand, he grasped that without their deep knowledge of the desert's politics and climate, he could never have reached this place. He started drawing pictures of the men and trying to learn the Arabic words for their belts, gowns, cloaks, headdresses, knives, daggers, and other details of their attire.

Sometimes he managed to draw while bobbing along on Zraigan's back. He turned in his saddle to watch the caravan winding through the desert behind him, and he sketched the line of camels and their riders, their profiles spiky with long guns and spears. It was difficult work, given that he had no control over his camel. "We were at the mercy of these desert ships and drifted about where they chose to carry us."

The mountains Church had seen in the distance the day before were growing closer. He wondered at the colors of the peaks, which were "of a beautiful dove tint with silvery grey rocks and chasms forming large luminous masses on their flanks." The sun carved the surfaces with light and shadow. "The ridges of the mountains were exquisitely rounded

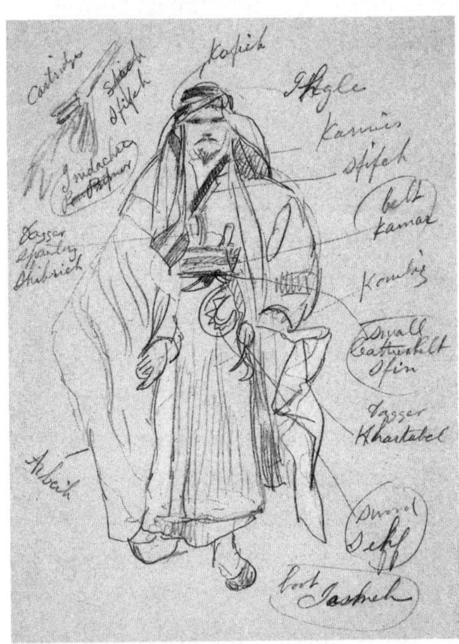

Arabian man sketched by Church, 1868

and the grading of the tints delicious. The flashing of the seams & precipices told tremendously."

Herman Melville had visited this region a decade earlier and condemned it as a hellscape of death that "compares with ordinary regions as skeleton with living & rosy man." Inhospitable to plant life and strewn with sharp rocks, the Judaean desert struck Melville as the "mere refuse & rubbish of creation." For Church no part of the natural world could be ugly. Every environment had its own character, color, and beauty, and he found their differences exhilarating. He had seen the cliff-lined Hudson, the low green jungles of the Río Magdalena, soaring Chimborazo, glittering icebergs, and now the unveiled face of the earth itself.

EIGHT DAYS AFTER THEY HAD set out, they rode across a stony wasteland until they entered a narrow pass. Emerging, they saw ahead of them a range of mountains with layers of differently colored rock in undulating stripes. To Church they looked like "soft tinted ribbons curving in and out to correspond with the irregularities of the slopes." Passionate about geology, he saw in these formations a creative force that had shaped a planet of stunning variety.

At the bottom of a gorge, Church and his friends dismounted and crossed to the far edge of a large flat rock. "There burst upon us one of the most stupendous views I have ever had the delight of witnessing." Below them stretched a deep valley that razored into the distance between the striped mountains. Eons of flood, wind, and rain had sculpted the mountainsides into chunky masses that glowed in the fiery afternoon sun. "I flung open my pocket sketchbook and drew the scene roughly[;] we then dashed down the path and seized another view and so on[,] sketching and running until we reached the narrow plain below." Abu Mousa, seeing Church's excitement, ordered his men to set up the night's camp right there.

An armed Bedouin guard shadowed Church all the next day, and the old sheikh ordered him not to stop to sketch without alerting him first. They were approaching the plains of El Arabah, where warring tribes often clashed. The caravan had encountered no strangers for days, but ahead lay an oasis that was the only source of water on the plains. "Our sheikh says he never encamps at the fountain on account of the danger of meeting parties of Hostile Arabs," Church noted in his journal. The Bedouin reloaded their guns. Abu Mousa cantered ahead on horseback, scaling the hills to scan for threats. After crossing the oasis, they rode over the plain for eight uneasy hours. Church could see the terrain ahead rising toward a series of craggy peaks. Somewhere among them, he knew, was Mount Hor, where Moses had buried his brother, Aaron, according to the Old Testament. As they began weaving their way into the mountains, Church spotted a tiny structure atop one peak—the tomb of Aaron.

The next day was a Sunday, and Church, Dodge, and Fowler spent it reading passages from the Old Testament set in this very place. Church could practically see the exiled Israelites passing him as they made their way to Mount Hor. In these wild mountains, his innate wonder at nature's drama was intensified by his belief that divine events had unfolded right here. Later, he tried to explain to Osborn how deeply this place had worked its way into his soul. He couldn't shake the haunting beauty of "sad—parched—forsaken Syria. There is poetry."

Petra lay only a few miles ahead, but Church couldn't resist climbing Mount Hor to see the shrine to Aaron. After an arduous ascent with a guide, he walked around what turned out to be a simple structure, then wandered off to gaze across the deep gorges. Kestrels and hawks soared and dipped on the currents. Suddenly Church saw, far in the distance, the outlines of a huge edifice cut into the face of a cliff. Petra.

He opened his spyglass. Now he could make out the details of a two-story façade encrusted with carved pediments and Corinthian capitals. He grabbed his sketchbook and began drawing, but the guide waved his arms wildly, indicating that someone might shoot at him from the valley below. Church complied out of respect while inwardly scoffing at the idea that he was in danger, but his guide knew that Bedouin roamed the valley, guarding the western entrance to Petra.

As they descended Mount Hor, Church noticed that the dominant colors didn't come from the plants, which were mostly greenish-gray shrubs that could survive extremes of heat and cold. Instead, the most vivid hues here were in the earth's bare surface. "I never beheld anything so beautiful in rocks," Church wrote in his journal. He insisted they were "indescribable" but described them anyway: "ribbons of graded tints crossed by bars—greenish—yellow orange purple all interlaced and following in the most exquisite manner the warm irregular surfaces of the rock." He noticed that some of the cliffs had caverns cut into them. These were tombs for the Nabataean dead. The first ones he saw had simple openings, but the closer they drew to Petra, the more ornate the entrances became.

At the edge of Petra, Church, Dodge, and Fowler rejoiced to see the tents of their caravan but were dismayed to find Abu Mousa surrounded by wild-looking men "screeching and yelling" who "appeared to be on the point of a fight." The men had propped their guns against the rocks in a gesture of goodwill, but the guns remained in easy reach. Compared to these frightening characters, Church conceded that the old sheikh seemed like "a saint."

That night, he was awakened repeatedly by shouts from the Petra Bedouin, and he woke the next morning to the same sound. Peering out through a gap in the tent, he made some quick oil studies, "fearful that I might be prevented by force from sketching."

After breakfast, he assembled his largest sketchbook, his paints and brushes, and his folding stool. Several of the Petra Bedouin were assigned to accompany him. They carried long guns and heavy clubs, and Church hoped that they would guard him rather than attack him. He asked Hene to tell them not to interfere with his work but to "stop when I stopped and move where I moved." After a hike of several miles, Church and the Bedouin entered a narrow canyon formed by tall cliffs of dark, undulating rock. A stream ran down the center, and the men were forced to hug the canyon wall as they sought dry ground. Above them, the walls sometimes veered together, blotting out the sky.

Suddenly, just visible between the dark canyon walls, Church saw a glowing façade of an ethereal rose color. It stood well over one hundred feet tall. Afterward he tried to convey the otherworldly sight: "You can imagine this fairy like temple blazing like sunlight among those savage black rocks." He marveled that "by contrast with the black precipices it shines as if it was self illuminating."

The building before him was Petra's most famous. It was known as Al-Khazneh, or the Treasury. Church had seen engravings of it, but they hadn't prepared him for the real thing. "The capitals are very rich and beautiful[;] among the ornaments of the frieze I observed grapes and pomegranate with appropriate leaves. Eagles were sculptured at the corners—also some animals[,] probably lions."

It was time to find out how the guards would react when they saw Church making an image of their city. He started with a black-and-white pencil sketch, surmising that an oil sketch might be too provocative. He shot a quick, appraising glance at the Bedouin. "I selected my view point—prepared my seat—took my portfolio from the Arab who carried it, opened it, and dashed at the subject with all fury to secure something at least before I could be interrupted." The Bedouin moved closer. One of them loomed over Church, trying to see what he was putting on paper. Church pointed at the building and then at his sketch, uttering one of the only Arabic words he knew—the word for "good."

To his intense relief, the Bedouin remained calm. "I wasn't shot—I wasn't disturbed—I was let alone." He continued sketching until it began to rain, and then the Bedouin took him back to the camp. "The next day when I attempted color—they were delighted." By the time the caravan left Petra on February 28, driven away by a snowstorm, Church had amassed a heap of pencil and oil sketches of Al-Khazneh and other Petra landmarks. He credited Hene's leadership for the success of the excursion. They returned across the desert to the port of Jaffa, and while they waited there for a steamer to Beyrout, Church sent Isabel a telegram saying she could expect him within days.

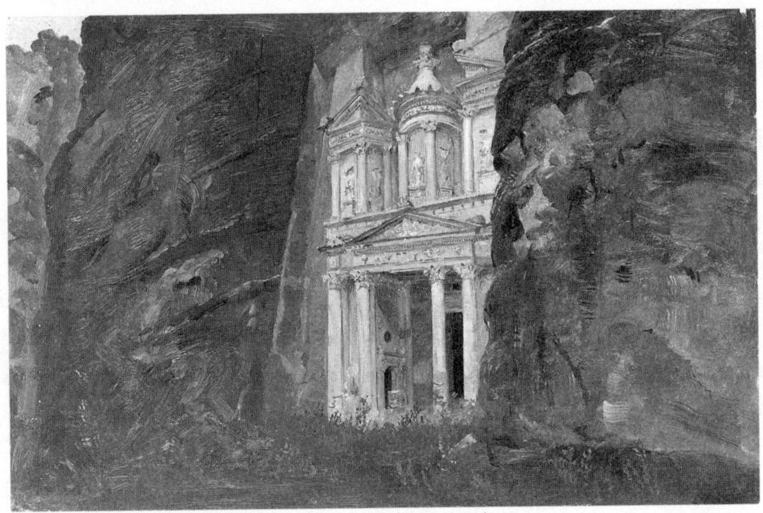

Oil sketch of Al-Khazneh in Petra by Church, 1868

After five weeks without him, she was relieved but impatient. "Even those few days seem long to wait," she sighed in her diary. When he finally arrived, she found him in wonderful spirits and "delighted with his trip." She thanked God for his safe return. "It is so <u>very</u> pleasant to have Fred back once more."

CHAPTER 21

"No Photographs"

A cold wind tore at Church's paper, but he held it down and continued to sketch. Despite a spell of miserable weather in Jerusalem, he was working outside at every opportunity. Isabel admired the way "dear conscientious Fred" never gave up.

Church always grew obsessed when he found a good subject, and the idea of a Jerusalem painting particularly appealed to him. Long a devout Christian, he was increasingly interested in architecture and ancient cultures, and he knew there was a great appetite in the United States for images of the Holy City—engravings, photographs, scrolling panoramas, and paintings. A Jerusalem painting from his brush would surely find a gallery audience and a buyer, as well as a market for engravings. Thanks to hyperbolic travelogues, more and more Americans were taking an armchair interest in the history of Jerusalem, where Western archaeologists were trying to pinpoint the precise locations of biblical events. Some Americans felt moved enough to make pilgrimages there—traveling from what they proudly considered the new Promised Land to the old. On the trip from Beyrout to Jerusalem, Isabel was embarrassed by one of her countrywomen, who insisted on attaching an American flag to her parasol and "taking possession as she called it of each place."

Isabel had come here in a humbler frame of mind. She simply wanted to walk where Jesus had walked and to pray at the places where he had suffered. She was aware that the archaeologists then at work in Jerusalem disagreed among themselves about where events had taken place, and she approached each holy site with conflicting emotions. At the Church of the Holy Sepulchre, held by many to be the site of Christ's tomb, she was "deeply impressed and awed," yet she did "not really believe that it was where our Saviour was laid." When she and her husband went to Bethlehem to tour the Church of the Nativity, built over the supposed location of the manger where Jesus was born, they were both "rather incredulous about this!" Still, in spite of her skepticism, she was swept up in the high emotions of the Christian pilgrims around her.

Isabel was just as interested in the customs of the Jews and Muslims. At the Wailing Wall she watched a Jewish man in a fur-trimmed velvet cap repeatedly "bow his head—clutch his fist—kiss the wall." She was amused by a small Jewish boy who stiffly imitated his elders' bowing, but saddened by the "poor old bent women" who "really seemed shaken with their genuine grief."

Not until Isabel spent a night on the Mount of Olives, east of the Old City, did she think she felt the presence of Jesus. Here, according to the Evangelists, Jesus had agonized over his impending betrayal before being seized and taken back to Jerusalem for crucifixion. Isabel and Church climbed to the top of the ridge and sat under a wizened olive tree. The air was cold, but the moon was shining. "Jerusalem lay spread out before us looking silvery and mysteriously grand," Isabel wrote. That night, they camped on the Mount of Olives, and Isabel discovered that she loved "tent life." She was again showing the sense of adventure Church had loved in her when they first met. After the disaster of losing Bertie and Emma, her days would always be tinged with anxiety and melancholy, but as they traveled through the Holy Land, Isabel's intrepid streak often prevailed.

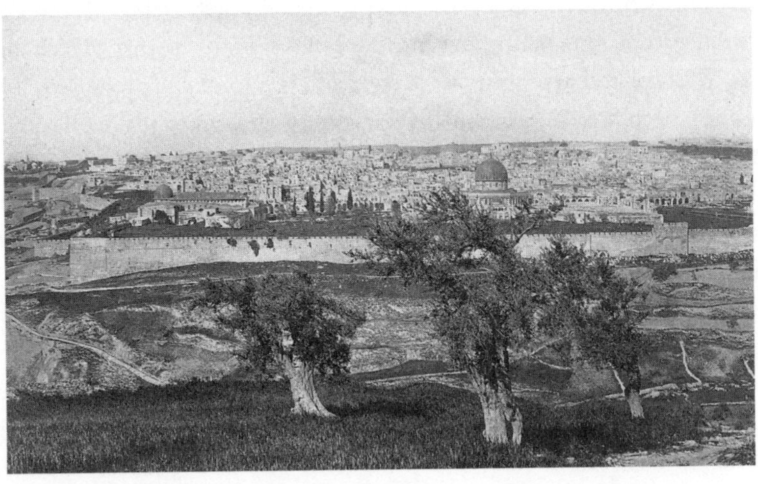

Jerusalem from the Mount of Olives, late nineteenth century

IN APRIL, FROM BEYROUT, CHURCH and Isabel traveled about fifty miles southeast to Damascus, one of the oldest cities in the world. Its strong biblical associations, most famously Saul's conversion to Christianity on the road to Damascus, appealed to the Churches, as did the city's imposing site at the foot of the snowcapped Anti-Lebanon mountains. Isabel found it difficult to be away from her little boy, who was in her mother's care in Beyrout, but she was enthusiastic about accompanying Church into the region, despite its possible dangers. As they approached Damascus along a river lined with poplars, hawthorns, and roses, she was enchanted by all the "fairy loveliness." Like many Americans and Europeans, she tended to reduce Ottoman Syria to a fairy tale. On the road she saw "turbaned turks—and picturesque costumed individuals of different nations; and swift little white donkeys—with crimson saddles & trappings and with their coats all cut into various patterns!" She was charmed by "gay, oriental, & picturesque" Damascus, with its huge old trees, covered bazaars, and Turkish bathhouses.

As they toured the city, Church and Isabel continued to gather ideas for their new house. The contrast between the simple exteriors of Syrian houses and their spectacular interiors intrigued them both. They entered one house whose door was so low that even the petite Isabel had to duck, but inside they found the house spacious and open, with marble courtyards, tiled mosaics, and fragrant orange trees. "All these rooms have fountains, dais's [*sic*], divans, mirrors etc. Walls & ceiling, highly and gorgeously decorated, and mirrors everywhere, amid the decorations, little bits of mirrors—doors & all wood work—inlaid with ivory & mother of pearl. At night by candle light, the effect must be quite splendid—One is reminded of Arabian nights tales."

Isabel was self-aware enough to realize how strange her Western features and clothes must appear to locals. When she and Church arrived in one village outside Damascus, "the women & children crowded around me, thinking me evidently just as remarkable looking a creature as I considered them." Yet of all the people she encountered on the trip, it was a British woman in her early sixties who seemed the most exotic. Jane Digby, Lady Ellenborough, had spent her entire adult life violating the principles by which Isabel lived: intellectual humility, sexual modesty, wifely submission, and maternal devotion. Digby attended the Protestant church in Damascus, but otherwise she lived a life of what Isabel termed "somewhat disgraceful notoriety."

Digby had become famous for cheating on and divorcing her neglectful first husband, after which she married three more times, had passionate affairs with a series of kings and aristocrats, gave birth in and out of wedlock, and abandoned most of her children. She had seen her favorite son die at the age of six when he fell over a banister and smashed his head on a marble floor. Devastated by her losses and betrayals, she had left Europe in 1853, when she was in her mid-forties, to travel through the Levant. On her way to the ruined city of Palmyra she had met a dashing Bedouin sheikh in his twenties. They had fallen in love and were married according to Islamic law, shocking family and friends who thought Jane couldn't shock them any further.

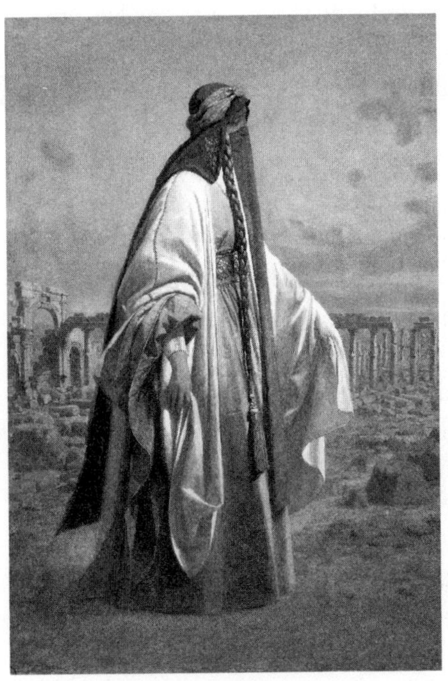

Jane Digby el-Mesreb in Syria,
by Carl Haag, 1859

After the marriage, Digby had built an elegant house in Damascus. When she wasn't galloping across the desert on a white horse beside her husband, she was sought out at home by Western and Arab artists, writers, and statesmen, including the Prince of Wales, who visited Damascus in 1862. Isabel had a mental image of a "bold grand looking lady," whose presence would be announced by "the rustle of massive silk."

Isabel and Church called on Jane Digby by appointment on May 2, 1868. In a fountain-filled garden whose marble pathways ran beneath trellises draped with blooming roses, they encountered a woman in a straw hat, a simple dress, and garden gloves who was arranging some vines. After a confused moment, Isabel realized with surprise that this was the famous Englishwoman they had come to meet. Digby showed Isabel and Church into the house, which was decorated with both European and Syrian elements—"a very agreeable and pretty combination," Isabel thought. She saw that their hostess's personal style was as eclectic as her house. Digby had dyed her long blond hair black and lined her famously striking blue eyes with kohl.

Isabel came away impressed with this woman who spent months each year riding with Bedouin men and camping in the desert. When Isabel herself rode into the desert north of Damascus so Church could paint the ruins of several biblical cities, she eyed their armed Bedouin guards with both anxiety and fascination. On their first day out, the men in the party had stopped to look at a strange heap on the ground: human remains. A sheikh told them that four men had recently been killed by Bedouin here. "I was _very_ much alarmed and I think the gentlemen were decidedly more serious after this," Isabel wrote. "Wild animals seemed as nothing compared to the fierce Bed[o]uin, mounted on thin swift steeds, and with their formidable looking spears etc."

When they reached the spectacular Roman ruins at Baalbek, Isabel spent several days resting while Church explored and sketched, but only after he had made sure Isabel was as comfortable as possible. She was feeling rather ill; she was contending with the early days of another pregnancy. Because the tents grew hot during the day, "Fred had an upper room—of a ruined castle near our encampment—cleaned and arranged for my comfort. I have to ascend to it on a ladder." From the windows, she admired the temple ruins that Church was sketching, and beyond them the mountains.

Once back in Beyrout, Church packed some crates with the treasures and souvenirs he had collected in Syria and arranged to ship them to his Tenth Street studio. "There are three to arrive from Beyrout," he informed Heade, joking that the customs duties would "be within $869,321,125,593,016801—I hope, at any rate, that you will have the kindness to see that my goods are not confiscated to pay charges." Then the Churches collected Freddie and Mrs. Carnes and bade farewell to their Beyrout friends. Not long after they had departed, the American consul wrote to Church, "Mrs. Dodge is already mourning over the depreciated quality of the puns and funny stories that pass current since your departure."

FROM BEYROUT, THE CHURCHES PLANNED to wind their way northwest for almost two thousand miles, with the Alps their ultimate destination. Church had painted mountain ranges in North and South America and now in Ottoman Syria, but he had never seen the Alps, a favorite setting for European and some American artists.

Their ship passed among the Greek islands, Isabel observed, on a "wonderfully blue sea." As they approached Constantinople, she rose early to watch the domes and minarets materialize above the cypress groves lining the water. They spent a week in the Ottoman capital, strolling through the mazelike bazaars and attending performances by "whirling" and "howling" dervishes. Then, steaming north up the Bosporus Strait separating Europe from Asia, they watched the city recede with a regret that curdled to misery as soon as they entered the churning, nausea-inducing Black Sea.

At Varna they boarded a train for Rustchuk, on the Danube, where they would catch a boat upriver. Isabel watched the landscape slip past and realized how much she had missed green meadows and tree-cloaked hills. Her eyes drank in the colors after months in deserts and bare mountains. On the crowded steamboat, Church secured a private room for Isabel and Freddie, but her mother "had to go down stairs with all the other ladies and children," while Church tried to snatch some sleep on a sofa in the noisy dining room. Passing from the Ottoman Empire into the Austro-Hungarian Empire, they did some sightseeing and shopping in Vienna and then traveled southwest to the Bavarian town of Berchtesgaden, a postcard of a village with white houses and thatched roofs set against a backdrop of snow-frosted Alpine peaks.

Church was once again walking in Humboldt's footsteps. The renowned naturalist had spent time in Berchtesgaden in April 1798 and had reportedly declared this region among the most beautiful in the world. The Königssee, a long lake carved by Ice Age glaciers, had drawn travelers to Berchtesgaden for centuries. "The most tremendous precipices line the lake—huge mountains plunge abruptly into the green waters," Church wrote to Osborn. Eagles scanned the lake's depths as they flew from crag to crag. Cowbells clanked from time to time in the hillside meadows. Church saw thunderheads piling up in a "delicious blue bloom" above rocky peaks that the sun burnished a "splendid warm gold." During the month he and his family stayed there, Church often made the three-mile trek from Berchtesgaden to the Königssee, sketching "12 to 15 hours daily," he told Osborn.

After so many days under the Syrian sun, Isabel enjoyed long walks with her mother and Freddie in the cool mountain air. It was a rainy summer, and Freddie, who had a new pair of galoshes, clomped along enthusiastically. "He has a little wood wagon which he drags after him, and which is his inseparable companion," Isabel reported to Church's mother. Church joined them on occasion, and they all rambled together through mossy forests and meadows dappled with forget-me-nots.

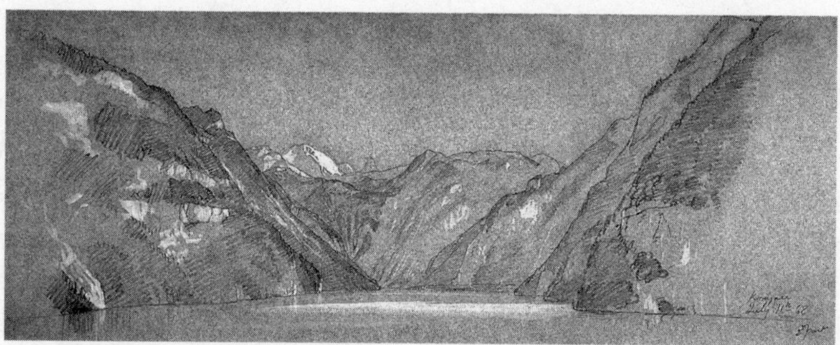

The Königssee in Bavaria sketched by Church, July 11, 1868

He sometimes worried about Freddie, who seemed less affectionate than Bertie had been. "Isabel is such a good mother to him," Church wrote to his own mother. "Still—good mothers do not always have good children. Otherwise I should have been the best of sons to you."

They had been abroad almost nine months, and both he and Isabel were growing homesick. Theddy had stoked their longing for the Farm with a newsy letter he penned in late May. The orchard trees were blooming and newborn calves were wobbling along behind their mothers. Church, usually so taciturn about his feelings, admitted, "We are both looking forward to the time when we shall set our feet on America, again. To tell the truth, I am not a little fidgetty [sic] when I think of the good friends and the humble home." He also yearned to see his mother, who was ailing again. In the end, though, like so many other artists before and since, he found it impossible to leave Europe without visiting Italy, which he had first glimpsed as a student in Cole's paintings.

On their way there, Church fell ill. He lost his appetite and felt exhausted, and he developed a strange boil on one of the fingers of his right hand. It soon became so painful he couldn't hold a paintbrush. By late September, when they reached Umbria, he was feeling somewhat better. He wrote to Osborn in a pensive mood. "The Alps disappointed us both—and I have no desire to revisit them," Church reflected. "You will perhaps raise your eyebrows when you hear my sweeping remarks about the Alps—but they have nothing which is not vastly exceeded by the Andes and lack many important features which make the Andes wonderful and exclusive." Even the Andes, however, were eclipsed by his new passion for the Middle East. "Syria, with its barren mountains and parched valleys, possesses the magic Key which unlocks our innermost heart."

ON OCTOBER 1, THEY REACHED Rome, where Cole had found his own magic key. He had made his first visit here in 1832, aware that the artists he most admired, Claude and Turner, had painted in its ethereal light. Standing in the Colosseum one day, Cole had looked up in awe at the stacked tiers of crumbling arches, overgrown with viburnum and acanthus. Suddenly, a sense of nature's immense power had so overwhelmed him that he saw the arena as the crater of a volcano "whose fires, long extinguished, had left the ribbed and blasted rocks to the wild-flower and the ivy." Nature, he grasped, would always triumph over human ambition.

During Church's stay in Rome, his thoughts turned repeatedly to Cole. "I believe him to be the best landscape painter that ever lived," he wrote to Osborn in November. "In profound poetic feeling he was far beyond Turner and equal to Claude and vastly superior to Claude in knowledge." A few weeks later Church again mentioned Cole: "I feel I should prefer to own one of Cole's best landscapes—in preference to any other landscape the world can furnish."

Rome, with its toppled marble statues, broken pillars crowned by flowers, and monumental arches recalling remote victories, had made many other sensitive people feel the way Cole had—thrillingly insignificant in the march of time. Byron had called Rome the "city of the soul." Shelley had written that it was "at once the Paradise / The grave, the city, and the wilderness." To Hawthorne it was "the city of all time, and of all the world!"

Church waited for a similar feeling to overtake him, but it never material-ized. For most American visitors, Rome was the oldest place they had ever been, but in Syria, Church had camped where the Israelites had camped centuries before the founding of Rome, and he had gazed over desert mountains and rifts formed millions of years earlier. To his eyes, Rome seemed raw and callow. The ruins weren't even made of solid marble, he noted scornfully. The ancient Romans had used brick and stucco, slapping a veneer of marble on top. "So much sham," he griped to Osborn. To Heade, he wrote, "I have no comments to make on Rome! I thereby distinguish myself from the crowd who scratch interminable letters about the 'Eternal City' as they delight to call it." Still, here they were, and he would try to make the best of it. He settled his family in a little house with a garden and a view that was pleasant enough, even if "the Tiber is not the Hudson."

Several of Church's closest friends from New York were in Rome that season to paint. Jervis McEntee was renting a studio within walking distance of the Churches' new house, and Church soon took the studio next door to McEntee's. McEntee and his wife were living only a few blocks away with their mutual friend Sanford Gifford, and the McEntees, the Churches, and Gifford began socializing regularly. Other acquaintances began calling on the Churches almost immediately. Church grew morose when he learned that it was customary for visiting Americans to make the rounds of the artists' studios. He wanted to be left alone to work on a large painting of Damascus he had started. "There are not many strangers in Rome as yet," he told Heade, "but a strong distant rumbling betokens a great rush this season."

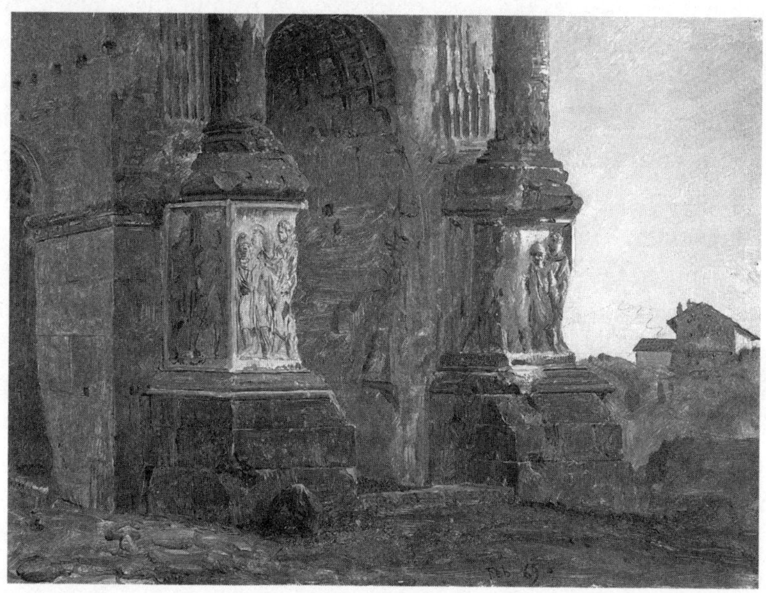

Oil sketch of the Arch of Septimius Severus by Church, February 1869

In late December, when Henry Wadsworth Longfellow—one of the rare welcome visitors—stopped by Church's studio, he pronounced the Damascus picture "highly poetical." Church joked to Osborn that Longfellow "must be wrong as the Saturday Review denies that I can paint a poetic picture." Church appreciated visits from erudite friends such as Longfellow, but he loathed the swarms of social callers who began to arrive at his studio in the afternoons.

When he got trapped by strangers, he tried to be polite, but privately he complained that it was "an intolerable bore to be obliged smilingly to submit to vapid compliments and foolish questions—I am compelled to give several lessons in geography . . . every day—and explain that there is a perceptible difference between black and white—that sea ports are seldom inland—that deserts are not necessarily flat plains of drifting sand, &c., &c., &c."

Church changed his routine to avoid interruptions, painting only during the morning hours, then going home for lunch before spending the afternoon with his family or out in the city. He was developing a taste for antique shops. "Rome has got to be the rubbish room of art in a great measure," Church reflected, but he loved hunting for gems among the junk. He wandered the streets until he saw a promising shop window, and then he spent hours inside poring over old pictures as a shopkeeper stood by naming the famous artists who had supposedly painted them. Although Church couldn't speak Italian and had to hire an interpreter to accompany him, he still enjoyed the ritual of haggling and prided himself on regularly paying a fraction of the asking price. Within a month he had purchased thirty paintings, many on religious themes, including the Nativity, the judgment of Solomon, and the martyrdom of various saints. "Among them is a genuine Claude—for the vendor told me so," he wrote to Osborn sardonically. "But really the picture is beautiful—I am never tired of looking at it." In addition to the purported Claude, he also bought paintings he thought might be by Correggio, Salvator Rosa, and Tiepolo, along with many other works whose provenance was unknown. Church had grand plans for his "old masters," as he liked to call them. "When I build again I intend to have one old room—with old furniture and old pictures— everything toned down 400 years back."

As a young man, Church had had eyes only for the natural world, but now that he was in his early forties and had seen much more of life and death, he was newly attuned to the value of human creations. He was becoming a cultural magpie. Wandering through Rome's churches and chapels in his first month there, he admired the painted angels and saints who floated through light-suffused skies. If he could have, he would have taken the frescoes from the very walls. Instead, he persuaded the Vatican's chief fresco artist to give him lessons. Renting a second studio, Church practiced fresco painting on one of its walls for hours every day. He found it "extremely agreeable to handle the colors," noting that "they have a luscious smoothness and crispness which is better than in oil." It was difficult to paint quickly on wet plaster before it dried, but Church had steady nerves and a confident hand thanks to decades of plein air oil sketching. His new teacher was so amazed at Church's skill that he invited him to work on a Vatican fresco in progress. Church daydreamed about becoming a fresco artist in the United States, but "of course in America—where we build in the morning and pull down in the evening[,] very few would be inclined to adorn their houses with immovable pictures." He teasingly offered to fresco Osborn's expensive new barn to entertain his cows.

Church was finally starting to enjoy Rome. One evening, he took a gorgeous torchlight tour of the Vatican sculpture gallery with Isabel, her mother, and Lockwood de Forest, a relative of Isabel's who was a talented young painter. When a cold snap settled over the city in late January 1869, Church laughed to see the normally languid Italians racing through the streets. "These Roman noses look like fiery beacons," he wrote to Osborn. "All the fountains are garnished with icicles and thick ice." Church felt revitalized in this bracing weather, and he thought Freddie looked "plump and rosy" and Isabel "vastly improved."

Church had so often in his younger years traveled solo, or with a male friend or two. In Rome, after a day of painting, he loved coming home to his own little family. He enjoyed having his mother-in-law around, with her excellent sense of humor and extra pair of hands to help Isabel. He was relieved to see that Freddie was displaying a more normal level of affection, throwing his arms around his parents' necks and calling them "Dear Mamma" and "Dear Papa." Freddie's presence "makes our Roman apartments seem more like home," Church told Osborn, and a new baby was due very soon.

In February, the weather suddenly turned springlike. Flowers burst forth in gardens and window boxes and carpeted the Campagna beyond the city. On the twenty-second, Isabel gave birth to a healthy boy, whom they named Theodore Winthrop Church. It was a weighty name for a tiny baby, and he was soon nicknamed Winnie.

THERE WAS JUST ONE MORE place Church felt he had to see before he took his family home. About a month after Winnie's birth, he traveled alone to the toe of Italy, where he boarded a ship for Greece. The passage from Messina to the Athenian seaport of Piraeus was the usual ordeal of nausea and vomiting. "Hor-ri-ble," he wrote to Osborn. "I was in an agony of disgust all the way." But Church loved Athens, a town so much smaller and tidier than Rome that it reminded him of New England. As he wandered around the Acropolis, he decided that his seasickness "was but a flea bite compared with the everlasting pleasure afforded by the sight of these ruins."

The Parthenon floated at the highest point of the Acropolis like a dense, bright cloud. Older than the Treasury at Petra, it appeared both eternal and fragile, colossal and buoyant. Church gazed and sketched and gazed again, trying to grasp how this ancient structure cast its spell. Huge chunks of fallen marble gleamed around him. Melville, wandering among them in 1857, had been reminded of thawing ice floes on the Hudson, and now, as Church painted on a brisk spring day, he thought of the invigorating snap of April in the Hudson Valley. The colors were so pure: white marble, blue sky, green fields in the distance. He made simple color notes on his drawings.

Church purchased some photographs of the Parthenon to consult along with his sketches when he got back to the States and could begin work on a full-scale painting, but he thought all the black-and-white images looked flat. "No photographs can convey even a faint impression of its majesty and beauty," he mused to Palmer. The waves of human cultures that had dashed against the Acropolis for two thousand years had shattered walls, pillars, and friezes, but the Parthenon's elemental divinity had outlasted them all—Byzantines, Franks, Ottoman Turks, Venetians, and the acquisitive British. There was something "God like" among these ruins, Church wrote, once again registering that divine, planetary vibration that bound the human to the eternal and made him feel most deeply alive.

The Parthenon also connected Church to the global birthplace of democracy just as his own country was recovering from the Civil War. He had rejoiced the previous November upon hearing of Grant's election as president; thanks to Field's transatlantic cable, Church's circle in Rome had learned of the outcome only hours after it was reported in the United States. "The election of Grant is very inspiriting," Church wrote Osborn. "Heaven help our country and bring us safely out of the confusion which at present prevails and make clear the turbid waters by settling the dirty politicians in the profoundest depths of oblivion."

Shortly before Church had traveled to Athens, Congress had approved the Fifteenth Amendment, which extended voting rights to Black men, and as he wandered the Acropolis, the amendment was winding its way through the ratification process. Pericles, the Athenian leader responsible for the construction of the Parthenon, had expanded democratic access to include poorer male natives of the city-state. The Parthenon, Church knew, was a potent symbol for nineteenth-century struggles for freedom, a linkage strengthened by the long literary afterlife of the Greek War of Independence, which had been waged against the Ottoman Empire in the 1820s. Church began to ponder how he should mine his sketches of the Parthenon for a future painting.

After two weeks of work at the Acropolis, he returned to Rome, which looked tawdrier than ever. "This dull heavy languid air is so different from the brilliant exhilarating atmosphere of Greece that I feel as if I never wanted to see Rome again," he wrote. All in all, the Old World—Europe—hadn't much impressed him, but the ancient worlds of Syria and Greece had transfixed and altered him. He would return to his "thin shelled" New York City with the enduring grandeur of Petra and the Parthenon fixed in his mind.

CHAPTER 22

"Like a Fever"

In May 1869, the Churches left Rome for Liverpool, stopping first in Paris, which looked gaudy to Church after the Acropolis, and then in London. They sailed in mid-June from Liverpool, and by early July he and Isabel were settled with two-year-old Freddie and four-month-old Winnie at the Farm. Their familiar little cottage brought them what no shimmering deserts or regal ruins could—contentment.

One evening soon after their return, Church sat down in the dining room to write to his sculptor friend Palmer. He reflected on his sojourn abroad and deemed it a success in every way. His adventures in Syria had filled his portfolio with images few other Americans had seen. His vision of nature had grown more nuanced, broadening to encompass arid lands and the traces of civilizations that had tried and failed to resist the assaults of time. He had seen firsthand how admired his work was both in Britain and on the Continent. Best of all, he and Isabel had rebuilt their shattered family. Now they were safely back in the embrace of a region Church had adored since his teenage years across the river at Cedar Grove. He exulted to Palmer, "Almost an hour this side of Albany is the Center of the World—I own it."

Osborn, who was planning to build a new townhouse on Park Avenue, proposed that Church join him in the project, so the Churches and the Osborns could live there together. They were as close as family—why shouldn't they occupy a double townhouse together? Church, although flattered, turned him down tactfully: "It's a terrible [*sic*] costly business living in New York." Church would keep his family at their peaceful perch on the Hudson, but he offered to help Osborn think through the design of the new house, pointing out that he had "just completed his architectural education at the Parthenon!!!!!"

Church was as happy as he had ever been. After almost a decade of marriage marked by love, tragedy, and adventure, he treasured Isabel deeply. "Can we appreciate how much we are indebted to our wives?" he mused. Similarly, when they found themselves apart in the coming years, Isabel addressed him as "My dear husband" and "My dearest boy." Eighteen years after their wedding, she would write, "I have no news for you—it is not news that I long for you inexpressibly. Take good care of your most precious self."

Their travels had changed them intellectually, spiritually, and aesthetically. For almost two years, they had reveled in the artistic and architectural achievements of ancient and modern cultures far from the Hudson Valley, and they had spent lavishly on art and decorative objects. Boxes and trunks from Beyrout and Constantinople and Rome and Naples kept arriving at Church's studio in the city and making their way up the Hudson. One of the boxes from Constantinople, Church reported to Osborn, contained "rugs—armour—stuffs—curiosities, etc. etc. etc., crowded in together and some of the other boxes have old clothes . . . stones from a house in Damascus, Arab spears—beads from Jerusalem—stones from Petra and 10,000 other things."

In August, Church received a shipment of three white donkeys from Syria. He was distressed to find that they had suffered at sea. "They had a passage of sixty-nine days, experienced one storm of great severity and were knocked about in a terrible manner as their bruised bodies show," he wrote Osborn. Once the donkeys had recovered, Isabel resumed her favorite pastime, judging one of them "the most delightful beast she ever rode."

In his hillside studio Church soon began a painting of a Syrian landscape, but he was too excited about being back home to spend much time indoors. He packed baskets of fruit and shipped them to family and friends. He raced around checking on the work of his hired hands, who were building a new icehouse, adding rooms to Cosy Cottage, and expanding the house in which his farmer lived. He also tore himself away repeatedly to take the train down to Manhattan. There he visited with Heade, inspected the antique paintings he had shipped from Rome, and looked for rooms to rent for the winter season.

The family's return to the Farm also brought a whirl of visits as they reunited with Church's parents and his sister Elizabeth as well as with the Coles, the Osborns, and the Nobles. Summing up his frenetic summer and autumn of 1869, Church wrote emphatically to Palmer, "I—have—not—been—idle."

Between all the guests and the two young Church boys, Cosy Cottage was full of life again. "Freddie marched in the other day with a huge mushroom in each hand," Church wrote. "He looked like a chubby giant with a pair of parasols—Isabel and I supped off those mushrooms and they were excellent."

Even with the prospect of added rooms, Cosy Cottage was starting to feel cramped. Church had written Osborn from Rome that "sometimes the desire to build attacks a man like a fever—and at it he rushes." Soon Church could hardly think about anything except designing a new home on the eighteen acres he had bought before going abroad.

But how and what to build? The wood-frame houses of upstate New York seemed quaint and flimsy to him after the handsome stone houses of Beyrout and Damascus. "Great conclusion arrived at in building is this," he wrote to Palmer. "Thick walls the first beauty—There can be no perfect building without thick walls." In every spare moment, Church sketched towers, windows, arches, and walls, often consulting with Isabel, whose eye and ideas he valued.

It was clear he would need a professional architect to advise him on the feasibility of his unusual schemes and to produce technical drawings. The Osborns had hired the celebrated Richard Morris Hunt to design their new townhouse on Park Avenue, but Church had qualms about working with a famous architect. "A young architect is more painstaking and more tractable than an old and popular one," he thought. Nevertheless, he hired the popular Hunt to work

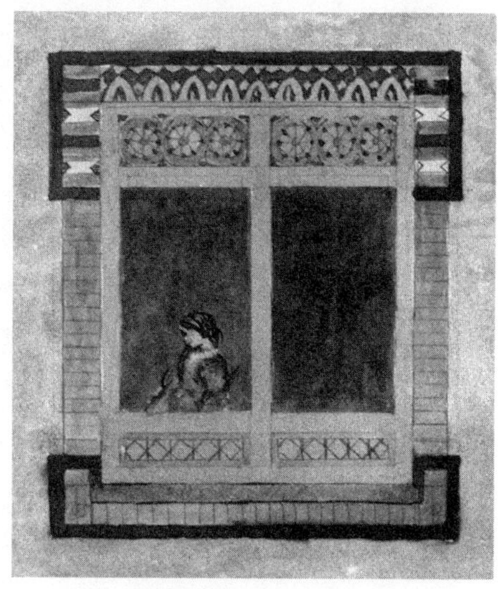

Window design by Church,
probably featuring Isabel

up a design. An early version was in the style of a French Renaissance château, not at all what Church was after, but a subsequent drawing pictured a villa with vaguely Moorish ornamentation, which was closer.

Church, still dissatisfied, turned to Calvert Vaux, the British-born architect who had partnered with Olmsted on Central Park and Brooklyn's Prospect Park. Vaux had spent years alongside the nation's preeminent landscape architect thinking about how built structures should be situated in their surroundings. He was also a sought-after and experienced designer of country houses, of which he insisted that "the design has to be adapted to the location, and the location to the design." Vaux was close to Church's good friend McEntee—Vaux was married to McEntee's sister—and Church and Vaux had an easy, friendly connection. They began trading ideas and sketches. Church hoped to break ground on the new house the following summer, but for now, he sketched and painted and dreamed.

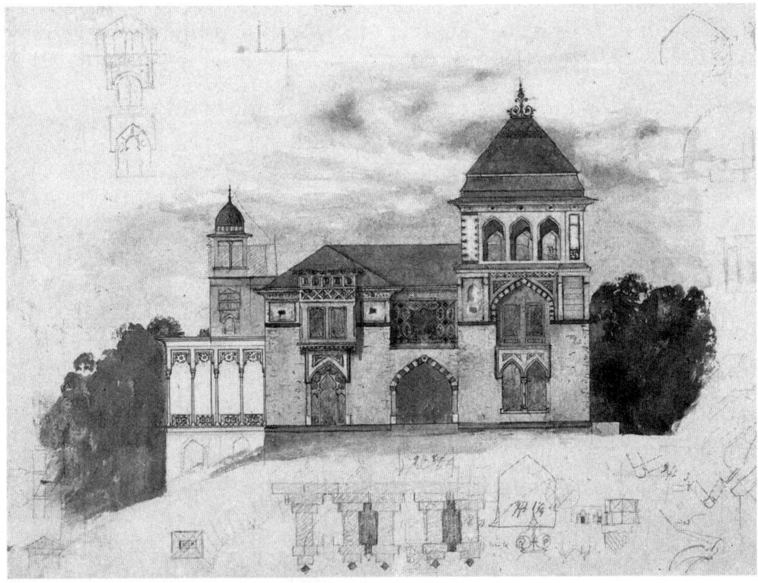

Sketch for the Olana villa's southwest façade by Vaux and Church, c. 1870

There was only one blight on these halcyon days. Church was in pain again. This time, it was his wrist, which was bothering him so much that he put off writing letters. He was not given to complaining, but he sometimes mentioned his ailment to let his correspondents know why his letters were so infrequent and telegraphic. "My wrist begins to cry out—so I had best stop—It is strange—but nothing I do hurts it so much as writing." He was grateful for one mercy: "Painting does not affect it in the least."

IN EARLY NOVEMBER 1869, CHURCH and Isabel moved Freddie and Winnie down to city lodgings on Fourth Avenue near Madison Square Park. One rainy evening toward the end of November, Church joined a crush of gentlemen entering a mansion at Madison and Twenty-Sixth Street. This was the headquarters of the Union League Club, a patriotic institution founded during the war. The mansion, owned by Leonard Jerome, a business partner of Cornelius Vanderbilt (and future grandfather of British prime minister Winston Churchill), was equipped with a large private theater. Church entered the theater and took a seat.

His fellow painters Whittredge, Kensett, McEntee, and Bierstadt were all present, as were Hunt, Olmsted, and Vaux. Also on hand were the leaders of civic institutions including Central Park, Columbia College, the National Academy of Design, and the New-York Historical Society. Nothing ambitious could be achieved in New York without money, and that had shown up, too, in the form of railroad magnates, stock speculators, manufacturing titans, and men who had simply inherited their fortunes. Around the room, fine cuff links and watch fobs threw off the first pale gleams of a dawning Gilded Age—the phrase with which Church's acquaintances Mark Twain and Charles Dudley Warner would christen the era in their satirical 1873 novel.

Presiding over the assembly was the legendary poet and publisher William Cullen Bryant, who was also the current president of the Century Association, the club to which Church and so many of his friends belonged. "Bryant looked like Homer," a fellow Centurion observed, with his balding head, bushy eyebrows, floating whiskers, and long white beard.

Gazing out over his august audience, the old man began to speak. New York, Bryant asserted, could now claim to be "the third great city of the civilized world," after London and Paris. It was the largest city in the United States, its population having tripled over the past three decades so that it now approached one million. With the completion of the transcontinental railroad in 1869, the city had become the gateway for people and goods moving across North America from Europe, and even on to China and back. Yet for all the efforts of its leading citizens, Bryant argued, the city remained better known for its conspicuous consumption, extreme inequality, and labor unrest than for its cultural achievements. Church concurred wholeheartedly. He would later describe New York to a friend as "Gotham that uneasy City where the roar of the Bears and Bulls drown[s] every sound pleasant to hear."

The men gathered at the Union League Club that night agreed it was time for New York to have an art museum worthy of the city's world stature. Bryant played on his listeners' prideful feelings. It was an embarrassment that so many smaller nations and poorer cities had famous art museums, he suggested. A great museum would give wealthy New Yorkers a place to share their extraordinary collections with their fellow citizens. It would allow American artists to learn from the art of Europe and give them ample room to display their own large works on significant subjects. And a museum would provide wholesome entertainment in a city bursting with tawdry attractions. Bryant's audience received these arguments with enthusiasm, and that night at the Union League Club the Metropolitan Museum of Art was born.

Church was elected to the organizing committee and soon joined three additional committees. He was already drowning in responsibilities, and he found himself constantly ill that winter, but he was too exhilarated by the museum work, the plans for the new house, and his family. Isabel was expecting another child in the spring. "The children are preposterously well—cheeks, chins, noses, all rosy—and their spirits are unquenchable," Church wrote Osborn just after New Year's of 1870. The ponds had frozen, and the skating was good. "The weather is splendid, mild, clear and quiet. Gorgeous sunsets and brilliant nights. I am painting small pictures."

IN APRIL 1870, ISABEL GAVE birth at Cosy Cottage to a baby boy, Louis Palmer Church. His first name was for Louis Legrand Noble, his middle name for Church's sculptor friend Erastus Dow Palmer. Church's excitement shone through in his letters announcing Louis's arrival. "The baby is a fine fellow—the other two are splendid—I am in high health and in never better spirits," he wrote to Palmer. The Farm seemed especially beautiful that spring. Watching Isabel as she rested on the grass under the blooming apple boughs in May, he thought the trees looked "like mountains of bridal bouquets" piled around her.

That same month, Church bought a hundred thousand bricks. He knew from his travels in Italy, Greece, Syria, and Egypt that even the mightiest structures raised by humans would eventually crumble, but he planned to enfold Isabel and the children in a dwelling as enduring and original as any ever seen on the Hudson. He had been moving walls and towers around in his mind for months as he tried to adapt architectural elements from the Holy Land. Persia had been too far east to visit in person, but Church reveled in the colors and patterns he found in illustrated books about Persian architecture and ornamentation. The design work was slow, but he loved it. "I enjoy this being afloat on a vast ocean," he told a friend, "or paddling along in the dreamy belief that I shall reach the desired port in due time."

By now, Vaux had produced a preliminary exterior drawing based in part on Church's suggestions. The mansion would have a tower, a central court hall flanked by several wings, and large windows to frame the spectacular river and mountain views. Church and Vaux continued to tinker with the floor plan, but they soon converged on a satisfying design. At the same time, work was being completed on a stable that incorporated living quarters for the masons and carpenters who would build the house. Church sent his farmer down to New York to find additional men to work on the house and grounds. At Castle Garden—precursor to Ellis Island as the main gateway for tens of thousands of immigrants arriving from Europe—Church's farmer offered work to some of the new arrivals, including a Swiss German man with experience growing grapes and orchard fruits. None of the hired hands spoke English, but Church managed to convey what he wanted done. Before long he had about fifteen laborers digging out a cellar on the hilltop with the aid of oxen so powerful that the men applauded as the animals hauled out huge stones. Every day Church strode energetically up and down the steep slope as he moved among Cosy Cottage, his hillside studio, and the construction site about five hundred feet farther up the hill.

One day in late June, three-and-a-half-year-old Freddie, who often played outside, was suddenly gone. Panicked, Church and Isabel enlisted farmhands and laborers to help scour the property, to no avail. Then they started along the roads toward the river and the train tracks. It was his farmer's son who finally found the little boy walking along a road, carefree and unharmed. He had decided he wanted to catch a train, as his father often did. Church told Osborn afterward that Freddie had "mounted on a stick and actually rode his imaginary steed four miles when he discovered he was on the wrong road. . . . He walked eight miles altogether." When the boy was brought home, he took a bedraggled bouquet of wildflowers out of his shirt and presented them to his mother. Freddie would perfect this pattern as a young man: embark on a harebrained escapade, distress his parents, and try to placate them with an apologetic offering.

AS THE NEW HOUSE SLOWLY rose, neighbors began wandering over to watch. Sometimes they found Church giving orders and trying to explain what he wanted. He joked to a friend about the challenge of conveying his vision to local craftsmen whose idea of a good building was "a brick school house or meeting house or jail." In October he wrote to Heade, "I have 9631201 problems in Architecture and construction given me to solve daily." But Church loved the challenge of creating a three-dimensional work of art, even as he continued to work in the medium that had made him wealthy and famous. He was painting a picture of Jerusalem on a commission from a former mayor of Hartford, who was reportedly going to pay $10,000 for it.

The vantage point Church had chosen was the Mount of Olives, and he was unfurling an extraordinary sky over the top half of a canvas more than seven feet long and four feet tall. Storm clouds as thick and angry as the ash exploding from his 1862 *Cotopaxi* billowed away from the city, chased off by a great light streaming from above. As Church painted, he was fired by his memories of the Holy City, but also by the beauty of the land and sky around him. He sometimes grabbed his paints and went out to try to capture the Hudson Valley. "We are having splendid Meteoric displays," he wrote Heade. "Magnificent sunsets and Auroras—red, green, yellow, and blue—and such—in profusion[;] I have actually been drawn away from my usual steady devotion to the new house to sketch some of the fine things hung in the sky."

Church finished *Jerusalem from the Mount of Olives* in November 1870 and put it on view at Goupil's the following April. He provided a numbered key to the scene, so that the crowds that gathered day after day could pick out the significant religious sites he had depicted. To some critics, the display smacked of commercialism, and Church's decision to show the picture at Goupil's instead of at the National Academy provoked the usual pique. But the *Herald* conceded that the picture contained "dazzling general effects," while a reviewer from a Hartford paper declared it "his best painting."

Church next launched himself on another commissioned picture, this one of the Parthenon. For the architectural details, he studied the photographs he had purchased in Athens, but for the colors he drew from his oil sketches and his memory. As he worked, a deep blue sky appeared on his canvas and the air took on the crystalline light of Greece. In the middle distance, he painted one small figure, who leaned against a broken slab of marble. Far beyond this figure, the Parthenon stood huge and radiant atop a field of ruins.

Sometimes when he had finished painting for the day, Church left his studio and walked up to where the walls of his new house were rising. This dwelling would be his Cedar Grove, where an artist-patriarch presided over peaceful domesticity. It would be his Parthenon, enduring long after frailer structures had collapsed. It would be his New Jerusalem, where his renewed family would worship their God even as they cherished the creations of other faiths. And it would be his cosmos in miniature, celebrating Humboldt's life and vision. Paintings from Church's travels—including his copy of Humboldt's portrait—would hang in every room. The objects he had collected on those travels would honor Humboldt's curiosity about global cultures. Books by Humboldt and his scientific followers would line the shelves of the library. Every window would frame a magnificent vista of trees, water, earth, and sky.

Church spent his days in a blissful blur of creativity. "I match every stone that is laid, examine every timber, direct almost everything—no matter how trivial," he told Osborn, "—and when night comes, I have out my portfolio and drawing board and work late and hard."

He loved to see his children flourishing in the countryside. "The three boys are as sturdy as possible," he wrote in the summer of 1871, "and I think enjoy existence as much as is permitted to our kind." With a watchful nursemaid, the boys explored the Farm on one of the donkeys, Winnie and Louis sitting in panniers to either side and Freddie riding in the middle, a scene Church found "highly picturesque." Another donkey pulled the boys' nursemaid in a little cart, and together they went on picnics.

On July 17, 1871, Isabel gave birth to a girl, her first since Emma. They named her Isabel Charlotte, for her mother and for Church's late sister. "We are all in an extasy [*sic*] over a pretty plump little baby girl," Church wrote to Osborn. She soon acquired a nickname: Downie. She was soft and gentle as a baby chick compared to her three boisterous older brothers, who were all under five years old when she was born. Beginning with Bertie in 1862, Isabel had given birth to six children in just under nine years.

CHAPTER 23

"A Model of Rank and File Citizenship"

Church knew how privileged he was to have a refuge in the countryside. His train route to New York City began among riverside meadows and groves. He disembarked among the hog pens, manure yards, and oil refineries that dominated the west side of Manhattan. From the train depot at Thirty-Third Street and Tenth Avenue, he faced a dismal walk of about forty minutes to his Tenth Street studio, unless he could find space on a horsecar somewhere along the route.

New York had only become denser, dirtier, and more dangerous in the twenty-five years since his arrival. The great green spaces of the new Central Park were open to all, but even the southern end of the park was far uptown—it began at Fifty-Ninth Street, out of reach for most New Yorkers, especially those in the packed tenements of Lower Manhattan. "Fever-nests," a recent public health report had branded the tenements. Yet many New Yorkers couldn't call even these unsanitary hovels home. An 1865 guidebook estimated that there were nearly thirty-one thousand homeless people—the "out-door poor."

Civic reformers were pushing for money and attention to be directed toward the city's needier residents. One of the most fervent was Frederick Law Olmsted, who advocated for green spaces open to all. After he and Vaux had overseen the creation of Central Park, Olmsted had thrown his energies into running the wartime U.S. Sanitary Commission, and then he and Vaux had collaborated on Prospect Park, across the East River in the city of Brooklyn. Now they were back at the helm of Central Park, which had been sadly mismanaged for the past several years by an administration composed of men whom Olmsted judged to be political hacks. In November 1871, he asked Church to consider serving as one of five commissioners who managed the city's parks and squares.

That he and Church were distant cousins was far less important to Olmsted than Church's reputation for integrity and his conscientious service to the new museum. It also meant a good deal that Vaux spoke highly of him. Olmsted confided to a friend that he saw Church as "a model of rank and file citizenship, but who in his special calling has earned the respect and regard of the community." Olmsted hoped that the appointment of an eminent artist would signal that the city prized "devotion to art and the study of Nature."

Church knew from his endless delight in country life how vital and restorative green space could be for city dwellers. His parents had taught him that as both a Christian and a citizen of a republic he must devote himself to the improvement of his community. Despite his already-punishing schedule, Church agreed to be nominated for a five-year term as a parks commissioner. On November 23, 1871, he was sworn in by Mayor A. Oakey Hall.

Thus began Church's life as a public servant. His primary duties included attending meetings, reviewing reports about the parks, and approving or denying expenditures. Now he would have to take the train down from the Farm to New York even more often; fortunately, within a week of his swearing-in, his train was pulling into Cornelius Vanderbilt's new Grand Central Depot. Rivaling any station in Europe for scale and majesty, it was a wrought-iron palace whose ceilings arched nearly a hundred feet above the tracks. Natural light poured through its glass-paneled roof during the day, and at night immense gas chandeliers threw a warm aura over the steam and smoke billowing from the locomotives.

For Church, it was an easy stroll south from the station down Park Avenue to the Osborns' luxurious new townhouse between Thirty-Fifth and Thirty-Sixth, where a guest room was always ready for him and Isabel. Inside the house, the walls were dense with paintings. Two of Church's great South American landscapes, *The Andes of Ecuador* and *Chimborazo*, spoke of the Osborns' long-standing admiration for his artistry and their pride in displaying his work among their treasures.

Church and Isabel had grown ever closer to W.H. and Virginia Osborn in recent years. With the war over, Osborn's responsibilities at the Illinois Central headquarters in Chicago had eased somewhat, and the family could spend more time in New York. Osborn wasn't as lighthearted and witty as Church; he was an authoritative man accustomed to dealing with presidents and generals. But he and Church had developed a warm rapport nonetheless. Osborn advised Church on travel logistics and financial matters; Church counseled Osborn on the Park Avenue townhouse and his new country house at Garrison, New York, across the Hudson from West Point. Church and Isabel invited the Osborns to the Farm; the Osborns encouraged the Churches to think of 32 Park as a second home. In 1870, Osborn tried to give Church a horse, a gesture so extravagant that Church didn't at first understand that it was a gift and, once he did, felt he couldn't accept it. "You

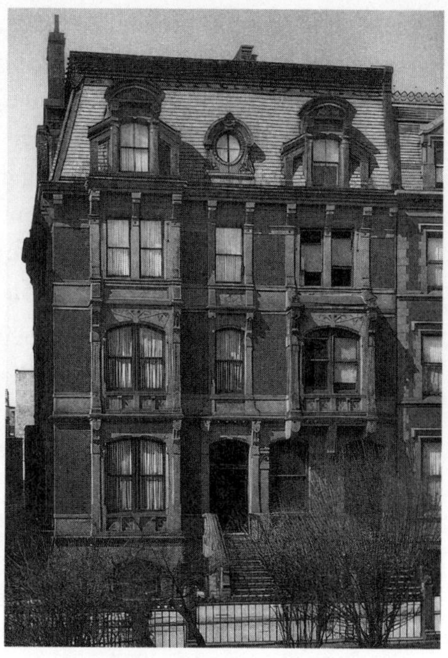

The Osborn residence at 32 Park Avenue, by Richard Morris Hunt

are always so kind that it becomes almost embarrasing [*sic*] to know what to say," he confessed to Osborn afterward. "I can do so little in return for your many kindnesses and favors."

IN HIS FIRST YEAR AS a commissioner, Church attended more than two dozen meetings at the Parks office opposite City Hall. On the far side of City Hall, the colossal New York and Brooklyn Bridge was under construction across the East River. When it was finally completed, it would soar almost three hundred feet above the river, but in late 1871, much of the work was still invisible. Day and night in enormous underwater structures called caissons, men were splitting boulders, bailing water, hauling mud, and trying to avoid "caisson disease," a painful and sometimes fatal condition brought on by ascending too rapidly to the surface.

While the bridge builders labored in dark, damp chambers deep in the river, Church and his fellow commissioners conducted the dry business that kept the city's parks and squares green and pleasant. They considered the grading of roads, the repair of broken pavement, and the laying of pipes in Central Park to create skating ponds. They authorized the purchase of sprinklers, scythes, mowing machines, lanterns, grass seed, trees, horse fodder, and innumerable other items. They agreed that dogs could enter parks only "when led by a chain or proper dog-string not exceeding five feet in length." On May 8, 1872, they approved the purchase—for the Central Park Menagerie—of three storks and a pelican for $100 and a kangaroo for $75.

Olmsted joined the commission in mid-1872 as president and treasurer, positioning himself to guide two major construction projects affecting Central Park—the new art museum and the American Museum of Natural History, which was going up on the west side of the park at West Seventy-Ninth Street. Vaux was collaborating on the design of both buildings with Jacob Wrey Mould, a British architect who had contributed many decorative elements and structures to Central Park. At one Parks meeting, Church introduced a resolution to begin work at the site recently chosen for the art museum, at the eastern edge of Central Park on Fifth Avenue in the sparsely settled eighties. All present voted in favor. New York was to have a permanent home for a world-class museum of art.

IN THE SPRING OF 1872, Church unveiled *The Parthenon* at Goupil's. The picture was a striking departure for him. He had chosen an angle and framing that omitted the Acropolis's ravishing backdrop of cerulean sea, distant islands, and mountains of the Peloponnese. Instead, he focused closely on the Parthenon and the scattered ruins around it. He painted the foreground in shadow, so that the sunlight bathing the Parthenon was all the more dazzling. The world's oldest symbol of democracy still stood triumphantly on its hilltop despite the ravages of time and war. Church underscored his allusive intent with the single small figure he had added among the ruins—a man wearing the garments adopted by many Greek men during and after the War of Independence. With this invocation of another people's nineteenth-century battle for democracy, Church gestured to the ongoing struggles in the United States to restore and strengthen democratic institutions after a devastating war.

The reviewers saw only Church's technical skill. Some praised him for the picture's simplicity and realism; others faulted him for the same thing. "It is the Parthenon without a soul," one critic carped. Church had been hearing similar complaints for years, but they seemed to be taking on a sharper tone. He adopted his usual approach to reviews, focusing his energies on what mattered most to him—his family, the new house, his next painting projects, and the plans for the new museum.

BY THAT FALL, THE BUILDERS had completed enough work that Church and Isabel could move the children from Cosy Cottage into the imposing new mansion on the hill, which Church, only half-joking, referred to as their "Feudal Castle." A relative who visited in October dubbed it a "Persian palace" and "the wonder of the world." The massive building was anchored at one corner by a four-story square tower so large that its first floor contained an ample parlor. The exterior walls were faced with pale brown stone, giving it a vaguely fortresslike air, but this austerity was quickly relieved as the eye traveled over the profusion of porches, balconies, windows, and doors that sprouted from the façade. The house was rather like Church himself—a bit reserved at first, but then relaxing to the point of playfulness. He had arranged polychrome bricks and tiles to create vibrant patterns that grew ever more ornate in the upper stories. Stacked layers of stencils danced along the cornices beneath a roofline enlivened by chimneys, towers, and gables. Even the roof, clad in small hexagonal tiles of multicolored slate, glinted where Church had interspersed gilt tiles.

Inside, the twelve-foot ceilings soared above the children's heads as they ran through patches of sun thrown by the first-floor windows. The heart of the house was the Court Hall, a large, cruciform room reminiscent of the interior courtyards the Churches had admired in Beyrout and Damascus. In the harsher climate of the Catskills, they couldn't leave this room open to the sky, but on its south side were large glass doors leading to the Ombra, a wide porch that offered a panorama of the Hudson and the Catskills—"one of the finest views of river & mountain in the country," as Church's friend McEntee described it in his diary. The windows framed the views as if they were paintings.

Church designed the dining room expressly for displaying the old paintings he had acquired in Rome. He omitted windows from its one long exterior wall and hung his paintings there instead. The family's living quarters were reached by a broad staircase that ascended from the Court Hall, and the second-floor bedrooms offered vertiginous views over the Hudson Valley. The children's nursery, with east-facing windows, was reached by a small staircase tucked near Isabel's bedroom.

Craftsmen would be working in the downstairs rooms for years to come. When the Osborns had been preparing to move into their new townhouse, Church sympathized about the ongoing chaos of construction in a letter to Osborn: "Of course the sound of the saw and the hammer continues—carpenters cling affectionately to their work and are as hard to oust from a new house as cats are from an old one. They have to be driven out inch by inch—but in fact the thousand little things—hinges, locks, knobs, &c., &c., require much time to dispose of."

Once the shell of the house was complete, Church turned to interior design, spending hours with British and French books on Middle Eastern architecture and design. He drew hundreds of sketches as he and Isabel discussed the details of woodwork, fireplaces, door panels, and paint colors. He mixed the paints for the interior colors himself.

Church borrowed liberally from French, Ottoman, Persian, Moorish, Armenian, and other traditions, repurposing ornamentation from domestic and sacred architecture to create an utterly original home. No other American had ever combined so many influences in one dwelling, and few had yet drawn on Middle Eastern motifs, which were only just beginning to reach American audiences. As Church tinkered with what he frequently described as his "Persian" home, he lumped cultural elements together casually, sometimes indiscriminately. Yet he admired the visual sophistication of these cultures so intensely that he wanted to spend the rest of his days surrounded by their borrowed radiance. In later years, Church worked with the painter and designer Lockwood de Forest to incorporate intricately carved furniture, mantelpieces, and screens sourced from Indian craftsmen at the workshop that de Forest established in Ahmedabad in 1881.

Reporters soon began to visit the unusual new house. They marveled at its towers and balconies, its inventively patterned walls and roof, and its awe-inspiring views of the Hudson and the Catskills. It was, one reporter wrote, "a bright open eyed house, presenting on the landscape sides an almost unbroken expanse of plate-glass windows." Young painters set up easels near the river below the house, shading their canvases with white umbrellas, a sight that made Church nostalgic for his early days of plein air painting. He told McEntee that he was hoping to paint outdoors again soon, if his wrist would only stop hurting.

When McEntee came for a visit at the new house, he noticed that his friend seemed "troubled." Church was feeling especially burdened by his frequent trips to the city. He never wavered in his passion for the new museum, but he was growing tired of his government duties on the parks commission. He wanted to spend his days painting landscapes, or designing stencils and balustrades. Instead, he was mired in bureaucratic squabbles and pestered by acquaintances seeking jobs. He told Osborn in early 1873 that he was "anxious to be rid of an office which I am not fitted for and which consumes so much of the time that might be more profitably employed on another sort of canvas." Osborn offered to see the mayor about relieving Church of his post. As luck would have it, Church's position on the commission was called into question that spring by an alderman who objected that his main residence was upstate. When the parks commissioners convened in May 1873, Church was no longer among them.

"Absolutely Startling"

A Bedouin man stood in Church's hillside studio. A burgundy keffiyeh covered the man's head and shoulders, and a striped cloak billowed around him. Church studied the drape of the man's clothes as he made some quick oil sketches.

It was late winter 1874. He had nearly completed a large picture on a subject drawn from his trip to Petra, and for scale and drama, he wanted to paint in several small human figures. Being nearly six thousand miles from the Bedouin men he had seen in Petra, however, Church prevailed upon a friend from Catskill to model. Benjamin Stone, a fellow painter, had a fierce, faraway gaze and a luxuriant beard. Church asked Stone to pose in some of the garments he had brought back from the Holy Land, and once he had gotten the sketches he needed, he thanked Stone with some gifts and went back to work on his big canvas.

The picture was unlike any other he had attempted. There was no sky in it, and, aside from a thicket of dusty-green shrubs, no landscape. Standing in his studio as ice floes choked the Hudson below, Church had imagined himself back at Petra, walking behind his Bedouin guides through the shadowy, winding canyon. Over and over he had relived the moment when that sun-struck façade had suddenly blazed forth at him. That was what he was trying to capture, that flashing instant of revelation when he had beheld Al-Khazneh—the majestic tomb known as the Treasury.

Church painted two tiny figures in the darkness to the left of the canyon's opening. In Petra, he had been afraid that his armed Bedouin guides might harm him when he began to paint. Now he harnessed the memory of

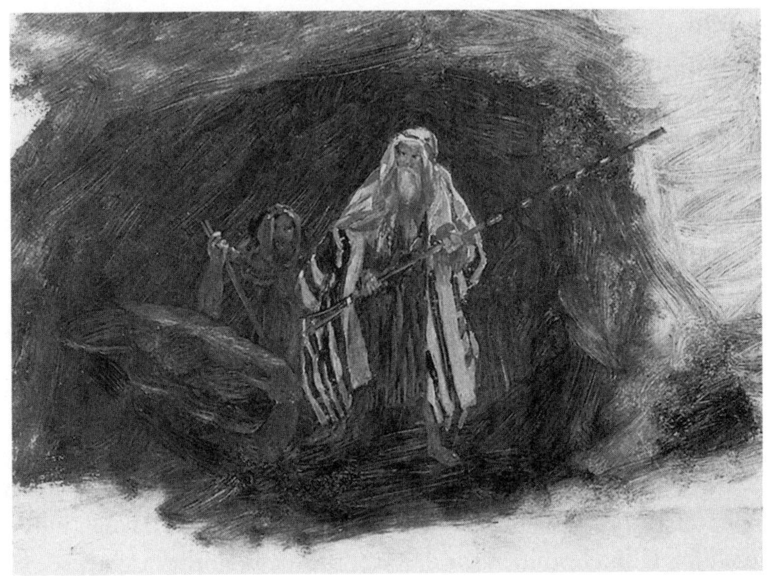

Church's oil sketch of his neighbor Benjamin Stone as a Bedouin, 1874

that fear. The two Bedouin he painted were lurking in the shadows, glints of metal hinting that they were armed. His treatment of the Treasury façade, by contrast, was bright and precise. The sun threw its intricacy into relief, an effect heightened by his painstaking depiction of every curve and corner. The capitals of the columns sprouted curls and leaflets, and the dentils on the soaring cornices were so clear they could be counted.

Church gave the picture a simple title—*El Khasné Petra*—but it depicted something complex and intangible. It was an emotional and spiritual portrait of what he had experienced at Petra: first fear, then reverence, awe, and a touch of melancholy. Human beings had the power to create astonishing beauty, but they would inevitably die, their names and lives unknown to those who came later to wander among their creations. Eventually their creations, too, would crumble and vanish. Go ahead, Church's new painting suggested, revel in the heights of human achievement, but always cultivate humility.

The painting was so different from what people expected of him. He decided not to chance a solo presentation at Goupil's, sending it instead to the crowded walls of the National Academy's annual exhibition, which would open in April.

After decades of renting space around the city, the academy had in the 1860s constructed its own building at the corner of Twenty-Third Street and Fourth Avenue. Designed as an airy Venetian palazzo, it looked as though the Ducal Palace had floated down and come to rest among the heavy brownstones and sign-plastered storefronts. Church had been associated with the academy for almost three decades, but he had shown a painting in the new building only in 1868, when *Niagara Falls* had been included in a show of American pictures recently returned from the Exposition Universelle in Paris.

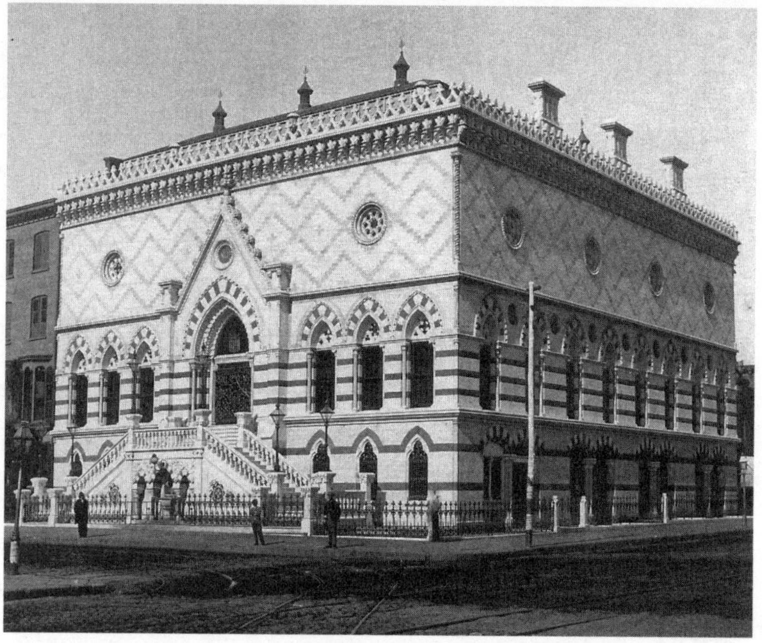

The National Academy of Design, by P. B. Wright

Now, six years later, he made his return with *El Khasné Petra*, a picture *The New York Times* called "absolutely startling." "There are few artists who would have attempted to cover so large a canvas with such very simple elements, but Mr. Church has made the essay, and can have no reason to repent of his temerity." The *Herald* appreciated the picture's symbolic power and emotional effect. "The ruins of the present call up to the mind vividly the story of the past and help us to recognize something of the glory of a civilization that has passed away, leaving monuments in presence of which the monuments we build seem frail and perishable indeed."

Nestled inside this universal message was a more personal meaning. Church had chosen to focus his Petra painting on the Treasury just as he and Isabel were settling into a treasury of their own, a place where they hoped to safeguard their children. Church didn't sell *El Khasné Petra*. Instead, he gave it to Isabel, and they hung it in a sitting room off the Court Hall that was Isabel's domain, above a fireplace whose surround was made of pink marble that echoed the color of the Treasury. Opposite, a full-length window framed a view of the Hudson.

THE SAME MONTH *EL KHASNÉ PETRA* went on display, a small but seismic exhibition opened in Paris, near the new opera house designed by Charles Garnier. Some of the pictures looked more like oil sketches than like finished paintings. One depicted a woman playing hide-and-seek with a little girl in a meadow whose plants were just blurry suggestions. The facial features of the woman and the girl were indicated by mere stabs of the brush. A seascape was even less polished, covered in horizontal smudges of paint, with a few diagonal slashes here and there. The only object in sharp focus was the rising sun, an orange ball hanging in a smoke-filled sky over an industrial harbor. A few strokes of orange brightened the sky and traced the reflection of the sun on the water, but otherwise the canvas was a blur of blue and gray. The title was *Impression, Sunrise*.

The picture of the mother and child was by Berthe Morisot, and the sunrise was by Claude Monet. They were two of thirty-one painters whose works were on view in a spring show organized by artists frustrated with the constraints of the tightly controlled annual Salon, an event sponsored by the French state. Not all the pictures were as loosely rendered as Morisot's and Monet's, but those that were drew the special notice of critics, who were divided in their reactions. "A vexatious mystification for the public," complained one, while another wrote of "slap-dash" brushstrokes and "palette-scrapings." But still another critic rejoiced at the works' originality. "These youths have a way of understanding nature which is neither boring nor banal. It is lively, sharp, light; it is delightful." The only appropriate term for these artists, he mused, was "Impressionists."

The new style would soon find acolytes among young American artists studying in France. When they and their paintings eventually reached the

United States, the art world that had nurtured Church, and which he had in turn helped bring to international prominence, would be upended. For now, however, the Paris show went unnoticed in New York.

CHURCH RELIED ON ISABEL IN a thousand ways. Like almost every other American woman of her generation and social class, she had no career of her own. Instead, she supported Church's career by running the household and caring for their children. She gave the servants instructions on meals and housekeeping, and she cut flowers for the dining table and gathered leaves to press as decorations for the nursery walls. Although she was usually deferential toward her self-confident and decisive husband, she could be insistent when she chose. On these occasions, Church submitted amiably to her wishes, especially when he encountered a certain "calm decided voice which admits of no appeal." He joked to a friend about "the terrorism caused by Mrs. Church's reproofs."

When Isabel found time to sit down at her desk, she replied to letters or perused volumes of sermons and spiritual essays, copying out passages that interested her. Plagued by chronically poor health, she derived peace and fortitude from religious readings. She devoted the rest of her limited energy to keeping her husband comfortable and happy. "His mind seems to require change as much as his body, and meeting fresh people diverts him," she told Virginia Osborn, her closest confidante. Both Church and Isabel loved having guests, whether for a meal, a weekend, or a longer stay. When she extended an invitation to McEntee and his wife, McEntee reflected in his journal that Isabel "must be lonely there and long for some congenial companion." Lovely as the estate was, if Church had business in the city and there were no guests, Isabel was left alone with the children and the household staff. McEntee suspected that even when Church was home, Isabel probably craved the novelty of friends.

The parade of guests began even before the new house was completed. The list was curated to include people who were fascinating yet unpretentious. Aside from the Osborns, the Churches' friends were mostly artists, writers, and clergymen. People who were "simply rich are blights on the fun of country life," Church wrote. "We wear our old clothes—ride in lumber wagons if we wish to—our children dress according to common sense dictation. We are not ashamed to offer our friends ham and eggs—in fact we are rather proud we have it to offer—and if we fall a little short in our fare at supper—we can usually recompence our hungry guests by a substantial sunset." So instead of playing host to Vanderbilts and Astors at dances and tea parties, they offered hikes and donkey-cart rides. Despite his wealth, Church still embraced the republican principles he had enshrined in so many paintings, especially self-reliance and the rejection of aristocracy.

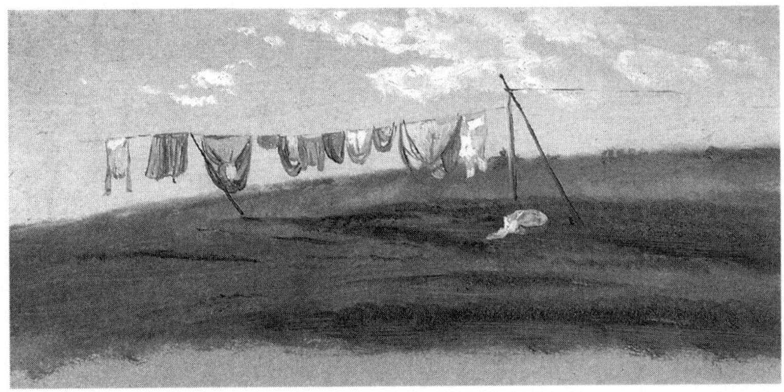

Oil sketch of drying laundry by Church, c. 1870

CHURCH WAS TAKING THE TRAIN to New York so often these days, he joked to Heade, he should apply for a job as a conductor so he could travel for free. When his friend Palmer ribbed him for swanning off to the city, Church invited him to come "on one of my trips and follow me around all day and half of the night and then if you can call it an idle time, I will ask you to try it again." In New York, Church was constantly on the move, meeting with dealers and patrons, purchasing things for the new house, and conferring with his fellow trustees of the Metropolitan Museum.

He also saw a great deal of his artist friends, especially Whittredge, Heade, Gifford, and McEntee. Church was far wealthier than all of them, and he frequently treated them to dinner at restaurants or invited them and their wives to the theater. Still, he could be insensitive about his privileged position. "He never knew what poverty was," Whittredge would recall years later. McEntee, who struggled to find buyers for his subtle landscape paintings, found Church's good fortune painful at times. "Church is very friendly to me," McEntee noted in his diary after one of their dinners. He "told me of the carpets he had bought today and lots of other things. He has plenty of money and cannot conceive the wretchedness I suffer from the lack of it."

W.H. and Virginia Osborn had no such complications in their relationship with the Churches. They continued to lavish gifts on Church and Isabel. For Christmas in 1874, they gave Isabel an extravagant sealskin cloak and muff. "Perhaps you can imagine how astonished Isabel was," Church wrote to Osborn. "I know your aversion to being thanked. I can only wait for opportunities." Church stayed with the Osborns when he came to the city on solo business trips, but sometimes he remained behind with the children—"the chicks," as he called them—and sent Isabel to enjoy its diversions and to spend time with Virginia Osborn. Each couple now had three sons and a daughter. Downie Church, at three years old, was the youngest in her family; the Osborns' daughter, Virginia, now twenty, was the oldest child in hers.

When W.H. and Virginia left for Europe in early 1875, the Churches and the Osborns were separated for several months. The oldest Osborn boy, Fairfield, remained at Princeton, while the two younger sons, Frederick and William, stayed with a relative in the city. W.H. and his daughter had become especially close as she reached adulthood, and he was a "proud and fond" father, Mrs. Osborn wrote. "He has spoken again and again of her bright quick appreciation of nature and art." In Italy, the younger Virginia frightened her parents by falling ill. She complained of a headache and a stiff neck, and they returned to Paris to consult doctors, one of whom diagnosed cerebral meningitis. Virginia died on May 8. The Osborns held a private funeral in their Paris rooms, and then they took their daughter's coffin home to be buried.

Less than two months later, seventeen-year-old Frederick Osborn drowned while swimming in the Hudson. The Osborns, like the Churches, had now lost two children in quick succession. Virginia and Isabel found a measure of solace in their friendship and in their faith. Their husbands, by contrast, didn't discuss their religious beliefs or their innermost feelings with each other in their frequent letters, but something had clearly changed in Osborn after the death of his children. A forceful, confident man who was used to being in control, he developed an anxious streak, as Mrs. Osborn tried to explain to one of her surviving sons: "It is a serious matter to have only two boys, one wants to know just where they are all the time."*

* The surviving Osborn sons would go on to positions of leadership in New York City. William Church Osborn became a prominent lawyer and served as a president of the Metropolitan Museum. His older brother Fairfield became a celebrated paleontologist (he named *Tyrannosaurus rex* in 1905) and served as a president of the American Museum of Natural History. Fairfield Osborn was also an influential eugenicist.

That year the Osborns, avoiding their empty house, joined the Churches for Christmas. Around this time, Church took dictation for a letter that Freddie wanted to send to Santa Claus. "I want some little sail boats to sail in the bath tub in the New House, and a little steam boat to play on the floor," he wrote, "—and two horses with wheels hitched up to a little waggon [*sic*]—And I want a little toy watch—and a little pitcher and a wooden toy knife—and a box of soldiers." Freddie was kind enough to mention the toys he thought his siblings would enjoy: "—and a little wagon for Downie to drag about the house, and a little toy chair for Louis and if it is too small for Downie—and a little pair of tongs and a shovel for me—And I would like a little bridge to put over the bath tub, a toy cow for Winnie and a toy watch too. And a little sled for Louis. And a little sled with two little horses for Downie to drag about the house. And a toy fox with wheels for Louis."

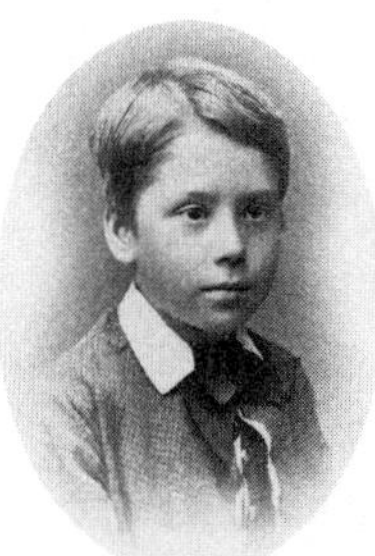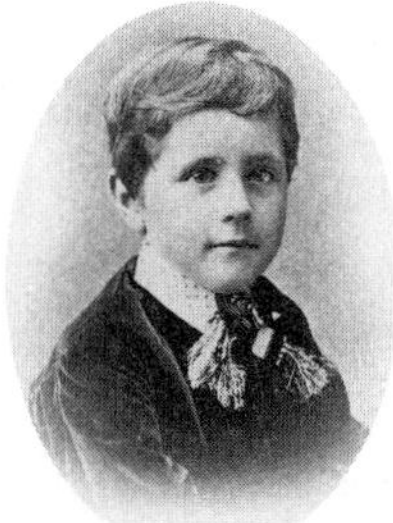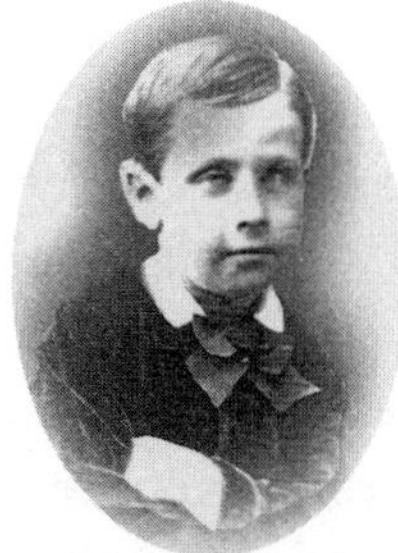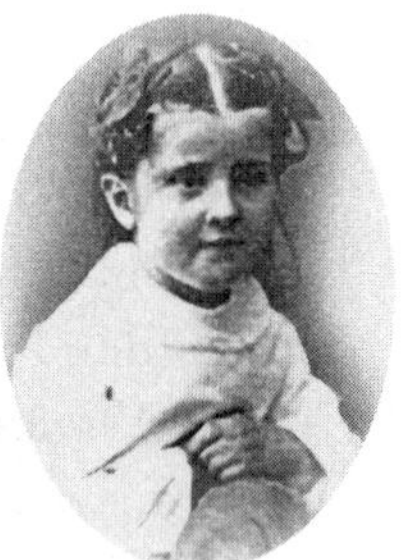

Freddie, Winnie, Louis, and Downie Church, c. 1875

The scene at the Churches' house on Christmas morning reminded Virginia Osborn of the holidays when she and her husband had watched their own four small children opening presents, but she concealed her sadness when she wrote of it afterward. The Churches "seemed so truly delighted to have us with them, that we felt as if we were giving as well as receiving pleasure," Mrs. Osborn told her mother. "Freddy Church reminded his mamma in the course of the day, that she had told him Santa Claus was poor this year, but he did not see any signs of it."

Frederic and Isabel had, in truth, been spending lavishly on the construction and furnishings of their new house, even as the art market was contracting in the wake of the financial panic that had swept the United States and Europe in 1873. Not long after Christmas, however, their circumstances suddenly changed. In February 1876, Church's father died at the age of eighty-two. Joseph Church had spent his whole life working, investing, and making money, as an obituary in the Hartford paper noted, adding that his son was the "eminent artist." When the estate was settled, Church inherited more than $80,000 in cash (at a time when a carpenter in New York City could expect to earn no more than $1,000 a year), and another $124,000 worth of investments and real estate. Church's mother and his surviving sister, Elizabeth, would continue to occupy the Hartford mansion, which, although stately in its New England way, was quaint compared to Frederic and Isabel's new hilltop villa.

CHAPTER 25

"This Glorious Country"

Even at fifty, after all his travels and achievements, Church was as awed by the natural world as he had been as a young man sketching at Cole's side. Church never stopped trying to capture the Hudson River and the ever-changing skies above it. "I cannot do it justice," he confided to a friend, urging him to come "see for yourself this glorious country where we reside."

As Church marked half a century on May 4, 1876, the United States was preparing to observe a milestone of its own: the centennial of the Declaration of Independence. On May 10, President Grant inaugurated the largest and longest celebration in the history of the nation. The high point in the many months of festivities would be the Fourth of July.

Americans had already started arguing about plans for the centennial in the 1860s. It was to be a world's fair, so that the United States could show people around the globe what it had achieved in its ten decades. Twenty-five years after the underwhelming American display at London's Great Exhibition of 1851, most people could agree that representatives of other countries ought to know about the innovations and triumphs of American art and industry. But which events and objects should be showcased? Who should be invited to participate in the American sections of the exhibition? What should the fair convey about the nation's recovery from the Civil War? Like Church, the United States was long past its youth, yet what kind of country it should aspire to be still provoked bitter disagreement. A world's fair offered a courtroom of sorts, where competing evidence could be weighed by a broad public.

First, however, Congress had to choose a host city. The Declaration of Independence had been signed in Philadelphia, but New Yorkers countered that their city was the most populous in the nation as well as the most economically and culturally significant. A few people tried to make a case for Boston, where so many consequential events in the Revolutionary War had unfolded, but no one outside the city took this idea too seriously. In the end, Philadelphia won the right to host the Centennial Exposition of 1876. While New Yorkers complained about the snub, the city's power brokers gathered to talk the matter over, and they soon began to lay plans for a separate New York centennial.

In Philadelphia, meanwhile, officials and private citizens had spent the next several years negotiating, squabbling, and finally cooperating on their plan. The London fair had covered twenty acres; the Philadelphia fair would cover ten times that. Exhibit halls had to be designed, built, and furnished with display cases and lighting. Fund drives were launched, and appeals for worthy submissions appeared in the papers. Invitations were extended to foreign governments to send their own exhibitions and delegations.

Just as had happened in New York's Metropolitan Fair of 1864, women were sidelined. A group of white women began to plan a pavilion where they could be sure their inventions and scientific research wouldn't be consigned to the least prominent display cases.

African American men and women were given still less encouragement by officials. Spurred by calls from Frederick Douglass and others, Black inventors, scientists, and artists decided to participate anyway.

AMONG THE GRANDEST BUILDINGS ERECTED on the Philadelphia fairgrounds was an art gallery for an international exhibition of painting and sculpture. Its organizers were confident that American artists would emerge looking as talented as any others in the world and American collectors as discerning. Fair officials appointed a Philadelphia engraver named John Sartain to oversee the selections for the American display. Sartain decided to feature works by both living and deceased American artists as well as foreign paintings from American collections. To help wade through the flood of anticipated submissions, he created a Committee on Selection composed of painters and sculptors from Boston, New York, and Philadelphia, the nation's three most important cities for the arts. Church's friend McEntee agreed to serve as one of the five committee members representing New York. He soon found himself attending weekly meetings and traveling up and down the coast by train as the committee worked to assemble the submissions in each city so they could make their decisions. "It is the most fatiguing work I ever did," McEntee complained in his journal.

Church wasn't interested in taking on committee work for the exposition, but he was amenable to sending a picture to Philadelphia; after all, he had done more than any other artist of his generation to foster international respect for American painting. He chose *Chimborazo*, completed in 1864 and currently hanging in the Osborns' townhouse. He was saving most of his best paintings for the centennial exhibition in New York.

It fell to McEntee to inform Osborn that *Chimborazo* had to be delivered to the selection committee for its judgment. Five weeks before the fair opened, however, Osborn objected to McEntee that Church, of all people, shouldn't have to submit his work to any committee. McEntee was bewildered by "how he thoroughly believed Church to be immensely beyond all other American artists." At least, McEntee noted in his journal, it was only Osborn who was being so "fussy." Church himself was "willing to do anything" the organizers needed, and he saw to it that *Chimborazo* made it to Philadelphia in time.

RAIN THREATENED THE OPENING CEREMONIES in Philadelphia on May 10. A sea of umbrellas bobbed above the massive crowd, blocking many fairgoers' sight lines toward the raised platform where several thousand dignitaries and honorees were taking their seats. The skies were clearing by the time President Grant arrived to the martial sounds of drumbeats and cornets and escorted by thousands of soldiers and sailors. The hero of the Union Army had come dressed in simple civilian clothes, the text of a brief speech tucked in his suit pocket.

The Centennial Exposition was meant to promote national healing and unity. From the Atlantic to the Pacific during that anniversary year, journalists and orators invoked the phrase inscribed on Senator Henry Clay's gravestone: "I know no North, no South, no East, no West." For Frederick Douglass, who had been invited to sit on the presidential platform during the opening ceremony, the nation's centennial arrived in a dark and bitter season. After all the bloodshed, after all the promises of support, the federal government was failing to protect the vulnerable millions it had liberated. "You turned us loose to the sky, to the storm . . . and, worst of all, you turned us loose to the wrath of our infuriated [former] masters," Douglass would rail a month later at the

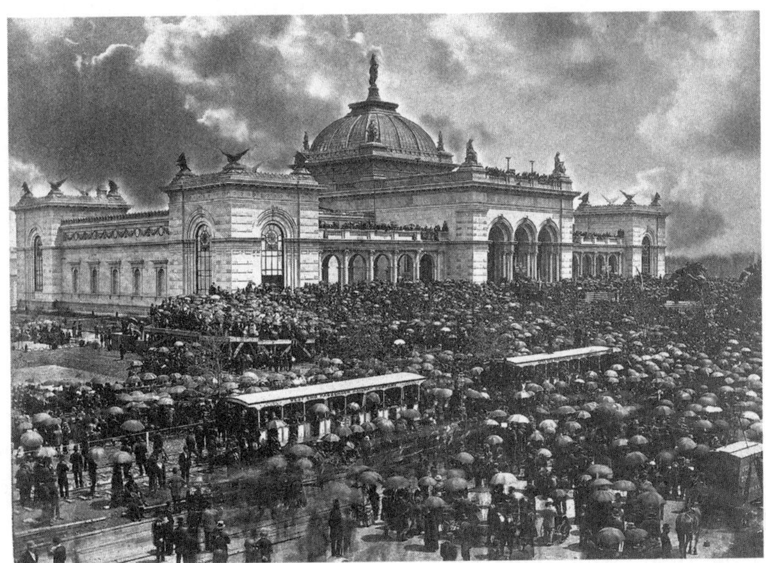

Opening day of the Centennial Exposition in Philadelphia, May 10, 1876

Republican National Convention. On May 10, Douglass almost didn't get to hear President Grant deliver his speech. The police guarding the entrance to the platform tried to bar his way, unable to comprehend that a Black man had been invited to join the honorees.

When Grant, after the usual congratulations and thanks, invoked the nation's history, he did not mention the Civil War, or the coordinated attacks in the South on Black people, who were being brutalized and murdered for trying to exercise their rights under the Fourteenth and Fifteenth Amendments. Instead, he spoke of the "great primal works"—of "felling forests" and "subduing prairies" and founding schools and churches.

When the fairgrounds were opened, a British dignitary expressed astonishment at the swift transformation of the muddy wasteland he had seen during a visit nine months earlier. "A change, such as can only be seen in America, had come over the locality since my visit," he reported. Enormous exhibition halls, grand hotels, and more than two hundred other buildings stood on landscaped grounds traversed by graceful avenues. A new train line that was linked to municipal and national railroads carried visitors to, from, and around the fair.

Fifty-six nations and colonies had sent items for exhibition, but unlike in London in 1851 or Paris in 1867, the Americans had had several years to pull together their attractions, and this time they didn't have to fit everything into the holds of ships to cross the Atlantic. The American tools and machines, which covered fourteen acres, provoked particular interest among foreign visitors, including the British, who were so proud of their Industrial Revolution. Americans had designed water pumps powerful enough to extinguish fires in tall buildings and compressors that could refrigerate beer and meat on a commercial scale. A new contraption used electricity to produce light and another transmitted the sound of human speech between rooms or even buildings. Presiding over it all was a steam engine forty feet tall that could produce power equivalent to more than fourteen hundred horses—enough to run the hundreds of other American machines.

The countless exemplars of American technological innovation at the Centennial Exposition discomfited some foreign representatives. One Briton warned Parliament that the United States had become a nation that would "influence the civilization of the Western World for ages to come."

BEFORE THE FAIR, THERE HAD been talk of importing Native American men, women, and children from sundry Western tribes and installing them in a five-acre reservation on the fairgrounds, so visitors could watch them cook, make tools, and sew clothes from animal skins. This would be interesting for white people, the organizers thought, and would at the same time show the Native participants who traveled to Philadelphia how vast and powerful the United States was.

The plan foundered for lack of congressional approval, but the Smithsonian Institution had sent representatives across the continent to collect Native artifacts. Visitors saw totem poles, weapons, tobacco pipes, cookware, beadwork, pottery, and papier-mâché mannequins dressed as Native people, including a warrior who was wearing what looked like a belt of human scalps. The main effect of this haphazard assemblage was to confirm the Euro-American view that Native peoples were stuck at a primitive phase of cultural development. The artifacts did at least convey some of the complexity of the peoples usually lumped together as "Indians," with objects—some correctly labeled—from the Tlingit, Haida, Paiute, Hopi, Navajo, Apache, and Sioux, among others.

It was the Sioux who dampened the cheerful mood of the centennial fair on the Fourth of July. That was the day the news reached the Northeast that General George Armstrong Custer had been killed in late June along with all his men—more than two hundred of them—during a federal campaign to seize Sioux territory in the gold-rich Black Hills of Dakota.

Also interrupting the Fourth of July program was Susan B. Anthony of the National Woman Suffrage Association, who stood up in Independence Hall immediately after the reading of the Declaration of Independence and presented the male officials with the "Declaration of the Rights of the Women of the United States." As the flustered men tried to restore order, women distributed copies of the pamphlet. Outside, Anthony read the new declaration to the assembled crowd. "While the Nation is buoyant with patriotism," she began, "and all hearts are attuned to praise, it is with sorrow we come to strike the one discordant note." Elizabeth Cady Stanton, who had helped write the document, later recalled that the timing of the protest was an implied condemnation of the Founding Fathers "and their male descendants for their injustice and oppression." At the close of its first century, the United States was far from being a glorious country for everyone.

NEW YORK, THWARTED IN ITS effort to host the Centennial Exposition, had organized elaborate celebrations of its own. On the night of July 3, some twenty thousand citizens marched in a torchlight procession, cheered on by tens of thousands more lining streets illuminated by gas lamps, Chinese lanterns, and bonfires. Flags and bunting hung from nearly every tenement, townhouse, hotel, and office building. At Union Square, twenty-five brass bands accompanied a chorus of six hundred voices in patriotic songs. Fireworks blazed over the rivers. At midnight, church bells began pealing.

The next day, the Fourth of July, crowds packed the Academy of Music near Union Square to hear an admired Congregational pastor named Richard Storrs assert that the greatness of the United States in 1876 was most abundantly manifest in New York. His argument was convoluted but daring. "This City, if any place on the continent, should have been the one where a reckless wickedness should have had sure prevalence, and reforming virtue the least chance of success." Yet New York was thriving; its citizens had "founded great institutions of beneficence . . . and turned the rocky waste to a pleasure-ground famous in the earth"—Central Park. There was "nowhere beneath the sun a city more ample in its moral securities." Once a vortex of depravity, New York was now teeming with generous, refined, civic-minded people, and—here Storrs reached his great conclusion—if the worst city in the United States was now a paragon, imagine the heights the rest of the nation must have attained.

Evidence for the claim of New York's ascent could be found only a few blocks away at the temporary home of the Metropolitan Museum of Art, where nearly seventy patrons and artists had joined forces to mount a triumphant display of the city's cultural riches. In late June, about 180 American and European paintings went on view, leaving bare patches on the parlor and ballroom walls of the island's finest homes. Among the prominent families who had sent pictures to the exhibition were the Osborns, Roosevelts, Morgans, Stebbinses, Dodges, Olyphants, and Havemeyers. John Taylor Johnston, a railroad executive who was president of the new museum, had loaned almost one hundred paintings, among them Church's two most famous North American landscapes: *Niagara Falls* and *Twilight in the Wilderness*. Hanging near the Church canvases was the greatest treasure of Johnston's collection, *The Slave Ship* by J. M. W. Turner.

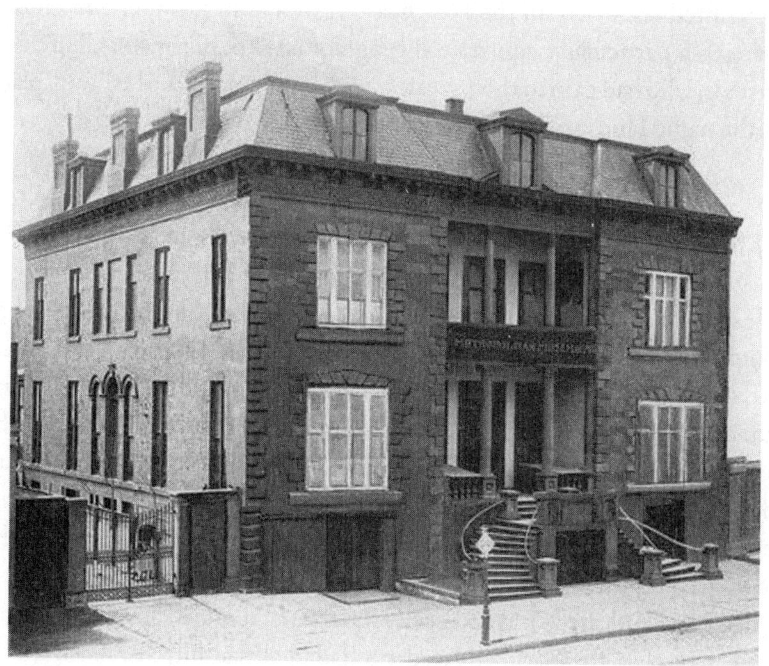

The Metropolitan Museum's temporary home on Fourteenth Street, c. 1875

For a second, larger show at the National Academy, Johnston and his committee had assembled nearly four hundred paintings, including six by Church. The eight Church paintings in the two shows marked him as a central figure in the New York Centennial, and they narrated his decades-long quest for new settings and subjects—North American forests and waterfalls, South American jungles and volcanoes, and ancient ruins in Greece and Syria.

At both exhibitions, American paintings shared the walls with works by acclaimed European artists. Among the Corots and Gérômes and Bouguereaus hung canvases by the late Cole and by seventy-nine-year-old Durand, and many of Cole's and Durand's heirs in the Tenth Street generation were likewise represented. The gifted John Frederick Kensett had died suddenly in his studio in 1872, but Church, Bierstadt, Cropsey, Gifford, McEntee, and Whittredge all had pictures in the 1876 New York shows.

Surveying their collective landscapes, a *New York World* critic mused that Cole, inspired by the Hudson River and its captivating scenery, had brought forth a whole school of American art, which could be called the "Hudson River School." It was meant as a compliment, at first—but the label ignored the wider interests and travels of the painters it lumped together, most of whom had painted elsewhere in the Northeast as well as in Europe. The Hudson River was a particularly constricted geographical boundary for Church and Bierstadt, who had earned their greatest acclaim for pictures of faraway places. But the name Hudson River School stuck.

EVEN AS THE NEW YORK art world celebrated the male painters inspired by Cole, it continued to keep its doors barred to his female heirs, who included Cole's own sister, Sarah, and his daughter Emily, a botanical painter whom Church was informally mentoring. In fifty years, the National Academy had elected only three women as associate members, none of whom was represented at the 1876 New York exhibitions. The first associate academician, Ann Hall, had been elected in 1828 and died in 1863, but the other two, Eliza Greatorex and Fidelia Bridges, had been elected much more recently and were actively painting. Neither had been welcomed in the main shows in New York and Philadelphia, and they had turned to the Women's Pavilion in Philadelphia instead.

The New York art world had been even less nurturing of African American painters. In 1869, the National Academy had finally admitted a Black student to its school. Charles Ethan Porter would become a lauded still-life painter;

Church would later number among his admirers. But neither Porter nor the accomplished African American landscape painter Robert Duncanson was represented in the collections of the wealthy lenders to the 1876 shows. In Philadelphia, however, Edmonia Lewis, a brilliant sculptor of African American and Ojibwe descent, had earned a spot for *The Death of Cleopatra*, which won her a medal; a few years later, Church noted with tacit approval that she had sculpted a bust of his friend Longfellow.

The Black landscape painter Edward Bannister also won a medal in Philadelphia, for *Under the Oaks*, a landscape the jury cited for its "wonderful closeness to nature." When Bannister went to the crowded committee room to pick up his medal, he heard someone ask, "What is that colored person in here for?" At the desk, he was chastised for taking up the official's time. People around him exchanged looks as he inquired about the prize for painting number 54. "What's that to you?" the official asked sharply. "I am interested in the report that *Under the Oaks* has received a prize; I painted the picture." Then, at least, the man apologized and "everyone in the room was bowing and scraping to me," Bannister recalled.

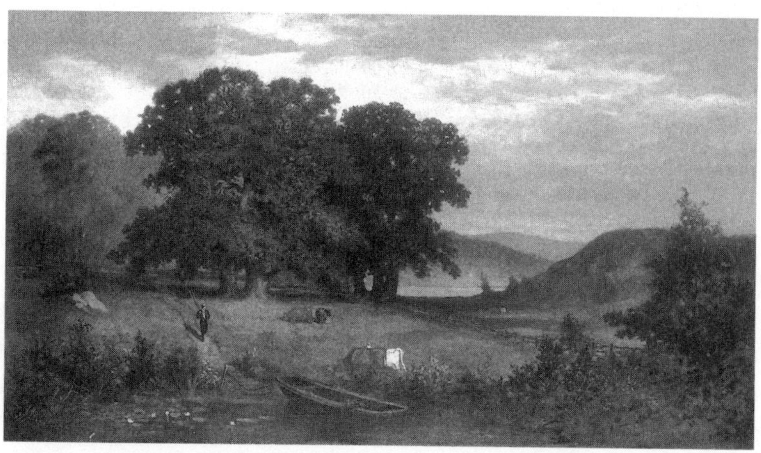

Edward Mitchell Bannister's *Oak Trees* of 1876 is thought
to be similar to his prize-winning *Under the Oaks* (now lost).

SLOWLY, PAINFULLY, THE ART WORLD was shifting. As it did, the pedestal on which Church had stood for years began to show cracks. He did receive a medal at Philadelphia, for *Chimborazo*. But that was an old picture, from another lifetime. Church was no longer a vigorous young artist who forded rivers and climbed volcanoes. In the summer of 1876, the *New York Evening Sun* published an item about the man he was becoming.

CHURCH, THE ARTIST, DISABLED.

A severe affliction has befallen Mr. Frederic E. Church, the artist. Some time ago he noticed in painting that his right wrist became fatigued much sooner than usual, but he paid little attention to it further than to shorten his hours of labor. Gradually the weakness increased, until he was finally obliged to forego painting with the hand. Since then all his work with the brush has been done with the left hand. The surgeons think that a sack of poisonous matter has formed in the wrist joint. To open it would be hazardous, as in such an event, the physicians say, the poison might permeate the whole system. It is possible that amputation may have to be resorted to finally. Mr. Church is in the prime of life. He lives in Greenport, Columbia county, N.Y., opposite Catskill, where he has a magnificent country seat.

Other papers also reported the news, and at the Century Association the next day, McEntee overheard some members discussing it. He and several others wrote to Church, who assured everyone that he did not face amputation. But it was true that his rheumatism was worsening. In his letters, Church often felt compelled to mention that he had difficulty holding a pen. "Wrist checks flow of ideas," he ended one note after just a few lines.

He tried to maintain hope. "I have a somewhat annoying and chronic trouble in my right wrist but the best surgeons assure me that it will never be worse," he wrote to an alarmed admirer. "And as I can use it without difficulty in painting I ought not to feel discouraged—especially as I am entirely free from pain."

I ought not to feel discouraged, he had written, as if reminding himself.

"A Very Big Skeleton"

With his body beginning to betray him, Church became nostalgic for the adventurous days when he had trekked through rugged landscapes, impressing his guides and companions with his vigor and grit. He longed for a respite from his responsibilities, longed to replace the confines of meeting rooms and the jostle of crowded sidewalks with deep forests and mountain lakes. Church had rarely faced a problem that he hadn't managed to overcome with careful consideration and discipline; now he clung to the hope that he could chase away the affliction in his wrist through force of will. To regain his health, he would pursue a change of climate and a new focus on physical conditioning.

In the fall of 1876, Church launched a series of annual camping trips to northern Maine, where he hadn't been for two decades. He loved traveling through the Northeast in this season. "When the autumn fires light up the landscape you will see Nature's palette set with her most precious and vivid colors." Delighted with his return to Maine after such a long absence, he persuaded three artist friends to go with him the following year: his Tenth Street friends Sanford Gifford and Horace Robbins, and Isabel's young relative Lockwood de Forest. They were joined by the engineer and writer Alexander Lyman Holley, who was penning a travel piece for *Scribner's Monthly*.

They did the first leg of the trip by train, then traveled by wagon as far into the woods as the old logging roads permitted. From there they hiked and canoed until they were near the base of Mount Katahdin. Church hadn't climbed Katahdin since his youthful trip with Winthrop two decades earlier, when he had been able to carry his own gear and was willing to sleep on the hard ground. This time, he hired several guides to carry most of the supplies. When they reached their campsite, the guides built sturdy lean-tos for sleeping.

Church relaxed into the familiar pleasures of camp life. He sketched and painted the changing moods of the lake. He regaled his friends with stories, jokes, and puns by the campfire, and he impressed them with his Yankee resourcefulness, as Holley reported in his article: "What things he can't make or mend, with the materials and tools at hand, I will not venture to state." On one occasion, Church soldered up a hole in a teapot by melting a metal paint tube together with birdshot in a spoon. As he had once done for Winthrop, he cooked freshly caught fish—Holley called this his "celebrated feat of baking a three-pound trout in hot ashes." When they climbed Katahdin, Church went off with one of the guides to explore the North Basin, an area he hadn't visited before.

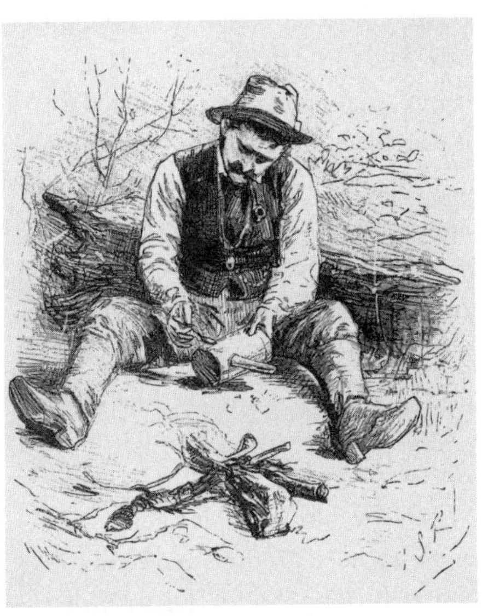

Church repairing the camp teapot,
Scribner's Monthly, May 1878

He corralled more friends when he returned in the autumn of 1878. This time it was his pastor at the First Presbyterian Church in Hudson, the Reverend George Yeisley; fifteen-year-old William Church Osborn, who had developed a passion for ornithology; and McEntee. Before the trip, Church offered McEntee some hard-earned packing advice, advising him to bring an "old winter suit warm flannels cardigan jacket two light Blankets Rubber coat a large rubber bag, or a piece of rubber cloth or other waterproof stuff." During the trip, McEntee marveled, "Church fixed my pipe with part of an old tin can, [a] bone of an owl's wing, some solder from a tin kettle, rosin from a spruce, a file and pair of scissors." They camped on a sandy beach at the edge of Lake Millinocket, in sight of Katahdin.

Later that fall, Church bought the property on which they had camped—a fifty-acre former farmstead on Lake Millinocket—and had some rustic structures built to accommodate his family and visitors. He wrote to an old friend in 1879 that Maine was a "good place to unbend the bow. This beau/bow is bent with lumbago today. Mrs. Church laughs . . . and says it gives me a comical, supercilious air. I don't feel either comic or supercilious." Church had persuaded Isabel to accompany him on the upcoming trip; Gifford brought his wife, Mary. McEntee, newly widowed and in mourning, also went along. One day, in acknowledgment of Church's enviable marriage, McEntee painted the name ISABEL on the side of the camp's canoe.

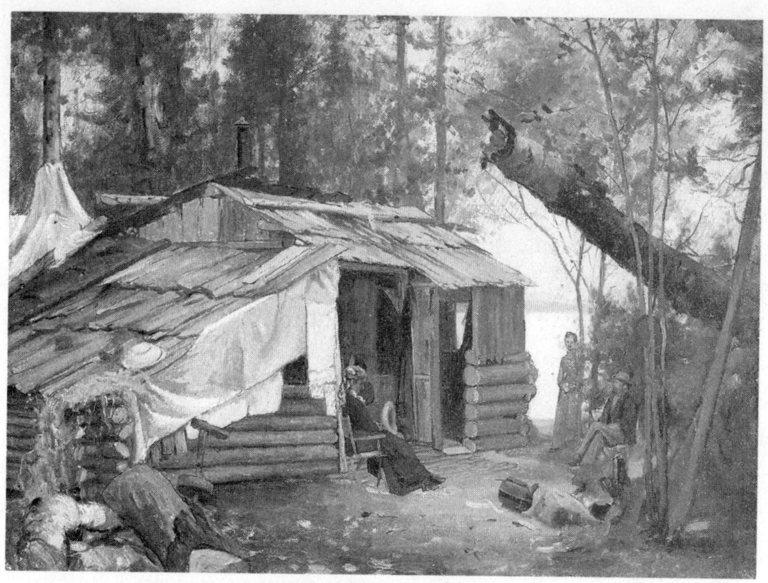

Church's camp at Lake Millinocket, Maine, by Jervis McEntee, c. 1879

ON THE AFTERNOON OF MARCH 30, 1880, Church stood waiting in the West Hall of the new Metropolitan Museum of Art with his fellow trustees. It was the moment they had been working toward for a decade. A band played as an invited audience of more than a thousand assembled in the hall. The city's wealthy and powerful men and their well-dressed families were arriving to celebrate the opening of the museum. The carriages of Astors, Chapins, Morgans, Tiffanys, Roosevelts, Stuyvesants, Van Rensselaers, and Vanderbilts rolled up from their mansions in Murray Hill, Gramercy Park, and Union Square. Passing the southern border of Central Park at Fifty-Ninth Street, they continued their journey so far northward that the unpaved portion of Fifth Avenue crunched under the carriage wheels. At

Eighty-Second Street, in front of the new museum building, they descended and streamed into the hall.

Despite the late-winter chill, people without invitations packed the walkways outside. They had come here on foot or, if they could afford the fare, had traveled by horsecar or on one of the new elevated trains that connected lower Manhattan to the Harlem River. The Third Avenue elevated line's Eighty-Fourth Street station was only a few blocks northeast of the new museum, which meant that New Yorkers without carriages could get to it, too. The promise of rapid transit was one reason the museum trustees had been open to siting the museum so far north, in a remote stretch of the island still dotted with farmhouses and shanties.

At 3:30 p.m., inside the building, the bandleader started his musicians on "Hail to the Chief," and everyone stood up. The women waved handkerchiefs and the men cheered while the museum's founding president, John Taylor Johnston, escorted Rutherford B. Hayes, the nineteenth president of the United States, to a seat on the platform. Hayes bowed and smiled, then sat down. This was the cue for the other dignitaries, including Church, to find their seats. Among those on the platform were Secretary of State William Evarts, Governor George B. McClellan of New Jersey, and Church's old friend Cyrus Field, who had been instrumental in acquiring a major collection of antiquities for the museum. Bierstadt was relegated to the audience, along with a few other artists who had been far less involved than Church.

Joseph H. Choate, a prominent lawyer and trustee, delivered the day's main speech. He pointedly reminded the other rich men present that their fortunes had been made on the backs of working-class New Yorkers. The wealthy owed it to them to help finance civic institutions such as the Metropolitan Museum. "Think of it, ye millionaires of many markets, what glory may yet be yours, if you only listen to our advice, to convert . . . railroad shares and mining stocks . . . into the glorified canvases of the world's masters, that shall adorn these walls for centuries."

The building, designed by Vaux and Mould, was a disappointment to those who were expecting an ornate, monumental edifice. The American answer to the great museums of Europe looked as though two large brick houses had backed up to either end of a giant greenhouse. The heavy monotony of the brick walls was unrelieved by the decorative stripes of gray and white granite used for the arches of the ogee windows. The siting of the building was equally unfortunate. Instead of stretching grandly along Fifth Avenue, the museum jutted sideways into the park at an awkward right angle to the street.

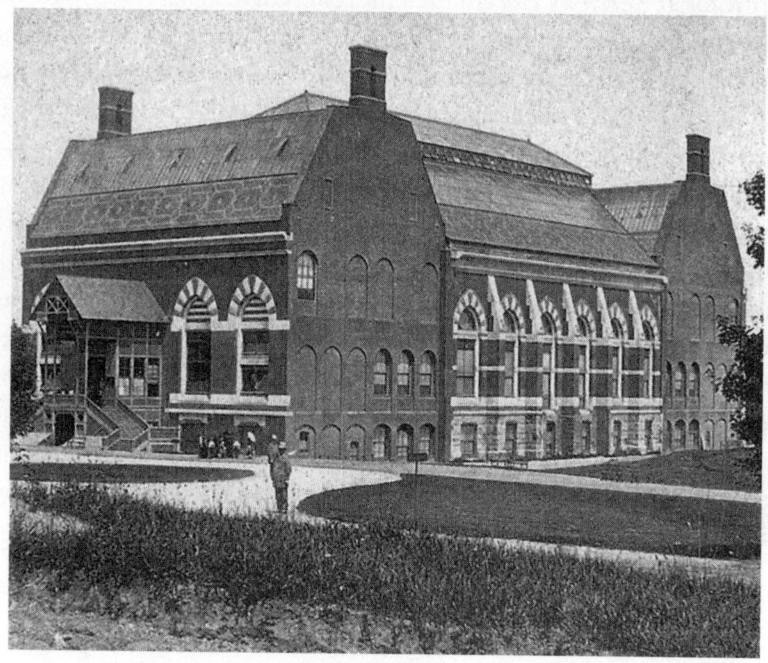

The Metropolitan Museum of Art, by Jacob Wrey Mould and Calvert Vaux, 1880

The New York Times generously called the building "unpretentious," and the *Art Journal* likened it to a plain jewelry casket whose chief function was to secure the treasures within. The art critic James Jackson Jarves was savage, however, charging that the new museum was "a forcible example of architectural ugliness, out of harmony and keeping with its avowed purpose . . . fit only for a winter garden or a railway depot." This wasn't fair; Jarves knew perfectly well that the brick walls had been left bare because they would become invisible when new wings were added in the future.

The collection inside was vast and varied. Some of it had been purchased expressly for the museum; the rest was on loan from collectors. There were antiquities from Cyprus and Egypt, ivory pieces from China and Japan, glassware from Venice, and porcelain from Limoges. The paintings were on the second floor, where, as at New York's centennial exhibitions, European and American works commingled. William H. Vanderbilt had been abroad when the loan collections were being assembled, but he had telegraphed the trustees to help themselves to any ten of his paintings they wanted to display.

A critic for *The Evening Post* admired the results of hanging Old Masters and contemporary European pictures alongside those by late and living Americans. "You walk through the two large western galleries and you feel that American art is not so bad after all, because you see that it stands up like a man by the side of its fellows and neither blushes nor faints."

Church had arranged for the loan of several of his paintings to the museum. In a way, though, these were not his most important contributions. Even as his health was deteriorating, he had devoted countless hours toward organizing the museum. Over and over, he had left his family, his studio, and his new house to travel to New York City for committee meetings. When most of the other trustees had pushed to situate the new museum at Forty-Second Street and Sixth Avenue, in a dense area close to the offices and clubs where they spent so many days and evenings, Church had advocated for a site where the museum, in careful collaboration with Central Park officials, would have room to expand. This new building was just the beginning.

CHURCH AND ISABEL WERE FILLING their own home upstate with so many works of art that they practically lived in a museum themselves, one journalist noted. "The whole house is a museum of fine arts, rich in bronzes, paintings, sculptures, and antique and artistic specimens from all over the world." Church was constantly purchasing new pieces from New York importers. On one such excursion, he "bought some Persian Brass work—two rugs—a three tined spear, Persian, an arabian coffee pot—an arabian table—a piece of Persian Embroidery—A Persian Battle Axe—A silk Turban—A moorish plate—et cetera."

Church and Isabel had finally settled on a name for their estate. At Christmas of 1879, Isabel had presented Church with an English translation of the ancient Greek scholar Strabo's *Geographica*. While perusing the work, one of them had come across a reference to a fortress that had once occupied a hill above a river in ancient Persia. The region where the fortress had stood, in today's Armenia, was thought by some to have been the location of the Garden of Eden. Church and Isabel borrowed the name of this fortress—Olanê— anglicized it, and began to call their estate Olana.

Church and Isabel had built their own Persian fortress on a hill above a river. Within it, they hoped to protect their four surviving children: Freddie, Winnie, Louis, and Downie. Freddie was now an adolescent, his brothers just a few years younger. The boys and their sister were becoming taller and stronger even as their father was increasingly weakened by his rheumatism and their mother suffered bouts of poor health. The children's rambunctiousness sometimes overwhelmed their frail mother and their prematurely aging father. When the weather permitted, Church and Isabel sent them out to play, and they explored the woods and meadows of Olana with the children of their parents' friends and neighbors. In winter, the children and their friends layered themselves in coats and shawls and sledded down the great hill or skated on the tree-lined lake that Church's men had dredged from the swamp.

In warmer months, windows and doors were propped open and the piazzas and porches became outdoor rooms. Summer days at Olana had a "suggestion of muslins," according to Susan Hale, a writer from Boston who was a favorite guest of the Churches. "Everywhere you look through vistas to shining oak boughs at hand, and dim, blue hills far beyond. . . . The air is all perfumed with wild grape and hay-like scents." Sometimes they climbed the back stairs and emerged in the gallery atop the tower, which overlooked four states at once: New York, Connecticut, Massachusetts, and Vermont.

The household often included Isabel's mother. "Old Grandma Carnes—you remember her at Beyrout, is a fine old war horse," Hale wrote to her sister, "—and she & Mr. Church keep up a constant fire of jokes; for he is always joking, and teasing her." The days at Olana ran on a regular schedule. At eight every morning a maid rang a triangle to call everyone to breakfast in the dining room, where they ate under the gaze of Church's painted saints from Rome. "Exquisite flowers arranged only by Mrs. Church are always on the table," Hale noted, "and every plate and pitcher and napkin is cho-

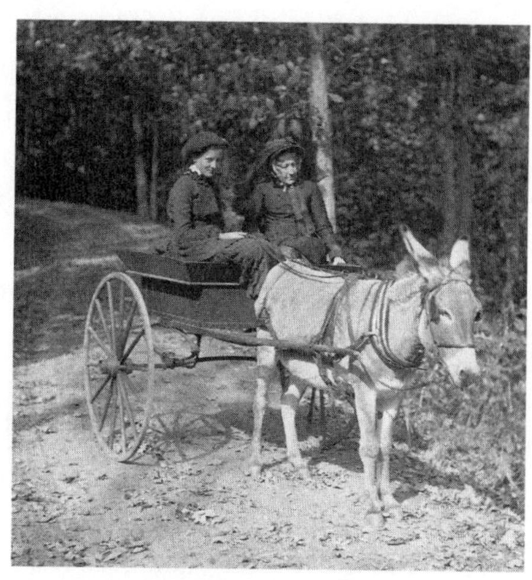

Downie and Mrs. Carnes at Olana with one of the Syrian donkeys, 1884

sen for its beauty or prettiness." After breakfast, it was Downie's job to fetch the Bibles for prayers and readings, and then everyone retired to their various occupations—painting, writing, studying—until lunch. Early afternoons were devoted to naps or reading, after which people changed into dinner dress and emerged to gather on the piazza and "talk, talk, talk until dinner at five-thirty."

The Church children adored animals, and Olana was home to dogs, peacocks, geese, cows, horses, pigs, and oxen. One day Church came up from the city with two parakeets and a black Persian kitten, the latter a gift from a friend. They named the kitten Cyrus after the founder of the first Persian Empire, and he stalked the grounds of his own Persian fortress terrorizing songbirds and field mice.

Downie became so attached to Cyrus that when Church sent an oil sketch of the cat to the friend who had given him to the family, he included his daughter's photograph. "As our little Downie—so we call her—cannot be separated from her cat I venture to enclose her photograph to go with the picture." The only girl and the youngest child, Downie was petted and admired by her parents and their guests alike. She would have stood out in a house full of older brothers even if she hadn't been so striking. Susan Hale described her as "a dream of beauty," while another visitor thought she was "simply the most beautiful girl I ever saw."

Church's extraordinary success as a painter, together with his inheritance from his father, meant that Downie and her brothers led lives very different from those of the children of most American artists—of most Americans, for that matter. The boys wore suits from Brooks Brothers, and Downie had a large collection of dolls. She sat for a portrait by the fashionable British painter Felix Moscheles the same year he painted President-elect Grover Cleveland. One of Downie's closest friends was J. P. Morgan's daughter Juliet, who came to stay at Olana one summer. Juliet's mother was Frances Tracy Morgan, sister of the late Annie Tracy, and Juliet's father owned several of Church's paintings. Susan Hale noted in a letter from Olana that Juliet's spectacular New York City mansion was lit by electricity. Olana did not have this latest convenience—few houses did yet, and the Churches preferred the glow of oil lamps and candles, anyway—but the family's lives were smoothed in many other ways by servants who did the cooking, laid the fires, and kept the enormous house clean.

Despite all the comforts, Church and Isabel permitted their children neither spiritual nor intellectual laziness. The daily Bible readings were mandatory, and the children studied with private tutors until they were old enough to go to the best boarding schools—St. Paul's in New Hampshire for the boys, and Miss Porter's in Connecticut for Downie. The children were often in earshot as their parents conversed with the writers, artists, naturalists, and explorers who were their constant guests. When the eminent writer Longfellow was approaching his seventy-fifth birthday, ten-year-old Downie wrote him a note and sent him a little present.

CHURCH'S AUTUMN TRIPS TO THE Maine woods hadn't restored his health. The pain was still at its worst when he was writing, and he struggled to manage his voluminous correspondence. Sometimes he was forced to ask Isabel to take dictation. Trying to make light of his difficulties, he told Palmer in one letter, "I am so ready to afflict you with so much verbosity" because Isabel was doing the actual writing.

Church's wrist was no longer the only part of his body troubling him. His knees were so stiff he had developed a limp. In August 1880, Isabel confided to Virginia Osborn that in recent weeks her husband had been "losing ground rapidly and getting more and more depressed." The following winter, McEntee ran into Church on the train to New York, after which McEntee wrote in his diary, "He looks badly and I do not believe he will live many years." Church was fifty-four.

It was all rather oppressive for the children, as Susan Hale observed. Downie had a melancholy air, and the boys sometimes stifled their laughter because the noise would have bothered their father. "You see there is a very big skeleton here which can't be kept in the closet—Mr. Church's constant suffering. It is the point on which all turns; his wife watches him so anxiously, the children are suppressed, draughts are avoided, pillows always at hand. He aches in every bone all the time with rheumatism, and . . . he cannot eat anything to agree with him. He is very thin, and easily tires."

Despite the pall of illness that hung over the house, Hale saw how important it was for Isabel and Church to have friends come stay at Olana. "It is terribly sad—this splendid house, a wonderful place he has created out of rough country land . . . the beautiful things with which he has surrounded himself. I suppose he cannot live long, and then—what! The boys wont [sic] care to keep this place, and who will buy it!"

Church was trying to be brave. "He never complains, or mentions any discomfort, but we all know it," Hale wrote. "He is very agreeable, and likes, I think, to talk and tell his stories, yet it seems like an effort for him to speak sometimes." Whenever Isabel heard Church making light of his condition, her spirits lifted. Any spark of humor was "always a good sign," Isabel told Virginia

Osborn. Church joked to Heade that he finally understood the genius of the human knee, now that he could not bend his own at will. Urging Palmer to join him in the therapeutic waters of Saratoga Springs, seventy-five miles north of Olana, Church wrote, "Rub all your joints and see if you cannot find a sore spot."

Church struck an optimistic note after his first visit to Saratoga Springs: "I think that the swelled joints are somewhat improved." But some days, his limbs were so stiff that he couldn't stand upright. The fingers of his right hand were contracting into a crooked gnarl, and he couldn't do up his buttons by himself. Isabel helped him dress. He began having massages twice every day, in the early morning and after dinner; they eased the pain at least a bit. Even at the height of summer, Church had a servant lay a fire in the sitting room. He was fielding suggestions from doctors, friends, even strangers who wrote to him with advice. He tried special mattresses and austere diets. His Tenth Street friend Whittredge later marveled at Church's inner strength. "He possessed remarkable courage and fortitude in his sufferings, never asking aid, nor permitting anybody to do anything for him which he could possibly do for himself."

The cold air of winter and early spring made Church ache all over. He and Isabel began to think about going farther afield in search of relief. They considered Florida, but Church worried about "its very changeable climate and its malarial atmosphere." W. H. Osborn recommended Southern California, but Church feared it would be too much like New York City in its relentless rush after inventions and riches. "The pioneers of Civilization are at the front with all new instruments of progress," he wrote of California. "They like the buzz and clatter—I for one have had enough of it for a time at least." Church and Isabel decided on Mexico instead, and Church began poring over books about its politics, art, and natural history. They grew excited about traveling again.

In March 1881, they left on a long journey that took them first to Chicago, then—in Osborn's private railroad car—to New Orleans, and from there by steamer to the Mexican port of Veracruz. They spent three weeks touring Mexico. "I like Mexico," Church told a friend afterward, "not only for its fine climates—its magnificent scenery—its picturesque people and Towns but especially for the dreamy, hazy conditions which pervade mind and nerves." Humboldt had traveled through Mexico in the early 1800s, and the volcanoes between Veracruz and Mexico City reminded Church of his own youthful expeditions on Humboldt's trail. He decided they would have to come back to Mexico for a much longer visit next time.

ON JULY 2, 1881, a delusional man named Charles Guiteau shot President James A. Garfield in a Washington train station. Garfield survived, but he was badly injured. In the following weeks the newspapers gave daily updates on his condition. The news dredged up memories of the dark days following Lincoln's assassination in 1865. For Church and Isabel, recollections of Lincoln's death were entwined with their grief for Bertie and Emma, who had died only weeks before the assassination.

Church did not usually discuss politics in his correspondence, but Guiteau's heinous act preoccupied him. After Garfield died on September 19 (of sepsis, not from his bullet wound), Church fixated on Guiteau's punishment. When Heade moved out of Church's Tenth Street studio to relocate to Washington that fall, Church wrote, "I am sorry to learn that you are going to overlook the Potomac. If you could bring yourself not to entirely ignore it—you might find some pretty bits along its shores." Church called for Guiteau to be hanged, punning darkly, "There are 50.000.000 people in suspense because he is not." On January 10, 1882, Church wrote to Heade, "It is possible that I may see Washington this winter, but I should prefer to wait until Giteau [*sic*] is under the daisies and Washington well aired—I should think all you Washingtonians would feel impelled to bury all your clothes and soak yourselves in the Potomac—above the City." Guiteau was convicted on January 25 and hanged on June 30 in front of 250 invited onlookers.

CHURCH'S PERSONAL TROUBLES CONTINUED UNABATED. His sister Elizabeth, now in her late fifties, had suffered an attack of some sort that had left her partially paralyzed. For years, she had been taking care of their elderly mother, who had gone blind; Church was now taking the train to Hartford every week to help look after them both. He had been trying to make progress on a commissioned painting, but wrote to his patron apologetically that he was stymied by his trips to Hartford and his anxiety over his sister's "very critical condition." Elizabeth made a partial recovery, but on July 17, 1883, his mother died.

Eliza Church's passing provoked conflicting emotions. When Church and Isabel visited the Osborns at their country house a few weeks later, Virginia observed that Church was "much more cheerful than he has been for a long time. His mother's peaceful death has relieved him from a terrible burden of anxiety." Yet Church, writing to Heade soon after, described her death as "an unspeakable loss to me."

That winter, he and Isabel escaped to Mexico again. "The Doctor forbids me a cold climate," Church explained to a friend. This time they stayed for almost half a year, settling in the Hôtel del Café Anglais in Mexico City, a lively establishment that was a favorite among visiting *norteamericanos*. From this base, they made excursions to surrounding towns, lakes, and mountains. Church especially loved Orizaba, a small town near the volcano Citlaltépetl, where he sketched the red-tiled roofs and handsome churches against their mountainous backdrop. Cuautla, a town south of Mexico City with a striking view of the volcano Popocatépetl, was another of his favorite places for sketching. In March 1884, he and Isabel had been in Cuautla for six sunny weeks when he wrote to Heade, "Air delicious but tends to laziness—would suit you."

When they returned to New York City, Mrs. Carnes noted that her son-in-law was not quite so gaunt and that Isabel looked "splendid." Church wrote happily to his Hartford friend Charles Dudley Warner, "Mrs. Church—for the first time since we were married—gained perfect health there." Thus began an almost unbroken series of winters in Mexico, at least for Church. Isabel wasn't quite as taken with the country as he was, and although she sometimes joined him, he often had to cajole a friend or two to accompany him instead. A few times, one of the children went along.

Church held Mexico up against the United States and found the latter wanting: "I hate heat, cold, flies, mosquitoes, low horizons, clapboards & shingles—green blinds—monotonous unpicturesque clothes—American Hotels and above all the heated, excited life of the States." He worried about the expansion of railroads, even as he enjoyed their convenience. By 1884, he and Isabel were able to travel by train from Mexico all the way home to Olana. Church predicted that railroads would lure hordes of Americans to Mexico, which in turn would become "the great winter resort of our people."

He exulted to Heade that Mexico had "everything to enchant the painter." He piled up pencil and oil sketches of houses, churches, flowers, and mountains. His letters brimmed with his old good cheer and energy. "Heade! There are the most picturesque things in this country I ever saw." To Palmer he wrote that he found it *all* fascinating: "the sky, the earth, the people, the beasts, birds & insects, the architecture . . . and the music here is exceptionally fine." In a letter to Osborn he enclosed a morning-glory seed, adding that the "flower is the most heavenly blue conceivable but so delicate that it cannot endure wind."

During one of his Mexican sojourns, Church took Isabel, Downie, and Susan Hale to a lake in the mountains that Humboldt had visited, and they all stood on a rock where Humboldt had supposedly stood. Church was forced to limp along slowly, but his enthusiasm was undimmed. Near the end of his third winter in Mexico, he crowed to Warner, "I seem to have recovered the spirits of the child—and feel the most ridiculous ambition to gird up my loins—get big canvasses and essay to paint great subjects."

CHAPTER 27

"Young Geniuses Fully Armed"

In the fall of 1884, Freddie started his freshman year at Princeton. Church had high expectations for his oldest son and namesake. Fred—as he was now called—had grown up to be a bright young man who made a good first impression on peers and elders alike. He was more sturdily built than his younger brothers, and he had a squarer jaw and broader face than his father. A graceful and powerful athlete, Fred excelled at the new game of American football. Off the field, he looked elegant in his Brooks Brothers suits. Mrs. Carnes thought her grandson was as "splendid looking [a] young fellow as you'd wish to see."

As the first child to arrive after Bertie and Emma died, Fred had been doted on by his parents. He had seen the world by the age of four. He had ridden camels and donkeys under Middle Eastern skies, crossed the Bosporus by steamer, and wintered in Rome. Early in his life, his parents had worried about his strange lack of affection, but it had proved to be a fleeting phase. Church frequently singled out his oldest son in letters. "Freddie is doing admirably and is happy," he wrote to McEntee in November 1878, when the boy was twelve, and then just after Christmas: "We are all well albeit the children are somewhat overcome by the Holiday festivities and unlimited candy. Freddie is here sedate as a judge—but with round red cheeks."

At the end of Fred's first year at St. Paul's School, when he was fourteen, Church received an upsetting letter from the headmaster, Henry Coit. "He knows of evil & corrupt ways," Coit warned Church. "He is not select in his companionship." Coit hinted at a budding, unspecified vice: "There is much in current literature that might be harmless to a man but would injure a boy." Church fired off an alarmed reply to Coit, who tried to reassure him but only made things worse. "The child will do his duty and come out all right, only now I am anxious at the early knowledge of evil."

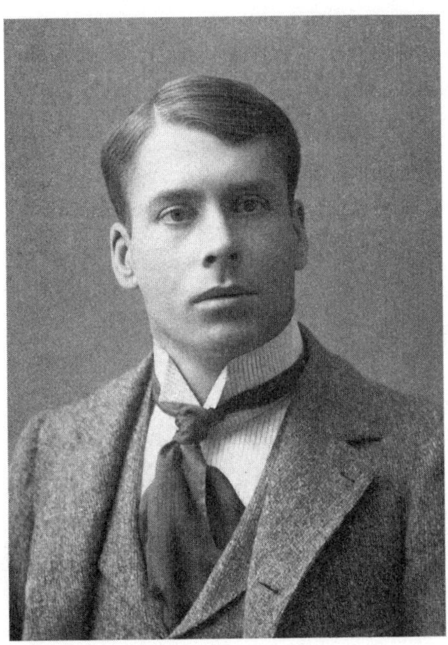

Fred Church at about
eighteen years old, c. 1885

In 1868, when Fred had been a baby, Isabel had learned of a scandal ruining another family's reputation and had mused to Church's mother, "A wild bad son, is indeed a terrible skeleton in a family." Now Church and Isabel began to worry about Fred. He had made it through St. Paul's, but he was starting to show a shocking carelessness with money. Right before Fred started at Princeton, Church had to settle a personal debt his son had run up with his tutor for $100, a considerable sum. When Church caught Isabel's mother preparing to send Fred $5 for his eighteenth birthday, he vetoed the plan, telling Mrs. Carnes she must send a present, not money.

At Princeton, Fred enrolled in the science track, which included courses in algebra, geometry, trigonometry, anatomy, botany, mineralogy, drafting, surveying, English, French, German, and oratory. Fred turned out to have an aptitude for drafting and surveying, and he produced a handsome plan of Olana as a class project. But he fell in with a set he later blamed for corrupting him, young men "who were dissipates and bad generally." By his second semester he was smoking and gambling. He began skipping class and missing exams. In his sophomore year he was kicked out of his cohort and held back.

Fred started his freshman year over, but he was soon playing billiards instead of going to class. A chemistry professor wrote to Church with details of Fred's lies and lack of discipline. Fred barraged his father with half apologies, excuses, and brazen requests for more money. After he was caught cheating, the Princeton authorities suspended him.

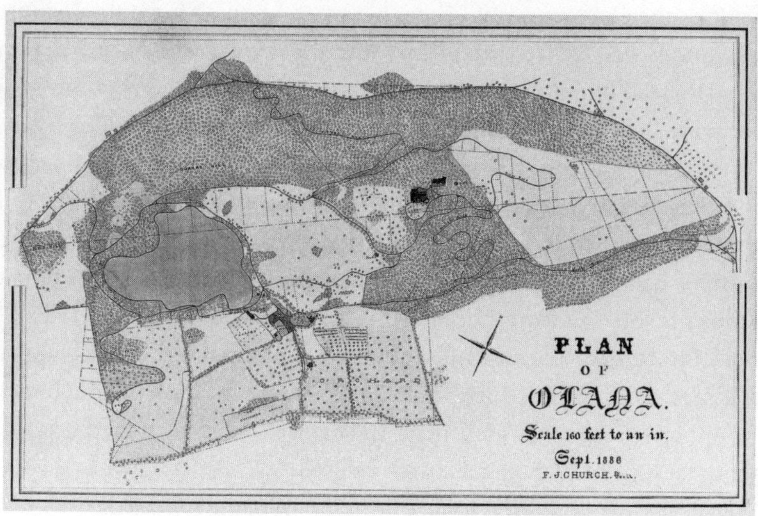

Plan of Olana drawn by Fred Church, September 1886

Church and Isabel were deeply distressed. Trying to find some strength and solace, Isabel copied out a line from Balzac in her notebook: "A mother's heart is an abyss, in whose depths forgiveness is always to be found." Church told Fred that his indebtedness had made his mother sick with worry. In a private conversation, Church tried to convey the long shadows that youthful misdeeds could cast over the rest of a man's life. He showed Fred a green plum whose shine had been rubbed off, saying that although that plum might one day ripen, the shine could never be restored. The image stuck in Fred's mind for years but had no effect on his behavior. He continued to borrow money from classmates. He found his studies boring and didn't have the self-discipline to soldier through the work. He invented excuses at every turn. He claimed that because his father had never been to college, he didn't understand how things worked there.

In January 1886, Isabel's mother died suddenly, leaving a void in the Churches' lives. For Church, Mrs. Carnes "was so much a part of ourselves that her death makes a break in our home circle which can never be closed." Isabel had been extremely close to her mother, and she struggled with her grief, prompting Fred to write to his father with unusual solicitude: "I think you & Mother had better go to N.Y. as soon as possible, being alone up in the country she must muse over her loss continually, while if she was in N.Y.[,] Downie & the Osborns would cheer her up. . . . I know it would do more to make Mother well & happy than anything else if you could only manage it."

Fred himself might have contributed to his mother's recovery, but instead he continued to cause her anguish. By the spring of 1887, he had left a further trail of unpaid bills, and Church told Fred that he would not be welcome at Olana that summer, nor would he be returning to Princeton in the fall. If Fred couldn't take college seriously, perhaps some exposure to the hard world beyond his coddled life would set him straight. Church arranged a long trip West for his son. He would be accompanied by a lawyer named John Pine, whom Osborn had recommended; Pine's job was to keep Church apprised of Fred's behavior. By late July, Fred and Pine were in Washington Territory, at the opposite end of the continent. In August, a homesick Fred begged his father to let him come home. Church refused.

Accepting his fate, Fred looked for employment in Seattle. His family connections and personal charm—he was praised by one new acquaintance for "his courteous, manly bearing"—landed him a steady job superintending a wharf for a warehousing business. Fred seemed to take to life in Seattle. He wrote to his father about the scenery in language that could have come from one of Church's labeled sketches—the mountains near Seattle "being of a superb rose color night & morning & snow-white in the day." But most of Fred's letters also contained appeals for money.

In the autumn of 1888, Church permitted Fred to visit Olana with his fiancée, a Seattle woman named Margaret McCleery. Church liked Margaret and was heartened by Fred's cheery reports about his new life. While Fred was visiting Olana, however, his Seattle employer, Charles Kittinger, discovered serious irregularities in Fred's bookkeeping. The enormous sum of $3,000 was missing. Kittinger later informed Church that because he liked Fred, he had decided to shield him from the wrath of the stockholders by putting up the missing money himself—"thereby saving Fred from arrest and disgrace." Kittinger suspected that Fred was stealing in order to gamble. He also told Church that Fred had taken up with a "Variety Actress" despite his engagement to Margaret McCleery, and that he had been seen drunk with the actress on more than one occasion.

After Fred had returned to Seattle—but before his father had learned about the embezzlement—Church was again besieged by requests for help. "I am at present as near rock bottom as I have ever been," Fred wrote his father in December. Learning that his son had borrowed money from yet another acquaintance, Church reprimanded him, intimating that Fred had traded on his father's fame and good standing. Fred lashed out angrily at this accusation: "If you had been dead or penniless I should have received it just the same.... When a fellow gets to be twenty-two[,] hasn't he some identity of his own?" But in the same letter Fred confessed that he couldn't pay his Brooks Brothers bill.

Church's lifelong tenacity in the face of obstacles was failing him. Fred presented an insoluble problem. Church and Isabel had probably been indulgent with the first child born to them after the deaths of Bertie and Emma, but Fred's behavior went beyond selfishness to verge on a kind of mental disorder. Nothing Church tried had the slightest effect. Isabel, unwell again, grew sicker with worry, and she confessed to another of their children that "a mother cannot have <u>such</u> a trouble, and keep well." There were long periods when an envelope bearing Fred's handwriting arrived every week, and Church was constantly forced to draft letters to his son's creditors. Isabel pleaded with Fred to reform his ways. But he just kept begging Church for more money and pressured his mother to try to influence his father. In the summer of 1889, Church sent the latest requested funds, along with an angry, heartbroken letter.

> I send you this money as a gift, not a loan. All of your drafts have been refused by me & I will honor no more of them. You have imposed on everyone you can. People now know you as you are and you <u>must</u> change your course or a felon's cell awaits you and you would not be saved by me, not if one dollar would keep you out of prison. God forbid that I should say you could never come home, but you cannot until you can come as a new man, having retrieved your place in the world. If I hear of any more of your evil-doings I shall be forced—out of justice to your brothers & sister—to disown you as my son.

Disgraced in Seattle by the embezzling scandal, Fred headed for the Olympic Peninsula, where he found work surveying land for agricultural development and timber harvesting. He was surrounded by mountains and lakes in a landscape as spectacular as any his father had ever explored, but all he could think about was how to exploit it. He toyed with the idea of investing in a copper mine and fantasized about making a fortune from timber. He staked a claim to 160 acres of government-owned forest, explaining excitedly to his mother how much he would make from its later sale, but within two years he was writing to the government land officer to say that a claim jumper had stolen his claim. Not daring to contact his father directly, Fred asked the land officer to write to Church about the loss, which the man refused to do.

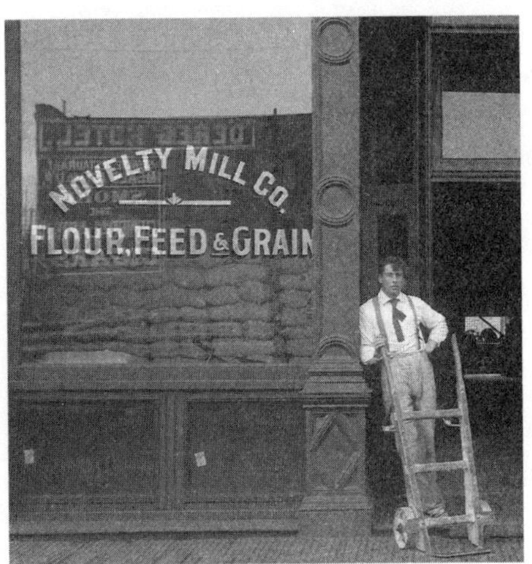

Fred Church at work in Seattle, c. 1893

Fred eventually returned to Seattle, working briefly for the Department of Parks before taking a job at a flour-milling business. Isabel tried to keep in touch with him, sending encouraging words that elicited a grateful reply for her faith in him. Fred fell in love again and got engaged, and although he was most often the author of his own troubles, he was visited by tragedy when his bride succumbed to a fatal intestinal illness a few months after the wedding. Upon hearing the news, Church sent what Fred thought was "the kindest letter he has ever written me & inclosed a check for $250."

But the money was not for Fred; it was so he could reimburse Virginia Osborn, who had quietly settled a doctor's bill for him. After that, Mrs. Osborn forwarded Fred's letters and telegrams to Church, but they agreed to conceal them from Isabel, who was too ill and too heartbroken about Fred to bear any more bad news.

Mrs. Osborn wrote to her daughter-in-law in despair. "I can never forget the dear little baby boy who took his first steps in our parlor in Paris. How sad we should have all felt it, if he had died then, but how much sadder this all is."

CHURCH ESCAPED INTO HIS WORK whenever his health and his other responsibilities permitted. As he grew older, his paintings had increasingly turned from political themes toward explorations of mortality and the passage of time. In 1877, he drew on his old South American sketches to paint a large canvas called *The River of Light*. The hard clarity of his earlier work gave way in this picture to a dreamy softness. The sun barely pierced the hazy air, its pale reflection stretching across the water in a path that beckoned the viewer into an indistinct distance. The painting was reminiscent of Thomas Cole's *Old Age*, the final picture in his 1840s series *Voyage of Life*. Church's other major paintings in these years were similarly contemplative. Drawing from his travels in Greece and Ottoman Syria, he depicted ancient architectural ruins against sweeping backdrops of sea and sky. These compositions spoke of the ephemerality of human life and even of whole civilizations, measured against the vast scale of the cosmos.

Now in his fifties, Church was, after Durand, the most prominent living member of the so-called Hudson River School. Church's association with this group derived from his strong early ties to Cole and the two decades he had been living and painting on his well-known Hudson River estate. In 1883, the critic Clarence Cook, a champion of younger artists such as Winslow Homer and Thomas Charles Farrer, declared it "time for the Hudson River School to at least begin to die." Church encountered this dismissive attitude when he tried to help the Cole family sell off some of Thomas Cole's paintings in the early 1880s. It depressed Church that the taste for Cole had passed. He wrote a friend in 1885, a year after Maria Cole's death, "Thomas Cole was an Artist for whom I had and have the profoundest admiration. If I were permitted to select three from among all the landscapes I have ever seen I shall certainly choose for one of them 'Desolation' the last of the five pictures by Cole."

Asher Durand, dean of the Hudson River School painters, died in September 1886, by which point the label had taken on a pejorative connotation. American critics and patrons were beginning to embrace the new style of painting known as Impressionism. The previous April, twelve years after the Paris exhibition that had given birth to the term *Impressionist*, the first major American show of French Impressionist paintings opened in New York with almost three hundred pictures, among them forty-eight Monets, thirty-eight Renoirs, seventeen Manets, and a corps of Degas ballerinas. Initial reactions ranged from disgust to delight. A reviewer for *The New York Times* complained, "There are some effects that look as though they were produced by gluing segments of the whites of hard boiled eggs over two-thirds of the canvas." The same writer went on to say, "One of the essentials to the appreciation of impressionist paintings is the beholder's getting as far away from them as practicable"—including by going around a corner into a different room. But a critic for *Harper's* praised Monet for his efforts "to note all the sheeny reflections and scintillations of sunlight upon moving water, and to fix all that is fleeting and fugitive in landscape effects."

As bold American collectors began to purchase French Impressionist works for their private galleries, American artists who were imbibing Impressionist ideas likewise drew attention. John Singer Sargent, who had studied in Paris and visited Monet at Giverny, was in particular demand for his vivid portraits. Another rising American was William Merritt Chase, who in the late 1880s began a series of paintings that captured daily scenes in Central Park, just as the French Impressionists had done in the Bois de Boulogne. A major inspiration for many of these new young artists was the rise of photography. Their paintings often strove to capture momentary impressions: the sudden tilt of a woman's head, or a man hurrying along a sidewalk. They also exuberantly explored the masses of color that photography—at least for now—could not capture.

Church was as fascinated by photography as he had been in his twenties and thirties when he was painting at Niagara Falls. A blaze of light, a sluice of chemicals, and suddenly an image was affixed to paper. Loved ones seemed present, even when they weren't. His four children, for example, lounging on the staircase at Olana—how different this carefree photographic image was from Church's memory of the wartime day Bertie had died, when Church had desperately sent for a portraitist to sketch a likeness before the little boy was buried.

It wasn't only people that photography could immortalize. It was Niagara in mid-plunge, the writhing vines of a jungle, an ancient ruin aglow at sunset. Church viewed the advent of photography not as a threat but with the enthusiasm of a man who cherishes every image of what he loves, and the object of Church's affection was the whole earth, in all its natural and cultural splendor. Since the 1840s, he had been painting landscapes that were miracles of technical achievement and inspired composition. He wasn't worried about the encroachment of photography because it could not do what he had done with oils and brushes.

Church was an avid collector of photographs, amassing close to two thousand images of landscapes, cities, villages, and ruins. But now, as the play of light and shadow began to fragment the canvases of younger painters, Church's extravagant, highly composed paeans to the natural world looked like relics of another age. In the spring of 1875 at Goupil's, a young critic had admired Church's "velvety vistas" and "gem-like vegetation" but found something disturbing about their style. "It is the kind of art which seems perpetually skirting the edge of something worse than itself, like a woman with a taste for florid ornaments who . . . dress[es] herself in a way to make quiet people stare," even though she is "really a very reputable person." The author of this eloquent insult was thirty-two-year-old Henry James.

Church had long been accustomed to criticism. It was part of being an artist. But now the criticism was coming from people who didn't share the experiences and references of his generation. His approach struck some younger artists as overly earnest. He had marveled in Humboldt's footsteps at the majestic scale and unity of nature, but the new generation had grown up with a Darwinian chill in the air. For them, nature was hardly unified; it was, as Darwin had demonstrated, cruel, random, and localized. The new generation had watched their elders wage the Civil War, a conflict marked by cruel, random, and localized violence. The idyll of an untrammeled, Edenic world was for old men—old painters.

Church, for his part, found the Impressionist style superficial. In an 1883 letter, he mocked "the sudden springing up of a crowd of young geniuses fully armed." These artists seemed to him too lazy to make a careful study of drawing, brushwork, and composition. They just picked up their brushes and hurled themselves at their paintings. He thought the simplicity of their technique, if one could call it that, confused viewers into thinking that every dabbler was a master. He predicted that this thin, sloppy style, which he called "rank in color" and "crude in effect," would not leave any mark on the history of art.

Meanwhile, he still had plenty of commissions. He joked to Palmer that he had promised new paintings to so many people that he might slip across the border to Canada. Or maybe he would "adopt some of the tactics of one of the numerous new schools and substitute slush for hard work." But those patrons still loyal to him loved the clarity and visual depth of his painting, and at almost sixty, he still fretted whenever he completed a commission about whether the buyer would like it.

In the summer of 1886, Church stood in his studio looking at incontrovertible evidence of his talent. *Niagara Falls* was back on his easel after three decades, sent by the Corcoran Gallery in Washington—then a private museum open to the public—following a botched restoration job. Streaks had appeared on the canvas, and in trying to remove them, the restorer had rearranged fragments of the sky into the water and moved a bit of the water into the sky. As Church assessed the damage, he fantasized about stuffing himself into a barrel and plunging over the Falls to "be swallowed up in the chaotic mess." But he worked diligently, until, standing back to survey his work, he decided the new sky was even better than the old.

But it wasn't only the painting Church had been trying to improve. His decades-long fascination with Niagara Falls had recently resulted in a measure of protection for the landmark itself. After more than a century of industrial blight, Canada and New York State had passed legislation creating parks on either side of the Falls. Olmsted, a key figure in this international effort, credited Church with having first proposed the idea in a speech Olmsted had attended at the Century Association more than a decade earlier. Church's reverence for nature had rippled out from his canvas to embrace the earth, rock, and water of Niagara itself.

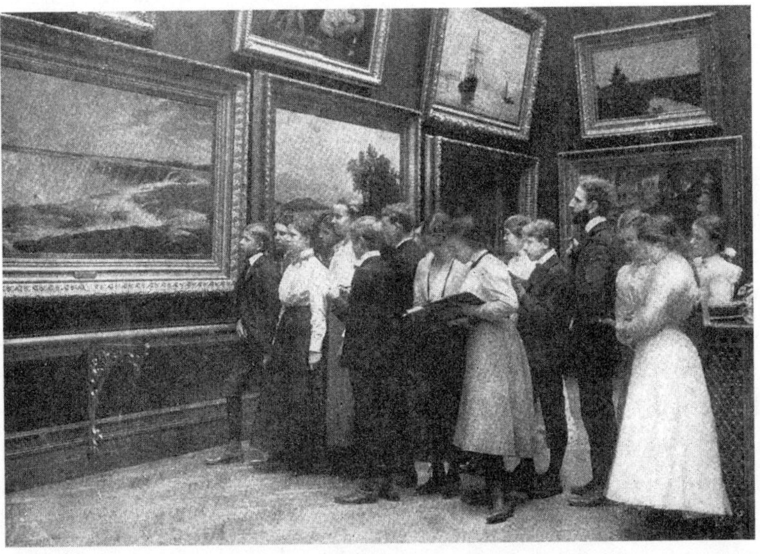

Students studying Church's *Niagara Falls* at the Corcoran Gallery of Art, 1890s

"His Beautiful Creations"

Church's painful debility was worsening year by year, improving only briefly when he went to Mexico each winter. He worked hard to conceal the depth of his suffering, especially when he and Isabel were hosting guests at Olana. As he sat writing a letter one day, he looked out the window and saw squirrels darting up the tree trunks, and he envied their agility.

He was still painting pictures now and then—mostly ethereal, elegiac portraits of light-bathed ruins and Mexican mountains and lakes. But he was at the mercy of his aching fingers and the rheumatic pain that throbbed through his whole frame. While his eye for details was as sharp as ever and his memory for what he saw in a landscape remained photographic, his body was stiffening and curling into unnatural shapes. "He is just a knotted skeleton," a family friend wrote in 1889, "all askew and covered with skin."

Yet there the glorious world was, moving and shining outside the arched windows of Olana. He painted whenever he felt up to it, but he turned increasingly to the design of the landscape, expressing himself not only in inches of canvas but in acres of earth. Inside, he and Isabel had juxtaposed art objects from myriad cultures, so that their relationships to one another changed as a person traversed the rooms. Outside, Church now designed winding drives that moved the onlooker from one exquisitely composed vista to another. "I can make more and better landscapes in this way than by tampering with canvas and paint in the Studio," he told Palmer.

Once, Church would have raced around the grounds and pitched in where he saw fit. Now he hired stronger, younger men to carry out his vision. To his Hartford friend Warner, he exulted, "I am busy Landscape Architecturing. I have nearly completed a cliff about a hundred feet in height." In the autumn of 1889, Church bought more than two thousand evergreen trees, adding them to the thousands of trees he had already planted over nearly three decades. He laid out new carriage drives, including one that gave visitors spectacular views of the Hudson and the Catskills as they rolled up to the villa. Just as he did in his paintings, Church was positioning landscape features to guide the viewer's eye from the foreground to the far distance. In letters and diaries, guests wrote of being moved to tears or robbed of breath by the sudden beauty of the prospect.

As he worked on Olana's landscape, Church kept sketching and painting, but his stiff knees discouraged him from walking down the hill to his free-standing studio. He had a new studio added to the western façade of the main house—a large, high-ceilinged room looking out over the river. Visitors entered the house through the front door, which was set into the eastern façade, and with the new studio completed, they now looked from the entrance hall down a long enfilade of open rooms toward a huge window framed in amber. It was like looking down the nave of a church.

Church ordered his hillside studio dismantled. He also gave up his space at the Tenth Street Studio Building after thirty years; most of his old friends there had already moved on. "If I can get my fingers untwisted," Church wrote Warner, "I may play painter in my new Studio—which has a most admirable light, indeed it is so perfect that it only lacks one thing—a Painter."

Yet his new studio did have a painter. Although he had started refusing commissions for landscapes, a friend had persuaded him to do an iceberg picture; Church joked to Palmer that he had agreed because "no sane person can call an Iceberg a landscape." He could see the ice-crusted Hudson River from his windows, and he could consult his studies from the 1859 trip with Noble. Inspired by his new studio, Church managed to work five or six hours a day. When he was done with *The Iceberg*, which showed a lone ship sailing past a massive floe, he painted a Mount Katahdin scene, then a Mexican landscape.

DESPITE THEIR HEALTH TROUBLES, THE Churches were still asking friends and acquaintances to visit. In June 1887, Mark Twain and his wife, Olivia Langdon Clemens, joined the Warners—Warner had coauthored *The Gilded Age* with Twain—in making the trip from Hartford to Olana. Almost thirty years earlier, Twain had marveled at *The Heart of the Andes* in St. Louis. Now he adapted easily to the slightly eccentric household of the artist himself. Twain came down to dinner in evening dress, but afterward vanished, reappearing in comfortable slippers with a pipe in his mouth. He sat down in the library and picked up a book. The next morning, Church and Isabel held their usual Bible reading, to which they always invited their guests. Twain made a show of having trouble finding his place in the Bible and handed the duty off to his wife.

One day during Twain's visit the whole house party toured the grounds, and in the evening they sat on a piazza overlooking the night-shrouded river. Twain began to tell stories. He "just let himself out," another guest wrote afterward. "He is the greatest circus I was ever at." Twain's thank-you note to Church called the visit "an ideal holiday, in a Garden of Eden without the Garden of Eden's unprotection from weather."

The Church children were jaded about the famous figures who visited Olana. In 1889, nineteen-year-old Louis complained to Sally Good (whom he would later marry), "There is another literary brick comeing [*sic*] here. . . . Will they never stop?" In person, however, Louis was well-behaved, as was Winthrop, who had started at Princeton in 1887. Eighteen-year-old Downie could be more openly disagreeable. Susan Hale thought Downie was immature and selfish, and she blamed the girl's parents: Church had been too strict, Isabel too doting. Hale thought Downie's good looks were "spoilt by the peevish expression of her mouth" and predicted she would "run her excellent father a merry jig before she is much older." Virginia Osborn also worried about Downie because she "smiles for all men alike, and she is quite [as] likely to take up with a Trapeze performer as anything else." Church had recently raged at a young man who had shown up at the door asking to see "Miss Downie." Church had ordered him to stay off the property—yet behind her father's back, Downie arranged to go for a drive with him. To everyone's relief, the suitor Downie chose to accept, Jeremiah Black, was a Princeton football player from an eminent Pennsylvania family of public officials and jurists. They married in February 1891, and their first child, a girl named Isabel, arrived that November.

Church could no longer manage the complexities of overseeing the estate. One of the children would need to step in. Fred was out of the question; Downie had moved away with her husband and started a family. Mature and reliable Winthrop, affectionately referred to as Dad by his siblings, was still at Princeton. That left Louis, the youngest boy, who had traveled widely in Europe but hadn't been much interested in college. Kind and conscientious, Louis often accompanied one or both of his parents when they sought winter relief in warmer climates. In 1891, twenty-one-year-old Louis agreed to take over management of Olana. Church insisted on paying him a salary.

IN 1895, CHURCH COMPLETED a simple, searing picture of Mount Katahdin. Across a lake, the peak rose above a forest touched with gold by the setting sun. Out on the water, a solitary figure paddled a canoe into the darkness cast across the water by tall evergreens. Church gave the picture to Isabel for her fifty-ninth birthday, with a poignant note: "Your old guide is paddling his canoe in the shadow, but he knows that the glories of the heavens and the earth are seen more appreciatively when the observer rests in the shade."

The shadows around Church were deepening. So many people he loved had died—Noble in 1882, his mother in 1883, his sister Elizabeth and his mother-in-law both in 1886, his friend McEntee in 1891. Then, in March 1894, W. H. Osborn, who had been almost as close to Church as a brother for three decades, had died. Church and Isabel joined Virginia Osborn in mourning.

Adding to Church's gloom were his frequent separations from Isabel. Rheumatism sent him to the dry air of the Mexican mountains every winter, but Isabel found more relief in relatively humid places, and for several years she had been going to Bermuda or to Palm Beach, Florida. In 1896, Church lamented to Warner, "Wife and I are vainly striving to find some place where we can both winter but this earth seems destitute of such an oasis."

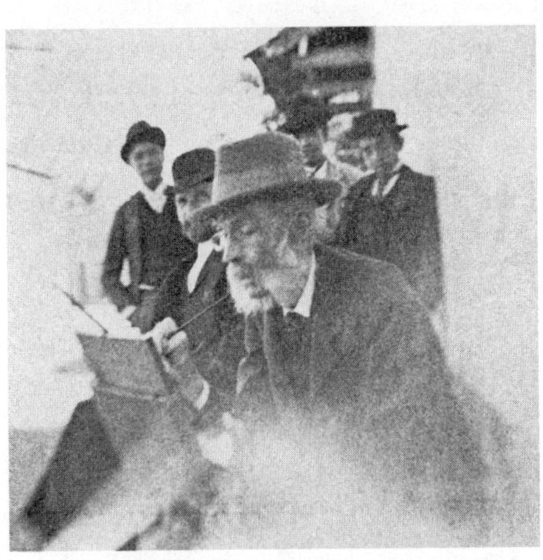

Church sketching in Mexico,
a paintbrush stuck through the gnarled
fingers of his damaged right hand

Still, he enjoyed his annual trips to Mexico, and he loved taking whichever friends he had persuaded to join him to see his favorite villages and churches and mountain views. He began spending much of his winter hiatus in Cuernavaca, a town southwest of Mexico City. "The whole town is a garden, and is almost buried in abundant masses of trees," Church's guidebook noted of Cuernavaca. In the dry mountain air, his pain eased, and he found the energy and inspiration to sketch and paint the town's vine-draped houses and elegant churches. In early 1897, he wrote Downie that he had been "sketching daily which I enjoyed as much as ever before in my life."

Throughout Mexico, Church had been rummaging happily in antique shops, just as he had done long ago in Rome, and again he had emerged with treasures. After one trip, Church told a friend that he had returned home "laden with Aztec and Toltec relics having bought the choicest articles from the collection of an old Priest." In 1893, Church gave two of those pieces—carved Toltec stone tiles—to the Metropolitan Museum of Art, where they were among the earliest pieces of ancient American art in any museum in the United States.*

Much as Church loved Mexico, he never stopped missing Isabel. In May 1899, a few days after Church's seventy-third birthday, they were reunited for the last time. Isabel had returned from Florida critically ill, and she lay dying in a quiet bedroom at the Osborns' townhouse. Church rushed to her side. Louis, Downie, and Winthrop also arrived in time to bid her goodbye. Louis described the deathbed scene to Sally Good: "The little Mother's life ended so peacefully and without pain that we have much to be thankful for." After a funeral service at the Osborns', Church and the children took the casket by train to Hartford, where she was buried next to Bertie and Emma. When Fred received the news of his mother's death, he began inquiring about his inheritance.

AFTER ANOTHER EMBEZZLING SCANDAL, FRED had retreated to the Olympic Peninsula to hunt and fish and live as cheaply as possible. He published several articles about his wilderness exploits in a new magazine called *Recreation*, which catered to the Teddy Roosevelt set—part-time adventurers looking for character-building excitement in the wilderness. One of Fred's pieces documented a dramatic run in a dugout canoe on the rapids of the Quinault River, a trip on which he and two friends were guided by several Native men hailing from the Quinault people.

Fred had brought along a camera, and he noted that the "Indians were all interested in the 'box that makes pictures.'" Thirty years earlier, his father had

---

* They now stand prominently in the museum's extensive exhibition of art from the ancient Americas and are described by the Met as being "among the finest examples of Mesoamerican stone relief sculpture" anywhere.

had a similar experience in Petra, when curious Bedouin guides had gathered around him as he sketched the Treasury. Like his father in Ottoman Syria, Fred was trying to capture the frontiers of the familiar world—familiar, at least, to the reading public back East. But in the few years since he had arrived, the Western frontier had all but vanished, thanks to speculators such as him and to federal policy toward Native peoples and lands. Washington Territory had gained statehood in 1889, the same year the Smithsonian Institution published a report about the near extinction of the North American buffalo at the hands of white men with guns. Soon, the U.S. Census had removed consideration of any frontier line from its statistics. Even Roosevelt glumly conceded that "the frontier proper has come to an end." At the World's Columbian Exposition in Chicago in 1893—the most ambitious fair in U.S. history—historian Frederick Jackson Turner had argued that the frontier, now closed, had been the defining force in the political, cultural, social, agricultural, and industrial history of the nation.

In April 1898, the U.S. government—spurred on by Roosevelt, now assistant secretary of the navy—declared war on imperial Spain in a quest for new territory, and with it new frontiers. By then, Fred had left Washington State on his own quest for a new frontier. He had set out for the Yukon, on the Canadian border with Alaska, a territory that the United States had bought from Russia in 1867. When a steamer filled with Yukon gold had docked in Seattle in mid-1897, it had sparked a gold rush, and Fred wanted in. Later, writing about his exploits for the ten-year reunion bulletin of his Princeton class of 1889—never mind that he hadn't graduated—Fred acknowledged he had gone "north with the other 49,999 chumps in the search for gold."

After giving up as a prospector, he turned westward again, this time heading for Hawaii just months after it was annexed by the federal government. In Honolulu, he remarried and took a job at a store that sold photographic supplies. He wrote to his father about a new kind of camera he was selling, with a lens that could revolve almost 180 degrees to take a panoramic landscape picture.

Through talent, discipline, bravery, and imagination, his father had created some of the most extraordinary landscape paintings in history. He had shown the cultural heights to which his nation could rise and the natural riches it should protect and cherish. His son's life was littered with get-rich-quick schemes, bad credit, pawnshops, and ruined landscapes. After the camera business went bust, Fred became a hotel manager in Honolulu.

HAVING BURIED ISABEL, CHURCH WENT home to Olana, where the children kept him company and friends paid condolence visits. Downie sorted through her mother's belongings, setting aside some dresses upon which she later drew to make a quilt. Church asked her to leave Isabel's camel-hair shawl so he could wrap himself in it and feel close to her. Seven months after his wife's death, he told Virginia Osborn, "I miss my dear Isabel as much as ever and often feel that it would have been a blessing if I could have passed away when she did." When his friend Warner proposed writing his biography, Church told him, "Of course there must be an allusion to the death of my beloved one and [to] her lovely character."

Louis took his father to Mexico again in early November 1899. Church had by now spent more than a dozen winters there. He was so debilitated he needed a wheelchair to transfer from one train to another, but still he enjoyed himself once he got to Mexico. Writing to Downie at least once a week, he filled his letters with praise of the architecture, people, climate, and scenery. After an excursion into the countryside near Cuernavaca, he sounded like a young painter again: "The show of wild flowers was enchanting. Superb blue morning glories enveloped the trees. The color of them was heavenly. . . . Large trees drooped under long clusters of great, white flowers and vines, shrubs and bushes glowed with blossoms of every color." But Church couldn't get to many of the wilder places he wanted to see and sketch. He could no longer mount a horse or a donkey, and the country roads were often too rough for any kind of carriage. He hired two local men to carry him on a chair lashed to two poles, and with their aid, he spent as much time outdoors as possible.

On March 1, 1900, Fred wrote to Church about some business dealings in which Fred had tried to involve him. He apologized, assuring his father, "I really & honestly want to please you in all things." Fred dispatched the letter to Downie's house in Pennsylvania, and she forwarded it to Church, who was in Cuernavaca

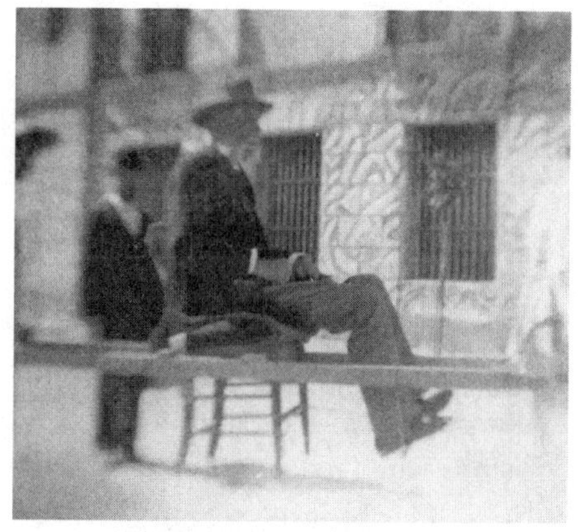

Church in Mexico, c. 1895

with his son Louis and Miles Graves, an old Hartford friend. By the time Fred's letter reached him, Church was dying. He had Bright's disease, an inflammation of the kidneys. In late March, Louis and Graves took Church to Mexico City, where they hastily arranged to have a special Pullman car attached to a train that was about to depart for New York. In Manhattan, Louis installed his father in the familiar surroundings of the Osborn mansion on Park Avenue. Downie and Winthrop joined Louis and Virginia Osborn in their vigil.

Lying in the same bed that Isabel had died in less than a year earlier, Church slept almost constantly for days. When he did wake up, he remained quiet but seemed cheerful. At times, he tried to order a carriage, or to get out of bed so he could go downstairs to supper. Although he was too weak to hold a fork properly, he refused to be fed by anyone else. Downie saw that he didn't understand he was dying. She recognized her father's "indomitable will," which persisted even as his physical strength abandoned him.

On April 7, Theddy Cole came down from Catskill to say goodbye to his old friend. Church died in his sleep later that day. One of his children cut a lock of his hair, brown shot through with silver, and slid it into an envelope.

THEY HELD CHURCH'S FUNERAL AT the Osborn house. Afterward, the children buried him in Hartford, next to Isabel, Bertie, and Emma. A Hartford newspaper omitted Fred in its coverage: "Three children survive."

As news of Church's death spread, dozens of obituaries and articles began to appear. They spoke of his towering talent, his personal integrity, his contributions to New York and the nation, and his courage in the face of danger and pain. "His fame was world-wide," the *New York Evening Post* wrote, "and his masterpieces are among the chief treasures of many famous collections." The *Boston Transcript* recalled him as "the last and greatest of all the American 'old masters'" and asserted that "his place is secure in the history of the arts." The *Transcript* also mentioned Church's famous sense of humor.

The New York Times trotted out the old rivalry with Bierstadt: "He had made his reputation before Bierstadt became famous. . . . Before he became known there were no landscape painters of prominence in this country." The *Times* noted that at the time of his death, Church's greatest days were behind him. "He produced very little work during the last score of years, and the fact that he was still alive has been almost forgotten by present day artists."

Worthington Whittredge, one of the last surviving painters from Church's Tenth Street circle, wrote a letter to Mrs. Osborn, which he asked her to share with the children. Throughout their long friendship, Whittredge recalled, he had always felt "something more than admiration" for Church, "—almost adoration for his great gifts whenever I have stood before his works."

"But I can hardly write what I feel at Church's death."

SIX WEEKS AFTER HER FATHER'S funeral, Downie traveled uptown to the Metropolitan Museum of Art. The museum looked markedly different from the day in 1880 when Church and his fellow trustees had sat on a platform listening to President Hayes at its opening. The original Vaux and Mould building had been swallowed by two newer wings, and an even grander edifice by Richard Morris Hunt, who had designed the Tenth Street Studio Building, was under construction along Fifth Avenue.

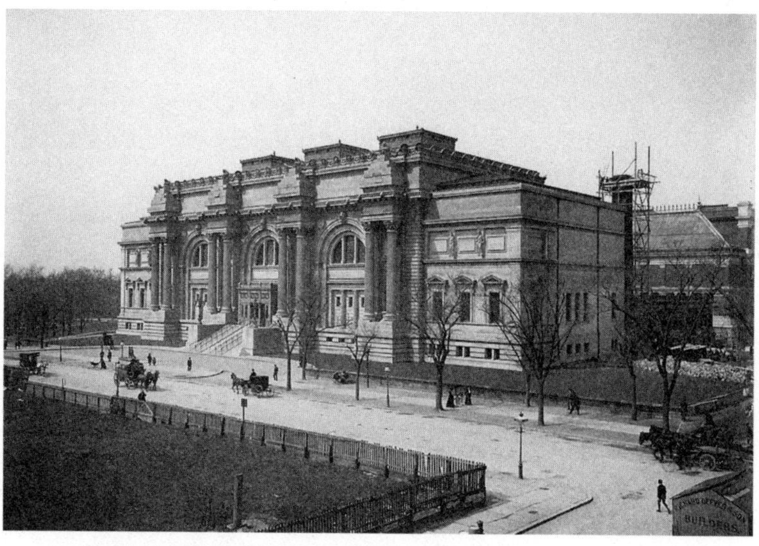

The Metropolitan Museum of Art, by Richard Morris Hunt, 1904

Inside, Downie entered a large, crowded gallery. There were more than a thousand people by her estimate, although this was only a private viewing. The exhibition wouldn't open to the public until the next day. Her father's paintings hung on the walls all around her. Afterward she wrote to Warner, "I was so overcome by the pictures seeing them together in that way—such <u>wonders</u>."

More than half a century earlier, Church had wandered through the memorial exhibition for Thomas Cole at the Art-Union gallery, following the arc of his mentor's life from one painting to the next. Now Church's own life, with all its far-flung odysseys and shifting visions of nature and humanity, was mapped out on the walls of the Metropolitan Museum. Every preoccupation of Church's mind and art shone from the fourteen canvases. There was his warning to his troubled nation in the blazing skies of *Twilight in the Wilderness*. His admiration for other cultures and his awe at the passage of time in *The Parthenon* and *El Khasné Petra*. And, above all, his wonder at the sublime powers of nature in *Niagara Falls*, *Cotopaxi*, and *The Heart of the Andes*.

For six months at the dawn of the twentieth century, it was the vigorous, masterly Church who dominated this hall of the great museum he had helped bring into being. "Years and years of suffering and never complaining," Whittredge mused to Virginia Osborn. "Years and years spent on his beautiful Creations and these we have, though we have lost him."

"A One-Man World's Fair"

Frederic Church died a very rich man. With the approval of Downie and Winthrop, he had stipulated in his will that Olana and its contents go to Louis. The rest of his estate was to be divided equally among Louis, Winthrop, and Downie—except for $50,000, which went into a trust whose interest income would pay Fred's expenses.

Shortly after Church's death, Louis married Sally Good, and they lived together at Olana until Louis died in 1943 at the age of seventy-three. Sally stayed on, but she lived lightly among the beautiful objects, not liking to disturb what had been arranged with so much thought and care. Attended by a few servants, she grew old at Olana. She was still living there in the winter of 1953 when a stranger drove up the carriage road.

The route to the house was long and steep. It twisted and turned as it rose, affording brief glimpses through the trees to the broad river below. The man approaching the house, David Huntington, was driving a 1949 Plymouth De Luxe. Only a bit of white and yellow trim relieved the dull maroon paint job. The car had never been waxed, and it reflected no light as it rolled up the drive.

The bare branches of the trees lining the drive shifted as Huntington passed beneath them, revealing more of the structure ahead. He found it difficult to make sense of what he was seeing—mansion, villa, castle? One huge wall looked as solid and blank as a fortress, presenting a stretch of yellow-brown stone so tall that a man standing on the ground would have to tip his head back to see the story above it. The windows up there had the defensive look of arrow slits. Much of the rest of the building seemed almost playful, all towers and verandas and windows. Many of the window surrounds culminated in a pointed arch.

Huntington was a Yale graduate student in art history, and he was excited to be here. He loved meeting new people and had a talent for putting them at ease—"charming and enthusiastic" was how an eminent statesman would later describe him in a speech. At thirty-one, Huntington was on the older side for a graduate student. In 1943, he had suspended his studies at Princeton to join the Army Air Forces. After the war, he went back to campus, but Princeton had become an oil-and-water swirl of carefree teenagers and worldly young men who had pulled their comrades from foxholes or burning airplanes. Huntington had returned to school physically unscathed but in mourning for his two closest friends, whom he had lost in the war. He graduated in 1947 with a degree in art and archaeology and went to work on a dig in England. After that he crossed the English Channel to tour the surviving architectural treasures of the bomb-blasted Continent.

Despite his travels, Huntington had never seen anything like the building that loomed above him as he shut his car door. "I went into the house absolutely bewildered by what I saw," he said. He was standing in a large central hall. To his left, a bit of pale sunlight struggled through two walls of windows, one set into the stone of the façade, the other perhaps twelve feet inside that, in an attempt to stave off the cold winds that blasted the hilltop in winter. To Huntington's right, a haze of warmer light filtered through an amber-papered window on the upper landing of a broad staircase. A huge Japanese scroll of the Buddha attaining nirvana hung above the lower flight of stairs, and in a wooden alcove nearby sat a golden Buddha. Next to this alcove someone had carefully arranged a sword, a shield, battle-axes, arrows, and spears. Symbols of peace and war coexisted strangely here. The hall was a kaleidoscope of dark and bright, of color and texture. The confusion Huntington had felt upon entering gave way to a rising, electric excitement.

Above his head, brightly stenciled patterns danced up the four peaked arches that framed the hall. Stuffed birds perched on a branch by the staircase. There were Persian rugs on the floor, mirrors and tapestries on the walls, sculptures and figurines on the tables. Winged Assyrian figures, carved and gilded, gleamed from dark wooden panels at each side of the landing, guarding the approach to the upper floor as if it were a temple or a tomb. Atop each of these panels, a tall bronze crane balanced on the back of a dragon-headed tortoise.

The place was frozen in time. It was as though the man who had built it had departed just a few minutes ago. To Huntington, it seemed like a "Noah's ark of all the world's culture," or "a one-man world's fair." He knew he had stumbled onto something important. Over the next months, his excitement would become more and more intense, developing into an obsession.

He walked into a small study. There was a fireplace in this room, a confection in dark wood and salmon-colored marble. A small wooden desk, intricately carved and decorated, sat in one corner. Almost every space on the walls not taken up by doors, windows, and furnishings was blanketed in oil paintings. Huntington recognized Niagara Falls in one; the picture felt overpowering to him, almost dangerous.

The largest and strangest painting in the room hung above the mantel. Much of the canvas was given over to the dark rock walls of a narrow canyon. The painting seemed to trap the viewer in the canyon's cold shadow. Up ahead, at the center of the canvas, the rocks opened toward a vertical ribbon of sunlight and the façade of an elaborate building of rose-colored stone. Directly across the room from this painting, a wide, floor-length window took up much of the wall. Beneath its pointed arch, Huntington could see dark hills and mountains on either side of the wide river. The composition of this natural scene, so precisely framed by the window, echoed that of the painting.

WHEN HUNTINGTON'S GRADUATE ADVISER HAD suggested he write his dissertation on a painter named Frederic Church, he had pretended to know the name. He went to the library, where he discovered that Church had once been celebrated in the United States and abroad. He struck Huntington as an intriguing subject for research, and that idea had brought him to this place—Olana.

Huntington had woken up that morning in mid-century America, where bold architects were creating houses with glass walls and flat roofs. But now he seemed to be in dozens of countries and centuries at once. A butterfly clung to one wall, trapped under a glass dome. A miniature Italian sarcophagus sat on a bookcase, surrounded by urns and bottles from the Middle East, India, and South America. A string of shells was draped around the shoulders of a Chinese vessel. A Roman chariot driver made of bronze whipped his horses as they raced across a red marble base. A Native American man, sculpted in plaster, knelt to the ground, a knife in one hand. Near him, cupids fed a unicorn on the painted surface of a Renaissance apothecary jar. A wooden chair in the Ottoman Turkish style, a Shaker rocking chair, a Victorian sofa, a French Empire table—it was an assortment of furniture suited to a gathering of cosmopolitan ghosts. Even the world's great spiritual traditions seemed to abide peacefully together in this place. There were the Buddhas in the central hall, a ceramic Madonna, an embroidered Jesus, painted Christian saints, a Koran stand with inlaid bone, a sculpture of Apollo, and an Aztec serpent god in stone.

As Huntington moved through the rooms, he had an eerie sensation. The objects around him seemed almost to be in motion. Their clashing differences and subtle similarities, the meteor streak of their journeys across space and time, were detonating what felt to him like a "spatial explosion." He sensed the presence of the creator of this spellbinding place, whose rooms, he later said, seemed "fraught with meaning and message." He was not simply inside the man's home, but inside his mind.

SALLY CHURCH—LOUIS'S WIDOW—WAS friendly but frail, with wide-set eyes and wispy white hair, which she wore swept back from her face. She had been born in July 1868, the same month the Fourteenth Amendment had granted citizenship to the formerly enslaved. She was now in her mid-eighties. It quickly became apparent to Huntington that she couldn't see or hear him well, and he realized that she also had a touch of dementia. "Sometimes," he later recalled, "she thought I was an opera singer from Hartford."

Huntington was polite and kind by nature, but his extraordinary experience in the house had left him impatient. He stayed as long as he felt he must and then took his leave. He began to drive away, but as members of her staff had instructed, he quickly parked in a spot she couldn't see from the windows. He walked to a courtyard behind the house and found the servants' entrance. He was ushered up the back stairs, through one door after another. The wooden staircase became steep and narrow, forcing awkward turns as he climbed toward the top of the house, with its strange roofline of towers and spires.

Here, the walls were plain: no pointed arches, no stenciled flowers, no gilt—just wooden slats and beams. Huntington emerged into a low-ceilinged attic. The detritus of the Church household lay all around him: broken chairs, Persian carpets, oil lamps, bird coops. Snowshoes and a toboggan hinted of red cheeks and snowy hillsides. Dozens of empty frames, still waiting for paintings, littered the room. Huntington saw cabinets and dressers and began tugging at their doors and drawers. Some were locked, but others opened at his touch.

"I was staggered," Huntington later recalled. There were tens of thousands of items—letters, sketches, unfinished oil paintings, canceled checks to Brooks Brothers. There were photographs of faraway places and others of smiling people in antiquated clothing posing on the porches downstairs. Some of the pictures confirmed Huntington's instinct about what he had seen as he moved through the house—the appearance of the rooms had barely changed since the days when Church lived here.

After his first visit, Sally Church's nephew, who was an executor of the estate, gave him permission to return to Olana for dissertation research. On these trips, he began to sort, catalog, and photograph the contents of the attic. He booked a room at a crumbling Greek Revival hotel in Hudson and ended up staying for ten weeks. After a series of false starts, he completed his dissertation on Frederic Church in 1960 and was awarded his Ph.D. the following year.

IN LATE OCTOBER 1963, PENNSYLVANIA Station—a soaring, light-flooded building celebrated upon its opening in 1910 as a Beaux-Arts master-piece—felt the first bite of a jackhammer. A giant crane sailed a stone eagle weighing fifty-seven hundred pounds to the ground. "Business leaders flanked the bird, posing for photographers," the *Times* reported. Having felled their prey, the men smiled at one another and the cameras. Enraged but helpless protesters bore witness to the events of the day, wearing the black armbands of mourners.

The following autumn, Huntington received a disturbing phone call from a Metropolitan Museum curator who knew about his obsession with Church. The man told him that Sally Church had died and the contents of the villa at Olana were to be auctioned. Huntington panicked. He jumped in his car and drove to Olana. Sally Church had died only weeks earlier, yet there were already white tags throughout the house—on furniture, rugs, sculptures, decorative objects, even on the butterflies pinned in their cases. The paintings were to be sold by a gallery in New York. Then the house and land would be sold.

Huntington's horror galvanized him. He decided to try to raise the money required to buy and preserve Olana in its entirety—house, collections, and several hundred acres of prime river real estate. He took a hotel room in Hudson and launched his campaign. He called or sent telegrams to everyone he could think of, struggling to mobilize support. He felt as if he were back in the war, a lone machine gunner in an Alpine pass trying to hold off an army—"waiting for help to come from behind, but nobody else was there yet."

Huntington's innate sociability and his scholarly expertise helped him win introductions to key figures in the museum world and on Wall Street. He brought a number of them to see Olana, but some found the place bizarre. One man told him, "If you get rid of the junk, it might be worth saving." In the United States in the 1960s, Victorian architecture struck many people as overwrought, even ghoulish, calling to mind Charles Addams's cartoons in *The New Yorker*. When a representative of Governor Nelson Rockefeller's office came to tour the place, she predicted that the governor wouldn't like it; he was a champion of Modernism. But she did leave Huntington with a glimmer of hope. Rockefeller cared deeply about New York history, and his family had had a strong connection to the Hudson Valley for generations, so he might be disposed to support the effort to save Olana. Soon, the governor's chief aide (and cousin), Sam Aldrich, joined Huntington in leading the campaign.

When Huntington wasn't showing visitors around Olana or sitting in the hotel in Hudson making phone calls, he was often in his car or on the train, which ran the same riverfront route Church had taken on his constant trips to and from New York City. After many arduous months, Huntington's efforts started to bear fruit. In late 1964 and early 1965, articles appeared in *The New York Times* and *Harper's* about the campaign to save Olana.

Huntington kept hammering away at his message. Olana was "the monument of Emerson's, Thoreau's, and Whitman's America," he argued. It represented Emerson's and Thoreau's worship of natural beauty and self-reliance, and Whitman's exuberant embrace of everything alien and new. The American nineteenth century stood on that hilltop.

Huntington organized benefit cruises to bring New Yorkers to Olana. He attended teas with socialites and meetings with local business leaders. Soon hundreds of people were filing through the house each month to peer into Church's world. Huntington began to garner support from talented and powerful people, among them Frederick Osborn, a prominent banker whose grandparents had been Church and Isabel's dearest friends. Osborn brought financial expertise, negotiation skills, and important connections. Celebrated artists and architects joined the cause, too—among them Lincoln Kirstein, the ballet impresario, and Philip Johnson, the architect who had in 1949 designed a most un-Victorian dwelling in Connecticut called the Glass House. A group of civic leaders agreed to form an organization to spearhead the fundraising, and they negotiated an extension on the deadline for raising the money required, which had been pegged at nearly half a million dollars.

Jacqueline Kennedy, widely known as an enthusiast of history and the arts, proved a vital ally, writing letters and making phone calls. When an exhibition of Church's work opened at the National Collection of Fine Arts (later part of the Smithsonian) before moving to Albany and then to New York, Mrs. Kennedy was honorary chairwoman of the opening-night dinner in Manhattan. She persuaded her brother-in-law Senator Robert F. Kennedy to lend his support to a bill in the New York State Legislature that would save Olana. Legislators enacted that bill with the encouragement of Governor Rockefeller.

When the signing ceremony was held at Olana in June of 1966, the governor made a dramatic entrance by helicopter. Olana was designated a state historic site. Later, a nonprofit organization was created to advocate for Olana and to foster educational programming at the site. Finally, this once-private retreat of extraordinary beauty had extended its embrace to everyone.

THE RESCUE AND PRESERVATION OF Olana spurred an ongoing reassessment of Church's work and legacy. In 1979, his painting *The Icebergs*—once thought to have been lost but then rediscovered at an English manor house turned boarding school—was auctioned at Sotheby's. The event drew international press attention when the winning bid came in at $2.5 million, the highest auction price earned up to that date by an American painting and the third highest for any painting in history. Only a Titian and a Velázquez had commanded more.

Today, hundreds of Church's pictures grace museums and private collections across the country, and his 1859 masterwork, *The Heart of the Andes*, hangs in the Metropolitan Museum of Art. *The Heart of the Andes* looks across the gallery past Leutze's *Washington Crossing the Delaware* to Bierstadt's *Rocky Mountains, Lander's Peak*, just as it did at the 1864 Metropolitan Fair. Over two thousand of Church's sketches, including more than five hundred virtuosic oil sketches, are held by the Cooper Hewitt, Smithsonian Design Museum in New York City.

All these works are the achievements of a painter who put the art of his young nation on the world map. They are the legacy of an adventurer who marveled along with Humboldt at the complexity of the cosmos. They are expressions of our shared capacity to feel most fully alive in the contemplation of a divine or universal power. They are offerings from an American who cared profoundly about his nation's experiment in self-government, and who harnessed his art to celebrate its virtues and warn of its fragility.

Up the Hudson River, Olana is a three-dimensional Church painting, composed from the elements he worshipped all his life: earth, stone, plants, water, sky, and the transfixing, metamorphic play of light across them all. Olana's gables and towers rise above the tree line, and overhead, the piled clouds link house and landscape to the heavens. Even before Church's death, some ventured that Olana might be the greatest masterpiece in a life filled with them.

From its heights, you can see the world.

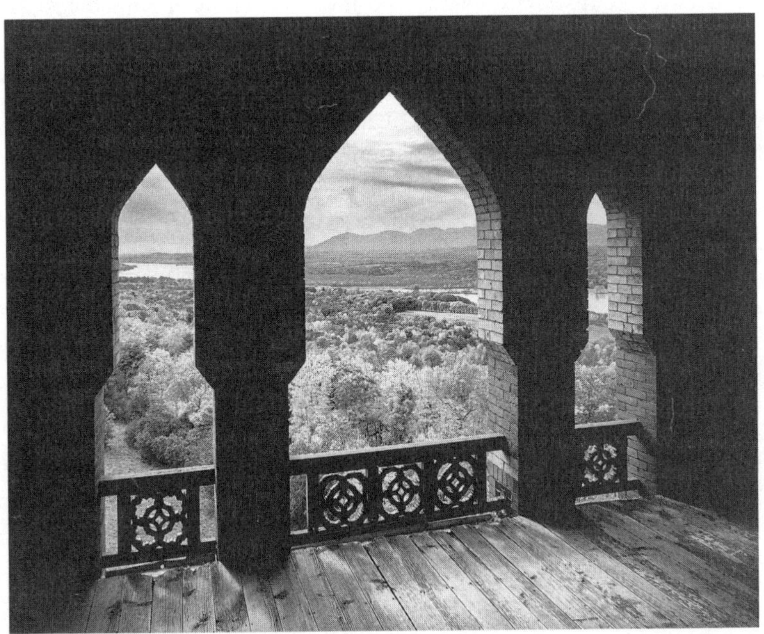

View from the Bell Tower at Olana today, by Peter Aaron

Acknowledgments

I first heard Frederic Church's name as a young girl, when my father told me about a place called Olana, which had been saved from destruction by visionary people galvanized by the loss of Pennsylvania Station. My father had stumbled across Olana in the early 1960s while stationed at West Point. Preferring historic houses to army duties, he explored the Hudson Valley on a little motorbike. Riding up a hilly road one day, he found himself before an imposing villa and suddenly realized he was on private property. I now know that Church's daughter-in-law, Sally Church, was still living there when my father accidentally joined the decades-long parade of trespassers that had begun while Church himself was still alive. I so wish I could show my father this book; he was cheering me on when I began it. My mother, Eleanor, and my sisters, Betsy, Elizabeth, and Jessica, have all kept up that chorus of encouragement, and I thank each of them, and their husbands and partners, too, for their support and love. My nieces and nephews (one of whom coined the collective noun *"neffuses"*) turned into fully fledged, delightful adults while I was off in the nineteenth century; I think they know how much I admire and adore them.

I have a staggering number of experts and friends to thank for their help at various stages of my research (although I'm certain to leave someone out by accident, for which I apologize). I want to start with a group of art historians who, through their personal generosity and their past research, made it possible for me to write *Glorious Country*. Franklin Kelly, Deputy Director and Chief Curator, National Gallery of Art (retired), has been unflaggingly supportive since the earliest stages of this project. His many published works on Church, his faith in my ability to capture Church's life story, our conversations, and his comments on the manuscript have all been vital.

Anyone writing on Church owes an enormous debt to Gerald L. Carr. His two-volume *Frederic Edwin Church: Catalogue Raisonné of Works of Art at Olana State Historic Site* is a feat of painstaking scholarship at which I marveled almost daily while researching *Glorious Country*. I simply could not have written my book without the *Catalogue Raisonné* and Carr's many other books and articles on Church. I'm also grateful for a full day of conversation we had about Church early in my research.

Tyler Green's brilliant writing on nineteenth-century U.S. landscape painters has shaped my understanding both of their art and of the literary and political culture in which they lived and worked. Green generously shared a wealth of original research that he hadn't yet published, and our conversations over the past several years have been some of the most intellectually exciting experiences of this whole adventure. I'm especially grateful for his detailed, probing comments on the manuscript, which sharpened and in some ways transformed the book.

Elizabeth Mankin Kornhauser, the Alice Pratt Brown Curator of American Paintings and Sculpture Emerita at the Metropolitan Museum of Art, likewise spoke with me many times about Church and his fellow landscape painters. Her work on Thomas Cole in particular has been foundational for my understanding of the American art world that Church entered as a young man. She answered frequent queries from me with generosity and good cheer, and she also read an early draft and gave me valuable comments.

Eleanor Jones Harvey, Senior Curator (19th-Century Art) at the Smithsonian American Art Museum, has likewise been supportive from the very beginning. Her writings on Church and his circle, especially on the Civil War era, have been indispensable, and she, too, kindly read a draft of the manuscript and gave me the benefit of her formidable knowledge of the era.

I'd also like to thank Linda Ferber, Senior Art Historian and Museum Director Emerita at the New York Historical, who spoke with me at length about Church and his artistic and personal relationship with Albert Bierstadt.

Kay Toll, a former board chair at Olana, first put the idea of a biography of Church in my head. The leadership at Olana, which is jointly run by the New York State Office of Parks, Recreation and Historic Preservation and the Olana Partnership, a nonprofit organization, assured me that if I did decide to write Church's biography, they would facilitate my access to the archives but otherwise leave me completely alone. For smoothing my research path, I'm especially grateful to Sean Sawyer, the Washburn and Susan Oberwager President of the Olana Partnership; Mark Prezorski, Senior Vice President and Landscape Curator of the Olana Partnership; and Amy Hausmann, the former Director of the Olana State Historic Site. Ida Brier, the longtime archivist at Olana until her recent retirement, is my hero. She patiently answered dozens of queries and educated me on the complexities of the extensive archives. Many other people associated with Olana have supported this project, including Mary Lawrie, Will Coleman, Maggie Dimock, Clare Flemming, Allegra Davis, Blakely Kralovec, Carolyn Keogh, Melanie Hasbrook, and Nicole Madden. The current cochairs of the Olana Partnership, Joe Baker and Robin Key, and immediate past chair, Peter Warwick, and his wife, Helen Warwick, have all offered their enthusiasm. Since the beginning of my project, no one associated with Olana has tried to influence what I wrote, nor did they see my manuscript until it was completed.

Many Church-related documents and artifacts are housed at the Bureau of Historic Sites and Parks of the New York State Office of Parks, Recreation and Historic Preservation. For their support and assistance, I thank former Commissioner of New York State Parks, Recreation and Historic Preservation Erik Kulleseid; Deputy Commissioner for Historic Preservation Daniel Mackay; Director of the Division for Historic Preservation Daniel McEneny; and Regional Director for the Taconic Region Linda Cooper, who is also Interim Director of the Olana State Historic Site. Thanks also to Daniel Bigler, Travis Bowman, Andrea Cerbie, Michele Phillips, Victoria Reisman, Kelli Smith, Sarah Stevens, and Mary Zaremski.

I spent a good deal of time across the Hudson River from Olana at the Thomas Cole National Historic Site, where I was warmly welcomed by Betsy Jacks, now the Executive Director Emerita (who kindly read my chapters on Church's time studying with Cole), as well as by her successor, Maura O'Shea; my gratitude also to Kate Menconeri, Amanda Malmstrom, and Jennifer Greim.

In September 2024, a scholars' conference on Church was convened at Olana by Betsy Kornhauser along with Tim Barringer and Jennifer Raab, both of Yale University; I thank the conveners for including me, and the participants for their illuminating presentations and conversations.

At the Albany Institute of History and Art, W. Douglas McCombs and Diane Shewchuk gave me a warm welcome to the Cole archives. Other scholars who have been generous with their time and research include the late David P. Schuyler; Christine Oaklander, who answered many questions about the Osborn family; Jonathan Palmer, formerly of the Vedder Research Library in Coxsackie, New York; Karen Zukowski, who taught me so much, both in conversation and through her extensive writings, about the Churches' life at Olana; Shannon Vittoria, formerly of the Met and now of LACMA, who kindly shared research on Church in Mexico done in collaboration with Kiki Barnes; Erin Monroe of the Wadsworth Atheneum; Philip Palmer of the Morgan Library & Museum; Ryan Hyman of Macculloch Hall Historical Museum; Shelby Mattice of the Bronck Museum at the Greene County Historical Society; Diane Galusha of the Historical Society of the Town of Middletown, New York; and Jim Andrews of Andes, New York.

The Cooper Hewitt, Smithsonian Design Museum, holds a spectacular collection of Church's pencil and oil sketches. For the opportunity to study them in person and for assisting me over and over with my research, I thank Caitlin Condell, Associate Curator and Head of the Drawings, Prints, and Graphic Design Department, and Casey Monroe, formerly the Senior Research Cataloguer, Frederic Edwin Church, at the Cooper Hewitt. My gratitude also to Mackenzie Jones and Janice Hussain for their assistance.

Many other friends and colleagues discussed my research with me and/or read drafts. Andrea Wulf is definitely my toughest critic, but she always manages to leave me laughing as she lets me know, with a directness I treasure, what is not working and why. Her generosity in sharing her time, ideas about writing, and vast knowledge of eighteenth- and nineteenth-century history have bettered my books and my life. For fifteen years my friend Scott Ellsworth and I have been exchanging ideas about nonfiction writing, and he has marked up many, many pages of my drafts. I am in awe of his work ethic and his creativity, and he is a deeply kind and generous friend who always knows how to encourage a flagging fellow writer. Maya Jasanoff has long been a source of wisdom and inspiration as I strive to craft nonfiction that is both rigorous and absorbing. Thomas Woltz, a virtuoso at friendship, has helped me understand landscape architecture, both as an art form and as an exacting profession, in ways that have deepened my understanding of nineteenth-century landscape architects— including Church's design of Olana. Howard Fish and I talked for many hours about writing. Bruce Crispell tackled a long draft and came back to me with astute suggestions. Beth Rundquist, a gifted painter and dear friend, read an early draft and gave me invaluable comments from an artist's perspective.

Carrie Rebora Barratt, Director of LongHouse Reserve and an expert on American art, generously took the time to read the book proposal and write a letter for my Guggenheim fellowship application. Pablo Navas Sanz de Santamaría, a Church scholar and former president of the Universidad de los Andes in Bogotá, commented on my chapters on Church's travels in the Andes. My dear friend and Hunter College colleague Gregory Mosher, a storied director and producer, read the manuscript with his brilliant eye for character and structure; we've been talking about the arts for ten years, and I've learned so much from him. Harold Holzer, another Hunter colleague and a leading authority on Abraham Lincoln, kindly and speedily read my chapters on the Civil War. Conrad Vispo shared on many occasions his expertise on historical weather data for New York State. The Carter family, who own Shirley Plantation in Virginia, have made the plantation's historical records available to researchers, and I thank Charles Carter for his guidance on accessing them. Brian Dewan pointed me toward some especially rich Church letters. Carol Hakim, an expert on the history of Lebanon, kindly read a chapter on the Church family's stay in Beirut. John Tresch and Barbara Cantalupo answered my queries about Poe and Church. Kerissa and Kemp Battle provided phenological data and pep talks. Sam Stout shared an unpublished memoir by an ancestor who attended school with Church in Hartford. Sara Cedar Miller helped me find Parks Department records for Church's tenure as a commissioner. Candice Hopkins of the Forge Project guided me on Indigenous historiography.

My gratitude also to Katie Adams, Edward Ball, and Amabel James for their comments and encouragement.

I'm also grateful to a number of busy and accomplished people for communicating with me about this project. I've admired Jean Strouse's books since before I met her at the Cullman Center for Scholars and Writers at the New York Public Library, which she directed for many years, and I'm grateful to her for a series of conversations about the joys and challenges of writing about painters and art. Erik Larson, a master of narrative nonfiction, took the time to speak with me about how he approaches research, plot structure, and character development; it was an incredibly generous thing to do.

A special thank-you to Valerie Paley, Senior Vice President and the Sue Ann Weinberg Director of the Patricia D. Klingenstein Library at the New York Historical. André Bernard, the former Vice President of the John Simon Guggenheim Memorial Foundation, became a valued sounding board, and I'm grateful to have come to count him as a friend. Susan Holloway Scott helped me decide to undertake a biography of Church in the first place. Geri Thoma and Bob Weil gave me early encouragement. Ron Chernow kindly passed on information about Church that he encountered while researching his biography of Mark Twain. Ted Widmer shared his expertise on nineteenth-century U.S. political history; Gail Buckman discussed Church's historical significance as an early and enthusiastic collector of photographs; and Mark Strieter went in person to confirm the species of a very particular tree. David L. Kennedy, Emeritus Professor and Senior Honorary Research Fellow in Roman Archaeology and History at the University of Western Australia, answered many questions about nineteenth-century Petra. Richard Drayton helped me with Jamaican meteorological records; Jamie Romm translated a passage in ancient Greek for me; Earle Shettleworth helped with my questions about nineteenth-century Maine; Annik LaFarge shared her research on Church's son Freddie; Ingo Schwarz shared his knowledge of Alexander von Humboldt; Mark Nesbitt of the Royal Botanic Gardens, Kew, and Heather Craddock, now of the National Archives, UK, helped me with a query about Jamaican botanical gardens. John Bigelow Taylor kindly gave me permission to reproduce images owned by his family, including a sketch by Church himself. I thank Jeff Cooley for a well-timed introduction, and Paul Worman for sharing a rare picture of Church at work. Andrew Solomon approached the launch of this book with creativity and generosity.

Members of the family of the late David Huntington, the art historian who in the 1960s led the campaign to save Olana, shared memories of him with me; for this I'm grateful to Dr. Huntington's wife, Trudy; his children Abby and Caleb; and his nephew Gordon Wyse.

Many dedicated librarians and archivists assisted me in my research. My thanks to Crystal Toscano of the New York Historical; Brynn White of the Century Association Archives Foundation; Eleanor Morgan of the Century Association Library; Helen Hewitt of Minterne House in the UK; Brian Ferree of the New York City Municipal Archives; Michelle McCarthy-Behler and John Cordovez of the New York Public Library's Manuscripts, Archives and Rare Books Division; Graham Greer of the Newberry Library; Keith Weimer of the University of Virginia Library; and Casey Machenheimer of Watkinson Library at Trinity College in Hartford.

I have wonderful colleagues in the Department of Urban Policy and Planning at Hunter College, and they have been extremely kind and patient, including through some challenging times (a side thank-you here to Lilli Link, MD, and Elizabeth Milbank, MD, who know how they helped). At

Hunter, I'm particularly indebted to Joe Viteritti, Jill Gross, John Chin, and Nick Bloom. Jennifer Raab, the former president of Hunter, made me feel very welcome at Hunter a decade ago and facilitated my research on this book (as she did for my last book); I also thank former provost Lon Kaufman and former dean Andy Polsky for their support. The Research Foundation of the City University of New York provided indispensable funding as I worked on the project, as did the John Simon Guggenheim Memorial Foundation.

I had fantastic research and editorial help on various aspects of *Glorious Country* from Helen Handelman (who came to my rescue at a particularly fraught time—thank you, Helen!), Emma Sargent, Tracey Van Dusen, and Casey Monroe; the latter brought his expertise on Church to the project, for which I'm especially grateful. My beloved friend and former student Rebecca Sunde offered early research assistance and constant moral support.

Byron Knief was a delightful and erudite companion on a trip in Church's footsteps through Colombia and Ecuador. Along with Byron, Carolina Barco generously helped launch us on our trip with ideas and contacts for our time in Colombia, where we enjoyed the warm hospitality of Pablo Navas Sanz de Santamaría and his wife, Gina; of Jaime Laserna and Esther de Laserna; and of Vivian Hughes. In Colombia, Andrés Trujillo was an excellent guide, and in Ecuador, Juan Fernando Durán threw himself into the project of tracing Church's travels in Humboldt's footsteps, with exciting results.

Ever since David Stark agreed to chair my dissertation at Columbia more than twenty-five years ago, he has been a mentor filled with curiosity, ideas, and encouragement, and he has become a treasured friend. I also want to thank two of my earlier teachers, Warren Heiser and Ginna Mashburn.

Other friends have buoyed me with their love and patience (and helped distract me when that's what I needed most), especially Joyce Robbins and Nitsan Chorev.

Scott Koniecko, president of the Beatrix Farrand Society on Mount Desert Island, Maine, introduced me to a community of people who love art, history, and books, among them Gilbert and Ildiko Butler, whom I thank for their hospitality as well as for their interest in Church and in the progress of this book. The much-missed Joan Davidson inspired me (as she did everyone lucky enough to know her) with her passion for the beauty and history of the Hudson Valley.

Sarah Chalfant of the Wylie Agency is a dream agent: smart, attentive, tough, and warm all at once. I can't believe my good fortune in having her in my corner on this project. My deep gratitude to Sarah as well as to Rebecca Nagel for all they have done over the past years, starting with getting my proposal into the hands of the legendary Nan Graham at Scribner. Nan immediately understood what I was hoping to do and recognized Church's political and cultural relevance to his own times and ours. Once I delivered the manuscript, I experienced Nan's preternatural ability to pinpoint what's missing in a narrative (and the many, many pages that should be excised). It has been a privilege to work with her. Thanks to Sabrina Pyun and Criss Moon for their good cheer and professionalism throughout the book's production. At Scribner, I'd also like to thank Dan Cuddy for managing a smooth production process, Steve Boldt for his extraordinarily attentive copyediting, and, for creating a gorgeous book inside and out, Jaya Miceli, Tristan Offit, and Kyle Kabel.

John Habich, one of the kindest, wisest, and most energetic people I've ever met, brought his insight and humor to an intensive edit of my manuscript that changed the way I will read and write for the rest of my life.

My deepest thanks go to my partner, Markley Boyer, who approaches each day with enthusiasm, conscientiousness, and a sparkling sense of adventure. He embraced the presence of Frederic Church in our lives, putting his astonishingly polymathic talents to work in innumerable ways to help bring this book into the world. Here is a partial list: Markley created beautiful maps of Church's travels; built a database to keep track of my illustrations; digitized seven thousand pages of Church-related correspondence; prepped dozens of images for print; took author photos; read the longest version of the manuscript; hiked all over the Northeast with me through landscapes Church had sketched and painted; introduced me to the joys of Church's beloved Maine (and the embrace of the extended Boyer family); organized trips for us in Church's footsteps to the Andes, Mexico, and the Middle East; endured a lightning storm on Cotopaxi with me and a grueling eighteen-mile round-trip hike to the top of a peak near Petra (and loved both); built me a writing cottage in the woods; rigged up a traveling office so I could keep working on car trips; built a book website; went to parties and concerts without me while I stayed home to write; encouraged me a thousand times when I was tired; and conversed with me almost every day for years about Church, art, U.S. history, writing, and the formatting of endnotes. No writer could possibly have a more loving, cheerful, talented, and patient partner.

This book is dedicated to you, Markley. Of course.

Notes

Unless otherwise noted, any correspondence cited in these endnotes comes from the Olana State Historic Site.

ABBREVIATIONS

AAA: Archives of American Art
CHSDM: Cooper Hewitt, Smithsonian Design Museum
OSHS: Olana State Historic Site
Palmer Papers: Erastus Dow Palmer Papers, McKinney Library, Albany Institute of History and Art
PUL: Princeton University Library
TCP: Thomas Cole Papers, New York State Library

PROLOGUE "Mr. Church Likes to Undertake the Impossible"

1 *policemen were called:* David C. Huntington, *The Landscapes of Frederic Edwin Church: Vision of an American Era* (George Braziller, 1966), 5.

2 *Two thousand arrived:* Kevin J. Avery, *Church's Great Picture:* The Heart of the Andes (Metropolitan Museum of Art, 1993), 36.

2 *Constructed of red brick:* Thomas Bailey Aldrich, "Among the Studios," in J. T. Trowbridge et al., eds., *Our Young Folks: An Illustrated Magazine for Boys and Girls* 1 (September 1865): 595.

2 *Over the door:* Annette Blaugrund, *The Tenth Street Studio Building* (Parrish Art Museum, 1997), 19.

2 *lawyers, bankers, doctors:* Businesses and residents on Tenth Street are listed in H. Wilson, ed., *Trow's New York City Directory* (John F. Trow, 1859).

2 *One critic wanted:* K.C., "The Heart of the Andes," *Christian Register*, January 14, 1860.

3 *"Your third visit":* Samuel L. Clemens, "To Orion Clemens, March 18, 1861, St. Louis, Mo.," in *Mark Twain's Letters, Volume 1: 1853–1866*, ed. Edgar Marquess Branch et al. (University of California Press, 1988), 116–20.

3 *"Church has the finest eye":* Louis Legrand Noble, *The Life and Works of Thomas Cole, N.A.* (Sheldon, Blakeman & Company, 1856), 364.

3　*He loved to hike:* H. W. French, *Art and Artists in Connecticut* (Charles T. Dillingham, 1879), 131.

3　*"with a rapidity":* William James Stillman, *The Autobiography of a Journalist* (Houghton Mifflin, 1901), 1:114–15.

3　*Then he spent:* Henry T. Tuckerman, *Book of the Artists: American Artist Life, Comprising Biographical and Critical Sketches of American Artists* (G. P. Putnam & Sons, 1867), 385–86.

4　*They compared him:* Elizabeth McKinsey, *Niagara Falls: Icon of the American Sublime* (Cambridge University Press, 1985), 249; and Huntington, *Landscapes*, 20.

4　*"Mr. Church likes":* "Twilight in the Wilderness," *World*, June 20, 1860.

4　*The same energy:* French, *Art and Artists*, 131.

4　*"He was fortune's favorite":* *The Autobiography of Worthington Whittredge, 1820–1910*, ed. John I. H. Baur (Brooklyn Museum Press, 1942), 28.

4　*"Mr. Church's capacity":* Charles Tracy, *The Tracy Log Book, 1855: A Month in Summer*, ed. Anne Mazlish (Acadia Publishing, 1997), 62.

4　*"boyish playfulness":* Anne Hampton Brewster, journal entry, December 12, 1868, box 4, folder 1, Anne Hampton Brewster Papers, Library Company of Philadelphia.

4　*"entirely unconscious":* Brewster, journal entry, February 12, 1869.

5　*"Christianity was above all":* Charles Dudley Warner, "An Unfinished Biography of the Artist" (1899), in Franklin Kelly, *Frederic Edwin Church* (National Gallery of Art, 1989), 198.

5　*"He is the only landscape-painter":* Eugene Benson, "Pictures in the Private Galleries of New York," *Putnam's Magazine* 6, no. 31 (July 1870): 84, quoted by John Davis, *The Landscape of Belief: Encountering the Holy Land in Nineteenth-Century American Art and Culture* (Princeton University Press, 1996), 174.

5　*"affords every variety":* Macaulay, "The Artist and the Convict," *Rochester Democrat and American*, June 12, 1862.

6　*visual-artist counterpart to the literary giants:* Huntington, *Landscapes*, 10.

6　*"Every appearance in nature":* Ralph Waldo Emerson, *Nature* (1836), chap. 4, "Language," reproduced in Tyler Green, *Emerson's* Nature *and the Artists* (Prestel, 2021), 74. Green makes a powerful case for the influence of Emerson's *Nature* on U.S. landscape painting in his introductory essay to this book as well as in his commentary on specific paintings throughout.

7　*a term coined in the 1870s:* Gerald L. Carr, *In Search of the Promised Land: Paintings by Frederic Edwin Church* (Berry-Hill Galleries, 2000), 107n2.

7　*"glorious country":* Church to Ogden Rood, May 16, 1875. Original in Ogden N. Rood Papers, Rare Book & Manuscript Library, Columbia University.

7　*"When you write":* [Edward Sheffield] Bartholomew to Church, March 11, 1856. Original in Wadsworth Atheneum Archive.

CHAPTER 1　"I Scarcely Dared Hope"

9　*"your own tall Majesty":* Warner, "Unfinished Biography," 189.

9　*It had green shutters:* Gerald L. Carr, *Frederic Edwin Church: Catalogue Raisonné of Works of Art at Olana State Historic Site*, 2 vols. (Cambridge University Press, 1994), 1:149.

9　*Even the privy:* John G. Waite Associates, "Thomas Cole House: Historic Structure Report" (Thomas Cole National Historic Site, 2019), 1:12. The cupola is visible in Frederic Church's sketch "Cedar Grove, Catskill," October 1848, OSHS.

10　*Church owed his presence here:* Daniel Wadsworth to Thomas Cole, May 8, 1844. Original in TCP.

10   *Wadsworth was one of Cole's:* Elizabeth Mankin Kornhauser, "Daniel Wadsworth and Elizabeth Hart Jarvis Colt: Connecticut's Leading Collectors of American Landscape Art," in *Tastemakers, Collectors, and Patrons: Collecting American Art in the Long Nineteenth Century,* ed. Linda S. Ferber and Margaret R. Laster (Penn State University Press and the Frick Collection, 2024), 68–69.

10   *"I scarcely dared hope":* Church to Thomas Cole, May 20, 1844. Original in TCP.

10   *"Gentlemen & Ladies":* All the drawings mentioned in this paragraph are reproduced in Carr, *Frederic Edwin Church,* 2: nos. 1–8.

11   *He often gazed:* John Butler Talcott, unpublished memoir, 8. I thank Sam Stout for sharing this memoir by his great-grandfather.

11   *asked him to draw pictures:* Warner, "Unfinished Biography," 177.

11   *"advised me with impressive seriousness":* Church to Jere Black, February 19, 1898.

11   *He decided he wanted:* Charles Freeman to Joseph Church, March 21, 1868.

11   *"mechanical genius":* Wadsworth to Cole, May 8, 1844.

11   *"had that aggressive trait":* *Autobiography of Worthington Whittredge,* 28.

11   *"We were wrecked":* Warner, "Unfinished Biography," 177–78.

11   *Mrs. Church wore simple gowns:* Elizabeth Church to Church, April 28, 1858.

12   *took off his hat:* Warner, "Unfinished Biography," 180.

12   *They both issued:* John K. Howat, *Frederic Church* (Yale University Press, 2005), 3.

12   *two sons had died:* Warner, "Unfinished Biography," annotation by Debora Rindge, 175.

12   *His father complained:* Charles Freeman to Joseph Church, January 17, 1860.

12   *"most delightful":* Church to Cole, May 20, 1844.

12   *"Be a good boy!":* Warner, "Unfinished Biography," 197.

13   *"beautiful and romantic":* Church to Cole, May 20, 1844.

13   *Esopus and Mohican:* Alf Evers, *The Catskills: From Wilderness to Woodstock* (Overlook Press, 1982), 10.

13   *The bones of mastodons:* Robert Titus and Johanna Titus, *The Hudson Valley in the Ice Age: A Geological History & Tour* (Black Dome Press, 2012), 178; *ancient sea creatures:* Robert Titus, *The Catskills: A Geological Guide,* 3rd ed. (Purple Mountain Press, 2004), 61ff.

13   *The Native American families:* Alan Taylor, *William Cooper's Town: Power and Persuasion on the Frontier of the Early American Republic* (Alfred A. Knopf, 1995), 34–40.

13   *Some locals believed:* Evers, *Catskills,* 227–34.

13   *One of the last Catskills witch doctors:* Evers, *Catskills,* 212–13.

14   *"city of pleasant faces":* Church to Aaron Goodman, February 5, 1849.

14   *museum opened the same summer:* Carr, *Frederic Edwin Church,* 1:85.

14   *Cole had grown up:* Alan Wallach, "Thomas Cole: Landscape and the Course of American Empire," in *Thomas Cole: Landscape into History,* ed. William H. Truettner and Alan Wallach (Yale University Press, 1994), 25.

14   *He had discovered the Catskills:* Wallach, "Thomas Cole," 23.

15   *In Italy, as he wandered:* Thomas Cole, journal, August 25, 1831, quoted by Louis Legrand Noble, *The Course of Empire, Voyage of Life, and Other Pictures of Thomas Cole, N.A.* (Cornish, Lamport, 1853), 135–36.

15   The Course of Empire: On *The Course of Empire,* see esp. Tim Barringer, "Thomas Cole's Atlantic Crossings," in Elizabeth Mankin Kornhauser and Tim Barringer, *Thomas Cole's Journey: Atlantic Crossings* (Metropolitan Museum of Art, 2018), 50–59.

15   *"the work of the highest genius":* James Fenimore Cooper to Louis Legrand Noble, January 6, 1849, quoted by Noble, *Course of Empire,* 225.

15   *Cole's landlord in Catskill:* Maureen Hart Hennessey, *Life at Cedar Grove* (Thomas Cole National Historic Site, 2011), 17.

15   *"glorious scenery"*: Thomas Cole to William A. Adams, April 23, 1834, quoted by Noble, *Course of Empire*, 184.

15   *Cole set up a painting studio*: National Park Service, *Thomas Cole National Historic Site: General Management Plan / Environmental Assessment* (Department of the Interior, 2004), 14.

16   *"a peculiar rising"*: Noble, *Course of Empire*, 409.

16   *His blue-gray eyes*: Noble, *Course of Empire*, 409.

16   *In a leather-bound account book*: Thomas Cole, account book entry, June 4, 1844, CV 553, series 4, box 2, folder 9, Cole Records, Thomas Cole Collection, Albany Institute of History and Art.

16   *his teacher quickly set him at ease*: Elizabeth B. Jacks, "Director's Foreword," in John Wilmerding, *Master, Mentor, Master: Thomas Cole & Frederic Church* (Thomas Cole National Historic Site, 2014), 3.

16   *sometimes he just perched*: See the sketch by Henry Cheever Pratt entitled "Cole Sketching," reproduced as plate 47 in Elizabeth Mankin Kornhauser, "Manifesto for an American Sublime: Thomas Cole's 'The Oxbow,'" in Kornhauser and Barringer, *Thomas Cole's Journey*, 71.

17   *"sow seed in the fields"*: Thomas Cole, *Lecture on Art* (c. 1845; repr., Thomas Cole National Historic Site, 2020), 1.

17   *"Genius has but one wing"*: Thomas Cole to John Falconer, February 1, 1848, quoted by Noble, *Course of Empire*, 379.

17   *disciplined daily sketching*: Carr, *Frederic Edwin Church*, 1:37.

17   *"Trees are like men"*: Thomas Cole, "Essay on American Scenery," *American Monthly Magazine* 1 (January 1836): 9.

17   *Church learned to capture*: For Church's tree sketches from this phase, see Carr, *Frederic Edwin Church*, 2: nos. 14–18.

17   *"very rude"*: Church to Theodore Cole, February 20, 1847, series 1, box 4, folder 4, Cole Family Letters: 1845–1855, TCP.

17   *He drew cows*: Carr, *Frederic Edwin Church*, 1:51.

17   *He drew horses*: Carr, *Frederic Edwin Church*, 1:51–52.

17   *His young charge*: Warner, "Unfinished Biography," 186.

CHAPTER 2   "What Are the Forms the Clouds Take"

19   *new litter of kittens*: Sarah Cole to Theodore Cole, c. 1845, quoted by Hennessey, *Life at Cedar Grove*, 58–59.

19   *Theddy and Mary sometimes*: Church to Theodore Cole, February 20, 1847.

19   *One warm summer day*: "Meteorological Observations for the Year 1844 Made Under the Directions of the University of the State of New York, at the Hudson Academy Situated in the City of Hudson in the County of Columbia," July 20, 1844. Church recorded the date of the trip in his account book, 1844–45, OSHS.

19   *They stayed there for five days*: Carr, *Frederic Edwin Church*, 1:37.

19   *"crimson bands interwoven"*: Cole, "Essay on American Scenery," 11.

20   *"whose color is too beautiful"*: Cole, "Essay on American Scenery," 11.

20   *"the Poet describes a sky"*: Thomas Cole, journal entry, February 22, 1840, series 2, box 4a, folder 1, TCP.

20   *"must know what are the forms"*: Cole, journal entry, February 22, 1840.

20   *Cole shared this passion for clouds*: I thank Tyler Green for this observation.

20   *"the most beautiful sunset"*: Quoted by Carr, *Frederic Edwin Church*, 1:46.

20   *"This cloud rests"*: Quoted by Carr, *Frederic Edwin Church*, 1:46.

20 *"broken into innumerable lines"*: Quoted by Carr, *Frederic Edwin Church*, 1:66.

20 *lit from within*: Carr, *Frederic Edwin Church*, 1:68.

20 *"Yea, and sometimes"*: Increase Mather, *The Voice of God, in Stormy Winds. Considered, in Two Sermons, Occasioned by the Dreadful and Unparallel'd Storm, in the European Nations. Novemb. 27th. 1703* (Boston: Printed by T. Green, for Nicholas Buttolph, 1704), 21.

20 *"prince of the power of the air"*: Ephesians 2:2.

20 *Private science academies*: James Rodger Fleming, *Meteorology in America, 1800–1870* (Johns Hopkins University Press, 1990), 19.

20 *Why did tornadoes spring up*: Fleming, *Meteorology*, 23ff.

21 *"the soul of all scenery"*: Cole, "Essay on American Scenery," 10.

21 *"gush of living light"*: Thomas Cole, journal entry, March 2, 1843, series 2, box 4a, folder 1, TCP.

21 *"needles of light"*: Quoted by Carr, *Frederic Edwin Church*, 1:73.

21 *he had to take his shoes*: Howat, *Frederic Church*, 10.

21 *on their way home*: Noble, *Course of Empire*, 364–65.

22 *"2 Bright light"*: Church, "Cloud Sketch, Catskill, New York," graphite on white wove paper, 1844, CHSDM.

22 *"Regrets that it will"*: Thomas Cole, journal entry, May 19, 1839, series 2, box 4a, folder 1, TCP.

22 *He thought that no sight*: Cole, "Essay on American Scenery," 10.

22 *"Theddy saw you arrive"*: Maria Cole to Thomas Cole, September 4, 1844, series 1, box 4, folder 3, Cole Family Letters: January 1844–November 1844, TCP.

23 *"The copper-hearted barbarians"*: Quoted by Kornhauser, "Manifesto for an American Sublime," 82. For a detailed study of Cole's Catskill Creek paintings, see H. Daniel Peck, *Thomas Cole's Refrain: The Paintings of Catskill Creek* (Cornell University Press, 2019). On Cole's opinion of the railroad built across Catskill Creek, see esp. Alan Wallach, "Thomas Cole's 'River in the Catskills' as Antipastoral," *Art Bulletin* 84, no. 2 (2002): 334–50.

23 *He wanted to tell stories*: Kornhauser, "Manifesto for an American Sublime," 76.

23 *"The most distinctive"*: Cole, "Essay on American Scenery," 5.

23 *He used his artistic gifts*: For analyses of Cole's warnings about industrialization, see, e.g., Kornhauser, "Manifesto for an American Sublime"; Wallach, "Thomas Cole's 'River'"; and Alan C. Braddock, "Directionality: The Art of Orientation," in *Implication: An Ecocritical Dictionary for Art History* (Yale University Press, 2023).

23 *"We are still in Eden"*: Cole, "Essay on American Scenery," 12. Cole gave his lecture on May 16, 1835; the essay was published the following year.

24 *quick oil sketches in the field*: On the role and evolution of oil sketches in American nineteenth-century art, see Eleanor Jones Harvey, *The Painted Sketch: American Impressions from Nature, 1830–1880* (Dallas Museum of Art, 1998).

24 *A British company*: Harvey, *Painted Sketch*, 26.

24 *purchased others during his stay in Catskill*: Frederic Church, account book, 1844–1845, OSHS.

24 *emerald pigment containing arsenic*: Lucinda Hawksley, *Bitten by Witch Fever: Wallpaper and Arsenic in the Victorian Home* (Thames & Hudson, 2016), 7, 64; and Victoria Finlay, *Color: A Natural History of the Palette* (Random House, 2004), 264–66. Paris green earned its name from its efficacy as a rodenticide in the rat-infested Parisian sewers.

24 *Cole would be able*: List of paints sent by Cole to Asher B. Durand in 1837, quoted by Harvey, *Painted Sketch*, 33.

25   *a swirl of rapids on Catskill Creek:* For the oil sketches Church did in these months, see Carr, *Frederic Edwin Church*, 2: nos. 37–42.

25   *the noise of katydids:* Maria Cole, diary entry, September 13, 1845, CV 553, series 2, box 1, folder 13, Maria Cole Diary 1835–45, Maria Cole and Bartow Family, Thomas Cole Collection, Albany Institute of History and Art.

25   *good light:* See Alexander Emmons to Church, October 27, 1844.

25   *He invited Theddy:* Church to Theodore Cole, February 20, 1847.

25   *he asked Church to take charge:* Thomas Cole to Maria Cole, March 3, 1845, series 1, box 4, folder 4, Cole Family Letters: 1845–55, TCP.

25   *probably Theddy:* Carr, *Frederic Edwin Church*, 1:55.

26   *Church called:* Carr, *Frederic Edwin Church*, 1:56.

26   *National Academy of Design:* On the founding of the National Academy, see esp. Carrie Rebora Barratt, "Mapping the Venues: New York City Art Exhibitions," in *Art and the Empire City: New York, 1825–1861*, ed. Catherine Hoover Voorsanger and John K. Howat (Metropolitan Museum of Art, 2000), 50ff; and Eliot Clark, *History of the National Academy of Design, 1825–1953* (Columbia University Press, 1954), 3–15.

26   *"These little pictures":* "Twentieth Annual Exhibition of the Academy of National Design [*sic*]," *Broadway Journal* 1, no. 18 (May 3, 1845).

26   *"my profession":* Quoted by Carr, *Frederic Edwin Church*, 1:59.

26   *His father, he learned:* Warner, "Unfinished Biography," 189.

26   *inspired by Cole:* Franklin Kelly, *Frederic Edwin Church and the National Landscape* (Smithsonian Institution Press, 1988), 6.

27   *Captain Joseph Wadsworth:* Kelly, *Frederic Edwin Church and the National Landscape*, 10.

27   *red, white, and blue:* Tyler Green (@tylergreenbooks), "I started working on Frederic Church," Instagram, May 17, 2021, https://www.instagram.com/p/CO-VfoOFlfH /?img_index=1.

27   *"The recollection of":* Church to Thomas Cole, October 17, 1846. Original in Detroit Institute of Arts Museum Archives.

28   *The Atheneum agreed:* Howat, *Frederic Church*, 16.

CHAPTER 3   "A Vast Amount of Good and Evil"

29   *"Nor must it be forgotten":* Charles Dickens, *American Notes, for General Circulation* (Harper & Brothers, 1842), 37.

29   *"It would be folly":* E. Porter Belden, *New-York: Past, Present, and Future* (G. P. Putnam, 1849), 76.

30   *"Let not the pleasure":* Warner, "Unfinished Biography," 107.

30   *"his extreme conscientiousness":* Warner, "Unfinished Biography," 197.

30   *Jervis McEntee:* "Jervis McEntee's Diary," *Archives of American Art Journal* 8, nos. 3 and 4 (July–October 1968): 1.

30   *"I thought it was like":* Anne Hampton Brewster, journal entry, February 12, 1869.

31   *"He thoroughly believes":* Valerie Balint, "Jervis McEntee and Church: Reflections on a Forty-Year Friendship," OSHS.

31   *"Oyster pie helps":* Church to Aaron Goodman, January 30, 1848.

31   *set his skies alight:* Joyce Zucker, "From the Ground Up: The Ground in 19th-Century American Pictures," *Journal of the American Institute for Conservation* 38, no. 1 (1999): 7.

31   *"CAUTION TO ARTISTS":* "Caution to Artists," *Bulletin of the American Art-Union* 2, no. 4 (July 1849): 27.

32   *doctors wondered:* Philip L. Cohen, "The Arthritis of Frederic E. Church," *Journal of Rheumatology* 24, no. 7 (1997): 1453–54.

32 *place four paintings:* Mary Bartlett Cowdrey, ed., "The American Art-Union," in *American Academy of Fine Arts and American Art-Union, Exhibition Record: 1816–1852* (New-York Historical Society, 1953), 2:70.

32 *"If his future career":* "The Art Union Pictures," *Literary World* 2, no. 39 (October 30, 1847): 303.

32 *"I don't mind":* Brewster, journal entry, December 12, 1868.

32 *mountain storm snapping:* Church, *Storm in the Mountains*, oil on canvas, 1847, Cleveland Museum of Art.

32 *gilded heavens:* Church, *View near Stockbridge, Mass.*, oil on canvas, 1847, private collection.

33 *president of the National Academy:* Thomas S. Cummings, *Historic Annals of the National Academy of Design* (George W. Childs, 1865), 188.

33 *The National Academy:* Edward Ruggles, *A Picture of New-York in 1848* (C. S. Francis & Co., 1848), 60.

33 *Thoreau . . . Melville:* William J. Dean, "Preface," in *The New York Society Library: 250 Years*, ed. Henry S. F. Cooper Jr. and Jenny Lawrence (New York Society Library, 2004), 8.

33 *Emerson delivered a speech:* Jerome Loving, *Walt Whitman: The Song of Himself* (University of California Press, 2000), 60.

33 *"a very fashionable place":* Ruggles, *Picture of New-York*, 60.

34 *These men made up: National Academy of Design Exhibition Record* (New-York Historical Society, 1943), 1:xi–xii; and Cummings, *Historic Annals*, 186.

34 *"That modest little canvass":* "Twentieth Annual Exhibition of the Academy of National Design [*sic*]," *Broadway Journal* 1, no. 17 (April 26, 1845).

34 *"on a level":* "Twentieth Annual Exhibition," *Broadway Journal* 1, no. 17.

34 *The Art-Union:* The Art-Union emerged out of an earlier organization known as the Apollo Association, itself the offspring of the Apollo Gallery, founded in 1838 by the artist James Herring. On the origins of the Art-Union, see Kimberly A. Orcutt, *The American Art-Union: Utopia and Skepticism in the Antebellum Era* (Fordham University Press, 2024); Barratt, "Mapping the Venues"; Charles E. Baker, "The American Art-Union," in *American Academy of Fine Arts*, ed. Cowdrey, vol. 1; Amanda Lett et al., *Perfectly American: The Art-Union & Its Artists* (Gilcrease Museum, 2011); and Rachel N. Klein, "Art and Authority in Antebellum New York City: The Rise and Fall of the American Art-Union," *Journal of American History* 81, no. 4 (March 1995).

34 *The grand prize for 1848:* Howat, *Frederic Church*, 25.

34 *Church's primary income:* Howat, *Frederic Church*, 23.

34 *"Gentlemen . . . I am sorry":* Church to the Art-Union, received by the latter April 10 [prob. 1849].

35 *building at 497 Broadway:* On the various homes of the Art-Union, see Barratt, "Mapping the Venues"; Baker, "American Art-Union"; Lett et al., *Perfectly American*; and Klein, "Art and Authority."

35 *The tableau changed by the hour:* "The Art Union and Its Friends," *Literary World* 3, no. 95 (November 25, 1848): 853.

35 *Walt Whitman—who occasionally joined:* Edward L. Widmer, *Young America: The Flowering of Democracy in New York City* (Oxford University Press, 1998), 147.

36 *Amorous behavior:* Klein, "Art and Authority," 1547n30.

36 *"the roar of Chariot Wheels":* Church to Goodman, December 17, 1849.

36 *new reservoir at Forty-Second Street:* Gerald T. Koeppel, *Water for Gotham: A History* (Princeton University Press, 2001), 275. On July 4, 1842, water from the Croton Reservoir entered the reservoir at Forty-Second Street for the first time.

36 *covered the hilly island:* See Eric W. Sanderson with Markley Boyer, *Mannahatta: A Natural History of New York City* (Harry N. Abrams, 2009).

36 *Giant circus-sign letters:* Philip B. Kunhardt Jr., Philip B. Kunhardt III, and Peter W. Kunhardt, *P. T. Barnum: America's Greatest Showman* (Alfred A. Knopf, 1995), 117.

36 *Lower Manhattan terminals:* Belden, *New-York*, 72.

36 *The central post office:* Belden, *New-York*, 73.

37 *free Black men:* Leslie M. Harris, *In the Shadow of Slavery: African Americans in New York City, 1626–1863* (University of Chicago Press, 2003), 5.

37 *slavery had been illegal:* Harris, *In the Shadow of Slavery*, 11.

37 *Southerners were allowed:* On this practice in pre–Civil War New York, see Jonathan Daniel Wells, *The Kidnapping Club: Wall Street, Slavery, and Resistance on the Eve of the Civil War* (Bold Type Books, 2020).

37 *Barnum purchased:* Kunhardt Jr., Kunhardt III, and Kunhardt, *P. T. Barnum*, 48ff.

38 *some as indentured servants:* Harris, *In the Shadow of Slavery*, 163.

38 *several men assaulted them:* David W. Blight, *Frederick Douglass: Prophet of Freedom* (Simon & Schuster, 2018), 204–5.

38 *"Persons who at a distance":* Frederick Douglass, "Colorphobia in New York!," *North Star*, May 25, 1849.

38 *Tens of thousands of immigrants:* Belden, *New-York*, 64. On the rise of the steamship industry in New York, see esp. T. J. Stiles, *The First Tycoon: The Epic Life of Cornelius Vanderbilt* (Alfred A. Knopf, 2009).

38 *The treaty Congress ratified:* Ron Chernow, *Grant* (Penguin, 2017), 58.

38 *He had gone to jail:* Laura Dassow Walls, *Henry David Thoreau: A Life* (University of Chicago Press, 2017), 207–13.

39 *influential Democratic Review:* Widmer, *Young America*, 3.

39 *"approaching political crisis":* Church to Goodman, November 5, 1848.

39 *"a good stirring up":* Church to Goodman, January 30, 1848.

39 *One National Academy official:* Cummings, *Historic Annals*, 203.

CHAPTER 4 "Blessed Are the Dead"

41 *low twenties all day:* "Meteorological Observations for the Year 1848, Made According to the Directions of the Regents of the University of the State of New York, at Union Hall Academy, Situated in the Town of Jamaica, Queens County," January 19, 1848.

41 *fanlight of red glass:* "Art Union and Its Friends," 853.

41 *In Hartford, they were praying:* Warner, "Unfinished Biography," 195.

41 *"I have no money":* Warner, "Unfinished Biography," 190.

42 *"better class":* Church to Goodman, January 30, 1848.

42 *"good-hearted":* Quoted by Justin Kaplan, *Walt Whitman: A Life* (Simon & Schuster, 1980), 96.

42 *Matteson reminded the men:* "Art Intelligence," *New York Evening Express*, January 21, 1848.

42 *Several evenings a week:* On the NAD's drawing classes, see Cummings, *Historic Annals*, 203; Clark, *History of the National Academy*, 25; and *Literary World* 3, no. 97 (December 9, 1848): 901. On drawing in nineteenth-century New York, see also Roberta J. M. Olson, *Drawn by New York: Six Centuries of Watercolors and Drawings at the New-York Historical Society* (New-York Historical Society, 2008).

43 *Dr. Collyer's Model Artistes:* "Scenes from Paradise," *New York Herald*, October 16, 1847.

43 *famous contemporary sculpture:* Robert Allen, *Horrible Prettiness: Burlesque and American Culture* (University of North Carolina Press, 1991), 92.

43 *"Adam's First Sight"*: "Scenes from Paradise."

43 *"Arrest of the Model Artists"*: "Arrest of the Model Artists—Rich Scene in Broadway," *National Police Gazette*, January 1, 1848.

43 *"The bronze is so near"*: "Nudity in Art," *Home Journal* 2, no. 204 (January 5, 1850): 2.

43 *"an indecent sculpture"*: Quoted in "Nudity in Art," 2.

44 *directors had generously yielded*: Cummings, *Historic Annals*, 207.

44 *reference to the recent scandals*: "The Life School," *New York Evening Express*, January 27, 1848.

44 *He had just encountered*: Warner, "Unfinished Biography," 196.

44 *"Have you thought"*: Warner, "Unfinished Biography," 197.

44 *Even the devout Cole*: Barringer, "Thomas Cole's Atlantic Crossings," 43–44.

44 *paintings on religious themes*: Carr, *Frederic Edwin Church*, 1:90.

45 *on January 31*: "Jottings on Art," *New York Evening Express*, February 7, 1848.

45 *new painting studio*: Thomas Cole, journal entry, December 25, 1846, series 2, box 4a, folder 1, TCP.

45 *"Oh, go away!"*: Noble, *Life and Works of Thomas Cole*, 395.

45 *girl, who had died*: Noble, *Course of Empire*, 375.

45 *thirteen below zero*: "Meteorological Observations for the Year 1848 Made Under the Directions of the University of the State of New York, at the Hudson Academy Situated in the City of Hudson in the County of Columbia," January 11, 1848.

45 *a series of paintings*: Thomas Cole, journal entry, January 1, 1848, series 2, box 4a, folder 1, TCP.

45 *"bilious attack"*: John Falconer to Jasper Cropsey, in "Thomas Cole Is No More: February 24, 1848," *American Art Journal* 15, no. 4 (1983): 75.

46 *"Pa, you're sick"*: Emily Cole quoted by Falconer to Cropsey, "Thomas Cole Is No More," 75.

46 *Communion of the Sick*: Falconer to Cropsey, "Thomas Cole Is No More," 75.

46 *"I want to be quiet"*: Quoted by Noble, *Life and Works of Thomas Cole*, 408.

46 *The sun was shining*: "Meteorological Observations for the Year 1848 Made Under the Directions of the University of the State of New York, at the Hudson Academy Situated in the City of Hudson in the County of Columbia," February 15, 1848.

46 *much of Catskill*: William Cullen Bryant, *A Funeral Oration, Occasioned by the Death of Thomas Cole: Delivered Before the National Academy of Design, New-York, May 4, 1848* (D. Appleton, 1848), 36.

46 *Cole's dog sat*: Falconer to Cropsey, "Thomas Cole Is No More," 75.

46 *"The Lord gave"*: Episcopal Church, *The Book of Common Prayer* (1846), 144.

47 *"I noticed the death"*: Charles Church to Joseph Church, March 15, 1848.

47 *"Do you sometimes"*: Warner, "Unfinished Biography," 197.

47 *The National Academy convened*: Cummings, *Historic Annals*, 205.

47 *He was liked and respected*: On Kensett and Durand, see John Paul Driscoll and John K. Howat, *John Frederick Kensett: An American Master* (W. W. Norton, 1985), 72; on Casilear and Durand, see Barbara Dayer Gallati, "Asher B. Durand's Early Career," in *Kindred Spirits: Asher B. Durand and the American Landscape*, ed. Linda S. Ferber (Brooklyn Museum, 2007), 58; on Cropsey and Durand, see Mishoe Brennecke, *Jasper F. Cropsey: Artist and Architect* (New-York Historical Society, 1987); on Gifford and Durand, see Kevin J. Avery, "Gifford and the Catskills," in *Hudson River School Visions: The Landscapes of Sanford R. Gifford*, ed. Kevin J. Avery and Franklin Kelly (Metropolitan Museum of Art, 2003), 32; on Inness and Durand, see Adrienne Baxter Bell, *George Inness and the Visionary Landscape* (George Braziller, 2015), 151; on McEntee and Durand, see Lee A. Vedder, "Jervis McEntee: Painter-Poet of the

Hudson River School," in *Jervis McEntee: Painter-Poet of the Hudson River School*, ed. Vedder (Samuel Dorsky Museum of Art, State University of New York at New Paltz, 2015), 16; on Whittredge and Durand, see *Autobiography of Worthington Whittredge*, 41; and on Church and Durand, see Carr, *Frederic Edwin Church*, 1:256.

48   *The Art-Union: Exhibition of the Paintings of the Late Thomas Cole, at the Gallery of the American Art-Union* (Snowden & Prall, 1848). The exhibition opened on March 27, 1848: Shannon Vittoria, "Chronology," in Kornhauser and Barringer, *Thomas Cole's Journey*, 257.

48   *earliest trees were starting to leaf:* "Meteorological Observations for the Year 1848, Made According to the Directions of the Regents of the University of the State of New York, at Union Hall Academy, Situated in the Town of Jamaica, Queens County," April 1848.

48   *On May 4, a warm day:* "Meteorological Observations for the Year 1848, Made According to the Directions of the Regents of the University of the State of New York, at the Institution for the Instruction of the Deaf & Dumb, New York City," May 4, 1848.

48   *women dressing in muslin:* "Our Window," *Putnam's Monthly* 10, no. 55 (July 1857): 130.

48   *At the Church of the Messiah:* "From Our New York Correspondent," *Semi-Weekly Union*, May 9, 1848.

48   *"a sound of lament":* Quoted by J. Gray Sweeney, "'Endued with Rare Genius': Frederic Edwin Church's *To the Memory of Cole*," *Smithsonian Studies in American Art* 2, no. 1 (1988): 65.

49   *A spring promised life:* On the symbolism in Church's tribute to Cole, see Sweeney, "'Endued with Rare Genius'"; and Franklin Kelly, "A Passion for Landscape," in *Frederic Edwin Church* (National Gallery of Art, 1989), 38.

49   *"Nor is thy dream":* Quoted by Sweeney, "'Endued with Rare Genius,'" 48.

49   *"This is a glorious landscape":* "The Academy of Design," *Evening Post*, March 13, 1848.

49   *cow in the foreground:* "Academy of Design," *Evening Post*.

50   *"Oh how comical":* Church to Goodman, December 17, 1849.

50   *"right good fun":* Church to Goodman, August 6, 1848.

50   *"All my hopes":* Church to Goodman, August 6, 1848.

50   *he reveled:* On Church's 1848 Vermont trip and painting topics, see esp. Carr, *Frederic Edwin Church*, 1:135–36.

50   *placid, optimistic images:* Kelly, *Frederic Edwin Church and the National Landscape*, 24. Relevant sketches include Carr, *Frederic Edwin Church*, 2: nos. 200, 203v, 204–9, 213–14, and 215r.

50   *"I sometimes go":* Church to Theodore Cole, September 11, 1848.

50   *"As you will never see":* Church to Theodore Cole, September 11, 1848.

CHAPTER 5   "A Sensation Wherever I Go"

53   *Church had worked:* On this painting see esp. Kelly, *Frederic Edwin Church and the National Landscape*, 22–24, and Christopher Kent Wilson, "The Landscape of Democracy: Frederic Church's 'West Rock, New Haven,'" *American Art Journal* 18, no. 3 (1986): 20–39.

53   *carefully numbered and labeled:* Wilson, "Landscape of Democracy," 21; Carr, *Frederic Edwin Church*, 2: no. 195r.

53   *opposition to tyrants:* Quoted by Wilson, "Landscape of Democracy," 33, and by Kelly, *Frederic Edwin Church and the National Landscape*, 23.

54   *Cole had once thought:* Kelly, *Frederic Edwin Church and the National Landscape*, 24.

54 *He hadn't sketched any men:* Kelly notes that Church's original sketch did "not include the mown hay, the men, or the carts, so the harvesting subject was deliberately added": Kelly, *Frederic Edwin Church and the National Landscape,* 22.

54 *West Rock, New Haven went on view: National Academy of Design Exhibition Record,* 1:80.

54 *"Church has taken his place":* "Fine-Art Gossip," *Bulletin of the American Art-Union* 2, no. 1 (April 1849): 20.

54 *"which it is the pride":* John Ruskin, *Modern Painters* (Wiley & Putnam, 1847), 1:xxv.

54 *"truth to nature":* Ruskin, *Modern Painters,* 1:411. On the reception of Ruskin's ideas in the United States, see esp. Franklin Kelly, "Turner and America," in *J. M. W. Turner,* ed. Ian Warrell (Metropolitan Museum of Art, 2007), 231–46.

54 *John Frederick Kensett:* John K. Howat, "Kensett's World," and John Paul Driscoll, "From Burin to Brush: The Development of a Painter," in John Paul Driscoll and John K. Howat, *John Frederick Kensett: An American Master* (W. W. Norton, 1985), 35, 61.

54 *Jasper Cropsey: National Academy of Design Exhibition Record,* 1:100–101.

55 *Sanford Gifford:* Ila Weiss, *Poetic Landscape: The Art and Experience of Sanford R. Gifford* (University of Delaware Press, 1987), 61.

55 *"without doubt among our best": Morning Courier and New-York Enquirer,* May 3, 1849, quoted by Wilson, "Landscape of Democracy," 21.

55 *"We should like":* Quoted by Warner, "Unfinished Biography," 198.

55 *"Oh! the miseries":* Church to Goodman, November 5, 1848.

55 *"in everybody's mouth":* "The National Academy of Design," *Bulletin of the Art-Union* 2, no. 2 (May 1849): 14.

55 *promotion to full membership:* Howat, *Frederic Church,* 29; and Cummings, *Historic Annals,* 216.

55 *youngest academician:* Wilson, "Landscape of Democracy," 22.

56 *performance of* Macbeth: Dennis Berthold, "Class Acts: The Astor Place Riots and Melville's 'The Two Temples,'" *American Literature* 71, no. 3 (1999): 429.

57 *letter in* The New York Herald: "Macready and Forrest," *New York Herald,* May 9, 1849; and Berthold, "Class Acts," 429.

57 *to plaster posters:* Philip Hone, *The Diary of Philip Hone, 1828–1851,* ed. Allan Nevins (Dodd, Mead, 1927), May 10, 1849, 2:867.

57 *"WORKINGMEN!":* Quoted by Berthold, "Class Acts," 430.

57 *Woodhull—a Macreadyite:* Edwin G. Burrows and Mike Wallace, *Gotham: A History of New York City to 1898* (Oxford University Press, 1998), 763.

57 *thick, clammy fog:* "Meteorological Observations for the Year 1848, Made According to the Directions of the Regents of the University of the State of New York at the Institution for the Instruction of the Deaf & Dumb, New York City," May 1848.

57 *picking up free tickets:* Burrows and Wallace, *Gotham,* 763.

58 *ten thousand people:* Burrows and Wallace, *Gotham,* 763.

58 *"vulgar, arrogant":* Hone, *Diary,* May 8, 1849, 2:866.

59 *"Although the lesson":* Hone, *Diary,* May 12, 1849, 2:869.

59 *Art-Union War:* Worthington Whittredge, a New York painter who later became one of Church's closest friends, dubbed it the Art-Union War, as quoted by Orcutt, *American Art-Union,* 115, from Worthington Whittredge, "The American Art Union," *Magazine of History* 7, no. 2 (February 1908): 65. On October 18, 1849, *The New York Herald* called it "the war of the Art-Unions," as quoted by Orcutt, *American Art-Union,* 176.

60 *brandished weapons:* On violence in Congress in the pre–Civil War era, see Joanne B. Freeman, *The Field of Blood: Violence in Congress and the Road to Civil War* (Farrar, Straus & Giroux, 2018).

60 *"designing men"*: George Washington, *Farewell Address: September 19, 1796* (T. Pomroy, 1812), 15.

60 *"a quiet, respectable man"*: "The Fugitive Slave Law," *New-York Daily Tribune*, October 3, 1850.

60 *"There is infamy"*: Ralph Waldo Emerson, "'Address to the Citizens of Concord' on the Fugitive Slave Law, 3 May 1851," in *Emerson's Antislavery Writings*, ed. Len Gougeon and Joel Myerson (Yale University Press, 1995), 53. Nell Irvin Painter has shown that Emerson directed a good deal of his concern about the new law toward the moral health of white people in a nation that tolerated the barbarism of slavery. On Emerson's writings on whiteness, Black people, and slavery, see Painter, *The History of White People* (W. W. Norton, 2010), 151–89.

61 *thousands of African Americans*: Burrows and Wallace, *Gotham*, 857.

61 *"The land will be filled"*: Quoted by Blight, *Frederick Douglass*, 242, from "The Fugitive Slave Law Illustrated," *Frederick Douglass' Paper* 4, no. 41 (October 2, 1851).

61 Twilight, *"Short Arbiter"*: On this painting, see esp. Kelly, *Frederic Edwin Church and the National Landscape*, 26–34.

61 *Church's painting was a warning*: For this interpretation, I am indebted to author and art historian Tyler Green (@tylergreenbooks): "With our foundational republicanism under threat," Instagram, November 4, 2024, https://www.instagram.com/p/DB8ykLsxF-o/?img_index=1.

62 *"full of dust"*: Church to Goodman, November 29, 1849.

62 *"When a notion"*: Church to Goodman, December 17, 1849.

62 *"the sublime melting"*: Cole, "Essay on American Scenery," 6.

62 *beech, hemlock, and birch*: William B. Leak and Mariko Yamasaki, "Tree Species Migration Studies in the White Mountains of New Hampshire," Research Paper NRS-19 (US Forest Service, Northern Research Station, 2012), 1.

62 *"most splendid country"*: [Church], "Mountain Views and Coast Scenery, by a Landscape Painter," *Bulletin of the American Art-Union* 8 (November 1850): 129. This account was published anonymously; Carr, in *Frederic Edwin Church*, 1:161, carefully evaluates the evidence that this was written by Church; see also Harvey, *Painted Sketch*, 66–67.

62 *Pesamkuk to the Wabanaki*: George Neptune, "Naming the Dawnland: Wabanaki Place Names on Mount Desert Island," *Chebacco: The Magazine of the Mount Desert Island Historical Society* 16 (2015): 97–98. On the name *Pemetic*, see Harald E. L. Prins and Bunny McBride, *Asticou's Island Domain: Wabanaki Peoples at Mount Desert Island, 1500–2000*, Acadia National Park Ethnographic Overview and Assessment (National Park Service, 2007), 1:i.

63 *"Isle des Monts Déserts"*: Quoted by Christopher Camuto, *Time and Tide in Acadia: Seasons on Mount Desert Island* (Countryman Press, 2011), epigraph.

63 *Church spent more than a month*: This was the first of a series of visits for Church, on which see esp. John Wilmerding, *The Artist's Mount Desert: American Painters on the Maine Coast* (Princeton University Press, 1995).

63 *He admired the "fine rich green"*: See Carr, *Frederic Edwin Church*, 1:184 and 2: no. 295.

63 *"amphibious islanders"*: [Church], "Mountain Views and Coast Scenery," 131.

63 *"land and seaward"*: Church to Goodman, August 17, 1850.

63 *"some shrewd Bostonian"*: [Church], "Mountain Views and Coast Scenery," 130.

64 *"There is no such picture"*: Quoted by Kelly, *Frederic Edwin Church and the National Landscape*, 36.

64 *he felt a mild despair*: Kelly, *Frederic Edwin Church and the National Landscape*, 36, quotes from Church's letter of August 1850 to the *Art-Union Bulletin*: "We . . . cannot

suppress a doubt that we shall neither be able to give the actual motion nor roar to any we may place upon canvas."

64 *He used fluid, swirling strokes:* John Wilmerding, *Maine Sublime: Frederic Edwin Church's Landscapes of Mount Desert and Mount Katahdin* (Cornell University Press, 2012), 38.

64 *The following spring:* Kelly, *Frederic Edwin Church and the National Landscape,* 36.

65 *sun hanging low:* Some commentators in Church's day and today believe it to be a sunrise—e.g., Franklin Kelly and Gerald L. Carr, *The Early Landscapes of Frederic Edwin Church, 1845–1854* (Amon Carter Museum, 1987), 116–17—but Tyler Green makes a persuasive argument that it is a sunset: Green (@tylergreenbooks), "With our foundational republicanism."

65 *Beacon, off Mount Desert Island: National Academy of Design Exhibition Record,* 1:80.

65 *"the sea and the shore":* Quoted by Kelly, *Frederic Edwin Church and the National Landscape,* 40.

CHAPTER 6 "In Your Own Secret Souls"

67 *He had positioned himself:* Carr, *Frederic Edwin Church,* 1:194, no. 312.

67 *In the decades after:* Barry Schwartz, "Social Change and Collective Memory: The Democratization of George Washington," *American Sociological Review* 56, no. 2 (1991): 223.

67 *The portico roof:* "Mount Vernon: Then & Now Photography," https://www.mount vernon.org/preservation/mount-vernon-ladies-association/mount-vernon-through -time/mount-vernon-then-now-photographs.

68 *"All wrong":* Quoted by Carr, *Frederic Edwin Church,* 1:194.

68 *The Century had been launched: The Century Association Yearbook* (Merrymount Press, 1940), 1, 92.

68 *"the most unspeakably respectable":* Quoted by Weiss, *Poetic Landscape,* 88.

68 *Cyrus Field and his wife, Mary:* Cyrus Field's wife and sister were both named Mary. Isabella Judson, one of Field's daughters, notes that it was "Mr. and Mrs. Field" who went on the 1851 trip with Church. See Isabella Field Judson, *Cyrus W. Field: His Life and Work* (Harper & Brothers, 1896), 39.

69 *dismissed the landscape as "uninteresting":* Frederick Law Olmsted, *Journeys and Explorations in the Cotton Kingdom* (S. Low, Son & Co., 1861), 142.

69 *But Olmsted saw:* Frederick Law Olmsted, *A Journey in the Seaboard Slave States: With Remarks on Their Economy* (Dix & Edwards, 1856), 59.

69 *Expanses of corn, wheat, and cotton:* On the crops grown at Shirley, see Robert James Teagle, "Land, Labor, and Reform: Hill Carter, Slavery, and Agricultural Improvement at Shirley Plantation, 1816–1866" (master's thesis, Virginia Polytechnic Institute and State University, 1998).

69 *Designed in the Georgian style:* Theodore R. Reinhart, ed., *The Archaeology of Shirley Plantation* (University Press of Virginia, 1984), 83.

69 *early eighteenth century:* Reinhart, *Archaeology of Shirley Plantation,* 19.

70 *Henry "Light-Horse Harry" Lee:* Emory M. Thomas, *Robert E. Lee: A Biography* (W. W. Norton, 1997), 23–24.

70 *"two little black boys":* Quoted by Teagle, "Land, Labor, and Reform," 24.

70 *his father was a director:* "Aetna Fire Insurance Company of Hartford," *Evening Post,* February 19, 1848. On Aetna's insurance policies on enslaved people, see Sharon Ann Murphy, *Investing in Life: Insurance in Antebellum America* (Johns Hopkins University Press, 2010), 308.

70   *He occasionally sold children:* Slave Record Book: Births 1822–1864, container 92, series K, microfilm, Shirley Plantation Collection 1650–1888, Records of Ante-Bellum Southern Plantations.

70   *He explained:* Teagle, "Land, Labor, and Reform," 22.

71   *"are the happiest people":* Quoted by Teagle, "Land, Labor, and Reform," 21.

71   *"God bless her":* Frederick Douglass, "A Day and a Night in Uncle Tom's Cabin," *Frederick Douglass' Paper*, March 4, 1853.

71   *copy of* Uncle Tom's Cabin: Church to Charlotte Church, October 17, 1854.

71   *"To you, generous, noble-minded":* Harriet Beecher Stowe, *Uncle Tom's Cabin* (John P. Jewett & Company, 1852), 2:314. The first installment of "Uncle Tom's Cabin" appeared in the *National Era* on June 5, 1851.

71   *"kind hospitality":* Church to Mary Carter, June 12, 1851. Original in Virginia Museum of Fine Arts Archives.

72   *"inhumanity":* Church to Rachel S. Jameson, April 25, 1867, reproduced in Theodore J. Holmes, *A Memorial of John S. Jameson, Sergeant in the 1st Conn. Cavalry, Who Died at Andersonville, Ga.* (n.p., c. 1867), 5, and quoted by Carr, *Frederic Edwin Church*, 1:276.

72   *"the most sublime of nature's works":* Thomas Jefferson, *Notes on the State of Virginia* (John Stockdale, 1787), 35.

72   *"But soon the fore part":* Herman Melville, *Moby-Dick, or, the Whale* (Harper & Brothers, 1851), 604.

73   *thousands of hibernating bats:* Alexander Clark Bullitt, *Rambles in the Mammoth Cave, During the Year 1844* (Morton & Griswold, 1845), 18.

73   *"I am telling":* Church to Cyrus Field, August 1851, quoted by Judson, *Cyrus W. Field*, 40.

73   *"Grand Moving Mirror":* "Grand Moving Mirror of American Scenery," *London Daily News*, May 7, 1851.

73   *Americans were widely:* On British views of the United States, see esp. chap. 1, "The Uneasy Cousins," in Amanda Foreman, *A World on Fire: Britain's Crucial Role in the American Civil War* (Random House, 2012).

73   *Dickens had been disgusted:* Dickens, *American Notes*, 295; see also Freeman, *Field of Blood*, 3–4.

73   *When he visited Congress:* Dickens, *American Notes*, 289–90.

74   *"We are a rude, clumsy people":* Horace Greeley, *Glances at Europe: In a Series of Letters from Great Britain, France, Italy, Switzerland, Etc., During the Summer of 1851* (Dewitt & Davenport, 1852), 25.

74   *contracted with suppliers:* Samuel Carter III, *Cyrus W. Field: Man of Two Worlds* (G. P. Putnam's Sons, 1968), 64.

74   *The federal government issued:* "Arrival of the American Frigate *St. Lawrence*," *Times* (London), March 14, 1851.

74   *"chariot, a flying machine, and a treadmill":* Quoted by Marcus Cunliffe, "America at the Great Exhibition of 1851," *American Quarterly* 3, no. 2 (1951): 119.

74   *the winning American entries:* "From Washington," *Norwich (CT) Evening Courier*, January 14, 1851.

74   *On May 1, Queen Victoria:* "The Opening of the Great Exhibition," *Times* (London), May 2, 1851.

74   *seating five thousand people:* Brenda Wineapple, *Ecstatic Nation: Confidence, Crisis, and Compromise, 1848–1877* (Harper Perennial, 2013), 79.

74   *the Koh-i-Noor diamond:* Greeley, *Glances at Europe*, 30.

75   *the contraption was rigged:* "The Great Exhibition," *Times* (London), May 3, 1851. See also William Dalrymple and Anita Anand, *Koh-i-Noor: The History of the World's Most Infamous Diamond* (Bloomsbury, 2017).

75 *American section resembled:* Greeley, *Glances at Europe,* 25.

75 *The British press gloated:* "A Hint for the American Non-Exhibitors," *Punch* 20 (1851): 246.

75 *small stuffed squirrel:* Robert Ellis, ed., *Official Descriptive and Illustrated Catalogue of the Great Exhibition of the Works of Industry of All Nations* (W. Clowes & Sons, 1851), 3:1434.

75 *autumn leaves:* Ellis, *Official Descriptive,* 3:1450–51, 3:1457.

75 *false teeth, hams, and cod-liver oil:* Ellis, *Official Descriptive,* 3:1433, 3:1437, 3:1449.

76 *"the gigantic bird":* "America in Crystal," *Punch* 20 (1851): 209.

76 *"desolate prairie":* Quoted by Charles T. Rodgers, *American Superiority at the World's Fair* (John J. Hawkins, 1852), 65, from *Times* (London), June 9, 1951.

76 *killing "savages":* Ellis, *Official Descriptive,* 3:1454.

76 *"Have you a difference":* Quoted by Rodgers, *American Superiority,* 65, from *Times* (London), June 9, 1951.

76 *"never move without one":* Quoted by Cunliffe, "America at the Great Exhibition," 116.

76 *Americans openly expressing:* Greeley, *Glances at Europe,* 75.

76 *Niagara Falls:* Ellis, *Official Descriptive,* 3:1460.

76 *surface of the moon:* Ellis, *Official Descriptive,* 3:1463.

76 *Council Medals:* "Industrial Exhibition of 1851," *New York Times,* October 29, 1851.

77 *one testimonial stated:* Gail Borden Jr., *The Meat Biscuit; Invented, Patented, and Manufactured* (D. Fanshaw, 1851), 11.

77 *Charles Rodgers:* Rodgers, *American Superiority.*

77 *perfect match:* Judson, *Cyrus W. Field,* 39.

77 *The Roman Republic:* Tyler Green and Beth Harris, "Landscape and the American Republic, Frederic Church's *Natural Bridge,*" Smarthistory, YouTube, June 4, 2022, https://www.youtube.com/watch?v=sYqdJ3B2LgA.

78 *Royal Academy of Arts:* Carr, *Frederic Edwin Church,* 1:196–97.

78 *After a visit:* Carr, *Frederic Edwin Church,* 1:204.

78 *Mount Katahdin:* Carr, *Frederic Edwin Church,* 1:207; and Theodore E. Stebbins Jr., "American Landscape: Some New Acquisitions at Yale," *Yale University Art Gallery Bulletin* 33 (Autumn 1971): 16.

79 *National Academy in May 1853: National Academy of Design Exhibition Record,* 1:80.

79 *what he feared would destroy it:* Tyler Green (@tylergreenbooks), "In 1852, Frederic Church completed his antebellum warning trilogy," Instagram, November 5, 2024, https://www.instagram.com/p/DB_XJKxxDbB/, makes this point about Church's 1852 canvas *Home by the Lake,* whose subject is closely related to that of *Mt. Ktaadn.*

79 *life insurance:* Judson, *Cyrus W. Field,* 52.

CHAPTER 7 "I Am Terrified"

81 *Church despaired:* Church to Eliza Church, April 28, 1853. Courtesy of the Winterthur Museum, Garden & Library, Joseph Downs Collection of Manuscripts and Printed Ephemera.

81 *freed its enslaved people:* Nancy P. Appelbaum, *Mapping the Country of Regions: The Chorographic Commission of Nineteenth-Century Colombia* (University of North Carolina Press, 2016), 12.

81 *Field was interested:* Judson, *Cyrus W. Field,* 52–53.

81 *They had spent nearly four years:* On Humboldt's trip to South America, see esp. Laura Dassow Walls, *The Passage to Cosmos: Alexander von Humboldt and the Shaping of America* (University of Chicago Press, 2009) and Andrea Wulf, *The Invention of Nature: Alexander von Humboldt's New World* (Alfred A. Knopf, 2015).

82 *"attempt to delineate nature"*: Alexander von Humboldt, *Cosmos: A Sketch of a Physical Description of the Universe*, trans. E. C. Otté (Henry G. Bohn, 1849), 1:xiv.

82 *"azure of the sky"*: Humboldt, *Cosmos*, 2:456.

83 *"boundless depth of feeling"*: Humboldt, *Cosmos*, 2:454.

83 *"the great enchantment"*: Humboldt, *Cosmos*, 2:456.

83 *"Are we not"*: Humboldt, *Cosmos*, 2:452; see also Walls, *Passage to Cosmos*, 245.

83 *"the nobler and grander"*: Humboldt, *Cosmos*, 2:454.

83 *other, older names*: Wade Davis, *Magdalena* (Bodley Head, 2020), 11.

84 *"novel and singular"*: Church to Eliza Church, April 28, 1853.

84 *"quaint and odd"*: Church to Elizabeth Church, April 29, 1853. Courtesy of Winterthur.

84 *"I can't sufficiently"*: Church to Charlotte Church, May 4, 1853. Courtesy of Winterthur.

84 *"to me it is"*: Church to Elizabeth Church, April 29, 1853.

84 *"monstrous size"*: Church to Eliza Church, April 28, 1853.

84 *skin shed by a scorpion*: Church to Charlotte Church, May 4, 1853.

84 *"Sometimes a little fellow"*: Church to Eliza Church, April 28, 1853.

85 *"I am very sorry"*: Church to Joseph Church, May 9, 1853. Courtesy of Winterthur.

85 *"Today I begin a diary"*: Frederic Church Diary, May–October 1853, May 2, OSHS.

85 *It had taken Humboldt and Bonpland*: Wulf, *Invention of Nature*, 89.

85 *refreshed scenery*: Church Diary, May 16, 1853.

85 *Thick, low clouds*: Church to Joseph Church, May 16, 1853. Courtesy of Winterthur.

85 *"I drink enormous quantities"*: Church to Joseph Church, May 9, 1853.

85 *Church saw coconuts*: Church to Eliza Church, May 25, 1853. Courtesy of Winterthur.

86 *"You can form"*: Church to Joseph Church, May 16, 1853. Courtesy of Winterthur.

86 *In* Cosmos: Humboldt, *Cosmos*, 2:452–53.

86 *"smothered in vines"*: Church, "Botanical Studies Along the Río Magdalena, Colombia," graphite on gray-green laid paper, May 1853, CHSDM.

86 *six-inch tarantula*: Church Diary, May 17, 1853.

86 *"I have been delighted"*: Church Diary, May 19, 1853.

87 *"chocolate trees"*: Church to Eliza Church, May 25, 1853.

87 *"singular and beautiful"*: Church to Eliza Church, May 25, 1853.

87 *"horrifying precipices"*: Quoted by Pablo Navas Sanz de Santamaría, *The Journey of Frederic Edwin Church Through Colombia and Ecuador: April–October 1853* (Villegas Editores, 2008), 70.

87 *"awful beyond all description"*: In a letter of September 21, 1801, Humboldt described this passage to his brother, Wilhem von Humboldt, as "über alle Beschreibung schlecht": Alexander von Humboldt, *Briefe Alexander's von Humboldt an seinen Bruder Wilhelm*, ed. Familie von Humboldt (J. G. Cotta'schen Buchhandlung, 1880), 334.

87 *flowering jacarandas, and ceiba trees*: Plant species of the region are documented by Camila Pizano et al., "'El Triunfo': Una Reserva Privada de Gran Importancia para la Conservación del Bosque Seco Tropical en Colombia," unpublished manuscript.

87 *sensitive plant*: Church Diary, May 31, 1853.

88 *"Our course was continually"*: Church to Joseph Church, June 9, 1853. Courtesy of Winterthur.

88 *There were no letters*: Church to Joseph Church, June 9, 1853.

88 *ten times as many people*: Church to Joseph Church, June 9, 1853. On the difficulty of ascertaining the population of Bogotá in the 1850s, see David Sowell, "Population Growth in Late-Nineteenth-Century Bogotá: Insights on a Demographic Dilemma," *Journal of Urban History* 38, no. 4 (June 11, 2012): 721.

89 *people were dressed*: Church to Joseph Church, June 9, 1853.

89   *middle of a political drama:* Matthew C. Hunter, "Graphic Making, Actuarial Knowing: Transfer and Countertransference in Frederic Edwin Church's South American Drawings," *West 86th: A Journal of Decorative Arts, Design History, and Material Culture* 23, no. 1 (Spring–Summer 2016): 59.

89   *controversial new constitution:* David Sowell, *The Early Colombian Labor Movement: Artisans and Politics in Bogotá, 1832–1919* (Temple University Press, 1992), 67; and M. C. Mirow, *Latin American Constitutions: The Constitution of Cádiz and Its Legacy in Spanish America* (Cambridge University Press, 2015), 153.

89   *"It is a spectacle":* Church Diary, June 6, 1853.

89   Cachacos *armed with guns:* Navas Sanz de Santamaría, *Journey of Frederic Edwin Church,* 74.

90   *"one of the wildest scenes":* Alexander von Humboldt, *Researches, Concerning the Institutions & Monuments of the Ancient Inhabitants of America: With Descriptions and Views of Some of the Most Striking Scenes in the Cordilleras!,* trans. Helen Maria Williams (Longman, Hurst, Rees, Orme & Brown, J. Murray & H. Colburn, 1814), 1:80.

90   *"dreadful roar":* Humboldt, *Researches,* 1:80.

90   *"I am terrified":* Church Diary, June 20, 1853.

90   *"sublimely picturesque":* Humboldt, *Researches,* 1:77.

90   *"At the top of the fall":* Church to Eliza Church, July 7, 1853. Courtesy of Winterthur.

91   *"enormously splendid":* Church Diary, June 22, 1853; and Navas Sanz de Santamaría, *Journey of Frederic Edwin Church,* 156.

91   *snow-crowned volcano:* Church, "Snowpeaks Tolima and Ruiz, from the Vicinity of Tequendama Falls, Colombia," graphite and white gouache on gray-green wove paper, June 20–30, 1853, CHSDM.

91   *In 1801, Humboldt:* Humboldt, *Researches,* 1:79.

91   *his joy was tempered:* Church to Eliza Church, July 7, 1853.

91   *"better than ever":* Church to Eliza Church, July 7, 1853.

92   *Church began to sketch:* Church to Eliza Church, July 7, 1853.

CHAPTER 8   "Unparalleled Magnificence"

93   *"as efficient as the majority":* Church to Eliza Church, July 7, 1853.

93   *"little horses":* Andrea Wulf, *The Adventures of Alexander von Humboldt* (Pantheon, 2019).

94   *"the most difficult passage":* Humboldt, *Researches,* 1:63.

94   *"big monks":* Mauricio Diazgranados, "A Nomenclator for the Frailejones (Espeletiinae Cuatrec., Asteraceae)," *PhytoKeys* 16 (August 21, 2012): 4.

94   *Church had felt the extremes:* Church to Elizabeth Church, July 23, 1853. Courtesy of Winterthur.

94   *"The plantain is so universal":* Church to Elizabeth Church, July 23, 1853.

95   *"resembled exceedingly an old man":* Church to Charlotte Church, July 30, 1853. Courtesy of Winterthur.

95   *"having luggage enough":* Church to Charlotte Church, July 30, 1853.

95   *Church sketched the elaborate cathedral:* See Church, "Cathedral at Popayán, Colombia," graphite on white wove paper, August 5, 1853, CHSDM.

95   *he could see the volcano:* Church to Charlotte Church, August 8, 1853. Courtesy of Winterthur.

95   *Residents lived in constant wariness:* Church to Charlotte Church, August 8, 1853.

95   *"marvellously beautiful and picturesque":* Church to Charlotte Church, August 8, 1853.

95   *"delicious"*: Church to Charlotte Church, August 8, 1853.

95   *"perched on the table"*: Church to Charlotte Church, August 8, 1853.

95   *up the slopes on foot*: Church to Charlotte Church, August 8, 1853.

95   *"grey ashes and rock"*: Church to Charlotte Church, August 8, 1853.

95   *"vaporous undulations"*: Church, "Puracé Volcano, Colombia and Mt. Sincholagua, Ecuador," graphite and white gouache on gray-green wove paper, August 9 and September 1853, CHSDM.

95   *barely take ten steps*: Church to Charlotte Church, August 8, 1853.

95   *"like a hot iron"*: Church to Charlotte Church, August 8, 1853.

96   *He set off with a guide*: Church to Charlotte Church, August 8, 1853.

96   *"Wherever we stopped"*: Church to Eliza Church, August 20, 1853. Courtesy of Winterthur.

96   *"the vallies [sic] of the Cordilleras"*: Humboldt, *Researches*, 1:53–54.

96   *"A view of such unparalleled magnificence"*: Church Diary, August 26, 1853.

96   *"Remember the ashy lights"*: Church, "Cotacachi from Otavalo, Ecuador," graphite, oxidized white gouache, and white gouache on white wove paper, August 29, 1853, CHSDM.

96   *Rafael Salas*: On Salas, see Xavier Puig Peñalosa, "Romanticismo y Pintura de Paisaje en el Ecuador Decimonónico: El Caso de Rafael Salas (1826–1906)," *Boletín de la Academia Nacional de Historia* 100, no. 207 (August 1, 2022): 13–49.

96   *Humboldt had tried*: Wulf, *Invention of Nature*, 100.

96   *"Having a guide"*: Church Diary, September 3, 1853.

97   *"Only think!"*: Church Diary, September 3, 1853.

97   *Humboldt had tried*: Wulf, *Invention of Nature*, 96.

97   *In the past three centuries*: Minard Hall and Patricia Mothes, "The Rhyolitic–Andesitic Eruptive History of Cotopaxi Volcano, Ecuador," *Bulletin of Volcanology* 70, no. 6 (April 2008): 676.

98   *they couldn't see much*: Church Diary, September 10, 1853.

98   *"grimly secludes itself"*: Church to Ramón Paez, September 11, 1866. Original in the AAA.

98   *He sketched this magnificent mountain*: Church Diary, September 12, 1853.

98   *"rears its white and lofty head"*: Church Diary, September 19, 1853.

99   *"They say that the scenery"*: Quoted by Judson, *Cyrus W. Field*, 54.

99   *Field was bringing back*: Judson, *Cyrus W. Field*, 56.

CHAPTER 9   "A True American"

101   *an illegal lottery*: Orcutt, *American Art-Union*, 176–88.

101   *record for an American landscape painting*: Carr, *Frederic Edwin Church*, 1:203.

101   A Country Home *and* A New England Lake: *National Academy of Design Exhibition Record*, 1:81.

101   *"unquestionably the finest"*: Church to E. P. Mitchell, December 14, 1854.

102   *the other four*: Debora Rindge, "Chronology," in Franklin Kelly, *Frederic Edwin Church* (National Gallery of Art, 1989), 162.

102   *On March 12, 1855*: "Sketchings," *Crayon* 1 (March 21, 1855): 186.

102   *Poole . . . Know-Nothings*: Elliott J. Gorn, "'Good-Bye Boys, I Die a True American': Homicide, Nativism, and Working-Class Culture in Antebellum New York City," *Journal of American History* 74, no. 2 (1987): 395.

102   *population of New York City*: The population of New York City was 60,000 in 1800 and 590,000 in 1850. By 1860 it would rise to nearly 1 million: Joseph J. Salvo and

Arun Peter Lobo, "Population," in *The Encyclopedia of New York City*, 2nd ed., ed. Kenneth T. Jackson (Yale University Press, 2010), 1018–20.

102 New York Times *charged:* "The Pugilists' Encounter," *New York Times*, March 9, 1855.

102 *academy, itself in financial straits:* Cummings, *Historic Annals*, 244–45.

102 *"excellent state of preservation":* "The Burial of William Poole," *New York Herald*, March 12, 1855.

102 I DIE A TRUE AMERICAN: "Burial of William Poole."

102 *funeral of Alexander Hamilton:* "The Funeral of Poole," *New York Times*, March 12, 1855.

103 *Few people showed up:* "National Academy of Design," *New York Times*, March 13, 1855.

103 *"many poor portraits":* "Sketchings," *Crayon* 1:186.

103 *over 4 million words:* George Templeton Strong, *The Diary of George Templeton Strong*, ed. Allan Nevins and Milton Halsey Thomas (Macmillan, 1952), preface, 1:v.

103 *"space smaller than usual":* Strong, *Diary*, March 18, 1855, 2:215.

103 *"warm, rich, hazy air":* Strong, *Diary*, March 18, 1855, 2:215.

103 *"strong, real, and true":* Strong, *Diary*, March 18, 1855, 2:216.

104 *painter and critic William James Stillman:* Stillman had briefly studied with Church in 1848 but soon quit; half a century later he would complain that Church had been too intensely focused on the details of nature: Howat, *Frederic Church*, 26–27.

104 *"American school":* "The Academy Exhibition—No. I," *Crayon* 1, no. 13 (March 28, 1855): 203, quoted by Howat, *Frederic Church*, 62.

104 *"the most remarkable and complete":* "Academy Exhibition—No. I."

104 *"this faculty of his":* "Academy Exhibition—No. I."

104 *"The atmospheric effects":* "National Academy of Design," *New York Times*, April 12, 1855.

104 *"CHURCH shows, this year":* "Exhibition of the National Academy of Design," *Knickerbocker* 45 (May 1855): 532.

104 *Boston Athenaeum's exhibition:* Howat, *Frederic Church*, 62.

105 *a spiritual awe:* The cultural critic Adam Badeau made this point in an 1859 essay: "Some quarrel with Mr. Church that he makes everything subordinate to effect: that is, that soul is more to him than body; but not so I. His pictures speak their meaning, have an influence, excite feelings, and even if sometimes his skies are impossible, or his foliage untrue, if he daguerreotypes not, gives no facsimile of nature, his works yet answer the higher purpose of awakening the same emotion which the sight of the landscape itself would inspire. This is art's noblest, truest function; not to imitate nature, but to rival it." "The National Academy of Design," in Adam Badeau, *The Vagabond* (Rudd & Carleton, 1859), 151–57.

105 *"We who can draw":* Church to Martin Johnson Heade, January 22, 1868. Original in the AAA.

105 *"drinking in large draughts":* Virginia Osborn to Amelia Sturges, February 19, 1857, quoted by Christine I. Oaklander, "Jonathan Sturges, W. H. Osborn, and William Church Osborn: A Chapter in American Art Patronage," *Metropolitan Museum Journal* 43 (2008): 181.

105 *He had recently raised:* Church to E. P. Mitchell, December 14, 1854.

105 *But he still roomed:* Church lived at 37 East Sixteenth Street "near 4th Avenue" (today's Park Avenue). See Church to Charlotte Church, June 11, 1855.

106 *"seemed a quivering haze":* "Frederic Church," *Harper's Weekly* 11, no. 545 (June 8, 1867): 364.

106 *"Magnificent, sultry-tropical"*: Strong, *Diary,* May 30, 1857, 2:338.

106 *"Let me stand with bare head"*: "Pictures Canvassed," *Harper's Weekly* 1, no. 22 (May 30, 1857): 339, quoted by Kelly, "Passion for Landscape," 50.

106 *"Rembrandt Peale said"*: Theodore Winthrop to Church, July 26, 1857.

CHAPTER 10 "Daring and Insolent Men"

107 *Church was thrown*: Tracy, *Tracy Log Book,* 62. The following account of the house party comes from this record, unless otherwise noted.

108 *named long ago by the Wabanaki*: Prins and McBride, *Asticou's Island Domain,* xi.

108 *Wiwonotonet, or "surrounded by mountains"*: Neptune, "Naming the Dawnland," 100; and Henry A. Raup, *Place Names of Mount Desert Island and the Cranberry Islands, Maine* (Mount Desert Island Historical Society, 2021), 168.

109 *"fresh as morning"*: Tracy, *Tracy Log Book,* 68.

109 *the energetic playfulness*: George William Curtis, "Theodore Winthrop: Obituary," *Atlantic,* August 1861, 11–12.

109 *died of starvation*: Theodore Winthrop, *The Life and Poems of Theodore Winthrop,* ed. Laura Winthrop Johnson (Henry Holt, 1884), 190.

110 *But Church went out*: Tracy, *Tracy Log Book,* 69.

111 *"These thoughts"*: Tracy, *Tracy Log Book,* 53.

112 *"They all declared"*: Tracy, *Tracy Log Book,* 121.

112 *he dined with them*: Church to George Warren, February 12, 1857. Original in the AAA.

112 *"Miss Annie Tracy"*: Joseph Hodges Choate to Carrie [Choate], December 13, 1857, in Edward Sanford Martin, *The Life of Joseph Hodges Choate: As Gathered Chiefly from His Letters* (Charles Scribner's Sons, 1920), 1:204.

113 *"great, ugly, three-tiered box"*: Theodore Winthrop, *Life in the Open Air, and Other Papers* (Ticknor & Fields, 1863), 3.

113 *"a compact, convenient, accessible"*: Winthrop, *Life in the Open Air,* 6.

113 *Thoreau, Winthrop's personal hero*: Winthrop, *Life and Poems,* 201.

113 *"The tops of mountains"*: Henry David Thoreau, "The Ascent of Ktaadn," *Sartain's Union Magazine* 3 (October 1848): 181.

113 *"Church of course"*: Theodore Winthrop to his mother, August 20, 1856, quoted by Winthrop, *Life and Poems,* 161.

113 *"totally at peace"*: Winthrop, *Life in the Open Air,* 66.

113 *"People talked as if"*: Winthrop, *Life in the Open Air,* 18.

114 *the two friends talked*: Winthrop, *Life in the Open Air,* 58.

114 *"What a pity"*: Winthrop, *Life in the Open Air,* 78.

114 *"mobile mushroom"*: Winthrop, *Life in the Open Air,* 73.

115 *"This was that Earth"*: Henry David Thoreau, "The Return Journey," *Sartain's Union Magazine* 3 (November 1848): 216–17.

115 *plein air studies*: Kelly, *Frederic Edwin Church and the National Landscape,* 71–74.

115 *Katahdin—"the greatest mountain"*: P. Thompson Davis et al., "Cosmogenic Exposure Age Evidence for Rapid Laurentide Deglaciation of the Katahdin Area, West-Central Maine, USA, 16 to 15 Ka," *Quaternary Science Reviews* 116 (May 15, 2015): 96.

115 *painting called* Sunset: Huntington, *Landscapes,* 75.

115 *Church could no longer view*: On the place of *Sunset* in Church's evolution, see esp. Kelly, "Passion for Landscape," 90–94.

CHAPTER 11 "Fidgety as a Wildcat"

117 *waved an umbrella:* Beaumont Newhall, *The Daguerreotype in America,* 3rd ed. (Dover, 1976), 69.

117 *almost since the invention:* Robert Hirsch, *Seizing the Light: A History of Photography* (McGraw Hill, 2000), 43.

118 *"beyond the power of man":* Ruskin, "Of Truth of Water," *Modern Painters,* 1:321.

118 *"He should not paint":* "Editor's Table: Exhibition of the National Academy of Design," *Knickerbocker* 45, no. 5 (May 1855): 532.

118 *to set about painting:* Church to Osborn, November 29, 1856. Original in PUL.

118 *"I wish to take":* Cole to Robert Gilmor, April 26, 1829, quoted by Ellwood C. Parry III, *The Art of Thomas Cole: Ambition and Imagination* (University of Delaware, 1988), 93.

119 *he would fail:* McKinsey, *Niagara Falls,* 202.

119 *He made notes:* McKinsey, *Niagara Falls,* 230.

119 *Cole kept trying:* "Catalogue," in Kornhauser and Barringer, *Thomas Cole's Journey,* 152–55.

119 *"By what mysterious power":* "Fragment of Notes Regarding Niagara Falls, [25–30 September 1848]," Papers of Abraham Lincoln Digital Library, https://papersof abrahamlincoln.org/documents/D200527.

119 *"Almost I fear":* Ralph Waldo Emerson, *Nature* (J. Munroe & Company, 1836), 12.

119 *"occult relation":* Emerson, *Nature,* 13.

120 *Cataract House:* Pierre Berton, *Niagara: A History of the Falls* (Anchor Canada, 2002), 72.

120 *Black employees risked:* On Cataract House employees and the Underground Railroad, see Karolyn Smardz Frost, "The Cataract House Hotel: Underground to Canada Through the Niagara River Borderlands," in *Harriet's Legacies: Race, Historical Memory, and Futures in Canada,* ed. Ronald Cummings and Natalee Caple (McGill-Queen's University Press, 2022).

120 *"fidgety as a wildcat":* Church to Goodman, September 2, 1858.

120 *went back out after supper:* Amelia Sturges to Mary Sturges, July 17, 1856.

120 *"I had only one friend":* Church to Goodman, September 24, 1858.

120 *"As there is but a step":* Church to Goodman, September 2, 1858.

122 *"universal and unqualified":* Church to Osborn, November 29, 1856.

122 *Just as Church intended:* Harvey, *Painted Sketch,* 67.

122 *"I shall commence":* Church to Osborn, February 23, 1857. Original in PUL.

122 *"hammering away":* Church to [Joseph B.?] Austin, March 5, 1857.

122 *agreed to pay him $2,500:* William, Stevens, Williams & Co. to Church, April 22, 1857.

123 *done something similar:* Ellwood C. Parry III, "Thomas Cole and the Problem of Figure Painting," *American Art Journal* 4, no. 1 (1972): 83.

123 *moving panoramas:* Kevin J. Avery, "'The Heart of the Andes' Exhibited: Frederic E. Church's Window on the Equatorial World," *American Art Journal* 18, no. 1 (1986): 60–65.

123 *"You pass from the bustle":* "Church's *Niagara,*" *New-York Daily Times,* May 21, 1857.

123 *"It is Niagara":* "The Fine Arts," *New York Herald,* May 31, 1857.

123 *"incontestably the finest":* *Albion,* quoted by *The Great Fall: Niagara. Painted by Frederic Edward [sic] Church* (Williams, Stevens, Williams & Co., 1857), 9.

123 *a biblical symbol:* Huntington, *Landscapes,* 71.

123 *The Kansas Territory:* James M. McPherson, *Battle Cry of Freedom: The Civil War Era* (Oxford University Press, 1988), 145ff.

123 *cheered slavery's apologists:* Alan Taylor, *American Civil Wars: A Continental History, 1850–1873* (W. W. Norton, 2024), 80–82.

124 Dred Scott *decision:* Wineapple, *Ecstatic Nation,* 90–91.

124 *thousands crowded:* "The Fine Arts," *New York Herald*, May 31, 1857.

124 *More than one thousand:* Carr, *Frederic Edwin Church*, 1:497.

124 *right to all profits:* Howat, *Frederic Church*, 73.

124 *Emerson, Irving:* On the reception of U.S. writers in the British press at mid-century, see Lelon Avalon Hill, "British Criticism of American Literature 1844–1860 as Reflected in *Littell's Living Age*" (master's thesis, University of New Mexico, 1940). On British reception of American art in the first half of the nineteenth century, see Tim Barringer, "A White Atlantic? The Idea of American Art in Nineteenth-Century Britain," *19: Interdisciplinary Studies in the Long Nineteenth Century*, no. 9 (November 9, 2009).

124 *Ruskin reportedly thought:* Tuckerman, *Book of the Artists*, 371.

124 *"remarkable picture":* Quoted by "Sketchings," *Crayon* 4 (September 1857), 282.

124 *"even this awful reality":* Quoted by "Sketchings," *Crayon* 4:282.

125 *"be studied by all":* Quoted by "Foreign Correspondence, Items, Etc.," *Crayon* 6 (May 1858), 174.

CHAPTER 12 "The Grandest Mountain in the World"

127 *He had also read:* Katherine Emma Manthorne, *Tropical Renaissance: North American Artists Exploring Latin America, 1839–1879*, New Directions in American Art (Smithsonian Institution Press, 1989), 78–79.

127 *Church had seen his friend Kensett:* I am indebted to Tyler Green for alerting me to the impact of Kensett's *Mount Washington from the Valley of Conway* on Church and other landscape painters.

128 *peaceful, agrarian vision:* Carol Troyen, "Retreat to Arcadia: American Landscape and the American Art-Union," *American Art Journal* 23, no. 1 (1991): 21.

128 *showed the painting in 1851:* "Programme of the Present Year," *Bulletin of the American Art-Union* 1 (April 1851): 17.

128 *Church was among them:* Driscoll and Howat, *John Frederick Kensett*, 66.

128 *"I long with an immense":* Winthrop to Church, July 26, 1857.

128 *"like a white cloud":* Church to Goodman, May 27, 1857.

128 *"grandest mountain":* Quoted by Howat, *Frederic Church*, 75.

128 *"the most terrible volcano":* Church to Goodman, June 24, 1857.

129 *"Snow peak dazzling":* Quoted by Carr, *Frederic Edwin Church*, 1:237–38.

129 *Cotopaxi had turned violent:* "Volcanic Eruption," *Flag of Our Union* (Boston), December 16, 1854.

130 *"The terror stricken faces":* Church to Warren, June 29, 1857.

130 *"Dark sullen purple":* Church sketch of Cotopaxi and Sincholagua, June 26, 1857, Carr, *Frederic Edwin Church*, 2: no. 379.

130 *"pinky warm":* Church sketch of Cotopaxi and Sincholagua, June 26, 1857.

130 *Church kept a diary:* Frederic Church, Sangay Diary, 1857, OSHS.

130 *"I had a little rat of a horse":* Church, Sangay Diary, July 9. The following account of the trip to Sangay is drawn from this diary.

CHAPTER 13 "All Earth's Riches"

135 *ship ran aground off Cuba:* Church to Goodman, September 3, 1857.

135 *second-floor studio:* On the Tenth Street Studio Building's layout and occupants, see Blaugrund, *Tenth Street Studio Building*.

135 *James Boorman Johnston:* Blaugrund, *Tenth Street Studio Building*, 17.

135 *about two dozen lucky artists:* Blaugrund, *Tenth Street Studio Building*, 23.

135 *Gignoux, Gifford:* Annette Blaugrund, "The Tenth Street Studio Building: A Roster, 1857–1895," *American Art Journal* 14, no. 2 (1982): 69–71.

135 *Worthington Whittredge: Autobiography of Worthington Whittredge*, 40–41; and Blaugrund, *Tenth Street Studio Building*, 134.

136 *continued to practice law:* H. Wilson, ed., *Trow's New York City Directory for the Year 1860* (John F. Trow, 1859), 921.

136 *Anna Mary Freeman:* Blaugrund, *Tenth Street Studio Building*, 23; and Shauna Martineau Robertson, "Anna Mary Freeman's Room: Women and Art in Antebellum America" (master's thesis, Brigham Young University, 2004), 63.

136 *inspiring a wave of sunsets:* I am indebted to Tyler Green for this observation.

136 *"very unpopular":* Heade to John Russell Bartlett, November 4, 1858. Original in the John Russell Bartlett Papers, John Carter Brown Library, Brown University. Heade told Bartlett he had just taken "one of the large studios on the ground floor." This letter is quoted by Theodore E. Stebbins Jr., *The Life and Work of Martin Johnson Heade: A Critical Analysis and Catalogue Raisonné* (Yale University Press, 2000), 21.

136 *"the most wonderful picture":* Quoted by Stebbins Jr., *Life and Work*, 22.

136 *"one of the most affable":* Quoted by Stebbins Jr., *Life and Work*, 21.

136 *broad mahogany staircase:* Aldrich, "Among the Studios," 596.

137 *items from his travels:* "Personal," *World*, December 7, 1860; "The Bostonian in New York," *New-York Daily Tribune*, May 12, 1861; and Aldrich, "Among the Studios," 597.

137 *huge chest of drawers:* "Personal," *World*, December 7, 1860.

137 *Cole's painting of Prometheus:* "Personal," *World*, December 7, 1860.

137 *A Chickering grand piano:* Church to Warren, February 12, 1857, and August 8, 1864. Courtesy of the Historical Society of Pennsylvania, Gratz Collection Painters & Engravers.

137 *"I love music too":* Church to Warren, April 24, 1856. Original in the Emmet Collection, Manuscript Division, New York Public Library.

138 *cups of hot chocolate:* M. E. W. Sherwood, "Frederick E. Church," *New York Times*, April 21, 1900.

138 *"He is famous":* Heade to Bartlett, November 4, 1858, partially quoted by Stebbins Jr., *Life and Work*, 21.

138 *portrait of Humboldt:* "Art in New York," *Boston Evening Transcript*, June 3, 1859; and "Letter from New York," *Press* (Philadelphia), June 6, 1859.

138 *copy of the 1802 portrait:* Eleanor Jones Harvey, *Alexander von Humboldt and the United States: Art, Nature, and Culture* (Princeton University Press, 2020), 345.

138 *nature was an intricate, dynamic web:* Wulf, *Invention of Nature*, 102.

138 *He saw with sudden clarity:* Wulf, *Invention of Nature*, 101.

139 *"painting of nature":* Wulf, *Invention of Nature*, 102.

140 *Church began to dream:* Church to Bayard Taylor, May 9, 1859. Original in the Division of Rare and Manuscript Collections, Cornell University.

140 *Church's friend Bayard Taylor:* Taylor to Humboldt, May 16, 1859.

140 *smoky yellow:* Notes made by Church on "Windmill in East Hampton, New York," graphite on white wove paper, July 29, 1858, CHSDM.

140 *He sketched a fishing vessel:* Church, "Fisherman by the Sea, East Hampton, New York," graphite on white wove paper, July–August 1858, and "Going Out to Sea, East Hampton, New York," graphite on white wove paper, July–August 1858, CHSDM.

140 *for three years:* Henry M. Field, *The Story of the Atlantic Telegraph* (Scribner's Sons, 1892), 18.

141 *spliced the ends:* John Steele Gordon, *A Thread Across the Ocean: The Heroic Story of the Transatlantic Cable* (Walker, 2002), 124.

141 *As they traveled apart:* John Mullaly, *The Laying of the Cable, or the Ocean Telegraph* (D. Appleton, 1858), 251; and Gordon, *Thread Across the Ocean*, 125.

141 *record the strength:* Mullaly, *Laying of the Cable*, 275, 281.

141 *The current coming from the* Agamemnon's *end:* Mullaly, *Laying of the Cable*, 308.

141 *From Newfoundland, Field telegraphed:* Gordon, *Thread Across the Ocean*, 134.

141 *"The Atlantic is dried up":* Quoted by Gordon, *Thread Across the Ocean*, 134.

141 *she wished she could confer:* Gordon, *Thread Across the Ocean*, 134.

141 *Queen Victoria to President Buchanan:* Field, *Story of the Atlantic Telegraph*, 198.

141 *the queen's words:* "Arrival of the Steam Frigate *Niagara*," *New York Herald*, August 16, 1858.

141 *Her Majesty congratulated:* Gordon, *Thread Across the Ocean*, 136–37.

141 *workers blasting rock:* "The Ocean Cable: The Metropolis in a Blaze of Glory," *New York Herald*, August 18, 1858.

142 *Frederick Law Olmsted:* "Ocean Cable."

142 *HONOR TO CYRUS W. FIELD:* "Ocean Cable."

142 *City Hall caught fire:* "The News," *New York Herald*, August 18, 1858.

142 *Tiffany and Co.:* "Caution," *New York Times*, August 28, 1858.

142 *Children wove through:* "The Cable Celebration," *New York Times*, September 1, 1858.

142 *Church's gallerists arranged:* Church to Goodman, September 24, 1858.

143 *reading a congratulatory note:* "Ocean Cable Celebration," *New York Times*, September 2, 1858.

143 *"I should think":* Church to Goodman, September 2, 1858.

143 *hailed as a hero:* "Cyrus W. Field," *Weekly Minnesotian*, September 18, 1858.

143 *Since September 1 no message:* Judson, *Cyrus W. Field*, 121.

143 *to inform the public:* "Card from Cyrus W. Field, Esq.—the Cable Not in Working Order," *New York Times*, September 25, 1858.

143 *"by the mile":* "Atlantic Telegraph Cable by the Mile," *New York Times*, October 8, 1858.

143 *notice in* The Evening Post: "Fine Arts," *New York Evening Post*, November 15, 1858. Church was also working on several smaller commissions: see Church to Hamilton Fish, December 12, 1858. Courtesy of the Hamilton Fish Papers, Manuscript Division, Library of Congress. And Church to Erastus Dow Palmer, December 27, 1858. Original in Vassar College Library.

143 *set for the end of April:* Avery, "'Heart of the Andes,'" 69n12.

144 *"The subject is new":* Theodore Winthrop, *A Companion to the Heart of the Andes* (D. Appleton, 1859), 6.

144 *"The globe itself":* Quoted by Avery, *Church's Great Picture*, 15.

144 *Winthrop recognized the vapors:* Winthrop, *Companion to the Heart of the Andes*, 25–28.

144 *erosive scouring of rock:* Winthrop, *Companion to the Heart of the Andes*, 17–21. On Church's interest in geology, see Rebecca Bedell, "Frederic Church and the Educational Enterprise," in *The Anatomy of Nature: Geology and American Landscape Painting, 1825–1875* (Princeton University Press, 2002).

144 *"All earth's riches":* Winthrop, *Companion to the Heart of the Andes*, 12.

144 *offering himself:* Winthrop, *Companion to the Heart of the Andes*, 43.

144 *a wayside cross:* Manthorne, *Tropical Renaissance*, 145–47.

144 *Church prized:* Harvey, *Alexander von Humboldt*, 354–56.

145 *Church unveiled:* Avery, "'Heart of the Andes,'" 69n12.

145 *he was much prouder:* "Art in New York," *Daily Evening Bulletin* (Philadelphia), February 5, 1866.

145 *"was more than a fashion":* "Frederic Edwin Church," *Harper's Weekly* 11, no. 545 (June 8, 1867): 364.

145 *"it beats any landscape":* Strong, *Diary*, May 7, 1858, 2:451.

145 *"the ravings of Ruskin"*: Strong, *Diary,* May 5, 1858, 2:450.

145 *envy and admiration:* "Art in New York," *Boston Evening Transcript.*

145 *Rembrandt Peale:* Rembrandt Peale to Church, December 15, 1859.

145 Harper's Weekly *fretted:* "The Heart of the Andes," *Harper's Weekly* 3, no. 127 (June 4, 1859): 355.

145 *Blodgett for $10,000:* Avery, *Church's Great Picture,* 34. In 1853, Leutze sold *Washington Crossing the Delaware* to businessman Marshall O. Roberts for $10,000: Jochen Wierich, *Grand Themes: Emanuel Leutze,* Washington Crossing the Delaware, *and American History Painting* (Penn State Press, 2012), 20.

146 *more recent commentators:* See, e.g., Angela Miller, *The Empire of the Eye: Landscape Representation and American Cultural Politics, 1825–1875* (Cornell University Press, 1996), 202–5; and Green, *Emerson's* Nature *and the Artists,* 79.

CHAPTER 14 "Our Beloved Union"

147 *Whittredge later recounted: Autobiography of Worthington Whittredge,* 29.

147 *Emma Carnes, a New Yorker:* Seventh Census of the United States, "1850 United States Federal Census for Emma Carnes," Records of the Bureau of the Census, Record Group 29, National Archives Microfilm Publication M432, 1,009 rolls (Washington, DC, National Archives), ancestry.com.

147 *Harvard in 1805: Quinquennial Catalogue of the Officers and Graduates of Harvard University: 1636–1910* (Harvard University, 1910), 171.

148 *exquisite marble sculpture:* Thomas Gold Appleton, *Life and Letters of Thomas Gold Appleton,* ed. Susan Hale (D. Appleton, 1885), 315.

148 *"His manners are polite":* Macaulay, "Artist and the Convict."

148 *"whole being was":* Sarah Osgood Tucker to Downie Church, May 16, 1900.

148 *unable to get into the building:* John F. Weir, *The Recollections of John Ferguson Weir, Director of the Yale School of the Fine Arts, 1869–1913,* ed. Theodore Sizer (New-York Historical Society, 1957), 45; and "Heart of the Andes," *Harper's Weekly,* 355.

148 *"glorious—magnificent!":* Quoted by Avery, *Church's Great Picture,* 37; see also Pierre Munroe Irving, *The Life and Letters of Washington Irving* (G. P. Putnam, 1864), 288–89, and "Letter from New York," *Press.*

148 *"the news touched me":* Church to Taylor, June 13, 1859. Original in the Division of Rare and Manuscript Collections, Cornell University.

148 *sailed with the giant canvas:* "Letter from New York," *Press.*

148 *"Her Majesty":* "The Heart of the Andes," *New York Herald,* July 17, 1859.

149 *"in every way a triumph":* "The Heart of the Andes," *London Daily News,* July 4, 1859.

149 *"On this American":* W. P. Bayley, "The 'Heart of the Andes,'" *Art-Journal,* September 1859, 298, quoted by Avery, *Church's Great Picture,* 39.

149 *"Coolly to make a trip":* "Church's 'Heart of the Andes,'" *Illustrated London News,* July 30, 1859.

149 *great cultural creations:* "Wonderful Development of American Art—Uprising of Enthusiasm," *New York Herald,* December 5, 1859.

149 *Arctic explorers:* Gerald L. Carr and David C. Huntington, *Frederic Edwin Church: The Icebergs* (Dallas Museum of Fine Arts, 1980), 38–41.

149 *his friend Noble:* "The Tip of *The Icebergs,*" in Eleanor Jones Harvey and Gerald L. Carr, *The Voyage of the* Icebergs: *Frederic Church's Arctic Masterpiece* (Dallas Museum of Art, 2002).

149 *"There are the dead":* Louis Legrand Noble, *After Icebergs with a Painter: A Summer Voyage to Labrador and Around Newfoundland* (D. Appleton, 1861), 167. Noble's book

was recently reprinted with a foreword by William L. Coleman, by Black Dome Press, 2022. The following account of the trip is drawn from Noble's work.

150 *"an Arab's tent"*: Noble, *After Icebergs*, 28.

151 *"fairly overflowed with fun"*: Noble, *After Icebergs*, 203.

151 *"like swallows round a barn"*: Noble, *After Icebergs*, 291.

151 *"burning of the water"*: Noble, *After Icebergs*, 91.

151 *"thou roving Ishmael"*: Noble, *After Icebergs*, 29.

152 *"Strange, supernatural"*: Quoted by Harvey and Carr, *Voyage of the* Icebergs, 47.

152 *"The painter gazes"*: Noble, *After Icebergs*, 140.

152 *nearly one hundred*: Harvey and Carr, *Voyage of the* Icebergs, 49.

153 *bright reds, yellows, and greens*: On Church's palette for *Twilight in the Wilderness*, see Kelly, "Frederic Edwin Church and the North American Landscape," appendix C, 388–99.

153 *the lakes and mountains of Maine*: Lockwood de Forest, a young painting student and distant relative by marriage of Church's, came to own the picture, and he noted that it depicted "the wilderness about Katahdin": Howat, *Frederic Church*, 101.

153 *"She is just what you would imagine"*: Virginia Osborn to Lucy Wheeler, January 14, 1860.

153 *By early January*: Church to T. G. Appleton, January 10, 1860.

153 *"Church has been successfully"*: "Correspondence of the *Transcript*," *Boston Evening Transcript*, January 10, 1860.

153 *"plain folks"*: Emma Carnes to Church, February 1, 1860, quoting Church's words back to him.

153 *Isabel confessed to her mother*: Emma Carnes to Church, January 20, 1860.

154 *"the light & joy"*: Emma Carnes to Church, January 20, 1860.

154 *Church's door was the only one*: "The Last Artists' Reception for the Season," *New-York Daily Tribune*, March 27, 1860.

154 *Baltimore collector*: Kelly, "Frederic Edwin Church and the North American Landscape," 293.

154 *"quite a tramp"*: Theodore Cole, diary entry, April 2, 1860, transcription by Raymond Beecher, November 30, 1979, from Thomson-Cole Manuscripts, Greene County Historical Society.

155 *farmer who had, in 1794*: Wynsant Brezie bought the land from John J. Van Rensselaer: Robert M. Toole, "Historic Landscape Report" (Olana State Historic Site, December 1996), 33.

155 *city of seven thousand*: Tom Lewis, *The Hudson: A History* (Yale University Press, 2005), 229.

155 *While Theddy hired*: Toole, "Historic Landscape Report," 44–46.

155 *He unveiled it*: Howat, *Frederic Church*, 99.

155 *For twenty-five cents each*: "Church's Latest Work," *New York Herald*, July 25, 1860.

155 *brilliant sunset*: Kelly, "Frederic Edwin Church and the North American Landscape," 103.

155 *"Mr. Church, like Turner"*: Quoted by Kelly, "Frederic Edwin Church and the North American Landscape," 281.

155 *Church's "best efforts"*: "Art in New York," *Daily Evening Bulletin*.

156 *One bald eagle*: Most scholars have made note of only one bald eagle in analyses of this picture (that in the dead tree), but a second bald eagle is instantly visible to anyone who has spent time observing the natural life of Maine's lakes and woods.

156 *With this painting*: I am indebted to Kelly, "Frederic Edwin Church and the North American Landscape," and Kelly, *Frederic Edwin Church and the National Landscape*, for his analysis of *Twilight in the Wilderness* as a commentary on wilderness; for a

recent critique and reappraisal, see Alan C. Braddock, "Nature: Wilderness Trouble," in *Implication*.

156   *darker biblical themes:* Kelly, *Frederic Edwin Church and the National Landscape*, 120–21.

156   *"happy to extricate":* Strong, *Diary*, December 19, 1859, 2:478.

157   *"the idea of an irrepressible conflict":* Richard Lathers, *Reminiscences of Richard Lathers: Sixty Years of a Busy Life in South Carolina, Massachusetts and New York*, ed. Alvan F. Sanborn (Grafton Press, 1907), 72.

157   *almost instantly famous:* On Lincoln's speech and its reception and impact, see esp. Harold Holzer, *Lincoln at Cooper Union: The Speech That Made Abraham Lincoln President* (Simon & Schuster, 2004); see also Harold Holzer, *Lincoln and the Power of the Press: The War for Public Opinion* (Simon & Schuster, 2014), 219–22.

157   *Lincoln won:* Holzer, *Lincoln and the Power*, 230.

157   *His candidacy unleashed:* For example, in New York on May 22, 1860, Henry S. Foote, a former governor of Mississippi, told a cheering crowd of Democrats, "Mr. Lincoln, if elected, will . . . bring on civil war, produce secession, discord, revolt, dissolution, the destruction of our free institutions": "The Presidential Campaign," *New York Herald*, May 23, 1860.

157   *That chilling phrase:* See, e.g., "The Campaign in Connecticut," *New York Herald*, April 2, 1860; "The Republican Press and the Republican Defeat in New England," *New York Herald*, April 8, 1860; "Legislative Acts / Legal Proceedings," *New York Herald*, April 16, 1860; "Disunion Plots," *New York Times*, May 10, 1860; and "Senator Davis's Platform," *New-York Daily Tribune*, May 10, 1860.

157   *dark night in the wilderness:* For interpretations of *Twilight in the Wilderness* as commenting on the impending Civil War, see esp. Kelly, *Frederic Edwin Church and the National Landscape*, 117–22, and Green, *Emerson's* Nature *and the Artists*.

158   *"Mt Desert":* The sketch is reproduced in Carr, *Frederic Edwin Church*, 2: no. 403, and see also 1:270–71.

158   *"Frederic has been desirous":* Elizabeth Church to Eliza Church, September 21, 1860.

CHAPTER 15   "The Rage of the Wicked"

159   *Church and Isabel returned:* Theodore Cole, diary entry, October 6, 1860.

159   *He asked Theddy:* On Church's work on the landscape, see Sean E. Sawyer, "Frederic Church's Place in the Country," in Barry Bergdoll, Sean E. Sawyer, and Thomas L. Woltz, *Olana: Frederic Church's Vision of Architecture and Landscape* (New York: Rizzoli Electa, 2026). On the recent restoration of Church's landscape design, see Thomas L. Woltz, "Restoring a Landscape Masterwork: Breathing New Life into Frederic Church's Living Work of Art," in *Frederic Church's Olana on the Hudson: Art, Landscape, Architecture,* ed. Julia B. Rosenbaum and Karen Zukowski (New York: Rizzoli Electa, 2018).

159   *tamper with slavery:* Lincoln to Alexander Stephens, December 22, 1860, in *The Complete Works of Abraham Lincoln*, ed. John G. Nicolay and John Hay (Francis D. Tandy Company, 1905), 6:85–86.

159   *New York City merchants:* John Strausbaugh, *City of Sedition: The History of New York City During the Civil War* (Twelve, 2016), 136.

159   *"fearful and horrible":* Quoted by Harold Holzer, *Lincoln President-Elect: Abraham Lincoln and the Great Secession Winter, 1860–1861* (Simon & Schuster, 2008), 46–47.

159   *He begged Winthrop:* Church to Winthrop, March 16, 1860. Original in the Ford Collection, New York Public Library.

159 *he wrote to his paint dealer:* Church to Thomas B. Lawson, January 11, 1860.

159 *"I sincerely hope":* John McClure to Church, December 4, 1860.

160 *Noble scoffed at the pretensions:* Charles Lanman, *Haphazard Personalities; Chiefly of Noted Americans* (Lee and Shepard Publishers, 1886), 224.

160 *strongly opposed to slavery:* Camille Ferri-Pisani, *Prince Napoleon in America, 1861: Letters from His Aide-de-Camp,* trans. Georges Joyaux (Indiana University Press, 1959), 232.

160 *he identified strongly:* Katherine E. Manthorne and John W. Coffey, *The Landscapes of Louis Rémy Mignot: A Southern Painter Abroad* (Smithsonian Institution Press, 1996), 10–11.

160 *oceanology, meteorology, and geology:* On the place of contemporary science in Church's creation of *The Icebergs,* see esp. David C. Huntington, "Introduction," in Carr and Huntington, *Frederic Edwin Church,* 9–19.

160 *"are obedient to law":* Matthew Fontaine Maury, *The Physical Geography of the Sea* (Harper & Brothers, 1859), 103.

161 *people dropped by:* "Art-Gossip," *New York Times* supplement, December 22, 1860, quoted by Harvey and Carr, *Voyage of the* Icebergs, 89.

161 *chalky white ground:* Zucker, "From the Ground Up," 8.

161 *Shouting and fistfights:* Strausbaugh, *City of Sedition,* 139.

161 *"The attitude of":* Frederick Douglass, "The Union and How to Save It," *Douglass' Monthly,* February 1861.

161 *hanged in effigy:* Edward L. Widmer, *Lincoln on the Verge: Thirteen Days to Washington* (Simon & Schuster, 2020), 324.

161 *Democratic Mayor Fernando Wood:* Strausbaugh, *City of Sedition,* 141.

161 *"peaceful and conciliatory":* "The Incoming Administration," *New York Times,* February 21, 1861.

161 *"many an assassin's knife":* Quoted by Widmer, *Lincoln on the Verge,* 336.

161 *"looked with curiosity":* Widmer, *Lincoln on the Verge,* 335.

162 *small contingent of soldiers:* Adam Goodheart, *1861: The Civil War Awakening* (Alfred A. Knopf, 2011), 137.

162 *"I go to put an end":* Winthrop to Theodore Woolsey, quoted by Winthrop, *Life and Poems,* 284.

162 *They and hundreds:* Emmons Clark, *History of the Seventh Regiment of New York, 1806–1889* (1890), 2:474.

162 *"taking the measure":* Theodore Winthrop, "The New York Seventh Regiment: Our March to Washington," *Atlantic Monthly,* June 1861, 744.

162 *"utterly united":* Winthrop, "New York Seventh Regiment," 745.

162 *Virginia had just:* "Stirring and Decisive News," *New York Herald,* April 19, 1861.

162 *Seventh Regiment was quartered:* Winthrop, *Life in the Open Air,* 263.

163 *"Church's New Picture":* *Harper's Weekly* 5, no. 225 (April 20, 1861): 242, quoted by Carr and Huntington, *Frederic Edwin Church,* 73.

163 *more than one hundred thousand:* Burrows and Wallace, *Gotham,* 869; and "The War[;] The Monster Meeting Yesterday," *New York Herald,* April 21, 1861.

163 *"For upwards":* "The War[;] The Monster Meeting."

163 *statue of George Washington:* Carr, *Frederic Edwin Church,* 1:275.

163 *flag had flown:* Erik Larson, *The Demon of Unrest: A Saga of Hubris, Heartbreak, and Heroism at the Dawn of the Civil War* (Crown, 2024), 457.

164 *In a letter to her sister-in-law:* Virginia Osborn to Lucy Wheeler, May 6, 1861.

164 *"Four weeks ago":* Osborn to Wheeler, May 6, 1861.

164 *donating the fees:* Kevin J. Avery, "'Rally 'Round the Flag': Frederic Edwin Church and the Civil War," *Hudson River Valley Review,* Spring 2011, 70.

164 *"you would as soon"*: "K. C.," "Church's Picture of 'The North,'" *Christian Register* (Boston), March 15, 1862.

164 *"Sonnet to F. E. C."*: Quoted by Huntington, *Landscapes*, 20.

164 *People flocked:* Quoted by Harvey and Carr, *Voyage of the* Icebergs, 62, from "From New York. From Our Own Correspondent. New York, May 2," *Springfield Daily Republican*, May 4, 1861.

164 *"There is a North"*: Proteus [pseud.], "There Is a North—Church's Last Work," *New-York Commercial Advertiser*, April 29, 1861.

164 *"None need be told"*: "American Art," *Knickerbocker*, July 1861, quoted by Gerald L. Carr, "Early Documentation of *The Icebergs*," in Harvey and Carr, *Voyage of the* Icebergs, 93.

165 *hopeful hour of dawn:* Doreen Bolger Burke, "Frederic Edwin Church and 'The Banner of Dawn,'" *American Art Journal* 14, no. 2 (1982): 39–46; Carr, *Frederic Edwin Church*, 1:277–78; and Avery, "'Rally 'Round the Flag.'"

165 *critics were dismissive:* E.g. "Art Items," *New-York Daily Tribune*, May 19, 1861.

165 *"the spacious firmament"*: Quoted by Mark E. Neely Jr. and Harold Holzer, *The Union Image: Popular Prints of the Civil War North* (University of North Carolina Press, 2000), 9.

165 *familiar beacon:* Burke, "Frederic Edwin Church," 44.

166 *sell the picture:* On Walters and *Twilight in the Wilderness*, see Kelly, "Frederic Edwin Church and the North American Landscape," 335–36.

166 *deputized by a friend:* Winthrop to George W. Curtis, May 15, 1861, reproduced in Ellsworth Eliot Jr., *Theodore Winthrop* (Yale University Library, 1938), 28.

166 *President Lincoln sitting:* Winthrop to Curtis, May 15, 1861.

166 *"Up towers"*: Winthrop to Curtis, May 15, 1861.

166 *Winthrop accepted an invitation:* Joshua E. Kastenberg, *The Blackstone of Military Law: Colonel William Winthrop* (Scarecrow Press, 2009), 80.

166 *"Afterward we must"*: Quoted by Goodheart, *1861*, 332.

166 *Butler promoted Winthrop:* Kastenberg, *Blackstone of Military Law*, 78.

166 *Butler had taken up his command:* Goodheart, *1861*, 299.

167 *three Black men:* Goodheart, *1861*, 298.

167 *"contraband of war"*: Goodheart, *1861*, 314.

167 *"center of the center!"*: Winthrop to Laura Winthrop Johnson, May 31, 1861, in Winthrop, *Life and Poems*, 289.

167 *"Voices of the Contraband"*: Winthrop, *Life in the Open Air*, 203–4.

168 *a scout named George Scott:* Benjamin Franklin Butler, *Autobiography and Personal Reminiscences of Major-General Benj. F. Butler: Butler's Book* (A. M. Thayer, 1892), 268.

168 *"We march at midnight"*: Winthrop to his mother, June 9, 1861, in Winthrop, *Life and Poems*, 291.

168 *When he jumped:* Butler to Mrs. Winthrop, June 13, 1861, quoted by Benjamin Franklin Butler, *Private and Official Correspondence of Gen. Benjamin F. Butler, During the Period of the Civil War* (Plimpton Press, 1917), 137.

168 *"some of the last"*: Laura Winthrop Johnson to Mrs. Benjamin Butler, June 1861, quoted by Butler, *Private and Official Correspondence*, 138.

168 *Church made a substantial donation:* I. E. Williams to Church, July 19, 1861.

168 *personal associations:* Eleanor Jones Harvey, *The Civil War and American Art* (Yale University Press, 2012), 37.

168 *It was modest:* "Cosy Cottage Historic Structure Report" (New York State Office of Parks, Recreation and Historic Preservation, 2001), 10.

168 *violent oil sketch:* Church, "Sunset over the Hudson Valley," oil on canvas-backed paper, July 1861, CHSDM.

169　*"When I think how"*: Church to Rachel S. Jameson, April 25, 1867.

169　*"your never to be forgotten"*: Church to Laura Winthrop Johnson, December 11, 1874.

CHAPTER 16　"A Moral Volcano"

171　*Church had lavished attention:* E.g., Church to W. H. Osborn, November 29, 1856.

171　*"How is baby????":* Church to Goodman, May 4, 1858.

171　*"You are fortunate":* Noble to Church, August 29, 1862.

171　*only the corn seemed unwell:* Rhinebeck (NY) Meteorological Register and Diary, June 1862, William L. Clements Library, University of Michigan.

171　*pregnancy was proving difficult:* Eliza Church to Church, October 31, 1862.

171　*"so delicate, so frail":* Virginia Osborn quoted by W. H. Osborn to Church, November 5, 1862.

171　*In early August, the crickets:* Rhinebeck (NY) Meteorological Register, August 1862.

172　*October 29:* Carr, *Frederic Edwin Church,* 1:273.

172　*"Saw Mrs. Churches":* Theodore Cole Diary, February 24, 1863.

172　*"You and Isabel must":* Eliza Church to Church, October 31, 1862.

172　*"I do want to see":* Eliza Church to Church, November 29, 1862.

172　*As president of the Illinois Central Railroad:* William K. Ackerman, *Historical Sketch of the Illinois-Central Railroad, Together with a Brief Biographical Record of Its Incorporators and Some of Its Early Officers* (Fergus Printing Company, 1890), 68.

173　*The railroad line:* Robert M. Sutton, "The Illinois Central: Thoroughfare for Freedom," *Civil War History* 7, no. 3 (September 1961): 279.

173　*"great castle of a House":* Osborn to Church, November 5, 1862.

173　*"Mr. Osborn sometimes lives":* Ferri-Pisani, *Prince Napoleon in America,* 233.

173　*William Church Osborn:* Oaklander, "Jonathan Sturges, W. H. Osborn," 194n79.

174　*"Nobody in this world":* Virginia Osborn quoted by W. H. Osborn to Church, November 5, 1862.

174　*men and supplies:* Sutton, "Illinois Central," 273.

175　*"They arrived, dead and alive":* Olmsted to Henry Whitney Bellows, June 3, 1862, quoted by Witold Rybczynski, *A Clearing in the Distance: Frederick Law Olmsted and America in the 19th Century* (Scribner, 1999), 210.

175　*"Negroes running helter skelter":* Quoted by Reinhart, *Archaeology of Shirley Plantation,* 157.

175　*"as if they had been":* Entry for July 24, 1862, in Edmund Ruffin, *The Diary of Edmund Ruffin,* ed. William Kauffman Scarborough (LSU Press, 1976), 2:386.

175　*"the property of Mr. Carter":* Entry for July 24, 1862, in Ruffin, *Diary of Edmund Ruffin.*

175　*preliminary Emancipation Proclamation:* Eric Foner, *The Fiery Trial: Abraham Lincoln and American Slavery* (W. W. Norton, 2011), 230–31.

176　*"If he postpone":* Strong, *Diary,* December 30, 1862, 3:284.

176　*"We shout for joy":* Frederick Douglass, "Emancipation Proclaimed," *Douglass' Monthly,* October 1862.

000　*"compels us to recognize":* Frederick Douglass, "The American Apocalypse: An Address Delivered in Rochester, New York, on 16 June 1861," Frederick Douglass Papers, https://frederickdouglasspapersproject.com/s/digitaledition/item/9084.

176　*British and American thinkers:* E.g., J. G., "On the Pernicious Influence of Inconsistencies in the Conduct of Christians," *Imperial Magazine; Or, Compendium of Religious, Moral, & Philosophical Knowledge,* November 1827, 1021; and George Payson, *Totemwell* (Riker, Thorne & Co., 1854), 153.

176　*expedition through Brazil:* Stebbins Jr., *Life and Work,* 61.

176   *The carriages of the wealthy:* Strong, *Diary,* November 13, 1862, 3:274.

176   *"crowded to overflowing":* Church to Joseph Church, January 30, 1863.

177   *"Extry!":* Strong, *Diary,* June 26, 1862, 3:233.

177   *dead belonged to immigrant families:* Burrows and Wallace, *Gotham,* 881.

177   *three different placards:* See photograph of 823 Broadway in Strong, *Diary,* vol. 3, plate preceding p. 241.

177   *The transport ships:* Strong, *Diary,* June 22, 1862, 3:231.

177   *Alexander Gardner and James Gibson:* Jeff L. Rosenheim, *Photography and the American Civil War* (Metropolitan Museum of Art, 2013), 7.

177   *"has not brought bodies":* "Brady's Photographs," *New York Times,* October 20, 1862. In a highly original reexamination of this exhibition, Sarah Lewis situates the Antietam photographs in relation to Brady's photographs of the so-called Circassian Beauties from Barnum's American Museum. See Sarah Lewis, *The Unseen Truth: When Race Changed Sight in America* (Harvard University Press, 2024), chap. 1, "Ungrounding."

177   *"a repulsive, brutal":* Oliver Wendell Holmes Sr., "The Doings of the Sunbeam," *Atlantic Monthly,* January 1863.

178   *Winslow Homer:* On Winslow Homer in the Civil War, see William R. Cross, "The Freedom of All Mankind" and "The Proof of a Poet" in *Winslow Homer: American Passage* (Farrar, Straus & Giroux, 2022); and Harvey, *Civil War and American Art,* 148–56.

178   *Church's friend Gifford:* On Sanford Gifford in the Civil War, see Harvey, *Civil War and American Art,* 113–29. On the Brady pictures as reportage, see Tyler Green, *Carleton Watkins* (University of California Press, 2020), 121.

178   *a few blocks away:* Green, *Carleton Watkins,* 118.

178   *in one day in May:* "Under Niagara—Church's New Picture of the Falls," *New York Times,* December 8, 1862; see also Jeremy Elwell Adamson, "Frederic Edwin Church's 'Niagara': The Sublime as Transcendence" (Ph.D. diss., University of Michigan, 1981), 568, and Carr, *Frederic Edwin Church,* 1:250.

179   *He was still not done:* Macaulay, "Artist and the Convict."

179   *He had learned:* Church to T. G. Appleton, November 16, 1863. Original in Massachusetts Historical Society.

179   *"To the World it seems":* Church to T. G. Appleton, November 16, 1863, quoted by Harvey, *Painted Sketch,* 90.

179   *"bolt from the sky":* Quoted by Blight, *Frederick Douglass,* 384.

179   *the rising sun:* David C. Huntington, "Church and Luminism," in *American Light: The Luminist Movement, 1850–1875,* ed. John Wilmerding (Harper & Row, 1980), 180.

179   *"Mr. Church is an artist":* "Cotopaxi," *New-York Daily Tribune,* March 24, 1863.

179   *"clearer than an opal":* "Art in New York," *Daily Evening Bulletin.*

179   *"To refine oil-color":* "Art in New York," *Daily Evening Bulletin.*

180   *"great battle-field":* Quoted by Katherine Manthorne, *Creation & Renewal: Views of Cotopaxi by Frederic Edwin Church* (Smithsonian Institution Press, 1985), 63; and Harvey, *Civil War and American Art,* 43.

180   *"war clouds":* "Mr. Church's *Cotopaxi,*" *New York Albion,* March 21, 1863, 141.

180   *"torn forever":* "Cotopaxi," *New-York Daily Tribune,* March 24, 1863.

180   *"heavy discharges of artillery":* Quoted from the *New American Cyclopaedia* in the pamphlet "Cotopaxi: Painted by Frederic E. Church" (1862).

180   *The allusion to Humboldt:* Harvey, *Civil War and American Art,* 45.

180   *also a prophecy:* Huntington, "Church and Luminism," 180.

180   *God sided with:* Huntington, *Landscapes,* 15.

CHAPTER 17 "The Nation's Future Greatness"

181 *studio on the first floor:* Aldrich, "Among the Studios," 596.

181 *peaceful Shoshone encampment:* Peter H. Hassrick, "Albert Bierstadt: Witness to a Changing West," in *Albert Bierstadt: Witness to a Changing West,* ed. Peter H. Hassrick (University of Oklahoma Press, 2018), 92.

181 *Bierstadt's studio was decorated:* "Domestic Art Gossip," *Crayon* 6 (November 1859): 349.

181 *"appropriate adjuncts":* [Albert Bierstadt], "Rocky Mountains 10 July 1859," *Crayon* 6 (September 1859): 287.

183 *Bierstadt was a far more literal:* I am profoundly indebted to Tyler Green for several conversations about Bierstadt and for his extensive and original interpretations of Bierstadt's place in articulating and supporting white imperialism across the North American continent. See esp. Tyler Green, *Claiming Yosemite: The California Genocide, the Civil War, and the Invention of National Parks* (Stanford University Press / Redwood Press, forthcoming).

183 *"Anglo-Saxon" culture:* Green, *Claiming Yosemite.*

183 *The pamphlet Bierstadt approved:* Green, *Claiming Yosemite.*

183 *"a city, populated":* Quoted by Linda S. Ferber, "Albert Bierstadt: The History of a Reputation," in Nancy K. Anderson and Linda S. Ferber, *Albert Bierstadt: Art and Enterprise* (Brooklyn Museum, 1990), 25.

183 *"This is a glimpse":* Quoted by Nancy K. Anderson, "'Wondrously Full of Invention': The Western Landscapes of Albert Bierstadt," in Anderson and Ferber, *Albert Bierstadt,* 77–78.

183 *meant for the Native people:* On images of Native Americans published in the North during the Civil War, see Scott Manning Stevens, "Other Homes, Other Fronts: Native America During the Civil War," in *Home Front: Daily Life in the Civil War North,* by Peter John Brownlee et al. (University of Chicago Press, 2013). On the violent conquest of the American West see esp. Peter Cozzens, *The Earth Is Weeping: The Epic Story of the Indian Wars for the American West* (Alfred A. Knopf, 2016); Ned Blackhawk, *The Rediscovery of America: Native Peoples and the Unmaking of U.S. History* (Yale University Press, 2023); and Elliott West, *Continental Reckoning: The American West in the Age of Expansion* (University of Nebraska Press, 2023).

183 *solo exhibition:* Quoted by Ferber, "Albert Bierstadt," 25.

183 *"This painting is destined":* Quoted by Anderson and Ferber, *Albert Bierstadt,* 194.

184 *Carleton Watkins at Goupil's:* Green, *Carleton Watkins,* 122.

184 *"has copyrighted nearly all":* "Fine Arts: National Academy of Design," *New York Times,* May 14, 1868, quoted by Maggie M. Cao, *The End of Landscape in Nineteenth-Century America* (University of California Press, 2018), 34.

185 *same fashionable gallery:* Howat, *Frederic Church,* 89.

185 *sympathetic to the Confederacy:* On British attitudes toward the Confederacy, see Foreman, *World on Fire.*

185 The North *became:* Carr, *Frederic Edwin Church,* 72; and Harvey, *Civil War and American Art,* 66.

185 *Franklin Expedition of 1845:* Harvey, *Civil War and American Art,* 46.

185 *"savages":* Quoted by Ken McGoogan, *Fatal Passage: The Untold Story of John Rae, the Arctic Adventurer Who Discovered the Fate of Franklin* (HarperPerennialCanada, 2001), 227. In 2024, the identity of one of the men whose corpse showed signs of cannibalism was confirmed via DNA analysis as Captain James Fitzjames, one of Franklin's senior officers: Douglas R. Stenton, Stephen Fratpietro, and Robert W.

Park, "Identification of a Senior Officer from Sir John Franklin's Northwest Passage Expedition," *Journal of Archaeological Science: Reports* 59 (September 24, 2024).

185 *Lady Franklin came: Court Journal*, June 21, 1863.

185 *"the best work":* "The Iceberg—Painted by Church," *London Morning Star*, June 22, 1863.

185 *"Mr. Church's power":* "Mr. Church's Picture of Icebergs," *Times* (London), July 3, 1863.

185 *"If General Meade":* Quoted by McPherson, *Battle Cry of Freedom*, 666.

186 *To Lincoln's frustration:* Holzer, *Lincoln and the Power of the Press*, 433.

186 *National Conscription Act:* Burrows and Wallace, *Gotham*, 887–88.

186 *On Saturday, July 11:* Burrows and Wallace, *Gotham*, 888. I'm indebted to Burrows and Wallace for the following account of what came to be called the Draft Riots.

186 *Around twelve hundred:* "The Draft," *New York Herald*, July 13, 1863.

186 *Some feared that:* Burrows and Wallace, *Gotham*, 884–86.

186 *recruitment of Black men:* Blight, *Frederick Douglass*, 388.

186 *company of firemen:* Burrows and Wallace, *Gotham*, 889.

186 *"the lowest Irish day laborers":* Strong, *Diary*, July 13, 1863, 3:335.

186 *Colored Orphan Asylum:* Strong, *Diary*, July 13, 1863, 3:336.

187 *precinct headquarters:* David M. Barnes, *The Draft Riots in New York, July, 1863: The Metropolitan Police, Their Services During Riot Week, Their Honorable Record* (Baker & Godwin, 1863), 117; and Barnet Schecter, *The Devil's Own Work: The Civil War Draft Riots and the Fight to Reconstruct America* (Walker, 2001), 148.

187 *Strong heard fire bells:* Strong, *Diary*, July 14, 1863, 3:337, 3:339.

187 *"If a quarter":* Strong, *Diary*, July 13, 1863, 3:336.

187 *pleading for soldiers:* Strong, *Diary*, July 13, 1863, 3:337.

187 *with special ferocity:* Harris, *In the Shadow of Slavery*, 283.

187 *Church and Isabel were upstate:* Church wrote from Hudson to John Frederick Kensett on July 13, 1863.

187 *was now married:* James P. Maher, ed., *Index to Marriages and Deaths in the New York World: 1860–1865* (Genealogical Publishing Company, 2006).

187 *"Annie wouldn't leave":* Lindley Miller to Mary Louisa Miller, July 18, 1863. Original in the Lindley Hoffman Miller Letters, Macculloch Hall Historical Museum Archives.

187 *Estimates would eventually range:* Burrows and Wallace, *Gotham*, 895.

187 *"Gramercy Park":* Strong, *Diary*, July 16, 1863, 3:340.

187 *"splendid walk":* Theodore Cole Diary, August 27, 1863.

188 *"I am overwhelmed":* Church to T. G. Appleton, November 16, 1863.

188 *"It has recently":* Quoted by Gerald L. Carr, "'The Land of Sacred Romance': To the Holy Land and Back," in *Frederic Church: A Painter's Pilgrimage*, ed. Kenneth J. Myers et al. (Detroit Institute of Arts, 2017), 46.

188 *"reaching without gap":* Ludlow, "Reminiscences of an Overlander, Part I," *Golden Era* (San Francisco), February 21, 1864, reprinted in Anderson and Ferber, *Albert Bierstadt*, 308.

188 *"the nicest possible compromise":* Ludlow, "Reminiscences of an Overlander."

188 *"garden of Eden":* Quoted by Anderson and Ferber, *Albert Bierstadt*, 178.

188 *"Mr. Bierstadt's name":* Quoted by Anderson and Ferber, *Albert Bierstadt*, 194.

189 *"And unlike MR. CHURCH'S":* "The New Pictures," *Harper's Weekly* 8, no. 376 (March 26, 1864): 195, quoted by Karl Kusserow, "The Trouble with Empire," in Karl Kusserow and Alan C. Braddock, *Nature's Nation: American Art and Environment* (Princeton University Art Museum, 2018), 126–27.

189 *His composition paid tribute:* I'm indebted to Tyler Green for pointing out the connection between these two paintings.

189 *"New York is stirred up"*: Church to Joseph Church, February 28, 1864.

189 *"a contagion of kindness"*: A Record of the Metropolitan Fair: In Aid of the United States Sanitary Commission, Held at New York, in April, 1864 (Hurd & Houghton, 1867), 7.

189 *He was also donating*: "The Metropolitan Fair," *New York Times*, April 22, 1864.

189 *"the busiest human ant-hill"*: Strong, *Diary*, April 4, 1864, 3:423.

190 *flags from the battlefield*: Strong, *Diary*, April 4, 1864, 3:423.

190 *uniform black dresses*: "The Metropolitan Fair," *New York Times*, April 4, 1864.

190 *first to lobby*: Record of the Metropolitan Fair, 13–14.

190 *women from Brooklyn*: Record of the Metropolitan Fair, 3.

190 *given their lives*: Record of the Metropolitan Fair, 2; and Strong, *Diary*, April 22, 1864, 3:431.

190 *"Mrs. Astor, Mrs. Belmont"*: Strong, *Diary*, April 4, 1864, 3:424.

190 *hundreds of paintings*: Catalogue of the Art Exhibition at the Metropolitan Fair, in Aid of the U.S. Sanitary Commission (J. F. Trow, 1864), 18.

190 *"great deal of curiosity"*: Record of the Metropolitan Fair, 98.

192 *Native "curiosities"*: "The Indian Home," *New York Evening Post*, April 2, 1864.

192 *When Ellie Strong*: "Report of the Treasurer of the Metropolitan Fair: In Aid of the United States Sanitary Commission" (1864), 3.

192 *the highest sum*: The Spirit of the Fair (J. F. Trow, 1864), 196.

192 *half that amount*: Spirit of the Fair, 196.

192 *offer of $25,000*: Anderson and Ferber, *Albert Bierstadt*, 173.

192 *"the relative merits"*: "Art in New York," *Daily Evening Bulletin*.

192 *"I don't think"*: Jervis McEntee, diary entry, March 16, 1876, from the Jervis McEntee Papers, 1850–1905, AAA.

CHAPTER 18 "Broken"

193 *In May 1864, Church moved*: Church to Joseph Church, April 15, 1864; and "Fine Arts," *New York Herald*, November 6, 1864.

193 *"Mother will be shocked"*: Church to Joseph Church, May 13, 1864.

193 *Bertie sometimes tugged*: Eliza Church to Joseph Church, June 11, 1864.

193 *hide-and-seek on a farm*: Charlotte to Joseph Church, September 12, 1864.

193 *five hundred thousand more soldiers*: Eugene Converse Murdock, *Patriotism Limited, 1862–1865: The Civil War Draft and the Bounty System* (Kent State University Press, 1967), 12.

193 *lost New York City*: Burrows and Wallace, *Gotham*, 903.

194 *Church finished* Chimborazo: "Fine Arts," *New York Herald*, November 6, 1864, 4.

194 *he entitled* Twilight: Church to J. S. Jenkins, January 23, 1865.

194 *symbol, variously, of renewal*: Tyler Green (@tylergreenbooks), "Frederic Church's final Emersonian sunset picture," Instagram, November 6, 2024, https://www.instagram.com/p/DCCDBytRQWy/?img_index=1.

194 *Church had started*: Carr, *Frederic Edwin Church*, 1:289.

194 *by February 15, 1865*: Murdock, *Patriotism Limited*, 12.

194 *In January, Church's lawyer*: John Gaul Jr. to Church, January 17, 1865.

194 *On March 6*: Burrows and Wallace, *Gotham*, 904; and "The Union Jubilee," *New York Times*, March 7, 1865.

194 *clear and frigid*: George B. Hodgsden, "Thermometrical Observations," March 6, 1865, New York Historical.

194 *"A Great and Happy Day"*: "The Union Jubilee," *New York Times*.

194 *He died on March 18*: Horace Robbins to Mary Robbins, March 21, 1865.

195   *"Poor Mr. Church"*: Robbins to Robbins, March 21, 1865.

195   *The next morning, Noble baptized:* Episcopal Diocese of Newark Church Records, Church of the Holy Trinity, Jersey City.

195   *She died eight days after:* "Deaths," *New York Times*, March 29, 1865. See also Carr, *Frederic Edwin Church*, 1:282.

195   *"change of scene":* Church to "Field" [probably James T. Fields], April 22, 1865. Original in the Huntington Library.

195   *British colony of Jamaica:* On Jamaican politics and culture in the nineteenth century, see esp. Tim Barringer and Wayne Modest, eds., *Victorian Jamaica* (Duke University Press, 2018).

195   *celebratory cannon fire:* Strong, *Diary*, April 10, 1865, 3:579.

195   *"Secessia is now conquered":* Strong, *Diary*, April 11, 1865, 3:582.

195   *"Up with the Black Flag":* Strong, *Diary*, April 15, 1865, 3:583.

195   *"as if some grand convulsion":* Quoted by Blight, *Frederick Douglass*, 319. On reactions to Lincoln's death, see Martha Hodes, *Mourning Lincoln* (Yale University Press, 2015).

196   *Sarah Hitchcock:* "Passenger List for the Steamship *Montezuma*, Port of New-York," September 16, 1865, National Archives Microfilm Publication M237, Records of the U.S. Customs Service, Record Group 36, National Archives, Washington, DC.

196   *"We all hope":* Theodore Cole Diary, April 22, 1865.

196   *poverty and racial tension:* Paton, "State Formation in Victorian Jamaica," and Tim Barringer, "Land, Labor, Landscape: Views of the Plantation in Victorian Jamaica," in Barringer and Modest, *Victorian Jamaica*, 125, 305.

196   *"Wreck and ruin":* William G. Sewell, *The Ordeal of Free Labor in the British West Indies* (Harper & Brothers, 1861), 174.

196   *"wretched place":* Horace Robbins to Mary Robbins, June 30, 1865. On the Churches' trip to Jamaica, see esp. Elizabeth Mankin Kornhauser and Katherine E. Manthorne, *Fern Hunting Among These Picturesque Mountains: Frederic Edwin Church in Jamaica* (Cornell University Press, 2010).

196   *"I have been intending":* Church to Charles Hart, March 31, 1865. Original in the AAA.

197   *"prematurely aged by sorrow":* "Art in New York," *Daily Evening Bulletin*.

197   *Hundreds of thousands of enslaved people:* Vincent Brown, *The Reaper's Garden: Death and Power in the World of Atlantic Slavery* (Harvard University Press, 2008), 267–68.

197   *allspice and mango trees:* Horace Robbins to Mary Robbins, May 18, 1865.

197   *Robbins noticed with relief:* Robbins to Robbins, May 18, 1865.

197   *From the house:* Robbins to Robbins, May 18, 1865.

198   *Lizards rushed away:* Church, "A Lizard, Jamaica," oil and graphite on paperboard, June 1865, CHSDM.

198   *he wore two gloves:* Horace Robbins to Mary Robbins, June 30, 1865.

198   *"some unusually ferocious monsters":* Church to Charles de Wolf Brownell, March 24, 1879, quoted by Jennifer Raab, "Details of Absence: Frederic Church and the Landscape of Post-Emancipation Jamaica," *Art History* 34, no. 4 (2011): 724.

199   *"He works away":* Horace Robbins to Mary Robbins, May 25, 1865.

199   *"very sad":* Robbins to Robbins, May 25, 1865.

199   *"I have stood":* Church to Theodore Cole, July 28, 1865.

199   *"Every day of my life":* Horace Robbins to Mary Robbins, June 30–July 5, 1865.

200   *Every decent plantation house:* Robbins to Robbins, May 18, 1865.

200   *seat of the colonial government:* Sewell, *Ordeal of Free Labor*, 182.

200   *"Poor Mr & Mrs Church":* Robbins to Robbins, May 25, 1865.

200   *Jamaica's British governor:* Robbins to Robbins, June 30, 1865.

200   *"The scenery is superb":* Church to Cole, July 28, 1865.

200 *In one direction:* Church to Joseph B. Austin, August 14, 1865.

200 *"I have accomplished":* Church to Cole, July 28, 1865.

200 *"Mrs. Church is fascinated":* Church to Cole, July 28, 1865.

200 *Hundreds of species:* Mark Nesbitt, "Botany in Victorian Jamaica," in Barringer and Modest, *Victorian Jamaica,* 210.

201 *Wardian case:* Sarah Whittingham, *Fern Fever: The Story of Pteridomania* (Frances Lincoln Adult, 2012), 18ff.

201 *"Mrs. Church is insane":* Church to Joseph B. Austin, August 14, 1865.

201 *"from 1/2 inch":* Church to Cole, July 28, 1865.

201 *"Notwithstanding this magnificent scenery":* Church to Cole, July 28, 1865.

201 *Merchants and shopkeepers:* "The Fall Trade—Extraordinary Commercial Activity," *New York Times,* September 16, 1865.

201 *"the number of negroes":* "Reports to the Freedmen's Bureau from Arkansas and Mississippi," *New York Herald,* September 16, 1865, 1.

201 *"Twenty-one negroes":* "The Press Despatch, Fortress Monroe," *New York Herald,* September 16, 1865.

201 *atrocities against Black people:* On white racism in the postwar era see esp. Eric Foner, *Reconstruction: America's Unfinished Revolution, 1863–1877* (Harper Perennial Modern Classics, 2014), and Manisha Sinha, *The Rise and Fall of the Second American Republic: Reconstruction, 1860–1920* (Liveright, 2024).

202 *"Eight Miles": New York Herald,* November 17, 1865.

202 *more than four hundred bodies:* Christine Chivallon and David Howard, "Colonial Violence and Civilising Utopias in the French and British Empires: The Morant Bay Rebellion (1865) and the Insurrection of the South (1870)," *Slavery & Abolition* 38, no. 3 (July 3, 2017): 541.

202 *a large Jamaica painting:* Church to Elizabeth Colt, September 13, 1866. Original in the Beinecke Rare Book Library, Yale University.

202 *Elizabeth Jarvis Colt:* On Colt, see Kornhauser, "Daniel Wadsworth and Elizabeth Hart Jarvis Colt," 71–77.

202 *"probably yet indulge":* Church to Colt, September 13, 1866.

202 *"grand and impressive":* "A New Tropical Landscape," *New York Evening Post,* September 10, 1870.

202 *The Vale of St. Thomas, Jamaica:* On this painting, see esp. Kornhauser, "Daniel Wadsworth and Elizabeth Hart Jarvis Colt," 75, and Kornhauser, "Frederic Edwin Church's Landscapes of Jamaica," in Kornhauser and Manthorne, *Fern Hunting,* 38–39.

203 *"Thank God afflictions":* Church to Colt, September 13, 1866.

203 *When Church wrote:* Church to Elizabeth Colt, October 20, 1866. Original in the Beinecke Rare Book Library, Yale University.

203 *"I know, by a like experience":* Elizabeth Colt to Church, October 26, 1866.

203 *"Only we—who have lost":* Church to Palmer, June 18, 1872. Original in Palmer Papers.

203 *"Dear Herbert":* March 18 and 26, 1893, in H. L. S. and L. H. S., *Phillips Brooks Year Book* (E. P. Dutton, 1894), 78, 86.

CHAPTER 19 "Fast Horses"

205 *Isabel's mother came up:* Church to Joseph Church, November 26, 1866.

205 *light poured through:* Church to Elizabeth Colt, October 20, 1866. Original in the Beinecke Rare Book Library, Yale University.

205 *"I am accomplishing":* Church to Osborn, January 1, 1866.

205 *"a snow plough":* Church to Heade, December 28, 1866. Original in the AAA.

205   *"accomplish four days"*: Church to Heade, December 28, 1866.

205   *His sister Charlotte*: Elizabeth Church to Church, May 27, 1858.

206   *"gets quite discouraged"*: Eliza Church to Joseph Church, September 29, 1866.

206   *Charlotte told a relative*: Edwin Church to Joseph Church, January 14, 1867; and H. C. Church to Joseph Church, December 3, 1866.

206   *"I am constantly thinking"*: Church to Joseph Church, November 26, 1866.

206   *poured his grief into painting*: Carr, *Frederic Edwin Church*, 1:311; and Allegra K. Davis, "'A Fitting Monument': Frederic Church and the Memorial Landscape," in *Afterglow: Frederic Church and the Landscape of Memory*, ed. Allegra K. Davis with contributions from Sean Sawyer and Rebecca Bedell (Hirmer, 2024), 44.

206   *a ruined church*: Carr, *Frederic Edwin Church*, 1:313.

206   *"You now have"*: Edward R. Janes to Church, January 19, 1867.

206   *"We are having"*: Church to Heade, April 5, 1867. Original in the AAA.

206   *"I superintended my own"*: Church to Osborn, March 26, 1867.

206   *"Mrs. C. has a digging fit"*: Church to Osborn, Hudson, June 13, 1867.

206   *"My young trees"*: Church to Erastus Dow Palmer, May 9, 1867. Original in Palmer Papers.

207   *He began to dream*: Toole, "Historic Landscape Report," 48.

207   *"I have nearly broken"*: Church to Osborn, Hudson, June 13, 1867.

207   *In recent decades*: Carr, "'Land of Sacred Romance,'" 50. Church also heard firsthand accounts of these places from his friend Bayard Taylor, the writer who had provided him with a letter to Humboldt about *The Heart of the Andes* in 1859. Taylor had traveled to the Holy Land in the 1850s and was a contributor to the growing American travel literature on Palestine and Ottoman Syria: Davis, *Landscape of Belief*, 43.

207   *"Just think of a series"*: Church to Osborn, January 6, 1868.

207   *"I am anxious"*: Church to Osborn, January 6, 1868.

207   *several newspapers*: Carr, "'Land of Sacred Romance,'" 51.

207   *"Any humble individual"*: Jervis McEntee to Bayard Taylor, March 1, 1868, quoted by Davis, *Landscape of Belief*, 168.

207   *McEntee and Gifford*: Weiss, *Poetic Landscape*, 114.

207   *Church picked the last grapes*: Church to Osborn, October 25, 1867.

207   *sailed for France*: "Passengers Arrived," *New York Times*, November 17, 1867.

208   *his fifth attempt*: Gordon, *Thread Across the Ocean*, 186.

208   *only American painter*: "Art Prizes at the Paris Exposition," *American Art Journal* 7, no. 8 (June 15, 1867): 116–17.

208   *"big and dirty"*: Church to [Edward?] Weeks, June 7, 1869.

208   *"Landscape Art in France"*: Church to Palmer, March 10, 1868. Original in Palmer Papers.

208   *Isabel admired the torchlights*: Diary of Isabel Mortimer Carnes Church, January 6, 1868, Isabel Mortimer Carnes Church Diary: January–June 1868, OSHS. Original at the New-York Historical Society.

208   *Peninsular and Oriental Hotel*: Moritz Busch, *Guide for Travellers in Egypt*, trans. W. C. Wrankmore (Trübner & Co., 1858), 32.

208   *"more than half oriental"*: Isabel Church Diary, January 4, 1868.

209   *"is the noisiest and dirtiest"*: Church to Osborn, January 6, 1868.

209   *"I have longed"*: Church to Osborn, January 6, 1868.

209   *"a perfect moonlight night"*: Isabel Church Diary, January 10, 1868.

209   *roses and almond trees*: Isabel Church Diary, February 21, 1868; and Church to Theodore Cole, January 30, 1868, CV553, series 2, box 1, folder 14, Thomas Cole Collection, Albany Institute of History and Art.

209 *"the loveliest blue sky"*: Church to Osborn, January 13, 1868.

209 *"We have enormous rooms"*: Church to Osborn, January 13, 1868.

209 *"The mode of living"*: Church to Osborn, January 13, 1868.

210 *South American scene*: Isabel Church Diary, February 3, 1868.

210 *acquaintances from New York*: Carr, "'Land of Sacred Romance,'" 51.

210 *"These white Bagdad donkeys"*: Church to Osborn, April 18, 1868.

210 *Church hired a man*: Church to Theodore Cole, January 30, 1868.

210 *"My wife is"*: Church to Osborn, April 18, 1868.

211 *"a connoisseur of donkeys"*: Church to Osborn, April 18, 1868.

211 *Occasionally, Isabel went*: Isabel Church Diary, February 14, 15, and 25, 1868.

211 *"Isabel enjoys herself"*: Church to Osborn, April 1, 1868.

211 *"They are awfully picturesque"*: Church to Heade, January 22, 1868. Original in the AAA.

211 *Church was intrigued*: Church to Osborn, January 13, 1868.

211 *vast central court*: Church to Osborn, January 13, 1868.

211 *"The Dwellings"*: Church to Palmer, March 10, 1868.

212 *"Here we are"*: Church to Heade, January 22, 1868. Original in the AAA.

212 *"You can't imagine"*: Church to Osborn, January 21, 1868.

212 *Alexander Fowler*: Carr, "'Land of Sacred Romance,'" 52.

212 *"Dear Fred!"*: Isabel Church Diary, February 6, 1868.

212 *the women failed*: Isabel Church Diary, February 7, 1868.

212 *Isabel was embarrassed*: Isabel Church Diary, February 10, 1868.

212 *"I should be most grateful"*: Isabel Church Diary, February 11, 1868.

212 *"a concentrated lump"*: Church to Theodore Cole, January 30, 1868.

212 *When he seemed fussy*: Isabel Church Diary, February 8, 1868.

212 *"You must feel"*: Isabel Church Diary, March 21, 1868.

212 *"When he is absent"*: Isabel Church Diary, March 21, 1868.

CHAPTER 20   "I Wasn't Shot"

213 *"till you have seen it"*: Letter of T. E. Lawrence to E. T. Leeds, February 1914, quoted by David Kennedy, "Travellers of 1857 to Petra," in *Refereed Proceedings of the First Conference on the Archaeology and Tourism of the Maan Governorate, 3rd–4th October 2017, Petra-Jordan*, ed. Zeyad M. Al-Salameen and Mohammad B. Tarawneh (Al-Hussein Bin Talal University, Maan, 2018), 188.

213 *abandoned to Bedouin tribes*: Tony Waltham, "The Sandstone Fantasy of Petra," *Geology Today* 10, no. 3 (1994): 105.

213 *hundreds of Europeans and some Americans*: On the numbers of Westerners who traveled to Petra in the decades after 1812, see Kennedy, "Travellers of 1857," 187.

213 *Few artists had yet*: The most prominent of the artists who reached Petra before Church was the Scottish painter David Roberts, who went there in the 1830s and created paintings that became widely known lithographs in the 1840s: Carr, "'Land of Sacred Romance,'" 50.

214 *Michail Hene*: Church to Palmer, March 10, 1868.

214 *"wild and lawless"*: Josias Leslie Porter, *A Handbook for Travellers in Syria and Palestine* (John Murray, 1868), 1:5.

214 *"no traveller should ever"*: Porter, *Handbook for Travellers*, 1:5.

214 *form of theft*: According to several mid-nineteenth-century British accounts, the Petra Bedouin resented the sometimes disrespectful and destructive behavior of Western tourists escorted to their city by Arab guides. The Bedouin were also angered by

the Arab guides, who negotiated generous payments for themselves while the Petra Bedouin saw their crops and pasturage damaged by the Arabs' camels and their own provisions depleted by the Arabs and Westerners. See, e.g., John Wilson, *The Lands of the Bible: Visited and Described in an Extensive Journey Undertaken with Special Reference to the Promotion of Biblical Research and the Advancement of the Cause of Philanthropy* (William Whyte, 1847), 1:301, 1:328–29, 1:332, 1:33–45; and Eliot Warburton, *The Crescent and the Cross, or, Romance and Realities of Eastern Travel* (Henry Colburn, 1846), 2:13–14. I am deeply grateful to Professor David Kennedy for sharing these sources as well as his expertise on nineteenth-century travelers to Petra.

214 *"some years ago"*: Church to Palmer, March 10, 1868.

214 *"I told Michail"*: Church to Palmer, March 10, 1868.

214 *meditated on the story*: Church to Palmer, March 10, 1868.

215 *Abu Mousa*: Frederic Church Petra Diary, February 15, 1868, OSHS.

215 *Church counted*: Church Petra Diary, February 15, 1868.

216 *"wild & lonely"*: Church Petra Diary, February 15, 1868.

216 *Church was discomfited*: Church Petra Diary, February 15, 1868.

216 *"It is no joke"*: Church Petra Diary, February 15, 1868.

216 *"Although in harmony"*: Church Petra Diary, February 15, 1868.

216 *The stench of creosote*: Church Petra Diary, February 15, 1868.

216 *"Strange sight"*: Church Petra Diary, February 15, 1868.

216 *"occasional cracks"*: Church Petra Diary, February 15, 1868.

216 *Rain forced the men*: Rev. David Stuart Dodge, "Visit to Petra," *New York Evangelist*, April 23, 1868.

217 *"seemed disposed"*: Church Petra Diary, February 17, 1868.

217 *"The motion"*: Church Petra Diary, February 18, 1868.

217 *drove his spear*: Church Petra Diary, February 18, 1868.

217 *"infinitely broken sides"*: Church Petra Diary, February 18, 1868.

217 *"strong purple shadows"*: Church Petra Diary, February 18, 1868.

217 *"Never saw so picturesque"*: Church Petra Diary, February 18, 1868.

218 *not to hurt him*: Church to Palmer, March 10, 1868.

218 *Sometimes he managed*: Carr, *Frederic Edwin Church*, 1:389.

218 *"We were at the mercy"*: Church Petra Diary, February 19, 1868.

218 *"The ridges of the mountains"*: Church Petra Diary, February 19, 1868.

219 *"compares with ordinary regions"*: Quoted by Davis, *Landscape of Belief*, 44.

219 *"mere refuse & rubbish"*: Quoted by Davis, *Landscape of Belief*, 44.

219 *"soft tinted ribbons"*: Church Petra Diary, February 20, 1868.

219 *a creative force*: Davis, *Landscape of Belief*, 174.

219 *"There burst upon us"*: Church Petra Diary, February 20, 1868.

219 *"I flung open"*: Church Petra Diary, February 20, 1868.

219 *An armed Bedouin guard*: Church Petra Diary, February 21, 1868.

219 *"Our sheikh says"*: Church Petra Diary, February 22, 1868.

220 *the exiled Israelites*: Church Petra Diary, February 22, 1868.

220 *"sad—parched—forsaken"*: Church to W. H. Osborn, July 29, 1868, quoted by Carr, *Frederic Edwin Church*, 1:326.

220 *guide waved his arms*: Church Petra Diary, February 24, 1868.

221 *"a saint"*: Church Petra Diary, February 24, 1868.

221 *"fearful that I might"*: Church Petra Diary, February 24, 1868.

221 *"stop when I stopped"*: Church to Palmer, March 10, 1868.

221 *"You can imagine"*: Church to Palmer, March 10, 1868.

221 *"by contrast with"*: Church to Osborn, April 1, 1868.

221　*"The capitals are very rich"*: Church Petra Diary, February 24, 1868.

221　*appraising glance*: Church to Palmer, March 10, 1868.

221　*"I selected"*: Church to Osborn, April 1, 1868.

222　*word for "good"*: Church to Osborn, April 1, 1868.

222　*"I wasn't shot"*: Church to Osborn, April 1, 1868.

222　*"The next day"*: Church to Osborn, April 1, 1868.

222　*"Even those few"*: Isabel Church Diary, March 10, 1868.

222　*"delighted with his trip"*: Isabel Church Diary, March 13, 1868.

222　*"It is so <u>very</u> pleasant"*: Isabel Church Diary, March 21, 1868.

CHAPTER 21　"No Photographs"

223　*"dear conscientious Fred"*: Isabel Church Diary, March 28, 1868.

223　*"taking possession"*: Isabel Church Diary, March 28, 1868.

223　*archaeologists then at work:* The Churches owned many volumes on biblical archaeology, and they toured the ongoing excavations under Jerusalem. On the archaeologists active in Jerusalem at the time of the Churches' visit, see Andrew Lawler, *Under Jerusalem: The Buried History of the World's Most Contested City* (Doubleday, 2021).

223　*"deeply impressed and awed"*: Isabel Church Diary, March 28, 1868.

224　*"rather incredulous"*: Isabel Church Diary, March 28, 1868.

224　*"bow his head"*: Isabel Church Diary, March 28, 1868.

224　*"Jerusalem lay spread"*: Isabel Church Diary, March 28, 1868.

225　*Church and Isabel traveled:* On Church and Isabel's trip to Damascus, see Isabel Church Diary, April 24–May 13, 1868; Davis, *Landscape of Belief*, 182–85; and Carr, "'Land of Sacred Romance,'" 55.

225　*"fairy loveliness"*: Isabel Church Diary, April 24, 1868.

225　*Like many Americans and Europeans:* The classic, field-forging study of the history and consequences of Orientalism in Western thought is Edward W. Said, *Orientalism* (Vintage, 1979). On Orientalism in late nineteenth-century American art and architecture, see Holly Edwards, *Noble Dreams, Wicked Pleasures: Orientalism in America, 1870–1930* (Princeton University Press, 2000).

225　*"turbaned turks"*: Isabel Church Diary, April 24, 1868.

225　*"All these rooms"*: Isabel Church Diary, April 24, 1868.

225　*"women & children"*: Isabel Church Diary, May [n.d.] 1868.

225　*"somewhat disgraceful notoriety"*: Isabel Church Diary, May 2, 1868.

226　*smashed his head:* Mary S. Lovell, *A Scandalous Life: The Biography of Jane Digby* (Fourth Estate, 1995), 133.

226　*Prince of Wales:* Lovell, *Scandalous Life*, 259.

226　*"bold grand looking lady"*: Isabel Church Diary, May 2, 1868.

226　*"very agreeable"*: Isabel Church Diary, May 2, 1868.

227　*"I was <u>very</u>"*: Isabel Church Diary, April 27, 1868.

227　*"Fred had an upper room"*: Isabel Church Diary, May [n.d.] 1868.

227　*"There are three"*: Church to Heade, October 9, 1868. Original in the AAA.

227　*"Mrs. Dodge is already"*: Consul J. Augustus Johnson to Church, July 7, 1868.

227　*"wonderfully blue sea"*: Isabel Church Diary, May 29, 1868.

228　*"whirling" and "howling" dervishes:* Isabel Church Diary, June 9, 1868.

228　*Isabel watched the landscape:* Isabel Church Diary, June [n.d.] 1868.

228　*"had to go down stairs"*: Isabel Church Diary, June [n.d.] 1868.

228　*had reportedly declared:* Carr, *Frederic Edwin Church*, 1:327. Humboldt scholars have not been able to pinpoint the origins of this supposed opinion, which appears in guidebooks to the region to this day: Robert Hoffmann, "Die Entstehung einer Legende. Alexander von Humboldts angeblicher Ausspruch über Salzburg," *HiN— Alexander von Humboldt im Netz. Internationale Zeitschrift für Humboldt-Studien* 7, no. 12 (April 26, 2006). I am grateful to Humboldt scholars Andrea Wulf and Ingo Schwarz for their assistance on this question.

228 *"The most tremendous"*: Church to Osborn, July 29, 1868.

228 *Cowbells clanked: A Handbook for Travellers in Southern Germany* (John Murray, 1873), 245.

228 *"delicious blue bloom"*: Church, "Mountains Near Berchtesgaden, Bavaria (Germany)," June–July 1868, graphite on light green wove paper, CHSDM.

228 *"12 to 15 hours"*: Church to Osborn, July 29, 1868.

228 *"He has a little"*: Isabel Church to Eliza Church, July 9, 1868.

229 *"Isabel is such"*: Church to Eliza Church, February 17, 1869.

229 *Theddy had stoked:* Theodore Cole to Church, May 24, 1868.

229 *"We are both"*: Church to Osborn, September 29, 1868.

229 *ailing again:* Church to Osborn, July 29, 1868.

229 *developed a strange boil:* Church to Osborn, September 29, 1868.

229 *"The Alps disappointed"*: Church to Osborn, September 29, 1868.

229 *"Syria, with its barren"*: Church to Osborn, September 29, 1868.

230 *"whose fires, long extinguished"*: Quoted by Noble, *Course of Empire*, 160.

230 *Nature, he grasped:* Theodore E. Stebbins Jr., *Lure of Italy: American Artists and the Italian Experience, 1760–1914* (Museum of Fine Arts, Boston, 1992), 45.

230 *"I believe him"*: Church to Osborn, November 9, 1868.

230 *"I feel I should"*: Church to Osborn, February 24, 1869, quoted by Wilmerding, *Master, Mentor, Master*, 31.

230 *"city of the soul"*: On Rome's allure for Byron and other travelers between 1770 and 1870, see John A. Pinto, *City of the Soul: Rome and the Romantics* (University Press of New England, 2016).

230 *"the Paradise / The grave"*: Percy Bysshe Shelley, *The Major Works* (Oxford University Press, 2003), 529.

230 *"the city of all time"*: Nathaniel Hawthorne, *The Marble Faun* (Hurst & Company, 1860), 90.

230 *"So much sham"*: Church to Osborn, November 4, 1868.

230 *"I have no comments"*: Church to Heade, October 9, 1868. Original in the AAA.

230 *"the Tiber is not"*: Church to Osborn, November 9, 1868.

231 *Church grew morose:* Church to Osborn, November 16, 1868.

231 *"There are not"*: Church to Heade, November 16, 1868. Original in the AAA.

231 *"highly poetical"*: Church to Osborn, January 1, 1869.

231 *"must be wrong"*: Church to Osborn, January 1, 1869.

232 *"an intolerable bore"*: Church to Osborn, January 13, 1869.

232 *"Rome has got"*: Church to Osborn, January 1, 1869.

232 *Although Church couldn't speak Italian:* Sanford Robinson Gifford to Elihu Gifford, November 2, 1868, Sanford Robinson Gifford Papers, 1840s–1900, series 1, box 1, AAA.

232 *"Among them is"*: Church to Osborn, November 16, 1868.

232 *he also bought paintings:* On the collection he brought home from Rome, see Karen Zukowski, "Historic Furnishings Report" (Olana State Historic Site, 2001), 748–64.

232 *"old masters"*: Church to Osborn, November 16, 1868.

232 *"one old room"*: Church to Osborn, November 16, 1868.

232 *Vatican's chief fresco artist:* Carr, *Frederic Edwin Church*, 1:304.

232 *"extremely agreeable"*: Church to Osborn, January 23 and 28, 1869.

233 *invited him to work:* Church to Osborn, January 13, 1869.

233 *"of course in America":* Church to Osborn, January 23 and 28, 1869.

233 *He teasingly offered:* Church to Osborn, January 1, 1869.

233 *Vatican sculpture gallery:* Lockwood de Forest, diary entry, Wednesday, December 30, 1868, Lockwood de Forest Papers, AAA.

233 *"These Roman noses":* Church to Osborn, January 23 and 28, 1869.

233 *"plump and rosy":* Church to Osborn, January 23 and 28, 1869.

233 *"Dear Mamma":* Church to Eliza Church, February 17, 1869.

233 *"makes our Roman apartments":* Church to Osborn, January 1, 1869.

233 *Flowers burst forth:* Church to Eliza Church, February 17, 1869.

233 *"Hor-ri-ble":* Church to Osborn, April 14, 1869.

234 *"was but a flea bite":* Church to Osborn, April 14, 1869.

234 *cast its spell:* Church to Osborn, April 14, 1869.

234 *Melville, wandering among them:* On February 11, 1857, Melville wrote in his journal that the ruins of the Parthenon looked like the frozen "North [Hudson] River breaking up." See Herman Melville, "February 4th [1857]," in *Journal Up the Straits*, ed. Raymond Weaver (Colophon, 1935), 113. On April 14, 1869, Church wrote to Osborn that the "the air is as bracing as that of the Catskills."

234 *"No photographs":* Church to Palmer, May 14, 1869. Original in Palmer Papers.

234 *"God like":* Church to Palmer, May 14, 1869. See also Carr, "'A Finer Perception of the Beautiful': Frederic Church and Classicism," in Myers et al., *Frederic Church*, 117–37.

234 *"The election of Grant":* Church to Osborn, November 9, 1868.

234 *Fifteenth Amendment:* Congress approved the amendment in February 1869, several months before Church went to Athens, and it was ratified in February 1870: Foner, *Reconstruction*, 446.

235 *"This dull heavy":* Church to Osborn, May 1, 1869.

235 *"thin shelled":* Church to Heade, January 22, 1868. Original in the AAA.

CHAPTER 22   "Like a Fever"

237 *Paris, which looked gaudy:* Church to [Edward?] Weeks, June 17, 1869.

237 *"Center of the World":* Church to Palmer, July 7, 1869. Original in Palmer Papers.

237 *"It's a terrible costly":* Church to Osborn, May 1, 1869.

238 *"just completed his architectural":* Church to Osborn, May 1, 1869.

238 *"Can we appreciate":* Church to Palmer, July 7, 1869.

238 *Isabel addressed him:* Isabel to Church, April 24 and May 9, 1878.

238 *"I have no news":* Isabel to Church, April 24, 1878.

238 *"rugs—armour—stuffs":* Church to Osborn, February 4, 1869.

238 *"They had a passage":* Church to Osborn, August 31, 1869.

238 *"the most delightful beast":* Church to Osborn, August 31, 1869.

238 *Syrian landscape:* Church to Austin, September 16, 1869.

238 *He packed baskets:* Church to Palmer, September 22, 1869. Original in Palmer Papers.

238 *He raced around:* Church to Palmer, September 22, 1869.

238 *"I—have—not":* Church to Palmer, September 22, 1869.

239 *"Freddie marched in":* Church to [Edward?] Weeks, October 13, 1869.

239 *"sometimes the desire":* Church to Osborn, November 9, 1868.

239 *"Great conclusion arrived at":* Church to Palmer, August 4, 1869. Original in Palmer Papers.

239 *often consulting with Isabel:* Karen Zukowski, "A New Jerusalem," in *Frederic Church's Olana*, 133.

239   *"A young architect":* Church to Osborn, November 9, 1868.

239   *An early version:* Hunt's sketch for a French Renaissance château is reproduced by James Anthony Ryan, "Frederic Church's Olana: Architecture and Landscape as Art," in Franklin Kelly, *Frederic Edwin Church* (National Gallery of Art, 1989), 133; Hunt's Moorish version is reproduced by Susan Stein, "Role and Reputation: The Architectural Practice of Richard Morris Hunt," in *The Architecture of Richard Morris Hunt,* ed. Susan Stein (University of Chicago Press, 1986), 113. See also Julia B. Rosenbaum, "Outside In: Space, Light, and the Artful Interior at Frederic Church's Olana," *Nineteenth-Century Art Worldwide* 20, no. 2 (2021), 6.

239   *turned to Calvert Vaux:* Francis R. Kowsky, *Country, Park & City: The Architecture and Life of Calvert Vaux* (Oxford University Press, 1998), 207.

240   *"the design has to be":* Quoted by Kowsky, *Country, Park & City,* 65.

240   *Vaux was close:* Kowsky, *Country, Park & City,* 64.

240   *halcyon days:* Church to Osborn, November 5, 1869.

240   *He was not given: Autobiography of Worthington Whittredge,* 29.

240   *"My wrist begins":* Church to [Edward?] Weeks, October 13, 1869.

241   *In early November:* Church to Osborn, November 5, 1869.

241   *leaders of civic institutions:* Winifred Eva Howe and Henry Watson Kent, *A History of the Metropolitan Museum of Art* (Metropolitan Museum of Art, 1913), 104.

241   *satirical 1873 novel:* Mark Twain and Charles Dudley Warner, *The Gilded Age: A Tale of To-Day* (American Publishing Company, 1873).

241   *president of the Century:* "Member Directory, 1847–1922: William Cullen Bryant," Century Association Archives Foundation, https://centuryarchives.org/member-directory/?PersonID=395.

241   *"Bryant looked like Homer":* Robert Underwood Johnson, quoted by the Literature Committee in the 1936 pamphlet "Incorporators of the Century, 1857," Century Association Archives Foundation, https://centuryarchives.org/member-directory/?PersonID=395.

241   *"the third great city":* Quoted by Howe and Kent, *History of the Metropolitan,* 107.

241   *approached one million:* Bureau of the Census, *A Compendium of the Ninth Census: June 1, 1870* (Government Printing Office, 1872), 76, https://www2.census.gov/library/publications/decennial/1870/compendium/1870e-05.pdf.

241   *"Gotham that uneasy City":* Church to Appleton, December 10, 1879.

242   *smaller nations:* Howe and Kent, *History of the Metropolitan,* 108.

242   *wholesome entertainment:* Howe and Kent, *History of the Metropolitan,* 111.

242   *Church was elected:* Howe and Kent, *History of the Metropolitan,* 123; and Church to Heade, March 7, 1870. Original in the AAA.

242   *"The children are preposterously":* Church to Osborn, January 2, 1870.

242   *"The baby is a fine fellow":* Church to Palmer, May 13, 1870. Original in Palmer Papers.

242   *"like mountains of bridal bouquets":* Church to Osborn, May 16, 1870.

242   *hundred thousand bricks:* Church to Osborn, May 16, 1870.

243   *"I enjoy this being afloat":* Church to Weir, June 8, 1871. Original in the AAA.

243   *preliminary exterior drawing:* Vaux to Church, May 16, 1870. Courtesy of the Bureau of Historic Sites, New York State Office of Parks, Recreation and Historic Preservation.

243   *At Castle Garden:* Church to Osborn, May 16, 1870.

243   *fifteen laborers digging:* Church to Palmer, August 11, 1870. Original in Palmer Papers.

243   *"mounted on a stick":* Church to Osborn, June 25, 1870.

244   *neighbors began wandering over:* Church to Osborn, October 31, 1870.

244   *"brick school house":* Church to Weir, June 8, 1871. Original in the AAA.

244   *"I have 9631201":* Church to Heade, October 24, 1870. Original in the AAA.

244   *pay $10,000 for it:* "Church's 'Jerusalem,'" *Hartford Daily Courant*, April 18, 1871.

244   *more than seven feet long and four feet tall:* Church to Heade, October 24, 1870.

244   *"Magnificent sunsets":* Church to Heade, October 24, 1870.

244   *crowds that gathered:* Huntington, *Landscapes*, 99.

244   *smacked of commercialism:* "Jerusalem, by Church," *New York Herald*, April 3, 1871.

244   *"dazzling general effects":* "Jerusalem, by Church," *New York Herald*.

244   *"his best painting":* "Church's 'Jerusalem,'" *Hartford Daily Courant*.

244   *Church next launched:* Church to Heade, January 6, 1871. Original in the AAA.

245   *his New Jerusalem:* On the Christian significance of Olana and its design, see Zukowski, "New Jerusalem."

245   *cosmos in miniature:* See Eleanor Jones Harvey, "Capturing the Cosmos," in Rosenbaum and Zukowski, *Frederic Church's Olana*.

245   *"I match every stone":* Church to Osborn, July 22, 1871. Original in the PUL.

245   *"The three boys":* Church to Osborn, July 22, 1871.

245   *"highly picturesque":* Church to Osborn, July 22, 1871.

245   *"We are all":* Church to Osborn, July 22, 1871.

CHAPTER 23   "A Model of Rank and File Citizenship"

247   *He disembarked among:* "The Grand Central Depot and the New Route," *New York Herald*, December 3, 1871.

247   *"Fever-nests":* *Report of the Council of Hygiene and Public Health of the Citizens' Association of New York upon the Sanitary Condition of the City* (D. Appleton, 1865), 103.

247   *"out-door poor":* Lewis Evens Jackson, *Walks About New York: Facts and Figures Gathered from Various Sources* (New-York Historical Society, 1865), 9.

247   *Now they were back:* Frederick Law Olmsted, *The Years of Olmsted, Vaux & Company: 1865–1874*, ed. David Schuyler et al. (Johns Hopkins University Press, 1992), 6:492; and *Minutes of the Proceedings of the Board of Commissioners of the Department of Public Parks: 1871–1872*, November 23, 1871, 235. See also Rybczynski, *Clearing in the Distance*, 310.

248   *"a model of rank and file citizenship":* Olmsted to Charles Loring Brace, November 24, 1871, quoted in Olmsted, *Years of Olmsted*, 6:493.

248   *five-year term:* Olmsted, *Years of Olmsted*, 6:493n1 and 6:494n3.

248   *On November 23:* *Minutes of the Proceedings*, 232.

248   The Andes of Ecuador *and* Chimborazo: Oaklander, "Jonathan Sturges, W. H. Osborn," 181.

249   *"You are always so kind":* Church to Osborn, August 8, 1870.

249   *New York and Brooklyn Bridge:* David McCullough, *The Great Bridge: The Epic Story of the Building of the Brooklyn Bridge*, 40th Anniversary Edition (Simon & Schuster, 2012), 337, 564.

249   *enormous underwater structures:* The Brooklyn caisson was launched in March 1870, and the New York caisson was launched in May 1871: McCullough, *Great Bridge*, 564–65.

249   *They considered:* *Minutes of the Proceedings*, 241, 247.

250   *"when led by a chain":* *Minutes of the Proceedings*, 241, 79.

250   *Central Park Menagerie:* *Minutes of the Proceedings of the Board of Commissioners of the Department of Public Parks, 1872–1873*, 376.

250   *Jacob Wrey Mould:* On Mould's work in Central Park, see esp. Francis R. Kowsky and Lucille Gordon, *Hell on Color, Sweet on Song: Jacob Wrey Mould and the Artful Beauty of Central Park* (Empire State Editions, 2023), 96ff.

250 *Church introduced a resolution:* Minutes of the Proceedings . . . 1872–1873, 559.

250 *He had chosen:* Kevin J. Avery, "'The Finest Edifice on the Finest Site in the World': Church's *Parthenon*," in Myers et al., *Frederic Church*, 173, offers a useful comparison of Church's 1871 *Parthenon* and Gifford's 1880 *Ruins of the Parthenon*.

250 *wearing the garments:* Avery, "'Finest Edifice,'" 169; and Michael Skafidas, "Fabricating Greekness: From Fustanella to the Glossy Page," in *The Fabric of Cultures: Fashion, Identity, and Globalization*, ed. Eugenia Paulicelli and Hazel Clark (Routledge, 2009).

250 *"It is the Parthenon":* Evening Mail, quoted by "Mr. Church's Latest Painting," *Hartford Daily Courant*, April 5, 1872.

251 *"Feudal Castle":* Church to Weir, June 8, 1871. Original in the AAA.

251 *"Persian palace":* Henry Mack, diary entry, October 30, 1872, Vedder Library, Greene County Historical Society.

251 *twelve-foot ceilings:* John G. Waite Associates, *Olana Historic Structure Report* (2001), 351.

251 *"one of the finest":* Quoted by David Schuyler, "Saving Olana," *Hudson River Valley Review* 32, no. 2 (2016): 4.

251 *The windows framed:* Julia B. Rosenbaum, "A World in View," in Rosenbaum and Zukowski, *Frederic Church's Olana*, 66; and Rosenbaum, "Outside In," 20.

251 *Church designed the dining room:* Church to Heade, November 25, 1874. Original in the AAA.

251 *The children's nursery:* Henry Mack, diary entry, October 30, 1872, Vedder Library, Greene County Historical Society.

252 *Craftsmen would be working:* Church to Palmer, August 9, 1870. Original in Palmer Papers.

252 *"Of course the sound":* Church to Osborn, January 2, 1870.

252 *utterly original home:* See, e.g., Roger B. Stein, "Artifact as Ideology: The Aesthetic Movement in Its American Cultural Context," in *In Pursuit of Beauty: Americans and the Aesthetic Movement*, ed. Doreen Bolger Burke (Metropolitan Museum of Art, 1986), 24; and Mary Roberts, "Worlding on the Hudson: Frederic Church and Global Histories of Art," *Art History* 45, no. 3 (2022): 531.

252 *his "Persian" home:* E.g., Church to Amelia Edwards, September 2, 1877. Original in the Somerville College Library, Oxford, England.

252 *Lockwood de Forest:* Karen Zukowski, *Creating the Artful Home: The Aesthetic Movement* (Gibbs Smith, 2006), 102. On de Forest's creative relationship with Indian craftsmanship, see Roberta A. Mayer, *Lockwood de Forest: Furnishing the Gilded Age with a Passion for India* (University of Delaware Press, 2009).

252 *Reporters soon began:* See, e.g., "Catskill," *New York Commercial Advertiser*, July 22, 1875, 1; and [Martha Lamb], "Homes of America, Part V," *Art Journal* 2 (1876): 245–48.

252 *"a bright open eyed":* F[rancis] N[ichols] Zabriskie, "'Old Colony' Papers: An Artist's Castle, and Our Ride Thereto," *Christian Intelligencer* (New York), September 10, 1884, 2, quoted by Rosenbaum, "Outside In," 20.

252 *Young painters:* Church to McEntee, July 20, 1873. Original in the AAA.

252 *He told McEntee:* Church to McEntee, September 2, 1873. Original in the AAA.

252 *"troubled":* Jervis McEntee, diary entry, September 17, 1873, reprinted in "Jervis McEntee Diary," *Archives of American Art Journal* 8, nos. 3 and 4 (1968): 21.

253 *"anxious to be rid":* Church to Osborn, February 23, 1873.

253 *called into question:* Carr, "'Land of Sacred Romance,'" 59, 63n55.

CHAPTER 24 "Absolutely Startling"

255 *A burgundy keffiyeh:* Lynne Zacek Bassett, *Costume and Custom: Middle Eastern Threads at Olana* (Olana Partnership, 2018), 16, fig. 13.

255 *he thanked Stone:* Benjamin Stone, diary entry, March 16, 1874, transcript courtesy of the Greene County Historical Society.

255 *There was no sky:* Jennifer Raab, *Frederic Church: The Art and Science of Detail* (Yale University Press, 2015), 157.

255 *ice floes choked the Hudson:* "Ice Bound," *Hartford Daily Courant*, January 17, 1874; "New York," *Hartford Daily Courant*, January 27, 1874; and "The Ice Crop," *New York Herald*, February 3, 1874.

256 *His treatment of the Treasury:* For an insightful analysis of this painting, see esp. "Vertical Light," in Raab, *Frederic Church*.

256 *The capitals of the columns:* Raab, *Frederic Church*, 148.

257 *Venetian palazzo:* On the National Academy's new building, designed by Peter Bonnett Wight, see esp. Sophie Lynford, *Painting Dissent: Art, Ethics, and the American Pre-Raphaelites* (Princeton University Press, 2022), 133–41.

257 *show of American pictures:* Strong, *Diary*, February 18, 1868, 4:189.

257 *"absolutely startling":* "The Academy of Design," *New York Times*, April 13, 1874.

257 *"The ruins of the present":* "The Academy of Design," *New York Herald*, April 20, 1874.

258 *they hung it in a sitting room:* Zukowski, "New Jerusalem," 152.

258 *One depicted a woman:* Berthe Morisot, *Cache-cache*, oil on canvas, 1873, private collection, reproduced in Sylvie Patry and Anne Robbins, eds., *Paris 1874: The Impressionist Moment* (Yale University Press, 2024), 11, no. 106.

258 *A seascape:* Claude Monet, *Impression, Sunrise*, 1872, oil on canvas, Musée Marmatton Monet, Paris, reproduced in Patry and Robbins, *Paris 1874*, 196–97, no. 98.

258 *artists frustrated:* Anne Robbins, "1874: An Impressionist Exhibition, or an 'Eclectic' One?," in Patry and Robbins, *Paris 1874*, 108.

258 *Not all the pictures:* Robbins, "1874," 108–9. On reactions to this show, see also Sebastian Smee, *Paris in Ruins: Love, War, and the Birth of Impressionism* (W. W. Norton, 2024), 299–308.

258 *"A vexatious mystification":* Émile Cardon, *La Presse*, April 29, 1874, quoted by Catherine Méneux, "The New Painting: A Mixed Critical Response," in Patry and Robbins, *Paris 1874*, 208.

258 *"slap-dash" brushstrokes and "palette-scrapings":* Quoted and translated by John Rewald, *The History of Impressionism* (Museum of Modern Art, 1961), 319–20; and Louis Leroy, "The Exhibition of the Impressionists," *Le Charivari*, April 25, 1874, reprinted and translated by John Rewald, *The History of Impressionism*, 4th ed. (Secker & Warburg, 1973), 318–24. It should be noted that Leroy's review was satirical and poked fun both at the paintings and at the imagined reactions of a conservative visitor to the exhibition.

258 *"These youths":* Jules-Antoine Castagnary, "Exposition du boulevard des Capucines—Les impressionistes," *Le Siècle* (Paris), April 29, 1874, quoted and translated by Rewald, *History of Impressionism*, 330.

258 *"Impressionists":* Castagnary, "Exposition du boulevard," 330.

259 *"calm decided voice":* Church to Palmer, May 28, 1875. Original in Palmer Papers.

259 *"the terrorism caused":* Church to Ogden Rood, May 16, 1875. Original in Rare Book & Manuscript Library, Columbia University Library.

259 *"His mind seems":* Isabel Church to Virginia Osborn, August 17, 1880. Original in the New-York Historical Society.

259 *"must be lonely there"*: Jervis McEntee, diary entry, October 27, 1872, reprinted in "Jervis McEntee Diary," *Archives of American Art Journal* 8, nos. 3 and 4 (1968): 8.

259 *"simply rich are blights"*: Church to Rood, May 16, 1875. Original in Rare Book & Manuscript Library, Columbia University Library.

260 *he joked to Heade:* Church to Heade, March 8, 1875. Original in the AAA.

260 *"on one of my trips"*: Church to Palmer, March 22, 1875. Original in Palmer Papers.

260 *"He never knew"*: *Autobiography of Worthington Whittredge*, 28.

260 *"Church is very friendly"*: Jervis McEntee, diary entry, October 17, 1876, reprinted in "Jervis McEntee Diary, 1874–1876," *Archives of American Art Journal* 31, no. 1 (1991): 18.

261 *"Perhaps you can imagine"*: Church to Osborn, December 27, 1874. Courtesy of PUL.

261 *"the chicks"*: Church to Palmer, August 9, 1876. Courtesy of the Albany Institute of History and Art.

261 *"proud and fond"*: Virginia Osborn to Mary Sturges, May 10, 1875, series I, box 1, folder 7, Osborn Family Papers, New-York Historical Society.

261 *cerebral meningitis:* Noted by Virginia Osborn in her scrapbook for daughter Virginia, [n.p.], Osborn Family Papers, New-York Historical Society.

261 *The Osborns held:* Osborn to Sturges, May 10, 1875.

261 *Frederick Osborn drowned:* "By Mail and Telegraph," *New York Times*, July 3, 1875.

261 *"It is a serious matter"*: Virginia Osborn to Fairfield Osborn, May 14, 1876.

262 *"I want some"*: Frederic Joseph Church to Santa Claus [c. 1873–76].

262 *"seemed so truly"*: Virginia Osborn to Mary Sturges, December [n.d., 1875], series I, box 1, folder 7, Osborn Family Papers, New-York Historical Society.

263 *"eminent artist"*: "Death of Joseph Church," *Hartford Courant*, February 15, 1876.

263 *Church inherited:* Zukowski, *Historic Furnishings Report*, 4n26. On the average wages of carpenters in New York in 1876, see Nelson W. Aldrich, *Wholesale Prices, Wages, and Transportation: Report by Mr. Aldrich from the Committee on Finance, March 3, 1893* (Government Printing Office, 1893), 1293.

CHAPTER 25 "This Glorious Country"

265 *"I cannot do it"*: Church to Ogden Rood, May 16, 1875. Original in Rare Book & Manuscript Library, Columbia University Library.

266 *cover ten times that:* Robert C. Post, ed., *1876: A Centennial Exhibition* (National Museum of History and Technology, Smithsonian Institution, 1976), 22.

266 *African American men and women:* See esp. Mitch Kachun, "Before the Eyes of All Nations: African-American Identity and Historical Memory at the Centennial Exposition of 1876," *Pennsylvania History: A Journal of Mid-Atlantic Studies* 65, no. 3 (1998): 300–323, and Philip S. Foner, "Black Participation in the Centennial of 1876," *Phylon* 39, no. 4 (1978): 283–96.

266 *Sartain decided to feature:* Kimberly Orcutt, *Power & Posterity: American Art at Philadelphia's 1876 Centennial Exhibition* (Penn State University Press, 2017), 38. For my treatment of the centennial art exhibitions in Philadelphia and New York, I am indebted to Orcutt's meticulous research and analysis.

266 *Committee on Selection:* Orcutt, *Power & Posterity*, 39–40.

267 *"most fatiguing work"*: Jervis McEntee, diary entry, March 31, 1876, reprinted in "Jervis McEntee Diary, 1874–1876," *Archives of American Art Journal* 31, no. 1 (1991): 14, quoted by Orcutt, *Power & Posterity*, 45.

267 *"how he thoroughly"*: Jervis McEntee, diary entry, March 31, 1876, 14. On this episode, see Orcutt, *Power & Posterity*, 44.

267 *"willing to do anything"*: Jervis McEntee, diary entry, April 14, 1876, reprinted in "Jervis McEntee Diary, 1874–1876," *Archives of American Art Journal* 31, no. 1 (1991): 14.

267 *several thousand:* Post, *1876*, 13.

267 *"I know no North"*: Kachun, "Before the Eyes of All Nations," 306–7; see, e.g., Charles Holland Kidder, ed., *Burley's United States Centennial Gazetteer and Guide* (S. W. Burley, 1876), 201; "Our Centennial!," *Los Angeles Daily Star*, July 6, 1876; and "Historical Address, by Hon. W. T. Avery," in *Addresses, Historical and Patriotic, Centennial and Quadrennial, Delivered in the Several States of the Union: July 4th, 1876–1883*, ed. Frederick Saunders (E. B. Treat, 1893), 559.

267 *"You turned us loose"*: Douglass, "Looking the Republican Party Squarely in the Face," address delivered at the Republican National Convention, June 14, 1876, Cincinnati, OH, *Douglass Papers*, ser. 1, 440–41, quoted by Blight, *Frederick Douglass*, 577.

268 *Douglass almost didn't get:* Kachun, "Before the Eyes of All Nations," 308–9.

268 *attacks in the South:* See esp. "The Politics of Depression," in Foner, *Reconstruction*; "Vindication," in Chernow, *Grant*; and Sinha, *Rise and Fall*, 266ff.

268 *"great primal works"*: Quoted in *General Grant: His Life and Services* (Cameron & Ferguson, 1885), 80.

268 *"A change"*: "Report of Colonel Sir Herbert Sandford, R.A., Executive Commissioner," in *Reports on the Philadelphia International Exhibition of 1876: Presented to Both Houses of Parliament by Command of Her Majesty* (George E. Eyre & William Spottiswoode, 1877), I:xxxix.

269 *more than fourteen hundred horses:* The Corliss engine typically ran at fourteen hundred horsepower but could be ramped up to twenty-five hundred: Philip T. Sandhurst, *The Great Centennial Exhibition* (P. W. Ziegler & Company, 1876), 265.

269 *"influence the civilization"*: John Anderson, "Machines and Tools for Working Metals, Wood, and Stone," in *Reports on the Philadelphia International Exhibition*, 1:236.

269 *five-acre reservation:* Robert A. Trennert, "The Indian Role in the 1876 Centennial Celebration," *American Indian Culture and Research Journal* 1, no. 4 (1976): 8–10.

269 *Visitors saw:* James D. McCabe, *The Illustrated History of the Centennial Exhibition* (National Publishing Company, 1876), 555–56; Trennert, "Indian Role," 11; and Judy Braun Zegas, "North American Indian Exhibit at the Centennial Exposition," *Curator: The Museum Journal* 19, no. 2 (1976): 166–68. By prearrangement, these artifacts passed after the exposition into the collection of the Smithsonian Institution: Post, *1876*, 77.

269 *The main effect:* Zegas, "North American Indian Exhibit," 171.

269 *The artifacts did:* Trennert, "Indian Role."

270 *Custer had been killed:* Wineapple, *Ecstatic Nation*, 556; West, *Continental Reckoning*, 418; and Blackhawk, *Rediscovery of America*, 348–51.

270 *Susan B. Anthony:* This episode is described in Kathleen Barry, *Susan B. Anthony: A Biography* (New York University Press, 2020), 276–78.

270 *"While the Nation"*: Ann D. Gordon, ed., *The Selected Papers of Elizabeth Cady Stanton and Susan B. Anthony: National Protection for National Citizens, 1873 to 1880* (Rutgers University Press, 1997), 3:234.

270 *"and their male descendants"*: *Eighty Years and More (1815–1897): Reminiscences of Elizabeth Cady Stanton* (European Publishing Company, 1898), 310. Stanton had decided not to attend the event with Anthony.

270 *On the night of July 3:* "The City in Gala Dress," *New-York Tribune*, July 4, 1876.

270 *"This City"*: "A Second Century Begun," *New York Times*, July 5, 1876.

271 *nearly seventy: Catalogue of the New York Centennial Loan Exhibition* (National Academy of Design, 1876), n.p.

271 *about 180:* Orcutt, *Power & Posterity*, 176.

271   *John Taylor Johnston:* Catalogue of the New York Centennial Loan Exhibition (Metropolitan Museum of Art, 1876), 14–20.

271   *The Slave Ship:* Catalogue of the New York Centennial (Metropolitan Museum of Art), 17.

272   *nearly four hundred:* Catalogue of the New York Centennial (National Academy of Design), n.p.

272   *"Hudson River School":* Carr, In Search of the Promised Land, 107n2.

272   *Church was informally mentoring:* Amanda Malmstrom, "'Catskill China Painter': The Art of Emily Cole," in The Art of Emily Cole, ed. Kate Menconeri and Amanda Malmstrom (Thomas Cole National Historic Site, 2024), 14; and Amanda Malmstrom, "'Live and Breathe the Soft Air': Emily Cole's Garden-to-Plate Art Practice and an Expanded Legacy of the Thomas Cole National Historic Site," in Emily Cole: Ceramics, Flora & Contemporary Responses, ed. Kate Menconeri and Amanda Malmstrom (Thomas Cole National Historic Site, 2025), 10–11.

272   *Women's Pavilion:* Greatorex was heavily involved with the Women's Pavilion, as were her two daughters: Katherine Manthorne, Restless Enterprise: The Art and Life of Eliza Pratt Greatorex (University of California Press, 2020), 218ff.

272   *admitted a Black student:* Hildegard Cummings, Charles Ethan Porter: African-American Master of Still Life (New Britain Museum of American Art, 2007), 20. The first African American painter to be elected to membership in the National Academy was Henry Ossawa Tanner, named an associate in 1909 and a full academician in 1927. On Tanner, see esp. Anna O. Marley, ed., Henry Ossawa Tanner: Modern Spirit (University of California Press, 2012).

273   *Church would later number:* Cummings, Charles Ethan Porter, 42–43. Church's visits to Porter's studio are mentioned in "An Artist Who Deserves Fame," Hartford Daily Times, September 11, 1879, and "The Artist Porter," Hartford Daily Courant, April 28, 1880. As Cummings, Charles Ethan Porter, 101, notes, Church apparently offended Porter in the 1870s by referring to a work of his as "the most unconscious piece of painting he had ever seen."

273   *Robert Duncanson:* On Duncanson's career, see esp. Naurice Frank Woods Jr., Race and Racism in Nineteenth-Century Art: The Ascendency of Robert Duncanson, Edward Bannister, and Edmonia Lewis (University Press of Mississippi, 2021), and Joseph D. Ketner, The Emergence of the African-American Artist: Robert S. Duncanson, 1821–1872 (University of Missouri Press, 1993).

273   *Edmonia Lewis:* Orcutt, Power & Posterity, 74; and Church to Mr. [Thomas G.] Appleton, October 28, 1880. Courtesy of Harvard University Library.

273   *"wonderful closeness to nature":* Quoted by Woods Jr., Race and Racism, 107–8.

273   *"What's that to you?":* Quoted by Woods Jr., Race and Racism, 108.

274   *"Church, the Artist, Disabled":* "Church, the Artist, Disabled," Evening Sun, June 3, 1876.

274   *McEntee overheard:* McEntee Diary, June 4 [1876], 16.

274   *did not face amputation:* "Personal," Evening Post, June 6, 1876.

274   *"Wrist checks flow":* Church to Palmer, September 21, 1875. Courtesy of the Albany Institute of History and Art.

274   *"And as I can":* Church to Edwin L. Doolittle, June 5, 1876. Courtesy of Harvard University Library.

CHAPTER 26   "A Very Big Skeleton"

275   *In the fall of 1876:* Carr, Frederic Edwin Church, 1:405.

275   *"When the autumn fires":* Church to McEntee, September 23, 1874. Original in the AAA.

275 *Alexander Lyman Holley:* American Institute of Mining, Metallurgical, and Petroleum Engineers, *Memorial of Alexander Lyman Holley* (American Institute of Mining, Metallurgical, and Petroleum Engineers, 1884).

276 *"What things he can't":* Alexander Lyman Holley, "Camps and Tramps About Ktaadn," *Scribner's Monthly* 16, no. 3 (1878): 36.

276 *Church soldered up:* Holley, "Camps and Tramps," 36.

276 *"celebrated feat":* Holley, "Camps and Tramps," 44.

276 *"old winter suit":* Church to McEntee, August 31, 1878. Original in the AAA.

276 *"Church fixed my pipe":* Jervis McEntee, diary entry, September 27, 1878, from the Jervis McEntee Papers.

276 *edge of Lake Millinocket:* Jervis McEntee, diary entry, September 6, 1878, from the Jervis McEntee Papers.

276 *Church bought:* Carr, *Frederic Edwin Church,* 1:405.

276 *"good place to unbend":* Church to Austin, August 27, 1879.

277 *the name* ISABEL: Jervis McEntee, diary entry, September 16, 1879, from the Jervis McEntee Papers.

277 *A band played:* "The New Museum Opened," *New York Times,* March 31, 1880.

277 *The carriages of Astors:* "The New Museum Opened."

277 *unpaved portion of Fifth:* See Morrison H. Heckscher, "The Metropolitan Museum of Art: An Architectural History," *Metropolitan Museum of Art Bulletin* 53, no. 1 (1995): 18, fig. 19.

278 *Eighty-Fourth Street station:* H. I. Latimer, *Manhattan Railway: Official Map and Guide to All the Elevated Railways in New York City* (1881), Library of Congress, https://www.loc.gov/item/98688705/.

278 *Rutherford B. Hayes:* "The New Museum Opened."

278 *Cyrus Field:* "The Metropolitan Museum of Art," *Evening Post,* March 31, 1880; Howe and Kent, *History of the Metropolitan,* 256; and Judson, *Cyrus W. Field,* 289–90.

278 *"Think of it":* Choate, quoted by the *Tenth Annual Report of the Trustees of the Association* (May 1880), 21, and by Roy Rosenzweig and Elizabeth Blackmar, *The Park and the People: A History of Central Park* (Cornell University Press, 1992), 358.

278 *Vaux and Mould:* Heckscher, "Metropolitan Museum of Art," 16, observes, "Though it is now hard to distinguish the role each played in the design, Vaux should probably be credited with the overall conception and plan and Mould with the architectural ornament and most of the drawings."

278 *gray and white granite:* Heckscher, "Metropolitan Museum of Art," 75, and 74, fig. 107. One wall of the original building can still be seen inside the Met today.

279 *"unpretentious":* "A Metropolitan Museum," *New York Times,* March 30, 1880; and "Metropolitan Museum of Art," *Art Journal* 6 (July 1880): 181.

279 *"a forcible example":* Quoted by Heckscher, "Metropolitan Museum of Art," 18.

279 *Jarves knew:* James Jackson Jarves, "American Museums of Art," *Scribner's Monthly* 18 (1879): 405–8.

279 *The collection:* On the early years of assembling the collection, see esp. Katharine Baetjer, "Buying Pictures for New York: The Founding Purchase of 1871," *Metropolitan Museum Journal* 38 (2003): 169–81, and Katharine Baetjer and Joan R. Mertens, "The Founding Decades," in *Making the Met, 1870–2020,* ed. Andrea Bayer and Laura D. Corey (Metropolitan Museum of Art, 2020).

279 *Cyprus and Egypt:* "Metropolitan Museum of Art," *Art Journal* 6: 182.

279 *The paintings:* "Metropolitan Museum," *New York Times.*

279 *William H. Vanderbilt:* Howe and Kent, *History of the Metropolitan,* 192.

280 *"You walk through":* Howe and Kent, *History of the Metropolitan,* 190, quoting the *New York Evening Post,* March 29, 1880.

280 *Church had advocated: Minutes of the Proceedings . . . 1872–1873*, 559.

280 *"The whole house":* F. N. Zabriskie, "'Old Colony Papers.' An Artist's Castle and Our Ride Thereto," *New York Christian Intelligencer*, September 10, 1884, quoted by Ryan, "Frederic Church's Olana," 143.

280 *"bought some Persian":* Church to Palmer, November 14, 1878. Courtesy of the Albany Institute of History and Art.

280 *reference to a fortress:* Strabo, *The Geography of Strabo: Literally Tr., with Notes*, trans. W. Falconer and Hans Claude Hamilton (H. G. Bohn, 1854), 2:270. I am grateful to classicist James Romm for sharing his insight into the original Greek phrase used by Strabo.

280 *Garden of Eden:* See, e.g., A. N. Sherwin-White, "Lucullus, Pompey and the East," in *The Cambridge Ancient History, Volume IX: The Last Age of the Roman Republic, 146–43 B. C.*, ed. J. A. Crook et al. (Cambridge University Press, 1994), 255.

280 *Church and Isabel borrowed:* This connection was made by Carr, *Frederic Edwin Church*, 1:395, who discovered the reference to "Olanê" in the Churches' copy of Falconer and Hamilton, *Geography of Strabo*, 2:270.

281 *"suggestion of muslins":* Susan Hale to Lucretia P. Hale, June 29, 1884.

281 *"Everywhere you look":* Hale to Hale, June 29, 1884.

281 *"Old Grandma Carnes":* Susan Hale to Lucretia P. Hale, July 6, 1884.

282 *One day Church:* Emma Carnes Diary, August 26, 1882, OSHS.

282 *"a dream of beauty":* Susan Hale to "Jack" [Edward Everett Hale Jr.], October 13, 1889.

282 *"simply the most beautiful":* Kate Bradbury to Amelia Edwards, December 24, 1889.

282 *The boys wore suits:* E.g., bill of sale of March 24, 1883, OSHS.

282 *collection of dolls:* Hale to Hale, July 6, 1884.

282 *She sat for a portrait:* The year was 1884: Felix Moscheles, *Fragments of an Autobiography* (Harper & Brothers, 1899), 238.

282 *Juliet's father owned:* Jean Strouse, *Morgan: American Financier* (Random House, 2014), 227, notes that Morgan had Church's painting *Near Damascus* over the sideboard in his dining room.

282 *lit by electricity:* Susan Hale to Lucretia Hale, July 13, 1884.

282 *studied with private tutors:* See, e.g., Susan Hale to "Jack" [Edward Everett Hale Jr.], June 29, 1884; Mrs. Carnes also mentions "the children's tutor": Emma Carnes Diary, June 6, 1882.

283 *Longfellow was approaching:* Church to Longfellow, February 23, 1882. Original in Harvard University Library.

283 *"I am so ready":* Church to Palmer, March 14, 1878. Courtesy of the Albany Institute of History and Art.

283 *"losing ground rapidly":* Isabel Church to Virginia Osborn, August 17, 1880. Original in the New-York Historical Society.

283 *"He looks badly":* Jervis McEntee, diary entry, February 7, 1881, from the Jervis McEntee Papers.

283 *stifled their laughter:* Susan Hale to "Jack" [Edward Everett Hale Jr.], July 24, 1884.

283 *"You see there":* Hale to Hale, July 6, 1884.

283 *"always a good sign":* Susan Hale to Lucretia Hale, July 25, 1884.

284 *"Rub all your joints":* Church to Palmer, June 10, 1883. Original in Palmer Papers.

284 *"I think that":* Church to Palmer, June 10, 1883.

284 *he couldn't do up:* Church to Osborn, February 11, 1885. Original in the PUL.

284 *He began having massages:* Church to Palmer, August 1, 1880. Original in Palmer Papers.

284 *He was fielding:* E.g., Dr. Mary A. Carpenter to Church, August 7, 1886.

284 *special mattresses and austere diets:* Church to Palmer, August 1, 1880.

284 *"He possessed remarkable courage":* *Autobiography of Worthington Whittredge,* 29.

284 *"its very changeable climate":* Church to Goodman, March 26, 1884.

284 *"The pioneers of Civilization":* Church to Appleton, May 1, 1883. Original in the Massachusetts Historical Society.

284 *Church and Isabel decided on Mexico:* Church to Appleton, February 7, 1881; Church to Appleton, February 17, 1881. Originals in the Massachusetts Historical Society.

284 *Osborn's private railroad car:* Church to Appleton, February 7, 1881.

284 *"I like Mexico":* Church to Appleton, May 1, 1883.

284 *reminded Church of his own:* Church to Warner, March 27, 1892.

285 *Charles Guiteau shot:* Candice Millard, *Destiny of the Republic: A Tale of Madness, Medicine, and the Murder of a President* (Doubleday, 2011), 150–53.

285 *After Garfield died:* For an account of Garfield's assassination and subsequent medical (mis)treatment, see Millard, *Destiny of the Republic.*

285 *"50,000,000 people":* Church to Heade, December 22, 1881. Original in the AAA.

285 *"It is possible":* Church to Heade, January 10, 1882. Original in the AAA.

285 *hanged on June 30:* Millard, *Destiny of the Republic,* 282–85.

285 *help look after them:* Virginia Osborn to Henry Fairfield Osborn, August [n.d.] 1883. Courtesy of Winterthur.

285 *"very critical condition":* Church to Mrs. Billings, October 17, 1881. Original in the Billings Mansion Archives.

285 *his mother died:* Emma Carnes Diary, July 17, 1883.

286 *"much more cheerful":* Osborn to Osborn, August [n.d.] 1883.

286 *"an unspeakable loss":* Church to Heade, September 9, 1883. Original in the AAA.

286 *"The Doctor forbids":* Church to Appleton, May 1, 1883.

286 *Hôtel del Café Anglais:* Thomas Allibone Janvier, *The Mexican Guide* (Charles Scribner's Sons, 1886), 27.

286 *where he sketched:* Carr, *Frederic Edwin Church,* 2: nos. 609–15.

286 *"Air delicious":* Church to Heade, March 2, 1884. Original in the AAA.

286 *"splendid":* Emma Carnes Diary, May 15, 1884.

286 *"perfect health":* Church to Warner, August 16, 1884.

286 *"I hate heat":* Church to Heade, September 9, 1885. Original in the AAA.

286 *expansion of railroads:* Church to Warner, December 27, 1884.

286 *all the way home:* Church to Palmer, May 24, 1884. Original in Palmer Papers.

286 *"the great winter resort":* Church to Heade, September 9, 1883.

286 *"everything to enchant":* Church to Heade, March 2, 1884.

286 *"Heade!":* Church to Heade, March 2, 1884.

286 *"the sky, the earth":* Church to Palmer, February 26, 1885. Original in Palmer Papers.

287 *"flower is the most heavenly":* Church to Osborn, February 11, 1885.

287 *Humboldt had supposedly:* Susan Hale to Lucretia P. Hale, March 17, 1886, in *The Letters of Susan Hale,* ed. Caroline P. Atkinson (Marshall Jones Company, 1919).

287 *"I seem to have recovered":* Church to Warner, March 2, 1885.

CHAPTER 27 "Young Geniuses Fully Armed"

289 *freshman year at Princeton:* Church to Palmer, September 10, 1884. Original in Palmer Papers.

289 *"splendid looking":* Emma Carnes Diary, November 3, 1884.

289 *"Freddie is doing admirably":* Church to McEntee, November 29, 1878. Original in the AAA.

289 *"We are all well"*: Church to McEntee, December 28, 1878. Original in the AAA.

289 *"He knows of evil"*: Henry A. Coit to Church, June 27, 1881.

290 *"The child will"*: Coit to Church, July 9, 1881.

290 *"A wild bad son"*: Isabel Church to Eliza Church, July 9, 1868.

290 *Church had to settle*: W. N. Scudder to Church, July 9, 1884.

290 *telling Mrs. Carnes*: Emma Carnes Diary, September 29, 1884.

290 *the science track*: Catalogue of the College of New Jersey, Princeton, Year 1885–86 (Princeton Press, 1885).

290 *"who were dissipates"*: Frederic Joseph Church to Church, June 13, 1887.

290 *he was kicked out*: H. B. Cornwall to Church, October 23, 1885.

290 *playing billiards*: Church to Church, June 13, 1887.

290 *A chemistry professor*: H. B. Cornwall to Church, December 24, 1885.

290 *Fred barraged his father*: Frederic Joseph Church to Church, January 26, 1886.

291 *"A mother's heart"*: Isabel Church, notebook, c. 1885, OSHS.

291 *Church told Fred*: Mentioned in Church to Church, June 13, 1887.

291 *He showed Fred*: Frederic Joseph Church to Church, August 24, 1895.

291 *He invented excuses*: Cornwall to Church, December 24, 1885.

291 *he didn't understand*: Frederic Joseph Church to Church, August 30, 1887.

291 *"was so much a part"*: Church to Warner, January 18, 1886.

291 *"I think you"*: Church to Church, January 26, 1886.

292 *Church told Fred*: Frederic Joseph Church to Church, June 21, 1887.

292 *Osborn had recommended*: Osborn to Church, July 4, 1887.

292 *Washington Territory*: John B. Pine to Church, July 24, 1887.

292 *homesick Fred begged*: Church to Church, August 30, 1887.

292 *"his courteous, manly"*: Job P. Lyon to Church, February 1, 1893. On Fred's time in Seattle, see Gerald L. Carr, *"Niagara & Baalbek*: Two Recently Rediscovered Paintings by Frederic Edwin Church," *American Fine Art Magazine* 37 (January/February 2018): 34–43.

292 *"being of a superb rose color"*: Frederic Joseph Church to Church, January 14, 1888.

292 *Church liked Margaret*: Church to Palmer, September 11, 1888. Original in Palmer Papers.

292 *serious irregularities*: Charles Kittinger to Church, October 16, 1889.

292 *"thereby saving Fred"*: Kittinger to Church, October 16, 1889.

292 *"Variety Actress"*: Kittinger to Church, October 16, 1889.

292 *"I am at present"*: Frederic Joseph Church to Church, December 20, 1888.

293 *"If you had been dead"*: Church to Church, December 20, 1888.

293 *"a mother cannot"*: Isabel Church to one of her children, May 26, 1889.

293 *Isabel pleaded*: Frederic Joseph Church to Church, July 7, 1889.

293 *But he just kept begging*: See Frederic Joseph Church to Kittinger, July 28, 1889; Frederic Joseph Church to Isabel Church, June 29, 1889.

293 *"I send you this money"*: Church quoted by Frederic Joseph Church to Kittinger, July 28, 1889.

293 *He toyed with the idea*: Frederic Joseph Church to Church, September 19 and October 12, 1889.

293 *He staked a claim*: Frederic Joseph Church to Isabel Church, November 12 and November 13, 1891.

294 *the man refused*: George G. Mills to Frederic Joseph Church, August 16, 1891.

294 *Fred eventually returned to Seattle*: Frederic Joseph Church to Church, January 8, 1893.

294 *a grateful reply*: Frederic Joseph Church to Isabel Church, October 29, 1891.

294 *"the kindest letter"*: Frederic Joseph Church to Virginia Osborn, May 16, 1894.

294 *settled a doctor's bill*: Church to Osborn, May 16, 1894.

294 *"I can never forget"*: Virginia Osborn to Loulu Osborn, n.d. (probably August 22, 1895).

294 The River of Light: On this painting, also called *Morning in the Tropics*, see esp. Franklin Kelly, "Frederic Edwin Church," in Franklin Kelly, *American Paintings of the Nineteenth Century* (Princeton University Press, 1996), 63–66. I'm also grateful to Dr. Kelly for a conversation about this painting.

295 *"begin to die"*: Quoted by Kevin J. Avery, "A Historiography of the Hudson River School," in *American Paradise: The World of the Hudson River School*, with John K. Howat et al. (Metropolitan Museum of Art, 1987), 6. When he made this comment, Cook was writing in 1883 about an 1878 exhibition of work by the Society of American Artists. See Clarence Cook, "Art in America in 1883," *Princeton Review* 11 (May 1883): 314. On Cook's significance as an art critic and champion of the American Pre-Raphaelites, see Lynford, *Painting Dissent*, and Sophie Lynford, "Patrons of Reform: Collecting the American Pre-Raphaelites," in Ferber and Laster, *Tastemakers, Collectors*.

295 *Church encountered*: Church to Theodore Cole, February 16, 1882.

295 *"Thomas Cole was"*: Church to John D. Champlin, September 11, 1885. Original in the AAA.

295 *a pejorative connotation*: Avery, "Historiography," 6.

295 *first major American show*: Leanne M. Zalewski, *The New York Market for French Art in the Gilded Age, 1867–1893* (Bloomsbury, 2023), 134. On this exhibition, see Sue Roe, *The Private Lives of the Impressionists* (Harper Collins, 2006), 256–65, and Michael Leja, "Monet's Modernity in New York in 1886," *American Art* 14, no. 1 (2000): 51.

295 *"There are some effects"*: "French Impressionists," *New York Times*, May 28, 1886.

295 *"One of the essentials"*: "French Impressionists."

295 *"to note all"*: Theodore Child, "A Note on Impressionist Painting," *Harper's New Monthly Magazine* 74, no. 440 (1887): 314.

296 *visited Monet at Giverny*: Jackie Wullschläger, *Monet: The Restless Vision* (Knopf Doubleday, 2024), 260. Two recent works examine the demand for Sargent's portraits in London and the United States, respectively: Jean Strouse, *Family Romance: John Singer Sargent and the Wertheimers* (Farrar, Straus & Giroux, 2024), and Natalie Dykstra, *Chasing Beauty: The Life of Isabella Stewart Gardner* (Mariner, 2024).

296 *William Merritt Chase*: Helene Barbara Weinberg, "Cosmopolitan and Candid Stories, 1877–1915," in *American Stories: Paintings of Everyday Life, 1765–1915*, ed. Helene Barbara Weinberg and Carrie Rebora Barratt (Metropolitan Museum of Art, 2009), 164–65.

296 *explored the masses of color*: Wullschläger, *Monet*, 34.

296 *Church was an avid collector*: See William L. Coleman, "What Was Photography to Frederic Church?," in David Hartt et al., *Terraforming: Olana's Historic Photography Collection Unearthed* (Olana Partnership, 2023).

296 *"perpetually skirting"*: Henry James, "On Some Pictures Lately Exhibited, *Galaxy* 20 (July 1875): 89–97, reprinted in *American Art 1700–1960: Sources and Documents*, ed. John W. McCoubrey (Prentice Hall, 1965), 168; quoted by Raab, *Frederic Church*, 9.

297 *cruel, random, and localized*: Stephen Jay Gould, "Church, Humboldt, and Darwin: The Tension and Harmony of Art and Science," in Franklin Kelly, *Frederic Edwin Church* (National Gallery of Art, 1989), 104–5. On the reception of Darwin in the United States, see esp. Randall Fuller, *The Book That Changed America: How Darwin's Theory of Evolution Ignited a Nation* (Penguin, 2018).

297 *"the sudden springing"*: Church to Charles Parsons, April 23, 1883. Original in the Missouri Historical Society.

297   *"rank in color"*: Church to Goodman, December 3, 1885.

297   *He joked:* Church to Palmer, October 21, 1885. Original in Palmer Papers.

297   *he still fretted:* Church to Goodman, December 9, 1885.

297   Niagara Falls *was back:* Sarah Cash, "'Encouraging American Genius': Collecting American Art at the Corcoran Gallery of Art," in *Corcoran Gallery of Art: American Paintings to 1945*, ed. Sarah Cash (Corcoran Gallery of Art, 2012), 30.

297   *"be swallowed up"*: Church to Palmer, August 6, 1886. Original in Palmer Papers.

298   *credited Church:* Howat, *Frederic Church*, 172–73.

CHAPTER 28   "His Beautiful Creations"

299   *As he sat:* Church to Mrs. John Gaul Jr., January 8, 1888.

299   *"He is just"*: Kate Bradbury to Amelia Edwards, December 27, 1889.

299   *"I can make"*: Church to Palmer, October 18, 1884. Original in Palmer Papers.

299   *"I am busy"*: Church to Warner, August 15, 1887.

300   *two thousand evergreen trees:* Toole, *Historic Landscape Report*, 71.

300   *"If I can"*: Church to Warner, December 4, 1890. Original in the New-York Historical Society.

300   *"no sane person"*: Church to Palmer, December 28, 1890. Original in Palmer Papers.

300   *five or six:* Church to Palmer, April 19, 1891. Original in Palmer Papers.

301   *Twain came down:* Robert Bush, "Grace King and Mark Twain," *American Literature* 44, no. 1 (March 1972): 34.

301   *"the greatest circus"*: Quoted by Ron Chernow, *Mark Twain* (Penguin Press, 2025), 384.

301   *"an ideal holiday"*: Samuel Clemens to Church, June 11, 1887, quoted by Chernow, *Mark Twain*, 385.

301   *"There is another"*: Louis Church to Sally Good, December 12, 1889.

301   *started at Princeton:* Carr, *"Niagara & Baalbek,"* 40, notes that Winthrop graduated with the class of 1891.

301   *Susan Hale thought:* Susan Hale to "JB," March 27, 1886.

301   *"spoilt by the peevish"*: Susan Hale to "Jack" [Edward Everett Hale Jr.], October 13, 1889.

301   *"smiles for all men"*: Hale (writing of Virginia Osborn) to "Jack," October 13, 1889.

301   *Dad:* E.g., Louis Church to Sally Good, May 12, 1900.

302   *"Your old guide"*: Quoted by Howat, *Frederic Church*, 182.

302   *Bermuda or to Palm Beach:* Carr, *Frederic Edwin Church*, 1:467–68.

302   *"Wife and I"*: Church to Warner, September 20, 1896.

302   *"The whole town"*: Janvier, *Mexican Guide*, 295.

303   *"sketching daily"*: Church to Isabel [Downie] Church Black, February 14, 1897.

303   *"laden with Aztec"*: Church to Brownell, July 20, 1892.

303   *two of those pieces:* On Church's relationship with the Met, see Elizabeth Kornhauser, "Global Collecting and the Metropolitan Museum of Art," in *Frederic Church: Global Artist*, ed. Tim Barringer et al. (Yale University Press, 2026).

303   *"The little Mother's life"*: Louis Church to Sally Good, May 16, 1899.

303   *he began inquiring:* Church to Isabel [Downie] Church Black, November 25, 1899.

303   *He published several articles:* F. J. Church, "Letter," *Recreation* 5, no. 6 (1896): 334–45; "A Day with Quinault Trout," *Recreation* 6, no. 6 (1897): 451–53; and "Shooting the Rapids of the Quinault," *Recreation* 9, no. 3 (1898): 186.

303   *"Indians were all"*: Church, "Shooting the Rapids," 189.

304   *North American buffalo:* For a useful discussion of William Hornaday's 1889 Smithsonian Institution report, "The Extermination of the American Bison," see Alan C.

Braddock, "Icon of Extinction and Resilience," in Kusserow and Braddock, *Nature's Nation*, 254ff.

304   *"the frontier proper":* Quoted by Daniel Immerwahr, *How to Hide an Empire: A History of the Greater United States* (Farrar, Straus & Giroux, 2019), 62.

304   *Turner had argued:* Erik Larson, *The Devil in the White City: Murder, Magic, and Madness at the Fair That Changed America* (Vintage, 2004), 286.

304   *war on imperial Spain:* Immerwahr, *How to Hide an Empire,* 65–73.

304   *Fred had left Washington State:* F. J. Church, letter, in *The Decennial Record of the Class of 1889, No. 4: Princeton University; 1889–1899* (Princeton Press, 1899), 29.

304   *When a steamer:* Pierre Berton, *The Klondike Fever: The Life and Death of the Last Great Gold Rush* (Basic, 2003), 107.

304   *"north with the other 49,999 chumps":* Church, letter, in *Decennial Record,* 30.

305   *Church asked her:* Church to Isabel [Downie] Church Black, July 18, 1899.

305   *"I miss my dear":* Church to Virginia Osborn, December 7, 1899.

305   *"Of course there must":* Church to Warner, October 31, 1899.

305   *"The show of wild flowers":* Church to Isabel [Downie] Church Black, November 13, 1899.

305   *chair lashed to two poles:* Church to Heade, September 10, 1898. Original in the AAA.

305   *"I really & honestly":* Frederic Joseph Church to Church, March 1, 1900.

306   *He had Bright's disease:* Isabel [Downie] Church Black Diary, May 19, 1900.

306   *special Pullman car:* "Seriously Ill. Mr. Church Returns Hurriedly to New York," *Mexican Herald,* March 24, 1900.

306   *Lying in the same bed:* Susan Hale to "Caroline," April 13, 1900.

306   *seemed cheerful:* Church Black Diary, May 19, 1900.

306   *"indomitable will":* Church Black Diary, May 19, 1900.

306   *On April 7, Theddy Cole:* Downie to Emily Cole, April [1900], CV 553, series 3, box 1, folder 16: Emily Cole (1858–1900), Thomas Cole Papers, Albany Institute of History and Art. I'm grateful to Amanda Malmstrom of the Thomas Cole National Historic Site for sharing this letter with me.

306   *"Three children survive":* "Frederic Edwin Church," unknown Hartford paper, April 7, 1900, OSHS.

306   *"His fame was world-wide":* "Frederick [*sic*] E. Church," *Evening Post,* April 9, 1900.

306   *"the last and greatest":* *Boston Transcript,* April 9, 1900, OSHS.

306   *"He had made":* "Frederic E. Church Dead," *New York Times,* April 8, 1900.

307   *"something more than admiration":* Whittredge to Virginia Osborn, April 10, 1900.

308   *"I was so overcome":* Isabel [Downie] Church Black to Warner, May 27, 1900.

308   *mapped out on the walls:* *Paintings by Frederic E. Church, N.A.: Special Exhibition at the Metropolitan Museum of Art, May 28 to October 15* (Metropolitan Museum of Art, 1900).

308   *"Years and years":* Whittredge to Osborn, April 10, 1900.

EPILOGUE   "A One-Man World's Fair"

309   *The rest of his estate:* Will of Frederic Edwin Church, 1899, OSHS.

310   *"charming and enthusiastic":* August Heckscher, audio recording of remarks delivered January 22, 1966, OSHS.

310   *Army Air Force:* "Memorials: David Carew Huntington '45," *Princeton Alumni Weekly,* February 8, 1991, 39.

310   *Huntington had never seen:* David Huntington, audio recording of remarks delivered January 22, 1966, OSHS.

310 *"I went into the house":* Charles B. Hosmer Jr., oral history interview with David C. Huntington, 1988, typescript copy, David C. Huntington Papers, OSHS, reproduced in Dorothy Heyl, ed., *The Campaign to Save Olana* (pub. by author, 2009), 5.

310 *Next to this alcove:* All the household objects described in the following pages are documented in Zukowski, *Historic Furnishings Report.*

310 *"one-man world's fair":* Huntington interview in Heyl, *Campaign to Save Olana,* 37.

311 *the picture felt overpowering:* Huntington interview, 36.

312 *"spatial explosion":* Huntington, audio recording of remarks, January 22, 1966.

312 *"fraught with meaning":* Huntington interview, 36.

312 *inside his mind:* Huntington interview, 33.

313 *staying for ten weeks:* Huntington interview, 6.

313 *awarded his Ph.D.:* Huntington interview, 8–9.

313 *"Business leaders flanked":* "Demolition Starts at Penn Station," *New York Times,* October 29, 1963.

313 *The man told him:* Huntington interview, 10.

313 *"waiting for help":* Huntington interview, 14.

314 *"If you get rid":* Huntington interview, 28.

314 *Charles Addams's cartoons:* David Schuyler, "The Preservation of Olana," in Rosenbaum and Zukowski, *Frederic Church's Olana,* 16.

314 New York Times *and* Harper's: Foster Hailey, "Fund Drive Is Begun to Save Estate on Hudson," *New York Times,* November 12, 1964; and Russell Lynes, "Persia on the Hudson," *Harper's* 230, no. 1377 (1965): 30–34.

314 *"Emerson's, Thoreau's, and Whitman's America":* Huntington, *Landscapes,* 125.

315 *exhibition of Church's work:* Schuyler, "Saving Olana," 20–21.

315 *She persuaded her brother-in-law:* Schuyler, "Preservation of Olana," 193.

315 *Only a Titian:* Rita Reif, "Frenzied Market for Major Art: $2.5 Million for 'Icebergs,'" *New York Times,* November 18, 1979.

Sources and Bibliography

Note: The titles and dates of the historical newspapers and periodicals I have consulted regarding particular events and people appear in the Notes.

Manuscript Collections

ALBANY INSTITUTE OF HISTORY AND ART
Erastus Dow Palmer Papers
Thomas Cole Collection

CENTURY ASSOCIATION, NEW YORK CITY
Board of Managers & Monthly Meeting Minutes

COOPER HEWITT, SMITHSONIAN DESIGN MUSEUM
Frederic Edwin Church Collection

COLUMBIA UNIVERSITY, RARE BOOK AND MANUSCRIPT LIBRARY
Ogden N. Rood Papers

CORNELL UNIVERSITY, DIVISION OF RARE AND
MANUSCRIPT COLLECTIONS, CARL A. KROCH LIBRARY
Bayard Taylor Papers

HISTORICAL SOCIETY OF PENNSYLVANIA, PHILADELPHIA
Frederic Edwin Church Letters

LIBRARY COMPANY OF PHILADELPHIA
Anne Hampton Brewster Papers

MACCULLOCH HALL HISTORICAL MUSEUM, MORRISTOWN, NJ
Lindley Hoffman Miller Letters

MASSACHUSETTS HISTORICAL SOCIETY, BOSTON
Appleton Family Papers

MISSOURI HISTORICAL SOCIETY ARCHIVES, ST. LOUIS
Charles Parsons Papers

NATIONAL ARCHIVES, WASHINGTON, DC
Records of the Bureau of the Census, Record Group 29

NEW YORK HISTORICAL, PATRICIA D. KLINGENSTEIN LIBRARY
American Art-Union Records
Osborn Family Papers

NEW YORK PUBLIC LIBRARY, MANUSCRIPTS, ARCHIVES AND
RARE BOOKS DIVISION
Emmet Collection
Ford Collection

NEW YORK STATE LIBRARY, MANUSCRIPTS AND SPECIAL COLLECTIONS
Thomas Cole Papers

OLANA STATE HISTORIC SITE, NEW YORK STATE OFFICE
OF PARKS, RECREATION AND HISTORIC PRESERVATION
Series 1. Correspondence of Frederic Edwin Church to Others
Series 2. Correspondence of Others to Frederic Edwin Church
Series 3. General Correspondence
Series 4. Diaries and Travel Notes of Frederic Edwin Church
Series 5. Works of Art by Frederic Edwin Church
Series 6. Certificates and Awards of the Church Family
Series 7. Miscellaneous Personal Material of Frederic Edwin Church
Series 8. Miscellaneous Personal Material of the Church Family
Series 9. Manuscripts—Poetry and Prose
Series 10. Art Exhibit Materials
Series 11. Art Criticism and Artist Biography
Series 12. Calling Cards and Greeting Cards
Series 13. Other Published Materials
Series 14. Financial Material of Frederic Edwin Church
Series 15. Financial Material of the Church Family
Series 16. Works of Other Artists
Series 17. Maps
Series 18. Photographs
Series 19. Album of the Carnes Family
Series 20. Genealogical Information
Series 21. Magazines and Newspapers
Series 22. Sheet Music and Music Books
Series 23. Additions to the Papers
Series 24. Herbaria and Miscellaneous Dried Plant Material
David Huntington Papers
Published Materials, 1845–1900

SMITHSONIAN INSTITUTION, ARCHIVES OF AMERICAN ART, WASHINGTON, DC
Frederic Edwin Church Papers
Jervis McEntee Papers
Lockwood de Forest Papers
Sanford Robinson Gifford Papers

THOMAS COLE NATIONAL HISTORIC SITE, CATSKILL, NY
Papers of the Cole Family

UNIVERSITY OF VIRGINIA LIBRARY, CHARLOTTESVILLE, VA
Shirley Plantation Records

VEDDER RESEARCH LIBRARY, FLORENCE COLE VINCENT MEMORIAL COLLECTION, COXSACKIE, NY
Theodore Cole Diary, 1857–60

WINTERTHUR MUSEUM, GARDEN AND LIBRARY, WINTERTHUR, DE
Frederic Edwin Church Letters

Digital Collections

Century Association Archives Foundation. Member Directory, 1847–1922. https://century archives.org/member-directory/.
Frederick Douglass Papers Digital Edition. Frederick Douglass Papers Project. Indiana University–Purdue University Indianapolis. https://frederickdouglasspapersproject .com/s/digitaledition.
Legacies of British Slavery Database. Center for the Study of the Legacies of British Slavery. Department of History, University College London. https://www.ucl.ac.uk/lbs/search/.
"Minutes of Proceedings of the Board of Commissioners of the Central Park," 1859–69. Historical Reports, Press Releases, and Minutes of the New York City Department of Parks and Recreation. https://www.nycgovparks.org/news/reports/archive.
"Minutes of Proceedings of the Board of Commissioners of the Department of Public Parks," 1870–74. Historical Reports, Press Releases, and Minutes of the New York City Department of Parks and Recreation. https://www.nycgovparks.org/news/reports/archive.

Weather Records

Anonymous. "Rhinebeck (NY) Meteorological Register and Diary." 1850–68. Unpublished manuscript. William L. Clements Library, University of Michigan.
Hodgsden, George B. "Thermometrical Observations." 1854–75. Unpublished manuscript. Patricia D. Klingenstein Library, The New York Historical.
Regents of the University of the State of New York. "Meteorological Observations for the Year 1844 Made Under the Directions of the University of the State of New York, at the Hudson Academy Situated in the City of Hudson in the County of Columbia." Unpublished manuscript. New York State Archives.

Regents of the University of the State of New York. "Meteorological Observations for the Year 1848 Made Under the Directions of the University of the State of New York, at the Hudson Academy Situated in the City of Hudson in the County of Columbia." Unpublished manuscript. New York State Archives.

Regents of the University of the State of New York. "Meteorological Observations for the Year 1848, Made According to the Directions of the Regents of the University of the State of New York, at the Institution for the Instruction of the Deaf & Dumb, New York City." Unpublished manuscript. New York State Archives.

Regents of the University of the State of New York. "Meteorological Observations for the Year 1848, Made According to the Directions of the Regents of the University of the State of New York, at Union Hall Academy, Situated in the Town of Jamaica, Queens County." Unpublished manuscript. New York State Archives.

City Directories

Doggett, John, and Charles R. Rode. *The New York City Directory for 1847–1848*. Doggett & Rode, 1848.

Doggett, John, and Charles R. Rode. *The New York City Directory for 1852–1853*. Doggett & Rode, 1853.

Wilson, H., ed. *Trow's New York City Directory for the Year Ending May 1, 1856*. John F. Trow, 1855.

Wilson, H., ed. *Trow's New York City Directory for the Year Ending May 1, 1860*. John F. Trow, 1859.

Published Works

PRIMARY SOURCES

Aldrich, Nelson W. *Wholesale Prices, Wages, and Transportation: Report by Mr. Aldrich from the Committee on Finance, March 3, 1893*. Government Printing Office, 1893.

American Institute of Mining, Metallurgical, and Petroleum Engineers. *Memorial of Alexander Lyman Holley*. American Institute of Mining Engineers, 1884.

Appleton, Thomas Gold. *Life and Letters of Thomas Gold Appleton*. Edited by Susan Hale. D. Appleton, 1885.

Atkinson, Caroline P., ed. *The Letters of Susan Hale*. Marshall Jones Company, 1919.

Badeau, Adam. *The Vagabond*. Rudd & Carleton, 1859.

Barnes, David M. *The Draft Riots in New York, July, 1863: The Metropolitan Police, Their Services During Riot Week, Their Honorable Record*. Baker & Godwin, 1863.

Belden, E. Porter. *New-York: Past, Present, and Future; Comprising a History of the City of New-York, a Description of Its Present Condition and an Estimate of Its Future Increase*. 2nd ed. G. P. Putnam, 1849.

Bierstadt, Albert. *The Rocky Mountains*. No pub., 1866.

Borden, Gail, Jr. *The Meat Biscuit; Invented, Patented, and Manufactured*. D. Fanshaw, 1851.

Bryant, William Cullen. *A Funeral Oration, Occasioned by the Death of Thomas Cole: Delivered Before the National Academy of Design, New-York, May 4, 1848*. D. Appleton, 1848.

Bullitt, Alexander Clark. *Rambles in the Mammoth Cave, During the Year 1844*. Morton & Griswold, 1845.

Busch, Moritz. *Guide for Travellers in Egypt and Adjacent Countries Subject to the Pasha*. Translated by W. C. Wrankmore. Trübner & Co., 1858.

Butler, Benjamin Franklin. *Autobiography and Personal Reminiscences of Major-General Benj. F. Butler: Butler's Book*. A. M. Thayer, 1892.

Butler, Benjamin Franklin. *Private and Official Correspondence of Gen. Benjamin F. Butler, During the Period of the Civil War*. Plimpton Press, 1917.

Catalogue of the Art Exhibition at the Metropolitan Fair, in Aid of the U.S. Sanitary Commission. J. F. Trow, 1864.

Catalogue of the College of New Jersey, Princeton, Year 1885–86. Princeton Press, 1885.

Catalogue of the New York Centennial Loan Exhibition. Metropolitan Museum of Art, 1876.

Catalogue of the New York Centennial Loan Exhibition. National Academy of Design, 1876.

Clark, Emmons. *History of the Seventh Regiment of New York, 1806–1889*. No pub., 1890.

Clay, Henry. *Speech at the Lexington Mass Meeting*. George F. Nesbitt, 1847.

Clemens, Samuel L. "To Orion Clemens 18 March 1861, St. Louis, Mo." In *Mark Twain's Letters, Volume 1: 1853–1866*, edited by Edgar Marquess Branch, Michael Barry Frank, Kenneth M. Sanderson, Harriet E. Smith, Lin Salamo, and Richard Bucci. University of California Press, 1988.

Cole, Thomas. "Essay on American Scenery." *American Monthly Magazine* 1 (January 1836): 1–12.

Cole, Thomas. *Lecture on Art*. Thomas Cole National Historic Site, 2020 (c. 1845).

Cummings, Thomas S. *Historic Annals of the National Academy of Design, New York Drawing Association, Etc., with Occasional Dottings by the Way-Side, from 1825 to the Present Time*. George W. Childs, 1865.

The Decennial Record of the Class of 1889, No. 4: Princeton University; 1889–1899. Princeton Press, 1899.

Dickens, Charles. *American Notes, for General Circulation*. Harper & Brothers, 1842.

Douglass, Frederick. *Which Greeley Are We Voting for?: An Address Delivered in Richmond, Virginia, on July 24, 1872*. Frederick Douglass Papers Digital Edition. Frederick Douglass Papers Project. https://frederickdouglasspapersproject.com/s/digitaledition/item/18481.

Ellis, Robert, ed. *Official Descriptive and Illustrated Catalogue of the Great Exhibition of the Works of Industry of All Nations*. Vol. 3. W. Clowes & Sons, 1851.

Emerson, Ralph Waldo. "'Address to the Citizens of Concord' on the Fugitive Slave Law, 3 May 1851." In *Emerson's Antislavery Writings*, edited by Len Gougeon and Joel Myerson. Yale University Press, 1995.

Emerson, Ralph Waldo. *Nature*. J. Munroe & Company, 1836.

Episcopal Church. *The Book of Common Prayer, and Administration of the Sacraments: And Other Rites and Ceremonies of the Church, According to the Use of the Protestant Episcopal Church in the United States of America, Together with the Psalter, or the Psalms of David*. John B. Perry, 1846.

Exhibition of the Paintings of the Late Thomas Cole, at the Gallery of the American Art-Union. Snowden & Prall, 1848.

Falconer, John. "'Thomas Cole Is No More': A Letter from John Falconer to Jasper Cropsey, February 24, 1848." *American Art Journal* 15, no. 4 (1983): 74–77.

Ferri-Pisani, Camille. *Prince Napoleon in America, 1861: Letters from His Aide-de-Camp*. Translated by Georges Joyaux. Indiana University Press, 1959.

Field, Henry M. *The Story of the Atlantic Telegraph*. Scribner's Sons, 1892.

French, Harry W. *Art and Artists in Connecticut*. Charles T. Dillingham, 1879.

General Grant: His Life and Services. Cameron and Ferguson, 1885.

Greeley, Horace. *Glances at Europe: In a Series of Letters from Great Britain, France, Italy, Switzerland, Etc., During the Summer of 1851. Including Notices of the Great Exhibition, or World's Fair*. Dewitt & Davenport, 1852.

A Handbook for Travellers in Southern Germany. John Murray, 1873.

Hawthorne, Nathaniel. *The Marble Faun*. Hurst & Company, 1860.

H. L. S. and L. H. S., eds. *Phillips Brooks Year Book*. E. P. Dutton, 1894.

Holmes, Theodore J. *A Memorial of John S. Jameson, Sergeant in the 1st Conn. Cavalry, Who Died at Andersonville, Ga*. No pub., 1867.

Hone, Philip. *The Diary of Philip Hone, 1828–1851*. Edited by Allan Nevins. Dodd, Mead, 1927.

Humboldt, Alexander von. *Briefe Alexander's von Humboldt an Seinen Bruder Wilhelm*. Edited by Familie von Humboldt. Verlag der J. G. Cotta'schen Buchhandlung, 1880.

Humboldt, Alexander von. *Cosmos: A Sketch of a Physical Description of the Universe*. Vols. 1 and 2. Translated by E. C. Otté. Henry G. Bohn, 1849.

Humboldt, Alexander von. *Researches, Concerning the Institutions & Monuments of the Ancient Inhabitants of America: With Descriptions and Views of Some of the Most Striking Scenes in the Cordilleras!* Translated by Helen Maria Williams. 2 vols. Longman, Hurst, Rees, Orme & Brown, J. Murray & H. Colburn, 1814.

Irving, Pierre Munroe. *The Life and Letters of Washington Irving*. Vol. 4. G. P. Putnam, 1864.

Jackson, Lewis Evens. *Walks About New York: Facts and Figures Gathered from Various Sources*. New-York Historical Society, 1865.

Janvier, Thomas Allibone. *The Mexican Guide*. Charles Scribner's Sons, 1886.

Jefferson, Thomas. *Notes on the State of Virginia*. John Stockdale, 1787.

J.G. "On the Pernicious Influence of Inconsistencies in the Conduct of Christians." In vol. 9 of *The Imperial Magazine; Or, Compendium of Religious, Moral, & Philosophical Knowledge*, edited by S. Drew. Caxton Press, 1827.

Judson, Isabella Field. *Cyrus W. Field: His Life and Work, 1819–1892*. Harper & Brothers, 1896.

Kidder, Charles Holland, ed. *Burley's United States Centennial Gazetteer and Guide*. S. W. Burley, 1876.

Lanman, Charles. *Haphazard Personalities; Chiefly of Noted Americans*. Lee & Shepard Publishers, 1886.

Lathers, Richard. *Reminiscences of Richard Lathers: Sixty Years of a Busy Life in South Carolina, Massachusetts and New York*. Edited by Alvan F. Sanborn. Grafton Press, 1907.

Latimer, H. I. *Manhattan Railway: Official Map and Guide to All the Elevated Railways in New York City*. No pub., 1881.

Martin, Edward Sanford. *The Life of Joseph Hodges Choate: As Gathered Chiefly from His Letters*. Vol. 1. Charles Scribner's Sons, 1920.

Mather, Increase. *The Voice of God, in Stormy Winds. Considered, in Two Sermons, Occasioned by the Dreadful and Unparallel'd Storm, in the European Nations. Novemb. 27th. 1703*. Boston: Printed by T. Green, for Nicholas Buttolph, 1704.

Maury, Matthew Fontaine. *The Physical Geography of the Sea*. Harper & Brothers, 1859.

McCabe, James D. *The Illustrated History of the Centennial Exhibition*. National Publishing Company, 1876.

Melville, Herman. *Journal up the Straits*. Edited by Raymond M. Weaver. Colophon, 1935.

Melville, Herman. *Moby-Dick, or, the Whale*. Harper & Brothers, 1851.

Moscheles, Felix. *Fragments of an Autobiography*. Harper & Brothers, 1899.

Mullaly, John. *The Laying of the Cable, or the Ocean Telegraph; Being a Complete and Authentic Narrative of the Attempt to Lay the Cable Across the Entrance to the Gulf of St. Lawrence in 1855, and of the Three Atlantic Telegraph Expeditions of 1857 and 1858*. D. Appleton, 1858.

National Academy of Design Exhibition Record: 1826–1860. 2 vols. New-York Historical Society, 1943.

Niagara. The Great Fall. By Frederic Edward [sic] Church. Williams, Stevens, Williams & Co., 1857.

Nicolay, John G., and John Hay, eds. *Complete Works of Abraham Lincoln*. Vol. 6. Francis D. Tandy Company, 1905.

Noble, Louis Legrand. *After Icebergs with a Painter: A Summer Voyage to Labrador and Around Newfoundland.* D. Appleton, 1861.

Noble, Louis Legrand. *The Course of Empire, Voyage of Life, and Other Pictures of Thomas Cole, N.A., with Selections from His Letters and Miscellaneous Writings: Illustrative of His Life, Character, and Genius.* Cornish, Lamport & Co., 1853.

Noble, Louis Legrand. *The Life and Works of Thomas Cole, N.A.* Sheldon, Blakeman & Company, 1856.

Olmsted, Frederick Law. *A Journey in the Seaboard Slave States: With Remarks on Their Economy.* Dix & Edwards, 1856.

Olmsted, Frederick Law. *Journeys and Explorations in the Cotton Kingdom.* S. Low, Son & Co., 1861.

Olmsted, Frederick Law. *The Papers of Frederick Law Olmsted.* Vol. 6. *The Years of Olmsted, Vaux & Company: 1865–1874.* Edited by David Schuyler, Jane Turner Censer, Carolyn F. Hoffman, and Kenneth Hawkins. Johns Hopkins University Press, 1992.

Paintings by Frederic E. Church, N.A.: Special Exhibition at the Metropolitan Museum of Art, May 28 to October 15. Metropolitan Museum of Art, 1900.

Payson, George. *Totemwell.* Riker, Thorne & Company, 1854.

Porter, Josias Leslie. *A Handbook for Travellers in Syria and Palestine.* Vol. 1. John Murray, 1868.

Quinquennial Catalogue of the Officers and Graduates of Harvard University: 1636–1910. Harvard University, 1910.

A Record of the Metropolitan Fair: In Aid of the United States Sanitary Commission, Held at New York, in April, 1864. Hurd & Houghton, 1867.

Report of the Council of Hygiene and Public Health of the Citizens' Association of New York upon the Sanitary Condition of the City. D. Appleton, 1865.

Report of the Treasurer of the Metropolitan Fair: In Aid of the United States Sanitary Commission. 1864.

Reports on the Philadelphia International Exhibition of 1876: Presented to Both Houses of Parliament by Command of Her Majesty. Vol. 1. G. E. Eyre and W. Spottiswoode, 1877.

Rodgers, Charles T. *American Superiority at the World's Fair.* John J. Hawkins, 1852.

Ruffin, Edmund. *The Diary of Edmund Ruffin.* Vol. 2. Edited by William Kauffman Scarborough. LSU Press, 1976.

Ruggles, Edward. *A Picture of New-York in 1848.* C. S. Francis, 1848.

Ruskin, John. *Modern Painters.* Vol. 1. Wiley & Putnam, 1847.

Sandhurst, Philip T. *The Great Centennial Exhibition.* P. W. Ziegler & Company, 1876.

Saunders, Frederick, ed. *Addresses, Historical and Patriotic, Centennial and Quadrennial, Delivered in the Several States of the Union: July 4th, 1876–1883.* E. B. Treat, 1893.

Sewell, William G. *The Ordeal of Free Labor in the British West Indies.* Harper & Brothers, 1861.

Shelley, Percy Bysshe. *The Major Works.* Oxford University Press, 2003.

Stillman, William James. *The Autobiography of a Journalist.* Vol. 1. Houghton Mifflin, 1901.

Stowe, Harriet Beecher. *Uncle Tom's Cabin.* 2 vols. John P. Jewett, 1852.

Strabo. *The Geography of Strabo: Literally Tr., with Notes.* Translated by W. Falconer and Hans Claude Hamilton. H. G. Bohn, 1854.

Strong, George Templeton. *The Diary of George Templeton Strong.* Edited by Allan Nevins and Milton Halsey Thomas. 4 vols. Macmillan, 1952.

Thoreau, Henry David. *The Maine Woods.* Edited by William Ellery Channing and Sophia E. Thoreau. Ticknor & Fields, 1864.

Tracy, Charles. *The Tracy Log Book, 1855: A Month in Summer.* Edited by Anne Mazlish. Acadia Publishing, 1997.

Tuckerman, Henry T. *Book of the Artists: American Artist Life, Comprising Biographical and Critical Sketches of American Artists.* G. P. Putnam & Sons, 1867.

Twain, Mark, and Charles Dudley Warner. *The Gilded Age: A Tale of To-Day.* American Publishing Company, 1873.

Warburton, Eliot. *The Crescent and the Cross, or, Romance and Realities of Eastern Travel.* Vol. 2. Henry Colburn, 1846.

Warner, Charles Dudley. "An Unfinished Biography of the Artist (1899)." In Franklin Kelly, with Stephen Jay Gould, James Anthony Ryan, and Debora Rindge, *Frederic Edwin Church.* National Gallery of Art, 1989.

Weir, John F. *The Recollections of John Ferguson Weir, Director of the Yale School of the Fine Arts, 1869–1913.* Edited by Theodore Sizer. New-York Historical Society, 1957.

Whittredge, Worthington. *The Autobiography of Worthington Whittredge, 1820–1910.* Edited by John I. H. Baur. Brooklyn Museum Press, 1942.

Wilson, John. *The Lands of the Bible: Visited and Described in an Extensive Journey Undertaken with Special Reference to the Promotion of Biblical Research and the Advancement of the Cause of Philanthropy.* Vol. 1. William Whyte, 1847.

Winthrop, Theodore. *A Companion to the Heart of the Andes.* D. Appleton, 1859.

Winthrop, Theodore. *The Life and Poems of Theodore Winthrop.* Edited by Laura Winthrop Johnson. Henry Holt, 1884.

Winthrop, Theodore. *Life in the Open Air, and Other Papers.* Ticknor & Fields, 1863.

SECONDARY SOURCES

Ackerman, William K. *Historical Sketch of the Illinois-Central Railroad, Together with a Brief Biographical Record of Its Incorporators and Some of Its Early Officers.* Fergus Printing Company, 1890.

Adamson, Jeremy Elwell. "Frederic Edwin Church's 'Niagara': The Sublime as Transcendence." Ph.D. diss., University of Michigan, 1981.

Allen, Robert. *Horrible Prettiness: Burlesque and American Culture.* University of North Carolina Press, 1991.

Anderson, Nancy K., and Linda S. Ferber. *Albert Bierstadt: Art and Enterprise.* Brooklyn Museum / Hudson Hills Press, 1990.

Appelbaum, Nancy P. *Mapping the Country of Regions: The Chorographic Commission of Nineteenth-Century Colombia.* University of North Carolina Press, 2016.

Avery, Kevin J. *Church's Great Picture: The Heart of the Andes.* Metropolitan Museum of Art, 1993.

Avery, Kevin J. "'The Finest Edifice on the Finest Site in the World': Church's *Parthenon.*" In *Frederic Church: A Painter's Pilgrimage,* by Kenneth John Myers, Kevin J. Avery, Gerald L. Carr, and Mercedes Volait. Detroit Institute of Arts and Yale University Press, 2017.

Avery, Kevin J. "Gifford and the Catskills." In *Hudson River School Visions: The Landscapes of Sanford R. Gifford,* edited by Kevin J. Avery and Franklin Kelly. Metropolitan Museum of Art, 2003.

Avery, Kevin J. "'The Heart of the Andes' Exhibited: Frederic E. Church's Window on the Equatorial World." *American Art Journal* 18, no. 1 (1986): 52–72.

Avery, Kevin J. "'Rally 'Round the Flag': Frederic Edwin Church and the Civil War." *Hudson River Valley Review,* Spring 2011, 66–103.

Baetjer, Katharine. "Buying Pictures for New York: The Founding Purchase of 1871." *Metropolitan Museum Journal* 38 (2003): 169–81.

Baetjer, Katharine, and Joan R. Mertens. "The Founding Decades." In *Making the Met, 1870–2020,* edited by Andrea Bayer and Laura D. Corey. Metropolitan Museum of Art, 2020.

Baker, Charles E. "The American Art-Union." In *American Academy of Fine Arts and American Art-Union, Exhibition Record: 1816–1852*, vol. 1, edited by Mary Bartlett Cowdrey. New-York Historical Society, 1953.

Balint, Valerie. "Jervis McEntee and Church: Reflections on a Forty-Year Friendship," Olana State Historic Site, September 24, 2015.

Barratt, Carrie Rebora. "Mapping the Venues: New York City Art Exhibitions." In *Art and the Empire City: New York, 1825–1861*, edited by Catherine Hoover Voorsanger and John K. Howat. Metropolitan Museum of Art, 2000.

Barringer, Tim. "Land, Labor, Landscape: Views of the Plantation in Victorian Jamaica." In *Victorian Jamaica*, edited by Tim Barringer and Wayne Modest. Duke University Press, 2018.

Barringer, Tim. "Thomas Cole's Atlantic Crossings." In Elizabeth Mankin Kornhauser and Tim Barringer, *Thomas Cole's Journey: Atlantic Crossings*. Metropolitan Museum of Art and Yale University Press, 2018.

Barringer, Tim. "A White Atlantic? The Idea of American Art in Nineteenth-Century Britain." *19: Interdisciplinary Studies in the Long Nineteenth Century*, no. 9 (November 2009): 1–26.

Barringer, Tim, Elizabeth Mankin Kornhauser, and Jennifer Raab, eds. *Frederic Church: Global Artist*. Yale University Press, 2026.

Barringer, Tim, and Wayne Modest, eds. *Victorian Jamaica*. Duke University Press, 2018.

Barry, Kathleen. *Susan B. Anthony: A Biography*. New York University Press, 2020.

Bassett, Lynne Zacek. *Costume and Custom: Middle Eastern Threads at Olana*. Olana Partnership, 2018.

Bedell, Rebecca. *The Anatomy of Nature: Geology and American Landscape Painting, 1825–1875*. Princeton University Press, 2002.

Bell, Adrienne Baxter. *George Inness and the Visionary Landscape*. George Braziller, 2015.

Bergdoll, Barry, Sean E. Sawyer, and Thomas L. Woltz. *Olana: Frederic Church's Vision of Architecture and Landscape*. Rizzoli Electa, 2026.

Berthold, Dennis. "Class Acts: The Astor Place Riots and Melville's 'The Two Temples.'" *American Literature* 71, no. 3 (1999): 429–61.

Berton, Pierre. *The Klondike Fever: The Life and Death of the Last Great Gold Rush*. Basic, 2003.

Berton, Pierre. *Niagara: A History of the Falls*. Anchor Canada, 2002.

Blackhawk, Ned. *The Rediscovery of America: Native Peoples and the Unmaking of U.S. History*. Yale University Press, 2023.

Blaugrund, Annette. "The Tenth Street Studio Building: A Roster, 1857–1895." *American Art Journal* 14, no. 2 (1982): 64–71.

Blaugrund, Annette. *The Tenth Street Studio Building: Artist-Entrepreneurs from the Hudson River School to the American Impressionists*. Parrish Art Museum, 1997.

Blight, David W. *Frederick Douglass: Prophet of Freedom*. Simon & Schuster, 2018.

Braddock, Alan C. "Icon of Extinction and Resilience." In Karl Kusserow and Alan C. Braddock, *Nature's Nation: American Art and Environment*. Princeton University Art Museum, 2018.

Braddock, Alan C. *Implication: An Ecocritical Dictionary for Art History*. Yale University Press, 2023.

Brennecke, Mishoe. *Jasper F. Cropsey: Artist and Architect*. New-York Historical Society, 1987.

Brown, Vincent. *The Reaper's Garden: Death and Power in the World of Atlantic Slavery*. Harvard University Press, 2008.

Burke, Doreen Bolger. "Frederic Edwin Church and 'The Banner of Dawn.'" *American Art Journal* 14, no. 2 (1982): 39–46.

Burrows, Edwin G., and Mike Wallace. *Gotham: A History of New York City to 1898*. Oxford University Press, 1998.

Bush, Robert. "Grace King and Mark Twain." *American Literature* 44, no. 1 (March 1972): 31–51.

Camuto, Christopher. *Time and Tide in Acadia: Seasons on Mount Desert Island*. Countryman Press, 2011.

Cao, Maggie M. *The End of Landscape in Nineteenth-Century America*. University of California Press, 2018.

Carr, Gerald L. "Early Documentation of *The Icebergs*." In *The Voyage of the* Icebergs: *Frederic Church's Arctic Masterpiece*, by Eleanor Jones Harvey and Gerald L. Carr. Dallas Museum of Art, 2002.

Carr, Gerald L. *Frederic Edwin Church: Catalogue Raisonné of Works of Art at Olana State Historic Site*. 2 vols. Cambridge University Press, 1994.

Carr, Gerald L. *In Search of the Promised Land: Paintings by Frederic Edwin Church*. Berry-Hill Galleries, 2000.

Carr, Gerald L. "'The Land of Sacred Romance': To the Holy Land and Back." In *Frederic Church: A Painter's Pilgrimage*, by Kenneth John Myers, Kevin J. Avery, Gerald L. Carr, and Mercedes Volait. Detroit Institute of Arts and Yale University Press, 2017.

Carr, Gerald L. "*Niagara & Baalbek*: Two Recently Rediscovered Paintings by Frederic Edwin Church." *American Fine Art Magazine*, no. 37 (February 2018): 34–43.

Carr, Gerald L., and David C. Huntington. *Frederic Edwin Church: The Icebergs*. Dallas Museum of Fine Arts, 1980.

Carter, Samuel, III. *Cyrus W. Field: Man of Two Worlds*. G. P. Putnam's Sons, 1968.

Cash, Sarah. "'Encouraging American Genius': Collecting American Art at the Corcoran Gallery of Art." In *Corcoran Gallery of Art: American Paintings to 1945*, edited by Sarah Cash. Corcoran Gallery of Art, 2012.

Chernow, Ron. *Grant*. Penguin Press, 2017.

Chernow, Ron. *Mark Twain*. Penguin Press, 2025.

Chivallon, Christine, and David Howard. "Colonial Violence and Civilising Utopias in the French and British Empires: The Morant Bay Rebellion (1865) and the Insurrection of the South (1870)." *Slavery & Abolition* 38, no. 3 (July 3, 2017): 534–58.

Clark, Eliot. *History of the National Academy of Design, 1825–1953*. Columbia University Press, 1954.

Cohen, Philip L. "The Arthritis of Frederic E. Church." *Journal of Rheumatology* 24, no. 7 (1997): 1453–54.

Coleman, William L. "Foreword." In Louis Legrand Noble, *After Icebergs with a Painter*. Black Dome Press, 2022.

Coleman, William L. "What Was Photography to Frederic Church?" In David Hartt, Sean E. Sawyer, William L. Coleman, and Corey Keller, *Terraforming: Olana's Historic Photography Collection Unearthed*. Olana Partnership, 2023.

Cosy Cottage Historic Structure Report. New York State Office of Parks, Recreation and Historic Preservation, 2001.

Cozzens, Peter. *The Earth Is Weeping: The Epic Story of the Indian Wars for the American West*. Alfred A. Knopf, 2016.

Cross, William R. *Winslow Homer: American Passage*. Farrar, Straus & Giroux, 2022.

Cummings, Hildegard. *Charles Ethan Porter: African-American Master of Still Life*. New Britain Museum of American Art, 2007.

Cunliffe, Marcus. "America at the Great Exhibition of 1851." *American Quarterly* 3, no. 2 (1951): 115–26.

Dalrymple, William, and Anita Anand. *Koh-i-Noor: The History of the World's Most Infamous Diamond*. Bloomsbury, 2017.

Davis, Allegra K. "'A Fitting Monument': Frederic Church and the Memorial Landscape." In *Afterglow: Frederic Church and the Landscape of Memory*, edited by Allegra K. Davis with contributions from Sean Sawyer and Rebecca Bedell. Hirmer, 2024.

Davis, John. *The Landscape of Belief: Encountering the Holy Land in Nineteenth-Century American Art and Culture*. Princeton University Press, 1996.

Davis, P. Thompson, Paul R. Bierman, Lee B. Corbett, and Robert C. Finkel. "Cosmogenic Exposure Age Evidence for Rapid Laurentide Deglaciation of the Katahdin Area, West-Central Maine, USA, 16 to 15 Ka." *Quaternary Science Reviews* 116 (May 15, 2015): 95–105.

Davis, Wade. *Magdalena*. Bodley Head, 2020.

Dean, William J. "Preface." In *The New York Society Library: 250 Years*, edited by Henry S. F. Cooper Jr. and Jenny Lawrence. New York Society Library, 2004.

Diazgranados, Mauricio. "A Nomenclator for the Frailejones (Espeletiinae Cuatrec., Asteraceae)." *PhytoKeys* 16 (August 21, 2012): 1–52.

Driscoll, John Paul. "From Burin to Brush: The Development of a Painter." In John Paul Driscoll and John K. Howat, *John Frederick Kensett: An American Master*. W. W. Norton, 1985.

Dykstra, Natalie. *Chasing Beauty: The Life of Isabella Stewart Gardner*. Mariner, 2024.

Edwards, Holly. *Noble Dreams, Wicked Pleasures: Orientalism in America, 1870–1930*. Princeton University Press, 2000.

Eliot, Ellsworth, Jr. *Theodore Winthrop*. Yale University Library, 1938.

Evers, Alf. *The Catskills: From Wilderness to Woodstock*. Revised and updated ed. Overlook Press, 1982.

Fleming, James Rodger. *Meteorology in America, 1800–1870*. Johns Hopkins University Press, 1990.

Foner, Eric. *The Fiery Trial: Abraham Lincoln and American Slavery*. W. W. Norton, 2011.

Foner, Eric. *Reconstruction: America's Unfinished Revolution, 1863–1877*. Updated ed. Harper Perennial Modern Classics, 2014.

Foner, Philip S. "Black Participation in the Centennial of 1876." *Phylon* 39, no. 4 (1978): 283–96.

Foreman, Amanda. *A World on Fire: Britain's Crucial Role in the American Civil War*. Random House, 2012.

Freeman, Joanne B. *The Field of Blood: Violence in Congress and the Road to Civil War*. Farrar, Straus & Giroux, 2018.

Frost, Karolyn Smardz. "The Cataract House Hotel: Underground to Canada Through the Niagara River Borderlands." In *Harriet's Legacies: Race, Historical Memory, and Futures in Canada*, edited by Ronald Cummings and Natalee Caple. McGill-Queen's University Press, 2022.

Fuller, Randall. *The Book That Changed America: How Darwin's Theory of Evolution Ignited a Nation*. Penguin, 2018.

Gallati, Barbara Dayer. "Asher B. Durand's Early Career." In *Kindred Spirits: Asher B. Durand and the American Landscape*, edited by Linda S. Ferber. Brooklyn Museum, 2007.

Goodheart, Adam. *1861: The Civil War Awakening*. Alfred A. Knopf, 2011.

Gordon, Ann D., ed. *The Selected Papers of Elizabeth Cady Stanton and Susan B. Anthony: National Protection for National Citizens, 1873 to 1880*. Vol. 3. Rutgers University Press, 1997.

Gordon, John Steele. *A Thread Across the Ocean: The Heroic Story of the Transatlantic Cable*. Walker, 2002.

Gorn, Elliott J. "'Good-Bye Boys, I Die a True American': Homicide, Nativism, and Working-Class Culture in Antebellum New York City." *Journal of American History* 74, no. 2 (1987): 388–410.

Gould, Stephen Jay. "Church, Humboldt, and Darwin: The Tension and Harmony of Art and Science." In Franklin Kelly, with Stephen Jay Gould, James Anthony Ryan, and Debora Rindge, *Frederic Edwin Church*. National Gallery of Art, 1989.

Green, Tyler. *Claiming Yosemite: The California Genocide, the Civil War, and the Invention of National Parks*. Stanford University Press / Redwood Press, forthcoming.

Green, Tyler. *Emerson's* Nature *and the Artists: Idea as Landscape, Landscape as Idea*. Prestel, 2021.

Hall, Minard, and Patricia Mothes. "The Rhyolitic–Andesitic Eruptive History of Cotopaxi Volcano, Ecuador." *Bulletin of Volcanology* 70, no. 6 (2008): 675–702.

Harris, Leslie M. *In the Shadow of Slavery: African Americans in New York City, 1626–1863*. University of Chicago Press, 2003.

Harvey, Eleanor Jones. *Alexander von Humboldt and the United States: Art, Nature, and Culture*. Princeton University Press, 2020.

Harvey, Eleanor Jones. *The Civil War and American Art*. Yale University Press, 2012.

Harvey, Eleanor Jones. *The Painted Sketch: American Impressions from Nature, 1830–1880*. Dallas Museum of Art, 1998.

Harvey, Eleanor Jones. "The Tip of *The Icebergs*." In Eleanor Jones Harvey and Gerald L. Carr, *The Voyage of the* Icebergs: *Frederic Church's Arctic Masterpiece*. Dallas Museum of Art, 2002.

Harvey, Eleanor Jones, and Gerald L. Carr. *The Voyage of the* Icebergs: *Frederic Church's Arctic Masterpiece*. Dallas Museum of Art, 2002.

Hassrick, Peter H. "Albert Bierstadt: Witness to a Changing West." In *Albert Bierstadt: Witness to a Changing West*, edited by Peter H. Hassrick. University of Oklahoma Press, 2018.

Hawksley, Lucinda. *Bitten by Witch Fever: Wallpaper and Arsenic in the Victorian Home*. Thames & Hudson, 2016.

Heckscher, Morrison H. "The Metropolitan Museum of Art: An Architectural History." *Metropolitan Museum of Art Bulletin* 53, no. 1 (1995): 1–80.

Hennessey, Maureen Hart. *Life at Cedar Grove*. Thomas Cole National Historic Site, 2011.

Heyl, Dorothy, ed. *The Campaign to Save Olana*. Self-published, 2009.

Heyrman, Christine Leigh. *American Apostles: When Evangelicals Entered the World of Islam*. Hill & Wang, 2015.

Hill, Lelon Avalon. "British Criticism of American Literature 1844–1860 as Reflected in *Littell's Living Age*." Master's thesis, University of New Mexico, 1940.

Hirsch, Robert. *Seizing the Light: A History of Photography*. McGraw Hill, 2000.

Hodes, Martha. *Mourning Lincoln*. Yale University Press, 2015.

Hoffmann, Robert. "Die Entstehung einer Legende. Alexander von Humboldts angeblicher Ausspruch über Salzburg." *HiN—Alexander von Humboldt im Netz. Internationale Zeitschrift für Humboldt-Studien* 7, no. 12 (2006).

Holzer, Harold. *Lincoln and the Power of the Press: The War for Public Opinion*. Simon & Schuster, 2014.

Holzer, Harold. *Lincoln at Cooper Union: The Speech That Made Abraham Lincoln President*. Simon & Schuster, 2004.

Holzer, Harold. *Lincoln President-Elect: Abraham Lincoln and the Great Secession Winter, 1860–1861*. Simon & Schuster, 2008.

Howat, John K. *Frederic Church*. Yale University Press, 2005.

Howat, John K. "Kensett's World." In John Paul Driscoll and John K. Howat, *John Frederick Kensett: An American Master*. W. W. Norton, 1985.

Howat, John K., Kevin J. Avery, Oswaldo Rodriguez Roque, Doreen Bolger Burke, and Catherine Hoover Voorsanger. *American Paradise: The World of the Hudson River School*. Metropolitan Museum of Art, 1987.

Howe, Winifred Eva, and Henry Watson Kent. *A History of the Metropolitan Museum of Art.* Metropolitan Museum of Art, 1913.

Hunter, Matthew C. "Graphic Making, Actuarial Knowing: Transfer and Countertransference in Frederic Edwin Church's South American Drawings." *West 86th: A Journal of Decorative Arts, Design History, and Material Culture* 23, no. 1 (Spring–Summer 2016): 56–78.

Huntington, David C. "Church and Luminism." In *American Light: The Luminist Movement, 1850–1875,* edited by John Wilmerding. Harper & Row / National Gallery of Art, 1980.

Huntington, David C. *The Landscapes of Frederic Edwin Church: Vision of an American Era.* George Braziller, 1966.

Immerwahr, Daniel. *How to Hide an Empire: A History of the Greater United States.* Farrar, Straus & Giroux, 2019.

Jacks, Elizabeth B. "Director's Foreword." In John Wilmerding, *Master, Mentor, Master: Thomas Cole & Frederic Church.* Thomas Cole National Historic Site, 2014.

John G. Waite Associates. *Olana Historic Structure Report.* 2001.

John G. Waite Associates. *Thomas Cole House: Historic Structure Report.* Vol 1. Thomas Cole National Historic Site, 2019.

Kachun, Mitch. "Before the Eyes of All Nations: African-American Identity and Historical Memory at the Centennial Exposition of 1876." *Pennsylvania History: A Journal of Mid-Atlantic Studies* 65, no. 3 (1998): 300–323.

Kaplan, Justin. *Walt Whitman: A Life.* Simon & Schuster, 1980.

Kastenberg, Joshua E. *The Blackstone of Military Law: Colonel William Winthrop.* Scarecrow Press, 2009.

Kelly, Franklin. *American Paintings of the Nineteenth Century, Part I.* With Nicolai Cikovsky Jr., Deborah Chotner, and John Davis. National Gallery of Art and Oxford University Press, 1996.

Kelly, Franklin. *Frederic Edwin Church and the National Landscape.* Smithsonian Institution Press, 1988.

Kelly, Franklin. "Frederic Edwin Church and the North American Landscape, 1845–60." Ph.D. diss., University of Delaware, 1985.

Kelly, Franklin. "A Passion for Landscape: The Paintings of Frederic Edwin Church." In Franklin Kelly, with Stephen Jay Gould, James Anthony Ryan, and Debora Rindge, *Frederic Edwin Church.* National Gallery of Art, 1989.

Kelly, Franklin. "Turner and America." In *J. M. W. Turner,* edited by Ian Warrell. Metropolitan Museum of Art, 2007.

Kelly, Franklin, and Gerald L. Carr. *The Early Landscapes of Frederic Edwin Church, 1845–1854.* Amon Carter Museum, 1987.

Kelly, Franklin, with Stephen Jay Gould, James Anthony Ryan, and Debora Rindge. *Frederic Edwin Church.* National Gallery of Art, 1989.

Kennedy, David. "Travellers of 1857 to Petra." In *Refereed Proceedings of the First Conference on the Archaeology and Tourism of the Maan Governorate, 3rd–4th October 2017, Petra-Jordan,* edited by Zeyad M. Al-Salameen and Mohammad B. Tarawneh. Al-Hussein Bin Talal University, Maan, 2018.

Ketner, Joseph D. *The Emergence of the African-American Artist: Robert S. Duncanson, 1821–1872.* University of Missouri Press, 1993.

Klein, Rachel N. "Art and Authority in Antebellum New York City: The Rise and Fall of the American Art-Union." *Journal of American History* 81, no. 4 (1995): 1534–61.

Koeppel, Gerald T. *Water for Gotham: A History.* Princeton University Press, 2001.

Kornhauser, Elizabeth Mankin. "Daniel Wadsworth and Elizabeth Hart Jarvis Colt: Connecticut's Leading Collectors of American Landscape Art." In *Tastemakers, Collectors, and*

Patrons: Collecting American Art in the Long Nineteenth Century, edited by Linda S. Ferber and Margaret R. Laster. Penn State University Press and the Frick Collection, 2024.

Kornhauser, Elizabeth Mankin. "Frederic Edwin Church's Landscapes of Jamaica." In Elizabeth Mankin Kornhauser and Katherine E. Manthorne, *Fern Hunting Among These Picturesque Mountains: Frederic Edwin Church in Jamaica*. Cornell University Press, 2010.

Kornhauser, Elizabeth Mankin. "Manifesto for an American Sublime: Thomas Cole's 'The Oxbow.'" In Elizabeth Mankin Kornhauser and Tim Barringer, *Thomas Cole's Journey: Atlantic Crossings*. Yale University Press, 2018.

Kornhauser, Elizabeth Mankin, and Tim Barringer, with Dorothy Mahon, Christopher Riopelle, and Shannon Vittoria. *Thomas Cole's Journey: Atlantic Crossings*. Yale University Press, 2018.

Kornhauser, Elizabeth Mankin, and Katherine E. Manthorne. *Fern Hunting Among These Picturesque Mountains: Frederic Edwin Church in Jamaica*. Cornell University Press, 2010.

Kowsky, Francis R. *Country, Park & City: The Architecture and Life of Calvert Vaux*. Oxford University Press, 1998.

Kunhardt, Philip B., Jr., Philip B. Kunhardt III, and Peter W. Kunhardt. *P. T. Barnum: America's Greatest Showman*. Alfred A. Knopf, 1995.

Kusserow, Karl. "The Trouble with Empire." In Karl Kusserow and Alan C. Braddock, *Nature's Nation: American Art and Environment*. Princeton University Art Museum, 2018.

Larson, Erik. *The Demon of Unrest: A Saga of Hubris, Heartbreak, and Heroism at the Dawn of the Civil War*. Crown, 2024.

Larson, Erik. *The Devil in the White City: Murder, Magic, and Madness at the Fair That Changed America*. Vintage, 2004.

Lawler, Andrew. *Under Jerusalem: The Buried History of the World's Most Contested City*. Doubleday, 2021.

Leak, William B., and Mariko Yamasaki. *Tree Species Migration Studies in the White Mountains of New Hampshire*. Research Paper NRS-RP-19. US Forest Service, Northern Research Station, 2012.

Leja, Michael. "Monet's Modernity in New York in 1886." *American Art* 14, no. 1 (2000): 51–79.

Lett, Amanda, Patricia Hills, Peter John Brownlee, and Randy Ramer. *Perfectly American: The Art-Union & Its Artists*. With Duane H. King. Gilcrease Museum, 2011.

Lewis, Sarah. *The Unseen Truth: When Race Changed Sight in America*. Harvard University Press, 2024.

Lewis, Tom. *The Hudson: A History*. Yale University Press, 2005.

Lovell, Mary S. *A Scandalous Life: The Biography of Jane Digby*. Fourth Estate, 1995.

Loving, Jerome. *Walt Whitman: The Song of Himself*. University of California Press, 2000.

Lynford, Sophie. *Painting Dissent: Art, Ethics, and the American Pre-Raphaelites*. Princeton University Press, 2022.

Lynford, Sophie. "Patrons of Reform: Collecting the American Pre-Raphaelites." In *Tastemakers, Collectors, and Patrons: Collecting American Art in the Long Nineteenth Century*, edited by Linda S. Ferber and Margaret R. Laster. Penn State University Press and the Frick Collection, 2024.

Maher, James P., ed. *Index to Marriages and Deaths in the New York World: 1860–1865*. Genealogical Publishing Company, 2006.

Malmstrom, Amanda. "'Catskill China Painter': The Art of Emily Cole." In *The Art of Emily Cole*, edited by Kate Menconeri and Amanda Malmstrom. Thomas Cole National Historic Site, 2024.

Malmstrom, Amanda. "'Live and Breathe the Soft Air': Emily Cole's Garden-to-Plate Art Practice and an Expanded Legacy of the Thomas Cole National Historic Site." In *Emily*

Cole: Ceramics, Flora & Contemporary Responses, edited by Kate Menconeri and Amanda Malmstrom. Thomas Cole National Historic Site, 2025.

Manthorne, Katherine. *Creation & Renewal: Views of Cotopaxi by Frederic Edwin Church*. Smithsonian Institution Press, 1985.

Manthorne, Katherine. *Restless Enterprise: The Art and Life of Eliza Pratt Greatorex*. University of California Press, 2020.

Manthorne, Katherine. *Tropical Renaissance: North American Artists Exploring Latin America, 1839–1879*. Smithsonian Institution Press, 1989.

Manthorne, Katherine E., and John W. Coffey. *The Landscapes of Louis Rémy Mignot: A Southern Painter Abroad*. Smithsonian Institution Press, 1996.

Marley, Anna O., ed. *Henry Ossawa Tanner: Modern Spirit*. University of California Press, 2012.

Mayer, Roberta A. *Lockwood de Forest: Furnishing the Gilded Age with a Passion for India*. University of Delaware Press, 2009.

McCoubrey, John W., ed. *American Art 1700–1960: Sources and Documents*. Prentice Hall, 1965.

McCullough, David. *The Great Bridge: The Epic Story of the Building of the Brooklyn Bridge*. 40th Anniversary Edition. Simon & Schuster, 2012.

McGoogan, Ken. *Fatal Passage: The Untold Story of John Rae, the Arctic Adventurer Who Discovered the Fate of Franklin*. HarperPerennialCanada, 2001.

McKinsey, Elizabeth. *Niagara Falls: Icon of the American Sublime*. Cambridge University Press, 1985.

McPherson, James M. *Battle Cry of Freedom: The Civil War Era*. Oxford University Press, 1988.

"Memorials: David Carew Huntington '45." *Princeton Alumni Weekly*, February 8, 1991, 39.

Millard, Candice. *Destiny of the Republic: A Tale of Madness, Medicine, and the Murder of a President*. Doubleday, 2011.

Miller, Angela. *The Empire of the Eye: Landscape Representation and American Cultural Politics, 1825–1875*. Cornell University Press, 1996.

Mirow, M. C. *Latin American Constitutions: The Constitution of Cádiz and Its Legacy in Spanish America*. Cambridge University Press, 2015.

Murdock, Eugene Converse. *Patriotism Limited, 1862–1865: The Civil War Draft and the Bounty System*. Kent State University Press, 1967.

Murphy, Sharon Ann. *Investing in Life: Insurance in Antebellum America*. Johns Hopkins University Press, 2010.

Myers, Kenneth John. "'Evangel in Art': Frederic Church and Christianity." In Kenneth John Myers, Kevin J. Avery, Gerald L. Carr, and Mercedes Volait, *Frederic Church: A Painter's Pilgrimage*. Detroit Institute of Arts and Yale University Press, 2017.

Myers, Kenneth John, Kevin J. Avery, Gerald L. Carr, and Mercedes Volait. *Frederic Church: A Painter's Pilgrimage*. Detroit Institute of Arts and Yale University Press, 2017.

National Park Service. *Thomas Cole National Historic Site: General Management Plan / Environmental Assessment*. Department of the Interior, 2004.

Navas Sanz de Santamaría, Pablo. *The Journey of Frederic Edwin Church Through Colombia and Ecuador: April–October 1853*. Villegas Editores, 2008.

Neely, Mark E., Jr., and Harold Holzer. *The Union Image: Popular Prints of the Civil War North*. University of North Carolina Press, 2000.

Neptune, George. "Naming the Dawnland: Wabanaki Place Names on Mount Desert Island." *Chebacco: The Magazine of the Mount Desert Island Historical Society* 16 (2015): 92–108.

Nesbitt, Mark. "Botany in Victorian Jamaica." In *Victorian Jamaica*, edited by Tim Barringer and Wayne Modest. Duke University Press, 2018.

Nevins, Allan, and Milton Halsey Thomas. "Preface." In George Templeton Strong, *The Diary of George Templeton Strong*, edited by Allan Nevins and Milton Halsey Thomas. 4 vols. Macmillan, 1952.

Newhall, Beaumont. *The Daguerreotype in America*. 3rd ed. Dover, 1976.

Nye, David E. *America as Second Creation: Technology and Narratives of New Beginnings*. MIT Press, 2004.

Oaklander, Christine I. "Jonathan Sturges, W. H. Osborn, and William Church Osborn: A Chapter in American Art Patronage." *Metropolitan Museum Journal* 43 (2008): 173–94.

Olson, Roberta J. M. *Drawn by New York: Six Centuries of Watercolors and Drawings at the New-York Historical Society*. With Alexandra Mazzitelli. New-York Historical Society, 2008.

Orcutt, Kimberly A. *The American Art-Union: Utopia and Skepticism in the Antebellum Era*. Fordham University Press, 2024.

Orcutt, Kimberly. *Power & Posterity: American Art at Philadelphia's 1876 Centennial Exhibition*. Penn State University Press, 2017.

Painter, Nell Irvin. *The History of White People*. W. W. Norton, 2011.

Parry, Ellwood C., III. *The Art of Thomas Cole: Ambition and Imagination*. University of Delaware, 1988.

Parry, Ellwood C., III. "Thomas Cole and the Problem of Figure Painting." *American Art Journal* 4, no. 1 (1972): 66–86.

Paton, Diana. "State Formation in Victorian Jamaica." In *Victorian Jamaica*, edited by Tim Barringer and Wayne Modest. Duke University Press, 2018.

Patry, Sylvie, and Anne Robbins, eds. *Paris 1874: The Impressionist Moment*. Yale University Press, 2024.

Peck, H. Daniel. *Thomas Cole's Refrain: The Paintings of Catskill Creek*. Cornell University Press, 2019.

Peñalosa, Xavier Puig. "Romanticismo y Pintura de Paisaje en el Ecuador Decimonónico: El Caso de Rafael Salas (1826–1906)." *Boletín de la Academia Nacional de Historia* 100, no. 207 (2022): 13–49.

Pinto, John A. *City of the Soul: Rome and the Romantics*. With Colin B. Bailey. University Press of New England, 2016.

Pizano, Camila, Roy González-M., Angélica Díaz-Pulido, Juan Pablo Gómez, and Hernando García. "'El Triunfo': Una Reserva Privada de Gran Importancia para la Conservación del Bosque Seco Tropical en Colombia." Unpublished manuscript. n.d.

Post, Robert C., ed. *1876: A Centennial Exhibition*. National Museum of History and Technology, Smithsonian Institution, 1976.

Prins, Harald E. L., and Bunny McBride. *Asticou's Island Domain: Wabanaki Peoples at Mount Desert Island, 1500–2000*. Acadia National Park Ethnographic Overview and Assessment. National Park Service, 2007.

Raab, Jennifer. "Details of Absence: Frederic Church and the Landscape of Post-Emancipation Jamaica." *Art History* 34, no. 4 (2011): 714–31.

Raab, Jennifer. *Frederic Church: The Art and Science of Detail*. Yale University Press, 2015.

Raup, Henry A. *Place Names of Mount Desert Island and the Cranberry Islands, Maine*. Mount Desert Island Historical Society, 2021.

Reinhart, Theodore R., ed. *The Archaeology of Shirley Plantation*. University Press of Virginia, 1984.

Rewald, John. *The History of Impressionism*. 4th ed. Secker and Warburg, 1973.

Rindge, Debora. "Chronology." In Franklin Kelly, with Stephen Jay Gould, James Anthony Ryan, and Debora Rindge, *Frederic Edwin Church*. National Gallery of Art, 1989.

Roberts, Mary. "Worlding on the Hudson: Frederic Church and Global Histories of Art." *Art History* 45, no. 3 (2022): 518–44.

Robertson, Shauna Martineau. "Anna Mary Freeman's Room: Women and Art in Antebellum America." Master's thesis, Brigham Young University, 2004.

Roe, Sue. *The Private Lives of the Impressionists*. Harper Collins, 2006.

Rosenbaum, Julia B. "Outside In: Space, Light, and the Artful Interior at Frederic Church's Olana." *Nineteenth-Century Art Worldwide* 20, no. 2 (2021).

Rosenbaum, Julia B. "A World in View." In *Frederic Church's Olana on the Hudson: Art, Landscape, Architecture*, edited by Julia B. Rosenbaum and Karen Zukowski, with Larry Lederman. Rizzoli Electa, 2018.

Rosenbaum, Julia B., and Karen Zukowski, eds. *Frederic Church's Olana on the Hudson: Art, Landscape, Architecture*. With Larry Lederman. Rizzoli Electa, 2018.

Rosenheim, Jeff L. *Photography and the American Civil War*. Metropolitan Museum of Art, 2013.

Rosenzweig, Roy, and Elizabeth Blackmar. *The Park and the People: A History of Central Park*. Cornell University Press, 1992.

Ryan, James Anthony. "Frederic Church's Olana: Architecture and Landscape as Art." In Franklin Kelly, with Stephen Jay Gould, James Anthony Ryan, and Debora Rindge, *Frederic Edwin Church*. National Gallery of Art, 1989.

Rybczynski, Witold. *A Clearing in the Distance: Frederick Law Olmsted and America in the 19th Century*. Scribner, 1999.

Said, Edward W. *Orientalism*. Vintage, 1979.

Sanderson, Eric W. *Mannahatta: A Natural History of New York City*. With Markley Boyer. Harry N. Abrams, 2009.

Sawyer, Sean E. "Frederic Church's Place in the Country," in Barry Bergdoll, Sean E. Sawyer, and Thomas L. Woltz, *Olana: Frederic Church's Vision of Architecture and Landscape*. New York: Rizzoli Electa, 2026.

Schecter, Barnet. *The Devil's Own Work: The Civil War Draft Riots and the Fight to Reconstruct America*. Walker, 2001.

Schuyler, David. "The Preservation of Olana." In *Frederic Church's Olana on the Hudson: Art, Landscape, Architecture*, edited by Julia B. Rosenbaum and Karen Zukowski, with Larry Lederman. Rizzoli Electa, 2018.

Schuyler, David. "Saving Olana." *Hudson River Valley Review* 32, no. 2 (2016): 2–26.

Schwartz, Barry. "Social Change and Collective Memory: The Democratization of George Washington." *American Sociological Review* 56, no. 2 (1991): 221–36.

Sherwin-White, A. N. "Lucullus, Pompey and the East." In *The Cambridge Ancient History, Volume IX: The Last Age of the Roman Republic, 146–43 B.C.*, edited by J. A. Crook, Andrew Lintott, and Elizabeth Rawson. Cambridge University Press, 1994.

Sinha, Manisha. *The Rise and Fall of the Second American Republic: Reconstruction, 1860–1920*. Liveright, 2024.

Skafidas, Michael. "Fabricating Greekness: From Fustanella to the Glossy Page." In *The Fabric of Cultures: Fashion, Identity, and Globalization*, edited by Eugenia Paulicelli and Hazel Clark. Routledge, 2009.

Smee, Sebastian. *Paris in Ruins: Love, War, and the Birth of Impressionism*. W. W. Norton, 2024.

Sowell, David. *The Early Colombian Labor Movement: Artisans and Politics in Bogotá, 1832–1919*. Temple University Press, 1992.

Sowell, David. "Population Growth in Late-Nineteenth-Century Bogotá: Insights on a Demographic Dilemma." *Journal of Urban History* 38, no. 4 (June 11, 2012): 720–30.

Stanton, Elizabeth Cady. *Eighty Years and More (1815–1897): Reminiscences of Elizabeth Cady Stanton*. European Publishing Company, 1898.

Stebbins, Theodore E., Jr. "American Landscape: Some New Acquisitions at Yale." *Yale University Art Gallery Bulletin* 33 (Autumn 1971): 7–25.

Stebbins, Theodore E., Jr. *The Life and Work of Martin Johnson Heade: A Critical Analysis and Catalogue Raisonné*. Yale University Press, 2000.

Stebbins, Theodore E., Jr. *The Lure of Italy: American Artists and the Italian Experience, 1760–1914*. With William H. Gerdts, Erica E. Hirschler, Fred S. Licht, and William L. Vance. Museum of Fine Arts, Boston, 1992.

Stein, Roger B. "Artifact as Ideology: The Aesthetic Movement in Its American Cultural Context." In *In Pursuit of Beauty: Americans and the Aesthetic Movement*, edited by Doreen Bolger Burke. Metropolitan Museum of Art, 1986.

Stein, Susan. "Role and Reputation: The Architectural Practice of Richard Morris Hunt." In *The Architecture of Richard Morris Hunt*, edited by Susan Stein. University of Chicago Press, 1986.

Stenton, Douglas R., Stephen Fratpietro, and Robert W. Park. "Identification of a Senior Officer from Sir John Franklin's Northwest Passage Expedition." *Journal of Archaeological Science: Reports* 59 (September 24, 2024).

Stevens, Scott Manning. "Other Homes, Other Fronts: Native America During the Civil War." In Peter John Brownlee, Sarah Burns, Diane Dillon, Daniel Greene, and Scott Manning Stevens, *Home Front: Daily Life in the Civil War North*. University of Chicago Press, 2013.

Stiles, T. J. *The First Tycoon: The Epic Life of Cornelius Vanderbilt*. Alfred A. Knopf, 2009.

Strouse, Jean. *Family Romance: John Singer Sargent and the Wertheimers*. Farrar, Straus & Giroux, 2024.

Strouse, Jean. *Morgan: American Financier*. Random House, 2014.

Sutton, Robert M. "The Illinois Central: Thoroughfare for Freedom." *Civil War History* 7, no. 3 (September 1961): 273–87.

Sweeney, J. Gray. "'Endued with Rare Genius': Frederic Edwin Church's 'To the Memory of Cole.'" *Smithsonian Studies in American Art* 2, no. 1 (1988): 45–71.

Taylor, Alan. *American Civil Wars: A Continental History, 1850–1873*. W. W. Norton, 2024.

Taylor, Alan. *William Cooper's Town: Power and Persuasion on the Frontier of the Early American Republic*. Alfred A. Knopf, 1995.

Teagle, Robert James. "Land, Labor, and Reform: Hill Carter, Slavery, and Agricultural Improvement at Shirley Plantation, 1816–1866." Master's thesis, Virginia Polytechnic Institute and State University, 1998.

Thomas, Emory M. *Robert E. Lee: A Biography*. W. W. Norton, 1997.

Titus, Robert. *The Catskills: A Geological Guide*. 3rd ed. Purple Mountain Press, 2004.

Titus, Robert, and Johanna Titus. *The Hudson Valley in the Ice Age: A Geological History & Tour*. Black Dome Press, 2012.

Toole, Robert M. *Historic Landscape Report*. Olana State Historic Site, December 1996.

Trennert, Robert A. "The Indian Role in the 1876 Centennial Celebration." *American Indian Culture and Research Journal* 1, no. 4 (1976): 7–13.

Troyen, Carol. "Retreat to Arcadia: American Landscape and the American Art-Union." *American Art Journal* 23, no. 1 (1991): 21–37.

Vedder, Lee A. "Jervis McEntee: Painter-Poet of the Hudson River School." In *Jervis McEntee: Painter-Poet of the Hudson River School*, edited by Lee A Vedder. Samuel Dorsky Museum of Art, State University of New York at New Paltz, 2015.

Vittoria, Shannon. "Chronology." In Elizabeth Mankin Kornhauser and Tim Barringer, *Thomas Cole's Journey: Atlantic Crossings*. Metropolitan Museum of Art, 2018.

Wallach, Alan. "Thomas Cole: Landscape and the Course of American Empire." In *Thomas Cole: Landscape into History*, edited by William H. Truettner and Alan Wallach. Yale University Press / National Museum of American Art, Smithsonian Institution, 1994.

Wallach, Alan. "Thomas Cole's 'River in the Catskills' as Antipastoral." *Art Bulletin* 84, no. 2 (2002): 334–50.

Walls, Laura Dassow. *Henry David Thoreau: A Life*. University of Chicago Press, 2017.

Walls, Laura Dassow. *The Passage to Cosmos: Alexander von Humboldt and the Shaping of America*. University of Chicago Press, 2009.

Waltham, Tony. "The Sandstone Fantasy of Petra." *Geology Today* 10, no. 3 (1994): 105–11.

Weinberg, Helene Barbara. "Cosmopolitan and Candid Stories, 1877–1915." In *American Stories: Paintings of Everyday Life, 1765–1915*, edited by Helene Barbara Weinberg and Carrie Rebora Barratt. Metropolitan Museum of Art, 2009.

Weiss, Ila. *Poetic Landscape: The Art and Experience of Sanford R. Gifford*. University of Delaware Press, 1987.

Wells, Jonathan Daniel. *The Kidnapping Club: Wall Street, Slavery, and Resistance on the Eve of the Civil War*. Bold Type Books, 2020.

West, Elliott. *Continental Reckoning: The American West in the Age of Expansion*. University of Nebraska Press, 2023.

Whittingham, Sarah. *Fern Fever: The Story of Pteridomania*. Frances Lincoln Adult, 2012.

Widmer, Edward L. *Lincoln on the Verge: Thirteen Days to Washington*. Simon & Schuster, 2020.

Widmer, Edward L. *Young America: The Flowering of Democracy in New York City*. Oxford University Press, 1998.

Wierich, Jochen. *Grand Themes: Emanuel Leutze,* Washington Crossing the Delaware, *and American History Painting*. Penn State Press, 2012.

Wilmerding, John. *The Artist's Mount Desert: American Painters on the Maine Coast*. Princeton University Press, 1995.

Wilmerding, John. *Maine Sublime: Frederic Edwin Church's Landscapes of Mount Desert and Mount Katahdin*. Cornell University Press, 2012.

Wilmerding, John. *Master, Mentor, Master: Thomas Cole & Frederic Church*. Thomas Cole National Historic Site, 2014.

Wilson, Christopher Kent. "The Landscape of Democracy: Frederic Church's 'West Rock, New Haven.'" *American Art Journal* 18, no. 3 (1986): 20–39.

Wineapple, Brenda. *Ecstatic Nation: Confidence, Crisis, and Compromise, 1848–1877*. Harper Perennial, 2013.

Woltz, Thomas L. "Restoring a Landscape Masterwork: Breathing New Life into Frederic Church's Living Work of Art." In *Frederic Church's Olana on the Hudson: Art, Landscape, Architecture*, edited by Julia B. Rosenbaum and Karen Zukowski, with Larry Lederman. Rizzoli Electa, 2018.

Woods, Naurice Frank, Jr. *Race and Racism in Nineteenth-Century Art: The Ascendency of Robert Duncanson, Edward Bannister, and Edmonia Lewis*. University Press of Mississippi, 2021.

Wulf, Andrea. *The Invention of Nature: Alexander von Humboldt's New World*. Alfred A. Knopf, 2015.

Wulf, Andrea. *The Adventures of Alexander von Humboldt*. With Lillian Melcher. Pantheon, 2019.

Wullschläger, Jackie. *Monet: The Restless Vision*. Knopf Doubleday, 2024.

Zalewski, Leanne M. *The New York Market for French Art in the Gilded Age, 1867–1893*. Bloomsbury, 2023.

Zegas, Judy Braun. "North American Indian Exhibit at the Centennial Exposition." *Curator: The Museum Journal* 19, no. 2 (1976): 162–73.

Zucker, Joyce. "From the Ground Up: The Ground in 19th-Century American Pictures." *Journal of the American Institute for Conservation* 38, no. 1 (1999): 3–20.

Zukowski, Karen. *Creating the Artful Home: The Aesthetic Movement.* Gibbs Smith, 2006.

Zukowski, Karen. *Historic Furnishings Report.* Olana State Historic Site, 2001.

Zukowski, Karen. "A New Jerusalem." In *Frederic Church's Olana on the Hudson: Art, Landscape, Architecture*, edited by Julia B. Rosenbaum and Karen Zukowski, with Larry Lederman. Rizzoli Electa, 2018.

Illustration Credits

Illustrations within text

CHAPTER 1

Unknown maker, *Frederic E. Church*, 1844, daguerreotype, 3⅝ × 3⅛ in., New York State Office of Parks, Recreation and Historic Preservation, Olana State Historic Site (OSHS), OL.1992.6

Mathew B. Brady, *Thomas Cole*, c. 1845, half-plate daguerreotype on silver-coated copper plate, 4¾ × 3½ in., National Portrait Gallery, Smithsonian Institution, Gift of Edith Cole Silberstein, NPG.76.11

Thomas Cole, *Portrait of the Artist's Wife*, c. 1836–48, graphite with white watercolor on light brown paper, 12½ × 9⁵⁄₁₆ in., Museum of Fine Arts, Boston, MA, Gift of Maxim Karolik for the M. and M. Karolik Collection of American Watercolors and Drawings, 1800–1875, 55.716

Frederic Edwin Church, *Hickory Tree*, June 1844, graphite on white paper, 9¼ × 6⅝ in., OSHS, OL.1980.1464

CHAPTER 2

Once-known maker, *Portrait of Reverend Louis L. Noble*, n.d., daguerreotype on leather-covered case, 3½ in. × 6¼ in. × ¾ in. (open), Thomas Cole National Historic Site Archives, Catskill, NY, Gift of Edith Cole Silberstein, Box 2

Frederic Edwin Church, *Cloud Sketch, Catskill, New York*, August 1844, graphite on white wove paper, 4⅝ × 7⁷⁄₁₆ in., Cooper Hewitt, Smithsonian Design Museum (CHSDM), Gift of Louis P. Church, 1917-4-1413

Unknown maker, *Thomas Cole Sketch Box*, c. 1835–45, hinged mahogany box, oil paint, and brass, 2½ × 18 × 14 in., Collection Bronck Museum, Greene County Historical Society, Gift of Edith Cole Silberstein, 64.11.4

Frederic Edwin Church, *Portrait of Thomas Cole* (detail), c. 1845, pencil on paper, 6⅞ × 6 in., John Wilmerding Collection, promised gift to the National Gallery of Art

CHAPTER 3

Unknown maker, *Eliza Church*, 1855–60, wood, leather, glass, copper plate, velvet and brass, 3¼ × ⅝ × 3⅝ in., OSHS, OL.1999.135

Austin Augustus Turner, *Jervis McEntee*, 1860s, albumen silver print from glass negative, 3¹¹⁄₁₆ × 2 in., The Metropolitan Museum of Art, The Albert Ten Eyck Gardner Collection, Gift of the Centennial Committee, 1970, 1970.659.560

George Belton Moore, *The New York Society Library, Frederick Diaper, Architect*, c. 1840, lithograph, 8⅜ × 13½ in., The New York Historical, 76236

Unknown maker, *Room of the American Art-Union*, n.d., The New York Historical, AA-U Records, Newspaper Clippings

William England, *Barnum's American Museum, New York City*, 1858, photograph

Samuel J. Miller, *Frederick Douglass*, 1847–52, daguerreotype, 5½ × 4⅛ in., The Art Institute of Chicago, Major Acquisitions Centennial Endowment, 1996.433

CHAPTER 4

Mathew B. Brady, *Asher Brown Durand*, 1845–50, half plate daguerreotype, gold toned, Library of Congress, Prints and Photographs Division, Daguerreotype Collection, DAG no. 157

Frederic Edwin Church, *Cedar Grove, Catskill*, October 1848, pencil on paper, 6¾ × 10¼ in., OSHS, OL.1980.1413

CHAPTER 5

Unknown maker, *Joseph Church*, 1840–60, wood, leather, glass, copper plate, velvet and brass, 3¾ × ⅞ × 4¾ in., OSHS, OL.1999.136

Unknown maker, *Astor Place Theatre, with surroundings* (detail), 1831–1900, lithograph, 7 × 9½ in., The New York Public Library, The Miriam and Ira D. Wallach Division of Art, Prints and Photographs: Print Collection, 1659137

James Posselwhite, after a miniature by Robert Thorburn, *William Charles Macready*, 1843, engraving on paper, 9⁵⁄₁₆ × 7½ in., Victoria and Albert Museum, Given by the British Theatre Museum Association, S.582-2015

Unknown maker, *Edwin Forrest*, 1840–60, ninth-plate daguerreotype, Harvard University, Harvard Theatre Collection, TC-37

CHAPTER 6

Mathew B. Brady, *Cyrus West Field*, c. 1860, salted paper print, 17¹³⁄₁₆ × 14⅛ in., National Portrait Gallery, Smithsonian Institution, NPG.80.294

Frederic Edwin Church, *Sketch of Shirley Plantation*, June 12, 1851, University of Virginia, Albert and Shirley Small Special Collections Library, included in a letter to Mary Carter

Read & Co. Engravers & Printers, *The Crystal Palace in Hyde Park for Grand International Exhibition of 1851*, 1851, colored engraving on paper

John Adams Whipple, *The Moon*, 1851, salted paper print, 7⁹⁄₁₆ × 6 in., Princeton University Art Museum, Robert O. Dougan Collection, Gift of Warner Communications, Inc., x1982-340

CHAPTER 7

Friedrich Georg Weitsch, *Portrait of Alexander von Humboldt*, 1806, oil on canvas, 49½ × 36½ in., Staatliche Museen zu Berlin, 1861 Transfer from the Crown's Possession, A II 828

Frederic Edwin Church, *Botanical Sketches from the Río Magdalena, Colombia*, April–May 1853, graphite and oxidized white gouache on gray-blue wove paper, 8⁷⁄₁₆ × 11⅛ in., CHSDM, Gift of Louis P. Church, 1917-4-129

Unknown maker, *Plaza Mayor de Bogotá, Colombia*, 1846, Art Collection 4, Alamy Stock Photo

Frederic Edwin Church, *Tequendama Falls near Bogotá, Colombia*, June 20–30, 1853, graphite and white gouache on tan wove paper, 18⅜ × 12½ in., CHSDM, Gift of Louis P. Church, 1917-4-260

CHAPTER 8
Unknown maker, *Ecuador. San Francisco de Quito*, 1850, PRISMA ARCHIVO, Alamy Stock Photo
Frederic Edwin Church, *Shadows on Chimborazo at Sunrise*, September 13–19, 1853, graphite on white wove paper, 4¹³⁄₁₆ × 7¹⁵⁄₁₆ in., CHSDM, Gift of Louis P. Church, 1917-4-127

CHAPTER 9
Unknown maker, *George Templeton Strong*, illustration from *The Diary of George Templeton Strong*, 1860, photograph, The New York Historical, 71367
Sergei Levitsky, *W. H. Osborn*, n.d., photograph, Osborn Family
André Adolphe-Eugène Disdéri, *Virginia Osborn*, 1860s, carte-de-visite photograph, Sturges Family Descendants

CHAPTER 10
Frederic Edwin Church, *Eagle Lake Viewed from Cadillac Mountain, Mt. Desert Island, Maine*, 1850–60, oil and graphite on paperboard, 11⁹⁄₁₆ × 17½ in., CHSDM, Gift of Louis P. Church, 1917-4-324
Unknown maker, *Theodore Winthrop* (detail), c. 1860, albumen silver print, 6 × 4¾ in., Archives of American Art, Smithsonian Institution, Miscellaneous photographs collection, circa 1845–1980, AAADCD_item_2473
Frederic Edwin Church, *Loch Annie, Mt. Desert Island*, 1855, Private Collection, NY, Photography © John Bigelow Taylor
Unknown maker, *Anne Tracy*, c. 1860, oil portrait, Courtesy Anne Sidamon-Eristoff, Photography © John Bigelow Taylor

CHAPTER 11
Platt D. Babbitt, *Niagara Falls from Prospect Point*, c. 1850–59, daguerreotype, 6⁹⁄₁₆ × 8½ in., OSHS, OL.1981.606
Charles Bierstadt, *Cataract House from Goat Island, Niagara N.Y.*, 1866–1903, stereograph on card mount (one side), Library of Congress, Prints and Photographs Division, LOT 11556-4
Frederic Edwin Church, *Horseshoe Falls and Terrapin Tower, Niagara River, Canada*, October 1856, graphite and white gouache on brown wove paper, 10¾ × 12¼ in., CHSDM, Gift of Louis P. Church, 1917-4-33-b
Unknown maker, *Frederic Church*, c. 1860, photograph, OSHS, OL.1986.628

CHAPTER 12
Unknown maker, *John Frederick Kensett in his studio*, c. 1866, photographic print, 6⅝ × 4⁵⁄₁₆ in., Archives of American Art, Smithsonian Institution, Miscellaneous photographs collection, circa 1845–1980, 2968
Frederic Edwin Church, *Chimborazo through Rising Mist and Clouds, Ecuador*, June–July 1857, oil and graphite on off-white paperboard, 13⁹⁄₁₆ × 21¼ in., CHSDM, Gift of Louis P. Church, 1917-4-824
Frederic Edwin Church, *Cotopaxi Erupting*, June 26, 1857, graphite and gouache on paper, 11¼₁₆ × 21¹¹⁄₁₆ in., OSHS, OL.1977.131
Frederic Edwin Church, *Sangay Erupting, Ecuador*, July 1857, oil and graphite on tan paperboard, 9 × 14⁵⁄₁₆ in., CHSDM, Gift of Louis P. Church, 1917-4-402

CHAPTER 13

Unknown maker, *Worthington Whittredge*, 1856, carte-de-visite photograph, Smithsonian Libraries and Archives, Cartes de visite portraits of nineteenth century artists, SIL-SIL7-343-033a

Unknown maker, *Tenth Street Studio Building, 15 (then 51) West 10th Street, New York, New York*, c. 1875, albumen print, 16 × 12¹¹⁄₁₆ in., Library of Congress, Prints and Photographs Division, Unprocessed in PR 13 CN 2010:100, P1979.620

Unknown maker, *Martin J. Heade at the Tenth Street Studio Building*, 1869, wood engraving in *Frank Leslie's Illustrated Newspaper*, January 23, 1869, pp. 296–97

Verlag von L. Haase & Co., *Alexander von Humboldt*, 1857, carte-de-visite photograph, 4½ × 3¾ in., The Picture Art Collection, Alamy Stock Photo

Alexander von Humboldt and Aimé Bonpland, *Géographie des plantes Équinoxiales: Tableau physique des Andes et Pays voisins*, from *Essai sur la géographie des plantes*, 1805, hand-colored print, 24 × 36 in., Biodiversity Heritage Library

Edward Anthony, *Broadway on a Rainy Day*, 1859, albumen silver print, 3¼ × 6⁵⁄₁₆ in. The Metropolitan Museum of Art, Warner Communications Inc. Purchase Fund, 1980, 1980.1056.1

Glass, Elliot, & Co., Tiffany & Co., *Tiffany's Transatlantic Cable Souvenir*, 1858, submarine cable sample, 4 × ½ in., National Museum of American History, from Silver Creations, Ltd. and Lanello Reserves Inc., 312154

CHAPTER 14

Unknown maker, *Battle Harbour, Labrador*, c. 1860, photograph on cardboard, 5¾ × 8½ in., OSHS, OL.1981.331.2

Frederic Edwin Church, *Floating Iceberg, Canada*, June–July 1859, oil and graphite on tan paperboard, 7½ × 14¹³⁄₁₆ in., CHSDM, Gift of Louis P. Church, 1917-4-296-a

George A. Baker, *Isabel Carnes Church*, c. 1860, oil on canvas, 27 × 22⅛ in., OSHS, OL.1981.3.a

Once-known photographer, *Theodore A. Cole*, n.d., photograph, 4¼ × 2½ in., Thomas Cole National Historic Site Archives, Catskill, NY, Box 4

Frederic Edwin Church, *Frederic & Isabel Church at Mount Desert Island*, c. 1860–62, pencil on paper, 8 × 5 in., OSHS, OL.1980.1603

CHAPTER 15

Unknown maker, *Theodore Winthrop*, c. 1861–62, photograph of a print on paper, 4¹⁄₁₆ × 2⁷⁄₁₆ in., National Portrait Gallery, Smithsonian Institution, NPG.83.7.BB

John Wood, *The Capitol [as] a barrack, "National Guard" D.C. Militia, Capt. Tate*, May 13, 1861, salted paper print, 11⁵⁄₁₆ × 13⅝ in., Library of Congress, Prints and Photographs Division, LOT 12251, p. 51

Frederic Edwin Church, *Our Banner in the Sky*, 1861, oil paint over a lithographic print on paper, 7⁹⁄₁₆ × 11⅜ in., OSHS, OL.1976.29

Mathew B. Brady, *Abraham Lincoln, head-and-shoulders portrait, facing left*, April 6, 1861, photographic print, Library of Congress, Prints and Photographs Division, PRES FILE - Lincoln, Abraham--Portraits--Meserve no. 66

Unknown maker, *A Group of "Contrabands"*, c. 1862, albumen silver print on stereo card (one side), Library of Congress, Prints and Photographs Division, LOT 4172-A, no. 203

CHAPTER 16

Louis Palmer Church, *Cosy Cottage*, c. 1890, photographic print, 3¹⁵⁄₁₆ × 5⅞ in., OSHS, OL.186.59.2

John Coates Browne, *Col. Osborne* [sic], *Gen. Burnside, Gen. Anderson, W. Denning, JCB 1865*, 1865, albumen silver print, 5⁵⁄₁₆ × 7⅝ in., The J. Paul Getty Museum, 84.XM.480.30

George Gardner Rockwood, *Emma Carnes Holding Herbert Church*, 1863, photograph, 4 × 2⁵⁄₁₆ in., OSHS, OL.1996.117

Alexander Gardner, *View on Battlefield of Antietam*, September 1862, albumen silver print on card mount, 4½ × 5¹⁵⁄₁₆ in., Library of Congress, Prints and Photographs Division, LOT 4197

CHAPTER 17

Albert Bierstadt, *The Rocky Mountains, Lander's Peak*, 1863, oil on canvas, 73½ × 120¾ in., The Metropolitan Museum of Art, Rogers Fund, 1907, 07.123

Albert Bierstadt, *Shoshone Man*, 1859, photograph, Idaho State Historical Society, 68-44-1

Napoleon Sarony, *Albert Bierstadt*, c. 1870, albumen silver print, 3⅝ × 2⁵⁄₁₆ in., National Portrait Gallery, Smithsonian Institution, Gift of Larry J. West, NPG.2007.23

Unknown maker, *"The Heart of the Andes" by Frederic Church, as exhibited at the Metropolitan Sanitary Fair*, 1864, stereograph (one side), The New York Historical, Manuscripts Collection, negative number 61263

Bierstadt Brothers, *Picture Gallery, Metropolitan Fair, N.Y., 1864*, 1850–1930, albumen silver stereograph (one side), The New York Public Library, The Miriam and Ira D. Wallach Division of Art, Prints and Photographs: Photography Collection, b11708071

CHAPTER 18

Freeman Studio, Kingston, Jamaica, *Isabel Carnes Church*, 1865, tintype, 4¼ × 3 × ⅛ in., OSHS, OL.1992.10.1

Freeman Studio, Kingston, Jamaica, *Frederic Edwin Church*, 1865, tintype, 4¼ × 3 × ⅛ in., OSHS, OL.1992.7.1

Frederic Edwin Church, *A Lizard, Jamaica*, June 1865, oil and graphite on paperboard, 12 × 5¹³⁄₁₆ in., CHSDM, Gift of Louis P. Church, 1917-4-712-b

Frederic Edwin Church, *View of the Palisadoes near Kingston, Jamaica*, May–September 1865, oil and graphite on paperboard, 12¹⁄₁₆ × 10³⁄₁₆ in., CHSDM, Gift of Louis P. Church, 1917-4-394-b

CHAPTER 19

Unknown maker, *Charlotte Church*, c. 1867, ferrotype photograph, OSHS, OL.2000.264

Maison Bonfils, *View of Beirut*, 1867–99, albumen silver print, Library of Congress, Prints and Photographs Division, LOT 13550, no. 172

Attributed to Felix Bonfils, *Isabel Mortimer Carnes Church and Her Son, Frederic Joseph, on a donkey in Beirut*, 1868, carte-de-visite photograph, 4⅞ × 3⅜ in., OSHS, OL.1984.447

Attributed to Felix Bonfils, *Frederic Edwin Church and His Son, Frederic Joseph, on a camel in Beirut*, 1868, carte-de-visite photograph, 4⅞ × 3⅜ in., OSHS, OL.1984.446

CHAPTER 20

Unknown maker, *Michail Hene*, n.d., photograph, OSHS, OL.1982.194

Frederic Edwin Church, *Crouching Dromedary*, February–March 1868, oil and graphite on tan paperboard, 11¹³⁄₁₆ × 18½ in., CHSDM, Gift of Louis P. Church, 1917-4-492

Frederic Edwin Church, *Arabian Man*, probably February 1868, graphite and white gouache on gray wove paper, 10¹³⁄₁₆ × 7¹¹⁄₁₆ in., CHSDM, Gift of Louis P. Church, 1917-4-1312-b

Frederic Edwin Church, *Al-Khazneh, Petra*, February–March 1868, oil and graphite on tan paperboard, 12¹⁵⁄₁₆ × 20 in., CHSDM, Gift of Louis P. Church, 1917-4-485-a

CHAPTER 21

Frank Mason Good, *Jerusalem from Mt. of Olives*, c. 1860s–70s, photographic print, 6 × 8¹¹⁄₁₆ in., OSHS, OL.1981.673.24

Carl Haag, *Portrait of Jane Digby el-Mesreb, the wife of Sheikh Mijuel el-Mesreb*, 1859, watercolor, 42½ x 29½, Tareq Rajab Museum

Frederic Edwin Church, *View of the Königssee, Bavaria (Germany)*, July 11, 1868, graphite and white gouache on blue wove paper, 11⅞ × 17¼ in., CHSDM, Gift of Louis P. Church, 1917-4-563-a

Frederic Edwin Church, *Arch of Septimius Severus, Rome*, February 1869, oil and graphite on off-white paperboard, 11⅛ × 15³⁄₁₆ in., CHSDM, Gift of Louis P. Church, 1917-4-567

CHAPTER 22

Frederic Edwin Church, *Sketch with female figure in double window*, n.d., 35 mm slide of watercolor on paper, OSHS, OL.1993.19.91_D2

Frederic Edwin Church, *Sketch for the Southwest façade of the Residence at Olana*, c. 1870, watercolor, ink, graphite on paper, 13 × 21¹⁵⁄₁₆ in., OSHS, OL.1984.40

CHAPTER 23

Unknown maker, *Osborn and Sturges Residence, 32 Park Avenue, designed by Richard Morris Hunt*, c. 1870 photograph, Osborn Family

CHAPTER 24

Frederic Edwin Church, *Two Bedouins*, March 1874, oil and graphite on thick paperboard, 12½ × 17¹⁵⁄₁₆ in., CHSDM, Gift of Louis P. Church, 1917-4-761

Maurice Stadtfeld, *View of the National Academy of Design*, n.d., in P. B. Wright, *The National Academy of Design. Photographs of the New Building* (New York: S. P. Avery, 1866), plate 1. Courtesy of the National Academy of Design

Frederic Edwin Church, *Laundry Hung Out to Dry*, 1865–75, oil on white paperboard, 8⅛ × 11 in., CHSDM, Gift of Louis P. Church, 1917-4-327-a

Frank Forshew, *Frederic Joseph Church*, August 1875, carte-de-visite photograph, 4⅛ × 2½ in., OSHS, OL.1992.12; *Theodore Winthrop Church*, c. 1870–80, photographic print on cardboard, 4½ × 2½ in., OSHS, OL.1994.43.A or OL.1994.43.B; *Louis Palmer Church*, August 1875, carte-de-visite photograph, 4⅛ × 2½ in., OSHS, OL.1992.35.A or OL.1992.35.B; *Isabel Charlotte (Downie) Church*, August 1875, carte-de-visite photograph, 4⅛ × 2½ in., OSHS, OL.1992.42

CHAPTER 25

Centennial Photographic Company (unknown maker), *Opening Day, "The Orators," Centennial International Exhibition of 1876, Philadelphia*, 1876, albumen silver print, Free Library of Philadelphia

Unknown maker, *The Douglas Mansion at 128 West 14th Street*, c. 1875, photograph printed in Winifred E. Howe, *A History of the Metropolitan Museum of Art* (New York: The Metropolitan Museum of Art, 1913), p. 163, The Metropolitan Museum of Art, Thomas J. Watson Library

Edward Mitchell Bannister, *Oak Trees*, 1876, oil on canvas, 33⅞ × 60¼ in., Smithsonian American Art Museum, Gift of H. Alan and Melvin Frank, 1983.95.155

CHAPTER 26

Unknown maker, *Don Cathedra on "Soft Sawder"*, 1878, engraving in A. L. Holley, "Camps and Tramps About Ktaadn," *Scribner's Monthly Magazine* 16 (May 1878), p. 33

Jervis McEntee, *Church's Camp in Maine*, c. 1879, oil on canvas, 12¼ × 17 in., OSHS, OL.1981.43.a
Unknown maker, *View of The Metropolitan Museum of Art*, 1880, stereograph (one side), The Metropolitan Museum of Art, Gift of Herbert Mitchell, 1995, 1995.114.1
Robert and Emily de Forest, *Isabel Charlotte (Downie) Church and Emma Carnes*, October 11, 1884, photograph, 11 × 9⅜ in., OSHS, OL.1982.1520

CHAPTER 27
Unknown maker, *Frederic Joseph Church*, c. 1885, albumen print, 2½ × 4 in., OSHS
Frederic Joseph Church, *Plan of Olana*, September 1886, paper, ink, and watercolor, 22⅛ × 36¼ in., OSHS, OL.1984.39.A.B
Unknown maker, *Frederic Joseph Church in Seattle*, c. 1893–94, photographic print, 7⅞ × 9⅞ in., OSHS, OL.1982.1385
Unknown maker, *Students in front of Niagara*, c. 1890s, photograph, Special Collections Research Center, The George Washington University, Corcoran Gallery of Art and Corcoran College of Art + Design Archives, Series 1 subseries 1, Box: 3, flat box: 1, Folders: 18-19, COR0005.3-RG

CHAPTER 28
Sylvester Baxter, *Frederic Church in Mexico*, photograph, n.d. Courtesy of Paul Worman.
Unknown maker, *Frederic Church in Mexico*, c. 1895, photograph, OSHS, David C. Huntington Archive, Series 18, Subseries B, Box 1, Folder 15
Unknown maker, *View facing southwest showing main facade and Wing D*, 1904, photograph, 2 × 2 in., The Metropolitan Museum of Art, Thomas J. Watson Library, DSVH003014

EPILOGUE
Peter Aaron/OTTO, *View from the Olana Bell Tower*, photograph © Peter Aaron

Color images

Unless otherwise noted, color images are by Frederic Church.

FIG. 1 Thomas Cole, *View on the Catskill—Early Autumn*, 1836–37, oil on canvas, 39 × 63 in., The Metropolitan Museum of Art, New York, Gift in memory of Jonathan Sturges by his children, 1895, 95.13.3
FIG. 2 *The Catskill Creek*, 1845, oil on panel, 11⅞ × 16 in., OSHS, OL.1980.1873
FIG. 3 Charles Herbert Moore, *Untitled (Cedar Grove)*, 1868, oil on canvas mounted on board, 5⅞ × 9¼ in., Thomas Cole National Historic Site, Gift of Edith Cole Silberstein, TC.2000.4
FIG. 4 *The Charter Oak at Hartford*, c. 1846, oil on canvas mounted on masonite, 24 × 34¼ in., Florence Griswold Museum, Gift of The Hartford Steam Boiler Inspection and Insurance Company, 2002.1.29
FIG. 5 *To the Memory of Cole*, 1848, oil on canvas, 31¾ × 47⅝ in., Private Collection
FIG. 6 *West Rock, New Haven*, 1849, oil on canvas, 27⅛ × 40⅛ in., New Britain Museum of American Art, John Butler Talcott Fund, 1950.10
FIG. 7 *Twilight, "Short Arbiter 'Twixt Day and Night"*, 1850, oil on canvas, 32¼ × 48 in., Collection of the Newark Museum of Art, Purchase 1956 Wallace M. Scudder Bequest Fund, 56.43
FIG. 8 *Mt. Ktaadn*, 1853, oil on canvas, 36¼ × 55¼ in., Yale University Art Gallery, Stanley B. Resor, B.A. 1901, Fund, 1969.71

FIG. 9 *The Natural Bridge, Virginia*, 1852, oil on canvas, 38 × 33 in., Courtesy of The Fralin Museum of Art at the University of Virginia, Gift of Thomas Fortune Ryan, 1912, photography by Mark Gulezian/QuickSilver

FIG. 10 *Niagara* (orig. *Niagara Falls*), 1857, oil on canvas, 40 × 90½ in., The National Gallery of Art, Corcoran Collection (Museum Purchase, Gallery Fund), 2014.79.10

FIG. 11 *The Heart of the Andes*, 1859, oil on canvas, 66⅛ × 120³⁄₁₆ in., The Metropolitan Museum of Art, New York, Bequest of Margaret E. Dows, 1909, 09.95

FIG. 12 *Twilight in the Wilderness*, 1860, oil on canvas, 40 × 64 in., The Cleveland Museum of Art, Mr. and Mrs. William H. Marlatt Fund, 1965.233

FIG. 13 *Iceberg near Cape Race, Canada*, June 21, 1859, graphite and white gouache on light brown paper, 4½ × 8¼ in., CHSDM, Gift of Louis P. Church, 1917-4-319-a

FIG. 14 *Iceberg Under Cloudy Skies, Canada*, June–July 1859, brush and oil, graphite on tan paperboard, 12 × 20¹⁄₁₆ in., CHSDM, Gift of Louis P. Church, 1917-4-305-b

FIG. 15 *The Icebergs*, 1861, oil on canvas, 64½ × 112½ in., Dallas Museum of Art, Gift of Norma and Lamar Hunt, 1979.28

FIG. 16 *Twilight over Cat Harbour, Canada*, June or July 1, 1859, oil and graphite on paperboard, 6½ × 10⁹⁄₁₆ in., CHSDM, Gift of Louis P. Church, 1917-4-831

FIG. 17 *Sunset over the Hudson Valley, Hudson, New York*, July 1861, brush and oil on canvas backed with paper, 7⁹⁄₁₆ × 11¹⁵⁄₁₆ in., CHSDM, Gift of Louis P. Church, 1917-4-791

FIG. 18 *Cotopaxi from near Ambato, Ecuador*, 1853, graphite, brush and white gouache on tan wove paper, 4¹³⁄₁₆ × 7⅝ in., CHSDM, Gift of Louis P. Church, 1917-4-120

FIG. 19 *Cotopaxi Erupting, Viewed from Quito, Ecuador*, June 1857, oil and graphite on tan paperboard, 6¹⁵⁄₁₆ × 11⅜ in., CHSDM, Gift of Louis P. Church, 1917-4-773

FIG. 20 *Cotopaxi*, 1862, oil on canvas, 48 × 85 in., Detroit Institute of Arts, Founders Society Purchase, Robert H. Tannahill Foundation Fund, Gibbs-Williams Fund, Dexter M. Ferry Jr. Fund, Merrill Fund, Beatrice W. Rogers Fund, and Richard A. Manoogian Fund, 76.89

FIG. 21 *Color Swatch for Some of the Principal Rooms of the First Story, Olana*, c. 1872–74, oil and graphite on paper, 13⅞ × 10⅞ in., OSHS, OL.1982.759

FIG. 22 Peter Aaron/OTTO, *Court Hall, Olana*, photograph © Peter Aaron

FIG. 23 *The Parthenon*, 1871, oil on canvas, 44½ × 72⅝ in., The Metropolitan Museum of Art, New York, Bequest of Maria DeWitt Jesup, from the collection of her husband, Morris K. Jesup, 1914, 15.30.67

FIG. 24 *El Khasné Petra*, 1874, oil on canvas, 60½ × 50¼ in., OSHS, OL.1981.10

FIG. 25 *El Río de Luz (The River of Light)*, 1877, oil on canvas, 54⅜ × 84⅛ in., The National Gallery of Art, Gift of the Avalon Foundation, 1965.14.1

FIG. 26 *Mount Katahdin from Millinocket Camp*, 1895, oil on canvas, 26½ × 42¼ in., Portland Museum of Art, Maine, Gift of Owen W. and Anna H. Wells in memory of Elizabeth B. Noyce, 1998.96

FIG. 27 Peter Aaron/OTTO, *Olana at Sunrise*, photograph © Peter Aaron

Index

About the Author

Victoria Johnson is a writer and Professor of Urban Policy and Planning at Hunter College (CUNY), where she teaches on cultural policy, philanthropy, and New York City history. She is the author of *American Eden: David Hosack, Botany, and Medicine in the Garden of the Early Republic*, which was a finalist for the 2018 National Book Award for Nonfiction, the 2018 Los Angeles Times Book Prize in Biography, and the 2019 Pulitzer Prize for History. The book was also a *New York Times* Notable Book of the Year and was shortlisted for the 2019 Cundill History Prize. Johnson has held fellowships from the Guggenheim Foundation and the Cullman Center for Scholars and Writers at the New York Public Library. She holds a doctorate in sociology from Columbia University, as well as an undergraduate degree in philosophy from Yale. Her website is gloriouscountry.org.